New York Stock Exchange

Constitution and Rules

July 15, 1965

The Official Constitution and Rules of the New York Stock Exchange. Reprinted from the New York Stock Exchange Guide.

CONTENTS

Cross-references in the text to paragraph numbers above ¶ 4000 refer to other sections of the full New York Stock Exchange Guide.

A Telephone Directory to Exchange departments and personnel and a list of Exchange Services start on page 901 in Volume 1 of the New York Stock Exchange Guide.

11 Wall Street • New York, N. Y. 10005

Published for the New York Stock Exchange
by Commerce Clearing House, Inc.

NYSE GUIDE

TABLE OF CONTENTS

Volume 1

Directory

Volume 2

Constitution and Rules

Volume 3

Related Laws and Regulations

(Compiled and Edited by Commerce Clearing House, Inc.)

TABLE OF CONTENTS

Volume 1

Directory

Volume 2

Constitution and Rules

Volume 3

Related Laws and Regulations

(Compiled and Edited by Commerce Clearing House, Inc.)

NEW YORK STOCK EXCHANGE
CONSTITUTION

. . . the full text of the Exchange's Constitution, together with references to related information in the Rules of the Board of Governors . . .

TABLE OF CONTENTS

Contents

Constitution of the New York Stock Exchange
ARTICLE I
Title—Objects—Definitions

¶ 1001   Title

SEC. 1. The title of this Association shall be the "NEW YORK STOCK EXCHANGE."

¶ 1002   Objects

SEC. 2. Its objects shall be to furnish exchange rooms for the convenient transaction of their business by its members; to furnish other facilities for its members and allied members; to maintain high standards of commercial honor and integrity among its members and allied members; and to promote and inculcate just and equitable principles of trade and business.

¶ 1003   Definitions

SEC. 3. Unless the context requires otherwise, the terms defined in this Section shall, for all purposes of the Constitution, have the meanings herein specified:

Member

(a) The term "member" means a member of the Exchange, and does not include within its meaning an allied member of the Exchange.

Membership

(b) The term "membership" refers to the members of the Exchange, and does not refer to the allied members.

Member firm

(c) The term "member firm" means a firm, transacting business as a broker or a dealer in securities, at least one of whose general partners is a member of the Exchange or which has the status of a member firm by virtue of permission given to it by the Board of Governors pursuant to the provisions of Section 13(a) of Article IX.

Allied member

(d) The term "allied member" means:

(i) a general partner in a member firm who is not a member of the Exchange and who has become an allied member as provided in Article IX, or

[The next page is 1051-3.]

(*ii*) a holder of voting stock in a member corporation who is not a member of the Exchange and who has become an allied member as provided in Article IX.

The term "allied member" does not include within its meaning the estate of a deceased person which is a general partner in a member firm or is a holder of voting stock in a member corporation, nor does the term "allied member" include within its meaning a limited partner in a member firm or the holder of non-voting stock in a member corporation.

Non-member

(e) The term "non-member" means a party not a member and not an allied member of the Exchange; it includes within its meaning a limited partner in a member firm who is not a member of the Exchange, and it also includes a stockholder in a member corporation who is not either a member of the Exchange nor the holder of voting stock in such corporation.

Member corporation

(f) The term "member corporation" means a corporation, transacting business as a broker or dealer in securities, approved by the Board of Governors as a member corporation, having at least one member of the Exchange who is a director thereof and a holder of voting stock therein. A corporation shall cease to be a member corporation if the approval of the Board of Governors is withdrawn or if it shall cease to transact business as a broker or dealer in securities or to have a member of the Exchange as a director thereof and holder of voting stock therein, unless the corporation has the status of a member corporation by virtue of permission given to it by the Board of Governors pursuant to the provisions of Section 13(b) of Article IX.

Voting stock

(g) The term "voting stock" means stock in a corporation the holders of which are entitled to vote for the election of the directors of such corporation.

Non-voting stock

(h) The term "non-voting stock" means stock of any class in a corporation other than voting stock.

Holder of voting stock

(i) The term "holder" when used with reference to voting stock of a member corporation means a person who is both the beneficial owner and record holder of such stock, except that in the case of a deceased holder, the term means the estate of such holder.

Holder of non-voting stock

(j) The term "holder" when used with reference to non-voting stock of a member corporation means

    (a) a person who is both the beneficial owner and record holder of such stock, or

    (b) the estate of such person, or

    (c) the trustee or trustees of a trust, or

(d) the trustee or trustees of any stock bonus, pension, disability, death benefit, profit-sharing, supplemental unemployment benefit plan or any other employee benefit plan established for the benefit of such member corporation, or

(e) a corporation organized exclusively for charitable purposes.

Amendments.
December 4, 1958.
July 5, 1957.
March 7, 1963.

ARTICLE II
Government

¶ 1051   **Board of Governors**

The government of the Exchange shall be vested in a Board of Governors, each member of which shall be a citizen of the United States, and which shall be composed as hereinafter set forth.

Composition of Board

The Board of Governors shall consist of the following: The Chairman of the Board of Governors, who shall be a member of the Exchange; the President of the Exchange, who shall not engage in any other business during his incumbency and who, if a member of the Exchange at the time of his election, shall promptly thereafter dispose of his membership; thirteen members residing and having their principal places of business within the Metropolitan area of the City of New York, of whom not less than seven shall be general partners of member firms or holders of voting stock in member corporations engaged in a business involving direct contact with the public and of whom not less than ten shall spend a substantial part of their time on the Floor of the Exchange; six members or allied members residing and having their principal places of business within the Metropolitan area of the City of New York who shall be general partners in member firms or holders of voting stock in member corporations engaged in a business involving direct contact with the public, of whom five shall be allied members and one a member of the Exchange; nine members or allied members of the Exchange residing and having their principal places of business outside of such Metropolitan area who shall be general partners in member firms or holders of voting stock in member corporations engaged in a business involving direct contact with the public, of whom not less than two shall be members of the Exchange; and three representatives of the public.

Eligibility for re-election

No Governor elected by the membership of the Exchange, except the Chairman of the Board, who has served part or all of two consecutive terms as a Governor, shall be eligible for election as a Governor, other than as Chairman of the Board, except after an interval of at least two years.

Duties of non-member Governors

Each non-member of the Exchange elected to the Board of Governors shall by the acceptance of the position of Governor be deemed to have agreed to uphold the Constitution of the Exchange.

Rights of allied member and non-member Governors

Each allied member and non-member elected to the Board of Governors shall have the right to go upon the Floor of the Exchange but shall not have the right to transact business thereon and shall have only such other rights as are specifically granted to Governors by the Constitution. No such Governor shall incur any obligation under Article XVI nor shall the family of such a Governor acquire any rights or privileges thereunder.

ARTICLE III

The Board of Governors

¶ 1101 Duties and Powers

SEC. 1. The Board of Governors shall be vested with all powers necessary for the government of the Exchange, the regulation of the business conduct of members, allied members, member firms and member corporations of the Exchange and the promotion of the welfare, objects and purposes of the Exchange and in the exercise of such powers may adopt such rules, issue such orders and directions and make such decisions as it may deem appropriate.

Penalties

The Board of Governors may prescribe and impose penalties for the violation of rules adopted pursuant to the Constitution and for neglect or refusal to comply with orders, directions or decisions of the Board or for any offense against the Exchange the penalty for which is not specifically prescribed by the Constitution.

Delegation of powers—Review

The Board of Governors may delegate such of its powers as it may from time to time determine, subject to the provisions of the Constitution, to the President, to other officers and employees of the Exchange, and to such committees, composed either of Governors or otherwise, as the Board may from time to time authorize; provided, however, that a member, allied member, member firm or member corporation affected by a decision of any officer, employee or committee acting under powers delegated by the Board may require a review by the Board of such decision, by filing with the Secretary of the Exchange a written demand therefor within 10 days after the decision has been rendered.

Delegation in emergency

Whenever it shall appear to the Board of Governors that an emergency exists, it may delegate all of its powers, for such period as it may determine, to a Special Committee, to be composed of Governors, a majority of whom shall be members of the Exchange.

[*Also see Article* XVIII (¶ 1831-1833).]

¶ 1102 Meetings

SEC. 2. Regular meetings of the Board of Governors shall be held at such times as the Board may designate by resolution, and special meetings of the Board shall be held on the call of the Chairman of the Board, the President, or pursuant to the written request of six Governors.

The Board of Governors, except as otherwise specifically provided in the Constitution, may consider and take action upon any matter at any regular meeting or at any special meeting, even though such matter has not been referred to in the notice of such meeting.

Hearing or trial

Any hearing or trial before the Board of Governors may be adjourned, from time to time, by the Board in its discretion; but no Governor who shall not have been present at every meeting of the Board at which evidence is taken, or at which an accused member or allied member or a person whose conduct is involved is heard, shall participate in the final decision.

Quorum

Except as otherwise specifically required by the Constitution with respect to the vote necessary for action to be taken by the Board of Governors, seven Governors shall be sufficient to constitute a quorum for any meeting of the Board of Governors, and any action taken pursuant to the vote of a majority of the Governors present at such meeting shall be deemed to be the action of the Board of Governors.

Procedure

The Board of Governors shall determine the manner and form by which its proceedings shall be conducted.

Participation in proceedings

No Governor shall be disqualified from participating in any meeting, action or proceeding of the Board of Governors by reason of being or having been a member of a committee which has made prior inquiry, examination or investigation of the subject under consideration. No person shall participate in the adjudication of any matter in which he is personally interested.

¶ 1103   Election of Officers—Contracts of Employment

President

SEC. 3. The Board of Governors, by the affirmative vote of a majority of the Governors then in office, shall elect the President of the Exchange to serve at the pleasure of the Board and shall fix his compensation.

Vice-Chairman

At its organization meeting following the annual election of the Exchange, the Board, by the affirmative vote of a majority of the Governors then in office, shall elect the Vice-Chairman of the Board who shall be a Governor and a member of the Exchange.

Representatives of public

Promptly after the annual election of the Exchange, the Board of Governors, on the nomination of the President, shall, by the affirmative vote of a majority of the Governors then in office, elect to the Board three representatives of the public, to hold office until the next annual election of the Exchange and until their successors are elected and take office.

Contracts of employment

By the affirmative vote of a majority of the Governors then in office, the Board of Governors may authorize any officer, on behalf of the Exchange, to enter into a contract of employment with any person for such period of time and upon such other terms and conditions as may be set forth in a written agreement which has been submitted to and authorized by the Board of Governors by such vote.

¶ 1104   Fees and Compensation

SEC. 4. The Board of Governors shall have control of the property and finances of the Exchange and shall be responsible for safeguarding the interests of the members of the Exchange in such property. It may fix the fees and compensation to be paid to the Governors, members of such committees as it may from time to time authorize, officers of the Exchange and the Trustees of the Gratuity Fund.

Appropriations

It shall annually appropriate the amounts to be expended in the administration of the Exchange in the ensuing year and may make such appropriations in such detail as it may deem desirable. It may at any time make additional appropriations and may increase or decrease any appropriation theretofore made. No expenditure in excess of the amount appropriated therefor shall be made without the prior approval of the Board.

Examination of accounts

The Board of Governors shall make or cause to be made such examination of the accounts and vouchers of the Exchange and of the Gratuity Fund as it may from time to time determine are required. It may employ auditors or accountants and may accept and adopt their reports as its examination.

¶ 1105   Adoption, Repeal, Amendment of Rules

SEC. 5. The Board of Governors may, by the affirmative vote of a majority of the Governors then in office, adopt, amend or repeal such rules as it may deem necessary or proper, including rules with respect to (a) the making and settling of Exchange Contracts, (b) the access of members to and the conduct of members upon the Floor of the Exchange and their use of Floor facilities, (c) insolvency of members, member firms and member corporations, (d) the formation of member firms and member corporations, the continuance thereof and the interests of members and allied members and other persons therein, (e) the partners, officers, directors, stockholders and employees of members, allied members, member firms and member corporations, (f) the offices of members, allied members, member firms and member corporations, (g) the business conduct of members, allied members, member firms and member corporations, (h) the business connections of members, allied members, member firms and member corporations, and their association with or domination by or over corporations or other persons engaged in the securities business, (i) capital requirements for members, member firms and member corporations, (j) the procedure for arbitration, and (k) transfers of memberships and disposition of the proceeds of such transfers.

¶ 1106   Supervision Over Members, Allied Members, Member Firms and Member Corporations

SEC. 6. The Board of Governors shall have general supervision over members, allied members, member firms and member corporations. It may examine into the business conduct and financial condition of members, allied members, member firms and member corporations. It shall have supervision over partnership and corporate arrangements and over all offices of such members, firms and corporations, whether foreign or domestic, and over all persons employed by such members, firms and corporations, and may adopt such rules with respect to the employment, compensation and duties of such employees as it may deem appropriate. The Board may require that transactions in securities admitted to dealings upon the Exchange shall be executed upon the Exchange. It shall have supervision over all matters relating to the collection, dissemination and use of quotations and of reports of prices on the Exchange and shall have power to approve or disapprove any application for ticker service to any non-member, or for wire, wireless, or other connection between any office of any member of the Exchange, member firm or member corporation and any non-member, and may require the discontinuance of any such service or connection. It shall have the power to approve or disapprove of any connection or means of communication with the Floor and may require the discontinuance of any such connection or means of communication. It may disapprove of any member acting as a specialist, odd-lot dealer or odd-lot broker.

¶ 1107   Listing of Securities

SEC. 7. The Board of Governors may approve applications for the listing of securities and the admission of securities, including securities on a "when issued" or "when distributed" basis, to dealings upon the Exchange, and may suspend dealings in such securities and may remove the same from listing.

¶ 1108   Corners

SEC. 8. Whenever in the opinion of the Board of Governors a corner
has been created in a security admitted to dealings on the Exchange, or a
single interest or group has acquired such control of a security so admitted that
the same cannot be obtained for delivery on existing contracts except at prices
and on terms arbitrarily dictated by such interest or group, the Board may
postpone the time for deliveries on Exchange Contracts therein, and may from
time to time further postpone such time or may postpone deliveries until
further action by the Board, and may at any time by resolution declare that
if such security is not delivered on any contract calling for delivery thereof
at or before the time to which delivery has been postponed or which has been
fixed by the Board for such delivery, such contract shall be settled by the
payment to the party entitled to receive such security or by the credit to
such party of a fair settlement price as agreed by the parties to the contract,
or if the parties to any contract which is to be settled on the basis of such
fair settlement price do not agree with respect thereto, such fair settlement
price and the date for the payment of the same may be fixed by the Board.
The Board before fixing the same shall give the parties to the contract which
is to be settled on the basis thereof an opportunity to be heard either before
the Board or before a committee authorized for the purpose. Any such committee shall report the testimony together with its conclusions thereon to the
Board which may act upon such report without further hearing or may accord the parties a further hearing before acting thereon.

¶ 1109   Removal and Disqualification of Governors

Absence

SEC. 9. If a Governor shall have been absent from three consecutive
regular meetings of the Board of Governors without having been excused by
the Chairman of the Board, the Board may, by the affirmative vote of a majority of the Governors then in office, remove such Governor and declare the
position theretofore held by him to be vacant.

Change in status

Any Governor qualified for office by reason of being a member of the
Exchange who shall cease to be a member shall thereupon cease to be a
Governor and his office shall thereupon become vacant.

Any Governor qualified for office by reason of being an allied member of
the Exchange who shall cease to be an allied member shall thereupon cease
to be a Governor and his office shall thereupon become vacant, except that if
such Governor shall cease to be an allied member by virtue of the termination of his membership as provided in Section 12 of Article XI then he shall
cease to be a Governor and his office shall become vacant only if he shall
cease for a period of thirty consecutive days to be an allied member.

If the Board shall determine that any Governor qualified for office by
reason of residing within or outside of the Metropolitan area of the City of
New York, or by reason of having his principal place of business within or
outside of such Metropolitan area, or by reason of being a general partner in
a member firm or a holder of voting stock in a member corporation engaged
in a business involving direct contact with the public, has as a result of a
change in his residence or place of business, or the status of his firm or

[The next page is 1057-3.]

corporation, lost such qualifications, the Board may, by the affirmative vote of a majority of the Governors then in office, remove such Governor and declare the position held by him to be vacant; provided, however, that with respect to a Governor in the class designated as "members residing and having their principal places of business within the Metropolitan area of the City of New York" the Board may not remove such a Governor for the sole reason of a change in the status of his firm or corporation, unless after such change in status the number of Governors in that class who are general partners in member firms or holders of voting stock in member corporations engaged in a business involving direct contact with the public is less than the number required by the provisions of Article II.

If the Board shall determine that any Governor elected in the class designated as "members residing and having their principal places of business within the Metropolitan area of the City of New York" who has spent a substantial part of his time on the Floor of the Exchange has ceased to do so and if the Board shall determine that, after such change, the total number of Governors in such class who spend a substantial part of their time on the Floor of the Exchange is less than the number required by the provisions of Article II, the Board may, by the affirmative vote of a majority of the Governors then in office, remove such Governor and declare the position held by him to be vacant.

Chairman, President, Trustee of Gratuity Fund

In the event of the refusal or failure of the Chairman of the Board, the President, a Governor of the Exchange, or a Trustee of the Gratuity Fund to discharge his duties, or for any cause deemed sufficient by the Board of Governors, the Board may, by the affirmative vote of a majority of the Governors then in office, remove such Officer, Governor or Trustee and declare his office or position to be vacant.

¶ 1110   Vacancies in Board

SEC. 10. Any vacancy in the office of a Governor of any class elected by the membership, other than in the office of the Chairman of the Board, shall be filled by the affirmative vote of a majority of the Governors then in office, unless the Board shall determine that the vacancy need not be filled until the next annual election. Prior to filling such vacancy, the Board shall request the Nominating Committee to submit to the Board the name of a person recommended by the Nominating Committee to fill such vacancy. Any person to be eligible to fill such vacancy must meet the qualifications for election in the class of Governors in which the vacancy exists, so that upon his election the composition of that class shall be as provided in Article II. A Governor so elected shall serve until the next annual election of the Exchange and until his successor is elected and takes office.

Any vacancy in the office of a Governor elected as a representative of the public shall be filled by the Board, upon the nomination of the President, by the affirmative vote of a majority of the Governors then in office.

¶ 1111   Interpretation of Constitution and Rules

SEC. 11. The Board of Governors shall have power to interpret the Constitution of the Exchange and all rules adopted pursuant thereto. Any interpretation made by it shall be final and conclusive.

¶ 1112   Indemnification

SEC. 12. The Exchange shall indemnify any person made a party to any
action, suit, claim or proceeding, whether civil or criminal, by reason of the
fact that he, his testator or intestate, is or was a Governor, a member of any
committee authorized by the Constitution or by the Board of Governors,
a Floor Official, a Trustee of the Gratuity Fund, a Trustee of the Special Trust
Fund, an officer or employee of the Exchange, or a director, officer or employee of any corporation a majority of the stock of which is held by the
Exchange against all liability incurred and all expenses (including attorney's
fees) reasonably and necessarily incurred in connection with the defense of
any such action, suit, claim or proceeding, or in connection with any appeal
therein, or in connection with any settlement thereof approved in writing by
the Exchange, unless it shall be judicially determined (either in such action,
suit or proceeding or in an action, suit or proceeding brought to enforce this
indemnity) that such person is liable to the Exchange, the Special Trust Fund
or to any such corporation for negligence or was guilty of willful misconduct
in the performance of his duties to the Exchange, the Special Trust Fund
or any such corporation. The foregoing right of indemnification shall not
exclude any other right to which any such person may be entitled. The
Board of Governors, in its discretion, may indemnify any of the above persons
or any other person who serves the Exchange in an official or representative
capacity against all liability and expense incurred in connection with the
defense of any action, suit, claim or proceeding or in connection with any
appeal therein or any settlement thereof.

Amendments.
December 4, 1958.
July 30, 1964.

ARTICLE IV
Chairman of the Board of Governors

¶ 1151   Presiding Officer

SEC. 1. The Chairman of the Board shall be the presiding officer of the Board of Governors and may preside at meetings of the Exchange whenever he shall so elect.

¶ 1152   Special Meetings

SEC. 2. The Chairman of the Board may call special meetings of the Exchange and of the Board of Governors. He shall call special meetings of the Exchange upon the direction of the Board of Governors or upon the written request of one hundred members, and special meetings of the Board upon the written request of six Governors.

¶ 1153   Appointment of Tellers

SEC. 3. The Chairman of the Board shall appoint tellers with respect to voting by members under Articles VII and XVIII.

¶ 1154   Member of Committees

SEC. 4. The Chairman of the Board shall be *ex officio* a member of any committee authorized by the Board.

¶ 1155   Vacancy in Office

SEC. 5. In case a vacancy shall occur in the office of Chairman of the Board, the Vice-Chairman of the Board shall succeed to the office of Chairman, to hold office until the next annual election of the Exchange and until his successor is elected and takes office.

¶ 1156   Appointment of Committees

SEC. 6. The Chairman of the Board shall, subject to the approval of the Board, appoint the members of all committees which may from time to time be authorized by the Board to consider matters pertaining to the administration of the Exchange and the policies of the Exchange concerning members, member firms and member corporations and shall fill all vacancies in such committees; and the Chairman of the Board may make any such appointment *ad interim* until the next regular meeting of the Board.

ARTICLE V
Vice-Chairman of the Board of Governors

¶ 1201   Duties

SEC. 1. The Vice-Chairman of the Board shall, in case of the absence or inability to act of the Chairman of the Board, assume all the functions and discharge all the duties of the Chairman of the Board and, in case of a vacancy in the office of Chairman of the Board, shall succeed to that office.

¶ 1202 Acting Chairman

SEC. 2. In case of the absence or inability to act of both the Chairman of the Board and the Vice-Chairman of the Board, the members of the Board of Governors who are members of the Exchange and in such order of priority as the Board may designate, or, in the absence of such designation, the senior available member of the Board of Governors who is a member of the Exchange, shall assume all the functions and discharge all the duties of the Chairman of the Board.

¶ 1203 Vacancy in Office

SEC. 3. In case a vacancy shall occur in the office of Vice-Chairman of the Board, the Board, by the affirmative vote of a majority of the Governors then in office, shall fill such vacancy by the election to such office of a Governor who is a member of the Exchange.

ARTICLE VI
President

¶ 1251 Chief Officer and Member of Committees

SEC. 1. The President shall be the chief officer and the chief executive officer of the Exchange, responsible for the management and administration of its affairs, and shall be the official representative of the Exchange in all public matters. By his acceptance of the office of President he shall be deemed to have agreed to uphold the Constitution of the Exchange. He shall, during his incumbency, be a member of the Board of Governors and *ex officio* a member of any committee authorized by the Board of Governors.

¶ 1252 Special Meetings

SEC. 2. The President may call special meetings of the Board of Governors.

¶ 1253 Appointment of Committees

SEC. 3. The President shall, subject to the approval of the Board, appoint the members of all committees which may from time to time be authorized by the Board to consider public matters and shall fill all vacancies in such committees; and the President may make any such appointment *ad interim* until the next regular meeting of the Board.

¶ 1254 Appointment of Officers

SEC. 4. Subject to the approval of the Board of Governors, the President shall appoint one or more Vice-Presidents, a Treasurer, a Secretary and such other officers of the Exchange, other than the Chairman of the Board and the Vice-Chairman of the Board, as he from time to time may determine are required for the efficient management and operation of the Exchange and fix the duties, responsibilities, terms and conditions of employment of such officers and, subject to like approval, he may terminate their employment at any time. All such officers shall be responsible to the President for the proper performance of their duties.

¶ 1255   Jurisdiction over Employees

SEC. 5. The President shall have power to appoint all other employees of the Exchange and to fix the duties, responsibilities, terms and conditions of their employment and to terminate their employment at any time.

¶ 1256   Appointment of Counsel and Other Advisers

SEC. 6. Subject to the approval of the Board of Governors, the President shall appoint general counsel for the Exchange and such other expert or professional advisers as may be desirable for the efficient administration of the Exchange. He may, subject to like approval, terminate any such appointment at his pleasure.

¶ 1257   Estimate of Income and Appropriations

SEC. 7. The President, or such other officer as he may designate, shall prepare and present to the Board at its first regular meeting in December of each year an estimate of the income of the Exchange for the succeeding calendar year and recommendations as to appropriations for expenses for said period. He may at any time recommend additional appropriations or the increase or decrease of any appropriations made by the Board and shall make reports and recommendations to the Board as to the financial policy of the Exchange.

¶ 1258   Acting President

SEC. 8. In case of the absence or inability to act of the President, or in case of a vacancy in the office of President, the Board of Governors may appoint the Chairman of the Board or such other person as it may designate as President *pro tem*, who shall assume all the functions and discharge all the duties of the President. In the absence of such designation by the Board, the senior available Vice-President shall assume all the functions and discharge all the duties of the President.

ARTICLE VII
Elections—Exchange Meetings

¶ 1301   Annual Election—Positions To Be Filled

SEC. 1. The annual election of the Exchange shall be held on the second Monday in May in each year. At such annual election there shall be elected by the membership, by ballot, a Chairman of the Board of Governors for the term of one year; and

Elections in 1960, 1963, 1966, etc.

At the annual election in the year 1951 and every third year thereafter:

Four members for the term of three years, residing and having their principal places of business within the Metropolitan area of the City of New York;

Two allied members for the term of three years, residing and having their principal places of business within the Metropolitan area of the City of New York who shall be general partners in member firms or holders of voting stock in member corporations engaged in a business involving direct contact with the public;

Three members or allied members for the term of three years, residing and having their principal places of business outside of such Metropolitan area who shall be general partners in member firms or holders of voting stock in member corporations engaged in a business involving direct contact with the public, of whom not less than one shall be a member of the Exchange;

Elections in 1961, 1964, 1967, etc.

At the annual election in the year 1952 and every third year thereafter:

Four members for the term of three years, residing and having their principal places of business within the Metropolitan area of the City of New York;

Two allied members for the term of three years, residing and having their principal places of business within the Metropolitan area of the City of New York who shall be general partners in member firms or holders of voting stock in member corporations engaged in a business involving direct contact with the public;

Three members or allied members for the term of three years, residing and having their principal places of business outside of such Metropolitan area who shall be general partners in member firms or holders of voting stock in member corporations engaged in a business involving direct contact with the public, of whom not less than one shall be a member of the Exchange;

Elections in 1962, 1965, 1968, etc.

At the annual election in the year 1953 and every third year thereafter:

Five members for the term of three years, residing and having their principal places of business within the Metropolitan area of the City of New York;

One allied member for the term of three years and one member for the term of three years, residing and having their principal places of business within the Metropolitan area of the City of New York who shall be general partners in member firms or holders of voting stock in member corporations engaged in a business involving direct contact with the public;

Three members or allied members for the term of three years, residing and having their principal places of business outside of such Metropolitan area who shall be general partners in member firms or holders of voting stock in member corporations engaged in a business involving direct contact with the public;

a Nominating Committee for the term of one year, to be composed of six members and three allied members of the Exchange; two Trustees of the Gratuity Fund for the term of three years; and persons to fill any vacancies which may exist in the Board of Governors or in the Trustees of the Gratuity Fund.

At each annual election there shall be elected in the class of Governors designated as "members residing and having their principal places of business within the Metropolitan area of the City of New York," such number of members who are general partners of member firms or holders of voting stock in member corporations engaged in a business involving direct contact with the public and such number of members who spend a substantial part of their time on the Floor of the Exchange as may be required so that, upon their election, the composition of that class of the Board shall be as provided in Article II.

Terms of office

The terms of office of the persons elected at each annual election shall commence at 3:30 p. m. on the seventh day after the date of their election and the Board of Governors shall meet promptly thereafter.

Amendment.
July 5, 1957.

¶ 1302   Nominating Committee

SEC. 2. The Nominating Committee shall be composed of six members and three allied members of the Exchange. No Governor shall be eligible to serve on the Nominating Committee nor shall any member of the Nominating Committee be eligible for election to the Nominating Committee for the ensuing year. Any vacancy in the Nominating Committee shall be filled by the remaining members thereof, who shall elect a person qualified to fill the vacancy. The Board of Governors shall have no control over or power with respect to the Nominating Committee.

¶ 1303   Meetings of Nominating Committee

SEC. 3. The Nominating Committee, during the month of March in each year, shall hold one or more meetings, to which all members, allied members and non-members who are limited partners in member firms or stockholders in member corporations shall be invited for the purpose of suggesting nominees for the offices and positions to be filled at the annual election of the Exchange. The Nominating Committee shall report to the Secretary of the Exchange, on the second Monday in April, nominees for such offices and positions. Each nominee shall be a person who, in the opinion of the Nominating Committee, is eligible for election to the office or position for which he is nominated. The Secretary of the Exchange shall, on receipt of the report of the Nominating Committee, post on the bulletin board and notify the members of the names of such nominees.

¶ 1304   Nominees by Petition and Arrangement of Ballot

SEC. 4. Members of the Exchange may propose by petition nominees for the offices or positions to be filled at the elections prescribed by this Article. Any such nominee must be endorsed by not less than forty members and no member shall endorse more than one nominee; provided, however, that one hundred members may, by petition, propose an entire ticket or any portion thereof. The petitions shall be filed with the Secretary of the Exchange in sealed envelopes within two weeks after the date fixed for the report of the Nominating Committee. The Nominating Committee and the Secretary of the Exchange shall open such envelopes and shall report to the Board of Governors the names of the persons nominated by petition who, if found eligible for election by the Board, shall be deemed nominees for such offices or positions. The names of all nominees shall be arranged in alphabetical order for each class of office or position and shall be reported to the Exchange promptly after the Board shall have passed upon the eligibility of the persons nominated by petition. The names of the persons nominated by the Nominating Committee shall be identified on the ballot by an appropriate legend or symbol.

Death, withdrawal or disqualification of nominees

In case of the death, withdrawal or disqualification, at any time in advance of the annual election, of a nominee proposed by the Nominating Committee for one of the offices or positions to be filled at such annual election, the Board of Governors, by the affirmative vote of a majority of the Governors then in office, may elect a person to the office or position for which such nominee was nominated, to hold office until the seventh day after the annual election of the Exchange in the succeeding year or may, in its discretion, direct that a special election of the Exchange be held to fill such office or position, but this shall not delay the election of persons to fill all other offices or positions. If such special election shall be directed, the Board shall determine the procedure for the same.

¶ 1305   Votes Required to Elect

SEC. 5. The nominees in each class of office or position to be filled at the annual election receiving the highest number of votes shall be declared elected to those offices and positions; provided, however, that in determining the results of an election in any class of Governors in which there are more nominees than there are offices to be filled

(1) the nominees in that class for any term of years in which the number of nominees does not exceed the number of offices to be filled shall first be declared elected;

(2) then, in any term or terms in which there are more nominees than there are offices to be filled, the nominees whose election would result in the required composition of that class of Governors provided in Article II, shall be declared elected in the order of the highest number of votes received by the remaining nominees in the class; a nominee whose election would not result in the required composition of that class of Governors shall not be declared elected, even though he receives more votes than a nominee whose election is necessary to bring about the required composition of that class.

For the purpose of determining the results of an election in which there are more nominees than there are offices to be filled in the class of Governors designated as "members residing and having their principal places of business within the Metropolitan area of the City of New York," the Nominating Committee, prior to the time when the names of nominees are reported to the Exchange in accordance with the provisions of Section 4 of this Article, shall advise the Secretary of the Exchange which of the nominees named by it for such class are general partners of member firms or holders of voting stock in member corporations engaged in a business involving direct contact with the public and which of the nominees named by it spend a substantial part of their time on the Floor of the Exchange. The Board of Governors, prior to such time, shall determine which of the nominees named by petition for such class of Governors are general partners of member firms or holders of voting stock in member corporations engaged in a business involving direct contact with the public and which of the nominees named by petition for such class of Governors spend a substantial part of their time on the Floor of the Exchange. The Board of Governors shall also determine the minimum number of nominees who are general partners of member firms or holders of voting stock in member corporations engaged in a business involving direct contact with the public and the minimum number of nominees who spend a substantial part of their time on the Floor of the Exchange whose election will be required in order that the composition of that class of Governors, after such election, shall be as provided in Article II.

Tie vote

In the case of a tie, the names of the nominees involved shall be referred to the Board of Governors who shall make a selection.

¶ 1306   Vacancies in Board

SEC. 6. The Nominating Committee, on receipt of a request from the Board of Governors for a recommendation of a person to fill a vacancy in office of a Governor, shall submit to the Board the name of a person recommended by the Nominating Committee to fill such vacancy, the person so recommended to have the qualifications for election prescribed in Section 10 of Article III.

¶ 1307   Postponement of Election

SEC. 7. If the Exchange is not open for business on the date of any election prescribed by this Article, such election shall be held on the next succeeding business day.

¶ 1308   Voting Privileges

SEC. 8. Each member of the Exchange in good standing shall be entitled to vote at any election or meeting of the Exchange. Each such member may vote in person or by absentee ballot at an election of the Exchange. Promptly after the names of all the nominees have been reported to the Exchange, the Secretary of the Exchange shall mail each member a ballot which, if executed personally by such member and received at the office of the Secretary prior to the close of business on the day of such election, shall for all purposes be considered as a vote cast by a member present in person.

Amendment.
March 3, 1960.

¶ 1309   Quorum

SEC. 9. When the Exchange shall be assembled for the transaction of business other than dealing in securities, a majority of all the members shall constitute a quorum.

ARTICLE VIII

Arbitration

¶ 1351   Controversies Arbitrated

SEC. 1. Any controversy between parties who are members, allied members, member firms or member corporations shall, at the instance of any such party, and any controversy between a non-member and a member or allied member or member firm or member corporation arising out of the business of such member, allied member, member firm or member corporation, or the dissolution of a member firm or member corporation, shall, at the instance of such non-member, be submitted for arbitration, in accordance with the provisions of the Constitution and the rules of the Board of Governors.

¶ 1352   Procedure and Costs

SEC. 2. The Board of Governors, in accordance with the provisions of Section 5 of Article III, shall adopt rules governing the procedure for arbitration through the facilities of the Exchange, which, among other matters, shall fix the maximum amount chargeable to the parties as costs to cover the expense of the hearings, which shall include the fees of the Arbitrators, and may from time to time amend, alter or repeal any rule so adopted.

¶ 1353   Arbitration Director

SEC. 3. The President, subject to the approval of the Board of Governors, shall designate one of the officers or other employees of the Exchange as Arbitration Director, and may also designate an employee of the Exchange as Assistant Arbitration Director, to act in the absence or inability to act of the Director. The Arbitration Director shall be charged with the duty of performing all ministerial duties in connection with matters submitted for arbitration pursuant to this Article.

¶ 1354   Arbitrators

Board of Arbitration

SEC. 4. Promptly after the annual election of the Exchange, the Chairman of the Board of Governors shall appoint, subject to the approval of the Board of Governors, a Board of Arbitration to be composed of fifteen arbitrators selected from members and allied members of the Exchange who are not members of the Board of Governors, to serve at the pleasure of the Board of Governors or until the next annual election of the Exchange and their successors are appointed and take office.

Panels of arbitrators

The Chairman of the Board of Governors shall from time to time appoint two panels of arbitrators, composed of persons who are residents of or have their places of business in the Metropolitan area of the City of New York, to serve until the next annual election of the Exchange and until their successors are appointed and take office. The first of such panels shall be composed of persons engaged in the securities business and the second of such panels shall be composed of persons not engaged in the securities business. The Chairman of the Board of Governors may likewise appoint panels similar to the panels above described to serve outside the City of New York.

¶ 1355   Member Controversies

SEC. 5. Any controversy between parties who are members, allied members, member firms or member corporations shall be submitted for arbitration to five Arbitrators, members of the Board of Arbitration provided for by Section 4 of this Article, and the decision of a majority of such Arbitrators shall be final. All such proceedings shall be held in the City of New York.

¶ 1356   Non-member Controversies

SEC. 6. Any controversy between a non-member and a member or allied member or member firm or member corporation, arising out of the business of such member, allied member, member firm or member corporation or the dissolution of a member firm or a member corporation shall, at the instance of such non-member, be submitted for arbitration to five Arbitrators. If the proceedings are to be held in the City of New York, the Arbitrators to hear and determine such a controversy shall be composed of five Arbitrators, to be selected by lot, by the Arbitration Director, as follows: one Arbitrator from the Board of Arbitration, one Arbitrator from the first of the panels and three Arbitrators from the second of the panels provided for by Section 4 of this Article; or, at the election of the non-member, to five Arbitrators, members of the Board of Arbitration. Arbitration proceedings pursuant to this Section shall be held in the City of New York, except as may be otherwise provided in the rules of the Board of Governors.

Proceedings held outside City of New York

If the proceedings are to be held outside the City of New York, such Arbitrators shall be selected, from panels appointed for service outside the City of New York, by lot, by the Arbitration Director, as follows: two Arbitrators from the first of such panels and three Arbitrators from the second of such panels provided for by Section 4 of this Article.

Majority decision final

The decision of a majority of the Arbitrators shall be final.

¶ 1357   Provisions Applicable to All Controversies

SEC. 7. All arbitration proceedings shall be conducted in such manner and pursuant to such rules as the Board of Governors shall from time to time adopt.

Power to decline use of facilities

The Board of Governors may decline in any case to permit the use of the arbitration facilities of the Exchange pursuant to this Article and may delegate such power in accordance with the provisions of Section 1 of Article III.

Dismissal of proceedings; assessment of costs

The Arbitrators in any case may at any time during the proceedings, and shall upon the joint request of the parties thereto, dismiss the proceedings and refer the parties to their remedies at law. In any arbitration proceeding, whether involving a member controversy or a non-member controversy, the Arbitrators may determine, subject to the rules of the Board of Governors, the amount chargeable to the parties as costs, to cover the expense of the hearings, and, upon the determination of such controversy, shall determine by whom such costs shall be borne or may in their discretion remit all or any part thereof. Where the expense of the hearings exceeds the amount chargeable to the parties as costs, such excess shall be borne by the Exchange.

No right of appeal

There shall be no appeal to the Board of Governors from a decision of the Arbitrators in any arbitration proceeding.

ARTICLE IX

Membership—Allied Membership—Member Firms— Member Corporations

¶ 1401   Members and Allied Members

SEC. 1. The membership of the Exchange shall consist of 1,366 members of the Exchange.

There may be an unlimited number of allied members.

Amendment.

January 4, 1962, effective April 1, 1963.

¶ 1402   Eligibility

SEC. 2. To be eligible for election as a member of the Exchange, a person must be at least twenty-one years of age and a citizen of the United States; any person elected shall have all the rights and privileges and shall be under all the duties and obligations of a member of the Exchange in accordance with the Constitution.

¶ 1403   Election, Reinstatement, Readmittance to Membership

SEC. 3. The affirmative vote of two-thirds of the Governors present at a meeting of the Board shall be necessary to elect to membership or to reinstate a member suspended for insolvency, except that the affirmative vote of two-thirds of the Governors then in office shall be required for the readmission of a person who has been expelled from the Exchange or declared ineligible for reinstatement or for the reinstatement of a member who has been suspended under Section 2 of Article XIII.

¶ 1404   Initiation Fee

SEC. 4. Upon election to membership, each member shall pay to the Exchange an initiation fee of seventy-five hundred dollars. The Board of Governors may remit any initiation fee payable upon the transfer of the membership of a person elected President of the Exchange, or upon the transfer of a membership to a person who shall have transferred his membership so as to qualify as President.

Amendment.

January 4, 1962.

¶ 1405   Non-payment of Initiation Fee

SEC. 5. If the initiation fee of a member is not paid on the day of his election, his election shall be void.

¶ 1406   Signing Constitution

SEC. 6. No person elected to membership shall be admitted to the privileges thereof until he shall have signed the Constitution of the Exchange. By such signature he pledges himself to abide by the same as the same has been or shall be from time to time amended, and by all rules adopted pursuant to the Constitution.

¶ 1407   Approval of Partnerships and Corporations

SEC. 7.   (a)

(1) No member shall form a partnership and no member, allied member or member firm shall admit any person to partnership in a member firm, without the prior approval of the Board of Governors.

(2) No member shall organize a member corporation and no member or allied member shall become a stockholder in a member corporation and no member corporation shall permit any person to hold any of its stock, without the prior approval of the Board of Governors.

Vote required

The affirmative vote of two-thirds of the Governors present at a meeting of the Board shall be necessary to grant any approval required by this Section.

Conditions of approval of member corporation

(b) The Board of Governors shall not approve a corporation as a member corporation unless:

(1) every director of such corporation is a holder of voting stock in the corporation and at least one of such directors is a member of the Exchange, and

(2) every holder of voting stock in such corporation is a member or allied member of the Exchange and is an officer or employee of such corporation who (unless he is in active government service or his health does not permit) actively engages in its business and devotes the major portion of his time thereto, except that such voting stock may be held by the estate of a deceased member or deceased allied member for such period as the Exchange may permit, and

(3) every holder of any other class of stock in such corporation is approved by the Board of Governors or is the estate of a deceased holder who has been so approved, and

(4) a primary purpose of such corporation is the transaction of business as a broker or dealer in securities, and

(5) such corporation complies with such additional requirements as the Board of Governors may from time to time prescribe.

Withdrawal of approval of member corporations

(c) Approval of a member corporation shall be withdrawn if

(1) any director of such corporation is not a holder of voting stock in such corporation; or

(2) any holder of voting stock in such corporation (except the estate of a deceased member or deceased allied member stockholder in such corporation) is not a member or allied member of the Exchange and an officer or employee of such corporation who, (unless he is in active government service or his health does not permit) actively engages in its business and devotes the major portion of his time thereto; or

(3) any non-voting stock in such corporation is held without the approval of the Board of Governors; or

(4) if in the opinion of the Board of Governors such corporation does not transact business as a broker or dealer in securities; or

(5) such corporation violates any of its, or any stockholder in such corporation violates any of his, agreements with the Exchange; or

(6) such corporation fails to comply with all the provisions of the Constitution of the Exchange and the rules and requirements of the Board of Governors and practices of the Exchange as the same may be amended from time to time.

Connection with former member corporation

(d) Without the consent of the Board of Governors no member or allied member shall be an officer, director, employee or stockholder of a corporation which, having been a member corporation, has ceased to be such for any reason.

Approval revocable

(e) The approval of a corporation as a member corporation constitutes only a revocable privilege and confers on the corporation no right or interest of any nature whatsoever to continue as a member corporation.

¶ 1408   General Partners and Holders of Voting Stock
Must Be Members or Allied Members

SEC. 8.   Unless permitted by the Board of Governors, no member or allied member of the Exchange shall have as a general partner in a member firm any person who is not a member or an allied member of the Exchange nor shall any member or allied member be the holder of voting stock in a member corporation unless all the holders of such stock are members or allied members of the Exchange or estates of deceased members or deceased allied members.

¶ 1409   Allied Membership

SEC. 9.   Any person, not a member of the Exchange, shall become an allied member of the Exchange by pledging himself to abide by the Constitution as the same has been or shall be from time to time amended, and by all rules adopted pursuant to the Constitution and by either

(a) becoming a general partner in a member firm, or

(b) becoming a holder of voting stock in a member corporation.

Such pledge to abide by the Constitution and Rules shall be made by written instrument filed with the Exchange in which the signer pledges himself as aforesaid.

¶ 1410   Rights and Privileges

SEC. 10.   Any person becoming an allied member shall have all the rights and privileges and shall be under all the duties and obligations of an allied member of the Exchange in accordance with the Constitution.

¶ 1411   Exclusion from Floor

SEC. 11.   Allied members shall have no right to go upon the Floor of the Exchange except as provided in Article II and in Section 14 of this Article.

¶ 1408   Art. IX

¶ 1412   Use of Facilities of Exchange

Sec. 12. The Exchange shall not be liable for any damages sustained by a member or an allied member or a member firm or a member corporation growing out of the use or enjoyment by such member, allied member, member firm or member corporation of the facilities afforded by the Exchange to members, allied members, member firms and member corporations for the conduct of their business.

¶ 1413   Death of Sole Exchange Member

General partner

Sec. 13. (a) The Board of Governors may, on the application of the surviving partners in a member firm whose only general partner who was a member of the Exchange has died, permit, notwithstanding the death of such member, a continuing partnership consisting of all of such surviving partners and no others (except that the estate of the deceased member may have an interest therein), to have the status of a member firm for such period as the Board of Governors may determine, under such conditions as it may fix. The Board in its discretion may, at any time during such period, withdraw such permission and upon such withdrawal such status shall terminate.

Director

(b) The Board of Governors may, on the application of the surviving holders of voting stock in a member corporation whose only director who was a member of the Exchange has died, permit, notwithstanding the death of such member, such corporation, if all of its voting stock is held by the surviving holders of voting stock of such corporation and no others (except that the estate of the deceased member may be a holder of such voting stock), to have the status of a member corporation for such period as the Board of Governors may determine, under such conditions as it may fix. The Board in its discretion may, at any time during such period, withdraw such permission and upon such withdrawal such status shall terminate.

¶ 1414   Alternates on Floor for Governors or Officers

Sec. 14. The Board of Governors may, by the affirmative vote of two-thirds of the Governors present at a meeting of the Board, extend to a member who is a Governor or who is an officer of one of the affiliated companies of the Exchange, the privilege of designating an alternate who shall have the power to transact in the place and stead of such member the usual business of such member on the Floor of the Exchange, under such conditions and to such extent as the Board may prescribe, but only at such times as such Governor or officer is prevented from transacting his usual business on the Floor by the duties imposed upon him by virtue of his acting as such Governor or officer. If such member is a general partner in a member firm, he may designate as such alternate one of his general partners, or if no general partner is ready and able to act, he and his partners may designate as such alternate a person approved by the Board. If such member is a limited partner in a member firm or if he has no partner, he may designate as such alternate a person approved by the Board. If such member is a holder of voting stock in a member corporation, he may designate as such alternate any other holder of voting stock in such corporation, or if no such other holder is ready and able to act, he and the other holders of such voting stock may designate as such alternate a person approved by the Board. If such member holds only non-voting stock in a member corporation he may designate as such alternate a person approved by the Board. Every contract made on the Floor by any alternate shall have the same force and effect as if it had been made by the member for whom he is acting; and a member for whom an alternate is acting shall be liable to the same discipline and penalties for any act or omission of such alternate as for his own personal act or omission.

Withdrawal of privilege

A majority of the members of the Board present at a meeting of the Board may withdraw such privilege for any cause or without cause.

¶ 1415   Alternates on Floor During National Emergencies

SEC. 15. The Board of Governors may, by the affirmative vote of two-thirds of the Governors present at a meeting of the Board, on the request of a member who, in time of national emergency for this country,

    (a) is on active duty in the armed forces of the United States, or

    (b) is on active duty in the armed forces of any nation or State which is then allied or associated with the United States, or

    (c) is engaged in any public service incident to the national defense,

authorize a general partner of such member or a holder of voting stock in the member corporation in which such member is a holder of voting stock to transact in the place and stead of such member the usual business of such member on the Floor of the Exchange, under such terms and conditions and to such extent as the Board may prescribe. Every contract made on the Floor by any alternate shall have the same force and effect as if it had been made by the member for whom he is acting; and a member for whom an alternate is acting shall be liable to the same discipline and penalties for any act or omission of such alternate as for his own personal act or omission.

Withdrawal of privilege

The Board of Governors may, by the affirmative vote of two-thirds of the Governors present at a meeting of the Board, withdraw such privilege for any cause or without cause.

Determination of existence of national emergency

The Board of Governors shall from time to time determine whether or not a national emergency for this country exists within the contemplation of this Section and whether or not a given activity is within its provisions.

[The next page is 1075.]

ARTICLE X

Dues and Fines—Charge on Net Commissions—Other Charges—Penalty for Non-payment

¶ 1451   Dues

Amount fixed by Board of Governors

SEC. 1. The dues payable by a member of the Exchange, exclusive of fines and of such other charges as may be imposed pursuant to the Constitution and of contributions under Article XVI, shall be fixed by the Board of Governors from time to time and shall not exceed One Thousand Five Hundred Dollars in any calendar year.

When payable

The dues shall be payable in advance on January 1, April 1, July 1, and October 1.

The amount of each installment shall be determined by the Board of Governors at least three days before the date on which the same is payable.

Exemption to members in armed forces

The Board of Governors may, on the request of a member who, in time of national emergency for this country,

> (a) is on active duty in the armed forces of the United States, or
>
> (b) is on active duty in the armed forces of any nation or State which is then allied or associated with the United States,

and who, in the determination of the Board, is not able to avail himself of the privileges provided in either Article IX, Section 15 or Article XV, Sections 11 and 12, exempt such member from the payment of dues, under such terms and conditions and to such extent as the Board may prescribe.

Determination of existence of national emergency

The Board of Governors shall from time to time determine whether or not a national emergency for this country exists within the contemplation of this Section and whether or not a given activity is within its provisions.

Allocation of dues

The dues for each quarter may be divided by the Board into two parts, one of which shall constitute the member's contribution to the current expenses of the Exchange for the quarter, as estimated by the Board, and the other of which shall constitute the member's contribution for the quarter towards the capital investment of the Exchange, which shall include advances to its subsidiaries to cover capital expenditures.

Amendment.
January 4, 1962, effective April 1, 1963.

¶ 1452   Charges

On net commissions

SEC. 2. The Board of Governors may, from time to time, fix and impose a charge upon members, member firms and member corporations, measured by their respective net commissions on transactions effected on the floor of the Exchange. Except as permitted by Sections 8 and 9 of this Article, the amount of such charge with respect to any transaction shall not, in any case, exceed one per cent of the difference between the gross commission charged by the member, member firm or member corporation on account of such transaction and the commissions payable by such member, firm or corporation to other members, member firms or member corporations on account of such transaction. Such charge shall be payable at such times and shall be collected in such manner as may be determined by the Board.

On odd lot purchase or sale

The Board of Governors may, from time to time, fix and impose a charge upon members, member firms and member corporations measured by their respective odd lot purchase and sales transactions as odd lot dealers on the floor of the Exchange. Except as permitted by Sections 8 and 9 of this Article, the amount of such charge shall not exceed ⅛th of one cent per share on any odd lot purchase or sale. Such charge shall be payable at such time and shall be collected in such manner as may be determined by the Board.

Amendments.
March 29, 1956.
July 30, 1964.

¶ 1453   Other Charges or Fees

SEC. 3. In addition to the dues and charges provided for by Sections 1 and 2 of this Article, the Board of Governors may, from time to time, fix and impose other charges or fees to be paid to the Exchange by members, member firms and member corporations for the use of equipment or facilities or for particular services or privileges granted.

¶ 1454   Dues on Transfer of Membership

SEC. 4. When a membership is transferred, the transferee shall pay to the transferor on the date of transfer the unexpired portion of the dues for the current quarter.

Amendment.
January 4, 1962, effective April 1, 1963.

¶ 1455   Penalty for Non-payment

SEC. 5. A member who shall not pay his dues, or a fine, or a contribution under Article XVI, or any other sums due to the Exchange, within forty-five days after the same shall become payable shall be reported by the Treasurer to the Chairman of the Board and, after written notice mailed to him of such arrearages, may be suspended by the Board of Governors until payment is made.

Should payment not be made within one year after payment is due, the membership of the delinquent may be disposed of by the Board, on at least ten days' written notice mailed to him at his address registered with the Exchange.

Amendment.
January 4, 1962, effective April 1, 1963.

¶ 1456   Suspension

Notice to Exchange

SEC. 6. Notice of the suspension of a member under the provisions of this Article shall be given to the Exchange.

Effect of suspension

A member suspended under the provisions of this Article shall be deprived, during the period of his suspension, of all rights and privileges of membership, but he may be proceeded against by the Board for any offense committed by him either before or after his suspension. No such suspension shall operate to bar or affect the payments provided for by Article XVI in the event of the death of the suspended member.

The suspension of a member under the provisions of this Article shall create a vacancy in any office or position held by him.

¶ 1457   Liability for Dues and Contributions
Until Transfer

SEC. 7. Notwithstanding the death or expulsion of a member, his membership until transferred shall continue liable for dues to the Exchange, as from time to time fixed by the Board of Governors, for contributions under the provisions of Article XVI, and for payments under Section 8 of this Article.

Amendments.
January 4, 1962, effective April 1, 1963.
July 30, 1964.

¶ 1458   Special Trust Fund Reimbursements

SEC. 8. In order to enable the Exchange to reimburse the Special Trust Fund referred to in Article XIX for payments made therefrom to provide assistance to customers as contemplated by Section 1 of that Article or to reimburse the Exchange for payments made directly by it to supplement the funds available through the Special Trust Fund, the Board of Governors may fix and impose such charge or charges upon members, member firms and member corporations as the Board deems appropriate notwithstanding any limitation on charges contained elsewhere in this Article; provided, however, that in no event shall the total of all charges imposed pursuant to this Section, plus the total of all contributions made by the Exchange to the Special Trust Fund, exceed $25 million in the aggregate. Any charge imposed under this Section shall remain in force for not longer than the period of time required to reimburse the Special Trust Fund and the Exchange as above provided.

Amendments.
July 30, 1964.
April 1, 1965.

¶ 1459   Recovery of "Haupt Expenditures"

SEC. 9. In addition to the dues and charges provided for by Sections 1, 2 and 3 of this Article, each member, member firm or member corporation shall, subject to the limitations provided below, pay to the Exchange with respect to transactions effected on and after February 1, 1964:

1. one-half of 1% of their respective net commissions on transactions effected on the floor of the Exchange, provided that the minimum payment in this regard for any period shall be

(a) in the case of a member firm or member corporation, at the rate of $750 a year per member general partner of such member firm or per member voting stockholder of such member corporation, and

(b) in the case of a member who is not a partner of a member firm or a stockholder of a member corporation, at the rate of $750 a year, and

(c) in the case of a member who is a limited partner of a member firm or a non-voting stockholder of a member corporation, at the rate of $750 a year, except that such member may claim credit against such minimum for any amount indirectly paid by him by reason of amounts paid under this Section by a member firm or member corporation in which he participates in the profits, and

2. one-sixteenth of one cent per share on their respective odd lot purchase and sale transactions as odd lot dealers on the floor of the Exchange.

Such charges shall be payable only until such time as the total paid or payable under this Section by all members, member firms and member corporations shall be determined by the Board of Governors to be approximately equal to the total Exchange Haupt expenditures as herein defined. The Board of Governors may for any period proportionately reduce the amount of such charges or suspend such charges entirely, in order to limit the charges paid or payable under this Section to the total Exchange Haupt expenditures.

The above charges shall be payable at such time and shall be collected in such manner as may be determined by the Board.

Any amount paid to the Exchange in 1963 by a member, member firm or member corporation with respect to his or its estimated portion of the total Exchange Haupt expenditures shall be credited against the charges payable by such member, member firm or member corporation under this Section, as such charges become due.

To the extent that any amount so paid in 1963 shall be found to exceed the amount which becomes payable by such member, member firm or member corporation under this Section, such excess shall be applied at that time against other charges payable to the Exchange, other than charges of a capital nature.

"Haupt expenditures" for the purposes of this Section shall be deemed to be the total of the amounts (not to exceed $12,000,000) which shall be expended or be payable by the liquidator of Ira Haupt & Co. ("Haupt") from funds made available by the Exchange for the payment or purchase of claims of securities customers of Haupt and for ordinary expenses of liquidation incidental thereto, not including, however, any portion of such funds which may be required to be expended to dispose of office space lease obligations of Haupt, and less such amounts, if any, as may be recovered by the Exchange in the final liquidation of Haupt.

This Section shall be deleted in its entirety from the Constitution on the first day of the month following determination by the Board of Governors that the total paid or payable under this Section by all members, member firms and member corporations approximately equals the Exchange Haupt expenditures.

Adopted January 30, 1964.

ARTICLE XI
Transfer of Membership—Termination of Allied Membership

¶ 1501   Transfer of Membership

SEC. 1. A transfer of membership may be made upon submission of the name of the candidate to the Board of Governors and the approval of the transfer by the affirmative vote of two-thirds of the Governors present at a meeting of the Board. Notice of the proposed transfer shall be posted on the bulletin board for at least ten days prior to transfer, which notice shall specify the date on which the proposed transfer will be considered by the Board of Governors. Consideration of a proposed transfer may be postponed from time to time by the Board. Notice of the date of such postponed consideration shall be posted promptly on the bulletin board.

Amendment.
January 4, 1962, effective April 1, 1963.

¶ 1502   Contracts on the Exchange by Transferors

SEC. 2. A member proposing to transfer his membership shall not after the posting of notice thereof make any contract on the Exchange for settlement on or after the date on which such proposed transfer will be considered by the Board, unless such member is a general partner in a member firm which will continue to be a member firm or is a holder of voting stock in a member corporation which will continue to be a member corporation, notwithstanding the completion of such transfer, in which case such member may make contracts on behalf of any member, member firm or member corporation whose status as such will continue subsequent to the date of the completion of such transfer. If a contract with such member is made after the posting of notice of the proposed transfer for settlement on or after the date on which such proposed transfer will be considered by the Board, it shall not, if such transfer is approved, be the basis of a claim against the proceeds of such transfer under sub-division *Third* of Section 3 of this Article. However, if such member is a general partner in a member firm which will continue to be a member firm or is a holder of voting stock in a member corporation which will continue to be a member corporation, notwithstanding the completion of such transfer, such a contract may be the basis of a claim under said sub-division *Third* of Section 3 against the proceeds of the subsequent transfer of the membership of any general partner in such firm or of any holder of voting stock in such corporation, including the transferee of such membership provided he is or becomes at the time of such transfer a general partner in such member firm or the holder of voting stock in such member corporation.

When contracts mature

All open Exchange Contracts of a transferring member and of his firm or corporation shall mature on the full business day preceding the date on which such proposed transfer will be considered by the Board, unless such firm or corporation will continue to be a member firm or member corporation notwithstanding the completion of such transfer, and if not settled before 2:15 p.m. of such preceding full business day, shall be closed out as in the case of an insolvency, unless the same are assumed or taken over by another member, member firm or member corporation.

Notice of transfer

Notice of a transfer to be made by the Board of Governors pursuant to the provisions of the Constitution shall be posted as in the case of a voluntary transfer and shall have the same effect with respect to open contracts and unmatured debts and obligations of the member or former member as in the case of a voluntary transfer.

Amendment.
January 4, 1962, effective April 1, 1963.

¶ 1503   Priorities in Disposition of Proceeds of
Transfer of Membership

Sec. 3.   Upon any transfer of a membership, whether made by a member
or his legal representatives or by the Board of Governors pursuant to the provisions of the Constitution, the proceeds thereof shall be applied by the
Exchange to the following purposes and in the following order of priority, viz.:

Due to Exchange

First.   The payment of such sums as the Board of Governors shall determine are or may become due to the Exchange from the member whose membership is transferred, from a member firm in which such member is a general
partner or from a member corporation any voting stock of which is held by
such member.

Due to Stock Clearing Corporation

Second. The payment of such sums as the Board of Governors shall determine are or may become due to Stock Clearing Corporation by such member, member firm or member corporation.

Allowed claims of members, member firms and member corporations

Third. The payment of such sums as the Board of Governors shall determine are due by such member, such member firm or such member corporation to other members, member firms or member corporations as a result of losses arising directly from the closing out under the Constitution and rules adopted pursuant thereto of contracts entered into in the ordinary course of business in the market on the Floor of the Exchange for the purchase, sale, borrowing or loaning of securities.

Claims not allowed priority

There shall not be allowed as entitled to priority in payment under this subsection any claim otherwise allowable under the foregoing paragraph, with respect to which the claimant, in the opinion of the Board of Governors, did not take promptly all other proper steps under the Constitution, the rules adopted pursuant thereto and practice of the Exchange to protect his rights and to enforce such claim when due.

Written statement of claim required

No claim asserted under this subsection *Third* shall be considered by the Board of Governors nor shall any member, member firm or member corporation asserting such a claim have any rights thereunder, unless a written statement of such claim shall have been filed with the Secretary of the Exchange prior to the transfer of the membership of the member against whom claim is being made.

Pro rata payment of claims

If the proceeds of the transfer of a membership are insufficient to pay in full all claims allowed under this subsection *Third*, payment shall be made pro rata upon all such allowed claims.

Expenses incurred by Exchange

Fourth. After provision for the payment of sums payable under subsections *First*, *Second* and *Third* hereof, there may, in the discretion of the Board of Governors, be deducted from the remaining proceeds, if any, and paid to the Exchange the amount of any unusual expenses incurred by the Exchange in connection with litigation involving the disposition of such proceeds, including counsel fees and disbursements and the cost of producing records pursuant to a court order or other legal process.

Surplus of proceeds

Fifth. The surplus, if any, of the proceeds of the transfer of a membership, after provision for the payment of sums payable under subsections *First*, *Second*, *Third* and *Fourth* hereof, shall be paid directly to the person whose membership is transferred, or to his legal representatives, upon the execution and delivery to the Exchange by him or them of a release or releases satisfactory to the Board of Governors, unless the Board, in its discretion, determines either (a) that the protection of the creditors of the member firm or member corporation or former member firm or former member corporation in which such member is or was last a general partner or a holder of voting stock requires the use of said surplus or any part thereof, or (b) that such surplus should be paid to such firm or corporation, in view of the fact that such member had expressly agreed, in the case of a partnership, in the partnership articles of such firm or, in the case of a corporation, in a writing filed with the Exchange, that such surplus shall be paid either by him or directly by the Exchange to such member firm or member corporation. In the event the Board makes either of such determinations, such surplus shall be paid to such firm or corporation, upon the execution and delivery to the Exchange by such member or such firm, or both, or by such member or such corporation, or both, of a release or releases satisfactory to the Board of Governors.

Prompt steps to protect rights required

No payment of such surplus under the provisions of this subsection *Fifth* shall be made to a member firm or to a member corporation or former member firm or former member corporation in which such member is or had previously been a general partner or a holder of voting stock, if such firm or corporation, in the opinion of the Board of Governors, did not take promptly all proper steps to protect and enforce its rights, or if the Board of Governors, in its sole discretion, shall determine that an unreasonable time has elapsed between the date when he ceased to be such a partner in such firm or the holder of voting stock in such corporation and the date of the transfer.

Agreements

Except as otherwise specifically provided for by the Constitution, no recognition or effect shall be given by the Exchange to any agreement or to any instrument entered into or executed by a member or his legal representatives which purports to transfer or assign such member's interest in his membership, or in the proceeds or any part thereof, or which purports to create any lien or other right with respect thereto, or which purports in any manner to provide for the disposition of such proceeds to a creditor of such member; nor shall payment of such proceeds be made by the Exchange to any agent or attorney-in-fact of a member except as may be permitted by the Rules of the Board of Governors in those cases in which (a) such agent or attorney-in-fact is acting solely for and on behalf of such member and is neither directly nor indirectly acting in his own behalf or in behalf of any third person or (b) is a general partner of such member or a holder of voting stock in a member corporation in which such member is the holder of voting stock.

Retention of proceeds

If the amount of any sum payable under the provisions of this Section 3 cannot for any reason be immediately ascertained and determined, the Board of Governors may, out of the proceeds of the membership, reserve and retain such amount as it may deem appropriate, pending determination of the amount so payable.

Amendment.
January 4, 1962, effective April 1, 1963.

¶ 1504   Membership of Deceased Member

SEC. 4. When a member dies, his membership may be disposed of by the Board of Governors.

¶ 1504   **Art. XI**

¶ 1505   Death of Sole Exchange Member

General partner

SEC. 5. (a) If, upon the death of a member who, at the time of his death, was a general partner in a member firm in which no other general partner is a member of the Exchange, the following conditions exist:

(1) the partnership articles of such firm provide for the continuance of the firm as a partnership of the surviving partners and no others (except that the estate of the deceased member may have an interest therein), and

(2) the deceased member shall have agreed in the partnership articles of such member firm that such continuing firm, if permitted by the Board of Governors to have the status of a member firm, shall be entitled to have the use of his membership from the date of his death until the termination of such status of such continuing firm or until a member of the Exchange be admitted to such firm as a general partner, and that, in so far as may be necessary for the protection of creditors of the continuing firm, and subject to the Constitution and Rules of the Exchange, the proceeds of his membership shall be an asset of the continuing partnership during such period, and

(3) such continuing partnership shall be permitted by the Board of Governors to have the status of a member firm,

then upon the transfer of the membership of such deceased member the proceeds thereof shall be applied to the same purposes and in the same order of priority as if such member had continued to be a member of the Exchange and a general partner in such continuing firm until the date of the termination of such status, or until a member of the Exchange is admitted to such firm as a general partner, whichever event occurs first.

Director

(b) If, upon the death of a member who, at the time of his death, was a director of a member corporation in which no other director is a member of the Exchange, the following conditions exist:

(1) the member corporation continues in business and all of its voting stock is held by the persons who held such stock prior to the death of such member and no others (except that the estate of the deceased member may be a holder of such voting stock), and

(2) the deceased member shall have agreed in a writing filed with the Exchange that such member corporation, if permitted by the Board of Governors to have the status of a member corporation, shall be entitled to have the use of his membership from the date of his death until the termination of such status of such corporation or until a member of the Exchange becomes a director of and a holder of voting stock in such corporation; and that, in so far as may be necessary for the protection of creditors of the corporation, and subject to the Constitution and Rules of the Exchange, the proceeds of his membership shall be an asset of the corporation during such period, and

(3) such corporation shall be permitted by the Board of Governors to have the status of a member corporation,

then upon the transfer of the membership of such deceased member the proceeds thereof shall be applied to the same purposes and in the same order of priority as if such member had continued to be a member of the Exchange and a director of and a holder of voting stock in such corporation until the date of the termination of such status, or until a member of the Exchange becomes a director of and a holder of voting stock in such corporation, whichever event occurs first.

¶ 1506   Membership of Expelled Member

SEC. 6. When a member is expelled or becomes ineligible for reinstatement, his membership may be disposed of by the Board of Governors.

Amendment.
January 4, 1962, effective April 1, 1963.

¶ 1507   Claims Against Deceased, Suspended or Expelled Member

SEC. 7. The death, expulsion or suspension of a member shall not affect the rights of creditors under the provisions of Section 3 of this Article.

¶ 1508   Claims by Former Members or Deceased Members

SEC. 8. The death, expulsion or suspension of a member or the transfer of his membership, or the suspension, retirement or dissolution of a member firm or member corporation shall not affect the rights of such member or his estate or of such member firm or member corporation under the provisions of Section 3 of this Article.

¶ 1509   Allied Membership Non-transferable

SEC. 9. An allied membership shall not be transferable.

¶ 1510   Death or Expulsion of Allied Member

SEC. 10. When an allied member dies or is expelled, his allied membership shall terminate.

¶ 1511   Election of Allied Member as President of Exchange

SEC. 11. When an allied member is elected President of the Exchange or is elected to membership in the Exchange, his allied membership shall terminate.

¶ 1512   Cessation of Status as General Partner or Holder of Voting Stock

SEC. 12. When an allied member (a) ceases to be a general partner in a member firm and does not forthwith become a general partner in another member firm or a holder of voting stock in a member corporation continuing the business of the first firm, or (b) ceases to be a holder of voting stock in a member corporation and does not forthwith become a holder of such stock in another member corporation or a general partner in a member firm continuing the business of the first corporation, his allied membership shall terminate.

¶ 1513   Non-payment of Fines by Allied Member

SEC. 13. When the Treasurer shall report to the Chairman of the Board that an allied member has neglected to pay a fine for forty-five days after the same became payable, the allied membership of such allied member shall terminate, unless the Board of Governors shall have granted an extension of time to pay such fine.

ARTICLE XII
Exchange Contracts

¶ 1551   Definition

SEC. 1. All contracts of a member of the Exchange or of a member firm or a member corporation with any member of the Exchange or with any member firm or any member corporation for the purchase, sale, borrowing, loaning or hypothecation of securities, or for the borrowing, loaning or payment of money, whether occurring on the Floor of the Exchange or elsewhere, shall be Exchange Contracts, unless made subject to the rules of another Exchange, or unless the parties thereto have expressly agreed that the same shall not be Exchange Contracts.

¶ 1552   Constitution and Rules Deemed Part of
                          Exchange Contracts

SEC. 2. The provisions of the Constitution of the Exchange and of the rules adopted pursuant thereto shall be a part of the terms and conditions of all Exchange Contracts and the By-Laws and the Rules of Stock Clearing Corporation approved by the Board of Governors shall be a part of the terms and conditions of every contract which is to be cleared or settled through Stock Clearing Corporation, and all such contracts shall be subject to the exercise by the Board of Governors and Stock Clearing Corporation of the powers with respect thereto vested in them by the Constitution and rules adopted pursuant thereto and by the By-Laws and the Rules of Stock Clearing Corporation, respectively.

¶ 1553   Deliveries Through Stock Clearing Corporation

SEC. 3. On every Exchange Contract delivery and payment shall be made through Stock Clearing Corporation as required by the By-Laws and Rules of Stock Clearing Corporation unless it is otherwise stipulated in the bid or offer, or it is otherwise mutually agreed by the parties to the contract, or Stock Clearing Corporation either in the particular instance or in pursuance of its By-Laws and Rules refuses to act in the matter.

Contracts of non-clearing members

A party to any such contract who is not a Clearing Member as defined in the By-Laws of Stock Clearing Corporation shall cause the transaction to be cleared or settled for him by a Clearing Member.

ARTICLE XIII

Insolvent Members—Suspension—Reinstatement

¶ 1601   Notice from Member—Suspension

SEC. 1.   A member who fails to perform his contracts, or is insolvent, shall immediately inform the Secretary of the Exchange in writing that he is unable to meet his engagements and prompt notice thereof shall be given to the Exchange. Such member shall thereby become suspended from membership until after having settled with his creditors he has been reinstated by the Board of Governors.

Suspension for insolvency on declaration

A member or allied member who is a partner in a member firm or a stockholder in a member corporation, which firm or corporation fails to perform its contracts, or is insolvent, shall immediately inform the Secretary of the Exchange in writing that his firm or corporation is unable to meet its engagements and prompt notice thereof shall be given to the Exchange. Such member firm or member corporation shall thereby become suspended as a member firm or as a member corporation and every member or allied member who is a general partner or holder of voting stock therein shall thereby become suspended from membership or allied membership, until after settlement has been made with his creditors and the creditors of such firm or corporation, the members have been reinstated and the suspensions of the allied members and the firm or corporation have been terminated by the Board of Governors.

¶ 1602   Notice from Exchange—Suspension

SEC. 2.   Whenever it shall appear to the Chairman of the Board that a member has failed to meet his engagements, or is insolvent, or the Chairman of the Board has been advised by the Board of Governors or by the Board of Directors of Stock Clearing Corporation that such member is in such financial condition that he cannot be permitted to continue in business with safety to his creditors or the Exchange, prompt notice thereof shall be given to the Exchange. Such member shall thereby become suspended from membership until after having settled with his creditors he has been reinstated by the Board of Governors.

Suspension by Exchange for insolvency

Whenever it shall appear to the Chairman of the Board that a member firm or member corporation has failed to meet its engagements, or is insolvent, or the Chairman of the Board has been advised by the Board of Governors or by the Board of Directors of Stock Clearing Corporation that such member firm or member corporation is in such financial condition that it cannot be permitted to continue in business with safety to its creditors or the Exchange, prompt notice thereof shall be given to the Exchange. Such member firm or member corporation shall thereby become suspended as a member firm or as a member corporation and every member or allied member who is a general partner or holder of voting stock therein shall thereby become suspended from membership or allied membership, until after settlement has been made with his creditors and the creditors of such firm or corporation, the members have been reinstated and the suspensions of the allied members and the firm or corporation have been terminated by the Board of Governors.

¶ 1603 Investigation of Insolvency

SEC. 3. Every member, allied member, member firm and member corporation suspended under the provisions of this Article shall immediately afford every facility required by the Board of Governors or a committee authorized thereby for the investigation of his or its affairs, and shall after notice to the Exchange of his or its suspension file with the Secretary of the Exchange a written statement covering all information requested, including a complete list of his or its creditors and the amount owing to each.

¶ 1604 Time Limit for Reinstatement

SEC. 4. If a member suspended under the provisions of this Article fails to settle with his creditors and the creditors of his member firm or of the member corporation in which he held or holds voting stock and apply for reinstatement within one year from the time of his suspension, or within such further time as the Board of Governors may grant, or fails to obtain reinstatement as hereinafter provided, his membership shall be disposed of by the Board of Governors.

Extension of time

The Board of Governors may, by the affirmative vote of a majority of the Governors then in office, extend the time of settlement for periods not exceeding one year each.

¶ 1605 Reinstatement of Insolvent Member—Vote Required

SEC. 5. When a member suspended under the provisions of this Article applies for reinstatement, notice thereof shall be given by the Secretary of the Exchange to the members by notifying each member of such application directly and through the weekly bulletin, and by posting notice upon the bulletin board at least one week prior to the consideration by the Board of Governors of said application. The applicant shall furnish to the Board a list of his creditors and, if he was a partner in a suspended member firm, a list of the creditors of such firm, and if he was a holder of voting stock in a suspended member corporation, a list of the creditors of such corporation, a statement of the amounts originally owing and the nature of the settlement in each case. If he furnishes satisfactory proof of settlement with all such creditors, the Board shall proceed to ballot upon his application. The affirmative vote of two-thirds of the Governors present at a meeting of the Board shall be required for his reinstatement, except that the affirmative vote of two-thirds of the Governors then in office shall be required for the reinstatement of a member suspended under Section 2 of this Article. Failing to receive the required vote, the applicant shall be entitled to be balloted upon at two subsequent regular meetings of the Board to be designated by him, provided however, that the three ballotings to which the applicant shall be entitled shall be within one year from the date of his suspension, or within such further extended time for settlement as may have been granted by the Board of Governors.

Termination of suspension by Board

The suspension under the provisions of this Article of an allied member, a member firm or a member corporation may be terminated at any time after settlement has been made with the creditors of such allied member and of his member firm or member corporation by the vote of two-thirds of the Governors present at a meeting of the Board of Governors except the affirmative vote of two-thirds of the Governors then in office shall be required to terminate such a suspension under Section 2 of this Article.

¶ 1606   Irregularities or Unbusinesslike Dealings

SEC. 6. Whenever the Board of Governors shall determine that a member suspended under the provisions of this Article has been guilty of irregularities or unbusinesslike dealing, such member may, by the affirmative vote of two-thirds of the Governors then in office, be declared ineligible for reinstatement.

¶ 1607   Disciplinary Measures During Suspension
for Insolvency

SEC. 7. A member or allied member of the Exchange suspended under the provisions of this Article may be proceeded against by the Board of Governors for any offense committed by him either before or after notice to the Exchange of his suspension in all respects as if he were not under suspension.

¶ 1608   Rights of Member Suspended for Insolvency

SEC. 8. A member suspended under the provisions of this Article shall be deprived during the term of his suspension of all rights and privileges of membership, except the right, if he has not been declared ineligible for reinstatement or has not also been suspended under the provisions of Article XIV, to have his business transacted at members' rates. His suspension shall create a vacancy in any office or position held by him. No such suspension shall operate to bar or affect the payments provided for by Article XVI in the event of the death of the suspended member. The suspension of an allied member under the provisions of this Article shall create a vacancy in any office or position held by him.

ARTICLE XIV

Expulsion and Suspension from Membership or from
Allied Membership—Disciplinary Proceedings

¶ 1651   Fraudulent Acts of Member
or Allied Member

SEC. 1. A member or allied member who shall be adjudged guilty, by the affirmative vote of a majority of the Governors then in office, of fraud or of fraudulent acts shall be expelled.

¶ 1652   Fraudulent Acts Prior to Admission to Membership
or Allied Membership

SEC. 2. Whenever the Board of Governors, by the affirmative vote of a majority of the Governors then in office, shall adjudge that a member prior to his application for membership, or an allied member prior to the approval

¶ 1606   **Art. XIV**

of him as a partner in a member firm or as a stockholder in a member corporation, had been guilty of a fraudulent or dishonest act and that the facts and circumstances thereof were not disclosed to the Exchange on his application for membership, or on the application for approval, as the case may be, such member or allied member shall be expelled.

¶ 1653   Fictitious Transactions—No Change in Ownership

SEC. 3. A member or allied member who shall be adjudged guilty, by the affirmative vote of a majority of the Governors then in office, of making a fictitious transaction or of giving an order for the purchase or sale of securities the execution of which would involve no change of ownership or of executing such an order with knowledge of its character may be suspended or expelled as the Board of Governors may determine.

¶ 1654   Demoralization of Market

SEC. 4. A member or allied member who shall be adjudged guilty, by the affirmative vote of a majority of the Governors then in office, of making any purchases or sales or offers of purchase or sale of securities for the purpose of upsetting the equilibrium of the market and bringing about a condition of demoralization in which prices will not fairly reflect market values, or of assisting in making any such purchases or sales or offers of purchase or sale with knowledge of such purpose, or of being, with such knowledge, a party to or of assisting in carrying out any plan or scheme for the making of such purchases or sales or offers of purchase or sale may be suspended or expelled as the Board of Governors may determine.

¶ 1655   Misstatements

SEC. 5. A member or allied member who shall be adjudged guilty, by the affirmative vote of a majority of the Governors then in office, of making a misstatement upon a material point to the Board of Governors or to a committee authorized thereby or to the Board of Directors of Stock Clearing Corporation or of making on his application for membership, or on the application for approval of him as a partner in a member firm or as a stockholder in a member corporation, a material misstatement to the Exchange may be suspended or expelled as the Board may determine.

¶ 1656   Violation of Constitution, Rules or Resolutions —Inequitable Conduct

SEC. 6. A member or allied member who shall be adjudged guilty, by the affirmative vote of a majority of the Governors then in office, of a violation of the Constitution of the Exchange or of a violation of a rule adopted pursuant to the Constitution or of a violation of a resolution of the Board of Governors regulating the conduct or business of members or allied members or of conduct or proceeding inconsistent with just and equitable principles of trade may be suspended or expelled as the Board may determine.

¶ 1657   Violation of Securities Exchange Act of 1934

SEC. 7. A member or allied member who shall be adjudged guilty, by the affirmative vote of a majority of the Governors then in office, of a wilful violation of any provisions of the Securities Exchange Act of 1934 or any rule or regulation thereunder shall be deemed to be guilty of conduct or proceeding inconsistent with just and equitable principles of trade and may be suspended or expelled as the Board of Governors may determine.

¶ 1658   Dealings Outside Exchange in Listed Securities

SEC. 8. Whenever the Board of Governors, by the affirmative vote of a majority of the Governors then in office, shall determine that a member or allied member is connected, either through a partner or otherwise, with another exchange or similar organization in the City of New York which permits dealings in any securities dealt in on the Exchange, or deals directly or indirectly upon such other exchange or organization, or deals publicly outside the Exchange in securities dealt in on the Exchange, such member or allied member may be suspended or expelled as the Board may determine; provided, however, that nothing herein contained shall be construed to prohibit any member, allied member, member firm or member corporation from, or to penalize any such firm or corporation for, acting as an odd-lot dealer or specialist or otherwise publicly dealing for his or its own account (directly or indirectly through a joint account or other arrangement) on another exchange located outside the City of New York (of which such member, allied member, member firm or member corporation is a member) in securities listed or traded on such other exchange.

¶ 1659   Failure to Testify or Produce Records

SEC. 9. Whenever the Board of Governors, by the affirmative vote of a majority of the Governors then in office, shall determine that a member or allied member has been required by the Board or any committee authorized thereby to submit his books and papers or the books and papers of his firm or of any partner or employee thereof or the books and papers of the member corporation in which he is a stockholder, or of any stockholder therein or officer, director or employee thereof to the Board or any such committee or to furnish information to or to appear and testify before or to cause any of his partners or employees or any stockholder in or any officer, director or employee of such member corporation to appear and testify before the Board or any such committee and has refused or failed to comply with such requirement, such member or allied member may be suspended or expelled as the Board may determine.

¶ 1660   Acts Detrimental to Welfare of Exchange

SEC. 10. A member or allied member who shall be adjudged guilty, by the affirmative vote of a majority of the Governors then in office, of any act which may be determined by the Board of Governors to be detrimental to the interest or welfare of the Exchange may be suspended for a period not exceeding five years.

¶ 1661   Failure to Testify or Produce Records
Before Other Exchanges

SEC. 11. If the Board of Governors, by the affirmative vote of a majority of the Governors then in office, shall determine that the interest and welfare of the Exchange or of the public will be served by facilitating the examination by the authorities of another exchange of any transaction in which a member or allied member of the Exchange has been concerned and that the testimony of such member or allied member, his partners or employees, or the stockholders in or the officers, directors or employees of the member corporation in which he is a stockholder or his books and papers or the books and papers of his firm or any partner therein or the books and papers of such member corporation or of any stockholder therein are material to such examination and shall direct such member or allied member to appear and testify or to cause any of such persons to appear and testify or to produce such books and papers before the authorities of such other exchange, and such member or allied member shall refuse or fail to comply with such direction, he may be suspended for a period not exceeding five years.

¶ 1662   Vote Necessary to Suspend or Expel

SEC. 12. Except as otherwise specifically provided in Sections 1 and 2 of this Article, the penalty of suspension may be inflicted and the period of suspension determined by the affirmative vote of a majority of the Governors then in office and the penalty of expulsion may be inflicted by the affirmative vote of two-thirds of the Governors then in office.

¶ 1663   Fine, Censure or Remission of Penalty

SEC. 13. In any case in which the Board of Governors may impose the penalty of suspension or expulsion, or the penalty of suspension for a period not exceeding five years, the Board, by the affirmative vote of a majority of the Governors then in office, may in lieu of such penalty impose a fine of not exceeding $10,000 or may direct that the guilty member or allied member be censured by the Chairman of the Board or may remit or reduce any such penalty on such terms and conditions as the Board shall deem fair and equitable.

Amendment.
December 3, 1964, effective January 1, 1965.

¶ 1664   Procedure, Trial and Penalty

SEC. 14. An accusation, charging a member or an allied member before the Board of Governors with having committed an offense, shall be in writing; it shall specify the charge or charges against such member or allied member with reasonable detail, and shall be signed by the person or persons making the charge or charges. A copy of such charge or charges shall be served upon the accused member or allied member either personally, or by leaving the same at his office address during business hours, or by mailing it to him at his place of residence. He shall have ten days from the date of such service to answer the same, or such further time as the Board may deem proper. The answer shall be in writing, signed by the accused member or allied member, and filed with the Secretary of the Exchange. Upon the answer being filed, or if the accused shall refuse or neglect to make answer as hereinbefore required, the Board shall, at a regular or special meeting thereafter, proceed to consider the charge or charges; if such meeting be a special meeting, notice of the object thereof shall be sent to all Governors. Notice of such meeting shall be sent to the accused; he shall be entitled to be personally present thereat, and shall be permitted in person to examine and cross-examine all the witnesses produced before the Board and also to present such testimony, defense or explanation as he may deem proper. After hearing all the witnesses and the accused, if he desires to be heard, the Board shall determine whether the accused is guilty of the offense or offenses charged. If it determines that the accused is guilty, the Board may fix and impose the penalty and a written notice of the result shall be served upon said member or allied member in the manner hereinbefore provided. The findings of the Board shall be final and conclusive.

¶ 1665 Summary Proceedings

SEC. 15. If the Board of Governors shall determine that the maximum penalty to be inflicted upon a member or allied member shall be limited to suspension for a period not exceeding sixty days, or to a fine not exceeding $2,000 for each violation of any provision of the Constitution or of any rule adopted by the Board of Governors or for conduct contrary to an established practice of the Exchange, the Board may proceed summarily and the method of procedure required by Section 14 of this Article shall not apply. In such cases the accused shall be summoned before the Board, informed of the nature of the accusation against him and afforded an opportunity for explanation by personal or other testimony. In any such proceeding the Board, by the affirmative vote of a majority of the Governors then in office, may determine the guilt and fix the fine or period of suspension to be imposed as a penalty.

Delegation of power

In accordance with the provisions of Section 1 of Article III, the Board of Governors may delegate to a committee authorized by the Board the power to impose penalties not exceeding a fine of $1,000 for each violation of any provision of the Constitution or of any rule adopted by the Board of Governors or for conduct contrary to an established practice of the Exchange. In any proceeding before such a committee, the method of procedure required by Section 14 of this Article shall not apply.

Maximum fine

The total fine imposed upon any member, allied member, member firm or member corporation in any one proceeding under the provisions of this Section shall not exceed $10,000.

Amendment.
December 3, 1964, effective January 1, 1965.

¶ 1666 Responsibility of Member or Allied Member for Acts of Firm or Corporation

SEC. 16. A member or allied member of the Exchange who is a general partner in a member firm or a stockholder in, or an officer or director of a member corporation is liable to the same discipline and penalties for any act or omission of such firm or corporation as for his own personal act or omission. The Board of Governors, by the affirmative vote of a majority of the Governors then in office, may relieve him from the penalty therefor or may remit or reduce such penalty on such terms and conditions as the Board shall deem fair and equitable.

¶ 1667 Disapproval of Business Connections

SEC. 17. Whenever it shall appear to the Board of Governors that a member or allied member is a partner in a partnership, a stockholder, officer or director in or employee of a corporation, or has an office or headquarters, or is individually or through any member of his member firm or through any stockholder in his member corporation interested in a partnership, corporation or business, or has any business connection whereby the interest or good repute of the Exchange may suffer, the Board may require the member or allied member to dissolve any such partnership or to sever all connection therewith (whether or not such partnership is a member firm) or require the member or allied member to sever all connection with the corporation (whether or not it is a member corporation) and cease to be a stockholder, officer or director therein or employee thereof or may require the discontinuance of such business, office or headquarters or business connection, as the case may be.

¶ 1668   Notice of Penalties

SEC. 18. Notice shall be given to the Exchange of the suspension or expulsion of a member or an allied member under the provisions of this Article. Similar notice of any other penalty imposed under this Article shall be given to the Exchange when so directed by the affirmative vote of a majority of the Governors then in office.

¶ 1669   Effect of Suspension or Expulsion of Members

SEC. 19. When a member is suspended by the Board of Governors under the provisions of this Article, such member shall be deprived during the term of his suspension of all rights and privileges of membership, but he may be proceeded against by the Board for any offense other than that for which he was suspended. No such suspension shall operate to bar or affect the payments provided for by Article XVI in the event of the death of the suspended member.

Termination of rights and privileges

The expulsion of a member shall terminate all rights and privileges arising out of his membership except such rights as he may have under the provisions of Sections 3 and 8 of Article XI.

Vacancy created

The suspension or expulsion of a member under the provisions of this Article shall create a vacancy in any office or position held by him.

¶ 1670   Effect of Suspension or Expulsion of Allied Members

SEC. 20. When an allied member is suspended by the Board of Governors, under the provisions of this Article, he may be proceeded against by the Board for any offense other than that for which he was suspended.

Vacancy created

The suspension or expulsion of an allied member under the provisions of this Article shall create a vacancy in any office or position held by him.

¶ 1671   Professional Counsel Excluded

SEC. 21. No person shall have the right to be represented by professional counsel in any investigation or hearing before the Board of Governors or any committee authorized thereby.

ARTICLE XV

Commissions and Service Charges

¶ 1701   Obligation To Charge or Collect Commissions

Sec. 1.   Commissions shall be charged and collected upon the execution of all orders for the purchase or sale for the account of members or allied members or of parties not members or allied members of the Exchange, of securities admitted to dealings upon the Exchange and these commissions shall be at rates not less than the rates in this Article prescribed; and shall be net and free from any rebate, return, discount or allowance made in any shape or manner, or by any method or arrangement direct or indirect. No bonus or percentage or portion of a commission, whether such commission be at or above the rates herein established, or any portion of a profit except as may be specifically permitted by the Constitution or a rule adopted by the Board of Governors, shall be given, paid or allowed, directly or indirectly, or as a salary or portion of a salary, to a clerk or person for business sought or procured for any member or allied member of the Exchange or member firm or member corporation.

Commissions on other exchanges

Notwithstanding the provisions of this Article, any member of the Exchange or member firm or member corporation holding a membership or associate membership in another exchange located in the United States, or holding a membership or associate membership in a Canadian exchange, or registered with a Canadian exchange as being entitled to a return of commission from members of said exchange, may in respect of transactions made on such other exchange charge the rates of commission prescribed by such other exchange.

¶ 1702   Commissions on Stocks, Rights and Warrants

Sec. 2. STOCKS, RIGHTS AND WARRANTS (hereinafter referred to as "stocks")

To non-members and to allied members

(a) On business for non-members and allied members, including joint account transactions in which any such person is interested:

(1) On stocks selling at $1.00 per share and above commissions shall be based upon the amount of money involved in a single transaction and shall be not less than the rates hereinafter specified:

(i) Subject to the provisions of paragraphs 2(a)(1)(iii), 2(d), and 2(f), on each single transaction not exceeding 100 shares, in a unit of trading; a combination of units of trading; or a combination of a unit or units of trading plus an odd lot.

Commission
2% on first $400 of money involved plus
1% on next $2,000 of money involved plus
½% on next $2,600 of money involved plus
1/10% on money involved above $5,000
plus $3.00

(ii) On odd lots (less than a unit of trading) same rates as paragraph (1) above, less $2.00, subject to the provisions of paragraphs 2(a)(1)(iii), 2(d), and 2(f).

(iii) Notwithstanding the foregoing:

(a) when the amount involved in a transaction is less than $100, the minimum commission shall be as mutually agreed;

(b) when the amount involved in a transaction is $100 or more, the minimum commission charge shall not exceed $1.50 per share or $75 per single transaction, but in any event shall not be less than $6 per single transaction.

(2) On stocks selling below $1.00 per share commissions shall be on a per share basis and shall be not less than the following:

Price per Share	Rate per Share
	cents
1/256 of $1	0.1
1/128 of $1	0.15
1/64 of $1 and above but under 2/32 of $1	0.5
2/32 of $1	0.5
Over 2/32 of $1 but under 8/32 of $1	1.0
8/32 of $1 and above but under 1/2 of $1	2.0
1/2 of $1 but under 5/8 of $1	3.0
5/8 of $1 but under 3/4 of $1	3.75
3/4 of $1 but under 7/8 of $1	4.5
7/8 of $1 but under $1	5.25

Notwithstanding the foregoing, when the amount involved in a transaction is less than $100, the commission shall be as mutually agreed; when the amount involved is $100 or more, the minimum commission shall be not less than $6 or the rate per share, whichever is greater.

To members on clearance

(b) On business for members of the Exchange when a principal is not given up, commissions shall be based on a rate per share as follows:

(1) On stocks selling at $1.00 per share and above, the commission rate per share shall be not less than the following:

Price per Share	Rate per Share
	cents
$ 1 and above but under $ 2	2.0
$ 2 and above but under $ 5	2.25
$ 5 and above but under $ 10	3.5
$ 10 and above but under $ 20	6.2
$ 20 and above but under $ 40	7.3
$ 40 and above but under $100	7.7
$100 and above but under $150	8.7
$150 and above but under $200	9.0
$200 and above	10.0

(2) On stocks selling below $1.00 per share, the commission rate per share shall be not less than the following:

Price per Share	Rate per Share
	cents
1/256 of $1	0.05
1/128 of $1	0.1
1/64 of $1 and above but under 2/32 of $1	0.2
2/32 of $1	0.375
Over 2/32 of $1 but under 8/32 of $1	0.5
8/32 of $1 and above but under ½ of $1	0.75
1/2 of $1 and above but under $1	0.8

(3) Notwithstanding the foregoing, when the amount involved in a transaction is less than $10, the commission shall be as mutually agreed.

To members on "give-up"

(c) On business for members of the Exchange when a principal is given up, commissions shall be based on a rate per share as follows:

(1) On stocks selling at $1.00 per share and above, the commission rate per share shall be not less than the following:

Price per Share	Rate per Share
	cents
$ 1 and above but under $ 2	1.25
$ 2 and above but under $ 5	1.40
$ 5 and above but under $ 10	2.10
$ 10 and above but under $ 20	3.10
$ 20 and above but under $ 40	3.65
$ 40 and above but under $100	3.85
$100 and above but under $150	4.35
$150 and above but under $200	4.50
$200 and above	5.00

(2) On stocks selling below $1.00 per share, the commission rate per share shall be not less than the following:

Price per Share	Rate per Share
	cents
1/256 of $1	0.05
1/128 of $1	0.1
1/64 of $1 and above but under 2/32 of $1	0.1
2/32 of $1	0.25
Over 2/32 of $1 but under 8/32 of $1	0.25
8/32 of $1 and above but under ½ of $1	0.5
1/2 of $1 and above but under $1	0.5

(3) Notwithstanding the foregoing, when the amount involved in a transaction is less than $10, the commission shall be as mutually agreed.

Odd lots

(4) Notwithstanding the provisions of sub-sections (1), (2) and (3) of this paragraph (c), the commission rates in stocks, when the amount

¶ 1702   **Art. XV**   © 1959, Commerce Clearing House, Inc.

dealt in is less than the unit of trading, shall be not less than 1¢ per share on stocks selling below $10 per share, and 2¢ per share on stocks selling at $10 per share or more.

Definition of single transaction

(d) For the purpose of this Section 2

(1) In respect of stocks selling at $1.00 per share and above, a single transaction shall be deemed to include all purchases or sales for one account, of a single security, pursuant to a single order

(i) amounting to 100 shares of a security in which the unit of trading is 100 shares

(ii) amounting to less than the unit of trading

(iii) amounting to 100 shares or less in one transaction or a series of transactions, pursuant to a single order entered at a single price or at the market, of a security in which the unit of trading is less than 100 shares. If such series of transactions includes an execution in an amount of less than the unit of trading and the order was at a price not more than the usual odd lot differential away from the limit on the full lot order, such odd lot transaction may be deemed to be a part of the single transaction;

(2) in respect of stocks selling at less than $1.00 per share, a single transaction shall be deemed to include all purchases or sales for one account, of a single security, pursuant to a single order, irrespective of the size of the order.

Determining amount involved in transaction

(e) In determining the amount involved in a transaction, commissions and taxes shall be disregarded.

Special rates

(f) Notwithstanding the rates prescribed elsewhere in this Section 2, the commission rates to members, allied members and non-members upon stocks which, pursuant to call or otherwise, are to be redeemed within twelve months shall be such rates as may be mutually agreed upon, provided, however, that such rates shall apply to transactions in any specific stock only after announcement to that effect has been made by the Exchange, and provided, further, that the Board of Governors may determine special rates on any or all such securities.

Amendments.
March 5, 1959—effective March 30, 1959.
April 3, 1958—effective May 1, 1958.
October 29, 1953—effective November 9, 1953.

(See Rule 380 [¶ 2380] Special Commission Rates—Rights and Warrants Selling Below 50¢.)

¶ 1703   Commission on Bonds

SEC. 3. BONDS.

To non-members and to allied members

(a) On business for non-members and allied members, including joint account transactions in which any such person is interested, the commission rates shall be not less than the following:

Price per $1,000 of Principal	Rate per $1,000 of Principal
Selling at less than $10.................	$ .75
Selling at $10 and above but under $100..	1.25
Selling at $100 and above...............	2.50

To members on clearance

(b) On business for members of the Exchange when a principal is not given up, the commission rates shall be not less than the following:

Price per $1,000 of Principal	Rate per $1,000 of Principal
Selling at less than $10.................	$ .50
Selling at $10 and above but under $100..	.62½
Selling at $100 and above...............	1.25

To members on "give-up"

(c) On business for members of the Exchange when a principal is given up, the commission rates shall be not less than the following:

Price per $1,000 of Principal	Rate per $1,000 of Principal
Selling at less than $10.................	$ .25
Selling at $10 and above but under $100..	.37½
Selling at $100 and above...............	.75

Special rates

(d) Notwithstanding the foregoing, the commission rates to members, allied members or non-members upon obligations of the United States, Puerto Rico, Philippine Islands and States, Territories and Municipalities therein; upon obligations of any international authorities in which the United States is a participant; upon bonds or notes having five years or less to run; and upon bonds or notes which, pursuant to call or otherwise, are to be redeemed within twelve months, shall be subject to rates as may be mutually agreed upon; provided, however, that the Board of Governors may determine special rates on any or all such securities.

Amendment.
March 29, 1956.
March 7, 1963.

¶ 1704   Clearing Charges

SEC. 4. When a member or member firm or member corporation having made or caused to be made a contract for his or its own account on the Floor of the Exchange for the purchase or sale of stock arranges to have such contract cleared by another member or member firm or member corporation, such clearing member or member firm or member corporation shall charge and collect from such executing member or member firm or member corporation a clearing charge therefor, for the combination of the receipt and the delivery of the stock involved, which charge, if purchase and sale are effected on the same business day, shall be computed at rates not less than those set forth in the following schedule:

¶ 1704   Art. XV

(a) Price per share	Rate per share
	cents
50¢ and above but under $ 1	0.30
$ 1 and above but under $ 5	0.75
$ 5 and above but under $10	1.00
$10 and above but under $50	2.75
$50 and above	3.00

If such purchase and sale are not effected on the same business day then such clearing charge shall be computed at one and one-half times the rates specified above.

(b) With respect to such stocks selling at less than 50¢ per share, such clearing charge shall be as mutually agreed.

¶ 1705 Special Rates on "When Issued" or "When Distributed" Transactions

SEC. 5. *"When issued" or "when distributed" securities, and rights and warrants whether issued, "when issued" or "when distributed".*—Notwithstanding the other provisions of this Article XV, when Rights or Warrants are admitted to dealings upon the Exchange, whether on an issued or "when issued" or "when distributed" basis, and when other securities are admitted to such dealings on a "when issued" or "when distributed" basis, the Board of Governors may determine special minimum rates of commission on any and all transactions in such rights, warrants or other securities, giving notice thereof to the membership. Unless special rates have been so determined, the minimum rates of commissions prescribed in this Article XV shall apply.

¶ 1706 Dealings in Securities of Original Issue

SEC. 6. If a member of the Exchange or member firm or member corporation engages in transactions in which the member or firm or corporation is acting as a dealer in securities of original issue, the rates of commission prescribed in this Article shall not apply to such transactions if not made on the Exchange; provided, however, that such transactions shall be subject to such regulations as the Board of Governors may from time to time prescribe.

¶ 1707 Proposition To Violate Commission Schedules

SEC. 7. No member, allied member, member firm or member corporation shall make a proposition for the transaction of business at less than the minimum rates of commission prescribed in this Article.

¶ 1708 Rebates to Members Not To Be Shared with Non-members

SEC. 8. Any return, rebate, discount or allowance of commissions resulting from an order given by a member or member firm or member corporation and payable by a member or member firm or corporation of another exchange in connection with the execution of such order shall be collected by the member or member firm or member corporation giving such order and may not be shared with a non-member of the Exchange.

¶ 1709   Service Charges

SEC. 9. Members of the Exchange, member firms and member corporations shall make and collect, in addition to minimum prescribed commissions, such other minimum charges with respect to accounts and services as the Board of Governors may from time to time prescribe. Except as may be specifically permitted by a rule adopted by the Board of Governors, such charges shall be net and free from any rebate, return, discount or allowance made in any shape or manner, or by any method or arrangement direct or indirect, and no bonus or percentage of such charges, whether such charges be the minimum charges prescribed by the Board or greater charges, shall be given, paid, or allowed, directly or indirectly, or as a salary or portion of a salary to a clerk or to any member of the Exchange, member firm or member corporation, or to any other person, firm or corporation for business sought or procured for any member of the Exchange, member firm or member corporation.

¶ 1710   Commission Rates to Member Firms and
                        Member Corporations

SEC. 10. A member firm and a member corporation shall be entitled to have its business transacted at the rates of commission prescribed for members.

Branch house or office

The privilege provided for under this Section shall extend to a branch house or branch office only when conducted under the same name as the parent firm or corporation and when the partners and their respective interests therein are identical with the partners and their respective interests in the parent firm.

Members as limited partners or non-directors

A member who is a limited partner in a firm does not thereby confer any of the privileges of the Exchange on such firm, and a member who is not a director of a member corporation and a holder of voting stock therein does not confer any of the privileges of the Exchange on such corporation, and on all business done for such firm by a limited partner who is a member of the Exchange and on all business done for such corporation by a member of the Exchange who is not holder of voting stock in such corporation commissions must be charged and collected at rates not less than the rates prescribed in this Article.

¶ 1711   Special Circumstances—Individual Member

SEC. 11. Notwithstanding any other provisions of this Article XV, when, in time of national emergency for this country, a member of the Exchange, who is not a general partner in a member firm or a holder of voting stock in a member corporation and whose principal business is that of executing orders on the Floor of the Exchange for other members, member firms, or member corporations,

(1) is on active duty in the armed forces of the United States, or

(2) is on active duty in the armed forces of any nation or State which is then allied or associated with the United States, or

(3) is engaged in any public service incident to the national defense,

the Board of Governors may permit another member, member firm or member corporation to pay to such member an amount not in excess of 50% of the minimum commissions applicable where a principal is given up, on transactions effected by such other member, member firm or member corporation on the Floor of the Exchange during the absence from the Floor of such member solely by reason of his engaging in any of the activities above mentioned, if the execution of such transactions would otherwise be part of the usual business of such absentee member, provided that all arrangements or agreements whereby such payments are made or are to be made have been submitted to and approved by the Board of Governors.

Determination of existence of national emergency

The Board of Governors shall from time to time determine whether or not a national emergency for this country exists within the contemplation of this Section and whether or not a given activity is within its provisions.

¶ 1712 Special Circumstances—Member Firms or Member Corporations

SEC. 12. Notwithstanding any other provisions of this Article XV, when, in time of national emergency for this country, a member of the Exchange who is a general partner in a member firm or a holder of voting stock in a member corporation,

(1) is on active duty in the armed forces of the United States, or

(2) is on active duty in the armed forces of any nation or State which is then allied or associated with the United States, or

(3) is engaged in any public service incident to the national defense,

the Board of Governors may permit an agreement between the member firm or member corporation in which the member engaging in any of the activities above mentioned is a general partner or a stockholder and another member, member firm or member corporation, providing in substance that, on transactions executed on the Floor of the Exchange by such other member, member firm or member corporation, for such first mentioned firm, or corporation the commissions chargeable by the executing member, member firm or member corporation shall be less than the minimum commissions otherwise prescribed as applicable to transactions effected on the Floor of the Exchange for other members where a principal is given up; provided that (1) such commissions so chargeable shall not be less than 50% of the minimum commissions so prescribed, (2) the transactions with respect to which such reduced commissions are charged were executed at a time when the absent member was absent from the Floor solely by reason of engaging in any of the activities above mentioned, (3) such transactions would otherwise in general have been effected by such absent member as a part of his usual business, and (4) such agreement has been submitted to and approved by the Board of Governors.

Determination of existence of national emergency

The Board of Governors shall from time to time determine whether or not a national emergency for this country exists within the contemplation of this Section and whether or not a given activity is within its provisions.

ARTICLE XVI

The Gratuity Fund

¶ 1751   Initial Contribution

SEC. 1. Every person who shall become a member of the Exchange shall pay to the Trustees of the Gratuity Fund the sum of fifteen dollars before he shall be admitted to the privilege of membership.

¶ 1752   Contribution on Death of Member

SEC. 2. Each member of the Exchange, by signing the Constitution pledges himself to make, upon the death of a member of the Exchange, a voluntary gift to the family of such deceased member in the sum of fifteen dollars, which shall be paid by the member at quarterly periods on the dates on which dues to the Exchange are to be paid. The Treasurer of the Exchange shall pay over quarterly to the Treasurer of the Gratuity Fund all amounts collected from members under this Article.

Amendment.
January 4, 1962, effective April 1, 1963.

¶ 1753   Amount of Gratuity

SEC. 3. The faith of the Exchange is hereby pledged to pay, within one year after proof of death of any member, out of the money collected under the provisions of this Article, the sum of twenty thousand dollars, or so much thereof as may have been collected, to the persons named in the next Section as therein provided, which money shall be a voluntary gift from the other members of the Exchange, free from all debts, charges or demands whatever.

¶ 1754   Distribution to Beneficiaries

Widow

SEC. 4. Should the member die leaving a widow and no child or children and no issue of a deceased child or children, then the whole sum shall be paid to such widow for her own use.

Widow and issue

Should the member die leaving a widow and a child or children or the issue of a deceased child or children, then one-half shall be paid to the widow for her separate use. The remaining one-half shall be paid to and divided among the child or children and the issue of any deceased child or children, such issue to take per stirpes and not per capita. If any such child or issue shall be a minor, his or her share shall be paid to his or her duly appointed guardian of the property.

Issue

Should the member die leaving a child or children or the issue of a deceased child or children and no widow, then the whole sum shall be paid to the children and such issue as directed in the preceding paragraph to be done with the moiety.

Collateral beneficiaries

Should the member die leaving neither widow, child nor issue of a child, then the whole sum shall be paid to the same persons who would, under the laws of the State of New York, take the same by reason of relationship to the deceased member had he owned the same at the time of his death; and if there be no such person, then the amount applicable under Section 3 of this Article in such case shall be held by the Trustees of the Gratuity Fund for the general purposes of that Fund.

Adopted children

The words "child" and "children" where used in this Section shall, for the purposes of this Article, be deemed to include an adopted child or children of the deceased member, provided, however, that such adoption shall have been in such manner and form that it will be recognized as valid by the Courts of the State of New York; the word "issue" where so used shall, for such purposes, be deemed not to include an adopted child or children.

Minors

In case any person entitled to any gratuity shall be under age and have no guardian entitled to receive payment at the maturity thereof, the Trustees may, in their discretion, deposit such money with the Bank of New York or the United States Trust Company as the property of, and in trust for, such minor; and in like manner if any person apparently entitled to any payment fails to claim it, or has disappeared or cannot be found after reasonable inquiry, the Trustees may deposit the presumptive share of such person in either of said Trust Companies to the credit of "The Trustees of the Gratuity Fund of the New York Stock Exchange, in trust," to the end that it may be paid to such person, if afterwards found, or otherwise to the parties who may subsequently establish their right thereto; a similar discretion shall apply in the case of any dispute between claimants for a gratuity or a portion thereof.

Proof of rights

In all cases a certified copy of the proceedings before a Surrogate or Judge of Probate shall be accepted as proof of the rights of the claimants, shall be deemed ample authority to the Exchange to pay over the money, shall protect the Exchange in so doing, and shall release the Exchange forever from all further claims or liability whatsoever.

¶ 1755 Limitation of Liability

SEC. 5. Nothing herein contained shall ever be taken or construed as a joint liability of the Exchange or its members for the payment of any sum whatever; the liability of each member, at law or equity, being limited to the payment of fifteen dollars only on the death of any other member, and the liability of the Exchange being limited to the payment of the sum of twenty thousand dollars, or such part thereof as may be collected, after it shall have been collected from the members, and not otherwise. Nevertheless, prior to the collection from the members of the amount of any gratuity payable under the provisions of this Article, the Trustees may, in their discretion, advance out of the Gratuity Fund (either capital or accumulated income) to the person or persons entitled thereto, the whole or any part of such gratuity; and, in every such case, the amount so advanced shall be repaid to the Gratuity Fund from the payments by the members when collected.

¶ 1756   Gratuities Not Assignable, Nor Part of Estate

SEC. 6. Nothing herein contained shall be construed as constituting any estate *in esse* which can be mortgaged or pledged for the payment of any debts; but it shall be construed as the solemn agreement of every member of the Exchange to make a voluntary gift to the family of each deceased member, and of the Exchange, to the best of its ability, to collect and pay over to such family the said voluntary gift.

¶ 1757   Reduction in Amounts To Be Paid by Members

SEC. 7. As of the close of each quarter in each year, the Trustees of the Gratuity Fund shall, provided the net worth of the Gratuity Fund has been determined (as hereinafter provided) to be in excess of the sum of five hundred thousand dollars, pay to the Treasurer of the Exchange out of the Gratuity Fund (either capital or accumulated income) a sum equal to the lesser of (1) the entire amount of such excess, or (2) such part of such excess as shall equal the aggregate of all amounts paid or payable by members under this Article in respect of deaths of members of the Exchange occurring during such quarter. As and when such sums are received by the Treasurer of the Exchange they shall be credited proportionately against such amounts so paid or payable.

Determination of "net worth"

The "net worth" of the Gratuity Fund shall be determined by the Trustees at a meeting in the last month of each quarter and shall be that amount by which, as of the close of the month preceding, the total assets (including cash, accounts receivable and investments stated at their market values but exclusive of accrued interest and accrued dividends) exceeded all known liabilities.

¶ 1758   Benefits to Members Only

SEC. 8. The provisions of Sections 2, 3, 4, 5 and 6 of this Article XVI shall not extend to the family of any deceased former member whose connection with the Exchange shall have been severed prior to his death by the transfer of his membership whether such transfer shall have been made by the member or his legal representatives or by the Board of Governors pursuant to the Constitution, or who has been expelled, but shall extend to the family of a deceased member who was suspended at the time of his death.

ARTICLE XVII

The Trustees of the Gratuity Fund

¶ 1801   Duties

SEC. 1. The execution of the provisions of the preceding Article, and the management and distribution of the Fund created thereunder shall be under the charge of a Board of Trustees, acting as agent for the Exchange, to be known as "The Trustees of the Gratuity Fund," and to consist of the Chairman of the Board of Governors and six members of the Exchange elected by the membership.

Vacancies

In case of a vacancy occurring among the six elected Trustees, the Board of Governors, at its next regular meeting thereafter, shall proceed to fill the same until the next annual election of the Exchange.

¶ 1802   Investment of Funds

Sec. 2. The Fund may be retained by the Trustees partially or wholly in the form of cash or, in the discretion of the Trustees, may be invested in securities which are legal investments for trust funds under the laws of the State of New York. Any securities held by the Trustees which cease to be such legal investments may, nevertheless, in the discretion of the Trustees, be retained by them.

Securities held by the Trustees may be in coupon or registered form. Securities held in registered form shall be registered in the name of "The Trustees of the Gratuity Fund of the New York Stock Exchange," but without specifying the individual names of such Trustees, and may be disposed of and assigned by any four of such Trustees.

¶ 1803   Organization of Trustees

Sec. 3. On the first Monday after the annual election of the Exchange, or as soon thereafter as may be practicable, the Trustees of the Gratuity Fund shall organize by electing a Chairman, and a Secretary and Treasurer of the Gratuity Fund, who shall serve for one year and until their successors are elected and take office. The offices of Secretary and Treasurer may be held by the same person.

¶ 1804   Meetings of Trustees

Sec. 4. Regular meetings of the Trustees shall be held at such times as the Trustees may designate by resolution. The Chairman may call a special meeting at any time; he shall call a meeting at the request of two Trustees. At a meeting four Trustees shall constitute a quorum.

¶ 1805   Duties of Chairman

Sec. 5. It shall be the duty of the Chairman to preside at meetings; he shall vote on all questions; he shall present to the Board of Governors in January of each year a report of the condition of the Fund, with a statement by the Treasurer of receipts and disbursements.

¶ 1806   Duties of Secretary

Sec. 6. It shall be the duty of the Secretary to keep regular minutes of the proceedings of the Trustees, and to give notice of meetings.

¶ 1807   Duties of Treasurer

Sec. 7. It shall be the duty of the Treasurer to receive and sign vouchers for all moneys paid to the Trustees, which he shall deposit in such institutions as they may direct, to his credit as "Treasurer of the Gratuity Fund of the New York Stock Exchange."

Custody of securities

He shall have the custody of all securities belonging to the Fund, subject to the examination and control of the Trustees.

Accounts

He shall keep, or cause to be kept, proper books of account.

Claims

He shall receive and keep a record of all claims for payment under Article XVI, and present the same to the Trustees for their action; when allowed and approved by the Trustees, he shall pay the same; but no such payment shall be made until directed by the Trustees.

Investments

He shall make such investments for the Fund as may be ordered by the Trustees, and report the same to the Trustees at the next regular meeting.

Books and reports

His books shall always be open to the inspection of any Trustee, and he shall make to the Chairman an annual statement of receipts and disbursements.

Compensation of Treasurer

He shall receive out of the Fund such compensation per annum as may be fixed by the Trustees and approved by the Board of Governors of the Exchange.

¶ 1808   Counsel

SEC. 8. The Trustees shall have power at their discretion to consult and employ legal counsel; they shall be authorized to make disbursements out of the Fund to defray necessary expenses.

¶ 1809   Vacancies in Offices

SEC. 9. In case of a vacancy occurring in the office of Chairman, or Secretary and Treasurer, the Trustees shall forthwith proceed to fill the same for the unexpired term. In case of the temporary absence or inability to act of either the Chairman, or Secretary or Treasurer, the Trustees shall have power to appoint one of their number to act in his stead *pro tem*.

¶ 1810   Examination of Fund

SEC. 10. The Board of Governors of the Exchange shall, at all times, have the right to direct the production before it of the securities belonging to the Fund, the Secretary's book of minutes and the Treasurer's books of account.

Annual examination

It shall be the duty of the Board of Governors to make an annual examination of the condition of the Fund; and it shall have the right at any time to make or cause to be made such additional examination thereof as it may deem proper.

ARTICLE XVIII

Emergency Committee

¶ 1831   Vesting Powers of Board of Governors
in Emergency Committee

SEC. 1. In the event that an attack as herein defined occurs and a quorum of the Board of Governors is not available and able to meet together or if the Board of Governors determines that an attack may be imminent, then, notwithstanding the provisions of any of the other Articles of the Constitution or of the rules and regulations of the Board of Governors, all the rights, powers and duties of the Board of Governors of the Exchange shall immediately vest in an Emergency Committee and continue to be so vested during the Period of Emergency.

Definitions

The term "attack" for the purpose of this Article XVIII means and includes any attack or series of attacks by an enemy or foreign nation causing, or which may cause, substantial damage or injury to civilian property or persons anywhere in the United States in any manner by sabotage or by the use of bombs, shellfire, or atomic, radiological, chemical, bacteriological or biological means, or other weapons or processes.

The term "Emergency Committee" for the purpose of this Article XVIII shall mean a Committee of seven members composed as provided in Sec. 2 of this Article.

The term "Period of Emergency" for the purpose of this Article XVIII shall mean the period commencing with the vesting of the powers of the Board in the Emergency Committee and ending on the date fixed by (a) the Board of Governors in office at the inception of the emergency or (b) by a majority vote of the membership or (c) by the Emergency Committee. On the date so fixed all of the Committee's powers shall revert to the Board of Governors.

If there are any vacancies in the Board of Governors on the date the Emergency Committee's powers are to revert to the Board of Governors, the Emergency Committee may make such provisions as it deems advisable for the election, by the members of the Exchange, of persons to fill such vacancies and may, in connection therewith, fix the time, place and manner of nominating persons to fill such vacancies and the time, place and manner of holding the election.

Amendment.

Adopted March 1, 1962.

¶ 1832   Composition of Emergency Committee

SEC. 2. The Emergency Committee shall, at the inception of the Period of Emergency, be composed of the following seven Governors who are available and able to meet together—the Chairman of the Board of Governors, the Vice-Chairman of the Board of Governors, the President of the Exchange, and the four senior members of the Board of Governors other than the Public Governors. If any of the foregoing are not available or able to meet together, vacancies shall be filled from other members of the Board in order of their seniority. If there are not seven members of the Board of Governors available and able to meet together, vacancies shall be filled in the order of their seniority, from the class of former Governors composed of members and allied members who retired from the Board of Governors at the last annual election. If all of the vacancies cannot be filled from that class, they shall be filled in order of seniority, from the class of former Governors composed of members and allied members who retired at the next to the last annual election, and so on until there are seven such Governors or former Governors available and able to meet together.

The seniority of a Governor or former Governor for the purpose of this Article XVIII shall be determined by the length of time he has served as a Governor (including service as Chairman of the Board) whether or not his terms of service have been consecutive.

After the Emergency Committee has been initially constituted as above provided, the Committee shall fill any vacancies which occur by appointing Governors or former Governors who are members or allied members of the Exchange, may increase the number of such Governors and former Governors who constitute the Committee, and thereafter may reduce such number provided the number is not reduced below seven. In filling vacancies and in adding members to the Committee, seniority shall not control. The Emergency Committee may remove any member of the Committee with or without cause.

In the event that at any time during the emergency there are less than three members of the Committee available and able to meet together the vacancies shall automatically be filled in the same manner as the Committee was originally constituted.

Amendment.

Adopted March 1, 1962.

¶ 1833   Meetings of Emergency Committee

SEC. 3. Meetings of the Emergency Committee shall be held at such times and places as the Committee may designate by resolution and special meetings of the Committee shall be held on the call of any member of the Committee. A member of the Emergency Committee calling a meeting shall attempt to give notice thereof by making such reasonable efforts as circumstances may permit to notify each Committee member of the meeting. Such notification may be oral, written or by publication and specify the purposes thereof. Failure of any member of the Committee to receive actual notice of a meeting of the Committee shall not affect the power of the Committee members present at such meeting to exercise the powers of the Emergency Committee.

Three members of the Emergency Committee shall be sufficient to constitute a quorum for any meeting of that Committee, and any action taken pursuant to the vote of a majority of the members of the Committee present at a meeting shall be deemed to be the action of the Committee, even though the Constitution requires a specified vote by the members of the Board of Governors had that action been taken by the Board.

Any action by an Emergency Committee shall be valid and binding as if taken by the Board of Governors if such Committee certifies that it is the properly constituted Emergency Committee even though it may subsequently develop that at the time of such action the Committee was not a duly qualified Emergency Committee.

If the Emergency Committee elects a person to an office which it believes to be vacant, the acts of such newly elected officer shall be valid and binding although it may subsequently develop that such office was not in fact vacant.

Amendment.
Adopted March 1, 1962.

ARTICLE XIX
Special Trust Fund
¶ 1841   Terms and Conditions

SEC. 1. The Board of Governors is hereby authorized on behalf of the Exchange to establish a trust, to be known as the Special Trust Fund, upon the terms and conditions set forth in this Section.

The principal of the trust shall consist of contributions made thereto by the Exchange as authorized from time to time by the Board of Governors, such principal and any net income accumulated thereon being hereinafter sometimes referred to as "the Fund."

The Fund shall, except as otherwise provided in this Section, be used solely for the purpose of providing direct or indirect assistance to customers of a member, member firm or member corporation threatened with loss of their money or securities because such member, member firm or member corporation, in the opinion of the Trustees of the Special Trust Fund, is insolvent or is in such financial condition that he or it may be unable without assistance to meet his or its obligations to such customers, but shall be used only to the extent, if any, and in the manner determined by the Trustees of the Special Trust Fund.

The Trustees of the Special Trust Fund shall consist of those persons who at any given time are Governors of the Exchange.

The Fund shall be kept separate and apart from any funds or other assets of the Exchange.

The net income realized on the Fund shall be added to and become a part of the Fund, except that whenever the net worth of the Fund is determined (as hereinafter provided) to be in excess of the sum of ten million dollars, the Trustees of the Special Trust Fund may apply the net income realized on the Fund in any calendar year thereafter, or so much thereof as they may determine, to the uses and purposes to which the Fund may be applied on termination of the Fund as hereinafter provided. The "net worth" of the Fund shall be determined by the Trustees of the Special Trust Fund and shall be that amount by which as of the close of the preceding calendar year, the total assets of the Fund (including cash, accounts receivable and investments stated at their market values but exclusive of accrued interest and accrued dividends) exceeded all its known liabilities.

Unless sooner terminated as hereinafter provided, the Special Trust Fund shall terminate twenty-one years after the death of the last surviving member alive on July 30, 1964 ; provided, however, that this limitation shall be void and of no effect if the Special Trust Fund may legally exist for a longer period of time or in perpetuity, in which event the Special Trust Fund shall exist for such longer period or in perpetuity. Upon termination, the Fund shall be transferred, conveyed, and paid over to such person, partnership, association or corporation, other than any member, member firm, member corporation or the Exchange, for such uses and purposes similar or related to the purposes for which the Fund was established, as the Trustees of the Special Trust Fund, in their sole and absolute discretion, shall determine, or, in the event the Trustees shall determine that no such similar or related purpose can be found, to such charitable uses and purposes as the Trustees, in their sole and absolute discretion, shall determine.

No member, member firm or member corporation, no customer of any such member, member firm or member corporation and no other person shall in any event have any claim or right of action, at law or in equity, whether for an accounting or otherwise, against the Exchange, the Trustees of the Special Trust Fund, or any other person, or against the Fund, as a result of any action taken or the failure to act by the Trustees in the exercise of their discretion. Whether or not expenditures from the Fund shall be made in any particular case and, if so, in what manner, to whom and to what extent, shall at all times remain exclusively within the sole and absolute discretion of the Trustees of the Special Trust Fund.

The Special Trust Fund may be retained partly or wholly in the form of cash or may be invested and reinvested in such securities as the Trustees may from time to time deem appropriate, notwithstanding the provisions of any law governing the investment of trust funds by fiduciaries.

The Trustees of the Special Trust Fund may pledge any or all of the securities in the Fund to secure the repayment of any borrowing effected by the Trustees, the proceeds of which are to be used to provide direct or indirect assistance to customers.

Any action taken by a majority of the Trustees of the Special Trust Fund then in office shall contitute action on behalf of the Special Trust Fund.

The trust shall not be subject to amendment, modification or revocation in any manner which would permit the Special Trust Fund or the net income thereon to be applied to uses and purposes other than those set forth in this Section. The trust may otherwise be amended, modified or revoked by the Board of Governors acting pursuant to an amendment of this Article adopted in accordance with Article XX.

The Board of Governors shall authorize the Chairman of the Board of Governors and the President of the Exchange to execute a deed of trust, incorporating the substance of the above provision of this Section and such other provisions for the administration of the Trust as the Board of Governors may deem appropriate.

¶ 1842 Additional Funds

SEC. 2. To supplement the funds available for the purposes for which the Special Trust Fund may be used, the Board of Governors may authorize the borrowing from time to time on behalf of the Exchange of additional funds in such amounts as the Board may determine. In anticipation of the possible need for such additional funds, the Board may authorize the obtaining on behalf of the Exchange of an appropriate indemnity bond or bonds or standby credit arrangements, all on such terms and conditions as the Board may determine.

Amendment.
July 30, 1964.

ARTICLE XX
Amendment of the Constitution

¶ 1851 Procedure

Action by Board

Every proposed amendment to the Constitution must be presented in writing at a regular meeting of the Board of Governors or at a special meeting expressly called for the purpose of receiving it. Upon presentation every proposed amendment shall be laid upon the table for at least two weeks and the Secretary of the Exchange shall promptly cause a copy thereof to be delivered to each Governor. After any such proposed amendment shall have lain upon the table for two weeks, action thereon shall be taken at the next regular meeting of the Board of Governors or at a special meeting expressly called for the purpose of acting thereon, or action thereon may be postponed by the Board of Governors within the limitations of this Article. Before approving or submitting any proposed amendment the Board of Governors may make such changes therein as it may deem necessary or appropriate to carry out the intention of such proposed amendment or to make it conform to other provisions of the Constitution or any applicable Federal or State Law.

Methods of proposing amendments

Amendments may be proposed in the following manner:

  a—By one or more Members of the Board of Governors.

  b—By the signed petition of not less than one hundred and seventy-five members of the Exchange setting forth the proposed amendment and filing the same with the Secretary of the Exchange who shall present it to the Board of Governors at the next regular meeting of the Board. After the expiration of not less than two weeks following the presentation of such proposed amendment to the Board of Governors, the Board may direct that it be submitted with or without the approval of the Board, to the Membership for vote by ballot, provided however that in any case the Board of Governors shall, within seven weeks after such proposed amendment has been presented to the Board, direct such submission to the Membership.

Action by membership

Any such proposed amendment when approved by the affirmative vote of a majority of the Governors then in office or submitted as directed in Subsection (b) above, shall be posted on the bulletin board and submitted to the membership for vote by ballot. The time for balloting shall expire at the end of the two weeks' period following the approval or submission of the proposed amendment by the Board of Governors, unless by the end of such period less than a majority of the then members have participated in the balloting in which event the time for balloting shall be extended for an additional two weeks. If at the end of such two weeks' or four weeks' period, as the case may be, the number of members participating in the balloting exceeds one-half of the number of memberships then outstanding, and such proposed amendment has been approved by the affirmative vote of a majority of the ballots which express a determinable preference for or against the proposed amendment, it shall thereupon become a part of the Constitution. Unless adopted as above provided, any such proposed amendment shall not be effective for any purpose.

Amendment of Article XVI

No amendment to the Constitution shall ever be made which will impair in any essential particular, the obligation of each member to contribute, as provided in Article XVI, to the provision for the families of deceased members.

Renumbered July 30, 1964.

ARTICLE XXI

Liability Under Previous Constitution

¶ 1901   Constitution Prior to General Amendment in 1953

The provisions of the Constitution of the Exchange in force immediately prior to the effective date of the general amendment of the Constitution in 1953 shall be superseded hereby, except that such amendment shall not affect the liability of any member, allied member or member firm of the Exchange for any offense theretofore committed, or any rights or liabilities theretofore acquired or incurred.

Renumbered July 30, 1964.

NEW YORK STOCK EXCHANGE
GENERAL RULES

... definitions of terms used throughout the rules of the Board of Governors; miscellaneous rules and policies; rules governing access to and communication with the Floor ...

TABLE OF CONTENTS

Definitions of Terms

RULES OF BOARD OF GOVERNORS

General Rules

Definitions of Terms

¶ 2001   Effect of Definitions

Rule 1. Unless the context requires otherwise, the terms defined in Rules
        2 to 25 [¶¶ 2002—2025], inclusive, shall, for all purposes of the Rules,
have the meanings therein specified.

¶ 2002   "Member," "Membership," "Member Firm," etc.

Rule 2. The terms "member," "membership," "member firm," "allied
        member," "non-member," and "member corporation" shall have the
meanings specified in Section 3 of Article I of the Constitution [¶ 1003] and the
terms "voting stock," "non-voting stock," and "holder," when used with respect
to a member corporation, shall also have the meanings specified in Section 3
of Article I of the Constitution [¶ 1003].

The term "member organization" includes "member firm" and "member
corporation." The term "participant" when used with reference to a member
organization includes general and limited partners of a member firm and
holders of voting and non-voting stock in a member corporation.

¶ 2003   "Security"

Rule 3. The term "security" or "securities" includes stocks, bonds, notes,
        certificates of deposit or participation, trust receipts, rights, war-
rants and other similar instruments.

¶ 2004   "Stock"

Rule 4. The term "stock" includes voting trust certificates, certificates of
        deposit for stocks, rights, warrants, and other securities classified for
trading as stocks by the Exchange, except when used with reference to stock
in a member corporation, or in a corporation for which application has been
made for approval as a member corporation.

¶ 2005   "Bond"

Rule 5. The term "bond" includes debentures, notes, certificates of deposit
        for bonds, debentures or notes, and other securities classified for
trading as bonds by the Exchange.

¶ 2006   "Floor"

Rule 6. The term "Floor" means the Floor of the Exchange.

¶ 2007   "Exchange Ticket"

Rule 7. The term "exchange ticket" means exchange ticket as prescribed in
        the Rules of Stock Clearing Corporation [¶ 3304].

Amendments.
September 3, 1964.

¶ 2008   **"Delivery"**

Rule 8. The term "delivery" means the delivery of securities on Exchange contracts, unless otherwise stated.

¶ 2009   **"Branch Office Manager"**

Rule 9. The term "branch office manager" means a registered representative in charge of a branch office.

¶ 2010   **"Registered Representative"**

Rule 10. The term "registered representative" means an employee engaged in the solicitation or handling of listed or unlisted business in securities, or other similar instruments; or in the trading of listed or unlisted securities, or other similar instruments, for the account of or as a representative of his employer; or in the sale of listed or unlisted securities on a dealer or principal basis for his employer; or in handling international securities arbitrage operations of his employer; or in the solicitation of subscriptions to investment advisory or to investment management service furnished on a fee basis by his employer; or one to whom has been delegated general supervision over the foreign business of his employer. The term "registered representative" does not apply to individuals who are engaged solely in the solicitation or handling of business in, or the sale of, cotton, grain or other commodities, provided their duties in such respect require their registration with a recognized national cotton or commodities exchange.

¶ 2011   **"The Exchange"**

Rule 11. The term "the Exchange," when used with reference to the administration of any rule, means either the Board of Governors or the officer, employee or committee to whom appropriate authority to administer such rule has been delegated by the Board pursuant to the provisions of Section 1 of Article III of the Constitution [¶ 1101].

¶ 2012   **"Business Day"**

Rule 12. Except as may be otherwise determined by the Exchange as to particular days, the term "business day" means any day on which the Exchange is open for business; provided, however, on any business day that the banks, transfer agencies and depositories for securities in New York State are closed:

(1) Deliveries or payments ordinarily due on such a day (exclusive of "cash" contracts made on such a day) shall be due on the following business day;

(2) such a day shall not be considered as a business day in determining the day for settlement of a contract, the day on which stock shall be quoted ex-dividend or ex-rights, or in computing interest on contracts in bonds or premiums on loans of securities; and

(3) the right to mark to the market, to make reclamation, or to close contracts under Rule 284 [¶ 2284] (other than "cash" contracts made on such a day) shall not be exercised on such a day.

For list of holidays on which the Exchange will not be open for business. see ¶ 2051.10.

Amendments.
January 21, 1954.

¶ 2013   Definitions of Orders

Rule 13

All or None Order

A market or limited price order which is to be executed in its entirety or not at all, but, unlike a fill or kill order, is not to be treated as cancelled if not executed as soon as it is represented in the Trading Crowd. The making of "all or none" bids or offers in stocks is prohibited and the making of "all or none" bids or offers in bonds is subject to the restrictions of Rule 61.

Alternative Order—Either/Or Order

An order to do either of two alternatives—such as, either sell (buy) a particular stock at a limit price or sell (buy) on stop. If the order is for one unit of trading when one part of the order is executed on the happening of one alternative, the order on the other alternative is to be treated as cancelled. If the order is for an amount larger than one unit of trading, the number of units executed determines the amount of the alternative order to be treated as cancelled.

At the Close Order

A market order which is to be executed at or as near to the close as practicable.

At the Opening or at the Opening Only Order

A market or limited price order which is to be executed at the opening of the stock or not at all, and any such order or the portion thereof not so executed is to be treated as cancelled.

Day Order

An order to buy or sell which, if not executed, expires at the end of the trading day on which it was entered.

Do Not Reduce or "DNR" Order

A limited order to buy, a stop order to sell or a stop limit order to sell which is not to be reduced by the amount of an ordinary cash dividend on the ex-dividend date. A do not reduce order applies only to ordinary cash dividends; it should be reduced for other distributions such as when a stock goes "ex" a stock dividend or ex rights.

Fill or Kill Order

A market or limited price order which is to be executed in its entirety as soon as it is represented in the Trading Crowd, and such order, if not so executed, is to be treated as cancelled. For purposes of this definition, a "stop" is considered an execution.

Good 'Til Cancelled Order (GTC) or Open Order

An order to buy or sell which remains in effect until it is either executed or cancelled.

Immediate or Cancel Order

A market or limited price order which is to be executed in whole or in part as soon as such order is represented in the Trading Crowd, and the portion not so executed is to be treated as cancelled. For the purposes of this definition, a "stop" is considered an execution.

Limit, Limited Order or Limited Price Order

An order to buy or sell a stated amount of a security at a specified price, or at a better price, if obtainable after the order is represented in the Trading Crowd.

Market Order

An order to buy or sell a stated amount of a security at the most advantageous price obtainable after the order is represented in the Trading Crowd.

"Not Held" Order

A "not held" order is a market or limited price order marked "not held," "disregard tape," "take time," or which bears any such qualifying notation.

An order marked "or better" is not a "not held" order.

Orders Good Until a Specified Time

A market or limited price order which is to be represented in the Trading Crowd until a specified time, after which such order or the portion thereof not executed is to be treated as cancelled.

Percentage Order

A market or limited price order to buy (or sell) a stated amount of a specified stock after a fixed number of shares of such stock have traded.

Scale Order

An order to buy (or sell) a security which specifies the total amount to be bought (or sold) and the amount to be bought (or sold) at specified price variations.

Sell "Plus"—Buy "Minus" Order

A market order to sell "plus" is a market order to sell a stated amount of a stock provided that the price to be obtained is not lower than the last sale if the last sale was a "plus" or "zero plus" tick, and is not lower than the last sale plus the minimum fractional change in the stock if the last sale was a "minus" or "zero minus" tick. A limited price order to sell "plus" would have the additional restriction of stating the lowest price at which it could be executed.

A market order to buy "minus" is a market order to buy a stated amount of a stock provided that the price to be obtained is not higher than the last sale if the last sale was a "minus" or "zero minus" tick, and is not higher than the last sale minus the minimum fractional change in the stock if the last sale was a "plus" or "zero plus" tick. A limited price order to buy "minus" would have the additional restriction of stating the highest price at which it could be executed.

Stop Order

A stop order to buy becomes a market order when a transaction in the security occurs at or above the stop price after the order is represented in the Trading Crowd. A stop order to sell becomes a market order when a transaction in the security occurs at or below the stop price after the order is represented in the Trading Crowd.

Stop Limit Order

A stop limit order to buy becomes a limit order executable at the limit price, or at a better price, if obtainable, when a transaction in the security occurs at or above the stop price after the order is represented in the Trading Crowd. A stop limit order to sell becomes a limit order executable at the limit price or at a better price, if obtainable, when a transaction in the security occurs at or below the stop price after the order is represented in the Trading Crowd.

Switch Order—Contingent Order

An order for the purchase (sale) of one stock and the sale (purchase) of another stock at a stipulated price difference.

Time Order

An order which becomes a market or limited price order at a specified time.

Adopted.
May 20, 1965, effective May 21, 1965.

[The next page is 2551.]

Miscellaneous Rules

¶ 2021   Disqualification of Governors on Listing of Securities

Rule 21. No member of the Board of Governors or of any committee authorized by the Board shall vote at any meeting of the Board or of any such committee, or participate in its deliberations (except to the extent of testifying at the request of the Board or of such committee) with respect to the admission of a security to the List or to dealings upon the Exchange or with respect to the approval of any plan for the distribution of any listed security, if he has directly or indirectly a substantial interest in such security or in such plan. Without limiting the foregoing, such a member shall be deemed to have such an interest if:

(1) Such security or any other security of the same issuer is one in the distribution of which he or his member organization is participating or to his knowledge has within six months prior thereto participated, as or on behalf of an underwriter or a member of a selling syndicate or group; or

(2) he or any participant in his member organization is an officer or director (or person occupying a similar status or performing similar functions) or a voting trustee of the issuer of such security or of any corporation which to his knowledge controls or is controlled by the issuer of such security; or

(3) he or his member organization or any participant therein owns directly or indirectly more than 1% of such security or of any class of stock of the issuer, or of any corporation which to his knowledge controls the issuer of such security; or

(4) he or his member organization or any participant therein to his knowledge holds directly or indirectly any substantial contract, option, or other privilege entitling him to purchase such security; or to his knowledge within six months prior thereto has directly or indirectly purchased (other than through the exercise of a right to subscribe) such security from the issuer or an underwriter thereof at a price below the market price.

¶ 2022   Disqualification of Governors Because of Personal Interest

Rule 22. No member of the Board of Governors or of any committee authorized by the Board shall participate (except to the extent of testifying at the request of such Board or of such committee) in the investigation or consideration of any matter relating to any member, allied member or member organization with knowledge that such member, allied member or member organization is indebted to such governor or committee member, or to his member organization or any participant therein, or that he, his member organization or any participant therein is indebted to such member, allied member or member organization, excluding, however, any indebtedness arising in the ordinary course of business out of transactions on any exchange, out of transactions in the over-the-counter markets, or out of the lending and borrowing of securities.

¶ 2023   New York Local Time

Rule 23. The Exchange shall conform to local New York City time.

¶ 2024   Change in Procedure to Conform to Changed Hours of Trading

Rule 24. Whenever a Rule of the Board of Governors prescribes an hour, time or period of time at, before or within which an act shall be done, the Exchange may, in the event that the hours of trading on any day are changed pursuant to the provisions of Rule 51 [¶2051], temporarily prescribe another hour, time or period of time for the performance of such act, which may be on a day subsequent to that on which the hours of trading are so changed.

¶ 2025   Cost of Production of Records

Rule 25. The cost to the Exchange of producing, pursuant to court order or other legal process, records relating to the business or affairs of a member, allied member or member organization may, in the discretion of the Exchange, be required to be paid to the Exchange by such member, allied member or member organization, whether such production is required at the instance of such member, allied member or member organization or at the instance of any other party.

¶ 2026   Publication of Proposed Amendments of Commission Rates

Rule 26. When a proposed amendment to Article XV of the Constitution relating to rates of commissions or other charges, has been presented to the Board, the text of such amendment shall be posted on the bulletin board, distributed to the membership and publicly announced at least 30 days before action thereon is taken by the Board of Governors.

Adopted.
February 19, 1959.

[The next page is 2575.]

Access to and Communication with Floor

(Rules and Policies Administered by The Floor Department.)

¶ 2035   Floor Employees To Be Registered

Rule 35. No employee of a member or member organization shall be admitted to the Floor unless he is registered with and approved by the Exchange, and upon compliance of both the employer and employee with such requirements as the Exchange may determine.

● ● ● *Supplementary Material:*

.10 **Telephone and other Floor clerks' tickets.**—No telephone clerk will be admitted to the Floor unless he carries a ticket issued by the Exchange. Each telephone clerk may have one, and only one, ticket.

The following types of tickets may be issued and the charges therefor will be billed on statements rendered by the Exchange, as indicated:

Bond Clerk	$42.50 Quarterly
Special Bond Clerk	80.00 Quarterly
Specialist Clerk	30.00 Quarterly
Stock Clerk	30.00 Quarterly
Relief Clerk	5.00 Annually

(The charge for a relief clerk's ticket is $5.00 per year or any part thereof. In the case of the issuance of a new relief clerk's ticket, this charge will appear on the next quarterly statement. Annual charges for the renewal of such tickets for the subsequent year will be billed on the December 31st statement.)

A description of the various types of tickets follows:

(1) *Bond Clerks' tickets* admit holders to the Bond Room only. The number of tickets of this type issued to any member or member organization is limited to the combined number of telephone spaces rented by the member or member organization and the number of members active in the Bond Room.

(2) *Special Bond Clerks' tickets* admit holders to the Bond Room only. The issuance of each ticket of this kind is subject to the prior approval of the Exchange. Special Bond Clerks' tickets may be cancelled by the Exchange at any time.

(3) *Specialist Clerks' tickets* admit holders to the areas behind the stock trading posts. They are issued only to employees of members holding specialist spaces. The tickets also admit the holders to the telephone booths along the walls of the stock trading rooms, but only to relieve stock clerks employed by the same member or member organization during the absence of the stock clerks.

(4) *Stock Clerks' tickets* admit holders to the telephone booths along the walls of the stock trading rooms. They are issued only to employees of members or member organizations renting telephone spaces. The tickets also admit the holders to the areas behind the stock trading posts but only to relieve specialist clerks employed by the same member or member organization during the absence of the specialist clerks.

(5) *Relief Clerks' tickets* admit holders to any location regularly occupied by a bond clerk, special bond clerk, specialist clerk, or stock clerk, only for the purpose of relieving a regular clerk during his absence from the Floor at lunch time, vacation periods, etc. For admission to the cafeteria relief clerks must present tickets which may be purchased at the Information Desk.

A member or member organization desiring to obtain a telephone clerk's ticket for an employee must make written application on a form which may be obtained from The Floor Department.

If the issuance of the ticket applied for is approved, the application and agreement remain in force until the cancellation of the ticket either by notice of the applicant to the Exchange or by notice of the Exchange to the applicant.

The application, in the absence of any notice of cancellation of the ticket either by the applicant or the Exchange, is regarded as authority to the Exchange to bill the applicant at the current rate for the type of ticket specified.

The applicant must, upon notice of cancellation either from the applicant to the Exchange or from the Exchange to the applicant, immediately surrender the ticket issued.

The right of the clerk to exercise the privilege granted by the ticket is contingent upon his passing an annual physical examination by the medical clinic located in the Exchange building. Failure to present himself for such examination when notified by the medical clinic may result in the cancellation of the ticket.

The ticket is valid until the end of the fourth calendar year following the date of its issuance.

A charge of $5 will be made for the issuance of a duplicate ticket to replace a ticket which has been lost.

A member or member organization employing telephone clerks should have at least one relief clerk and may have as many as two relief clerks for each clerk holding other types of tickets.

If a ticket of one kind is outstanding in the name of an individual no different kind of ticket will be issued in the same name unless and until the first ticket is surrendered for cancellation.

All tickets cancelled before expiration must be surrendered to The Floor Department. On expiration all tickets must be surrendered to The Floor Department.

.20 Regulations pertaining to Telephone and other Floor clerks.—All telephone clerks and specialists' clerks of members and member organizations must be at their booths or posts on the Floor at 9:30 a. m. or such earlier time as may be set by the Exchange in view of unusual circumstances.

Each member or member organization having a telephone space on the Floor must keep at least one clerk on the Floor for fifteen minutes (or such longer period as may be set by the Exchange because of unusual circumstances) following the close of the market each day or until all reports due said member or member organization have been received, whichever time is later.

Telephone clerks or other employees of members and member organizations are not allowed to be upon or to cross the trading area of the Floor for any purpose during the period between ten minutes preceding the opening of the market and five minutes following the close of the market.

Member organizations that borrow or lend securities on the Floor must keep their telephone clerks on the Floor until their loans have been renewed.

Telephone clerks are, however, forbidden to attend meetings of the Loan Crowd for any purpose.

Telephone and other Floor clerks who, because of illness or injury, are relieved from duty by the medical clinic located in the Exchange building, must report to that clinic before returning to duty. Clerks who, because of illness or injury, are absent for more than two days, without having previously reported to the medical clinic located in the Exchange building, must likewise report to that clinic before returning to duty.

Members and member organizations should instruct their telephone clerks that they must keep a day's supply of stationery on hand, and that arrangements should be made for this stationery to be delivered to the Exchange either after the close by the employer's messengers or before 9:30 a.m. by the telephone clerks.

Telephone and other Floor clerks may not make bids or offers nor may any clerk interfere with any order during its transmission.

.30 **Clerks' badges.**—Each telephone or other Floor clerk must wear an identifying badge while on the Floor. The badge must bear:

(1) The clerk's name;

(2) a description of the type of ticket held;

(3) the name of the employer;

(4) in the case of specialist clerks, the number of the post at which the clerk is regularly stationed.

In addition, each type of badge must be of a distinctive color, i.e.,

Bond Clerk's ....Blue
Special Bond Clerk's ....Orange
Specialist Clerk's ....Red
Stock Clerk's ....Yellow
Relief Clerk's ....Green

Badges must be ordered through the Exchange. Between the time of ordering a badge and the time of delivery the clerk will be required to wear a temporary badge of the proper type. Temporary badges are the property of the Exchange and must be surrendered as soon as the new badge is issued.

The use of altered or mutilated badges is prohibited.

.40 **Personnel available to specialist units on the Floor.**—Each specialist unit shall have: (1) at least one regular specialist clerk for every Post space assigned to a member of the unit, and (2) an adequate number of relief clerks to provide proper service during the absence of regular clerks.

Each specialist unit having insufficient office personnel available for the Floor in an emergency situation shall, within such reasonable period of time as the Exchange shall determine, make arrangements with other specialists or with its clearing firm to assure that proper service will be rendered to members and member organizations should an emergency situation arise.

¶ 2036 Wire Connections Between Exchange and Members' Offices

Rule 36. No member or member organization shall establish or maintain any telephonic or other wire connection between his or its office and the Exchange without the approval of the Exchange. The Exchange may grant or withhold such approval, without being obliged to assign any reason or cause for its action. It may cause to be disconnected any such connection or may deprive any member or member organization of the privilege of using any public telephone or means of communication installed by the Exchange for the use of members or member organizations.

● ● ● *Supplementary Material:*

.10 Installation of private telephone lines to Exchange.—The Telephone Company will not recognize any order for the installation or disconnection of a private telephone line between the Floor and the office, whether main or branch, of a member or member organization, nor for the installation or disconnection of a telephone quotation line, except such orders as are issued by the Exchange directly to the Telephone Company.

Requests for private telephone lines between offices and the Floor should be sent to The Floor Department. Requests for quotation wire service should be sent to the Ticker, Quotations and Telephone Department. Members or member organizations who desire such installations or disconnections should present their requests sufficiently in advance of the desired effective date to avoid any inconveniences resulting from insufficient notice to the Telephone Company.

.20 Sub-letting spaces on Floor.—No member or member organization may, without specific permission of the Exchange, sub-let to another member or member organization any telephone or specialist space on the Floor.

.30 Members' badges.—All members who execute orders on the Floor must be provided with an identification badge and must wear the same while on the Floor.

Every member's badge must contain his name, a firm or corporate name and a number.

If the member is a participant in a member organization having no office in New York City, or if he is not a participant in a member organization, the name of the organization with whom he makes his office must be shown, preceded by the word "at." The name of his clearing organization, if different, may not be shown, except by specific permission of the Exchange.

¶ 2037 Visitors

Rule 37. Visitors shall not be admitted to the Floor of the Exchange except by permission of an Officer of the Exchange.

¶ 2038 Communications

Rule 38. Communications or announcements shall not be posted on the bulletin board without the consent of the Chairman of the Board, the President, or a person authorized by the Exchange to give such consent.

NEW YORK STOCK EXCHANGE
DEALINGS AND SETTLEMENTS

. . . included are all the rules of the Board of Governors affecting exchange contracts, together with related material either explaining or extending the scope of the rules . . .

TABLE OF CONTENTS
Making and Settling of Exchange Contracts

Contents

Dividends, Interest, Rights, etc.

Contents   © 1957, Commerce Clearing House, Inc.

Delivery Dates on Exchange Contracts

Contracts for Sale of Stock (Rules 64, 65)

Nature of Contract	Delivery Date	Remarks
Cash	Due on the day of the contract.	Transactions made at or before 2:00 P.M. are due before 2:30 P.M.; those made after 2:00 P.M. are due within 30 min. after sale. (Rule 177.)
Regular Way	Due on the fourth business day following the day of the contract, except odd lots of less than 100-share-unit stocks sold by a specialist and/or odd-lot dealer in such stocks, which are due on the fourteenth day following the day of the contract. (Rule 65(b) and 85(d)3.)	
Seller's Option...	Due on the date of expiration of the option, which may not be less than five business days nor more than sixty days. If due date is a day other than a business day, delivery shall be due on the next succeeding business day unless otherwise agreed. (Rule 178.)	Seller may deliver earlier by giving written notice, on or after the day when delivery would have been due if the contract had been made "regular way," of intention to make delivery on next business day following such notice. (Rule 179(a).) Written contracts must be exchanged. (Rule 137.)
When Issued and When Distributed (Rule 63).	Due as determined by Exchange.	Written contracts on transactions not cleared through Stock Clearing Corporation must be exchanged. (Rule 137.)

Contracts for Sale of U. S. Government Bonds (Rule 66)

(Obligations of any international authorities in which the United States is a participant and securities guaranteed by the United States Government as to principal and interest are classed as United States Government bonds.)

Nature of Contract	Delivery Date	Remarks
Cash	Due on the day of the contract.	Transactions made at or before 2:00 P.M. are due before 2:30 P.M.; those made after 2:00 P.M. are due within 30 min. after sale. (Rule 177.)
Regular Way ...	Due on the first business day following the day of the contract.	
Seller's Option...	Due on the date of expiration of the option, which may not be less than two business days nor more than sixty days. If due date is a day other than a business day, delivery shall be due on the next succeeding business day unless otherwise agreed. (Rule 178.)	Seller may deliver earlier by giving written notice, on or after the day when delivery would have been due if the contract had been made "regular way," of intention to make delivery on next business day following such notice. (Rule 179(a).) Written contracts must be exchanged. (Rule 137.)
When Issued and When Distributed (Rule 63).	Due as determined by Exchange.	Written contracts on transactions not cleared through Stock Clearing Corporation must be exchanged. (Rule 137.)

Contracts for Sale of Convertible Bonds Dealt in Pursuant to Rule 67

(Bonds bearing warrants or subscription privileges are classed as convertible bonds. Bonds on which the conversion or subscription privilege has expired are not classed as convertible bonds.)

Nature of Contract	Delivery Date	Remarks
Cash	Due on the day of the contract.	Transactions made at or before 2:00 P.M. are due before 2:30 P.M.; those made after 2:00 P.M. are due within 30 min. after sale. (Rule 177.)
Regular Way	Due on the fourth business day following the day of the contract.	
Seller's Option...	Due on the expiration of the option, which may not be less than five business days nor more than sixty days. If due date is a day other than a business day, delivery shall be due on the next succeeding business day unless otherwise agreed. (Rule 178.)	Seller may deliver earlier by giving written notice, on or after the day when delivery would have been due if the contract had been made "regular way," of intention to make delivery on next business day following such notice. (Rule 179(a).) Written contracts must be exchanged. (Rule 137.)
When Issued and When Distributed (Rule 63).	Due as determined by Exchange.	Written contracts or transactions not cleared through Stock Clearing Corporation must be exchanged. (Rule 137.)

Contracts for Sale of Other Bonds, Including Convertible Bonds Dealt in Pursuant to Rule 68

(Bonds bearing warrants or subscription privileges are classed as convertible bonds. Bonds on which the conversion or subscription privilege has expired are not classed as convertible bonds.)

Nature of Contract	Delivery Date	Remarks
Cash	Due on the day of the contract.	Transactions made at or before 2:00 P.M. are due before 2:30 P.M.; those made after 2:00 P.M. are due within 30 min. after sale. (Rule 177.)
Regular Way	Due on the fourth business day following the day of the contract.	
Regular Way—Delayed Delivery...	Due on the seventh day following the day of the contract. If due date is a day other than a business day, delivery shall be due on the next succeeding business day unless otherwise agreed. (Rule 178.)	Seller may deliver without advance notice except that such delivery shall not be made before the fourth business day following the day of the contract. (Rule 179(b).)
Seller's Option...	Due on the date of expiration of the option, which may not be less than eight nor more than sixty days. If the due date is a day other than a business day, delivery shall be due on the next succeeding business day unless otherwise agreed. (Rule 178.)	Seller may deliver earlier by giving written notice, on or after the day when delivery would have been due if the contract had been made "regular way," of intention to make delivery on next business day following such notice. (Rule 179(a).) Written contracts must be exchanged. (Rule 137.)
When Issued and When Distributed (Rule 63).	Due as determined by Exchange.	Written contracts on transactions not cleared through Stock Clearing Corporation must be exchanged. (Rule 137.)

[The next page is 2625.]

Chart

Dealings and Settlements

Making and Settling of Exchange Contracts

(Rules and Policies Administered by The Floor Department.)

¶ 2045   Application of Rules

Rule 45. Rules 46 to 294 [¶¶ 2046—2294], inclusive, shall apply to all Exchange Contracts made on the Exchange and, to the extent determined by the Exchange to be applicable, to Exchange Contracts not made on the Exchange.

¶ 2046   Floor Officials—Appointment

Rule 46. The President, with the approval of the Board of Governors, shall from time to time designate as Floor Officials such number of Governors and other members active on the Floor as he may determine, who shall perform such duties as are prescribed by the Rules of the Board or as may be designated by the Board.

¶ 2047   Floor Officials—Unusual Situations

Rule 47. Floor Officials shall have power to supervise and regulate active openings and unusual situations that may arise in connection with the making of bids, offers or transactions on the Floor.

Dealings upon the Exchange

¶ 2051   Hours for Business

Rule 51. Except as may be otherwise determined by the Board of Governors as to particular days, the Exchange shall be open for the transaction of business on every business day, excluding Saturdays, from 10:00 a. m., when it shall be officially announced to be open, until 3:30 p. m., when it shall be officially announced to be closed.

The Chairman, Vice-Chairman and the senior Floor Governor or in the absence from the Floor of any of them, the next senior Floor Governor present on the Floor acting by a majority shall have the power to suspend trading in all securities whenever in their opinion such suspension would be in the public interest. A special meeting of the Board of Governors to consider the continuation or termination of such suspension or closing the market shall be held as soon thereafter as a quorum of Governors can be assembled.

Amendment.
March 19, 1964.

● ● ● **Supplementary Material:**

.10 **Holidays.**—The Board has determined that the Exchange will not be open for business on New Year's Day, Washington's Birthday, Decoration Day, Independence Day, Labor Day, Election Day, Thanksgiving Day, Christmas Day. (In addition, the Exchange has traditionally been closed on Good Friday by special action, taken annually, by the Board of Governors.)

The Board has also determined that, when any holiday observed by the Exchange falls on a Saturday, the Exchange will not be open for business on the preceding Friday unless unusual business conditions exist, such as the ending of a monthly or the yearly accounting period.

¶ 2052   Dealings on Floor—Hours

Rule 52. Dealings upon the Exchange shall be limited to the hours during
          which the Exchange is open for the transaction of business; and no
member shall make any bid, offer or transaction upon the Floor before or after
those hours, except that loans of money or securities may be made after the
official closing of the Exchange.

¶ 2053   Dealings on Floor—Securities

Rule 53. Only securities admitted to dealings on an "issued," "when issued,"
          or "when distributed" basis shall be dealt in upon the Exchange.

¶ 2054   Dealings on Floor—Persons

Rule 54. No member shall, while on the Floor, make a transaction in any
          security admitted to dealings on the Exchange with any allied
member or non-member except the following: a person authorized to transact
business on the Floor pursuant to Section 14 or 15 of Article IX of the Constitution [¶¶ 1414, 1415], an officer or employee of the Exchange authorized to
close contracts pursuant to Rule 284 [¶ 2284], or an officer or employee of
the Exchange or of Stock Clearing Corporation engaged in carrying out arrangements approved by the Exchange to facilitate the borrowing and lending of money.

● ● ● *Supplementary Material:*

.10   Officers and employees of Exchange authorized to close contracts pur-
      suant to Rule 284 [¶ 2284].—

GEORGE M. CRABTREE	The Floor Department
THEODORE E. JENSEN	The Floor Department
JOHN L. LESNIEWSKI	The Floor Department
OTTO LOWE, JR.	Director, Department of Floor Procedure
JEREMIAH J. O'DONOHUE	Assistant Director, Department of Floor Procedure
J. WILLIAM O'REILLY	Director, The Floor Department
BRUCE E. PAINE	Assistant Director, Department of Floor Procedure

¶ 2055   Unit of Trading—Stocks and Bonds

Rule 55. The unit of trading in stocks shall be 100 shares, except that in the
          case of certain stocks designated by the Exchange the unit of trad-
ing shall be such lesser number of shares as may be determined by the Exchange, with respect to each stock so designated.   The unit of trading in
bonds shall be $1,000 original principal amount thereof, except that a unit of
trading of more than $1,000 may be designated by the Exchange for specific
issues of bonds.

   Amendment.
   October 18, 1962.

¶ 2056   Unit of Trading—Rights

Rule 56. Except as otherwise designated by the Exchange, transactions in
          rights to subscribe shall be on the basis of one right accruing on
each share of issued stock and the unit of trading in rights shall be 100 rights.

[The next page is 2641.]

Auction Market—Bids and Offers

(Rules and Policies Administered by The Floor Department.)

¶ 2061 Recognized Quotations

Rule 61. The recognized quotations shall be public bids and offers in lots of one trading unit or multiples thereof.

Round lots—Odd lots

Bids or offers for less than the unit of trading shall specify the principal amount of the bonds or number of shares of stock covered by the bid or offer.

More than one unit

All bids and offers for more than one trading unit shall be considered to be for the amount thereof or any lesser number of units except that bids and offers "all or none" may be made in bonds when the number of units specified in such bid or offer is fifty or more.

● ● ● *Supplementary Material:*

.10 **Less than trading unit.**—A transaction in an amount less than the unit of trading does not take bids or offers from the Floor.

.20 **More than trading unit—Uneven amounts.**—A transaction in more than the unit of trading but not a multiple thereof (such as 175 shares, 225 shares or $10,500 principal amount of bonds) takes bids and offers from the Floor, affects "stop" orders, may be published on the tape and in the sales sheet and is not considered a special transaction. A bid or offer for any such amount is considered to be either for the amount thereof or for lesser amounts in the unit of trading except in bonds where a bid or offer is made "all or none."

¶ 2062 Variations

Rule 62. Bids or offers in stocks above one dollar per share shall not be made at a less variation than ⅛ of one dollar per share; in stocks below one dollar but above ½ of one dollar per share, at a less variation than 1/16 of one dollar per share; in stocks below ½ of one dollar per share, at a less variation than 1/32 of one dollar per share; and in bonds at a less variation than ⅛ of 1% of the principal amount; provided that the Exchange may fix variations of less than the above for bids and offers in specific issues of securities or classes of securities.

● ● ● *Supplementary Material:*

.10 **Government bonds, etc.—Variations.**—The Exchange has directed that bids and offers in bonds of the United States, Puerto Rico, of States, Territories and Municipalities therein, obligations of any international authorities in which the United States is a participant, and securities guaranteed by the United States Government as to principal and interest, must be made in variations of not less than 1/32 of 1%.

.20 **"Part-redeemed" bonds—Bids and offers.**—Bonds which have been redeemed or repaid in part are designated as "part-redeemed" bonds; and bids and offers shall be made on the basis of a percentage of the original principal amount thereof.

¶ 2063   "When Issued"—"When Distributed"

Rule 63. Bids and offers in securities admitted to dealings on a "when issued" basis shall be made only "when issued," i. e., for delivery when issued as determined by the Exchange.

Bids and offers in securities admitted to dealings on a "when distributed" basis shall be made only "when distributed," i. e., for delivery when distributed as determined by the Exchange.

● ● ● *Supplementary Material:*

.10 **"When issued" and "when distributed" orders.**—When dealings in a stock on a "when issued" or "when distributed" basis are suspended, and dealings of the same stock are continued on a "regular way" basis, all orders in the hands of the specialists and odd-lot dealers for the purchase or sale of the stock on a "when issued" or "when distributed" basis will expire at the close of business on the day before such dealings on a "when issued" or "when distributed" basis are suspended, unless otherwise directed by the Exchange.

¶ 2064   100-Share-Unit Stocks

Rule 64. Bids and offers in *stocks* admitted to dealings on an "issued" basis shall be made only as follows, and may be made simultaneously as essentially different propositions, but when made without stated conditions shall be considered to be "regular way":

(1) "Cash," i. e., for delivery on the day of the contract;

(2) "regular way," i. e., for delivery on the fourth business day following the day of the contract;

(3) "seller's option," i. e., for delivery within the time specified in the option, which time shall be not less than five business days nor more than sixty days following the day of the contract; except that the Exchange may provide otherwise in specific issues of stocks or classes of stocks;

and, except that beginning with the fourth business day preceding the final day for subscription, bids and offers in rights to subscribe shall be made only "next day," i. e., for delivery on the next business day following the day of the contract; and shall be made only for "cash" on the final day for subscription.

¶ 2065   Less Than 100-Share-Unit Stocks

Rule 65. (a) Stocks having a unit of trading of less than 100 shares, not assigned by the Exchange for dealings by the use of cabinets as provided in Rule 85 [¶ 2085], shall be dealt in as provided in Rule 64 [¶ 2064].

(b) Anything contained in the Rules to the contrary notwithstanding, the following rule shall apply to deliveries of less than 100-share-unit stocks dealt in pursuant to this rule:

Unless otherwise directed by the Exchange, an odd lot of stock sold by an odd-lot dealer for his own account shall be delivered on the fourteenth day following the day of the contract, and may be delivered on any business day prior thereto, except that delivery shall not be made before the fourth business day following the day of the transaction, unless otherwise agreed.

¶ 2066 U. S. Government Securities

Rule 66. Bids and offers in *securities of the United States Government* admitted to dealings on an "issued" basis shall be made only as follows, and may be made simultaneously as essentially different propositions, but when made without stated conditions shall be considered to be "regular way":

(1) "Cash," i. e., for delivery on the day of the contract;

(2) "regular way," i.e., for delivery on the business day following the day of the contract;

(3) "seller's option," i. e., for delivery within the time specified in the option, which time shall be not less than two business days nor more than sixty days following the day of the contract, except that the Exchange may provide otherwise in such securities.

¶ 2067 Convertible Bonds

Rule 67. Bids and offers in *convertible bonds* admitted to dealings on an "issued" basis (unless designated by the Exchange to be dealt in pursuant to Rule 68 [¶ 2068]) shall be made only as follows, and may be made simultaneously as essentially different propositions, but when made without stated conditions shall be considered to be "regular way":

(1) "Cash," i. e., for delivery on the day of the contract;

(2) "regular way," i.e., for delivery on the fourth business day following the day of the contract;

(3) "seller's option," i. e., for delivery within the time specified in the option, which time shall be not less than five business days nor more than sixty days following the day of the contract, except that the Exchange may provide otherwise in specific issues of bonds or classes of bonds.

¶ 2068 Other Bonds

Rule 68. Bids and offers in *bonds* admitted to dealings on an "issued" basis which are not subject to the provisions of Rule 66 [¶ 2066] or Rule 67 [¶ 2067] (including such convertible bonds as are designated by the Exchange to be dealt in pursuant to this Rule) shall be made only as follows, and may be made simultaneously as essentially different propositions, but when made without stated conditions shall be considered to be "regular way":

(1) "Cash," i. e., for delivery on the day of the contract;

(2) "regular way," i. e.. for delivery on the fourth business day following the day of the contract; provided that the seller shall be permitted (unless the buyer specified "fourth day" when making his bid) to state at the time of closing the transaction on the Floor that the bonds are sold for "delayed delivery," in which event delivery shall be due on the seventh day following the day of the contract;

(3) "seller's option," i. e., for delivery within the time specified in the option, which time shall be not less than eight days nor more than sixty days following the day of the contract, except that the Exchange may provide otherwise in specific issues of bonds or classes of bonds.

● ● ● *Supplementary Material:*

.10 **"Delayed Delivery" and "Fourth Day" trades.**—In bonds which may be dealt in "delayed delivery" a member having a "delayed delivery" sell order may accept the best "regular way" bid even if there is a prior "fourth day" bid. A member having a "fourth day" buy order may accept the best "fourth day" offer even if there is a prior "delayed delivery" offer.

The privilege of designating a contract as having been made "delayed delivery" rests entirely with the seller who must notify the buyer at the time of the transaction that it is made "delayed delivery." If the seller does not so notify the buyer the contract is regarded to have been made "fourth day."

¶ 2069   Disagreement, "Fourth Day" or "Delayed Delivery"

Rule 69. (a) In case of a disagreement as to whether a transaction in bonds was made "fourth day" or "delayed delivery," the transaction shall be considered to have been made "delayed delivery," provided (1) that the purchasing member cannot establish by witness or otherwise that he made a "fourth day" bid, and (2) the discrepancy is discovered before 2:15 p. m. of the business day following the day of the transaction.

(b) If the discrepancy is discovered after the hours specified in paragraph (a) the members shall determine their responsibility by mutual agreement, except that when a "delayed delivery" comparison has been exchanged by the parties the transaction shall be considered to have been made "delayed delivery."

(c) If the discrepancy is discovered before the hours specified in paragraph (a) and the purchasing member has reported the transaction to his customer as having been made "fourth day," a corrected report shall be rendered immediately unless the member made the transaction on a "fourth day" order.

(d) When as a result of such disagreement, either member clears the transaction for his own account, he shall assume the cost of any additional stamp taxes necessary and may not charge any commission, except with the concurrence of his customer after the latter has been given a full statement of the facts. He shall enter upon his office records a statement (which shall be preserved for at least three years) of the circumstances which led to the clearing of the transaction in this way.

¶ 2070   Below Best Bid—Above Best Offer

Rule 70. When a bid is clearly established, no bid or offer at a lower price shall be made.

When an offer is clearly established, no offer or bid at a higher price shall be made.

Amendments.
April 21, 1955, effective June 1, 1955.

¶ 2071   Precedence of Highest Bid and Lowest Offer

Rule 71. The highest bid and the lowest offer shall have precedence in all cases.

¶ 2072 Priority and Precedence of Bids and Offers

Rule 72. I. *Bids*.—Where bids are made at the same price, the priority and precedence shall be determined as follows:

Priority of first bid

(a) When a bid is clearly established as the first made at a particular price, the maker shall be entitled to priority and shall have precedence on the next sale at that price, up to the number of shares of stock or principal amount of bonds specified in the bid, irrespective of the number of shares of stock or principal amount of bonds specified in such bid.

Precedence of bids equaling or exceeding amount offered

(b) When no bid is entitled to priority under paragraph (a) hereof, (or when a bid entitled to priority or precedence has been filled and a balance of the offer remains unfilled), all bids for a number of shares of stock or principal amount of bonds equaling or exceeding the number of shares of stock or principal amount of bonds in the offer or balance, shall be on a parity and entitled to precedence over bids for less than the number of shares of stock or principal amount of bonds in such offer or balance, subject to the condition that if it is possible to determine clearly the order of time in which the bids so entitled to precedence were made, such bids shall be filled in that order.

Precedence of bids for amounts less than amount offered

(c) When no bid is entitled to priority under paragraph (a) hereof (or when a bid entitled to priority or precedence has been filled and a balance of the offer remains unfilled) and no bid has been made for a number of shares of stock or principal amount of bonds equaling or exceeding the number of shares of stock or principal amount of bonds in the offer or balance, the bid for the largest number of shares of stock or greatest principal amount of bonds shall have precedence, subject to the condition that if two or more such bids for the same number of shares of stock or principal amount of bonds have been made, and it is possible to determine clearly the order of time in which they were made, such bids shall be filled in that order.

Simultaneous bids

(d) When bids are made simultaneously, or when it is impossible to determine clearly the order of time in which they were made, all such bids shall be on a parity subject only to precedence based on the size of the bid under the provisions of paragraphs (b) and (c) hereof.

Sale removes bids from Floor

(e) A sale shall remove all bids from the Floor except that if the number of shares of stock or principal amount of bonds offered exceeds the number of shares or principal amount specified in the bid having priority or precedence, a sale of the unfilled balance to other bidders shall be governed by the provisions of these Rules as though no sales had been made to the bidders having priority or precedence.

Subsequent bids

(f) After bids have been removed from the Floor under the provisions of paragraph (e) hereof, priority and precedence shall be determined, in accordance with these Rules, by subsequent bids.

¶ 2072   Continued
Bids in called securities

(g) Notwithstanding the provisions of this Rule and of sub-section (c) of Rule 85 [¶ 2085], the Exchange may, when all or any part of an issue of securities is called for redemption, require that all bids at the same price in the called securities shall be on a parity and that no bidder shall be entitled to more than the amount of his bid.

Transfer of priority, parity and precedence

(h) A bid may be transferred from one member to another and, as long as that bid is continued for the same account, it shall retain the same priority, parity and precedence it had at the time it was transferred.

II. *Offers.*—Where offers are at the same price the priority, parity and precedence shall be determined in the same manner as specified in the case of bids. An offer may be transferred from one member to another and, as long as that offer is continued for the same account, it shall retain the same priority, parity and precedence it had at the time it was transferred.

● ● ● *Supplementary Material:*

.10   **Precedence of bids and offers.**—The following examples explain the operations of Rule 72 [¶ 2072]:

(Note: For the purpose of these examples, it is assumed that all bids and offers are at the same prices; where an item is marked * it is assumed the bidder or offerer has clearly established priority pursuant to paragraph I(a) of Rule 72 [¶ 2072])

I.

Bids	Offers
A — 100*	D — 200
B — 100	
C — 100	

B was definitely ahead of C. A gets 100 under paragraph I(a) and B gets 100 under paragraph I(b).

II.

Bids	Offers
A — 100*	F — 1000
B — 200	
C — 400	
D — 300	
E — 500	

A receives 100 under paragraph I(a); E receives 500 under paragraph I(c); and C receives 400 under paragraph I(b).

III.

Bids	Offers
F — 1200	A — 100*
	B — 200
	C — 400
	D — 300
	E — 500

A sells 100 under paragraph I(a); E sells 500 under paragraph I(c); C sells 400 under paragraph I(c); B and D match for 200 under paragraph I(b), unless one of them can establish clearly that he made his offer before the other.

¶ **2072.10   Rule 72**   © 1961, Commerce Clearing House, Inc.

IV.

Bids	Offers
A — 500	F — 700
B — 400	
C — 300	
D — 200	
E — 100	

Bids were made simultaneously and under paragraph I(d) are on a parity. A receives 500 under paragraph I(c), and B, C and D match for 200 under paragraph I(b).

V.

Bids	Offers
E — 900	A — 1100
	B — 1000
	C — 900
	D — 500

Offers were made simultaneously and under paragraph I(d) are on a parity. A, B and C match for 900 under paragraph I(b).

VI.

Bids	Offers
A — 100*	F — 700
B — 400 ⎫ Bid	
C — 400 ⎬ simultaneously	
D — 300	
E — 200	

A receives 100 under paragraph I(a). Under paragraph I(d), B and C are on a parity and under paragraph I(c) have precedence because of largest number of shares. B and C match for 400 and the remaining 200 goes to the one who lost the match.

VII.

Bids	Offers
E — 600	A — 400 ⎫ Offered
	B — 400 ⎬ simultaneously
	C — 400 ⎭
	D — 200

Under paragraph I(d), A, B and C are on parity and under paragraph I(c) have precedence as to amount over D. A, B and C match for 400. Losers of first match should match for balance of 200 shares.

.20 Splitting.—When two or more bids on a parity have an opportunity to "match" for a lot of stock, the members making such bids may, by agreement, "split" the lot among themselves unless any other member in the Crowd objects. The same principles apply to offers.

> For example: A bids for 200, B for 200, C for 100. A and B are on a parity. D offers 200. A and B may agree to "split" the amount offered and take 100 shares each, unless C objects, in which event A and B must "match" for 200 shares.

.30 Free bonds.—The preceding examples [.10], with respect to precedence of bids and offers in 100-share-unit stocks and stocks traded in in units of less than one hundred shares at the active Posts, apply in principle to precedence of bids and offers in free bonds.

¶ 2073 "Seller's Option"

Rule 73. On offers to buy "seller's option" at the same price, the longest option shall have precedence; on offers to sell "seller's option" at the same price, the shortest option shall have precedence.

¶ 2074 Publicity of Bids and Offers

Rule 74. A claim by a member who states that he had on the Floor a prior or better bid or offer shall not be sustained if the bid or offer was not made with the publicity and frequency necessary to make the existence of such bid or offer generally known at the time of the transaction.

¶ 2075 Disputes as to Bids and Offers

Rule 75. Disputes arising on bids or offers, if not settled by agreement between the members interested, shall be settled, if practicable, by a vote of the members knowing of the transaction in question; if not so settled, they shall be settled by a Floor Official.

● ● ● *Supplementary Material:*

.10 Discrepancies as to amount.—When there is no dispute regarding a transaction except as to the amount traded in and neither party can produce a witness, the transaction must be considered to have been for the smaller amount.

¶ 2076 "Crossing" Orders

Rule 76. When a member has an order to buy and an order to sell the same security, he shall, except as provided in Rule 85(e)1 [¶ 2085], publicly offer such security at a price which is higher than his bid by the minimum variation permitted in such security before making a transaction with himself.

(*See* ¶ 2085.10 *and Rule* 91 [¶ 2091].)

● ● ● *Supplementary Material:*

.10 "Crossing" bonds.—When a "cross" is made in a free bond at a bid or offered price which has been established publicly, the bidders and offerors must determine their rights in accordance with Rule 72 [¶ 2072].

¶ 2077 Prohibited Dealings and Activities

Rule 77. No member shall offer publicly on the Floor:

    (1) To buy or sell securities "on stop" above or below the market;
    (2) to buy or sell securities "at the close";
    (3) to buy or sell dividends;
    (4) to bet upon the course of the market; or
    (5) to buy or sell privileges to receive or deliver securities.

¶ 2078 Sell and Buy Orders Coupled at Same Price

Rule 78. An offer to sell coupled with an offer to buy back at the same or at an advanced price, or the reverse, is a prearranged trade and is prohibited. This rule applies both to transactions in the unit of trading and in lesser and greater amounts.

¶ 2073   Rule 73

¶ 2079   Bids and Offers—Binding

Rule 79. All bids made and accepted, and all offers made and accepted, in accordance with Rules 45 to 85 [¶ 2045-2085], 116 to 119 [¶ 2116-2119], and 122 and 123 [¶ 2122, 2123], shall be binding.

¶ 2079A   Miscellaneous Requirements on Stock and Bond Market Procedures

● ● ● *Supplementary Material:*

.10   Request to make better bid or offer.—When a broker does not bid or offer at the limit of an order which is better than the currently quoted price in the security and is requested by his principal to bid or offer at such limit, he should either do so or forthwith return the order.

.20   Bids and offers on tape.—A request to have a bid or offer published on the tape must be recorded by the Supervisor at the Post on the form provided for this purpose. Each such request must be made on a separate slip. A reasonable interval must elapse between the publishing of successive bids or offers in the same security. No bid or offer in bonds may be published after the market has closed.

.30   One or two points or more away from last sale.—All transactions in stocks at the active Posts which are made (a) at one point or more away from the last previous sale when such previous sale is under $20 per share or (b) at two points or more away from the last previous sale when such previous sale is at $20 per share or over, may not be published on the tape without the prior approval of a Floor Official. When such a transaction is an opening sale it will be accompanied when published on the tape by the symbol "OPD," meaning "opened" and when such a transaction occurs after an opening sale it will be accompanied by the symbol "SLD," meaning "sold."

The purpose of these symbols is to indicate that such transactions may not be in their proper order on the tape with relation to transactions in other stocks made at or about the same time owing to a possible delay in the publication of such transactions due to the necessity of obtaining the prior approval of a Floor Official.

The term "one point or more" or the term "two points or more" as used herein is the net difference between the price of the current sale and the price of the last previous sale after taking into consideration a dividend or other distribution when the stock sells "ex-dividend" or "ex-distribution." For instance, if the opening sale in such stock is at 48 "ex-dividend" ½, and the last previous sale was at 50, the net difference would be regarded as 1½ points and approval for publication would not be required. If the opening transaction is at 20½ "ex-dividend" ¼ and the last previous sale was at 19¾, the net difference would be regarded as one point and in this case approval for publication would be required.

Bond Market Procedures

.40   Transactions at wide variations.—Before making transactions in bonds at wide variations from previous prices, members must consult a Floor Official. In certain cases the Floor Official may require that bonds be offered or bid for on the tape before making a trade, but such offers or bids may not be placed on the tape except upon the instructions of the Floor Official. If any doubt exists whether bonds may be bid for or offered at given prices, a Floor Official should be consulted. This applies also to orders placed in the cabinets.

.50 Quotation cards.—Quotation cards are maintained in free bonds for the information and guidance of members, containing the bids and offers in each such bond.

Notations of bids and offers at the market will be permitted to be placed on the quotation cards but shall be removed immediately after the opening sale of the bonds and in any event not later than 10:15 a.m.

After 10:15 a.m. a member having a market order will be permitted to have a notation of his bid or offer placed on the quotation card only when the spread between the best bid and the best offer is more than one-half point and such member agrees: (1) to allow the quotation clerk to quote his bid or offer at the price of the last sale or better, except that a Floor Official may permit otherwise, and (2) to trade on his bid or offer, whichever the case may be.

There shall be NO obligation on other members to regard such an order as other than a LIMITED order at the price of the last sale.

Members are requested to notify the clerks immediately when their orders are cancelled or executed.

When a member who is not regularly active in the Crowd leaves after having made a bid or offer which is noted on the quotation card, the clerk is instructed to cancel the notation.

.60 Transactions within the ring.—All transactions in the Bond Crowd MUST take place within the ring on the Floor. Reporters have been instructed NOT to take a record of transactions made away from that area.

.70 Reporters.—After the market closes the reporters are required to take any sales which occurred before the closing and are then required to leave the Crowd.

¶ 2080 Transmission of Names of Bidders, Offerors, Buyers or Sellers

Rule 80. The name of a bidder, offeror, buyer or seller on the Floor of the Exchange shall not be transmitted from the Floor except that:

(1) The name of a specialist bidding or offering for an account in which he has a direct or indirect interest may be transmitted from the Floor, provided it is made clear that the specialist is acting for his own account and not for the "book"; and

(2) a member or member organization may send to his or its office a written report containing the name of the opposite party to the transaction, solely for the purpose of processing the transaction.

Amendments.
November 19, 1953, effective November 24, 1953.

[The next page is 2661.]

Cabinet Dealings

(Rules and Policies Administered by The Floor Department.)

¶ 2085   Cabinet Securities

Stocks

Rule 85. (a) Ten-share-unit stocks assigned by the Exchange for dealings by the use of cabinets shall be dealt in at a location designated for the purpose, except that when exigencies require, a Floor Official may permit dealings at the same location, without the use of cabinets.

Bonds

(b) The Exchange shall designate those bonds which are to be dealt in by the use of cabinets.

Sequence of orders

(c) Bids and offers in securities dealt in by the use of cabinets shall be written on cards, which shall be filed in the cabinets in the following sequence:

    (1) According to price, and

    (2) According to the time received at the cabinet.

Orders in such securities shall be filled according to the bids and offers filed in the cabinets, in the sequence indicated above, except that oral bids and offers in such securities may be made if not in conflict with bids and offers in the cabinets.

(See .30-.43, below, regarding "Cabinet Bonds."

.20; .70, below, regarding "short" orders in cabinet bonds and stocks.

.50, below, regarding "Cabinet Securities—Order Forms."

.60, below, regarding Oral "Bids and Offers."

¶ 2120.10 regarding "Sending Orders to Specialists."

¶ 2123.55 regarding "G. T. C. Orders—Semiannual Confirmations."

¶ 2123.75 regarding "Marking Sell Orders 'Long' or 'Short'.")

Ten-share-unit stocks

(d) In addition to other applicable rules, the following rules shall apply to *ten-share-unit stocks* dealt in by the use of cabinets:

    (1) No order shall be filed in the cabinets unless it bears the name of a specialist registered in such stocks on whom responsibility for the execution of the order shall rest.

    (2) Members registered as specialists in such ten-share-unit stocks shall be required to register with the Exchange as odd-lot dealers in said stocks.

    (3) Unless otherwise directed by the Exchange, an odd lot of stock sold by an odd-lot dealer for his own account shall be delivered on the fourteenth day following the day of the contract, and may be delivered on any business day prior thereto except that delivery shall not be made before the fourth business day following the day of the transaction, unless otherwise agreed.

¶ 2085   Continued

"Cabinet" bonds

(e) In addition to other applicable rules, the following rules shall apply to *bonds* dealt in by the use of cabinets:

(1) When a member has filed a bid or offer in the cabinets pursuant to an order entrusted to him and thereafter he receives a commission order on the opposite side, he may "cross" such orders without making any further bids or offers, provided (i) the bid or offer which he so accepts has been filed in the cabinets for a reasonable period of time, and (ii) he announces to the crowd before accepting his own bid or offer, his intention so to do. This applies only when the member acts as broker on both sides and not when he acts on either side for his own account, or for any account in which he, his member organization or any participant therein is directly or indirectly interested, in which event Rule 91 [¶ 2091] shall apply. "Cabinet" bonds shall not be opened by a "cross" whether "regular way" or otherwise, until reasonable notice has been given to members maintaining bids or offers in the cabinets in said bonds one point or less from the last sale in the bonds.

(*See* .10, *below, regarding* " 'Crossing' Bonds.")

Placing cards in cabinet

(2) Every card placed in the cabinets shall bear a definite price and no mark or identification shall be placed thereon to indicate it is other than a limited order at the price, except that:

(A) Market orders specifically marked as such may be placed in the cabinets but shall be removed immediately after the opening sale of the bonds and in any event not later than 10:15 a. m.

(B) When the spread between the best bid and the best offer in the cabinets is more than one-half point, orders representing market orders may, after 10:15 a. m., be kept or placed in the cabinets provided a DEFINITE price is placed thereon. Such price shall be the last sale or better, except that a Floor Official may permit otherwise. In this event, the fact that a card represents a market order may be indicated by a distinguishing mark placed thereon by the broker, but there shall be NO obligation on other members to regard it as other than a LIMITED order at the price appearing on the card.

"Cash" or "seller's option"

(3) Notwithstanding the provisions of Rule 67 [¶ 2067] and Rule 68 [¶ 2068], members who file "regular way" bids in the cabinets, shall be given an opportunity to bid for bonds offered "cash" or "seller's option." Such opportunity shall be given to all bidders in the sequence in which their bids appear in the cabinets. The same principle shall apply to "regular way" offers when "cash" or "seller's option" bids are made.

● ● ● *Supplementary Material:*

.10   **Procedure in "crossing" bonds.**—A "cross" must take place as nearly as possible in the center of the ring provided for that purpose and a member making the "cross" must proceed as follows:

Immediately prior to bidding or offering, he must raise his arm and simultaneously announce the full name of the security to be "crossed" at least twice, and with an audibility sufficient under the circumstances to make his intention to "cross" generally known. He must immediately thereafter bid and offer as required in Rule 76 [¶ 2076] in an equally audible and public manner.

(*See* ¶ 2091 *regarding members taking or supplying securities for own account.*)

.20 "Short" orders in inactive stocks.—Short orders entrusted to a specialist at Post 30 shall be executed in the same manner as provided in ¶ 2123.71. The specialist shall be responsible for changing the limits on any short orders entrusted to him which he places in the cabinet assigned to such stock.

Cabinet Bonds

.30 Absence from crowd.—During the absence (whether temporary or otherwise) of a member regularly stationed in the crowd, he must authorize another member to act for him with respect to orders placed in cabinets by him. If, during his absence, another member offers to trade upon such orders, the authorized representative must consummate the trade without delay and must charge a commission.

.32 Bids and offers binding.—When a member removes a card from the cabinets and informs either the member who caused it to be inserted or the representative of the latter that the bid or offer is accepted, the bid or offer may not be withdrawn and the transaction must be consummated. (*See* .70, *below.*)

.33 Cancellation of orders.—When orders in the cabinets are cancelled, the card must be removed by the members entering such orders or by their representatives.

.34 Changing price limits.—When changes in price limits are made on a subsequent date in open orders already filed in the cabinets the date on such orders must be changed at the same time by the members entering such orders or by their representatives.

.35 Clerks restricted.—Cabinet clerks may not give any information regarding trades before they have been consummated nor make any change whatever in the price, date, designation or symbol with respect to orders in the cabinets. They may, however, reduce the amount of an order when it is partially executed.

.36 Closing cabinets.—The cabinets are closed when the market closes.

.37 Month, week and G. T. C. orders.—Month orders in the cabinets are cancelled on the last business day of each month. Week orders in the cabinets are cancelled on the last business day of each week. In order to retain their relative positions at the opening on the next business day thereafter, such orders must be renewed and filed in the cabinets after the close of the market on the day of cancellation, but not later than one hour after the close of the market. G. T. C. orders remaining in the cabinets will retain their status.

.38 Recognition of better bids and offers.—When a member removes a card from the cabinets, representing an order to buy, for the purpose of consummating a transaction with the member who caused the card to be inserted,

¶ **2085.38   Cabinet Bonds.**—Continued

a higher bid than that represented by the card made before the transaction is consummated must be recognized and accepted.   The same principle applies to selling orders when a lower offer is made.

.39   Responsibility for orders.—All orders filed in the cabinets must bear the name of a member regularly stationed in the Crowd.

Members are responsible for all cards bearing their names in the cabinets.

.40   "Seller's option" orders.—All selling orders on a "seller's option" basis filed in the cabinets, must be written on special cards which may be obtained at the office of the Superintendent of the Bond Floor.   These cards must be filed in the same manner as other "cabinet" bond orders, except that a shorter option at a given price takes precedence over a longer option at the same price.

.41   Special bids and offers.—Special bids or offers, such as for bonds "ex" a given coupon, bonds in particular denominations, etc., must not be placed in the cabinets except with the consent of a Floor Official.

.42   "Stop orders."—"Stop orders" may not be placed in the cabinets.

.43   "Stopping" bonds.—Bonds may not be "stopped" against bids or offers in the cabinets except by agreement of both members concerned (not their clerks).

.50   Cabinet securities—Order forms.—Orders for ten-share-unit stocks or for bonds dealt in by the use of cabinets must be written on special order forms which may be procured from the Exchange, and must be in the following colors:

White for day orders   Salmon for month orders (Bonds)
Blue for week orders (Bonds)   Yellow for G. T. C. orders.

.60   Oral bids and offers.—Rule 85(c), above, permits oral bids and offers to be made when not in conflict with bids and offers filed in the cabinets. Oral bids and offers at the same price as those filed in the cabinets are not considered to be in conflict but the written orders in the cabinets have precedence over the oral bids and offers.

.70   "Short" orders in bonds assigned to cabinets.—Short orders may be placed in bonds assigned to cabinets.   The execution of such orders is subject to the rules in regard to short selling and the members placing such orders in the cabinets shall be responsible for changing the limits on short orders so placed.   Employees of the Exchange may not be used to change the limits on such orders.

When a member accepts an offer marked "short," which has been placed in the cabinets, the offer may not be withdrawn, but if the price of the offer is in violation of such short selling rules, the price may be changed by the seller before a trade is consummated, to conform to such rules.   The buying member, however, shall not be bound to trade at the changed price, and may withdraw his acceptance.

Any change in the price at which a short order in bonds may be offered shall be deemed to constitute the cancellation of the order at the old price and the entry of a new order at the new price, and such new order shall be subject to the priority of any orders already filed in the cabinet at that price.

(*See* ¶ 2079A.40, *"Transactions at wide variations."*)

[The next page is 2681.]

¶ **2085.39   Rule 85**

Members Dealing for Their
Own Accounts

(Rules and Policies Administered by The Floor Department.)

¶ 2091   Taking or Supplying Securities Named in Order

Rule 91.   No member, whether acting as a specialist or otherwise, who has accepted for execution, personally or through his member organization or a participant therein, an order for the purchase of securities shall fill such order by selling such securities for any account in which he, his member organization or a participant therein has a direct or indirect interest or having so accepted an order for the sale of securities shall fill such order by buying such securities for such an account, except as follows:

Missing the market

(a) A member who neglects to execute an order may be compelled to take or supply for his own account or that of his member organization the securities named in the order;

"Crossing" for own account

(b) A member may take the securities named in the order provided (1) he shall have offered the same in the open market at a price which is higher than his bid by the minimum variation permitted in such securities, and (2) the price is justified by the condition of the market, and (3) the member who gave the order shall directly, or through a broker authorized to act for him, after prompt notification, accept the trade;

(c) A member may supply the securities named in the order provided (1) he shall have bid for the same in the open market at a price which is lower than his offer by the minimum variation permitted in such securities, and (2) the price is justified by the condition of the market, and (3) the member who gave the order shall directly or through a broker authorized to act for him, after prompt notification, accept the trade;

"On order"

(d) A member acting as a broker is permitted to report to his principal a transaction as made with himself when he has orders from two principals to buy and to sell the same security and not to give up, such orders being executed in accordance with Rule 76 [¶ 2076], in which case he must add to his name on the report the words "on order."

● ● ● *Supplementary Material:*

.10   **Confirmation of transactions.**—When a member or member organization is notified to send a representative to a post for the purpose of confirming a transaction with another member who has elected to take or supply for his own account the securities named in an order entrusted to him, the member or member organization so notified or a member representing the notified party must respond promptly. The transaction must then be either confirmed or rejected with a member and not with a clerk. The representative must initial the memorandum record of the specialist which shows the details of the trade and return it to the specialist. The specialist must keep such memoranda records for a period of one year.

¶ 2091   Continued

.20 Principal transactions against orders in specialists' possession.—A specialist occasionally may effect a transaction as principal against an order which had been entered for an account carried by the specialist's organization or serviced by someone at his organization. In such cases, it is desirable that all specialists follow a uniform procedure. The customer for whom the order had been entered should be contacted promptly. The fact that the stock has been taken or supplied as principal against his order should be explained to him so that he may then accept or reject the transaction.

¶ 2092   Limitations on Members' Trading Because of Customers' Orders

Rule 92. (a) No member shall (1) personally buy or initiate the purchase of any security on the Exchange for his own account or for any account in which he, his member organization or a participant therein, is directly or indirectly interested, while such member personally holds or has knowledge that his member organization or a participant therein, holds an unexecuted market order to buy such security in the unit of trading for a customer, or (2) personally sell or initiate the sale of any security on the Exchange for any such account, while he personally holds or has knowledge that his member organization or any participant therein, holds an unexecuted market order to sell such security in the unit of trading for a customer.

(b) No member shall (1) personally buy or initiate the purchase of any security on the Exchange for any such account, at or below the price at which he personally holds or has knowledge that his member organization or any participant therein, holds an unexecuted limited price order to buy such security in the unit of trading for a customer, or (2) personally sell or initiate the sale of any security on the Exchange for any such account at or above the price at which he personally holds or has knowledge that his member organization or any participant therein, holds an unexecuted limited price order to sell such security in the unit of trading for a customer.

(c) The provisions of this Rule shall not apply (1) to any purchase or sale of any security in an amount of less than the unit of trading made by an odd-lot dealer to offset odd-lot orders for customers, or (2) to any purchase or sale of any security upon terms for delivery other than those specified in such unexecuted market or limited price order.

¶ 2093   Trading for Joint Account

Rule 93. (a) No member while on the Floor shall, without the prior approval of a Floor Official, initiate the purchase or sale on the Exchange of stock for any account in which he, his member organization or a participant therein is directly or indirectly interested with any person other than such member organization or participant therein.

(b) The provisions of this Rule shall not apply to any purchase or sale (1) by a member for a joint account maintained solely for effecting *bona fide* domestic or foreign arbitrage transactions, or (2) by an odd-lot dealer or a specialist for any joint account in which he is expressly permitted to have an interest or participation by Rule 94 [¶ 2094].

¶ **2091.20   Rule 91**

¶ 2094 Specialists' or Odd-Lot Dealers' Interest in Joint Accounts

Rule 94. (a) A specialist or odd-lot dealer, who is not a general partner or a holder of voting stock in a member organization, shall neither directly nor indirectly acquire or hold any interest or participation in any joint account for buying or selling on the Exchange any stock in which such specialist or odd-lot dealer is registered, except a joint account with a member who is not a general partner or a holder of voting stock in a member organization or with a member organization.

(b) A specialist or odd-lot dealer, who is a general partner or a holder of voting stock in a member organization and such organization, shall neither directly nor indirectly acquire or hold any interest or participation in any joint account for buying or selling on the Exchange any stock in which such specialist or odd-lot dealer is registered, except a joint account in which such member organization is a participant with a member who is not a general partner or the holder of voting stock in a member organization or with another member organization.

(*See* ¶ 2314.26.)

¶ 2095 Discretionary Transactions

Rule 95. (a) No member while on the Floor shall execute or cause to be executed on the Exchange any transaction for the purchase or sale of any stock with respect to which transaction such member is vested with discretion as to (1) the choice of security to be bought or sold, (2) the total amount of any security to be bought or sold, or (3) whether any such transaction shall be one of purchase or sale.

(b) The provisions of paragraph (a) of this Rule shall not apply (1) to any discretionary transaction executed by such member for any *bona fide* cash investment account or for the account of any person who, due to illness, absence or similar circumstances, is actually unable to effect transactions for his own accounts; provided that such member shall keep available for inspection a detailed record of any such transaction and the grounds for exercising such discretion and shall file with the Exchange regular reports as required, or (2) to any transaction permitted by Rule 93 [¶ 2093] for any account in which the member executing such transaction is directly or indirectly interested.

● ● ● *Supplementary Material:*

.10 **Discretionary transactions.**—Every member who, while on the Floor has executed or caused to be executed any discretionary transaction described in clause (1) of paragraph (b) of Rule 95, above, must report such transactions, when requested, to the Floor Department on a form which may be obtained from that department, giving the following information:

(1) The name and type of each account for which any such transaction was executed.

(2) The name and amount of each stock purchased or sold under such discretion during the period mentioned.

(3) If for a margin account, the grounds for exercising such discretion with respect to each account.

¶ 2095.10   Continued

Only those members who have reportable information should submit reports.

Reports should be made by the individual members and not by the member organizations.

Transactions in bonds should not be reported.

No report should be made with respect to transactions permitted by Rule 93 [¶ 2093] for any account in which the member executing such transactions is directly or indirectly interested.

Reports should not include discretionary transactions effected upon orders originated in the office or "off" the Floor.

.20   Originating orders in discretionary accounts.—Specialists should not originate orders in the stocks in which they are registered for any accounts over which they may have discretion.

¶ 2096   Limitation on Members' Trading Because of Options

Rule 96.   No member while on the Floor shall initiate the purchase or sale on the Exchange for his own account or for any account in which he, his member organization or any participant therein is directly or indirectly interested, of any stock in which he holds or has granted any put, call, straddle or option, or in which he has knowledge that his member organization or any participant therein holds or has granted any put, call, straddle or option.

[The next page is 2701.]

Specialists, Odd-Lot Brokers, and Registered Traders

(Rules and Policies Administered by The Floor Department.)

¶ 2099   Round-Lot Transactions of Odd-Lot Dealer and Broker

Rule 99.   No odd-lot dealer or his relief or associate odd-lot broker shall effect while on the Floor of the Exchange purchases or sales of any security in which such odd-lot dealer is registered, for any account in which such odd-lot dealer, his member organization or any participant therein is directly or indirectly interested, unless such dealings are reasonably necessary to permit the odd-lot dealer to act as such in such security, or, if also registered as a specialist in such security, to act as a specialist.

Adopted.

April 16, 1964, effective June 1, 1964.

¶ 2100   Round-Lot Transactions of Odd-Lot Dealer or Broker Affecting Odd-Lot Orders

Sales

Rule 100.   (a) When an odd-lot dealer or his relief or associate odd-lot broker determines to sell a round-lot, he shall give the order to the specialist or another member not associated with the odd-lot dealer for execution, if the transaction would establish the price for the execution of odd-lot orders the dealer or his relief or associate odd-lot broker holds and make the dealer a buyer on balance.

Purchases

(b) When an odd-lot dealer or his relief or associate odd-lot broker determines to buy a round-lot, he shall give the order to the specialist or another member not associated with the odd-lot dealer for execution, if the transaction would establish the price for the execution of odd-lot orders the dealer or his relief or associate odd-lot broker holds and make the dealer a seller on balance.

Exception to Paragraphs (a) and (b) Above

(c) If unusual circumstances exist, such as unusual activity in a stock with a corresponding increase in the number of orders being received and a need for effecting an unusual number of off-setting round-lot transactions, the off-setting orders may, with the approval of a Floor Official, be handled by the odd-lot dealer or his relief or associate odd-lot broker.   A record should be kept of the circumstances.

Specialist as Principal

(d) The approval of a Floor Official is required for transactions described in paragraphs (a) and (b) when the specialist acts as a principal on the opposite side of the transaction and such transaction is at a price more than one-eighth point away from the previous sale.

¶ 2100 Continued

Transactions of Specialist—Odd-Lot Dealer

(e) If an odd-lot dealer and a specialist in a security deal for the same account such specialist or odd-lot dealer may not effect, without the approval of a Floor Official, a transaction for any account in which they, their member organization, or any participant therein has a direct or indirect interest that would have an effect described in paragraphs (a) or (b) above.

Stop Orders

(f) An odd-lot dealer or his relief or associate odd-lot broker may not, without the approval of a Floor Official, effect a transaction or cause a transaction to be effected for the account of the odd-lot dealer which would elect any odd-lot stop order held by such odd-lot dealer or his relief or associate odd-lot broker.

Adopted.

April 16, 1964, effective June 1, 1964.

¶ 2101   Registration of Odd-Lot Dealers and Brokers

Rule 101. No member shall act as an odd-lot dealer or odd-lot broker on the Floor in a security unless such member is registered as an odd-lot dealer or an odd-lot broker in such security with the Exchange and unless the Exchange has approved of his so acting as an odd-lot dealer or odd-lot broker and has not withdrawn such approval; provided, however, that the Exchange may exempt relief odd-lot brokers from the provisions of this Rule upon such conditions as it may prescribe.

● ● ● *Supplementary Material:*

.10   Qualifications.—A member who applies to register as an odd-lot dealer or broker is required to pass an Odd-Lot Examination prescribed by the Exchange. See ¶ 2345.15 for procedures for examination. Applications for this examination should be submitted to the Floor Department.

¶ 2102   Options of Odd-Lot Dealers

Rule 102. No odd-lot dealer, no member organization of which he is a participant and no participant in such organization shall acquire, hold, or grant, directly or indirectly, any interest in any put, call, straddle or option in any stock in which such odd-lot dealer is registered.

¶ 2103   Registration of Specialists

Rule 103. No member shall act as a specialist on the Floor in any security unless such member is registered as a specialist in such security with the Exchange and unless the Exchange has approved of his so acting as a specialist and has not withdrawn such approval; provided, however, that the Exchange may exempt relief specialists from the provisions of this Rule, upon such conditions as it may prescribe.

If the Exchange shall have found any substantial or continued failure by a specialist to engage in a course of dealings for his own account to assist in the maintenance, so far as practicable, of a fair and orderly market, the registration of such specialist shall be subject to suspension or cancellation by the Exchange in one or more of the stocks in which he is registered.

Amendment.
September 16, 1964, effective January 4, 1965.

● ● ● *Supplementary Material:*

.10   Registration of specialists.—Four classes of specialists have been established, namely, (1) regular specialists, (2) relief specialists, (3) associate specialists, and (4) temporary specialists. No member is permitted to act as regular specialist, relief specialist or associate specialist unless he is registered with the Exchange. No registration is required for temporary specialists, but no member is permitted to act as such unless authorized by a Floor Official.

Registration applies only to individual members, and not to member organizations. Consequently each Floor member of a specialist organization who expects to act as regular specialist, relief specialist or associate specialist at any time must register individually.

All members of the Exchange registered as regular specialists, or odd-lot dealers or odd-lot brokers will be required to pay a quarterly registration fee of $75.00 and all members registered as relief or associate specialists will be required to pay a quarterly registration fee of $2.50.

Notice of all new applications for registration as regular or relief specialist will be posted on the bulletin board. Approval will not be given on any such application until one week from the date of receipt thereof, except that, if circumstances require immediate action, temporary approval may be given. Members wishing to make representations with respect to any application should file their comments with the Department of Floor Procedure during the period when notice is posted.

Notice of applications for registration as associate specialists will not be posted.

Before registration as a specialist, a member is required to pass a Specialist's Examination prescribed by the Exchange. See ¶ 2345.15 for procedures for examination. Applications for this examination should be submitted to the Floor Department.

¶ 2104   Dealings by Specialists

Rule 104.   No specialist shall effect on the Exchange purchases or sales of any security in which such specialist is registered, for any account in which he, his member organization or any participant therein is directly or indirectly interested, unless such dealings are reasonably necessary to permit such specialist to maintain a fair and orderly market, or to act as an odd-lot dealer in such security.

Functions of Specialists

.10   Regular specialists.—Any member who expects to act regularly as specialist in any listed stock and to solicit orders therein must be registered as a regular specialist.

The function of a member acting as regular specialist on the Floor of the Exchange includes, in addition to the effective execution of commission orders entrusted to him, the maintenance, in so far as reasonably practicable, of a fair

¶ 2104.10 Continued

and orderly market on the Exchange in the stocks in which he is so acting. This is more specifically set forth in the following:

(1) The maintenance of a fair and orderly market implies the maintenance of price continuity with reasonable depth, and the minimizing of the effects of temporary disparity between supply and demand.

(2) In connection with the maintenance of a fair and orderly market, it is commonly desirable that a member acting as specialist engage to a reasonable degree under existing circumstances in dealings for his own account when lack of price continuity, lack of depth, or disparity between supply and demand exists or is reasonably to be anticipated.

(3) Transactions on the Exchange for his own account effected by a member acting as specialist must constitute a course of dealings reasonably calculated to contribute to the maintenance of price continuity with reasonable depth, and to the minimizing of the effects of temporary disparity between supply and demand, immediate or reasonably to be anticipated. Transactions not part of such a course of dealings are not to be effected.

(4) A specialist's quotation, made for his own account, should be such that a transaction effected thereon, whether having the effect of reducing or increasing the specialist's position, will bear a proper relation to preceding transactions and anticipated succeeding transactions.

(5) Transactions on the Exchange for his own account of a member acting as specialist are to be effected in a reasonable and orderly manner in relation to the condition of the general market, the market in the particular stock and the adequacy of the specialist's position to the immediate and reasonably anticipated needs of the market. The following types of transactions to establish or increase a position are not to be effected except when they are reasonably necessary to render the specialist's position adequate to such needs:

(A) a purchase at a price above the last sale in the same session;

(B) the purchase of all or substantially all the stock offered on the book at a price equal to the last sale, when the stock so offered represents all or substantially all the stock offered in the market; and when a substantial amount of a stock is offered at a price equal to the last sale price the purchase of more than 50% of all the stock offered;

(C) the supplying of all or substantially all the stock bid for on the book at a price equal to the last sale, when the stock so bid for represents all or substantially all the stock bid for in the market; and when a substantial amount of a stock is bid for at a price equal to the last sale price, the supplying of more than 50% of all the stock bid for; and

(D) failing to reoffer or rebid where necessary after effecting transactions described in (A), (B) and (C) above.

Transactions of these types may, nevertheless, be effected with the approval of a Floor Official or in less active markets where they are an essential part of a proper course of dealings and where the amount of

¶ **2104.10**   **Rule 104**

stock involved and the price change, if any, are normal in relation to the market.

(6) Transactions on the Exchange by a specialist for his own account in liquidating or decreasing his position in a specialty stock are to be effected in a reasonable and orderly manner in relation to the condition of the general market, the market in the particular stock and the adequacy of the specialist's positions to the immediate and reasonably anticipated needs of the market and in this connection, unless he has the prior approval of a Floor Official, he should avoid:

(A) liquidation of all or substantially all of a position by selling stock at prices below the last different price or by purchasing stock at prices above the last different price unless such transactions are reasonably necessary in relation to the specialist's overall position in the stocks in which he is registered;

(B) failing to maintain a fair and orderly market during liquidation;

(C) failing to re-enter the market where necessary, after effecting transactions described in (A) above.

(7) When inquiry is made of a specialist as to the price at which a block of stock may be sold, the specialist may advise the broker of the "clean up" price for the block. However, the specialist may not specify the amount that would be purchased by the book and the amount that he would take as a dealer. If, as a result of this inquiry, the block is sold and the specialist participates as a dealer at the "clean up" price, he should also execute at the same price the executable buy orders held by him except for the amount of the block which can be executed at the current bid, whether such bid is for orders held by him or for the account of the specialist or both. The same principle applies in the event an inquiry is made with respect to an order to purchase a block of stock.

(8) If a specialist has limit sell orders on his book at two or more different prices, he should not, as a dealer, purchase all of the stock from the book at the lowest limit price and then immediately purchase stock from the book at a higher limit price. He should in such a situation withdraw the offer and cross the entire amount of stock he is purchasing as a dealer at one price. The same principle applies in the event the specialist sells stock to limit orders on the book at two or more different prices.

.11 Participation at openings or reopenings.—A specialist should avoid participating as a dealer in opening or reopening a stock in such a manner as to upset the public balance of supply and demand as reflected by market and limited price orders, unless the condition of the general market or the specialist's position in light of the reasonably anticipated needs of the market makes it advisable to do so. He may, however, buy or sell stock as a dealer to minimize the disparity between supply and demand at an opening or reopening.

.12 LIFO transactions.—A member acting as a specialist may not effect transactions for the purpose of adjusting a LIFO inventory in a stock in which he is so acting except as a part of a course of dealings reasonably necessary to assist in the maintenance of a fair and orderly market.

¶ 2104 Continued

.13 Relief specialists.—Any member registered as a regular specialist must either (1) be associated with other members also registered as regular specialists in the same stocks, either through a partnership or a member corporation or a joint account, and arrange for at least one member of the group to be in attendance during the hours when the Exchange is open for business, or (2) arrange for the registration by at least one other member as relief specialist, who would always be available, in the regular specialist's absence, to take over the "book" and to service the market, so that there would be no interruption of the continuity of service during the hours when the Exchange is open for business.

The same obligations and responsibilities for the maintenance and stabilization of markets which rest upon regular specialists, rest also upon relief specialists while in possession of the "book."

A member will be permitted to register as a relief specialist for only one particular specialist or specialist group. Approval of the registration of a regular specialist as a relief specialist will be granted provided that the surrounding circumstances are such as to permit him to act in such relief capacity, and at the same time insure the adequate servicing of the stocks in which he is registered as a regular specialist and the proper performance of his dealer function therein.

.15 Associate specialists.—Any member who expects to act as assistant to a regular specialist in handling the "book," but does not expect either to solicit orders or to assist in the maintenance and stabilization of the market by purchases and sales for his own account, may be registered as an associate specialist.

The duties of an associate specialist are the execution of commission orders entrusted to the regular specialist, and rendering such other assistance as may be necessary either to the regular specialist or relief specialist.

An associate specialist is not responsible for the maintenance or stabilization of the market by purchases or sales for his own account. He is prohibited from handling the "book" or making any bid or offer unless either the regular specialist or a relief specialist is present.

.17 Temporary specialists.—In the event of an emergency, such as the absence of the regular and relief specialists, or when the volume of business in the particular stock or stocks is so great that it cannot be handled by the regular and relief specialists without assistance, a Floor Official may authorize a member of the Exchange who is not registered as a specialist or relief specialist in such stock or stocks, to act as temporary specialist for that day only.

A member who acts as a temporary specialist by such authority is required to file with The Floor Department, at the end of the day, a report showing (a) the name of the stock or stocks in which he so acted, (b) the name of the regular specialist, (c) the time of day when he so acted, and (d) the name of the Floor Official who authorized the arrangement. The necessary forms may be obtained at the money desk.

The Floor Officials will not give such authority for the purpose of permitting a member not registered as specialist or relief specialist habitually to relieve a regular specialist at lunch periods, etc.

¶ 2104.13   **Rule 104**   © 1964, Commerce Clearing House, Inc.

If a temporary specialist substitutes for a regular specialist, and if no regular or relief specialist is present, the temporary specialist is expected to assume the obligations and responsibilities of regular specialists for the maintenance and stabilization of the market.

Capital Requirements of Specialists
(effective January 4, 1965)

.20   Regular specialists.—

(1) A member registered as a regular specialist at an active post must be able to assume a position of 12 trading units in each common stock in which he is registered.

(2) A member registered as a regular specialist at an active post must be able to assume a position of 400 shares in each of the 100 share trading unit preferred stocks and of 100 shares in each of the 10 share trading unit preferred stocks in which he is registered.

(3) A member registered as a regular specialist at the inactive post must have, at all times, net liquid assets of $50,000.

In the event that two or more specialists are associated with each other and deal for the same specialist account, the above requirements shall apply to such specialists as one unit, rather than to each specialist individually.

.23   Relief specialists.—

(1) The requirements with respect to a member registered as a full-time relief specialist, i.e., one who may be called upon to act as a relief specialist for an entire business day, shall be, for a member already registered as a full-time specialist, net liquid assets of $50,000 or a joint account with the regular specialist in the stock; for all others, the requirement shall be, net liquid assets of $100,000 or a joint account with the regular specialist in the stock. Any joint account must be approved by the Department of Member Firms.

(2) There is no requirement with respect to a member registered as a part-time relief specialist, i.e., one who may be called upon to act as a relief specialist for less than the entire business day, usually for lunch periods, etc. Dealings effected by a part-time relief specialist while relieving the regular specialist must be made for the account of the regular specialist whom he is relieving.

Specialists may meet the above requirements either with their own capital or by availing themselves of the financing privileges provided by § 220.04(g) of Regulation T or § 221.3(o) of Regulation U of the Board of Governors of the Federal Reserve System [¶ 8121, 8218] which are explained at .30, below.

.30   Financing of specialists.—Under § 220.04(g) of Regulation T and § 221.3(o) of Regulation U of the Board of Governors of the Federal Reserve System [¶ 8121, 8218], a member may have his transactions as a specialist financed on a basis which is mutually satisfactory to the specialist and the creditor. He may finance such transactions by borrowing from a bank on terms which are mutually agreeable; he may have a member organization finance such transactions in a special account on a margin basis which is mutually satisfactory to the specialist and the carrying organization; or he may have a joint account with the carrying organization for the purpose of

¶ 2104.30   Continued

having his specialist transactions financed on a margin basis which is mutually satisfactory.

Each specialist who makes such an arrangement must inform The Floor Department of the name of the creditor and the terms of the arrangement. The Floor Department must be informed immediately by telephone of the intention: (1) to terminate or change an existing financing arrangement (confirmed subsequently in writing); or (2) to issue a margin call. (This Rule does not in any manner alter a member's notification requirements to the Department of Member Firms.) The specialist is required to submit to that Department on Form SPC (see .40, below) an initial report at such time as the arrangement becomes operative, and monthly reports thereafter.

.40 Reports on Form SPC.—Each specialist who arranges to have his specialist transactions carried by a member organization on a margin basis lower than that required by the Board of Governors of the Federal Reserve System for regular margin accounts, must file with The Floor Department a report on Form SPC, (1) as of the first date that such arrangement becomes operative, i.e., when the margin in the specialist's account first fails to meet the requirements of the Board of Governors of the Federal Reserve System for regular margin accounts, (2) as of the date previous to the first date that the arrangement becomes operative, and (3) monthly thereafter, as of the last ledger date of the month, including the month in which the arrangement first becomes operative.

Similar reports must be filed by each specialist who, for the purpose of financing his transactions as a specialist, arranges with a bank to have a loan value extended to him in an amount greater than that permitted for the financing of his non-specialist transactions.

General Instructions

The report of a joint account may be prepared and forwarded by any participant.

Forms may be obtained from The Floor Department. Reports should be filed with that Department as promptly as possible after the ledger date as of which the report is prepared.

Specific Instructions

ITEM I. Report in Item I the amount of money borrowed from banks under Section 3(o) of Regulation U to finance transactions effected as specialist, together with the total market value of the collateral to such borrowing and the excess of such total market value over the money borrowed.

ITEM II. Report in the respective categories in Item II the amounts required therein with regard to any account carried under Section 4(g) of Regulation T. The figures required under II(b) and II(d) should reflect the net credit balance *or* the net debit balance existing in the account as of the date of the report.

Deposits of cash or securities in the account should be considered in reporting amounts in Items II(a), (b) and (d).

.50 Income records.—Each specialist and specialist organization shall submit, for the confidential use of the Exchange, such information relating to his or its specialty business as may be requested by the Exchange.

Beginning with its next fiscal year, each specialist and specialist organization shall keep its records showing its commission income and dealer profit and loss in each of its specialty stocks so that they will be readily available when the Exchange requests them for its confidential use for the purpose of surveillance and study of specialists' operations.

Amendment.

September 16, 1964, effective January 4, 1965.

¶ **2104.40   Rule 104**   © 1964, Commerce Clearing House, Inc.

¶ 2104A   Specialists—General

● ● ● *Supplementary Material:*

.10 Specialist matching.—Specialists who deal separately for own account in the stocks in which they are registered, but have combined books in such stocks, are entitled to only one "match" against competing specialists and other members in the Crowd.

.20 Specialists exchanging names.—When purchasing stock for their own accounts from orders on the books, specialists must not "exchange names" and purchase such stock from the book of the other specialist. The same principle applies when specialists are selling stock to orders on the books.

.30 Specialists "stopping" stock on book.—A specialist must not "stop" stock for his own account on his own book or on the book of another member acting as specialist in the same stock.

.40 Short sales.—Members dealing for their own account are subject to the restrictions of the Commission's short selling rules. The statement in the second paragraph under "Functions of Specialists" (*see* ¶ 2104.13) that the function of a specialist includes "the maintenance, in so far as reasonably practical, of a fair and orderly market on the Exchange in the stocks in which he is so acting" shall apply only to the extent that the short selling rules of the Commission permit.

.50 Form 81 reports.—Every specialist (including relief specialists) must keep a record of purchases and sales initiated on the Floor, in stocks in which he is registered, for an account in which he has an interest. Such record must show the sequence in which each transaction actually took place and in so far as practicable the time thereof, and whether such transaction was at the same price or in what respect it was at a different price in relation to the immediately preceding transaction in the same stock. Specialists and relief specialists are required to report such transactions on Form 81, on periodic call from the Exchange. A separate form must be used for each stock involved.

Specialist units who operate on LIFO basis for valuing inventory are required to submit a report on Form 81 for the 30-day period prior to the end of the unit's year. This requirement is applicable to specialist units valuing inventory on a LIFO basis, whether they operate on a calendar or fiscal year basis.

In preparing reports, the instructions set forth below must be followed.

Dates.—All reports are to be based on trade (not blotter) dates.

Price designations.—In recording and reporting such transactions, if a transaction was effected at a price:

    (1) which was above the price at which the immediately preceding transaction in the stock took place on the Exchange, enter the designation + (plus);

    (2) which was below the immediately preceding price, enter the designation − (minus);

    (3) which was at the same price as the last sale, enter the designation 0 + (zero plus) or 0 − (zero minus) as the case may be.

¶ 2104A.50—Continued

These designations are to be entered in the column on the forms headed
"+ — 0+ 0—."

Symbols to be used in recording and reporting special types of transactions.—Transactions made:

(1) In error and to offset an error are to be designated "E";

(2) for bona fide arbitrage are to be designated "ARB"; and

(3) to effect or facilitate a distribution of securities (see SEC Regulations §§ 240.10b-6, 7, 8 [¶ 4330—4332]), or if such transactions and such distributions are made pursuant to the approval of the Exchange, are to be designated "R".

The above symbols should be placed on the form after the price of the stock.

Symbols to be used in recording and reporting opening positions.—The position at the opening in a stock is to be entered in the appropriate column on the form in connection with the first transaction in such stock that day. It is not necessary to record changes in positions in that stock for the remainder of that day. Indicate "short" positions with the symbol "S". Indicate "even" positions with the symbol "O".

Price, number of shares and time of transaction.—The price and the number of shares involved in each purchase and sale must be reported as nearly as practicable in the sequence in which the transactions occurred, including the time thereof.

Miscellaneous.—For the purpose of this report, "short" sales are those defined in the Securities and Exchange Commission's Regulation § 240.3b-3 [¶ 4235], but not including any sale exempted by paragraph (d) of Regulations § 240.10a-1 of the Securities and Exchange Commission [¶ 4324]. If a portion of a certain sale was "short" and the remainder was "long," the number of shares sold "short" and the number of shares sold "long" should be recorded in the appropriate columns of the form.

If the face of the form is not adequate for all reportable transactions, the record should be continued on the reverse side. If one copy of the form does not provide sufficient space to record all transactions, additional copies should be used, which should be numbered in series with the first copy of the form and they should be attached thereto.

Signature on reports.—Each report submitted by a member should bear his signature or that of a person authorized to submit the report for him. Reports submitted by a member organization should be signed by a general partner, or by an officer who is a holder of voting stock or other person authorized to sign.

Forms.—Forms may be obtained from the Mailing Division, 11 Wall Street, New York 5, N. Y.

Inquiries.—Inquiries in connection with these reports should be addressed to The Floor Department, 11 Wall Street, 10th Floor, telephone HAnover 2-4200, Extension 236 or 202.

¶ 2105   Specialists' Interest in Pools and Options

Rule 105.   No member acting as a specialist and no member organization in which such member is a participant or any other participant in such member organization shall be directly or indirectly interested in a pool dealing or trading in a stock in which such a member is a specialist, nor shall any such member, member organization or participant therein, directly or indirectly hold, acquire, grant or have an interest in any option to buy or sell or to receive or deliver shares of a stock in which such member is a specialist.

Amendment.
July 20, 1961.

¶ 2106   Taking Book or Order of Another Member

Rule 106. When a member temporarily takes the book of a specialist or an order from another member, he shall, while he is in possession of that book or order and for the remainder of the day, stand in the same relationship to the book or order as the specialist or other member himself.

¶ 2107   Specialist's Transactions off the Exchange

Purchaser

Rule 107. (a) A specialist may, with the prior approval of a Floor Governor, purchase off the Floor of the Exchange, for an account in which he is directly or indirectly interested, a block of a stock in which he is registered, without executing the purchase orders on his book at prices at or above the per share price paid by the specialist for such block.

No specialist who has purchased a block of stock as provided above shall bid for or purchase such stock on the Exchange for an account in which he is directly or indirectly interested:

(1) at a price above the preceding sale (i.e., a "plus" tick), or

(2) at a price above the next preceding different sale price (i.e., a "zero plus" tick)

until the number of shares sold for such accounts has equalled the number of shares in the block purchased for such accounts.

Specialist's Sales

(b) A specialist may, with the prior approval of a Floor Governor, sell off the Floor of the Exchange, for an account in which he is directly or indirectly interested, a block of a stock in which he is registered, without executing the selling orders on his book at prices at or below the per share price received by the specialist for such block.

Amendments.
Paragraph (a) was adopted May 21, 1953, effective June 1, 1953.
Paragraph (b) was adopted October 18, 1956, effective October 22, 1956.

● ● ● *Supplementary Material:*

.10 Specialist's transactions off the Exchange.—The approval of a Floor Governor to effect any purchase or sale as provided in Rule 107, above, will not be granted unless he shall have determined that the regular market on the Floor of the Exchange cannot, within a reasonable time and at a reasonable price or prices, absorb or supply the particular block of stock, and that the purchase or sale will aid the specialist in maintaining a fair and orderly market. In making such determination, the following factors may be taken into consideration, viz.:

¶ 2107.10—Continued

(1) Price range and the volume of transactions in such stock on the Floor of the Exchange during the preceding month;

(2) attempts which have been made to acquire or to dispose of the stock on the Floor of the Exchange;

(3) the existing condition of the specialist's book and Floor quotations with respect to such stock;

(4) the specialist's position in the stock;

(5) the apparent past and current interest in such stock on the Floor; and

(6) the number of shares and the current market value of the particular block of stock.

Any specialist who has effected a purchase or a short sale of a block of stock pursuant to Rule 107, above, shall submit to The Floor Department on Form 81 daily reports of all transactions in the stock effected on the Exchange for any account in which he is directly or indirectly interested, commencing with the time that the block purchase or block sale was effected and ending, (i) in the case of a block purchase at the time that the number of shares of the stock sold for such accounts has equalled the number of shares in the block purchased for such accounts, or (ii) in the case of a short sale at the time that the number of shares of the stock purchased for such accounts has equalled the number of shares in the block sold short for such accounts.

¶ 2108   Limitation on Members' Bids and Offers

On parity

Rule 108. (a) No bid or offer made by a member or made on an order for stock originated by a member while on the Floor to establish or increase a position in such stock for an account in which such member has an interest shall be entitled to parity with a bid or offer made on an order originated off the Floor.

On precedence based on size

(b) No bid or offer made by a member or made on an order for stock originated by a member while on the Floor to establish or increase a position in such stock for an account in which such member has an interest shall be entitled to precedence based on size over a bid or offer made on an order originated off the Floor.

Exceptions

(c) The provisions of paragraphs (a) and (b) shall not apply to bids or offers made:

(1) By an odd-lot dealer in a stock in which he is registered as an odd-lot dealer;

(2) to offset a transaction made in error;

(3) for bona fide arbitrage;

(4) pursuant to a limit order given to the specialist in that stock.

(*See* ¶ 2110.20-2110.27, *for "Interpretations and Instructions".*)

● ● ● *Supplementary Material:*

.10 **Combining own bids or offers with orders.**—When members combine bids or offers for own account with orders in their possession for the purpose of initiating or increasing a position and purchase or sell stock they

¶ **2107.10   Rule 107**

must, if the amount bought or sold is in excess of their orders, ask other members in the Crowd at the time who made bids or offers at the price of the transaction, including the specialists, if they have public orders. If such be the case, the member who bought or sold the stock must turn over to the other members on their public orders the amount in excess of his orders before retaining the remainder for his own account. This does not apply when the member is covering a short position or liquidating a long position for his own account.

¶ 2109   Limitation on "Stopping" Stock

Rule 109. (a) The privilege of "stopping" stock shall not be accepted by a member for an account in which such member or another member has an interest.

Exceptions

(b) The provisions of paragraph (a) shall not apply with respect to:

(1) An order originated off the Floor;

(2) an odd-lot dealer in a stock in which he is registered as an odd-lot dealer;

(3) a transaction made to offset a transaction made in error;

(4) a bona fide arbitrage;

(5) a "stop" from another member acting for an account in which such other member has an interest.

(*See* ¶ 2112.20-2112.27 *for "Interpretations and Instructions".*)

¶ 2110   Congregating in, Dominating Market and Effecting
               Purchases or Sales in Orderly Manner

Rule 110.   Members, while acting as Registered Traders on the Floor of the Exchange, who desire to purchase or sell stock for accounts in which they have an interest:

(1) Shall not congregate in a particular stock, and individually or as a group, intentionally or unintentionally, dominate the market in that stock;

(2) shall not effect such purchases or sales except in a reasonable and orderly manner and they shall not be conspicuous in the general market or in the market in a particular stock.

Amendment.
Amended May 21, 1964, and July 16, 1964, effective August 3, 1964.

● ● ● *Supplementary Material:*

.10   When establishing or increasing a position, no more than three Registered Traders may be in the trading Crowd for one stock at the same time unless an increase is approved in writing by a Floor Governor whenever, in his opinion, the presence of a larger number of Registered Traders would be constructive.

This limitation includes brokers who are attempting to execute orders for Registered Traders. In such cases, brokers must announce publicly that they are so acting for Registered Traders.

¶ 2110—Continued

.20 The provisions of this Rule apply to transactions in stocks and not to transactions in bonds.

.30 The provisions of this Rule shall not apply (1) to transactions effected by specialists in stocks or rights in which they are registered and (2) to transactions effected by rights specialists in a security which is the subject of the rights for the purpose of acquiring or liquidating a bona fide hedge position against the rights.

¶ 2111   Registered Traders

Rule 111. (a) No member shall initiate transactions, while on the Floor, for an account in which he has an interest unless such member is registered as a Registered Trader with the Exchange and unless the Exchange has approved of his so acting as a Registered Trader and has not suspended or withdrawn such approval.

(b) A member who applies to be registered as a Registered Trader is required:

(1) To establish that at the time of his registration he can meet an initial minimum capital requirement of $250,000 (effective January 1, 1965); and

(2) to pass a Registered Trader Examination prescribed by the Exchange.

(c) The provisions of Paragraph (a) of this Rule shall not apply to transactions made:

(1) by specialists or odd-lot dealers in the stocks in which they are registered;

(2) to offset a transaction made in error;

(3) for bona fide arbitrage; or

(4) when a Floor Official expressly invites a member or members to participate in a difficult market situation.

(d) Members may initiate transactions in bonds while on the Floor and the provisions of Paragraphs (a) and (b) of this Rule shall not apply to such transactions.

(e) Specialists in rights in which they are registered may effect transactions in the security which is the subject of the rights; and when such transactions are made for the purpose of acquiring or liquidating a bona fide hedge position against the rights, the provisions of Paragraph (a) and (b) of this Rule shall not apply.

Adopted.
May 21, 1964. Amended July 16, 1964, effective August 3, 1964.

● ● ● *Supplementary Material:*

.10 **Initial Minimum Capital Requirement.**—The initial minimum capital requirement shall be applicable to each individual who registers and shall be in addition to any and all other capital requirements of the Exchange.

.20 **Withdrawals.**—No withdrawals which will bring the capital below Exchange requirements shall be made.

¶ **2110.20**   **Rule 110**

.30 Maintenance Requirement.—There shall be a maintenance requirement of $175,000 for each Registered Trader. If the maintenance requirement falls below this amount and the capital is not raised to the required level within a reasonable period of time, his registration may be suspended or withdrawn.

¶ 2112   Restrictions on Registered Traders

Rule 112.   (a) No Registered Trader shall effect, while on the Floor of the Exchange, for an account in which he has an interest, "long" purchases of stock above the previous day's closing price on "plus" or "zero plus" ticks, except for "zero plus" tick purchases on the bid.

(b) No Registered Trader shall effect, while on the Floor of the Exchange, a transaction for an account in which he has an interest and execute an off-Floor order in the same stock during the same trading session.

(c) No Registered Trader shall, for an account in which he has an interest, while on the Floor of the Exchange:

(1) in establishing or increasing a position, retain priority over an off-Floor order; or

(2) in liquidating a position, have precedence based on size over an off-Floor order.

(d) Registered Traders shall meet the following stabilization tests, to be computed on a monthly basis:

(1) 75 percent measured by the tick test on the acquisition side.

(2) 75 percent measured by the tick test on the liquidation side except where the liquidating transaction is at a loss of not less than one-eighth of a point calculated on a "first in, first out" (FIFO) basis. Transactions, which are non-stabilizing, effected at a loss, will not be counted in computing the stabilizing percentage.

(3) Under the tick test, purchases on minus and zero minus ticks and sales on plus and zero plus ticks are stabilizing.

(e) The provisions of the above Paragraphs of this Rule shall not apply to transactions made:

(1) by specialists or odd-lot dealers in the stocks in which they are registered;

(2) to offset a transaction made in error;

(3) for bona fide arbitrage;

(4) in bonds; or

(5) by specialists in rights in which they are registered when effecting transactions in the security which is the subject of the rights for the purpose of acquiring or liquidating a bona fide hedge position against the rights.

Adopted.
May 21, 1964. Amended July 16, 1964, effective August 3, 1964.

● ● ● *Supplementary Material:*

Interpretations and instructions regarding Rules 108 [¶ 2108], 109 [¶ 2109], 110 [¶ 2110], 111 [¶ 2111], and 112 [¶ 2112].

¶ 2112—Continued

Interpretations and Instructions

.20 "On the Floor" and "Off the Floor."—(a) "On the Floor" or "On-Floor" means the trading Floor of the Exchange and the premises immediately adjacent thereto, such as the smoking rooms, the various entrances and lobbies of the 11 Wall Street, 18 New Street, 12 Broad Street and 18 Broad Street Buildings, and also means the telephone lobby in the first basement of 11 Wall Street and the Luncheon Club on the seventh floor (with the exception of the public telephones in the Luncheon Club). An off-Floor order for an account in which a member has an interest is to be treated as an on-Floor order if it is executed by the member who initiated it.

(b) In addition to transactions originated on the Floor by a Registered Trader for an account in which he has an interest, the following transactions are considered on-Floor trading for the purpose of Rules 108, 109, 110, 111 and 112 and subject to all the restrictions on Registered Traders:

(1) any transaction for a member organization:

(i) which results from an order entered off the Floor following a conversation with a member on the Floor who is a participant in the same member organization;

(ii) which results from an order entered off the Floor following the unsolicited submission from the Floor to the office of a quotation in a stock and the size of the market by a member who is a participant in the same member organization;

(iii) which results from an order entered off the Floor which is executed by a member on the Floor who is a participant in the same member organization and who had handled the order on a "not held" basis; provided, however, that the following are not on-Floor orders and such restrictions shall not apply to an order

(A) to sell stock for an account in which the member organization is directly or indirectly interested if, in facilitating the sale of a large block of stock, the member organization acquired its position on the Floor because the demand was not sufficient to absorb the block at a particular price or prices;

(B) to purchase or sell stock for an account in which the member organization is directly or indirectly interested if the member or his member organization was invited to participate on the opposite side of a block transaction by another member organization or participant therein because the market on the Floor could not readily absorb the block at a particular price or prices; or

(C) to purchase or sell stock for an account in which the member organization is directly or indirectly interested if the transaction is on the opposite side of a block order being executed by the member organization for the account of its customer and the transaction is made to facilitate the execution of such order; and

(iv) which results from an order entered off the Floor which is executed by a member on the Floor who is a participant in the same member organization and who has changed the terms of the order.

¶ 2112.20   **Rule 112**   © 1964, Commerce Clearing House, Inc.

(2) any transactions initiated off the Floor by a Registered Trader after such Trader has been on the Floor during the same day.

.21 Competition with odd-lot dealer.—A Registered Trader may compete with a bid or offer made by an odd-lot dealer or his representative in the crowd except a specialist handling an odd-lot dealer's order.

.22 Orders given out by Registered Traders.—(a) *To commission brokers.*— An on-Floor order given by a Registered Trader to a commission broker is subject to all the Floor Trading Rules. When a Registered Trader gives out an order on the Floor to another member:

    (1) To buy "long" stock,

    (2) to sell "short" stock,

    (3) to sell "long" stock, or

    (4) to buy to cover a "short" position,

the order must be so marked and indicated as being for an account in which the Registered Trader has an interest, unless it is exempt under the provisions of Rule 111(c), in order that the other member may know whether it may be entitled to priority, parity or precedence based on size.

(b) *To specialists.*—An on-Floor order given to a specialist by a Registered Trader has, after the intervention of two trades in the same stock, all the privileges of an off-Floor order except that it may not have the privilege of a "stop" and it is subject to the provisions of Rules 110 and 112.

.23 Pair-offs before opening.—A Registered Trader cannot acquire "long" stock by pairing off with a sell order before the opening, unless all off-Floor bids at that price are filled.

.24 Priority—Parity—Precedence.—(a) A Registered Trader, in establishing or increasing a position, may not retain priority over an off-Floor order and cannot have parity with or precedence based on size over such an order. A Registered Trader, in liquidating a position, may not have precedence based on size over an off-Floor order. These provisions shall not apply to a Registered Trader's off-Floor activities prior to his initial entry on the Floor during any trading session.

(b) A specialist in the stocks in which he is registered may retain priority on a bid but if bidding for his own account to establish or increase a position he cannot have parity with an off-Floor order or precedence based on size over such an order unless the transaction is exempted from Rule 108 (¶ 2108).

.25 Stops.—A Registered Trader who desires to buy "long" stock cannot acquire the stock through a "stop" unless all off-Floor bids at that price are filled or the transaction is exempted from Rule 109 (¶ 2109).

.26 Previous purchases by Registered Traders.—When requested, specialists should give information to the best of their ability as to previous purchases by Registered Traders.

.27 Size of offer.—Specialists should state the full size of the offer except in instances in which they believe the proper exercise of the brokerage function makes it inadvisable to do so.

Reports by Registered Traders of On-Floor Trading (Form 82-A)

.30 Registered Traders required to report.—Each Registered Trader is required to submit daily in accordance with the provisions set forth below,

¶ 2112.30—Continued

a report of all on-Floor Trading done by him on the previous day in stocks for an account in which he or his member organization has an interest; or if he has done no such trading, a report so stating.

A single form in duplicate must be used for reporting all transactions in an account, regardless of the number of stocks involved. The reports must also include all transactions executed on orders initiated or originated for such accounts by a member while on the Floor and all transactions which are considered on-Floor trading under the provision of ¶ 2112.20(b).

In preparing reports, the instructions set forth below must be followed.

Dates.—All reports are to be based on trade (not blotter) dates.

Price designations.—In recording and reporting such transactions, if a transaction was effected at a price:

(1) Which was above the price at which the immediately preceding transaction in the stock took place on the Exchange, enter the designation + (plus);

(2) which was below the immediately preceding price, enter the designation − (minus);

(3) which was at the same price as the last transaction, enter the designation 0 + (zero plus) or 0 − (zero minus) as the case may be.

These designations are to be entered in the column on the forms headed "Price & Tick."

Symbols to be used in recording and reporting the following types of transactions made by Registered Traders:

(1) In error and to offset an error are to be designated "E";

(2) for bona fide arbitrage are to be designated "ARB";

(3) resulting from "stopped" stock are to be designated "ST";

(4) where a member has "won" a "match" are to be designated "M";

(5) to effect or facilitate a distribution of securities (see SEC Regulations 240.10b-6, 7, 8 (¶ 4330-4332), or if such transactions and such distributions are made pursuant to the approval of the Exchange, are to be designated "R"; and

(6) purchases on their own bids on "plus" or "zero plus" ticks are to be designated "B".

The above symbols should be placed on the form after the price and tick of the stock.

Symbols to be used in recording and reporting opening positions.—The position at the opening in a stock is to be entered in the appropriate column on the form in connection with the first transaction in such stock that day. It is not necessary to record changes in positions in that stock for the remainder of that day. Indicate "short" positions with the symbol "S". Indicate "even" positions with the symbol "O".

Price, number of shares and time of transaction.—The price and the number of shares involved in each round-lot and odd-lot purchase and sale effected must be reported as nearly as practicable in the sequence in which the transactions occurred, including the time thereof.

¶ **2112.30   Rule 112**   © 1964, Commerce Clearing House, Inc.

Neutral transactions.—A Registered Trader desiring to exempt neutral transactions for an account in which he or his member organization has an interest from consideration in the computation of his monthly stabilizing percentage must report the trade date, number of shares, and price of the stock upon acquisition, as provided in Form 82-A. Only non-stabilizing transactions liquidated at a loss of not less than one-eighth of a point calculated on a "first in, first out" (FIFO) basis are neutral transactions. Failure of a Registered Trader to report the required information regarding neutral transactions may result in the inclusion of such transactions in the computation of his monthly stabilizing percentage.

Transactions not to be reported.—Transactions not effected on the Exchange.

Miscellaneous.—Odd-lot on-Floor trading transactions are to be included in the report on Form 82-A.

For the purpose of this report, "short" sales are those defined in the Securities and Exchange Commission's Regulation 240.3b-3 (¶ 4235), but not including any sale exempted by paragraph (d) of Regulation 240.10a-1 of the Securities and Exchange Commission (¶ 4324(d)). If a portion of a certain sale was "short" and the remainder was "long", the number of shares sold "short" and the number of shares sold "long" should be recorded in the appropriate columns of the form.

If the face of the form is not adequate for all reportable transactions, the record should be continued on the reverse side. If one copy of the form does not provide sufficient space to record all transactions, additional copies should be used, which should be numbered in series with the first copy of the form and they should be attached thereto.

Signature on reports.—Each report, including the duplicate of Form 82-A, submitted by a Registered Trader should bear his signature or that of a person authorized to submit the report for him.

Submission of reports.—Form 82-A in duplicate is to be sent to The Floor Department, 11 Wall Street, 10th Floor, as promptly as possible, but not later than 10 a. m. on the business day following the day covered by the report.

Forms.—Forms may be obtained from the Mailing Division, 11 Wall Street, New York 5, N. Y.

Inquiries.—Inquiries in connection with these reports should be addressed to The Floor Department, 11 Wall Street, 10th Floor, telephone HAnover 2-4200, Extension 236 or 202.

¶ 2113   Specialists' Public Customers

Rule 113.   (a) No specialist or member organization in which he is a participant shall accept an order for the purchase or sale of any stock in which he is registered as a specialist directly (1) from the company issuing such stock; (2) from any officer, director or 10% stockholder of that company; (3) from any pension or profit-sharing fund; (4) from any institution, such as a bank, trust company, insurance company, or investment company.

¶ 2113—Continued

(b) No order given to a specialist for the purchase or sale of a security in which he is registered as a specialist shall indicate in any way the account for which it is entered.

(c) Every specialist shall report to the Exchange such information as the Exchange may require with respect to transactions made in the stocks in which he is registered for any customer account not prohibited under section (a) which:

(1) is carried by his member organization; or

(2) is serviced by him or any participant or employee in his member organization; or

(3) is introduced by him or his member organization to another member organization on a disclosed basis.

Amendment.
September 16 and 17, 1964, effective January 4, 1965.

● ● ● *Supplementary Material:*

.10 **Form SPA.**—In accordance with the above rule, specialists are required to submit weekly reports on Form SPA. This form can be obtained at the Information Desk on the Floor.

.20 **"Popularizing" specialty stocks.**—It is contrary to good business practice for a specialist or his firm or any member or employee thereof to "popularize," either orally or in writing, any security in which he is registered.

¶ 2114   "One-Man" Specialist Units

Rule 114. Whenever a single "book" in a particular security is handled by only one member registered as a regular specialist in such security, such regular specialist shall, within such reasonable period of time as the Exchange shall determine, join with at least one other member registered as a regular specialist in such security, in such manner as the Exchange shall approve.

If the action required by the foregoing provisions of this Rule has not been taken within the reasonable period of time referred to above, the registration of such regular specialist in such security shall thereupon be cancelled.

Adopted.
May 21, 1964, effective June 1, 1964.

[The next page is 2731.]

Handling of Orders and Reports

(Rules and Policies Administered by The Floor Department.)

¶ 2115   Disclosure of Specialists' Orders Prohibited

Rule 115. No member acting as a specialist shall directly or indirectly disclose to any person, other than a Floor Official or other official of
the Exchange, any information in regard to the orders entrusted to him as
specialist, except that a specialist may disclose information contained in his
book for the purpose of demonstrating the methods of trading to visitors to
the Floor, provided that at the same time he makes the information so disclosed available to all members.

¶ 2115A   Orders at Opening or in Unusual Situations

● ● ● *Supplementary Material:*

.20 **Arranging an opening or price.**—Specialists and other members are not
permitted to hold or represent orders of members merely for the purpose
of arranging an opening or price except:

(1) In order to facilitate business and establish a fair opening price,
a specialist may hold a market order of another member, provided such
order is delivered to the specialist before the opening of the Exchange;
or, when unusual circumstances prevail, instead of holding such an order
of another member, the specialist may give up his own name with the
intention of changing the name after the opening, provided such procedure is limited to one side of the market; or

(2) when a Floor Official has determined that unusual circumstances
are present or apparent, and, in the interest of an orderly market, requests
specialists or other members to hold market and limited orders of members in order to assist in establishing a fair price.

a. In arranging an opening or reopening, a limited price order
to buy which is at a higher price than the security is to be opened
or reopened is to be treated as a market order. Similarly, a limited
price order to sell which is at a lower price than the security is to
be opened or reopened is to be treated as a market order.

b. Market orders shall have precedence over limited orders at
the opening or reopening of the market in a security. When the
price on a limited price order is the same as the price at which the
stock is to be opened or reopened, it may not be possible to execute
a limited price order at such price.

c. In arranging an opening or reopening, a specialist is required
to see that each market order he holds participates in the opening
transaction. If the order is for an amount larger than one unit of
trading, the size of the bid which is accepted or the offer which is
taken establishing the opening or reopening price shall be the amount
that a market order is entitled to participate in at the opening or
reopening.

"Pair-offs."—A specialist who, as provided in (1) above, holds a market order of another member or gives up his own name instead of holding the order, may, in arranging the opening, "pair-off" such an order against any order held by the specialist or by another member.

The member who leaves such an order with the specialist should, as promptly as possible after the opening of the stock, return to the Post. The specialist may either return the order slip to such member or retain it. In either case, the specialist must advise the member as to the broker and the name given up on the opposite side of the transaction, and the member should proceed as promptly as possible to confirm the transaction with the broker on the opposite side.

In the event that the specialist has given up his own name instead of holding a member's order, and, based upon such order, the specialist has effected a "pair-off" against an order of another member, the specialist should notify the member to whom he originally gave his own name of the broker and the name given up on the opposite side of the transaction. Such member should proceed as promptly as possible to confirm the transaction with the broker on the opposite side. If the specialist has effected the "pair-off" against an order which he handled as a broker, he should send a give-up notice to the member to whom he originally gave his own name.

"Stopping."—When a specialist has been unable to "pair-off" a market order which has been left with him, as provided in (1) above, he may, after the opening of the Exchange but before the opening of the stock, "stop" at the offer price any such market order to buy, or at the bid price any such market order to sell. In such cases, the specialist should notify the broker who left the order with him that the order is "stopped" and inform him of the price at which it is "stopped." In the event that the specialist is unable to execute the order at a better price, he should send for the broker who left such order with him, and allow the broker to consummate the transaction.

Establishing a fair price.—A specialist or other member who holds orders in order to assist in establishing a fair price, as provided in (2) above, should, after the establishment of such price, send for the members whose orders were held for that purpose. Such members should proceed as promptly as possible to confirm the transactions with the brokers on the opposite side.

Responsibility for losses.—A specialist or other member who makes an error in arranging an opening or establishing a fair price shall not be responsible for any loss involved if the member whose order has been held or represented neglects to endeavor to confirm the transaction.

In the event that a member endeavors to confirm a transaction resulting from an order left with the specialist as provided in (1) above, but is unable to do so because of an error made by the specialist in arranging an opening, the specialist shall be responsible for any loss which may be involved, except when:

(1) the broker who left such order fails to return to the Post within 30 minutes after the opening sale; or

(2) the broker who left such order returns to the Post within 30 minutes after the opening sale, but neglects to endeavor to confirm the transaction with the broker on the opposite side within 30 minutes after returning to the Post.

¶ **2115A.20   Rule 115**   © 1965, Commerce Clearing House, Inc.

Commissions.—Notwithstanding any of the foregoing provisions, commissions must be charged *in all cases* where:

(1) a member has made a bid or an offer as a result of an order in his possession and executes the order; or

(2) a member has "stopped" stock at a limit and has executed the order at a better price.

Precautions to avoid errors.—The possibility of confusion and errors will be substantially reduced if members who leave orders with specialists, as prescribed above, would make notations thereon of their names or badge numbers, and if specialists would make notations on orders which they return to members as to the brokers and the names given up on the opposite side.

Amendments.
Effective May 21, 1965.

¶ 2116   "Stop" Constitutes Guarantee

Rule 116. An agreement by a member to "stop" securities at a specified price shall constitute a guarantee of the purchase or sale by him of the securities at that price or its equivalent.

If an order is executed at a less favorable price than that agreed upon, the member who agreed to stop the securities shall be liable for an adjustment of the difference between the two prices.

• • • *Supplementary Material:*

.10 Reporting "stops."—Members and member organizations should report to their customers that securities have been "stopped" with another member only if the "stop" is unconditional and the other member had definitely agreed thereto.

.20 "Stopping" stock.—The privilege of stopping stock, other than rights, shall not be granted or accepted by a member in cases where the spread in the quotation is only the minimum variation of trading in the particular stock, except that a member who holds simultaneously an order to buy at the market and an order to sell the same stock at the market may stop such purchase and selling orders against each other and pair them off at prices and in amounts corresponding to those of the subsequent sales in the stock as they occur in the market. This exception will also apply when two members, one holding an order to buy at the market and the other holding an order to sell the same stock at the market, arrive in the Crowd at the same time.

For the purpose of the exceptions provided herein, a limited order to buy which is possible of execution at the prevailing offer price or a limited order

[The next page is 2733-3.]

to sell which is possible of execution at the prevailing bid price may be regarded as a market order.

.30 Restrictions on "stopping" stock.—No specialist may stop stock against the book or for his own account at a price at which he holds an order capable of execution at that price. However, he may stop stock:

   (1) in connection with an opening or reopening;

   (2) when there is a broker in the Crowd representing another order at the stop price;

   (3) when the specialist does not have an executable order at the stop price; or

   (4) when a broker makes an unsolicited request that a specialist grant him a stop if

      (a) the spread in the quotation is not less than twice the permitted minimum variation of trading in the stock;

      (b) after the granting of the stop the spread between the bid and offer is reduced;

      (c) the specialist does not reduce the size of the market following the stop; and

      (d) on the election of the stop the order or orders on the specialist's book entitled to priority will be executed against the stopped stock.

¶ 2117   Orders of Members To Be in Writing

Rule 117. No member on the Floor shall make any bid, offer or transaction for or on behalf of another member except pursuant to a written order. If a member to whom an order has been entrusted leaves the Crowd without actually transferring the order to another member, the order shall not be represented in the market during his absence.

● ● ● *Supplementary Material:*

.10 Absence from Crowd.—When a member keeps an order in his possession and leaves the Crowd in which dealings in the security are conducted, he is not entitled during his absence to have any bid, offer or transaction made in such security on his behalf or to have dealings in the security held up until he is summoned to the Crowd. To insure representation of an order in the market during his absence, a member must therefore actually turn the order over to another member who will undertake to remain in the Crowd. If a member keeps the order in his possession and during his absence from the Crowd the security sells at or through the limit of his order, he will be deemed to have missed the market.

.20 Re-opening contracts.—Transactions in securities made by a member when he has no order for the purchase or sale thereof must be consummated for the account of the member or his member organization and may not later be assumed by another account.

¶ 2118   Orders To Be Reduced on Ex-Date

Rule 118. When a security is quoted ex-dividend, ex-rights or ex-interest, the following kinds of orders shall be reduced by the value of the payment or rights on the day the security sells ex:

    (1) Open buying orders;

    (2) open stop orders to sell. (With open stop limit orders to sell, the limit, as well as the stop price, should be reduced.)

The following shall not be reduced:

    (1) Open stop orders to buy;

    (2) open selling orders.

Amendment.
Effective May 21, 1965.

● ● ● *Supplementary Material:*

.10   Reduction of orders—Odd amounts.—When the amount of a cash dividend or the cash value of a stock dividend or distribution is not equivalent to or is not a multiple of the fraction of a dollar in which bids and offers are made in the particular stock, orders shall be reduced by the next higher variation, i. e., when the variation is $\frac{1}{8}$ orders must be reduced by $\frac{3}{8}$ for a dividend of 30¢ per share, and by $1\frac{1}{8}$ for a dividend of $1.06¼ per share.

.20   Reduction of orders—Optional amounts.—When a dividend is payable at the option of the stockholder either in cash or securities, the stock will be ex-dividend the value of the cash or securities, whichever is greater.

.30   Responsibility for reduction of orders.—Open orders held by a specialist prior to the day a stock sells ex-dividend, ex-distribution or ex-rights must be reduced by the specialist by the value of the dividend, distribution or rights, unless he is otherwise instructed by the members or member organizations from whom the orders were received.

The following is the procedure with respect to orders in stocks selling "ex" on the first business day of May and of November:

    (1) The specialist shall be responsible for the reduction of orders which are properly confirmed or renewed on the last business day of April and of October.

    (2) The members or member organizations giving orders to the specialist shall be responsible for the reduction of orders which are received by the specialist on the first business day of May and of November.

¶ 2119   Change in Basis from "And Interest" to "Flat"

Rule 119. When a change in the basis of trading in bonds from "and interest" to "flat" becomes effective as determined by the Exchange, limited selling orders shall be raised in price by the amount of the accrued interest. This shall be done by the Floor broker to whom the order has been entrusted for execution.

The party who gave the order to sell shall be immediately notified that his order to sell at a price "and interest" is no longer valid and has for his protection been replaced by an equivalent order on the "flat" basis, pending his further instructions.

¶ 2120   Discretion to Employees, Forbidden

Rule 120. No member or member organization shall give to an employee on the Floor discretion to give orders for the purchase or sale of securities, nor shall any such employee exercise such discretion.

¶ 2121   Records of Specialists

Rule 121. Every specialist shall keep a legible record of all orders placed with him in the securities in which he is registered as a specialist and of all executions, modifications and cancellations of such orders, and shall preserve such record and all memoranda relating thereto for a period of at least twelve months.

● ● ● *Supplementary Material:*

.10   **Entry of orders on specialists' books.**—All orders given to specialists or to other members must be entered and treated according to the name appearing on the slip, even though such name may be that of a member who is known to be a participant in a member organization. Similarly, all reports, confirmations, inquiries, give-ups, calls for members to confirm trades, etc., must be made in the name appearing on the slip.

¶ 2122   Orders with More than One Broker

Rule 122. No member, member organization or any participant therein shall maintain with more than one broker, for execution on the Exchange, market orders or orders at the same price for the purchase or sale of the same security with knowledge that such orders are for the account of the same principal, unless specific permission has been obtained from a Floor Official.

¶ 2123   Record of Orders

Given Out

Rule 123. Every member shall preserve for at least twelve months a record of every order originated by him on the Floor and given to another member for execution, and of every order originating off the Floor, transmitted by any person other than a member or member organization, to such member on the Floor, which record shall include the name and amount of the security, the terms of the order and the time when such order was so given or transmitted; provided, however, that the Exchange may, upon application, grant exemptions from the provisions of this Rule.

Cancelled or Executed

Whenever a cancellation is entered with respect to such an order, or a report of the execution of such an order is received, there shall be preserved for at least twelve months, in addition to the record required by the foregoing paragraph, a record of the cancellation of the order or of the receipt of such report, which shall include the time of the entry of such cancellation or of the receipt of such report.

By Accounts

Before any such order is executed, there shall be placed upon the order slip or other record the name or designation of the account for which such order is to be executed. No change in such account name or designation shall be made unless the change has been authorized by the member or a general partner in his firm or an officer who is a holder of voting stock in his member corporation, who shall, prior to giving his approval of such change, be personally informed of the essential facts relative thereto and shall indicate his approval of such change in writing on the order.

• • • Supplementary Material:

.10 Orders originated on or transmitted to the Floor.—When giving out orders originating on the Floor, or transmitted by any person other than a member or member organization to members on the Floor, or when changing or cancelling orders previously given, members are required to do so in writing. This requirement, as well as the requirement as provided in Rule 123, above, relating to the keeping of records, may be met by preparing and retaining a duplicate of each such order given out and of any subsequent changes.

¶ 2123A   Miscellaneous Requirements

• • • Supplementary Material:

.10 Limited orders—Market orders.—If a member gives a specialist an order to sell stock at a limit and thereafter the specialist receives another order to sell at the market, the specialist must execute the market order below the limited order, unless he can execute them both at the same price. The same principle applies to orders to buy.

.20 Sending orders to specialists.—In view of the provisions of Section 11(b) of the Securities Exchange Act of 1934 [¶ 4342], members and member organizations must not transmit to specialists any orders except written market or limited price orders.

Members will facilitate business on the Floor by sending their orders to the specialists as early as possible before the opening, and by requesting their customers and correspondents to file G. T. C. orders wherever possible, rather than to repeat the same order each morning.

In the event of a change in a day order to an open order, such open order is considered to be a new order and must be added to the book after other orders previously received at the same price.

.22 Sending orders to odd-lot dealers.—So far as possible, odd-lot orders should be in the hands of odd-lot brokers on the Floor not later than 9:45 a.m.

.23 Use of order and report forms.—Members and member organizations who rent telephone spaces on the Floor may use at such spaces order forms, etc., bearing only their own name. In the case of a member organization, the name of the Exchange member may be used, if desired, provided the prior approval of the Exchange has first been obtained.

A member or member organization who rents no space may use forms bearing their own name in the telephone spaces of other members or member organizations with the permission of the Exchange, but if no such permission has been obtained such order slips may be used only for orders originated on the Floor.

A member who acts as a specialist and uses the report pad of another member or member organization, must have his own name placed on said pad in addition to the name of such other member or member organization.

The foregoing does not apply to members who assist other members temporarily or in an emergency, but only to those members who regularly use the pad of another member or member organization.

.24 Report forms.—Report forms used on the Bond Floor should be imprinted or rubber stamped with the name of the member, the member organization of which he is a general partner or a holder of voting stock, or both the name of the member and such organization. The use of plain paper for the purpose is not permitted.

Specialists' Responsibility for Orders and Reports

.31 Orders sent to specialists' representatives.—A member acting as a specialist is responsible for all orders which are given by members to any person designated by said specialist to receive orders for him. Every such specialist must designate a representative at his post to receive orders and cancellations for him. Every specialist or his representative must be at the post not later than 9:30 a. m. (or such earlier time as may be set by the Exchange because of unusual circumstances) and must remain on the Floor for at least fifteen minutes following the close of the market each day, (or such longer period as may be set by the Exchange because of unusual circumstances) and must not leave the Floor in any event before all reports have been sent out.

.32 Report not received.—If a report has not been received from a specialist on an order which he should have executed, the specialist is responsible for any loss which may be sustained up to and including the next opening price. The member or member organization giving the specialist the order is responsible for any further loss thereafter unless the order was for the account of an out-of-town member or member organization, in which case the foregoing loss should be borne jointly by the New York member or member organization and the out-of-town member or member organization.

If a member or member organization makes a written request of a specialist after the close for a report regarding the execution of an order, the specialist must definitely answer the inquiry before 9:30 a.m. of the following business day.

.33 Addressed order or order handed to specialist.—When a specialist receives and retains an order addressed to him for stock other than one in which he specializes, which is delivered by a page or through the tubes, or is handed to him by a member without the member saying anything in relation thereto, the specialist and the member are each responsible for one-half of any loss that may be occasioned thereby.

.34 Unaddressed order.—When a specialist receives and retains an unaddressed order, delivered by a page or through the tubes, for a stock other than one in which he specializes, the specialist is entirely responsible for any loss that may be occasioned thereby.

[The next page is 2737-3.]

¶ **2123A Specialists' Responsibility.—**Continued

.35 Erroneous statement.—When a member hands an order to a specialist and makes an erroneous statement to the specialist at the time as to amount, price or name of the stock, the member is entirely responsible for any loss that may be occasioned thereby.

.36 Legibility of orders.—In the preceding three paragraphs, it is assumed that the order was clearly written. If there is any question regarding clarity or legibility the matter should be referred to a Floor Official.

.37 Identity of stock.—When a member trades with a specialist the responsibility lies with the member as to the identity of the stock traded in.

.38 Reports, written and oral.—If a specialist accepts an order, and later informs a member in writing or orally that the order has been executed, the specialist is responsible for said execution if it has been covered by the tape.

If an order is received and executed by a specialist and he reports in writing or orally to a member that the order was not executed, the specialist cannot compel the member to accept a report subsequently.

.39 Duplicate reports.—Duplicate reports issued by specialists must have DUPLICATE (in large letters) prominently stamped on the face of the report.

.40 "Stop orders".—A specialist must not make a transaction for his own account in a stock in which he is registered that would result in putting into effect any stop order he may have on his book. However, a specialist may be party to the election of a stop order only when his bid or offer made with the approval of a Floor Official has the effect of bettering the market and when he guarantees that the stop order will be executed at the same price as the electing sale.

Broker's Obligation In the Handling of Certain Orders

.41 Market orders.—A broker handling a market order is to use due diligence to execute the order at the best price or prices available to him under the published market procedures of the Exchange.

.42 Limited orders.—A broker handling a limited price order is to use due diligence to execute the order at the limit price, or at a better price, if available to him under the published market procedures of the Exchange.

.43 At the close orders.—The acceptance of an "at the close" order by a broker does not make him responsible for an execution at the closing price. [See Rule 77.(2)]

.44 Not held orders.—A broker who has been given a not held order is to use brokerage judgment in the execution of the order, and if he exercises such judgment, is relieved of all responsibility with respect to the time of execution and the price or prices of execution of such an order.

A specialist may not accept a "not held" order.

.45   Erroneous reports.—Rule 411 [¶ 2411] provides that the price at which an order is executed shall be binding notwithstanding the fact that an erroneous report in respect thereto may have been rendered. As between brokers, when a purchase or sale has been reported in error, and a transaction has appeared on the tape at the price of the erroneous report and in a quantity equal to or exceeding the amount reported, the broker who made the error must render a corrected report not later than 11:00 a.m. on the second business day following the day of the transaction. If not so corrected the broker who made the error will be responsible for any resulting loss.

.50   Confirming G. T. C. orders entered on single order slips.—Members and member organizations who use single order slips when entering G. T. C. orders in the unit of trading on the Floor must confirm such orders by use of duplicate confirmation and receipt slips not later than the close of the business day following the entry of such single slip orders. Such orders not so confirmed will be cancelled without notice. Such single slip G. T. C. orders entered on the last two business days of April and October must, however, be confirmed on the last business day of those months in the same manner as other G. T. C. orders. (See paragraph following.)

.55   G. T. C. orders—Semiannual confirmations.—All orders in stocks in the unit of trading, except "day" orders, shall be entered with specialists only as G. T. C.

"Week" and "month" orders, and orders good until a specified date, may not be entered with specialists.

It shall be the responsibility of members and member organizations to cancel with the specialists those G. T. C. orders that expire at any time prior to the end of the six-month period.

G. T. C. orders expire at the end of the six-month period unless confirmed or renewed with the specialists on the last business day of such period. The six-month periods end on the last business day of the months of April and of October.

G. T. C. orders properly confirmed or renewed in the manner of their original entry, except as to partial execution or reduction in shares, are entitled to retain the same order of precedence on the specialist's book, and the specialist will be responsible for their proper entry. G. T. C. orders not so confirmed or renewed are automatically cancelled, and if entered later must be entered by the specialist in the order of their receipt.

All confirmations of cancellations of orders and confirmations or renewals of G. T. C. orders shall be dated and shall contain duplicate receipt stubs.

Specialists must return the receipt stubs of G. T. C. orders, cancellations and confirmations on the same day on which they are received; specialists must return the receipt stubs of semiannual confirmations or renewals not later than the opening of the following business day. Such receipts must be signed or stamped with the name of the specialist.

Specialists must remain on the Floor or have a representative thereon for one hour after the close on the last business day of each six-month period for the purpose of receiving confirmations and renewals of G. T. C. orders.

Receipt stubs of G. T. C. orders will be returned by hand to the telephone booths on the Floor of members and member organizations who have given such orders to specialists.

(See "Responsibility for Reduction of Orders" at ¶ 2118.30.)

60. Transmission of orders and reports.—Pages with green arm bands ("green diamond" pages), "carrier" pages, reporters, tubemen and supervisors are not permitted to leave their stations.

Squad pages assigned to trading posts may be used by members to carry orders, reports and cancellations of full lots only and to answer annunciator numbers.

Any order, report, cancellation, request for quotation or request for report may be dispatched through the pneumatic tubes, but may not (except to the extent indicated above) be carried by pages.

Members are requested to instruct their clerks to dispatch requests for quotations, reports, etc., through the tubes. Specialists are requested to instruct their clerks to return answers promptly by the same method.

All orders, reports, etc., sent through the tubes must be addressed to the brokers, firms or corporations for whom they are intended. Tube attendants have been instructed not to accept unaddressed slips for transmission.

The services of a broker should be utilized for the transmission of urgent orders or cancellations.

Floor reports of transactions may be dispatched to a member's office from the Floor by either of two methods, (1) sending a clerk or messenger holding a card of identification of the necessary kind to the Floor for the purpose of collecting such reports, or (2) sending the reports through the locked boxes of the Distributing Department of Stock Clearing Corporation.

The cards of identification which are necessary under the first method above-mentioned are (a) telephone or relief telephone clerks' tickets, (b) Stock Clearing Corporation passes, or (c) special "Floor" cards issued by The Floor Department. Holders of telephone or relief telephone clerks' tickets are admitted to the Floor during trading hours. But such persons are not permitted to perform any duties other than collecting reports if the member or member organization already has on the Floor a full complement of telephone clerks. Holders of Stock Clearing Corporation passes or special "Floor" cards are admitted to the Floor after the close.

When the second method above-mentioned is employed, manila envelopes of standard size and style must be used. A clearing member or member organization must use envelopes bearing his or its own name and clearing number; a non-clearing member or member organization must use envelopes bearing either his or its own name or the name and clearing number of the member or member organization who clears the transaction. The envelopes are collected at frequent intervals by Exchange employees and deposited

¶ **2123A.60**   Continued

in the locked boxes in Stock Clearing Corporation where they may be called
for by representatives of the member or member organization. Clearing
members or member organizations are already provided with such boxes;
additional boxes are available for the use of non-clearing members or member
organizations who desire to use envelopes bearing their own names and call
for their own reports. The standard envelopes which must be used for the
purpose are provided by the Exchange and no other type of envelope may
be used. They may be ordered in lots of 100 through The Floor Department,
the charge therefor being approximately at cost to the Exchange. The
envelopes have a natural expansion of one inch and should not be expanded
beyond that point as this makes it impossible to insert them in the locked boxes.

.65 Stabilizing orders.—Attention is directed to the provisions of Regulations
§§ 240.10b-6, 7, 8 of the Securities and Exchange Commission [¶ 4330—
4332] in the event a member is given an order for execution on the Exchange
and he knows that the order is for the purpose of pegging, fixing or stabilizing
the price of a security to facilitate an offering.

Short Sales

.71 Specialists.—A specialist who accepts an order to sell short will be
charged with seeing that the order is executed only when permitted
by the rules of the Securities and Exchange Commission.
(*See S. E. C. Regulation* § 240.10a-1 [¶ 4324] *and* ¶ 2440.)

Whenever the lowest price at which a short order may be executed is
altered by reason of a change in the last sale price, the order shall be regarded
as a new order at the new price and shall take its place on the specialist's
book as though it were a new order received at the time of the price change.

If a specialist accepts a short order at a limited price, such order shall
be entered on his books along with long stock in accordance with the usual
practice and rules of precedence.

Great care must be exercised by specialists in the handling of short
limited orders. Members entrusting short limited orders to specialists will
appreciate that such orders may not retain their precedence when the limit
at which they can be executed is changed as a result of the restrictions contained in such rules.

.72 Floor brokers.—The principles stated above regarding the handling of
short orders by specialists are applicable also to all Floor brokers. Such
brokers will be responsible for seeing that short orders are executed only
in conformity with such rules. When such a broker holds two or more selling
orders in the same security, the order of precedence outlined in .71, above,
for specialists shall govern.

.75 Marking sell orders "long" or "short."—Members and member organizations and their employees are requested, when marking sell orders "long"
or "short," to make such notations in the upper right hand corner of the order
slip.

.80 Identification of orders and cancellations.—All orders and cancellations
of orders must be dated.

When members cancel open orders, notation should be made on such
cancellations of the fact that an open order is being cancelled, so that the

specialist or other broker with both open and day orders will not be under the necessity of inquiring as to which order is cancelled.

Members should endeavor to have their customers and correspondents designate clearly whether their orders, including "stop" orders, are for the day or otherwise.

Amendments.
. Effective May 21, 1965.

¶ 2124 Odd-Lot Orders

Rule 124. (A) Any order to purchase or sell a security in an amount less than the unit of trading (an odd-lot order) which is transmitted for execution to a participant in a member organization engaged in the odd-lot business or his agent (a relief or an associate odd-lot broker) shall be executed, unless otherwise provided herein, at a price based on the price of a transaction in the round-lot market on the Floor of the Exchange, plus or minus a differential which shall be an amount deemed by the Exchange to be reasonable. (See Rule 125.)

Such odd-lot orders, unless otherwise provided under Section B, shall be executed in the manner described below. The term "first transaction," unless otherwise provided herein, shall be regarded as the first round-lot transaction to occur in the security following the receipt of the order at the trading post by the odd-lot dealer or his agent. The term effective transaction used herein refers to the round-lot transaction on which the execution of an odd-lot order shall be based.

Market Orders:

(1) A market order to buy shall be filled at the price of the first transaction, plus the differential.

(2) A market order to sell marked "long" shall be filled at the price of the first transaction, minus the differential.

(3) A market order to sell marked "short" shall be filled at the price of the first transaction which is higher than the last different round-lot price, minus the differential.

Limited Orders:

(1) *Buy Limited Orders.* The effective transaction for a limited order to buy shall be the first round-lot transaction which is below the specified limit by the amount of the applicable differential or by a greater amount. The order shall be filled at the price of the effective transaction, plus the differential.

(2) *Sell Limited Orders, Marked "Long."* The effective transaction for a limited order to sell marked "long" shall be the first round-lot transaction which is above the specified limit by the amount of the applicable differential or by a greater amount. The order shall be filled at the price of the effective transaction, minus the differential.

(3) *Sell Limited Orders, Marked "Short."* The effective transaction for a limited order to sell marked "short" shall be the first round-lot transaction which is above the specified limit by the amount of the applicable differential, or by a greater amount, *and which is also higher than the last different round-lot transaction (a "plus" or "zero-plus" tick)*. The order shall be filled at the price of the effective transaction, minus the differential.

New York Stock Exchange Guide

Rule 124 ¶ 2124

Stop Orders:

(1) *Buy Stop Orders.* A buy stop order shall become a market order when a round-lot transaction takes place at or above the stop price. The order shall then be filled at the price of the next transaction, plus the differential.

(2) *Sell Stop Orders, Marked "Long."* A sell stop order marked "long" shall become a market order when a round-lot transaction takes place at or below the stop price. The order shall then be filled at the price of the next transaction, minus the differential.

(3) *Sell Stop Orders, Marked "Short."* A sell stop order marked "short" shall become a market order when a round-lot transaction takes place at or below the stop price. The order shall then be filled at the price of the next transaction, which is higher than the last different round-lot price, minus the differential.

Stop Limited Orders:

(1) *Buy Stop Limited Orders.* A buy stop limited order shall become a limited order when a round-lot transaction takes place at or above the stop price. The order shall then be filled in the manner prescribed for handling a limited order to buy.

(2) *Sell Stop Limited Orders, Marked "Long."* A sell stop limited order marked "long" shall become a limited order when a round-lot transaction takes place at or below the stop price. The order shall then be filled in the manner prescribed for handling a limited order to sell, marked "long."

(3) *Sell Stop Limited Orders, Marked "Short."* A sell stop limited order marked "short" shall become a limited order when a round-lot transaction takes place at or below the stop price. The order shall then be filled in the manner prescribed for handling a limited order to sell, marked "short."

(B) *OTHER TYPES OF ORDERS*
(1) Buying on Offer—Selling on Bid

(a) *Buy on Offer.* An order to buy on the offer shall be filled at the round-lot offer price prevailing at the time the odd-lot broker receives the order, plus the differential.

(b) *Sell on Bid.* An order to sell on the bid marked "long" shall be filled at the round-lot bid price prevailing at the time the odd-lot broker receives the order, minus the differential. An order to sell on the bid marked "short" shall not be accepted.

(c) *Limited Order to Buy on the Offer.* A limited order to buy on the offer shall be filled at a price equal to the round-lot offer price prevailing at the time the odd-lot broker receives the order, plus the differential, but only if the offer price plus the differential is at or below the limit of the order. If the order can not be filled forthwith, it shall be cancelled and the originating member or member organization shall be informed regarding the quotation and the cancellation.

(d) *Limited Order to Sell on the Bid.* A limited order to sell on the bid marked "long" shall be filled at a price equal to the round-lot bid price prevailing at the time the odd-lot broker receives the order, minus the differential, but only if the bid price minus the differential is at or above the limit of the order. If the order can not be filled forthwith, it shall be cancelled and the originating member or member organization shall be informed regarding the quotation and the cancellation.

A limited order to sell on the bid marked "short" shall not be accepted.

(e) *Limited Order, "Immediate or Cancel."* A limited order to buy marked "Immediate or Cancel" shall be handled in the manner specified in (c) above for the handling of a limited order to buy on the offer. A limited order to sell marked "Immediate or Cancel" shall be handled in the manner specified in (d) above for the handling of a limited order to sell on the bid.

(f) *Limited Order, "With or Without Sale."* A limited order "With or Without Sale" shall be filled on an effective round-lot transaction, or an effective bid or offer, whichever occurs first after the odd-lot broker receives the order. The order shall be filled as follows:

i) If an effective round-lot transaction occurs first, a buy order shall be filled at the price of the effective transaction plus the differential and a sell order shall be filled at the price of the effective transaction minus the differential.

ii) If an effective bid or an effective offer occurs before an effective round-lot transaction takes place, a buy order shall be filled at the effective offer price plus the differential and a sell order shall be filled at the effective bid price minus the differential.

A limited order to sell "With or Without Sale" marked "short" shall not be accepted.

(2) Buying on Closing Offer—Selling on Closing Bids

(a) *Buy "On Close."* An order to buy "On Close" shall be filled at the price of the closing round-lot offer, plus the differential.

(b) *Sell "On Close."* An order to sell "On Close" marked "long" shall be filled at the price of the closing round-lot bid, minus the differential. An order to sell "On Close" marked "short" shall not be accepted.

(c) *Limited Order to Buy Marked "Or on Close."* A limited order to buy marked "Or on Close" which remains unfilled at the close of business on the Exchange, shall be filled at a price equal to the closing round-lot offer, plus the differential.

(d) *Limited Order to Sell Marked "Or on Close."* A limited order to sell marked "long" and marked "Or on Close" which remains unfilled at the close of business on the Exchange, shall be filled at a price equal to the closing round-lot bid, minus the differential. A limited order to sell marked "short" and marked "Or on Close" shall not be accepted.

(3) Discretionary Orders

A discretionary order must not be accepted by an odd-lot dealer.

(4) Orders Filled After the Close

At the request of a customer an order may be filled after the close at a price based on the closing round-lot bid or offer provided 1) the order was received prior to the close and could have been filled, in the case of a buy order, if a sale had occurred at the offer price and, in the case of a sell order, if a sale had occurred at the bid price, 2) the request is made within a reasonable time after the close and 3) nothing has occurred after the close which could affect the market value of the stock. The order shall be filled as follows:

(a) A buy order shall be filled at the price of the closing round-lot offer, plus the differential.

(b) A sell order marked "long" shall be filled at the price of the closing round-lot bid, minus the differential. A sell order marked "short" may not be accepted for filling after the close.

(5) Basis Price Order

An order may be filled at the "Basis Price" provided a Basis Price has been established and the order was received at least a half hour before the close of the market, and marked "On Basis" prior to the close of the market. "On Basis" market orders and "On Basis" limited price orders for which the Basis Price is effective shall be filled as follows.

(a) *Buy Order.* A buy order marked "Basis Price" shall be filled at the Basis Price plus the differential.

(b) *Sell Order.* A sell order marked "long" and marked "Basis Price" shall be filled at the Basis Price minus the differential. A sell order marked "short" may not be filled at the Basis Price.

(See ¶ 2124.10 for establishment of Basis Prices).

(6) "Seller's Option" Trade

A "seller's option" trade for delivery within not less than five business days nor more than thirty days following the day of the contract shall be filled at a price below the effective round-lot sale or bid by the amount of the applicable differential. An additional charge may be made if the stock involved is loaning at a premium. A contract for delivery in over thirty days may be made at a price mutually agreed upon.

If a "seller's option" odd-lot is part of an order to sell more than 100 shares "seller's option," the odd-lot dealer may fill the odd-lot at a price below the "seller's option" round-lot by the amount of the applicable differential, if the customer so requests at the time the order is entered.

(7) Cash Trades

If an odd-lot dealer agrees to fill an odd-lot order for cash, such order can be filled on a "regular way" round-lot transaction or on the bid in the case of an order to sell for cash, or on the offer in the case of an order to buy for cash. All such orders shall be filled at the applicable differential.

¶ **2124   Rule 124**

A cash odd-lot order which is a part of a cash order for more than the unit of trading, may be filled by the odd-lot dealer for cash at the applicable differential from the round-lot cash price, if the customer so requests at the time the order is entered.

• • • *Supplementary Material:*

.10 Basis Prices.—Basis Prices shall be established by joint agreement of odd-lot dealers in 100-share unit stocks where there has been no round-lot sale during the trading session, the spread between the closing bid and offer prices is two points or more and an odd-lot dealer has been given an "On Basis" order. The Basis Price must be reviewed and approved by a Floor Official.

.20 "Delayed Sale," "Sold Sale."—When a "delayed sale" or "sold sale" occurs (printed on the ticker tape followed by the symbol "SLD"), the odd-lot dealers shall make every effort to ascertain the approximate time the transaction took place. If there is some doubt as to whether or not this transaction in any way affects the execution of an odd-lot order, the firm that entered the order should be notified, informed of the circumstances, and given the opportunity to accept or reject a report based on the transaction.

.30 Sales Not Printed on the Tape.—The customer of the odd-lot dealer must accept a report based on a sale which took place on the Floor, but which, through error, was not printed on the tape, if the odd-lot dealer filled and reported the customer's order at the post at the time the sale occurred.

If the odd-lot dealer failed to fill the order at the time the sale occurred the customer should be offered the choice of accepting or refusing a report based on that sale.

.40 Orders to Be Reduced on Ex-Date.—Open buy limited orders and open stop orders to sell held by an odd-lot dealer prior to the day a stock sells ex-dividend, ex-distribution or ex-rights must be reduced by the odd-lot dealer by the value of the dividend, distribution, or rights, unless he is otherwise instructed by the members or member organizations from whom the orders were received. Except, if the amount of a stock dividend is 20% or more, the order shall be returned for instruction. (See Paragraphs 2118.10 and .20 for reduction of orders—odd amounts and optional amounts.)

Adopted.
April 16, 1964.
Effective June 1, 1964.

¶ 2125   Odd-Lot Differential

Rule 125.   Pending the completion of the odd-lot cost study and a determination by the Exchange of what is a reasonable differential, the differential shall be that imposed by the respective odd-lot dealers.

Adopted.
April 16, 1964.
Effective June 1, 1964.

[The next page is 2761.]

Publications of Transactions and Changes

¶ 2125A   Publication of Transactions

● ● ● *Supplementary Material:*

.10   **Duty of seller.**—It is the duty of the seller to notify the reporter in the Crowd of a sale. Members should promptly call the attention of reporters to any error on or omission from the tape.

.11   **Price not in dispute.**—The publication of a transaction on the tape may not be objected to if the price at which it was made is not in dispute.

.12   **"Seller" contract in bonds.**—No "seller" contract in bonds for more than seven days may be published without the approval of a Floor Official.

.13   **Registered as to principal.**—Transactions in bonds registered as to principal must be published on the tape and "sales sheet," * designated "Registered as to Principal."

.14   **"Fourth day"—"Delayed delivery."**—Transactions in bonds made for fourth day delivery and regular way delayed delivery may, upon a member's request, be published upon the tape and in the "sales sheet" * with a special mark designating them as such, but will otherwise be published without any special designation. The symbol "FD" must be used for fourth day delivery and "DD" for regular way delayed delivery.

.15   **Last sale.**—The phrase "last sale," when used in connection with bonds, means the last regular way trade either "Fourth Day" or "Delayed Delivery."

.16   **"Stopped" securities.**—Transactions in "stopped" securities may be published on the tape and in the "sales sheet" * unless objected to by a member. However, each "stopped" transaction not published on the tape during the trading session shall be (1) printed on the tape after the close and tabulated separately in the transactions reported in the "sales sheets," and (2) included in total volume for the day.

¶ 2125B   Publication of Changes, Corrections, Cancellations or Omissions and Verification of Transactions

● ● ● *Supplementary Material:*

.10   **Publication on the tape or in the "sales sheet."**—Publication of a change or a correction in a transaction which previously appeared on the tape, or publication of the cancellation of a transaction which previously appeared on the tape and which was properly rescinded, or publication of a transaction omitted from the tape may be made on the tape on the day of the transaction at the request of one of the parties thereto with the approval of a Floor Official. In the event such publications are not made on the tape on the day of the transaction, they may be published on the tape before 9:50 a.m. of the following business day or in the "sales sheet" * within seven calendar days of the date of the transaction at the request of one of the parties thereto with the

(* Reference herein to the "sales sheet" is to the list of transactions published by Francis Emory Fitch, Inc.)

¶ 2125B.10—Continued

approval of a Floor Official, provided the price of the transaction does not affect the high, low, opening or closing price of the security on the day of the transaction.

.11   Verification.—A transaction which may not be published on the tape or in the "sales sheet" * after the date of the transaction may be confirmed by the Department of Floor Procedure, upon the written request of one of the parties to the transaction, provided the department is able to verify the facts with the other party to the transaction. This written request must contain: the date on which the transaction was made and approximate time thereof; the name, amount and price of the security and the names of the participating brokers on the Floor.

.12   Mechanical and clerical errors.—Erroneous publications made on the tape due to mechanical trouble or to clerical errors may be corrected on the tape on the day of the transaction, or on the tape before 9:50 a.m. of the following business day, or in the "sales sheet" * within seven calendar days of the date of the transaction under the direction of the supervisor or official having jurisdiction.

.13   Other errors.—A correction in the amount of a transaction reported erroneously to a reporter by a party to the transaction, may be published on the tape on the day of the transaction, or on the tape before 9:50 a.m. of the following business day, or on the "sales sheet" * within seven calendar days of the date of the transaction with the approval of a Floor Official.

Members who wish to make requests to have publications made on the tape or in the "sales sheet" or to have verifications of transactions made, should first take up the matter as to procedure with a reporter in the Crowd where the security is dealt in or with the section supervisor at the post.

[The next page is 2771.]

(* Reference herein to the "sales sheet" is to the list of transactions published by Francis Emory Fitch, Inc.)

¶ **2125B.11**

Comparisons and Exchange of Contracts

(Rules and Policies Administered by The Floor Department.)

¶ 2131   Comparison—Requirements for Reporting Trades and Providing Facilities

Duty to Report Transactions

Rule 131. (a) It shall be the duty of every member to report each transaction made by him on the Floor as promptly as possible to his office, to the office of the member or member organization clearing for him or his member organization, or to the office of his principal, as the case may be, where adequate facilities to effect comparison are maintained.

Facilities for Comparison

(b) Every clearing member and member organization shall maintain adequate facilities for the comparison of transactions, and shall keep them available during such hours as to enable other members and member organizations reasonably to complete comparisons as required by the Rules.

Availability of Records

(c) It shall be the duty of every member to have available, at his office, his records with regard to transactions effected by him on the Floor in order to enable other members and member organizations with whom or for whom transactions were made to make inquiry concerning such transactions.

Availability of Representative

(d) Every member and member organization shall have a representative qualified to answer inquiries regarding orders and trades present in the office until at least 4:30 p.m. every business day.

Amendments.
September 26, 1963.

¶ 2132   Comparison—Cleared Transactions

Rule 132. Comparison of transactions in securities which are to be cleared through Stock Clearing Corporation shall be effected in the following manner:

(1) Each buying and selling clearing member shall send to Stock Clearing Corporation an exchange ticket, in respect of each purchase and each sale, on the business day following the day of the transaction, in the form, at the time and in the manner prescribed by the Rules of Stock Clearing Corporation.

(2) Each clearing member shall promptly verify with his or its records the contract lists received from Stock Clearing Corporation. Any changes or corrections thereon shall be made in the form, at the time and in the manner prescribed by the Rules of Stock Clearing Corporation.

(3) Each clearing member shall deliver to Stock Clearing Corporation a comparison notice with respect to his or its transactions in the form, at the time and in the manner prescribed by the Rules of Stock Clearing Corporation.

Amendments.
September 3, 1964.

[The next page is 2771-3.]

¶ 2133   Comparison—Non-cleared Transactions

Rule 133. Comparisons of transactions in securities which are not to be cleared through Stock Clearing Corporation and transactions which are not compared through the Clearing House Comparison service of Stock Clearing Corporation shall be effected in the following manner:

(1) Each selling member and member organization shall send to the office of the buyer in respect of each sale a comparison form in duplicate on the business day following the day of the transaction, but not later than the time prescribed by Stock Clearing Corporation for the delivery on that day of exchange tickets in respect to transactions to be cleared through Stock Clearing Corporation;

(2) The party to whom the comparison is presented shall retain the original, if it be correct, and immediately return the duplicate duly signed;

except that transactions for delivery on the business day following the day of the contract shall be compared, in the manner prescribed herein, no later than one hour and a half after the closing of the Exchange on the day of the transaction.

Amendments.
September 20, 1961; September 3, 1964.

¶ 2134   Differences and Omissions—Cleared Transactions
                              ("DK's")

Rule 134. (a) When a clearing member questions a transaction which appears on, or has been omitted from, his or its purchase contract list or sale contract list, such clearing member shall communicate that fact by telephone to the other party to the transaction as soon as possible, but not later than the opening of the Exchange on the second business day following the day of the transaction; and

(b) if the transaction is not promptly acknowledged by both parties, the transaction shall be reported to the executing Floor broker or brokers by the parties thereto as soon as possible, but in any event prior to the opening of the Exchange on the second business day following the day of the transaction; and

(c) the Floor broker or brokers to whom such a transaction is reported shall investigate it immediately.

Amendments.
September 3, 1964.

• • • *Supplementary Material:*

.10 Duplicate DK's.—All DK slips must be prepared in duplicate, and the member or member organization to whom a DK has been presented must indicate receipt thereof by stamping or signing the duplicate copy, and returning such copy to the member or member organization from whom the DK was received. This is solely for the purpose of providing a record of the fact that the DK has been received by the party to whom it was delivered.

New York Stock Exchange Guide   **Rule 134   ¶ 2134.10**

¶ 2135   Differences and Omissions—Non-cleared Transactions ("DK's")

Rule 135. (a) When a comparison of a transaction which is not to be cleared through Stock Clearing Corporation is received and the recipient has no knowledge of the transaction, the comparison shall be stamped "Don't know," dated and initialed by the person so marking the same, and the comparison form, so stamped, shall be returned immediately to the seller; and

(b) when the buyer has not received a comparison from the seller, or when comparison cannot be made because of a difference, the buyer shall communicate that fact by telephone to the seller as soon as possible, but not later than the opening of the Exchange on the second business day following the day of the transaction; and

(c) when a comparison form has been returned to the seller stamped "Don't know," or if, for any reason, comparison cannot be made, the parties shall, as soon as possible, but not later than the opening of the Exchange on the second business day following the day of the transaction, report the transaction to the executing Floor broker or brokers; and

(d) the Floor broker or brokers to whom such a transaction is reported shall investigate it immediately; provided, however, that, if the questioned transaction is one for delivery on the business day following the day of the transaction, it shall be handled as provided above and reported to the executing Floor broker or brokers as soon as possible, but in any event prior to the opening of the Exchange on the business day following the day of the transaction.

The provisions of this rule do not apply to transactions which are compared through the Clearing House Comparison service of Stock Clearing Corporation.

Amendments.
September 20, 1961.

● ● ● *Supplementary Material:*

.10   Sample "Don't know" stamp.—

```
┌─────────────────────────────────────────────┐
│                                               │
│                  DON'T KNOW                   │
│                                               │
│                 Jones & Smith                 │
│                                               │
│   Date . . . . . . . . . . . . . .   Per . . . . . . . . . . . .  │
│                                               │
└─────────────────────────────────────────────┘
```

¶ 2136   Comparison—Transactions Excluded from a Clearance

Rule 136. A transaction which was to be cleared through Stock Clearing Corporation, but which has been excluded for any reason from a clearance, and has not been compared through the Clearing House Comparison service of Stock Clearing Corporation, shall be compared, in the manner provided in Rule 133 (¶ 2133), as promptly as possible after the parties thereto have been advised that the transaction has been excluded from the clearance.

Amendments.
September 20, 1961.

¶ 2137   Written Contracts

Rule 137. On "seller's option" transactions in stocks, on "seller's option" transactions in bonds for more than seven days, and on all transactions made "when issued" or "when distributed," that are not cleared through Stock Clearing Corporation, written contracts in forms approved by the Exchange shall be exchanged not later than the second business day following the transaction.

Powers of attorney to employees

Such contracts must be signed by a member, a general partner or a duly authorized officer of a member organization; or the member or member organization may authorize one or more employees to sign them in the name of such member or member organization with the same effect as if the name of such member or member organization had been signed under like circumstances by such member, general partner or duly authorized officer of a member organization by executing and filing with the Exchange, in the form prescribed by it, a Power of Attorney or authorization for each person so authorized.

¶ 2137   Continued

Before the name of any member corporation is affixed to such a contract by an officer or employee thereof, the member corporation shall file with the Exchange in the form prescribed by it evidence that such officer or employee has been authorized to sign such contracts on behalf of the member corporation.

Liability

When written contracts have been exchanged, only the members or member organizations whose names have been so signed thereon shall be liable.

Amendment.∙
February 28, 1957, effective March 18, 1957.

¶ 2137A   Samples of Written Contracts

● ● ● *Supplementary Material:*

.10   "Seller's option" contract for bonds.—

$.........Bonds.   New York,.........19..

........have $\begin{cases} \text{SOLD to} \\ \text{PURCHASED of} \end{cases}$ ....

$........par value ....

Bonds at ....payable and deliverable ....,
either party having the right to call for deposits, according to the requirements of the Constitution and Rules of the New York Exchange; and on the failure of the party called upon to comply therewith, this contract shall mature, with the right and authority to the party not in default to close the contract in accordance with the Rules of the New York Stock Exchange.

....

.20   "Seller's option" contract for stock.—

..........Shares.   New York,.........19..

........have $\begin{cases} \text{SOLD to} \\ \text{PURCHASED of} \end{cases}$ ....

..................shares of the .... Stock of the

.... at .... per share

payable and deliverable ...., either party having the right to call for deposits, according to the requirements of the Constitution and Rules of the New York Stock Exchange; and on the failure of the party called upon to comply therewith, this contract shall mature, with the right and authority to the party not in default to close the contract in accordance with the Rules of the New York Stock Exchange.

....

¶ **2137A**   © 1961, Commerce Clearing House, Inc.

.30 "When Issued" or "When Distributed" contract.—

....
(Firm Name)

Date.......................

Sold to Purchased From	Quantity	Description of Security	Price

If this contract was made on a national securities exchange, it shall be subject to and governed by the requirements of such exchange, its constitution, rules, practices and interpretations thereof, relating to contracts between members of such exchange, as the same may be amended or modified from time to time.

If this contract was made elsewhere than on a national securities exchange, it shall be subject to and governed by the requirements of the National Association of Securities Dealers, Inc., its By-Laws, Rules of Fair Practice, Uniform Practice Code, rulings and interpretations thereof, as the same may be amended or modified from time to time.

This contract shall be settled and payment therefor made at such time and place, in such manner, and by the delivery of such securities and/or other property as the exchange or association to whose requirements this contract is subject in its sole discretion may determine, or shall be cancelled and thereafter shall be null and void if such exchange or association determines in its sole discretion that the plan or proposal pursuant to which the securities were to be issued or distributed has been abandoned or materially changed or that the securities which are the subject of the contract have been materially changed. During the pendency of this contract either party shall have the right to call for a mark to the market, and upon failure of the other party to comply therewith the party not in default may close this contract in accordance with the requirements of the exchange or association to whose requirements this contract is subject.

¶ 2138 **Give-Ups**

Time for Effecting

Rule 138. An original party to a transaction may give up to the other original party to said transaction, the names of other members or member organizations, but such giving up or the acceptance thereof shall not constitute a substitution of principals. Such give-ups shall be effected either at the time of the transaction or within one hour and a half after the time of the transaction; except that the time limit for effecting give-ups on any day shall be one hour after the closing of the Exchange on the day of the transaction. Give-ups

¶ 2138   Continued

effected at any time other than at the time of the transaction on transactions which are not to be cleared through Stock Clearing Corporation shall be in writing and delivered to the party on the other side of the transaction.

Give-Up Transactions in Securities Which Are to Be Cleared Through Stock Clearing Corporation

A clearing member so given up shall indicate the clearing number of the executing party on such forms, at such times, and in the manner prescribed by the Rules of Stock Clearing Corporation.

Duty of Comparison

The members or member organizations so given up shall have the same duty of comparison as original parties; and no original party shall refuse to compare with the members or member organizations given up as provided in this Rule.

In the event a give-up is not effected within the time limit specified in this Rule, the transaction shall be compared and cleared by the party who failed to give up.

● ● ● *Supplementary Material:*

.10   "Clearing number" defined.—The term "clearing number" means the Stock Clearing Corporation number assigned to a Clearing Member or the Commission Bill number assigned to a Non-Clearing Member.

Amendments.
September 3, 1964.

¶ 2139   Recording

Rule 139. When names are given up on transactions, members or member organizations so given up or receiving such give-ups shall immediately record such names on their blotters or other records, and shall use the names, so given up, on exchange tickets and comparisons, or when exchanging contracts.

Amendments.
September 3, 1964.

¶ 2140   Members Closing Contracts—Conditions

Rule 140. A member or member organization may close a contract as provided in Rule 283 [¶ 2283] in the event that:

(1) He or it has been advised that the other party to the contract does not recognize the contract; or

(2) the other party to the contract neglects or refuses to exchange written contracts pursuant to Rule 137 [¶ 2137].

¶ 2141   "Fail To Deliver" Confirmations

Rule 141. If delivery on a contract has not been made on the due date, either the buyer or the seller may, while such contract remains open, send to the other party, in duplicate, a "fail to deliver" confirmation.

When a "fail to deliver" confirmation is sent to a member or member organization, the party to whom the confirmation is presented shall retain the original, if it be correct, and promptly return the duplicate stamped and initialed; if such party has no knowledge thereof, the confirmation shall be stamped in the manner provided in Rule 135(a) [¶ 2135].

¶ 2142   Effect on Contracts of Errors in Comparison, etc.

Rule 142. No comparison or failure to compare, and no notification or acceptance of notification, such as notification of failure to receive or failure to deliver, shall have the effect of creating or of cancelling a contract, or of changing the terms thereof, or of releasing the original parties from liability.

¶ 2143   Stock Clearing Corporation Orders

Rule 143. Orders issued by Stock Clearing Corporation for the receipt or delivery of securities shall be binding and enforceable upon members or member organizations for whom Stock Clearing Corporation acts.

[The next page is 2791.]

Loans

(Rules and Policies Administered by The Floor Department.)

¶ 2151   **Delivery Day**

Rule 151.   Unless otherwise agreed, securities loaned shall be deliverable on the fourth business day following the day on which the loan is made.

¶ 2152   **Failure to Deliver**

Rule 152.   A loan of securities shall become a failure to deliver if the securities are not delivered when due, except that, unless it has been cleared through Stock Clearing Corporation, the contract may be cancelled by mutual consent.

¶ 2153   **Premiums and Interest**

Rule 153.   When securities are loaned, the premium payable by the borrower, or the interest payable by the lender, at such rates as are agreed upon, shall accrue on the day on which delivery from the lender to the borrower is due, whether or not such securities are delivered.

When securities are loaned for delivery on the day of contract, the premium at the rate agreed upon shall accrue on the day of contract and the three succeeding business days; the interest at the rate agreed upon shall accrue on the day of contract and shall continue to accrue at said rate up to but not including the day on which a change in rates established on the Floor becomes effective.

¶ 2154   **Renewal Premium**

Rule 154.   Unless otherwise agreed, all open loans of securities shall carry the renewal premium at the rate established on the Floor, which premium shall accrue on the fourth business day after the rate is established.

Premiums at the established renewal rates shall be paid for each business day on which the borrower has the use of the securities, but not including the day on which the return is due.

¶ 2155   **Renewal Interest Rate**

Rule 155.   Unless otherwise agreed, all open loans of securities shall carry the renewal interest at the rate established on the Floor, which interest shall accrue on the fourth business day after the rate is established and shall remain in effect on each subsequent day up to but not including the day on which a change in rates established on the Floor becomes effective.

Interest at the established renewal rate for loans of securities shall be paid for each calendar day on which the lender has the use of the money paid by the borrower, but not including the day on which the return is due.

¶ 2156   Premiums for One Day Only

Rule 156. An agreement to pay a premium because of a failure to deliver securities shall not change the nature of the contract, and premiums on each subsequent day shall be payable only by mutual agreement. When any such agreement has been made, the party failing to receive shall be regarded as having waived his right under Rule 284 [¶ 2284] to close out the contract on that day.

By mutual agreement a failure to deliver may be changed to a loan of securities, in which event the contract shall be subject to all of the Rules applying to loans.

¶ 2157   Premiums on Basis of Dollars

Rule 157. Premium rates on stock loans shall be established upon a basis of dollars per one hundred shares. Such premiums shall be quoted only at the following rates:

$ 1.00 per hundred shares
2.00 "   "   "
3.00 "   "   "
6.00 "   "   "
10.00 "   "   "
15.00 "   "   "
20.00 "   "   "

Higher rates shall be in multiples of $10.00.

¶ 2158   Settlement of Accrual Premiums or Interest

Rule 158. It shall not be necessary for the parties to loans of securities to confirm renewal rates or to send daily bills for premiums or interest. By mutual agreement, all accrued premiums or interest may be paid when the securities are returned, but in any event settlement for premiums and interest shall be made at least once a month.

¶ 2159   Loans Must Be Completed

Rule 159. Where a member or member organization has contracted to borrow money on collateral, the simple payment of interest by the borrower, without actually effecting or properly endeavoring to effect the loan, shall be held to be an evasion of the contract and is forbidden.

¶ 2160   Notice for Return

Rule 160. Notice for the return of loans of money shall be given before 12:15 p. m. of the business day on which the return is to be made.

Unless otherwise agreed, notice for the return of loans of securities shall be given before 3:45 p. m., and such return shall be made on the fourth business day following the day on which such notice is given.

A notice given pursuant to the provisions of this Rule shall be considered as in full force until delivery is made.

¶ 2161   Exchange Employees Not to Participate

Rule 161. No Floor employee of the Exchange shall take any part in the borrowing or lending of securities.

[The next page is 2805.]

Marking to the Market

(Rules and Policies Administered by The Floor Department.)

¶ 2165   Demands for Marking to the Market

Rule 165. The party who is partially unsecured by reason of a change in the market value of the subject of an Exchange contract, may demand from the other party the difference between the contract price and the market price. The party from whom such difference is demanded shall immediately either (1) pay the same directly or through Stock Clearing Corporation to the party who is partially unsecured, in which case the money so paid shall bear interest at the current renewal rate for call loans, except in the case of a loan of securities when the money so paid shall be considered part of such loan, or (2) deposit the same with Stock Clearing Corporation, if permitted by its By-Laws and Rules.

¶ 2166   Demands for Marking—Procedure

Rule 166. All demands for the difference between the contract price and the market price shall be made during the hours when the Exchange is open for business, shall be in writing and shall be delivered at the office of the party upon whom the demand is made and shall be complied with immediately.

¶ 2167   Deposits Through Clearing Members Only

Rule 167. If the party required to make a deposit with Stock Clearing Corporation is not a Clearing Member as defined in the By-Laws of Stock Clearing Corporation, he shall cause the deposit to be made for him by a Clearing Member. The cash so deposited with Stock Clearing Corporation shall be held by it subject to its By-Laws and Rules.

¶ 2168   Failure to Comply with Demand

Rule 168. If a party to a contract shall fail to comply with the provisions of Rule 165 [¶ 2165], the other party to such contract may cause the same to be closed as provided in Rule 284 [¶ 2284].

[The next page is 2821.]

Settlement of Contracts

*(Rules and Policies Administered by the
Department of Stock List.)*

¶ 2175 **Extension or Postponement of Contracts—
Power of Board**

Rule 175. Anything contained in the Rules to the contrary notwithstanding, the Board of Governors may extend or postpone the time for the performance of Exchange contracts whenever in its opinion such action is called for by the public interest or by just and equitable principles of trade.

¶ 2176 **Delivery Time**

Rule 176. Deliveries of securities (except as provided in Rule 177 [¶ 2177]) shall be due before 12:00 noon, unless Stock Clearing Corporation shall advance or extend the time within which securities deliverable through it may be delivered, in which event the time within which other securities may be delivered shall thereby be similarly advanced or extended.

¶ 2177 **Delivery Time—"Cash" Contracts**

Rule 177. Deliveries against transactions made for "cash" at or before 2:00 p.m. shall be due before 2:30 p.m. Deliveries against transactions made for "cash" after 2:00 p.m. shall be due within thirty minutes after the time of the transaction.

¶ 2178 **Contracts Due on Holidays or Saturdays**

Rule 178. All contracts which would otherwise fall due on a day other than a business day shall mature on the succeeding business day, unless otherwise agreed.

¶ 2179 **"Seller's Option"**

Rule 179. (a) When securities have been sold "seller's option," delivery shall be due on the day of the expiration of the option (unless such day is other than a business day, when Rule 178 [¶ 2178] shall apply) but may be made at the option of the seller on any business day prior thereto upon one day's written notice. Such notice must be given by the seller before 4:00 p.m. and may not be given until the day when delivery would have been due if the contract had been made "regular way."

Delivery—"Regular way delayed delivery"

(b) When securities have been sold "regular way delayed delivery," delivery may be made at the option of the seller on any business day prior to the day the contract is due, without advance notice, except that such delivery shall not be made before the fourth business day following the day of the contract.

Effect of notice

(c) A notice given pursuant to the provisions of this Rule shall be considered as in full force until delivery is made.

¶ 2180   Failure to Deliver

Rule 180. If securities due on any particular day are not delivered within the time specified in Rules 176 [¶ 2176] and 177 [¶ 2177] the contract may be closed as provided in Rule 284 [¶ 2284]. If not so closed, and in the absence of any notice or agreement, the contract shall continue without interest until the following business day; but in every case of non-delivery of securities, the party in default shall be liable for any damages which may accrue thereby. All claims for such damages shall be made promptly.

¶ 2181   Delivery by Certificate or Transfer—Personal Liability

Rule 181. The receiver of shares of stock shall have the option, prior to the date delivery is made, of requiring the delivery to be made either in certificates therefor or by transfer thereof; except that in cases where personal liability attaches to ownership, the seller shall have the right to make delivery by transfer.

The right to require receipt or delivery by transfer shall not obtain while the transfer books are closed.

¶ 2182   Charges on Transfer

Rule 182. If the transfer of securities entails any expense (such as transfer fees, additional taxes, etc.) which is not ordinarily payable on a sale of such securities, the expense shall be borne by the party at whose instance the transfer is made.

If delivery is made during the closing of the transfer books with an assignment executed as provided in Rule 202 [¶ 2202], 203 [¶ 2203], or 214 [¶ 2214], the expense of making transfer shall be borne by the party who first delivered the security during the closing of the transfer books.

The Exchange may in any particular case direct otherwise.

¶ 2183   Payment on Delivery

Rule 183. In all deliveries of securities, the party delivering shall have the right to require the purchase money to be paid upon delivery; if delivery is made by transfer, payment may be required at the time and place of transfer; provided, however, that payment on deliveries through Stock Clearing Corporation shall be made in conformity with its By-Laws and Rules.

¶ 2184   Damages Not To Be Deducted

Rule 184. Parties receiving securities shall not deduct from the purchase price any damages claimed for non-delivery, except with the consent of the party delivering the same.

¶ 2185   Denominations on Delivery

Rule 185. Unless otherwise agreed, stock certificates delivered in settlement of contracts in stocks:

  (1) In which the unit of trading is 100 shares, shall be for the exact amount of the trading unit or for smaller amounts aggregating the trading unit;

¶ **2180**   **Rule 180**

(2) in which the unit of trading is less than 100 shares, shall be for the exact amount of stock sold or for smaller amounts aggregating the amount sold, but no certificate delivered shall be for more than 100 shares;

(3) for less than the unit of trading, shall be for the exact amount of stock sold or for smaller amounts aggregating the amount sold.

¶ 2186   Bonds—Denominations on Delivery

Rule 186. Unless otherwise agreed, bonds delivered in settlement of contracts in bonds:

(1) in which the unit of trading is $1,000, shall be in denominations of $1,000 or $500 each, except that bonds in denominations of more than $1,000, when exchangeable without charge for $1,000 or $500 pieces, shall be deliverable;

(2) in which the unit of trading is more than $1,000, shall be in denomination of the unit of trading, or in larger denominations when exchangeable without charge for bonds in the unit of trading.

Amendments.
October 18, 1962; September 19, 1963.

¶ 2187   Bonds—Deliverability

Rule 187. Unless otherwise agreed, contracts in bonds, which are issuable either in coupon or registered form, may be settled by delivery of bonds in either form in the denominations permitted by Rule 186; provided, however, that such bonds shall be

(1) interchangeable, without charge;

(2) prepared in accordance with the engraving requirements of the Exchange; and

(3) exchangeable and transferable in the Borough of Manhattan, City of New York.

Amendments.
September 19, 1963.

● ● ● *Supplementary Material:*

.10 The Exchange will designate those issues which meet the foregoing requirements and may be dealt in and delivered interchangeably.

¶ 2188   "Small" Bonds—"Large" Bonds

Rule 188. Coupon bonds in denominations of less than $500 shall be designated as small bonds, and in denominations of more than $1,000, except as provided in Rule 186 [¶ 2186], as large bonds, and shall be a delivery only when dealt in specifically as such.

¶ 2189   Unit of Delivery

Rule 189. The buyer shall accept any portion of a lot of securities contracted for or due on a security balance if tendered in lots of one trading unit or multiples thereof, and may buy in the undelivered portion as provided

[The next page is 2823-3.]

in Rule 284 [¶ 2284] ; but on sales made "seller's option" or "regular way delayed delivery," the buyer shall not be required to accept, before the date of the expiration of the option, a portion of a lot of securities contracted for.

¶ 2190   Deliveries of Failures

Rule 190. On delivery of a failure to deliver item carried forward from a previous day the party making the delivery shall place upon the delivery ticket the words "Account Failure" giving the date on which delivery was originally due, and the date on which delivery is made.

¶ 2191   Foreign Currency Bonds

Rule 191. All contracts in bonds issued in foreign currencies shall be made and settled on the basis of the equivalent in United States currency fixed by the Exchange.

• • • *Supplementary Material:*

.10   Equivalent values.—(The Exchange has fixed £200 Sterling and 1,000 Cuban Pesos as the equivalent of $1,000.)

¶ 2192   "Part-paid" Securities

Rule 192. Securities which have been partly paid for on subscription shall be designated as "part-paid" securities.

The settlement price of contracts in "part-paid" securities shall be determined by deducting from the contract price the unpaid portion of the subscription price.

• • • *Supplementary Material:*

.10   **Method of computation.**—(To illustrate the method of computing the settlement price of "part-paid" securities, the following example is given:

If the subscription price on an issue of stock is $97 per share and $50-Paid receipts are dealt in ($47 per share remaining to be paid) and if a contract is made at $98½, the price at which the contract would be settled is $51½, i.e., $98½ less $47.)

¶ 2193   "Part-redeemed" Bonds

Rule 193. Unless otherwise directed by the Exchange, bonds which have been redeemed or repaid in part shall be designated as "part-redeemed" bonds.

Contracts in "part-redeemed" bonds shall be made and settled on the basis of a percentage of the original principal amount thereof.

• • • *Supplementary Material:*

.10   **Method of computation.**—(To illustrate the method of dealing and computing the settlement price of "part-redeemed" bonds, the following example is given:

A sale at 70 of a bond on which a principal payment of 25% has been made (reducing the principal of the bond to $750), would represent a sale of the $750 bond at a price of $700, being 70% of $1,000.)

¶ 2194   **Stamp Taxes**

Rule 194.   Each delivery of securities subject to tax on transfer or sale must
be accompanied by a sales ticket stamped in accordance with the
laws of the United States and the State of New York, except that in the case
of securities cleared or deliverable through Stock Clearing Corporation, sales
tickets so stamped shall be delivered in accordance with its By-Laws and Rules.

● ● ● *Supplementary Material:*

.10   **Tax bills for bond deliveries.**—Where sales tickets received with deliveries of coupon bonds cover a larger number of bonds than are due
to a particular client, brokers may deliver bonds to their clients with the following memorandum:

> "The bonds delivered herewith were purchased by us acting as your
> broker and are a part of a block of .... bonds
> purchased by us for which we hold tax bills.
>
> ...."
>
> **(Broker's stamp with clerk's initials)**

8-62
Report 66
Rules of Board—Settlement of Contracts
➡➡➡ *Administered by Department of Stock List.*
2825

¶ 2195 Assignments

Rule 195. (a) A certificate of stock, a registered bond, or other registered security shall be accompanied by a proper assignment, executed either on the certificate itself or on a separate paper, in which latter case there shall be a separate assignment for each certificate or bond.

Separate assignments

(b) A separate assignment shall contain provision for the irrevocable appointment of an attorney, with power of substitution and a full description of the security, and shall be in the form approved by the Exchange. The number of shares of stock or the principal amount of a bond shall be expressed in both words and numerals.

(*Form No. 2 or 3, page 2851. Special forms of assignment required in assigning registered certificates of the corporate stock of the City of New York which are obtainable at the office of the Comptroller of the City of New York.*)

¶ 2196 Power of Substitution

Rule 196. When the name of an individual or member organization has been inserted in an assignment, as attorney, a power of substitution shall be executed in blank by such attorney.

When the name of an individual or member organization has been inserted in a power of substitution, as substitute attorney, a new power of substitution shall be executed in blank by such substitute attorney.

When the name of Stock Clearing Corporation has been inserted in an assignment, as attorney, or in a power of substitution, as substitute attorney, a power of substitution shall be executed in blank by Stock Clearing Corporation as provided in Rule 200(e).

(*Form No. 1, page 2851.*)

Amendments.
Effective June 12, 1962.

¶ 2197 Alterations or Corrections

Rule 197. Any alteration or correction in an assignment, power of substitution, or other instrument shall be accompanied by an explanation on the original instrument, signed by the person, firm or corporation executing the same.

¶ 2198 Signatures

Rule 198. The signature to an assignment or power of substitution shall be technically correct, i.e., it shall correspond with the name as written upon the certificate in every particular without alteration or enlargement, or any change whatever, except that in the case of a firm "and" or "&," "Company" or "Co." may be written either way.

¶ 2199 Corporate Assignments

Rule 199. (a) A certificate in the name of a corporation (except as provided in paragraph (b) hereof) or an institution, or in a name with official designation, shall be a delivery only if the statement "Proper papers for transfer filed by assignor" is placed on the assignment and signed by the transfer agent.

Member corporations

(b) A certificate in the name of a member corporation shall be a delivery provided the assignment is executed either (1) by the manual signature of an officer of such member corporation, or other person, authorized pursuant to Rule 200(a) [¶ 2200], or (2) by the mechanically reproduced facsimile signature of an officer of such member corporation adopted in accordance with Rule 200(b) [¶ 2200], and the following statement appears on the assignment: "Authorizing resolutions filed with New York Stock Exchange."

(*See "Assignments by Member Corporations" at ¶ 2200.10.*)

Amendments.
September 17, 1953.

¶ 2200   Assignments—By Member Organizations

Member corporations—By authorized persons

Rule 200. (a) A member corporation may authorize one or more of its officers, or one or more other persons, who are either its employees or who are officers or employees of Stock Clearing Corporation, to assign registered securities in the name of the member corporation and on its behalf and to guarantee assignments, by filing with the Exchange, in the form prescribed by it, a certified copy of resolutions of its Board of Directors, authorizing such person or persons so to act.

Member corporations—By facsimile signature of officer

(b) A member corporation may assign securities registered in the name of such member corporation, and may execute powers of substitution, by means of a mechanically reproduced facsimile signature of an officer of such member corporation, provided the member corporation shall have (1) executed and filed with the Exchange, in the form prescribed by it, an agreement with respect to the use of such facsimile signature, (2) filed with the Exchange, in the form prescribed by it, a certified copy of resolutions of the Board of Directors of such member corporation authorizing the execution and filing with the Exchange of such agreement, and (3) complied with such other requirements as may be prescribed by the Exchange in connection with the use of facsimile signatures.

Members and member firms—By authorized persons

(c) A member or member firm may authorize one or more persons, who are either his or its employees or who are officers or employees of Stock Clearing Corporation, to assign registered securities in the name of such member or member firm and to guarantee assignments, with the same effect as if the name of such member or firm had been signed under like circumstances by such member or by one of the partners of the firm, by executing and filing with the Exchange, in the form prescribed by it, a separate Power of Attorney for each person so authorized.

¶ 2200   **Rule 200**   © 1962, Commerce Clearing House, Inc.

Members and member firms—By facsimile signature

(d) A member or member firm may assign securities registered in the name of such member or member firm, and may execute powers of substitution, by means of a mechanically reproduced facsimile signature, provided the member or member firm shall have executed and filed with the Exchange, in the form prescribed by it, an agreement with respect to the use of such facsimile signature and shall have complied with such other requirements as may be prescribed by the Exchange in connection with the use of facsimile signatures.

Stock Clearing Corporation—Powers of substitution by facsimile signature

(e) Stock Clearing Corporation may execute powers of substitution by means of a mechanically reproduced facsimile signature of an officer of such corporation, provided such corporation shall have (1) executed and filed with the Exchange, in the form prescribed by it, an agreement with respect to the use of such facsimile signature, (2) filed with the Exchange, in the form prescribed by it, a certified copy of resolutions of the Board of Directors of such corporation authorizing the execution and filing with the Exchange of such agreement, and (3) complied with such other requirements as may be prescribed by the Exchange in connection with the use of facsimile signatures.

Amendments.
Effective June 12, 1962.

● ● ● *Supplementary Material:*

Detailed Procedure To Be Followed in Effecting Appointments Pursuant to Rule 200 [¶ 2200].

.10 Assignments by member corporations.—A member corporation desiring to authorize officers or other persons for the purposes set forth in Rules 199(b) [¶ 2199] and 200(a), above, shall have adopted at a meeting of its Board of Directors resolutions, in the forms prescribed by the Exchange, authorizing such persons to act, and file certified copies of such resolutions with the Department of Stock List.

The resolutions authorize the officers or other persons named therein, in the name and on behalf of the corporation, to assign registered securities, to guarantee signatures and to make other necessary certifications or guarantees in connection with the transfer of securities.

The resolutions provide that any issuer of securities (whether or not listed on the Exchange), its transfer agents, and any bank, banker or trust company, in whatever capacity it may act, having received at any time from the Exchange or from the member corporation (1) notice of the filing with the Exchange of certified copies of the resolutions, supporting certificates and specimen signatures, and (2) facsimiles of the specimen signatures of the persons authorized by the resolutions, may at any time rely on any instrument or paper which has been signed in accordance with the resolutions prior to the receipt by them from the Exchange or from the member corporation of written notice of the revocation of the authorization.

Two forms of corporate resolutions are provided as follows:

(1) Resolutions authorizing officers of the member corporation (designated by titles) to act. These grant continuing authority to the

persons from time to time holding the offices designated, and become effective for those persons duly elected and certified by an Incumbency Certificate.

(2) Resolutions authorizing specific persons (other than officers) to act. These grant authority to the persons specifically named therein. Any subsequent authorization must be covered by a new set of resolutions.

A person authorized pursuant to this procedure will sign his name, over the designation "Authorized Signature," in conjunction with an imprint of the name of the member corporation, which may be in the form of a rubber stamp, and otherwise reading as follows:

JOHN JONES & CO., INC.

By (signed) Richard Roe

Authorized Signature

(Authorizing resolutions filed
with New York Stock Exchange)

Resolutions authorizing officers to act must be accompanied by an Incumbency Certificate, executed by the Secretary or an Assistant Secretary, as to the names of the persons duly elected to the offices of the member corporation designated by the resolutions and the genuine signatures of such persons.

Resolutions authorizing persons other than officers must be accompanied by a certificate of the Secretary or an Assistant Secretary, as to the genuine signatures of the persons authorized by the resolutions to act.

In either event, a legal opinion of the attorney for the member corporation that the member corporation has the power under its charter, by-laws and the laws of the state under which it is organized to confer the authority and power given by the resolutions, must be filed with the resolutions.

In filing resolutions (Other than Officers) the Exchange requires a covering letter stating that the person being authorized is an employee of the member corporation (or an officer or employee of Stock Clearing Corporation).

Cards, in form provided by the Exchange, containing specimens of the signatures to be used by the persons authorized also must accompany the resolutions, in order that the Exchange may have cards prepared bearing facsimiles of the signatures. These cards are sent by the Exchange to all transfer agents for listed securities together with notice of the filing of the certified resolutions, supporting certificates and specimen signatures with the Exchange. This procedure makes it unnecessary for member corporations to file resolutions or signature cards with transfer agents for listed securities. A supply of the signature cards issued by the Exchange will be sent the member corporation for its use in connection with transfers of unlisted securities.

Certified copies of resolutions and specimen signatures of those authorized should be filed with the Exchange two weeks in advance of the date the corporation is to become a member corporation (or two weeks in advance of the date a member corporation desires to have additional persons act), so that the signature cards may be sent out by the Exchange at the appropriate time.

¶ **2200.10   Rule 200**

Notification should be given the Exchange of the revocation of any authorization in the following manner:

(1) *Officers.* Whenever it is desired to revoke the authority previously given by resolution to an officer designated by title, a certificate to this effect, executed by the Secretary or an Assistant Secretary of the member corporation, should be filed with the Exchange.

Whenever there is a change in the identity of a person holding an office which has been designated by title in a resolution filed with the Exchange and it is desired to revoke the authority of the person leaving such office and to establish the authority of the person succeeding to such office, a certificate, executed by the Secretary or an Assistant Secretary of the member corporation, evidencing such change in the identity of the person holding such office should be filed with the Exchange. In addition a new Incumbency Certificate covering *all* officers of the member corporation who have authority to sign, executed by the Secretary or an Assistant Secretary of the member corporation, must be filed with the Exchange, together with a signature card containing a specimen of the signature of any newly authorized officer.

(2) *Persons Other Than Officers.* Whenever it is desired to revoke the authority previously given to any named person (other than an officer), a copy of the resolution of the Board of Directors of the member corporation revoking the authority previously given such person and stating that the authority previously granted the remaining named persons is being continued, must be filed. This must be certified by the Secretary or an Assistant Secretary of the member corporation.

Whenever it is desired to authorize a new person (other than an officer) to sign, whether or not such new person is being substituted for a person whose authority is being revoked, the Exchange must be furnished with a new Certificate as to Authorized Persons covering such new person who is being authorized to sign and all other persons (other than officers) who will continue to sign, together with the necessary certified copy of resolution granting authority to the new person.

In order to defray in part the expenses of the Exchange in preparing signature cards and notifying transfer agents, a charge will be made by the Exchange on the filing of the resolutions, at the rate of $90 for one person being authorized, and $40 for each additional person being authorized at the same time.

.20 Powers of attorney to employees.—A member or member firm desiring to appoint one or more employees for the purposes set forth in Rule 200(c), above, must execute and file with the Department of Stock List, in form prescribed by the Exchange, a separate power of attorney for each employee appointed, signed by either (1) all general and limited partners; or (2) designated partners constituting a Special Committee appointed for such specific purpose under the partnership articles of the firm. If it is desired to execute the document under (2) above, an appropriate provision, in form approved by the Exchange, must be included in the partnership articles, or an amendment thereto, signed by all partners of the firm, both general and limited. A suggested form of such provision may be obtained from the Exchange. These powers of attorney will be kept on file by the Exchange.

Two forms of power of attorney are provided, authorizing an employee to sign for the firm as follows:

Type A power—authorizes the employee to sign the firm name, i.e., "John Jones & Co."

Type B power—authorizes the employee to sign his name in conjunction with an imprint of the firm name, i.e., "John Jones & Co. By (Signed) Richard Roe, Attorney."

Only one type of power may be used at any one time by a firm in appointing attorneys for the firm.

A power of attorney filed with the Exchange must be accompanied by a specimen of the signature which will be used by the person appointed, together with a covering letter stating that the person being authorized is an employee of the member firm (or an officer or employee of Stock Clearing Corporation). On receipt of a power of attorney in proper form and a specimen signature, the Exchange will undertake to have cards prepared bearing facsimile signatures which will be furnished to transfer agents of all listed securities together with notice of the appointment.

A power of attorney is revocable by notice in writing to the Exchange and according to the provisions of the power transfer agents may rely on instruments executed by such attorneys until they receive written notice of revocation from the member or firm appointing the attorney or from the New York Stock Exchange.

The expenses of the Exchange in connection with the preparation of signature cards and notifying transfer agents are to be borne by the members and member firms availing themselves of this privilege. For this purpose, a charge is made on filing of the powers with the Exchange, at the rate of $90 for one power and $40 for each additional power filed at the same time.

If powers of attorney are executed under (1) above, arrangements should also be made for the addition of the signatures of any new partners (general or limited) to any powers on file with the Exchange, promptly after their admission to the firm.

.30 Machine imprinted facsimile signatures.—A member organization desiring to make use of a machine imprinted facsimile signature for the purposes set forth in Rule 200, above, must file with the Department of Stock List an agreement, in form prescribed by the Exchange. In the case of a member firm, the agreement must be signed by either (1) all general and limited partners; or (2) designated partners constituting a Special Committee appointed for such specific purpose under the partnership articles of the firm. If it is desired to execute the document under (2) above, an appropriate provision, in form approved by the Exchange, must be included in the partnership articles, or an amendment thereto, signed by all partners of the firm, both general and limited. A suggested form of such provision may be obtained from the Exchange. In the case of a member corporation, the agreement must be signed by an officer pursuant to resolutions, in form prescribed by the Exchange, of the Board of Directors of the corporation duly adopting the facsimile signature of a specified officer as the signature of the corporation and directing the filing of the agreement.

¶ **2200.30   Rule 200**   © 1962, Commerce Clearing House, Inc.

8-62
Report 66   Rules of Board—Settlement of Contracts   **2831**
➤➤➤ *Administered by Department of Stock List.*

In the agreement the member organization agrees to indemnify the Exchange, any issuer of securities (whether or not listed on the Exchange), its transfer agents and any bank, banker or trust company, in whatever capacity it may act, that has received from the Exchange, or from the member organization a specimen of the facsimile signature, from any loss or liability arising out of any act done in reliance upon the authenticity of the facsimile signature or one resembling or purporting to be such facsimile signature, when used as provided in the agreement.

In connection with the use by a member corporation of a mechanically reproduced facsimile signature, the member corporation must file with the Exchange a legal opinion of the attorney for the member corporation that the facsimile signature has been duly adopted by the member corporation, the agreement properly authorized, and the signature, the agreement and the resolutions are effective and binding upon the corporation under its charter, by-laws and the laws of the state under which it is organized.

The member organization must also file with the agreement an acknowledgment by their surety company of the issuance of a rider to their blanket bond to protect the member organization against loss resulting from their agreement, which may be in the form of a photostat of such rider.

Prior to the execution of an agreement, full details of the procedure to be followed by the member organization, and of the machine and signature plate to be used should be furnished the Department of Stock List so that the requirements for the use of machine signatures may be followed.

Upon approving the use of a particular facsimile signature by a member organization, the Exchange will send a notice to transfer agents for listed securities, together with a card containing a specimen of the facsimile signature, imprinted from the actual signature plate to be used by the member organization. The imprinting of the signature on the cards for the Exchange will be done by the member organization on its own machine, on cards furnished by the Exchange. A supply of the imprinted cards will be sent the member organization for their use in connection with transfers of unlisted securities.

The expenses of the Exchange in connection with the preparation of signature cards and notifying transfer agents are to be borne by the member organizations availing themselves of this procedure. For this purpose, a charge of $90 is made on the filing of the agreement with the Exchange.

If the agreement is executed under (1) above, arrangements should also be made for the addition of the signatures of any new partners (general or limited) to the agreement on file with the Exchange, promptly after their admission to the firm.

¶ 2201   Assignments—By Persons Since Deceased,
                    Trustees, Guardians, etc.

Rule 201. A certificate shall not be a delivery with an assignment or power of substitution executed by a: (1) person since deceased; (2) trustee or trustees, except trustees acting in the capacity of a board of directors of a corporation or association, in which case Rule 199(a) [¶ 2199] shall apply; (3) guardian; (4) infant; (5) executor; (6) administrator; (7) receiver in bankruptcy; (8) agent; or (9) attorney, except as provided in Rule 200(c) [¶ 2200].

¶ 2202   Assignments—By Insolvents

Rule 202. A certificate with an assignment or power of substitution executed by an insolvent shall be a delivery only during the closing of the transfer books, during which time such a certificate shall be a delivery only if held by others than the insolvent and if it is accompanied by an affidavit that the said certificate was so held on a date prior to the insolvency and the signature to the assignment or power of substitution is guaranteed as provided in Rule 209 [¶ 2209].

(*Form No.* 16, *pages* 2857—2858.)

¶ 2203   Assignments—By Dissolved Member Organizations

Rule 203. A certificate with an assignment or power of substitution executed by a member organization that has since ceased to exist shall be a delivery only during the closing of the transfer books, provided the execution of the assignment or power of substitution is properly acknowledged and the signature thereto is guaranteed as provided in Rule 209 [¶ 2209].

(*For firm—Form No.* 6 *or* 7, *pages* 2852—2854; *for corporation—Form No.* 15, *pages* 2856, 2857.)

¶ 2204   Assignments—By Continuing Member Organizations

Rule 204. A certificate with an assignment or a power of substitution executed by a member organization that has since dissolved or ceased to be a member organization and is succeeded by either:

(1) A member firm or firms having as general partners one or more of the general partners or holders of voting stock of the dissolved or former member organization; or

(2) a member corporation or corporations having as holders of voting stock one or more of the general partners or holders of voting stock of the dissolved or former member organization,

shall be a delivery only if the new member organization or one of the new member organizations, shall have signed the statement "Execution guaranteed" as of the date of or a date subsequent to the formation of the new member organization so signing.

¶ 2205   Assignments—Change in Member Organization Name

Rule 205. A certificate with an assignment or power of substitution executed by a member organization, the name of which has since been changed, shall be a delivery only if such member organization shall have signed the statement "Execution guaranteed" as of the date of or a date subsequent to the change in name.

¶ 2206   Joint Tenancy—Special Designation, etc.—Tenancy in Common

Rule 206. A certificate with an inscription to indicate joint tenancy, or with a qualification, restriction or special designation, shall not be a delivery.

A certificate with an inscription to indicate tenancy in common, shall be a delivery only if signed by all co-tenants.   •

¶ 2202   **Rule 202**

¶ 2207   Two or More Names

Rule 207. A certificate issued in the names of two or more individuals or firms shall be a delivery only if signed by all the registered owners.

¶ 2208   Married Women

Rule 208. A certificate in the name of a married woman shall be a delivery, except that, where applicable law limits the right of a married woman to transfer the certificate, such certificate shall be a delivery only when the assignment shall be executed jointly by husband and wife and acknowledged before a notary public or other qualified officer.

(NOTE: The laws of Texas, Arizona and New Mexico, and some foreign countries, restrict the rights of married women to transfer certificates.)
(Form No. 8, page 2854.)

Amendments.
Effective February 13, 1956.

¶ 2209   Signature Guarantee

Rule 209. Except with respect to registered securities of the United States Government, the signature to an assignment of a certificate not in the name of a member or member organization shall be guaranteed by a member or member organization, or by a commercial bank or trust company organized under the laws of the United States or of the State of New York and having its principal office in the vicinity of the Exchange. Each signature to a power of substitution executed by other than a member, member organization or Stock Clearing Corporation shall be guaranteed in like manner.

Amendments.
Effective June 12, 1962.

⊛ ● ● **Supplementary Material:**

.10 "Vicinity of the Exchange".—The Exchange has determined that the words "vicinity of the Exchange" shall mean that part of the Borough of Manhattan, City of New York, located south of Fulton Street.

¶ 2210   Member Signature Is Guarantee

Rule 210. An endorsement or guarantee of an assignment or power of substitution shall be a guarantee of the signature to such assignment or power of substitution, and shall be also a guarantee of the legal capacity and authority of the signer.

¶ 2211   Out-of-Town Member Executions

Rule 211. (a) A certificate with an assignment or power of substitution executed or guaranteed by a member or member organization not having in the vicinity of the Exchange an office at which settlement of Exchange contracts is regularly effected shall be a delivery only if such assignment or power of substitution shall be (1) guaranteed by a member or member organization having such an office in the vicinity of the Exchange or (2) stamped as follows by such member or member organization first delivering it:

"Delivered by ...."

(Name of resident member
or member organization.)

Guarantee by commercial bank or trust company

(b) A certificate with an assignment or power of substitution guaranteed by a commercial bank or trust company, as provided in Rule 209 [¶ 2209], shall be a delivery only if such assignment or power of substitution shall be (1) guaranteed by a member or member organization or (2) stamped as follows by the member or member organization first delivering it:

"Delivered by ...."
(Name of member or
member organization.)

(*See "Vicinity of the Exchange," at* ¶ 2209.10.)

¶ 2212 Guarantee by Insolvent

Rule 212. A certificate with an assignment or power of substitution guaranteed by an insolvent shall be a delivery only if reguaranteed as provided in Rule 209 [¶ 2209].

¶ 2213 Transfer Books Closed Indefinitely

Rule 213. The Exchange may in particular cases direct that assignments and powers of substitution on certificates of a company whose transfer books are closed indefinitely be properly acknowledged.
(*Forms Nos. 4 to 15, pages* 2852—2857.)

¶ 2214 Transferees in Error

Rule 214. A certificate of stock on which the name of a transferee has been filled in in error shall be a delivery during the closing of the transfer books, provided that:

(1) Statements as follows have been placed on the back of the certificate, signed and properly acknowledged:

(A) *By Transferee:*
"I (we) have no interest in the within certificate of stock."

(B) *and by Assignor:*
"Above power of attorney cancelled by me (us) and a new detached assignment and power issued in lieu of it."

(C) *and by Attorneys (if any):*
A separate statement as follows, with proper acknowledgment by each attorney:
"I (we) have no interest in the within certificate of stock, and within power of substitution dated ....
is hereby cancelled."
(*Acknowledgment Forms Nos. 13, 14 and 15, pages* 2855—2857.)
and,

(2) the registered owner shall have executed a separate detached assignment (*Form No. 2, page* 2851), and

(3) the papers shall have been presented to the Exchange and determined to be in order.

¶ 2215   Acknowledgments; Affidavits

Rule 215. Acknowledgments, affidavits, or depositions shall be executed before an officer having authority to take acknowledgments under the laws of the state in which such instruments are executed and shall bear the seal of the signing officer.

Any alteration or correction in an acknowledgment shall be properly noted by the signing officer.

¶ 2216   Assignments of "Rights"

Rule 216. Rules 195 to 215 [¶ 2195-2215], inclusive, shall apply to assignments of registered warrants for rights to subscribe, provided that warrants assigned by a trustee, guardian, executor, administrator, conservator, assignee, receiver in bankruptcy or a corporation shall be a delivery if permitted by the Exchange.

¶ 2217   Called Stock or Registered Bonds

Rule 217. Certificates of stock or registered bonds which are called for redemption shall not be a delivery after the record date fixed by the corporation for the purpose of the drawing for redemption, or the date of the closing of transfer books therefor, except when an entire issue is called for redemption and except in respect of transactions in called securities dealt in specifically as such.

¶ 2218   Called Coupon Bonds

Rule 218. Coupon bonds which are called for redemption shall not be a delivery on and after the date of availability, by publication or otherwise, of the serial numbers of the bonds drawn, except when an entire issue is called for redemption and except in respect of transactions in called bonds dealt in specifically as such.

¶ 2219   Proper Coupons, Warrants

Rule 219. Coupon bonds shall have securely attached proper coupons, warrants, etc., of the same serial numbers as the bonds. The money value of a coupon missing from a bond may be substituted by mutual consent of the parties to the contract.

Amendments.
Effective February 13, 1956.

¶ 2220   Bonds Registered as to Principal or for Voting Purposes Only

Rule 220. Coupon bonds which have been registered as to principal shall be a delivery only if registered to bearer, or, while the transfer books are closed, only if accompanied by a proper assignment for each bond.

Coupon bonds which have been "registered for voting purposes only" shall be a delivery only if such registration has been cancelled.

¶ 2221   Endorsed Bonds

Rule 221. A coupon bond bearing an endorsement of a definite name of a person, firm, corporation, association, etc., in conjunction with words of condition, qualification, direction or restriction, not properly pertaining thereto as a security, shall not be a delivery unless sold specifically as an "endorsed bond."

This rule shall also apply to bonds with coupons bearing such endorsements.

¶ 2222   Released Endorsed Bonds

Rule 222. A coupon bond bearing an endorsement indicating that the bond was deposited in accordance with a governmental requirement pertaining to banking institutions or insurance companies shall not be a delivery. If released, with such release acknowledged before an officer authorized to take acknowledgments, it may be delivered if sold specifically as a "released endorsed bond."

¶ 2223   Mutilated Bonds

Rule 223. A coupon bond which has become mutilated shall not be a delivery unless permitted by the Exchange.

¶ 2224   Mutilated Coupons

Rule 224. A bond bearing a coupon which has been mutilated as to the bond number or signature or which has been cancelled in error shall not be a delivery unless appropriate endorsement in the form required by the Exchange shall have been placed upon the reverse of the coupon.

The endorsement shall be signed on behalf of the obligor by an officer thereof or, under authorization from the obligor, on behalf of the Corporate Trustee or Paying Agent by a duly authorized officer thereof or other person authorized to sign on behalf thereof.

Amendments.
Effective March 30, 1962.

● ● ● *Supplementary Material:*

.10 **Mutilated Coupons.**—It is required that the following endorsement be placed upon the reverse of a coupon which has been mutilated as to bond number or signature:

> "This coupon belongs to Bond No...............
> and is a valid obligation of the obligor.
>
> ....
> ...."

In case a coupon has been cancelled in error, it is required that the following endorsement be placed upon the reverse of the coupon:

> "This coupon, belonging to Bond No............,
> cancelled in error; it is a valid obligation of the obligor.
>
> ....
> ...."

The endorsement shall be signed on behalf of the obligor by an officer thereof or, under authorization from the obligor, on behalf of the Corporate Trustee or Paying Agent by a duly authorized officer thereof or other person authorized to sign on behalf thereof.

The Department of Stock List shall be notified in writing by the obligor, Corporate Trustee or Paying Agent signing the endorsement, of the making of the endorsement, identifying the endorsed coupon and reciting the language of the endorsement. If the endorsement is by other than the obligor, such notification to the Exchange must include a certification that proper authorization to make the endorsement has been received from the obligor.

If the coupon has become detached from the bond, it shall be properly attached thereto.

¶ 2225   Delivery of Equivalent Securities

Rule 225. All contracts made in securities listed on the Exchange shall be subject to the condition that, unless otherwise specifically agreed between the parties, in the event that such securities become or are exchangeable for new or other securities under a plan or proposal relating to such securities, the Exchange may in its discretion direct that, upon admission to dealings of the new securities, settlement of such contracts, unless previously effected, may be made by delivery either of the securities contracted for or the equivalent in securities and cash or other property receivable under such plan or proposal.

[The next page is 2851.]

Forms Approved by the Exchange

(For Use in Conjunction with Rules 175-225 [¶ 2175-2225].)

1. **Power of Substitution.**

POWER OF SUBSTITUTION TO BE USED WHEN ATTORNEY HAS BEEN DESIGNATED IN AN ASSIGNMENT.

"I (*or we*) hereby irrevocably constitute and appoint ....my (*or our*) substitute to transfer the within named Stock under the foregoing Power of Attorney, with like Power of Substitution."

Dated ....

....

—————— ——————

2. **Assignment Separate from Certificate.**

For value received ....hereby sell, assign and transfer unto .... (   ) Shares of the .... Capital Stock of the .... standing in .... name on the books of said ....represented by Certificate No. .... herewith and do hereby irrevocably constitute and appoint .... attorney to transfer the said stock on the books of the within named Company with full Power of Substitution in the premises.

Dated ....

....

—————— ——————

3. **Assignment Separate from Bond.**

For value received .... hereby sell, assign and transfer unto .... one bond of the ....for .... ($), No. .... herewith, standing in .... name on the books of said .... and do hereby irrevocably constitute and appoint .... attorney to transfer the said bond on the books of the within named Company, with full Power of Substitution in the premises.

Dated ....

....

—————— ——————

4. Acknowledgment—When Assignment on a Certificate is Executed by an Individual.

State of ....⎫
⎬ *ss.*
County of ....⎭

On this .... day of .... 19..., before me a Notary Public for the County of .... personally appeared .... to me known, and known to me to be the individual named in the within Certificate, and who executed the foregoing Assignment and Power of Attorney, and acknowledged to me that he executed the same.

| SEAL | ....
....
_____ ....

5. Acknowledgment—When Power of Substitution is Executed by an Individual.

State of ....⎫
⎬ *ss.*
County of ....⎭

On this .... day of .... 19..., before me a Notary Public for the County of .... personally appeared .... to me known, and known to me to be the individual named in the foregoing Power of Attorney and who executed the foregoing Power of Substitution, dated .... 19..., and acknowledged to me that he executed the same.

| SEAL | ....
....
_____

6(a). Acknowledgment—When Assignment on a Certificate is Executed by a Firm.

State of ....⎫
⎬ *ss.*
County of ....⎭

On this .... day of .... 19..., before me a Notary Public for the County of .... personally appeared .... to me known, and known to me to be a member of (or authorized to sign under a Power of Attorney filed with the New York Stock Exchange for) the firm of .... named in the within certificate, and who executed the foregoing Assignment and Power of Attorney, and acknowledged to me that he executed the same as the act and deed of said firm.

| SEAL | ....
....

Note.—If used for a firm that has ceased to exist, omit the word "be" in third line and substitute the words "have been on .... 19...."

_____

Form 4

6(b). Acknowledgment—When Assignment on a Certificate is Executed by a Firm by Mechanically Reproduced Facsimile Signature.

State of ....⎫
                               ⎬ *ss.*
County of ....⎭

    On this .... day of .... 19..., before me a Notary Public for the County of .... personally appeared .... to me known, and known to me to be a member of the firm of .... named in the within certificate, and acknowledged to me that the foregoing Assignment and Power of Attorney was executed by the duly adopted mechanically reproduced facsimile signature of said firm as the act and deed of said firm.

....

| SEAL |

....

Note.—If used for a firm that has ceased to exist, omit the word "be" in third line and substitute the words "have been on .... 19...."

7(a). Acknowledgment—When Power of Substitution is Executed by a Firm.

State of ....⎫
                               ⎬ *ss.*
County of ....⎭

    On this .... day of .... 19..., before me a Notary Public for the County of .... personally appeared .... to me known, and known to me to be a member of (or authorized to sign under a power of attorney filed with the New York Stock Exchange for) the firm of .... named in the foregoing Power of Attorney, and who executed the foregoing Power of Substitution, dated .... 19..., and acknowledged to me that he executed the same as the act and deed of said firm.

....

| SEAL |

....

Note.—If used for a firm that has ceased to exist, omit the word "be" in third line and substitute the words "have been on .... 19...."

7(b).   Acknowledgment—When Power of Substitution is Executed by a Firm by Mechanically Reproduced Facsimile Signature.

State of ....⎫
⎬ *ss.*
County of ....⎭

On this .... day of .... 19..., before me a Notary Public for the County of .... personally appeared .... to me known, and known to me to be a member of the firm of .... named in the foregoing Power of Attorney, and acknowledged to me that the foregoing Power of Substitution, dated .... 19, ..., was executed by the duly adopted mechanically reproduced facsimile signature of said firm as the act and deed of said firm.

| SEAL | .... |

Note.—If used for a firm that has ceased to exist, omit the word "be" in third line and substitute the words "have been on .... 19...."

8.   Acknowledgment—For Wife and Husband for Assignment on a Certificate in Name of a Married Woman.

State of ....⎫
⎬ *ss.*
County of ....⎭

On this .... day of .... 19..., before me a Notary Public for the County of .... personally appeared .... and .... her husband, both of them known to me, and they severally acknowledged that they executed the foregoing Assignment and Power of Attorney, for the purpose therein mentioned.

| SEAL | .... |

9 and 10.   [Eliminated February 13, 1956.]

11.   Acknowledgment—When Separate Assignment is Executed by an Individual.

State of ....⎫
⎬ *ss.*
County of ....⎭

On this .... day of .... 19..., before me a Notary Public for the County of .... personally appeared .... to me known, and known to me to be the individual named in the annexed Certificate of Stock (*or Bond*) and who executed the foregoing Assignment and Power of Attorney, and acknowledged to me that he executed the same.

| SEAL | .... |

12(a). Acknowledgment—When Separate Assignment is Executed by a Firm.

State of ....⎫
                                      ⎬ *ss.*
County of ....⎭

On this .... day of .... 19..., before me a Notary Public for the County of .... personally appeared .... to me known, and known to me to be a member of (or authorized to sign under a power of attorney filed with the New York Stock Exchange for) the firm of .... named in the annexed Certificate of Stock (*or Bond*) and who executed the foregoing Assignment and Power of Attorney, and acknowledged that he executed the same as the act and deed of said firm.

| SEAL |

Note.—If used for a firm that has ceased to exist, omit the word "be" in third line and substitute the words "have been on .... 19...."

12(b). Acknowledgment—When Separate Assignment is Executed by a Firm by Mechanically Reproduced Facsimile Signature.

State of ....⎫
                                      ⎬ *ss.*
County of ....⎭

On this .... day of .... 19..., before me a Notary Public for the County of .... personally appeared .... to me known, and known to me to be a member of the firm of .... named in the annexed Certificate of Stock (*or Bond*) and acknowledged to me that the foregoing Assignment and Power of Attorney was executed by the duly adopted mechanically reproduced facsimile signature of said firm as the act and deed of said firm.

| SEAL |

Note.—If used for a firm that has ceased to exist, omit the word "be" in third line and substitute the words "have been on .... 19...."

13. Acknowledgment—For an Individual. (Cancellation of Assignment.)

State of ....⎫
                                      ⎬ *ss.*
County of ....⎭

On this .... day of .... 19..., before me a Notary Public for the County of .... personally appeared .... to me known, and known to me to be the individual described in and who executed the above Instrument, and acknowledged to me that he executed the same.

| SEAL |

14. Acknowledgment—For a Firm. (Cancellation of Assignment.)

State of ....⎫
⎬ *ss.*
County of ....⎭

On this .... day of .... 19..., before me a
Notary Public for the County of .... personally appeared
.... to me known, and known to me to be a
member of the firm of .... described in and who
executed the above Instrument, and acknowledged to me that he executed the
same as the act and deed of said firm.

| SEAL | ....
    ....

Note.—If used for a firm that has ceased to exist, omit the word "be" in third
line and substitute the words "have been on .... 19...."

15(a). Acknowledgment—When Assignment or Power of Substitution is
Executed by a Member Corporation.

State of ....⎫
⎬ *ss.*
County of ....⎭

On this .... day of ...., 19..., before me
personally came ...., to me known, who, being by
me duly sworn, did depose and say that he resides at ....
.... in ....;
that he is .... of ....,
the corporation described in and which executed the foregoing instrument;*
that he knows the seal of said corporation; that the seal affixed to said instrument is such corporate seal; that it was so affixed by order of the Board of
Directors of said corporation, and that he signed his name thereto by like order.

| SEAL | ....
    ....

*If the corporation has no corporate seal, omit the words after the asterisk and substitute
therefor the following: "that he signed his name thereto by order of the Board of Directors of
said corporation; and that the reason why no seal is affixed to said instrument is because the
corporation had no seal."

Note.—If used for a corporation that has ceased to exist, omit the word "is" in
the fifth line and substitute the word "was on ....,19...."

Form 14   © 1957, Commerce Clearing House, Inc.

15(b). Acknowledgment—When Assignment or Power of Substitution is Executed by a Member Corporation by Mechanically Reproduced Facsimile Signature.

State of ....⎫
                                  ⎬ ss.
County of ....⎭

On this .... day of ...., 19..., before me personally came ...., to me known, who, being by me duly sworn, did depose and say that he resides at ....
.... in ....;
that he is .... of ....,
the corporation described in and which executed the foregoing instrument;* that he knows the seal of said corporation; that the seal affixed to said instrument is such corporate seal; that it was so affixed by order of the Board of Directors of said corporation, and that the duly adopted, mechanically reproduced facsimile of his signature was affixed thereto by like order. ....

| SEAL |

....

*If the corporation has no corporate seal, omit the words after the asterisk and substitute therefor the following: "that the facsimile of his signature was affixed thereto by order of the Board of Directors of said corporation; and that the reason why no seal is affixed to said instrument is because the corporation had no seal."

Note.—If used for a corporation that has ceased to exist, omit the word "is" in the fifth line and substitute the words "was on ...., 19...."

16(a). Affidavit by a Member Firm as Holder of Security in Name of Insolvent.

State of ....⎫
                                  ⎬ ss.
County of ....⎭

.... being duly sworn, deposes and says: that he resides at ....; that he is a member of the firm of ....; that ....
.... shares of the ....stock of .... represented by certificate number .... were purchased by my said firm for value on .... without notice of the insolvency of and prior to the appointment of a Receiver for .... in whose name said certificate is registered and by whom said certificate was endorsed and that said shares were not received by my said firm in payment of an antecedent indebtedness.

Sworn to before me this⎫
.... day of⎬
.............., 19...⎭   ....

| SEAL |

Note.—If used for a power of substitution executed by an insolvent, substitute the words "who executed the foregoing Power of Substitution, dated ...., 19....," for the words in the eighth and ninth lines reading "in whose name said certificate is registered and by whom said certificate was endorsed."

16(b). Affidavit by a Member Corporation as Holder of Security in Name
of Insolvent.

State of ....⎫
                               ⎬ *ss.*
County of ....⎭

.... being duly sworn, deposes and
says: that he resides at ....; that he is
an officer, to wit .... of ....
a .... corporation (hereinafter called the "Corporation"); that .... shares of the ....
stock of .... represented by certificate number
.... were purchased by the Corporation for value on
.............................without notice of the insolvency of and
prior to the appointment of a Receiver for ....in whose name said
certificate is registered and by whom said certificate was endorsed and that
said shares were not received by the Corporation in payment of an antecedent
indebtedness.

Sworn to before me this⎫
.... day of ⎬
.............., 19 ...⎭   ....

SEAL

Note.—If used for a power of substitution executed by an insolvent, substitute
the words "who executed the foregoing Power of Substitution, dated
...................., 19....," for the words in the ninth and tenth
lines reading "in whose name said certificate is registered and by whom
said certificate was endorsed."

[The next page is 2871.]

Dividends, Interest, Rights, etc.

*(Rules and Policies Administered by the
Department of Stock List.)*

¶ 2235   **Ex-Dividend, Ex-Rights**

Rule 235. Transactions in stocks (except those made for "cash") shall be
ex-dividend or ex-rights on the third business day preceding the
record date fixed by the corporation or the date of the closing of transfer
books. Should such record date or such closing of transfer books occur upon
a day other than a business day, this Rule shall apply for the fourth preceding
business day.

Transactions in stocks made for "cash" shall be ex-dividend or ex-rights
on the business day following said record date or date of closing of transfer
books.

The Exchange may, however, in any specific case, direct otherwise.

*(See Rule 118 [¶ 2118] as to types of orders which shall or shall not be reduced
and ¶ 2118.10-.30 regarding reduction of orders, odd amounts, optional amounts
and responsibility.)*

¶ 2236   **Ex-Warrants**

Rule 236. Transactions in securities which have subscription warrants
attached (except those made for "cash") shall be ex-warrants
on the third business day preceding the date of expiration of the warrants,
except that when the date of expiration occurs on a day other than a business
day, said transactions shall be ex-warrants on the fourth business day preceding said date of expiration.

Transactions in securities made for "cash" shall be ex-warrants on the
business day following the date of expiration of the warrants.

The Exchange may, however, in any specific case, direct otherwise.

¶ 2237   **Buyer Entitled to Dividends, etc.**

Rule 237. Unless otherwise agreed, the buyer shall be entitled to receive all
dividends, rights and privileges, except voting power, accruing
upon securities purchased which are ex-dividend or ex-rights during the
pendency of the contract.

¶ 2238   **Charge for Delivery of Dividends or Rights**

Rule 238. For the delivery of stock dividends or rights or for the payment
of cash dividends pertaining to securities which the holder has
failed to transfer, a charge of not exceeding one per cent of such payment
or of the value of such stock dividends or rights delivered may be made by
the party making such delivery or payment, except by mutual consent of the
parties involved. For stock or scrip dividends or rights the charge shall be
computed on the fair market value thereof on the record date or date of
closing of transfer books.

No charge shall be made for collecting dividends or rights accruing
on securities deliverable on a contract.

Amendments.
Effective February 13, 1956.

New York Stock Exchange Guide   **Rule 238   ¶ 2238**

¶ 2239 Claims for Dividends, Rights, etc.

Rule 239. When the owner of a registered security claims dividends, interest, rights, etc., from the party in whose name the security is registered, the registered holder thereof may require from the claimant presentation of the certificate or bond, a written statement that he was the holder of the security at the time of the closing of the books, a guarantee against any future demand for the same and the privilege to record on the certificate or bond evidence of the payment by cash or due-bill.

¶ 2240 Excess Rights

Rule 240. In cases where members or member organizations on the last day for subscription have more rights to subscribe than they or their customers appear to be entitled to in accordance with the records of the members or member organizations, the excess amount of rights shall be sold in the best available market and the proceeds of such sales shall be held subject to the claims of the persons entitled to such rights to subscribe.

¶ 2241 Interest—Added to Contract Price

Rule 241. In settlement of contracts in bonds dealt in "and interest" there shall be added to the contract price interest on the principal amount at the rate specified in the bond, which shall be computed up to but not including the day on which delivery is due, except that in the case of contracts made "delayed delivery," such interest shall be computed only up to but not including the fourth business day following the day of the contract; and in the case of contracts made "seller's option," such interest shall be computed only up to but not including the day when delivery would have been due if the contract had been made "regular way."

¶ 2242 Computation of Elapsed Days

Rule 242. The amount of interest deemed to have accrued on contracts in accordance with Rule 241 [¶ 2241] shall be:

(1) On bonds (except bonds issued or guaranteed by the United States Government), that portion of the interest on the bonds for a full year, computed for the number of days elapsed since the previous interest date on the basis of a 360-day-year. Each calendar month shall be considered to be 1/12 of 360 days, or 30 days, and each period from a date in one month to the same date in the following month shall be considered to be 30 days.

(2) on bonds issued or guaranteed by the United States Government, that portion of the interest on the bonds for the current full interest period, computed for the actual number of days elapsed since the previous interest date on the basis of actual number of calendar days in the current full interest period. The actual elapsed days in each calendar month shall be used in determining the number of days in a period.

● ● ● *Supplementary Material:*

.10 **Computation of elapsed days.**—The following tables are given to illustrate the method of computing the number of elapsed days in conformity with Rule 242, above:

On bonds (except bonds issued or guaranteed by the United States Government):
From 1st to 30th of the same month to be figured as 29 days
From 1st to 31st of the same month to be figured as 30 days
From 1st to 1st of the following month to be figured as 30 days.

Where interest is payable on 30th or 31st of the month:
From 30th or 31st to 1st of the following month to be figured as 1 day
From 30th or 31st to 30th of the following month to be figured as 30 days
From 30th or 31st to 31st of the following month to be figured as 30 days
From 30th or 31st to 1st of second following month, figured as 1 month, 1 day.

On bonds issued or guaranteed by the United States Government:
From 15th of a 28-day month to the 15th of the following month is 28 days
From 15th of a 30-day month to the 15th of the following month is 30 days
From 15th of a 31-day month to the 15th of the following month is 31 days.

The six months' interest period ending:
January 15 is 184 days
February 15 is 184 days
March 15 is 181* days
April 15 is 182* days
May 15 is 181* days
June 15 is 182* days
July 15 is 181* days
August 15 is 181* days
September 15 is 184 days
October 15 is 183 days
November 15 is 184 days
December 15 is 183 days

*Leap Year adds 1 day to this period.

¶ 2243   Interest Computation—Fractions

Rule 243. In all transactions involving the payment of interest, fractions of a cent equalling or exceeding five mills shall be regarded as one cent; fractions of a cent less than five mills shall be disregarded.

¶ 2244   Bonds—"And Interest" Dealings

Rule 244. Bonds dealt in "and interest" shall continue to be dealt in on that basis until the Exchange directs otherwise.

¶ 2245   Income Bonds

Rule 245. Income bonds, unless otherwise directed by the Exchange, shall be dealt in "flat."

¶ 2246   Past Due Coupons

Rule 246. Bonds dealt in "flat" shall carry all past due and unpaid coupons, unless the Exchange directs otherwise.

¶ 2247   Payment of Interest or Principal on Bonds Dealt "Flat"

Rule 247. Bonds dealt in "flat" on which a payment of interest or principal is made shall be ex-interest or ex-principal as directed by the Exchange.

¶ 2248   Registered Bonds "And Interest," Due-Bills for Interest

Rule 248. When registered bonds dealt in "and interest" are delivered between the record date fixed for the purpose of determining holders entitled to receive interest and the interest payment date, a due-bill, signed by the party in whose name the bond stands, or by a member or member organization, for the full amount of the interest to be paid by the obligor, shall accompany the bond until interest is paid.

¶ 2249   Registered Bonds "Flat," Due-Bills for Interest

Rule 249. When registered bonds dealt in "flat" are delivered after the record date fixed for the purpose of determining holders entitled to receive an interest or principal payment, in settlement of a contract made prior to the date on which the issue of bonds is quoted "ex" by direction of the Exchange, a due-bill, signed by the party in whose name the bond is registered, or by a member or member organization, for the full amount of the interest or principal to be paid by the obligor, shall accompany the bonds.

The Exchange may, however, in any particular case, direct otherwise.

¶ 2250   Deliveries On or After Interest Dates

Rule 250. Bonds dealt in "and interest," delivered on or after the date on which interest is due and payable, shall be without the coupons due on such date, with adjustment for the cash value of the coupons in determining the accrued interest payable as provided by Rule 241 [¶ 2241].

Amendments.
Effective February 13, 1956.

¶ 2251   Cash Adjustment for Coupons

Rule 251. (a) In the settlement of contracts in bonds dealt in "and interest," when delivery is due prior to the interest-payment date and is made on or after the interest-payment date, and in the settlement of "delayed delivery" contracts in such bonds made prior to the fourth business day preceding the interest-payment date, for delivery on or after the interest-payment date, there shall be a cash adjustment for coupons paid during the pendency of the contract on the basis of the greatest net amount obtainable for the coupons either in United States currency or in other currencies converted at the exchange rate prevailing at 10:00 a.m. on the interest-payment date.

(b) In the settlement of "seller's option" contracts in bonds dealt in "and interest," made prior to the fourth business day preceding the interest-payment date for delivery on or after the interest-payment date, there shall be a cash adjustment for coupons paid during the pendency of the contract on the basis of the greatest net amount obtainable for the coupons either in United States currency or in other currencies converted at the exchange rate prevailing at 10:00 a.m., on the date delivery becomes due.

The greatest net amount obtainable for coupons in other currencies converted at the prevailing exchange rate may be demanded only if all bondholders have the option of collecting interest on the same basis.

Amendments.
Effective February 13, 1956.

[The next page is 2885.]

Due-Bills

*(Rules and Policies Administered by the
Department of Stock List.)*

¶ 2255   "Due-Bill," "Due-Bill Check" Defined

Rule 255. (a) The term "due-bill," as used in the Rules, means an assignment or other instrument employed for the purpose of evidencing the transfer of title to any dividend, interest or rights pertaining to securities contracted for, or evidencing the obligation of a seller to deliver such dividend, interest or rights to a subsequent owner.

(b) The term "due-bill-check," as used in the Rules, means a due-bill in the form of a check payable on the date of payment of a cash dividend, which prior to such date shall be considered as a due-bill, as defined in paragraph (a), for the amount of such dividend.

¶ 2256   Forms of Due-Bills

Rule 256. Due-bills shall be in form approved by the Exchange except that with specific permission of the Exchange certificates of less than the unit of trading issued after the record date, in the names of members or member organizations, may be accompanied by a special form of odd-lot due-bill. *(Form No. 17, 18, 19, 20, 21 or 22, pages 2901-2902.)*

¶ 2257   Deliveries After "Ex" Date

Rule 257. When a security is sold before it is ex-dividend or ex-rights, or is sold thereafter to and including the record date for "cash," and delivery is made too late to enable the buyer to obtain transfer in time to become a holder of record to receive the distribution to be made with respect to such security, the seller shall pay or deliver the distribution to the buyer in the following manner, unless otherwise directed by the Exchange:

(1) In the case of stock dividends or rights to subscribe, the seller shall deliver to the buyer, within four days after the record date, either the dividend or rights, or a due-bill for such dividend or rights.

(2) In the case of cash dividends, the seller shall deliver to the buyer, within four days after the record date, a due-bill-check for the amount of the dividend.

The same principle shall apply to the return of loans of securities after the record date.

¶ 2258   Due-Bills—Guaranty

Rule 258. A due-bill which is used pursuant to specific direction of the Exchange shall be signed by the holder of record entitled to receive the distribution from the issuer of the security. The signature shall correspond with the name on the face of the security to which the due-bill is attached. When executed by a non-member, it shall be guaranteed in the same manner as assignments of securities.

¶ 2259   Due-Bills—Redemption

Rule 259. When, by direction of the Exchange, a security is not ex-dividend
            or ex-rights, as the case may be, on the date such event would
ordinarily take place, and due-bills are required to accompany deliveries, the
due-bills shall be redeemable on the date fixed by the Exchange.

When due-bills are used without specific direction of the Exchange, by
reason of deliveries made too late to allow purchasers who are entitled to dividends or rights to effect a transfer of the securities, or otherwise, the due-bills
shall be redeemable on the date of payment or distribution of the dividend or
rights, except that in the case of rights to subscribe which are admitted to
dealings on the Exchange on a "when issued" basis, such due-bills shall be
redeemable on the date fixed by the Exchange for settlement of "when issued"
contracts in the rights.

When due-bills are used on deliveries of registered bonds pursuant to
Rules 248 [¶ 2248] and 249 [¶ 2249], the due-bills shall be redeemable on the
date of payment of the interest, except that in the case of registered bonds
dealt in "flat," which are delivered after the date on which the issue of bonds
is declared ex-interest by the Exchange, such due-bills shall be redeemable
on the date when delivery of the bonds is made, or on the date of payment of
the interest, whichever is later.

Due-bills shall be redeemed by the members or member organizations
by whom they are signed or guaranteed.

[The next page is 2901.]

Forms Approved by the Exchange

(For Use in Conjunction with Rules 255-259 [¶ 2255-2259].)

17. Due-Bill for Cash Dividend.

FOR VALUE RECEIVED, the undersigned, holder of record at the close of business on . . . . , of . . . . (   ) shares of . . . . Stock of . . . . , represented by Certificate No. . . . . , hereby assigns, transfers and sets over unto . . . .
. . . .
the cash dividend of . . . . ($) to which the undersigned is entitled.
Dated . . . .

. . . .

---

18. Due-Bill for Stock Dividend.

FOR VALUE RECEIVED, the undersigned, holder of record at the close of business on . . . . , of . . . . (   ) shares of . . . . Stock of . . . . , represented by Certificate No. . . . . , hereby assigns, transfers and sets over unto . . . .
. . . .
the . . . . (   ) shares of . . . . Stock of . . . . to which the undersigned is entitled as a stock dividend, and hereby irrevocably constitutes and appoints . . . . attorney to transfer the shares representing said stock dividend on the books of said corporation with full powers of substitution in the premises.
Dated . . . .

. . . .

---

19. Due-Bill for Stock Distribution.

FOR VALUE RECEIVED, the undersigned, holder of record at the close of business on . . . . , of . . . . (   ) shares of . . . . Stock of . . . . , represented by Certificate No. . . . . , hereby assigns, transfers and sets over unto . . . .
. . . .
the . . . . (   ) shares of . . . . Stock of . . . . to which the undersigned is entitled as a stock distribution, and hereby irrevocably constitutes and appoints . . . . attorney to transfer the shares representing said stock distribution on the books of said corporation with full powers of substitution in the premises.
Dated . . . .

. . . .

20. Due-Bill for Rights.

FOR VALUE RECEIVED, the undersigned, holder of record at the close of business on ...., of .... (   ) shares of .... Stock of ...., represented by Certificate No. ...., hereby assigns, transfers and sets over unto ....

....

the warrant and/or fractional warrant to which the undersigned is or may be entitled, evidencing the Right to Subscribe for ....

....

....

Dated ....

....

---

21. Due-Bill for Interest.

Due bearer .... dollars ($) representing the interest due ....
on (registered bond   ) No. .... (of the   )
    (certificate of deposit)   (representing)

....

....

for $, which interest is payable to holders of record on ....

....

Dated ....

....

---

22. Due-Bill for Odd-Lots.

....

Due Bearer the .... dividend declared by the ....to stockholders of record of .... on .... (   ) shares of their .... stock.

Dated ....

....

[The next page is 2911.]

Reclamations

*(Rules and Policies Administered by the
Department of Stock List.)*

¶ 2265   "Reclamation" Defined

Rule 265. The term "reclamation," as used in Rules 266 to 274 [¶ 2266—2274], inclusive, means a claim for the right to return, or to demand the return of, securities previously delivered and accepted.

¶ 2266   Time for Return

Rule 266. A security with an irregularity which has been delivered may be returned or reclaimed on the day of delivery up to 3:30 p. m. On a subsequent business day, delivery on reclamation shall be made before delivery time on such day.

¶ 2267   Returns Replaced Immediately

Rule 267. When a security is returned or reclaimed, the party who delivered it shall immediately either give the party presenting it the security in proper form for delivery in exchange for the security originally delivered or pay the current market value therefor. In the latter case, unless otherwise agreed, the party to whom the security is returned shall be deemed to be failing to deliver the security.

¶ 2268   Within 10 Days—Currency, in Market

Rule 268. Reclamation for an irregularity which affects only the currency of the security in the market shall be made within ten days from the day of original delivery.

¶ 2269   Endorsed Bonds

Rule 269. Reclamation on bonds bearing endorsements referred to in Rules 221 and 222 [¶ 2221, 2222] shall be made within ten days from the day of original delivery.

¶ 2270   Exchangeable Certificates

Rule 270. Reclamation, by reason of the fact that a form of certificate was delivered which was not a proper delivery, but which is exchangeable without charge for a certificate which is a delivery, shall be made within ten days from the day of original delivery.

¶ 2271   Without Limit—Wrong Security

Rule 271. Reclamation, by reason of the fact that the wrong security was delivered, may be made without limit of time.

¶ 2272   Lost or Stolen—Title Questioned

Rule 272. Reclamation, by reason of the fact: (1) That title to a security is called in question, or (2) that a security is reported to have been lost or stolen, or (3) that the transfer or payment of a security is prohibited or restricted by law or governmental authority, may be made without limit of time, and such security may be returned to the party who introduced it into the market.

¶ 2273   Partial Call

Rule 273. Reclamation, by reason of the fact that a called security was delivered, which was not a delivery under the provisions of Rule 217 or 218 [¶¶ 2217, 2218], may be made without limit of time and such security may be returned to the party who held it at the time such security ceased to be a delivery.

(Note: This Rule does not apply when an entire issue is called for redemption or when the securities involved were dealt in specifically as called securities.)

¶ 2274   Married Women

Rule 274. Reclamation, by reason of the fact that a certificate in the name of a married woman was delivered, which was not a delivery under the provisions of Rule 208 [¶ 2208] because applicable law limits the right of a married woman to transfer the certificate, may be made without limit of time.

Adopted.
Effective February 13, 1956.

¶ 2275   Special Cases

Rule 275. Notwithstanding the provisions of Rules 265 to 274 [¶¶ 2265-2274], inclusive, where there are equitable considerations, the Exchange may in particular cases direct otherwise, and may also issue special directions in circumstances not specifically covered by such Rules.

[The next page is 2925.]

Closing Contracts

(Rules and Policies Administered by The Floor Department.)

¶ 2281   **Disagreement on Contract**

Rule 281.   When a disagreement between members or member organizations arising from a transaction in securities is discovered, the money difference shall forthwith be established by purchase or sale or by mutual agreement.

¶ 2282   **Contracts of Insolvents**

Rule 282.   When an announcement is made of the suspension of a member or member organization pursuant to the provisions of Article XIII of the Constitution [¶¶ 1601-1608], members or member organizations having Exchange contracts with the suspended member or member organization for the purchase, sale or loan of securities shall, without unnecessary delay, proceed to close such contracts on the Exchange or in the best available market, except in so far as the By-Laws and Rules of Stock Clearing Corporation are applicable and provide the method of closing. Should such a contract not be closed as above provided, the price of settlement for the purpose of Section 3 of Article XI [¶¶ 1503] of the Constitution shall be fixed by the fair market value at the time when such contract should have been closed under this Rule.

¶ 2283   **Members Closing Contracts—Procedure**

Rule 283.   When Rule 140 [¶¶ 2140] permits the closing of a contract, an original party to the contract may close it, provided that notice, either written or oral, shall have been given to the other original party at least thirty minutes before such closing. If a member or member organization given up by an original party to a contract has been advised that the other party to the contract does not recognize it, or if the other party to the contract neglects or refuses to exchange written contracts, he or it shall promptly notify the original party who acted for him or it, who may then close the contract as herein provided.

¶ 2284   **Procedure for Closing Defaulted Contract**

Rule 284.   A contract in securities admitted to dealings on the Exchange which has not been fulfilled according to the terms thereof may be officially closed by an officer or employee of the Exchange authorized by the Exchange to close such contracts.

The ORDER to close such contract shall be delivered to the Exchange, and the member organization giving such ORDER shall deliver at the office of the member organization in default NOTICE of intention to make such closing. Every such ORDER and every such NOTICE shall be in writing, and shall state the name of the member organization giving the ORDER, the date of the original contract to be closed, the maturity date of such contract, and the name of the other party thereto.

With respect to contracts, other than "cash" contracts to be closed on the day of the contract, such NOTICE shall be delivered to the member organization in default prior to forty-five minutes after delivery time. Unless the Exchange directs otherwise, such ORDER shall be delivered to the Exchange between 2:15 and 2:30 p. m. and the contract shall not be closed before 2:35 p. m.

When a contract made for "cash" is to be closed on the day of the contract, the time of the transaction shall be stated on the NOTICE and the ORDER. Such NOTICE shall be delivered to the member organization in default prior to the delivery of the ORDER to the Exchange. Such ORDER shall be delivered to the Exchange between 2:30 and 2:45 p.m. in the case of transactions effected at or before 2:00 p.m. and within forty-five minutes after the transaction in the case of transactions effected after 2:00 p.m. No "cash" contract to be closed on the day of the contract shall be closed prior to five minutes after the delivery time for such contract.

The closing of a contract may be deferred by order of a Floor Official whenever in his opinion a fair market in which to close the contract is not available, and the Exchange may defer the closing of a contract if it determines that the default is due to the existence of a general emergency situation, but no such deferment shall relieve the party in default of any resulting damages.

¶ 2285   Notice of Intention to Successive Parties

Rule 285. Every member or member organization receiving notice that a contract is to be closed for his or its account because of non-delivery shall immediately re-transmit notice thereof to any other member or member organization from whom the securities involved are due. Every such re-transmitted notice shall be in writing and shall be delivered at the office of the member or member organization to whom it is addressed; it shall state the date of the contract upon which the securities are due from such member or member organization, and the name of the member or member organization who has given the original notice to close.

¶ 2286   Closing Portion of Contract

Rule 286. When notice of intention to close a contract, or re-transmitted notice thereof, is given for less than the full amount due, it shall be for not less than one trading unit.

¶ 2287   Liability of Succeeding Parties

Rule 287. The closing of a contract pursuant to the Rules of the Board of Governors shall be for the account and liability of each succeeding party in interest in such contract, and, in case notice that such contract will be closed has been re-transmitted, as provided in Rule 285 [¶ 2285], such closing shall also automatically close all contracts with respect to which such re-transmitted notice shall have been delivered prior to the closing.

Re-establishment of contract

If such re-transmitted notice is sent by a member or member organization before the contract has been closed, but is not received until after such closing, the member or member organization who sent the same may, unless other-

¶ 2285   Rule 285   © 1961, Commerce Clearing House, Inc.

wise agreed, promptly re-establish, by a new sale, the contract with respect to which such notice has been sent.

Payment of money difference

Any money difference resulting from the closing of a contract, or from the re-establishment of a contract as herein provided, shall be paid not later than 3:00 p. m. on the following business day to the member or member organization entitled to receive the same.

¶ 2288   Notice of Closing to Successive Parties

Rule 288. When a contract has been closed the member or member organization who closed the same, or who gave the order to close the same, shall immediately notify the member or member organization for whose account the contract was closed. Immediate notification shall be given to succeeding parties in interest and to other members or member organizations to whom re-transmitted notice, as provided for in Rule 285 [¶ 2285], has been sent. Statements of resulting money differences, if any, shall also be rendered immediately.

¶ 2289   Must Receive Delivery

Rule 289. When a member or member organization has given notice of intention to close a contract for non-delivery, or has re-transmitted notice thereof as provided in Rule 285 [¶ 2285], he or it must receive and pay for securities due upon such contract if tendered at his or its office prior to the closing of such contract.

If the person who, pursuant to Rule 284 [¶ 2284], has in hand the order to close is notified prior to the closing by a member or member organization that some or all of the securities (but not less than one trading unit) are in his or its physical possession and will be promptly delivered, then the order to close shall not be executed with respect to such securities, and the member or member organization who has given the original order to close shall accept and pay for such securities, if tendered promptly.

Damages for non-delivery

If such securities be not promptly tendered, the member or member organization who has stated that they would be promptly delivered shall be liable for any resulting damages.

● ● ● *Supplementary Material:*

.10 Notices to the Exchange.—Notices by the party giving the order, of cancellations or changes in quantity when given at or before 2:30 p. m., must be given to The Floor Department. After 2:30 p. m. such notices must be given to the person handling the order at the place on the Floor where the security is dealt in.

Notices by the party in default of physical possession of the securities and intention to make immediate delivery, when given at or before 2:30 p. m., must be given to The Floor Department. After 2:30 p. m. such notices must be given to the person handling the order at the place on the Floor where the security is dealt in.

¶ 2290　　Defaulting Party May Deliver After Notice of Intention to Close

Rule 290. A member or member organization who has received a notice of intention to close a contract, or re-transmitted notice thereof, may deliver the securities at the office of the member or member organization issuing such notice up to 2:30 p. m. He or it may deliver such securities after 2:30 p. m. if notice is given to the Exchange before the execution of the order that he or it has physical possession of the securities.

(*See* ¶ 2289.10, "*Notices to the Exchange.*")

¶ 2291　　Failure to Fulfill Closing Contract

Rule 291. When a contract is closed, any member or member organization accepting the bid or offer, and not complying promptly therewith, shall be liable for any damages resulting therefrom.

¶ 2292　Restrictions on Members' Participation in Transaction to Close Defaulted Contracts

Rule 292. No member or member organization, who for his or its own account has given an order to close a contract because of non-delivery, shall fill the order by selling for his or its own account, either directly or through a broker, the securities named therein; and no member or member organization shall knowingly enable or permit any other person on whose behalf the order to close because of non-delivery has been issued to fill such order by selling for his own account the securities named therein. If a member or member organization has issued an order to close because of non-delivery and, acting for another principal, supplies the securities named therein, he or it must make delivery in accordance with the terms of the contract thus created, and may not by consent or otherwise fail to make such delivery. The member or member organization for whose account a contract is being closed, or any succeeding member or member organization in interest, or any member or member organization to whom re-transmitted notice has been sent, shall not accept the bid or offer, unless such member or member organization is acting for a principal other than the one for whose account the contract is being closed.

¶ 2293　　Closing Contract in Unlisted or Suspended Securities

Rule 293. A contract in unlisted securities, or in securities which have been suspended from dealings on the Exchange, which has not been fulfilled according to the terms thereof may be closed in the best available market by the party thereto who is not in default. Otherwise, the provisions of Rules 284 to 290 [¶ 2284—2290], inclusive, shall be followed as nearly as possible.

¶ 2294　　　　　Default in Loan of Money

Rule 294. When a loan of money is not paid before 2:15 p. m. of the day upon which it becomes due, the borrower shall be considered as in default and the lender may, without notice, sell the securities pledged therefor, or so much thereof as may be necessary to liquidate the loan.

[The next page is 2941.]

Miscellaneous Floor Procedure

(Policies Administered by The Floor Department.)

¶ 2299A   Civil Defense Alarm Procedure

● ● ● *Supplementary Material:*

.10   In the event of a Civil Defense alarm in New York City the following procedure will be followed:

(a) If an alarm is in effect at the time the Exchange would normally be opened, the opening will be postponed until after the public all clear signal.

(b) If an alarm is given during the time the Exchange is open for business, the Floor sirens will be sounded, which shall automatically terminate all trading on the Floor. An appropriate notice will be published on the tape.

(1) The termination of trading under the circumstances shall have the same effect on bids and offers as a closing of the Exchange.

(2) Upon such termination of trading all open agreements to "stop" securities shall become effective. However, in the event that the alarm sounds after the opening of the Exchange, but prior to the time that a specialist is able (A) to establish a definite quotation in a stock, or (B) to arrange the opening price, the provisions of this paragraph shall not apply to market orders which have been accepted by the specialist before the opening of the Exchange for the purpose of arranging the opening. A specialist who has established a quotation in a stock shall "stop out" such market orders left with him before the opening of the Exchange, regardless of whether he has had the opportunity of informing the member who left such order with him that it was "stopped" at a particular price.

(3) If trading is resumed the same day, bidding and offering on the Floor at the re-opening shall be conducted as at any other opening, but for other purposes a trading session so interrupted shall be regarded as a single session.

(c) All day orders shall be regarded as good for the entire day regardless of any interruption of trading.

(d) A period of at least 10 minutes will be allowed between the public all clear signal and the opening or re-opening.

It is contemplated that as soon as possible after the public all clear signal is given, necessary notices concerning procedure will be published on the tape, including the time of re-opening, the time of final closing, etc.

¶ 2299B   Federal Agencies Exempt from Taxation

● ● ● *Supplementary Material:*

.10   The Bureau of Internal Revenue, in a ruling dated December 13, 1943, stated that the Bureau will not assert a liability for documentary stamp tax against the buyer or other party to the transaction in the case of a sale of stock by a governmental agency, provided:

(1) The governmental agency files with the Bureau and the Exchange a blanket certification that on all transactions on which the tax is paid by it, it will consider that it has paid the tax on behalf of the pur-

chaser and has been reimbursed by the purchaser for the affixation of the required tax stamps out of the proceeds of sale received by it, and an agreement that it is not entitled to and will not make a claim for refund of the taxes thus paid;

(2) the governmental agency furnishes to the Bureau and the Exchange an opinion of their counsel as to its authority to give such an agreement.

Unless otherwise stipulated in the offer, any sale made for the account of a Federal agency or instrumentality that has filed such a certification shall be a regular transaction and the selling broker will be required to provide the Federal tax in the customary manner.

The Exchange is in receipt of such blanket certification and opinion of counsel from the Alien Property Custodian, the Federal Deposit Insurance Corporation and the Reconstruction Finance Corporation.

The Department of Taxation and Finance of the State of New York, in a ruling dated July 18, 1946, stated that on sales of stock by a Federal agency, the payment of the New York stock transfer tax by the Federal agency, on behalf of the buyer of the stock, will discharge the buyer from liability for the tax imposed by Article 12 of the Tax Law, under an arrangement similar to that provided above.

Unless otherwise stipulated in the offer, any sale made for the account of a Federal agency or instrumentality that has filed such a certification shall be a regular transaction and the selling broker will be required to provide the New York State tax in the customary manner.

The Exchange is in receipt of such blanket certification and opinion of counsel from the Alien Property Custodian and the Reconstruction Finance Corporation.

The above must not be confused with a sale of securities for the account of an insolvent bank. Sales of stocks and bonds by insolvent banks (National and State) are not subject to Federal tax in those instances where the collection of the tax would operate to diminish the assets of such banks necessary for full payment to depositors, provided proper exemption certificates are attached to the securities when presented for transfer. However, the New York State Tax Commission has ruled that transfers of stock from the name of an insolvent bank are subject to the payment of the New York State stock transfer tax, regardless of whether the bank is a National or State bank. No conditions as to payment of tax need be made in a sale of this kind on the Floor. Such sales are not considered as special transactions and will be published on the tape. (See ¶ 3321.11.)

¶ 2299C   **After-Hours Employment of Stock
Exchange Employees**

● ● ● *Supplementary Material:*
(*See Rule* 350 [¶ 2350] *and* ¶ 2350.10.)

       © 1964, Commerce Clearing House, Inc.

NEW YORK STOCK EXCHANGE

ADMISSION OF MEMBERS—Allied Members and Member Organizations

... rules and policies of Board of Governors governing transfers of memberships, the formation of member organizations, admissions of members and allied members, corporate affiliates, and related matters ...

TABLE OF CONTENTS

Admission of Members

Transfers of Memberships—Admissions of Members, Allied Members, etc.

(Rules and Policies Administered by the Office of the Secretary.)

¶ 2301   Proposed Transfer of Membership

Rule 301. An offer or agreement by a member for the transfer of his membership may be made only in writing in such form as may from time to time be prescribed by the Exchange and shall be executed personally by such member or by his legal representatives, except that an attorney-in-fact of such member may execute such documents in his behalf only if the following conditions are complied with, viz.:

(1) The Exchange has approved the execution of the power of attorney running to such attorney-in-fact;

(2) the Exchange is satisfied as to the validity and continued effectiveness of such power of attorney; and

(3) the Exchange is satisfied that the holder of such power of attorney is acting thereunder solely as agent for the member and is neither directly nor indirectly acting in his own behalf or in behalf of any third person and that he is not a creditor of such member and does not directly or indirectly represent any person who is such a creditor, unless

(A) the holder of such power of attorney is the Secretary of the Exchange acting pursuant to a power executed by the member and approved by the Exchange in connection with an agreement made with respect to the financing of the purchase of the membership; or

(B) the holder of such power of attorney is a general partner or a holder of voting stock in a member organization in which such member is also a general partner or a holder of voting stock and has no financial interest in the transfer other than such as may arise by virtue of such attorney's interest in such member organization.

● ● ● *Supplementary Material:*

Qualifications

.10 Age and citizenship.—An applicant for membership in the Exchange must be at least twenty-one years of age and a citizen of the United States (Art. IX, Sec. 2 [¶ 1402]). If he is a naturalized citizen, he must present his naturalization papers.

.12 Experience.—A member who is to be active on the Floor is required to be indoctrinated under the guidance of an experienced Floor member for such period as may be necessary to acquaint him with Floor procedures. He is required to pass an examination before receiving the privilege of executing orders on the Floor without supervision.

An allied member or a member who intends to work in the office of a member organization is required to pass an examination before undertaking any active duties with the firm. In addition, a member or allied member who intends to assume supervisory responsibilities or who proposes to service customer accounts is required to pass an appropriate examination in these areas.

¶ 2301.12   Experience.—Continued

An allied member whose sole duty is on the Floor of the American Stock Exchange or another exchange will be permitted to meet examination requirements by passing a Floor examination given by the exchange of which the person is a member.

The procedures for applying for examination are the same as described in ¶ 2345.15.   Study outlines are published to assist in preparation for examination.

Procedure Regarding Election

.20 **Approval by Board of Governors.**—A transfer of a membership in the Exchange requires approval of the Board of Governors by the affirmative vote of two-thirds of the Governors present at a meeting of the Board.   (Art. XI, Sec. 1 (¶ 1501].)

Other pertinent provisions of the Constitution are as follows:

Eligibility for membership and procedure
on election .... Article   IX [¶ 1401-1416]
Dues .... Article   X [¶ 1451-1457]
Transfer of membership and disposition of
proceeds .... Article   XI [¶ 1501-1513]
Gratuity Fund—Payments and benefits.... Article XVI [¶ 1751-1758]

.21 **Bids and offers—Memberships.**—Agreements for the transfer of memberships are usually arranged through the Secretary of the Exchange who maintains a file of written bids for and offers of memberships. Although such agreements may be negotiated elsewhere, the final arrangements for the transfer of a membership must be consummated through the Office of the Secretary. In general, all documents relating to the transfer of a membership must be executed personally by the member. Under certain circumstances, however, a power of attorney running to a third person and authorizing him to act for the member in this connection may be recognized by the Exchange.

.22 **Deposit—Indemnity agreement.**—A candidate for membership must, immediately upon the execution of an agreement for the transfer of a membership (other than a transfer for a nominal consideration), deposit with the Secretary of the Exchange either (1) a certified check for twenty per cent of the agreed purchase price, or (2) a written guarantee (on a form supplied by the Exchange) by a member organization. The purpose of this is to indemnify, up to the amount of the deposit or guarantee, the prospective seller against any loss which he may sustain in the eventual price realized by him in the prompt resale and transfer of his membership in case the proposed purchaser repudiates his agreement or fails to deposit the balance of the purchase price and the initiation fee at the proper time. In the event that the applicant fails of election to membership, the deposit will be returned to him or the guarantee will become void, as the case may be.

.23 **Application for membership.**—In making application for membership, a candidate is required to sign a personal statement, on a form prescribed by the Exchange, giving, among other things, complete details as to his business history. He must arrange with the Medical Clinic located in the Exchange building for a physical examination. He must present letters of recommendation from at least three responsible persons.

.24 **Sponsors.**—An applicant for membership shall be sponsored by two members or allied members of the Exchange of at least one year's standing, who have known the applicant sufficiently well and over a long enough period of time that they can unqualifiedly endorse the applicant from their personal knowledge of him and of his business connections.

A casual social or business acquaintanceship is not sufficient basis to qualify a member or an allied member as a sponsor.

The sponsors are required to read and sign the candidate's application and, ordinarily, are also required to appear with an applicant at the time the application is presented for consideration.

.25 Appearance of applicant.—The applicant is required to appear personally at the time his application for membership is presented for consideration. The Office of the Secretary will advise the applicant of the date of such appearance at the time arrangements are entered into for the proposed transfer.

.26 Posting.—The Constitution provides that at least ten days must elapse between posting of a notice of a proposed transfer of membership and balloting by the Board of Governors (*Art. XI, Sec. 1* [¶ 1501]). Notice of a proposed transfer is posted on the bulletin board of the Exchange and published in the Weekly Bulletin of the Exchange upon the submission, in proper form, of *all* required documents. The notice is ordinarily posted *after* the appearance of the applicant.

.27 Payments to be made on day of election.—On the day on which the Board of Governors is scheduled to ballot on his application, the proposed member must deposit with the Exchange the balance of the purchase price of his membership, an initiation fee of $7,500 to the Exchange (*Art. IX, Sec. 4* [¶ 1404]), an initial contribution to the Gratuity Fund of $15 (*Art. XVI, Sec. 1* [¶ 1751]), and the unexpired portion of the transferor's dues for the then current quarter. (*Art. X, Sec. 4* [¶ 1454].)

.28 Signing Constitution.—No person elected to membership is admitted to the privileges of membership until he has signed the Constitution of the Exchange, thereby pledging himself to abide by the Constitution, as from time to time amended, and the rules adopted pursuant thereto. (*Art. IX, Sec. 6* [¶ 1406].)

Financial Arrangements Regarding Membership

.30 General.—The purchase of a membership may be financed in whole or in part as follows:

    I. By the applicant's own means (see .31);

    II. By gift to the applicant, accompanied by a release from the donor (see .32);

    III. By funds advanced as a subordinated loan (see .33); or

    IV. By funds advanced by a member organization accompanied by a release, the applicant simultaneously entering into an a-b-c agreement with the firm or corporation (see .34).

Financing arrangements which do not conform to one or more of the above will not be approved.

.31 I. Own means.—No special documents are required to be filed with the Exchange when an applicant finances the purchase of his membership, including the payment of the initiation fee, entirely with his own personal means. In his appearance as an applicant for membership, he is required to agree with the Exchange that he will not thereafter enter into any agreement whatsoever with reference to his membership unless the specific approval of the Exchange is first obtained.

¶ 2301 **Financial Arrangements Regarding Membership.**—Continued

.32 II. Gift under release.—If all or any part of the purchase price is being advanced to an applicant as a gift, the Exchange requires that the applicant file with the Exchange a general release from the donor to evidence the fact that the new member will be under no obligation to make any payment to the donor. A similar general release must be obtained from the transferor in the case of a transfer of a membership for a nominal consideration.

.33 III. Funds advanced as a subordinated loan.—If an applicant for membership borrows funds to be used for the purchase of a membership, the instrument evidencing his obligations must be in the form of a "subordination agreement" approved by the Exchange. Similarly, if a present member who originally financed the purchase of his membership in whole or in part with borrowed funds desires to refund his outstanding obligations, any new agreements must be in the approved form. Duplicate originals of all agreements executed in connection with such borrowings or refundings must be filed with the Exchange, and will be retained by the Exchange as part of its records.

The purpose of the required subordination agreement is to preclude the lender from asserting any claim against the membership or the proceeds of its transfer and to insure that such proceeds will first be applied to the payment of all claims entitled to priority under the provisions of Article XI of the Constitution [¶ 1501-1513].

In general, in order to be approved by the Exchange, the maturity of a subordination agreement must be not less than the respective periods of time below mentioned, according to the percentage of the total purchase price of the membership advanced under the subordination agreement:

Percentage of Purchase Price Advanced	*Minimum Time of Maturity*
80% or more	3 years
60% to 80%	2½ years
40% to 60%	2 years
20% to 40%	1½ years
less than 20%	1 year

All renewals of subordinated loans must be for a minimum period of one year. A subordination agreement for an amount substantially in excess of the then current market value of memberships will not be approved.

Subsection Fifth of Section 3 of Article XI of the Constitution [¶ 1503] expressly provides that the Exchange will not recognize any purported assignment of or attempted lien upon the proceeds or any part of the proceeds of the transfer of a membership, except as specifically provided in the Constitution; nor will the Exchange in general give effect to any power of attorney or direction to pay such proceeds or any part of the proceeds to any person except the member himself or, under the circumstances set forth in subsection Fifth of Section 3 of Article XI of the Constitution [¶ 1503], to his firm or corporation. (See Rule 302 [¶ 2302] regarding permissible powers of attorney.)

.34 IV. A-B-C agreement.—

Definition.—An a-b-c agreement is a form of arrangement entered into when it is intended that a portion of the risk of fluctuations in the value of a membership owned by a member of the Exchange, who is a general partner in a member firm or a holder of voting stock in a member corporation, shall rest with the partners of the firm or with the corporation rather than have the entire risk rest with the member individually. It should be noted a membership, even if it is the subject of an a-b-c agreement, remains a personal franchise vested solely in the member.

Terms of agreement.—Before entering into an a-b-c agreement, the firm or corporation must release the member from any obligation to repay the funds advanced, except under the terms of the agreement. Approved forms of releases are available in the Office of the Secretary. The member must agree that upon the dissolution of the member organization or his ceasing to be a participant therein, or upon his death or other contingencies, he or his legal representatives will comply with the terms of one of the three following options:

> (a) Retain his membership and pay to the partnership or corporation the amount necessary to purchase another membership; or

> (b) sell his membership and pay the proceeds over to the partnership or corporation; or

> (c) transfer his membership for a nominal consideration to a person designated by the partnership or corporation and satisfactory to the Board of Governors.

(The agreement should clearly state who shall be responsible for the payment of the initiation fee in the event of the exercise of option (a).)

The member must have the unqualified right, at all times, subject only to his making the agreed payment to his member organization, to retain his membership (i. e., to elect option (a)). The choice as to which of the other two options shall be exercised may rest with the member organization in case the member does not choose to keep his membership. Similarly, the member organization may be empowered to make the election of option (b) or option (c), if the member does not declare his election of option (a) within a specified reasonable time. The agreement must provide that the member will have at least 30 days to declare his election of option (a) computed from the date on which notice is specifically given, pursuant to the partnership articles, separate agreement, or otherwise, that the member organization will be dissolved or cease to be a member organization, or the member's status as a partner or stockholder will be terminated on a specified date. In the event of the death or incompetency of the member the period (at least 30 days) shall be deemed to expire ten days after the appointment of the legal representative or committee of the member. Any sums payable under option (a) or (b) must be payable to the member organization so as to be wholly available to its creditors.

Although the Exchange will not object to the inclusion, pursuant to Rule 301 [¶ 2301], in the partnership articles or separate agreement, of a power of attorney authorizing a general partner of the member or a holder of voting stock in the member corporation to execute documents on his behalf in connection with a sale or transfer of the membership after the expiration of the 30-day period above described, the Exchange reserves the right to pass upon the use of such power of attorney in any particular instance.

Inclusion in partnership articles or separate agreement.—In the case of firms, all a-b-c agreements must be incorporated in the partnership articles of

¶ 2301.34   Financial Arrangements Regarding Membership—Continued

the firm and in the case of corporations, all a-b-c agreements must be incorporated in a separate written agreement between the member and the corporation. Such articles and agreements must be submitted to and approved by the Exchange prior to becoming effective.

Standards for determining partners' interests.—An a-b-c agreement of a member firm, as a condition of approval, must conform to one of the three following standards:

Profit-and-loss basis.—All general partners must participate in the liquidation of the membership in the same proportions as they participate in firm profit and loss.

Capital basis.—All capital-contributing general partners, including the member whose membership is the subject of the agreement (whether or not such member is a capital-contributing partner) must participate in the liquidation in the same proportions as their respective contributions of capital. The member whose membership is the subject of the agreement must, under this standard, have a minimum participation of one-half of that which he would have if all general partners had an equal participation. The percentage interest which is not allocated to the member must be allocated to the other participants in proportion to their respective contributions of capital.

Capital-profit-and-loss basis.—All capital-contributing general partners, including the member whose membership is the subject of the agreement (whether or not such member is a capital-contributing partner) must participate in the liquidation in the same proportions as their respective participations in profit and loss. The member whose membership is the subject of the agreement must, under this standard, have a minimum participation of one-half of that which he would have if all general partners had an equal participation. The percentage interest which is not allocated to the member must be allocated to the other participants in proportion to their respective participations in profit and loss.

Standard for determining stockholders' interests.—An a-b-c agreement of a member corporation, as a condition of approval, must conform to the following standard:

All holders of voting stock must participate in the payments to be made to the corporation on the liquidation of the a-b-c agreement in the same proportion as their stock interests in the corporation.

Limited partners and holders of non-voting stock.—It is optional under any standard above described to include or exclude limited partners or holders of non-voting stock as participants. If limited partners are included when the Capital Basis Standard or the Capital-Profit-and-Loss Basis Standard is used, the minimum interest of the member may not be reduced by reason of such inclusion.

Larger participation for Exchange member.—It is optional to allocate to the member whose membership is the subject of the agreement a larger participation in the liquidation of the membership than the mathematical minimum under any standard above described. When this is done, the percentage interest which is not allocated to the member must be allocated to the other participants in proportion to their respective interests in profit and loss, to

¶ 2301.34   **Rule 301**

their respective contributions of capital, or to their respective stock interests, as the case may be.

Treatment on books.—When a membership is made the subject of an a-b-c agreement it must be placed on the books at the current market value, for determination of future profits or losses. Subsequent adjustments in percentage participations by reason of retirements, admissions, changes in profit-and-loss interests, contributions or withdrawal of capital, etc., or by reason of admission or retirement of a stockholder, or changes in the holdings of an existing stockholder, must be computed at the current market value of memberships at the time such events occur.

Non-conforming agreements.—An existing a-b-c agreement which does not conform to one or more of the requirements above described, having been entered into with the approval of the Exchange prior to the adoption of such requirements, may remain in effect without change until terminated by the dissolution of the member organization, the sale or transfer of the membership, or the death of the Exchange member, except that if the agreement is non-conforming in that the interests of the participants differ from the standards above described, and one of the participants dies or retires, the interest of such deceased or retiring partner or stockholder must be allocated to the other partners or stockholders in such proportions as to produce a greater degree of conformity.

For the purpose of these requirements, a merger or split-up of a firm in which the member and all participants in the a-b-c agreement become partners in a new firm, the extension of partnership articles, the entering into of substantially identical new partnership articles, the admittance of a new partner or the death or retirement of a partner, are not regarded *per se* as constituting the dissolution of a partnership.

.35 V. Other agreements.—Except as described above, an applicant must not execute any instrument nor enter into any agreement, oral or written, in regard to his membership or the funds advanced for the purchase of his membership. In his application for membership, the applicant must describe in detail the method by which he is financing the acquisition of his membership and must specifically agree that he will not thereafter make, without the specific approval of the Exchange, any change whatsoever in the initial financing arrangements except, without the use of borrowed money, the payment of principal and interest on a subordination agreement or the discharge of his obligations under an a-b-c agreement.

¶ 2302   Surplus of Proceeds of Membership Transferred

Rule 302. Payment of the surplus, if any, of the proceeds of the transfer of a membership shall be made only to the person or persons specified in subsection Fifth of Section 3 of Article XI of the Constitution [¶ 1503], except that payment of such proceeds may be made to an attorney-in-fact of the person whose membership has been transferred only if the following conditions are complied with, viz.:

(1) The Exchange has approved the execution of the power of attorney running to such attorney-in-fact;

(2) the Exchange is satisfied as to the validity and continued effectiveness of such power of attorney; and

(3) the Exchange is satisfied that the holder of such power of attorney is acting thereunder solely as agent for the person whose membership has been transferred and is not, directly or indirectly, acting in his own behalf or in behalf of any third person and that he is not a creditor of the person whose membership has been transferred and does not directly or indirectly represent any person who is such a creditor, unless the holder of such power of attorney is, or immediately preceding the transfer was, a general partner or a holder of voting stock in a member organization in which such member was also a general partner or a holder of voting stock and has no financial interest in such proceeds other than such as may arise by virtue of the fact that he is or was such a partner or such a stockholder.

● ● ● *Supplementary Material:*

.10 **Claims against proceeds of memberships.**—At the time a membership is posted for transfer, a member or member organization asserting claims for priority of payment out of proceeds of sale pursuant to Article XI of the Constitution [¶¶ 1501-1513] should promptly file a statement of such claim, in duplicate, with the Secretary of the Exchange. Forms for the filing of claims under subsection Third of Section 3 of Article XI [¶ 1503] may be obtained from the Office of the Secretary.

¶ 2303   Limitation on Access to Floor

Rule 303. The Board of Governors may, in its discretion, deny access to the Floor of the Exchange to a member, or may impose such conditions and limitations as it may determine with respect to his access thereto and the transactions which he may effect thereon, (1) if the Exchange has knowledge of the entry or filing against such member of legal process such as a judgment for the payment of money, or (2) if legal proceedings of any nature are instituted or if any legal process is served upon the Exchange purporting to attach, levy upon, encumber, or in any way effect any immediate or future disposition or transfer of the membership of such member or the proceeds of such transfer, or (3) if the then existing obligations or arrangements of such member with respect to the disposition of his membership or of the proceeds of the transfer thereof are not in accordance with the Constitution, Rules and practice of the Exchange.

● ● ● *Supplementary Material:*

.10 **Disposition of memberships.**—The Board of Governors may dispose of the membership of

    (1) A deceased member (*Art. XI, Sec. 4* [¶ 1504]) ;

    (2) an expelled member or a member ineligible for reinstatement (*Art. XI, Sec. 6* [¶ 1506]) ;

    (3) a member delinquent in payment of dues, fines, or contributions under Article XVI [¶ 1751-1758] or contributions under Section 16, Article IX [¶ 1416] or other sums due to the Exchange (*Art. X, Sec. 5* [¶ 1455]).

.20 **Designation of alternates.**—A member of the Exchange who, in time of national emergency for this country, is on active duty in the armed forces of the United States or of any nation or State which is then allied or associated with the United States, or who is engaged in any public service incident to the national defense, may make application to the Board of Governors for approval of one of his general partners or a holder of voting stock in the member corporation in which such member is a holder of voting stock to act as his alternate on the Floor of the Exchange. (*Art. IX, Sec. 15* [¶ 1415].) The procedure in submitting an application for approval of an alternate is, in general, the same as that followed by an applicant for membership.

[The next page is 3051.]

Partnerships—Corporations

*(Rules and Policies Administered by the
Office of the Secretary.)*

¶ 2311   Formation of or Admission to Member Organizations

Rule 311.   A member who proposes to form a member organization or to admit any person as a participant in a member organization or who proposes to become a participant in an organization for which application is made for approval as a member organization, shall notify the Secretary of the Exchange in writing before any such formation or admission, and shall submit such information as may be required by the Exchange.

(See Article IX [¶¶ 1401-1416] of the Constitution.)

¶ 2312   Notice of Changes Within Member Organizations

Rule 312.   (a) A member who is a general partner or a holder of voting stock in a member organization shall promptly give or cause to be given to the Secretary of the Exchange notice in writing (1) of the death or retirement of any other participant or officer, (2) of the dissolution of the member organization, or (3) of the fact that the member organization has ceased to transact business as a broker or dealer in securities.

(b) In addition, in the case of a member corporation, such member shall give similar notice (1) of any proposed change in the stockholdings, (2) of any proposed change in the directors or officers, (3) of any proposed change in the charter, certificate of incorporation, by-laws or other documents on file with the Exchange, or (4) of the happening of any of the events specified in subdivisions (1), (2) and (3) of subparagraph (c) of Section 7 of Article IX of the Constitution [¶ 1407].

(See Article IX [¶¶ 1401-1416] of the Constitution.)

● ● ● *Supplementary Material:*

.10   **Constitutional provisions.**—A member proposing to form a member organization, or to admit any person as a participant, is required to obtain the prior approval of the Board of Governors, and each general partner in a member firm, and each holder of voting stock in a member corporation is required to become an allied member of the Exchange. (Art. IX, Secs. 7 and 8 [¶¶ 1407, 1408].)

Reference should be made to Sections 9, 10, and 11 of Article IX [¶¶ 1409-1411], regarding the method of becoming an allied member and the rights and privileges of allied memberships, as well as Rules 311 to 319 [¶¶ 2311-2319], inclusive, relating to partnerships or to corporations.

.12   **Experience.**—A member who is to be active on the Floor is required to be indoctrinated under the guidance of an experienced Floor member for such period as may be necessary to acquaint him with Floor procedures. He is required to pass an examination before receiving the privilege of executing orders on the Floor without supervision.

An allied member or a member who intends to work in the office of a member organization is required to pass an examination before undertaking any active duties with the firm. In addition, a member or allied member who intends to assume supervisory responsibilities or who proposes to service

New York Stock Exchange Guide   **Rule 312   ¶ 2312.12**

¶ 2312.12 Continued

customer accounts is required to pass an appropriate examination in these areas.

An allied member whose sole duty is on the Floor of the American Stock Exchange or another exchange will be permitted to meet examination requirements by passing a Floor examination given by the exchange of which the person is a member.

The procedures for applying for examination are the same as described in ¶ 2345.15. Study outlines are published to assist in preparation for examination.

.14 Other business connections.—Rule 318 [¶ 2318] requires that every member and allied member who is a general partner in a member firm or a holder of voting stock in a member corporation must be actively engaged in the business of his member firm or member corporation and devote the major portion of his time thereto, and that without prior approval of the Exchange no such member or allied member shall become associated in any outside business. (See Rule 318 [¶ 2318] and ¶ 2318.10.)

.16 Application.—The papers required to be submitted prior to approval of the formation or admission of a member organization are as follows:

(1) Letter signed by Exchange member or proposed Exchange member giving name and address of proposed or existing organization, date of proposed formation or admission, and names of all proposed or present participants and officers;

(2) individual partners' or stockholders' applications executed by each non-member participant; and

(3) short form application executed by the present or proposed Exchange member.

The papers required to be submitted prior to approval of the admission of a non-member as a participant in an existing member organization are as follows:

(1) Letter signed by Exchange member stating name of proposed participant and proposed date of admission to member organization;

(2) a partner's or stockholder's application executed by the proposed participant.

The papers required to be submitted prior to approval of the admission of an Exchange member as a participant in an existing member organization are as follows:

(1) Letter signed either by an Exchange member who is a participant in the organization, or by an allied member of the organization and by the proposed Exchange member participant giving the proposed date of admission to the member organization and stating whether the member will be a general or limited partner, or a holder of voting or non-voting stock;

(2) short form application executed by the proposed Exchange member participant.

.18 Allied member pledge.—A proposed allied member must sign a statement in which he pledges himself to abide by the Constitution as from time to time amended and the Rules adopted pursuant thereto. (Art. IX, Sec. 9 [¶ 1409].) This pledge is included in the application to be executed by each proposed allied member.

.20 Allied member sponsors.—An applicant for approval as an allied member of the Exchange shall be sponsored by two members or allied members of the Exchange of at least one year's standing, who have known the applicant sufficiently well and over a long enough period of time that they can unqualifiedly endorse the applicant from their personal knowledge of him and of his business connections. **A casual social or business acquaintanceship is** not sufficient basis to qualify a member or an allied member as a sponsor. The sponsors should, if possible, not be participants in the organization which the applicant proposes to join. The sponsors are required to read and sign the proposed allied member's application.

Sponsors are not required in the following cases:

(1) An applicant for approval as either a limited partner or as a holder of non-voting stock;

(2) an applicant for approval as a general partner or holder of voting stock, if the applicant has been a member or allied member of the Exchange within one year of the date of the new application.

.22 Fee for consideration of application.—At the time an application for approval of a participant (other than a member of the Exchange) in a member organization is submitted, a fee of $100 is payable. In the event the number of applications involving the same organization and submitted at any one time exceeds 10, the maximum fee charged shall be $1,000. While the fee is payable at the time of submission, a member or member organization may request that the charge be placed on the regular quarterly statement from the Exchange.

No fee is charged for consideration of the following types of applications:

(1) An application of an Exchange member or proposed Exchange member to become a participant in a member organization;

(2) an application of an individual who has been a member of the Exchange or a participant in a member organization within three months of the date of the new application.

.24 Posting.—An application for approval of admission of a participant (other than a member of the Exchange) in an existing member organization, or for the approval of the formation and admission of a member organization, is ordinarily not acted upon by the Board of Governors until after notice of the application has been posted on the bulletin board of the Exchange and published in the Weekly Bulletin of the Exchange for a period of not less than two weeks. Such notice is posted upon submission in proper form of all required papers in connection with the application.

.26 Partnership agreements.—For information regarding the submission of copies of proposed partnership articles, see ¶ 2313.10.

.28 Corporate documents.—For information regarding the submission of copies of proposed or existing corporate documents and other agreements, see ¶ 2313.20.

[The next page is 3065.]

Partnerships—Corporations (Continued)

*(Rules and Policies Administered by the
Department of Member Firms.)*

¶ 2313   Submission of Partnership Articles—Submission
of Corporate Documents

Rule 313.   (a) All partnership articles and all amendments thereto shall be
submitted and be acceptable to the Exchange prior to becoming
effective.

(b) The charter or certificate of incorporation and all amendments thereto, the by-laws and all amendments thereto, forms of stock certificates and any
and all agreements or other documents and amendments thereto between a
member corporation and any of its stockholders or between any of the stockholders of a member corporation other than agreements relating to ordinary
securities and commodities transactions shall be submitted to and be acceptable to the Exchange prior to becoming effective.

● ● ● *Supplementary Material:*

Information Regarding Partnership Articles

.10   Submission of partnership agreements.—Drafts of partnership articles or
of changes in partnership articles proposed to be entered into in connection with the formation of a firm or the admission of a new partner should be
submitted to the Department of Member Firms at least one week in advance
of the date on which the application will be acted upon by the Board of Governors.   Drafts of other changes to be made in partnership articles should be
submitted in advance of their effective date.

The Exchange requires that a signed, photostatic or conformed copy of all
partnership articles, including any amendments and supplements thereto, as
executed, be filed with the Exchange.

(See ¶ *2312.10-2312.24 for procedure to be followed regarding approval of partners
and partnerships.)*

.12   Partner's equities; continuing interest of deceased partner.—For suggested provisions of partnership articles, see ¶ 2325.17, 2325.18.

.14   A-B-C agreements.—For suggested provisions of partnership articles, see
¶ 2301.34.

.16   Use and proceeds clause.—For required agreement to be included in
Partnership Articles, see ¶ 2314.20.

.18   Sole board member provision.—For information concerning sole board
member provisions, see Sections 13(a) and 13(b) of Article IX of the
Constitution [¶ 1413]. See, also, ¶ 2314.28.

Information Regarding Member Corporations

**.20   Submission by proposed member corporations of certificate of incorpora-
tion, by-laws and other corporate documents.**—Existing corporations
shall promptly submit certified copies (to the extent possible) of the foregoing
documents and corporations to be formed shall submit drafts thereof, prior to
the time they become effective, to the Department of Member Firms. Upon

the formation of a corporation or when an amendment to any of the foregoing documents becomes effective, a duly certified copy of the certificate of incorporation and by-laws shall be filed with the Department of Member Firms and signed, photostatic or conformed copies of the other documents shall be so filed.

(*See ¶ 2312.10-2312.24 for procedure to be followed regarding approval of corporations.*)

There shall also be submitted an opinion of counsel in form and substance satisfactory to the Exchange stating, among other things, that the corporation is duly organized and existing and that its stock is validly issued and outstanding and that the restrictions required by the Exchange on the transfer and issuance of its stock have been made legally effective.

(*See .22, below, for restrictions on corporations not incorporated under laws of the State of New York.*)

.21 **Provisions concerning disposition of stock.**—Each certificate of incorporation of a member corporation shall contain provisions that the corporation or its stockholders, or both, shall have a prior right to purchase, at a price at which it is proposed to be sold or at a stipulated or determinable price, the stock of any stockholder who:

    (1) Proposes to sell or dispose of any of his stock, or dies, or

    (2) has violated any agreement made by him with his member corporation or with the Exchange, or has been suspended or expelled from the Exchange.

Where the state of incorporation is unwilling to accept a certificate of incorporation, which contains a purchase option effective upon a stockholder's having violated any agreement made by him with the member corporation or with the Exchange, the Exchange will accept in lieu thereof a separate agreement signed by each stockholder in the member corporation.

Each stock certificate of a member corporation shall carry on its face a statement of such provisions or a full summary thereof.

.22 **Restrictions on corporations.**—Corporations not organized under the laws of the State of New York shall effectively subject themselves to the following restrictions and the opinion of counsel submitted to the Exchange at the time the corporation applies for approval as a member corporation shall set forth the extent to which the following restrictions have been made legally effective:

No dividend shall be declared or paid which shall impair the capital of the corporation nor shall any distribution of assets be made to any stockholder unless the value of the assets of the corporation remaining after such payment or distribution is at least equal to the aggregate of its debts and liabilities, including capital.

.23 **List of stockholders.**—In the case of existing corporations making application to become member corporations, a certified list of stockholders, giving the name, address and the number of shares of each class of stock held, shall be submitted to the Department of Member Firms, and in the case of corporations proposed to be organized similar information shall be given with

¶ 2313.21   **Rule 313**   © 1957, Commerce Clearing House, Inc.

respect to the persons who will be the stockholders when the corporation is organized.

(*See* ¶ 2312.10-2312.24 *for procedure to be followed regarding approval of stockholders.*)

.24 **Agreement with the Exchange.**—Every stockholder of a member corporation must agree with the Exchange that, so long as the corporation continues as a member corporation, he will not, without the prior written approval of the Exchange, transfer, sell, assign, pledge or otherwise create, or permit to be created, any lien, charge or encumbrance upon his stock in the corporation. Each stock certificate of a member corporation shall carry on its face a statement of such agreement or a full summary thereof.

The member corporation and all its stockholders must agree with the Exchange that if any of the voting stock in such corporation should at any time be acquired, held or owned by a person other than a member or allied member in good standing, or any of its non-voting stock should at any time be held by a person not approved by the Exchange, excepting in either case the estate of a deceased stockholder for such period as may be allowed by the Exchange, or if any stockholder should violate his said agreement, the corporation may be deprived by the Exchange of all the privileges of a member corporation.

¶ 2314   Fixed Interest in Business of Partner

Rule 314.   Every member and allied member in a member organization must have a fixed interest in its entire business.

● ● ● *Supplementary Material:*

.10 **Profits of partnership.**—If a limited partner is to receive a share in the profits of the partnership, it must be a percentage of the profits of the *entire* partnership.

.11 **Interest of members and allied members.**—

(1) Percentage interests of general partners must be fixed in advance.

(2) A partner's drawings against his interest in profits may be at the discretion of the firm.

(3) As between the partners or stockholders, any member or allied member, other than a sole Exchange member whose membership is not subject to an a-b-c agreement, may be guaranteed against loss by his other partners or stockholders.

(*See* ¶ 2301.34 *for information concerning a-b-c agreements.*)

(4) Salaries of members and allied members must be fixed in advance and shall not bear an unreasonable relationship to their respective interests in profits and losses or voting stock interests.

(5) Members and allied members shall have at least a 40% interest in that part of the Net Worth of the organization which is required by Rule 325—Capital Requirements.

"That part of Net Worth . . . required by Rule 325" shall be the total of the amounts required by the debit items of Rule 325 plus the greater of 1/20th of aggregate indebtedness or the basic dollar minimum fixed by the Exchange.

For the purposes of this provision the interest of members and allied members shall include:

[The next page is 3067-3.]

(A) In respect of a member partnership—the capital accounts of general partners, plus their shares of undistributed profits and less their share of undistributed losses, plus equities in their accounts covered by approved equities agreements and plus the market or fair value of any Exchange memberships owned by them and not recorded on the books, the proceeds of which are available for firm creditors.

(B) In respect of a member corporation—the book value (fair value of net assets applicable to each class of stock) of all capital stock held by holders of voting stock, all debentures held by them, all subordinated borrowings by the member corporation from them, and plus the market or fair value of any Exchange memberships owned by them and not recorded on the books but which are assets of the corporation.

The Exchange will expect that each member organization will meet this requirement when the organization is formed or admitted to membership and whenever the organization makes changes in its partnership agreement or corporate financial structure affecting the relationship of "general" to total capital, or in its subordinated borrowings.

(6) Additional compensation may be paid to holders of voting stock through the medium of a profit-sharing plan acceptable to the Exchange, provided that the terms of the plan are fixed in advance and are not changed more frequently than once every three months.

(7)(A) Each member or allied member in a member organization, other than a sole Exchange member whose membership is not subject to an a-b-c agreement, must receive or own either

(i) a percentage of the profits or of the voting stock and profits of the organization which is not less than the minimum set forth in the following schedule:

If the working capital of the member organization, exclusive of memberships and other fixed assets, is	Minimum percentage is
Under $ 10,000*	15%
$ 10,000 to 50,000*	10%
50,000 to 100,000	7½%
100,000 to 500,000	5%
500,000 to 1,000,000	3%
1,000,000 to 2,000,000	2%
2,000,000 to 5,000,000	1%
5,000,000 to 10,000,000	1/2 %
10,000,000 to 20,000,000	1/4 %
20,000,000 or more	1/8 %
30,000,000 to 50,000,000	1/16%†
50,000,000 to 75,000,000	1/32%†
75,000,000 or more	1/64%†

† Provided that stock equity, at the time of purchase (in the case of a member corporation) or capital contribution (in the case of a partnership) equals at least $25,000.

(* See Rule 325 [¶ 2325] for minimum capital requirements for member organizations.)
or;

¶ 2314.11   Continued

(ii) Where such general partner or voting stockholder is guaranteed $8,000 or more a year, by salary and/or participation, a lesser percentage than the minimum called for above—but not less than 1%, in respect of organizations with working capital of less than $2,000,000, and not less than ½ of the minimum called for above in respect of organizations with working capital of $2,000,000 or more; provided that an Exchange member who is a general partner or voting stockholder must be guaranteed $12,000 or more a year, by salary and/or participation, unless he has and maintains a minimum interest at least double that required in the foregoing schedule in (i) above; and provided,

(iii) That, notwithstanding the provisions of (i) or (ii) herein being applicable to such general partner, he may be charged with his proportion of net losses of the firm.

(B) The sole Exchange member of a member organization whose membership is not subject to an a-b-c agreement, must have and maintain a minimum interest in the profits and losses of the partnership or in voting stock and in profits of the corporation, regardless of the amount of his salary, at least double that required in the foregoing schedule in (i) above in respect of organizations with working capital of less than $30,000,000 and not less than ¼% in respect of organizations with working capital of $30,000,000 or more.

Non-conforming arrangements.—Non-conforming minimum interests of sole Exchange members which were approved prior to June 21, 1956, may remain in effect without change until terminated by the dissolution of the organization, the sale or transfer of the membership, or the death of the Exchange member, except that if one of the participants in profits or losses or holders of participating securities dies or retires, the interest of such deceased or retiring partner or stockholder must be allocated to the other partners or stockholders in a manner which will produce a greater degree of conformity.

For the purpose of these requirements, a merger or split-up of a firm in which the member and allied members become partners in a new firm, the extension of partnership articles, the entering into of substantially identical new partnership articles, the admittance of a new partner or the death or retirement of a partner, are not regarded per se as constituting the dissolution of a partnership.

If a member corporation has issued securities, other than voting stock, which participate in profits, each holder of voting stock shall have and maintain both in voting stock and in the total combination of all participating securities (including voting stock) an interest which is not less than the minimum specified in (A) or (B) above whichever is applicable.

(8) Member organizations may provide by agreement for a so-called "float" of net profits, not exceeding 15%, which "float" may remain unallocated until the close of an organization's calendar or fiscal year, at which time distribution thereof may be made to some or all of the general partners or to some or all of the holders of voting stock of the member organization in such manner as may be determined at the discretion of the partners or prescribed by the Board of Directors.

¶ **2314.11**   **Rule 314**   © 1961, Commerce Clearing House, Inc.

(9) In respect of partnerships, solely for the purpose of determining the rights of the partners, among themselves, partners' participations in the profits and losses in any firm investment account may be fixed in proportions which differ from their participation in other profits and losses of the firm, provided that each general partner has a fixed participation in such firm investment accounts and in the other income of the firm.

Member firms should consult their own counsel if the profit and loss interest in the firm investment account is to be different than that in the other income of the firm since substantial rights of the individual partners may be affected.

.12 Interest of limited partners and holders of non-voting stock (not members or allied members).—

(1) Interest on limited capital and preferential dividends on non-voting stock shall not exceed 8% per annum on the amount of the capital contribution or on the par value of the stock. The same 8% maximum limitation is equally applicable in respect of subordinated lenders of cash including debenture holders of a member corporation.

(*For information concerning subordinated lenders see ¶ 2325.20.*)

(2) In addition to interest on his capital contribution, a limited partner may receive a reasonable participation in the profits of the firm provided his percentage interest is fixed in advance and is not changed more frequently than once in every three months. A limited partner's participation in the profits of his firm should bear some reasonable relationship to his contribution to capital. In the case of a member corporation non-voting stock may be entitled, in addition to such maximum preferential dividends, to participate in additional dividends payable out of earnings or earned surplus simultaneously with or after the payment of dividends on the voting stock of such amounts and upon such terms as may be fixed in the Certificate of Incorporation and approved by the Exchange.

(3) Persons other than members, allied members, or those described in (a) and (b) below shall not be entitled to participate to an amount in excess of 45% of the direct or indirect profits of the member organization:

(a) Members or allied members who, at retirement age, have retired from the member organization and from business life.

(b) Widows of deceased or retired members or allied members

provided, however, that in any event the percentage of interest held by members and allied members shall not be lower than 45%.

(4) The capital interest of persons, other than members or allied members, shall be subject to the limitation set forth in ¶ 2314.11(5).

(5) Any limited partner may be guaranteed against loss by his other partners.

(6) In addition to his interest on his capital contribution, and in lieu of a participation in profits of the partnership, a limited partner may receive a reasonable dollar annual return, provided it is fixed annually in advance.

(7) A limited partner may share in losses of the partnership.

¶ **2314** Continued

.13 **Employee participation in partnership profits.**—With the prior permission of the Exchange a member firm may allocate participations in firm profits to selected employees of not more than 5% to any individual employee.

.14 **Interest of non-citizen participants.**—The combined capital interests and interests in profits of all participants of a member organization who are not United States citizens shall not exceed 45%.

.15 **Trusts.**—The following conditions are applicable to trusts which are proposed as limited partners or holders of non-voting stock of member organizations:

(1) The settlor or Testator of the trust must be or have been a stockholder or partner of the member organization or it's predecessor;

(2) Beneficiary (or Beneficiaries) of the trust must be either (a) related by blood or by marriage to the settlor or Testator or (b) an acceptable charity;

(3) Each trustee must be acceptable to the Exchange as a person of good character and reputation;

(4) A beneficiary or a trustee should not be engaged in the securities business, except in the firm with which the trust is associated; and

(5) The Exchange will impose no time limitation on trusts as limited partners or non-voting stockholders.

Information Common to Partnerships and Corporations

.20 **Required agreement by member.**—Each member who is a general partner or a holder of voting stock in a member organization shall specifically agree in the firm's partnership articles or in the case of a member corporation, in a document filed with the Exchange, that he contributes the use of his membership to the organization and that, insofar as may be necessary for the protection of creditors of the organization, and subject to the Constitution and Rules of the Exchange, the proceeds of the transfer of his membership shall be an asset of the member organization.

.22 **Gratuity payments to members.**—Only the persons specified in Article XVI of the Constitution [¶ 1751-1758] may share in Gratuity benefit payments. Therefore, there may be no oral understanding nor may provisions be embodied in partnership articles, in an agreement, a Will or in any other document which may have the effect of directly or indirectly defeating the purpose of said Article.

.24 **Floor commissions.**—All Floor commissions of an Exchange member who is a general partner or a holder of voting stock in a member organization must be for the account of the firm. Floor commissions earned by a limited partner or a holder of non-voting stock who is a member of the Exchange must be retained by him unless such a holder of non-voting stock is also a holder of voting stock, in which event commissions must be for the account of the member corporation.

.26 **Specialist trading.**—When an Exchange member general partner or holder of voting stock in a member organization is a specialist, his ordinary trading business as a specialist must be for the organization's account, or for a joint account in which his organization is permitted to participate under the provisions of Rule 94(b) [¶ 2094].

¶ **2314.13   Rule 314**

.28 Death of sole Exchange member partner or director.—For suggested provisions for inclusion in partnership articles or in the agreement with the Exchange to enable a member organization to apply, in accordance with Sections 13(a) and 13(b) of Article IX of the Constitution [¶ 1413], for permission to continue as a member organization following the death of its sole Exchange member partner or director, organizations should consult with the Department of Member Firms.

In each case involving the death of a sole Exchange member partner or director who, at the time of his death, (1) was in the active military or naval service of the United States, or (2) in time of war in which the United States is a belligerent, was in the active military or naval service of any nation or State which is a belligerent against one or more enemies of the United States, or (3) was occupied in any public service incident to the national defense, the Exchange will, after considering all the circumstances surrounding the particular case, prescribe a definite period during which the organization may have the status of a member organization.

In those cases involving the death of a sole Exchange member partner or director who, at the time of his death, was not engaged in war service as defined in (1), (2) and (3) above, the maximum period the Exchange will prescribe during which the organization may have the status of a member organization will not exceed sixty days from the date of the death of the sole Exchange member partner or director.

¶ 2315   Assignment, Transfer, etc., of Interest of Partner or Stock of Stockholder

Rule 315.   No partner or holder of stock of a member organization shall assign or in any way encumber his interest therein or transfer, sell, assign or in any way encumber or pledge his stock thereof, without the prior written approval of the Exchange.

(See ¶ 2313.24 for information re: agreement not to assign, transfer, etc. stock of a member corporation.)

● ● ● *Supplementary Material:*

.10   Consideration for the issuance of stock.—No stock shall be issued except for cash or such other consideration as may be approved by the Exchange.

.11   Classes of stock.—A member corporation may have such classes of stock with such preferences and restrictions as to voting and rights as to assets and dividends as it may see fit, subject to the limitation set forth at ¶ 2314.12, paragraph (1). But a non-voting stock shall be unqualifiedly a non-voting stock unless otherwise prescribed by the law of the State of Incorporation.

(See Rule 312 [¶ 2312] for notice requirements of proposed issuance, redemption etc. of stock of member corporation. Rule 320(d)(1) and (2) [¶ 2320] for restriction on issuance, transfer etc. of stock.)

.13   Par value of stock.—The voting and non-voting shares of stock of a member corporation shall have a stated par value.

.14   Capital stock and interest of members and allied members.—Not less than 25% of the total capital of a member corporation shall be in the form of capital stock.

¶ 2316   Minimum of Active Partners in Firms—Use of a Firm Name

Rule 316.   Except as may be otherwise permitted by the Exchange, no member or allied member shall conduct business under a firm name unless he has at least one partner nor shall any member firm doing business with the public have less than two general partners who are active in the firm's business; provided, however, that if by death or otherwise a member or allied member becomes the sole general partner in a firm, he may continue business under the firm name for such period as may be allowed by the Exchange.

(*See Rule 404 [¶ 2404] re carrying of accounts by individual members.*)

¶ 2317   Participant in One Member Organization

Rule 317.   No person shall at the same time be a participant in more than one member organization.

• • • Supplementary Material:

.10   The word "participant" includes general and limited partners of a member firm and holders of voting and non-voting stock of a member corporation. See Rule 2 [¶ 2002].

¶ 2318   Other Connections of Members and Allied Members

Rule 318.   Every member organization shall engage primarily in the transaction of business as broker or dealer in securities or commodities. With the prior approval of the Exchange, member organizations may engage in kindred activities.

Unless otherwise permitted by the Exchange every individual member must be actively engaged in the securities business and devote the major portion of his time thereto, and every member and allied member in a member organization must be actively engaged in the business of his organization and devote the major portion of his time thereto.

Without prior approval of the Exchange, no individual member and no member or allied member in a member organization shall become:

    (1) A partner in any non-member business organization;

    (2) an officer or employee of any non-member business corporation, firm or association;

    (3) an employee of any firm or individual engaged in business; or

    (4) associated with any outside securities, financial or kindred business.

Amendments.
December 19, 1955, effective January 4, 1956.
December 19, 1956, effective January 2, 1957.
April 21, 1960, effective May 2, 1960.

• • • Supplementary Material:

.10   The Board of Governors has determined upon the following permissible exceptions:

    (1) Director of corporation not in the securities business;

    (2) chairman of a board of directors of a corporation not in the securities business;

    (3) officer of personal holding company not publicly owned;

    (4) officer of operating company not in the securities business, if duties are nominal and not operational;

    (5) officer of an investment trust, open end or closed, if it is not self-managed and self-distributing;

(6) officer, for a reasonable period, of an operating company whose securities the firm underwrote, distributed or sponsored; and

(7) affiliations of members and allied members existing on December 31, 1956.

In respect of item (4) of Rule 318, above, the Board has determined that a financial interest in a securities or financial or kindred business, whether through stock ownership, or bonds, or loans of any nature, would constitute an "association", unless the ownership was nominal—not exceeding 5%—and the other securities or financial or kindred business were publicly owned.

The Board has determined that an individual member is "actively engaged in the securities business", as the phrase is used in Rule 318, when he is active as a Floor trader, specialist, so-called two dollar broker, or associated odd lot broker, or engaged in business with the public by servicing customers' accounts and introducing them to another member organization.

.11 Writing, Broadcasting and Speaking.—Policies pertaining to writing, broadcasting and speaking activities by members, allied members and other personnel of member organizations, are detailed in Supplementary Material to Rule 346 (¶ 2346) and under Rules 471, 472 and 473 (¶¶ 2471, 2472, 2473, 2474) and Supplementary Material.

Outside writing, broadcasting and speaking activities referred to in Rule 346 means activities other than those engaged in by a member, allied member or member organization in the conduct of his or its securities business.

¶ 2319   Fidelity Bonds

Rule 319. Each member firm doing business with the public and each member corporation shall carry fidelity bonds covering its general partners and employees or covering its officers and employees in such form and in such amounts as the Exchange may require.

Amendments.
December 19, 1955, effective January 4, 1956.
November 17, 1960, effective January 16, 1961.

● ● ● Supplementary Material:

Partner Coverage

.10 Each member partnership required to maintain minimum net capital under Rule 325 must have a fidelity bond (Stockbrokers Partnership Bond) covering general partners. The form of bond developed by the insurance industry in cooperation with the Exchange is the only form which has been approved by the Exchange. Specific Exchange approval is required for any variation from the form.

The required minimum coverage of the fidelity bond will vary with the type of business done by the member organization and with its minimum net capital requirement. These minimum coverages are set forth below:

Type of Business	Minimum Coverage
1. Firms which introduce business to another member organization on a disclosed basis but do not carry accounts....	$100,000
2. Firms which carry accounts for or do a principal business with non-members.	

Net Capital Requirement* Under Rule 325		Minimum Coverage
$ 50,000—	....	$ 200,000
50,000—$	100,000.............	300,000
100,000—	200,000.............	500,000
200,000—	300,000.............	600,000
300,000—	500,000.............	700,000
500,000—	1,000,000...........	800,000
1,000,000—	2,000,000...........	1,000,000
2,000,000—	3,000,000...........	1,500,000
3,000,000—	4,000,000...........	2,000,000
4,000,000—	6,000,000...........	3,000,000
6,000,000—	12,000,000...........	4,000,000
12,000,000—	25,000,000...........	5,000,000

*The highest net capital requirement during the preceding twelve months will govern.

Blanket Bond Coverage

11. A. *Basic Coverage.* Members and member organizations subject to minimum net capital under Rule 325 are required to have Brokers Blanket Bond coverage in amounts not less than the minimums prescribed above which apply both to partner coverage and blanket bond coverage.

B. *Specific Coverages.* In addition to this basic Brokers Blanket Bond coverage, members and member organizations are required to include the following minimum specific coverages with respect to: MISPLACEMENT, FRAUDULENT TRADING†, CHECK FORGERY and SECURITIES FORGERY.

    1. Individual members subject to net capital requirements who introduce accounts on a disclosed basis:

        Coverage: At least $100,000 with respect to each of the above categories.

    2. Member organizations which introduce accounts on a disclosed basis:

        Coverage: At least $100,000 with respect to each of the above categories.

    3. Member organizations which either (a) carry accounts for non-members or (b) do a principal business with non-members:

        Coverage: With respect to MISPLACEMENT and CHECK FORGERY—at least the amount of the basic bond minimum requirement.

                With respect to FRAUDULENT TRADING—at least $100,000 or 50% of the basic bond minimum requirement, whichever is greater, up to $500,000.

                With respect to SECURITIES FORGERY—at least $100,000 or 25% of the basic bond minimum requirement, whichever is greater, up to $250,000.

---

† Fraudulent trading coverage not required of individual members or partnerships having no employees.

General

.12 Each member organization will be expected to review carefully any need for coverage greater than that provided by the required minimums. Where experience or the nature of the business warrants additional coverage the Exchange expects the member organization to acquire it.

Each member and member organization required to carry the above forms of insurance shall advise the Exchange if such insurance is entirely or partially cancelled. Full details should be given in writing.

¶ 2320   Miscellaneous Restrictions on Corporate Members

Officers

Rule 320.   (a) No person shall be elected a director or appointed an officer of a member corporation without the prior written approval of the Exchange.

Ownership of stock

(b) Every director, principal officer and holder of voting stock will be required to own voting or non-voting stock, or both, in an amount approved by the Exchange.

Number of stockholders

(c) The Exchange may limit the number of stockholders of any or all classes.

Corporate changes to be approved by Exchange

(d) A member corporation shall not without the prior written approval of the Exchange:

(1) Reduce its capital or purchase or redeem any class of its stock or in any way amend its charter, certificate of incorporation or by-laws, and the Exchange may at any time in its discretion require the corporation to restore or increase capital or surplus, or both.

(2) Issue or transfer any shares of any class of its stock.

(3) Issue any bonds, notes or other instruments evidencing funded indebtedness of the corporation.

(4) Amend, modify or cancel any agreement made by it or any of its stockholders relating to the management of the corporation or the issue or transfer of securities of the corporation (other than agreements relating to ordinary securities and commodities transactions).

(See Rule 312 [¶ 2312].)

¶ 2321 Formation of Corporate Affiliates

Rule 321. A member firm comprised of two or more general partners or a member corporation may, with the prior written approval of the Exchange, form an affiliated company.

• • • Supplementary Material:

Information Regarding Affiliated Companies of Member Organizations

.10 Authority to form.—A member organization will be required to show adequate reason for desiring an affiliate.

.11 Form of organization.—An affiliate shall be an incorporated company, the liability of whose stockholders is limited.

.12 Name.—The name of the corporate affiliate and the name of the member organization must be sufficiently different to prevent confusion. The mere addition of "Inc." may not be sufficient.

.13 Capitalization.—Not less than 25% of the total capital of the corporate affiliate shall be in the form of capital stock. The members and allied members in the member organization or the member organization itself shall at all times own beneficially at least 40% of the total capitalization of the corporate affiliate. Such ownership shall comprise all the voting stock (except as otherwise approved by the Exchange) and may include non-voting stocks, debentures and subordinated borrowings.

Holders of non-voting stock, debentures and/or notes, who are not members or allied members of the Exchange, may not receive in the aggregate in excess of 45% of the direct or indirect profits of the corporate affiliate.

.14 Classes of stock.—A corporate affiliate shall have but one class of voting stock, but may have one or more classes of capital stock.

Except where otherwise specifically required by law, sole voting control must under all circumstances be vested in the holders of the voting stock. No stock of any class or kind shall be issued without approval of the Exchange.

.15 Participating securities—Fixed interest of members and allied members.
—Since Rule 314 provides that each member and allied member in a member organization must have a fixed interest in its entire business, it follows that the fixed interest of each member and allied member must extend to the member organization's corporate affiliate. When any of the corporate affiliate's participating stock is owned by the members and allied members in the member organization, such holdings must at all times be distributed among such members and allied members in approximately the same proportions as their respective interests in the profits of the member organization. When a member or allied member's interest in the member organization is changed, a corresponding change must be made in his participating interest in the affiliate.

11-64
Report 95

Rules of Board—Partnerships—Corporations
➥ Administered by Department of Member Firms.

3075

.16 Holding by estate of decedent.—If a deceased general partner's capital in the member firm continues for a stated period of time at the risk of the continuing or successor partnership under the provisions of the partnership agreement in effect at the time of his death, his holdings of participating securities of the corporate affiliate may be permitted to be held by his estate for the same period of time, provided that voting rights of any such securities, while held by the estate, shall be covered by a voting trust agreement under which a general partner of the member firm shall be the voting trustee. In the event the estate of the deceased general partner becomes a limited partner in the member firm, the voting stock included within such securities must either be sold to the affiliate company, the member firm or the surviving general partners or be converted into a non-voting security, subject to the approval of the Exchange.

In the event of the death of a holder of voting stock in a member corporation who is also a holder of any securities issued by a corporate affiliate, such securities held by such decedent in the affiliate may, unless the Exchange shall otherwise determine, be held by his estate for the same reasonable period of time as his holdings of member corporation voting stock.

.17 Non-voting stockholders.—Each holder of non-voting stock of the corporate affiliate must be approved by the Exchange. The definitions of "holder" of stock—voting and non-voting—of a member corporation, as set forth in Article I of the Constitution, also apply to "holder" of corporate affiliate voting and non-voting stock.

If, under the laws governing incorporation, non-voting securities are given rights to vote under certain circumstances, the opinion of counsel required under .35 below, shall state the circumstances under which the holders of non-voting securities are entitled to vote. The Exchange may, in specific instances, permit the issuance of a non-voting security where the statutory voting rights of the non-voting security are limited.

The Exchange will reserve the right to approve or disapprove the ratio of capital between voting and non-voting securities and to limit the number of security holders, any such limitation to depend upon the circumstances involved in each case.

.18 Employees.—With the prior permission of the Exchange, employees may be permitted to own participating securities providing such holdings do not exceed 5% of all participating securities in the case of one employee.

.19 Submission of corporate documents.—The charter or certificate of incorporation of the corporate affiliate and all amendments thereto, its by-laws and all amendments thereto, forms of stock certificates and other securities issued or to be issued by the corporate affiliate and any and all agreements or other documents and amendments thereto between a member organization, its partners or stockholders and the proposed corporate affiliate, its stockholders or employees shall be submitted and be acceptable to the Exchange prior to becoming effective.

.20 Agreement of security holders.—Each holder of securities issued by a corporate affiliate must agree in writing with the corporation that whenever such holder (1) proposes to sell or dispose of any such securities, (2) retires from the member organization, (3) dies, (4) is declared incompetent or (5) terminates his employment with the member organization and the affiliate, the member organization, the members and allied members therein, the corporate affiliate or its stockholders, or all of them, shall have the prior right to purchase such holder's securities at the price at which they are proposed to be sold or at a price to be determined by a prescribed formula and, further, that so long as the corporation continues as a corporate affiliate such holder will not, without the prior approval of the Exchange, transfer, sell, assign, pledge or otherwise create, or permit to be created, any lien, charge or encumbrance upon his securities in the corporation.

The corporate affiliate and/or the holders of its securities must further agree with the Exchange that, if any of the corporate affiliate's voting stock which is not held by its parent member organization should at any time be acquired, held or owned by a person other than a member or allied member in good standing, or any of its other securities should at any time be held by a person not approved by the Exchange, or if any security holder should violate the agreement entered into by him pursuant to the foregoing paragraph, the member organization may be required by the Exchange to sever any and all connections with the corporate affiliate.

.21 Severance of connection with affiliate.—The Exchange may at any time require that the member organization and the partners or stockholders thereof sever all connections with the corporate affiliate and dispose of all stock and other interests therein; and each member organization and the partners or stockholders thereof shall enter into an agreement with the Exchange so providing. At any time after directing such severance, the Exchange may require the member organization to change its name if the Exchange finds that the name of the former corporate affiliate may be confused with the name of such member organization.

.22 List of stockholders.—A list of stockholders of the corporate affiliate and the number of shares of each class of stock held shall be submitted to the Department of Member Firms.

.23 Directors, officers and employees.—A person shall not be elected a director or appointed an officer without the prior specific approval of the Exchange and shall retain such position only so long as he shall continue to be approved by the Exchange. The directors and the President and Executive Vice President of a corporate affiliate should be members or allied members in the member organization in good standing and each other officer who is not a member or allied member shall file an RE-1 Form with the Exchange. No employee whose duties with the corporate affiliate correspond to those of a registered representative shall be employed by such affiliate unless such person has been and is continued to be approved by the Exchange as a registered representative. With the approval of the Exchange, an employee may function with both the member organization and the affiliate.

.24 Changes in capital structure or stock ownership.—No change shall be made in the capital structure of a corporate affiliate or in the ownership of its stock without the prior approval of the Exchange.

.25 Capital requirements.—The Exchange will not prescribe capital requirements for a corporate affiliate. However, the Exchange will require a pro forma balance sheet of the affiliate to be filed with it before any action is taken on a member organization's application to form such an affiliate. The Exchange may, however, require the submission of subsequent balance sheets.

.26 **Reports.**—Unless otherwise specifically requested by the Exchange, a corporate affiliate will not be required to file with the Exchange weekly reports on commitments.

.27 **Endorsement or guarantee.**—No member organization or member or allied member thereof shall endorse or guarantee any obligations of the organization's corporate affiliate or voluntarily assume directly or indirectly any of the liabilities of any such affiliate.

No affiliate shall become liable jointly, or jointly and severally, with any member organization with which it is affiliated or any member or allied member in any such organization.

.28 **Banking commitments.**—A corporate affiliate's banking and other commitments, loans and obligations shall be kept separate and distinct from those of the organization with which it is affiliated, and neither the organization nor any of its partners or stockholders shall assume any liability for the obligations of the corporate affiliate.

.29 **Customers' positions.**—A corporate affiliate shall not hold or carry (except in connection with items pending consummation) any accounts, securities, commodities, moneys, balances, equities, or commitments for customers, other than joint accounts in which the affiliate is interested with brokers, dealers or financial institutions. A corporate affiliate will not be permitted to act as broker.

.30 **Functions of an affiliate.**—A corporate affiliate may be formed to do an underwriting or dealer business. It may also be formed to do an investment advisory business or any other business acceptable to the Exchange, so long as such business does not include dealings on an agency basis. If an affiliate is formed to do an underwriting business, the Exchange will prefer that the member organization cease all underwriting activities. The Exchange might make exceptions to this policy depending upon the circumstances involved. However, if an affiliate is formed to do a dealer business, the Exchange will not object to the member organization also doing a similar type of business. The Exchange will not object to an affiliate being formed for speculative purposes.

.31 **Offices.**—A corporate affiliate will be permitted, under the conditions set forth in Rule 343 [¶ 2343] and ¶ 2343.10, 2343.11 to occupy the same quarters as those of the member organization. Every office of an affiliate must be approved by the Exchange. (*See* ¶ 2342.10 *re annual fee.*)

.32 **Books and records.**—A corporate affiliate shall keep books and records separate and distinct from those of the member organization with which it is affiliated and such books and records shall, upon request, be made available to inspection by the Exchange. However, such books and records may be maintained by the member organization.

.33 **Advertising.**—The advertising of a corporate affiliate shall be subject to the same supervision as that of member organizations. (*See Rules* 471, 472 [¶ 2471, 2472].)

.34 **Transactions between member organizations and corporate affiliates.**—A corporate affiliate will not be prohibited by the Exchange from having cash or margin brokerage transactions effected for its account by the member organization. Non-member commissions must be charged on all such transactions. If a member organization carries the account of its own affiliate, the amount of the debit balance in the affiliate's account is to be charged to the member organization's working capital and no value is to be given to the securities in such account in computing the member organization's working capital.

.35 Conditions to be complied with after organization of corporate affiliate but prior to commencement of business.—No corporate affiliate shall commence business after its organization without the prior written approval of the Exchange. Before giving such approval there shall be submitted to the Exchange an opinion of counsel, in form and substance satisfactory to the Exchange, stating (1) that the affiliate is duly organized and existing, (2) that the stock of the affiliate has been duly and validly issued and is fully paid and non-assessable, (3) the extent to which the restrictions hereinabove set forth with respect to voting control, ownership of participating securities, change in capital structure and transfer and pledge of stock have been made legally effective, and (4) the extent to which the stockholders may be individually liable for the obligations of the corporation.

.36 New issues.—The provisions of Section 11(d)(1) of the Securities and Exchange Act of 1934, relating to the extension or maintenance of credit in connection with new issues, will apply to transactions by a member organization in new issues in the distribution of which its affiliate participated with the same force and to the same extent as if the member organization itself had participated in the distribution of such new issues.

.37 Disclosure.—In connection with any transactions which the member organization may have had with its customers, or any recommendation which the member organization may make to its customers involving securities underwritten, distributed or sold by its affiliate, full disclosure shall be made by the member organization to its customers of the interest of the affiliate in such securities at that time.

.38 Off-board transactions.—Except in respect of the so-called Exempt List of Guaranteed and Preferred Stocks, listed in ¶ 2394.10, an affiliate must obtain Exchange permission before effecting a transaction in a listed stock off the Floor of the Exchange. An affiliate may participate in a secondary distribution of a listed stock only if the Exchange has approved participation therein by members and member organizations. (*See Rule* 393 [¶ 2393] *and* 2393.10-2393.11 *for information re secondary distribution.*)

NEW YORK STOCK EXCHANGE
OPERATION OF MEMBER ORGANIZATIONS

. . . rules of Board of Governors regulating the operations of member organizations and individual members . . .

TABLE OF CONTENTS

Contents   © 1965, Commerce Clearing House, Inc.

Operation of Member Organizations

Capital Requirements

*(Rules and Policies Administered by the
Department of Member Firms.)*

¶ 2325   Capital Requirements for Member Organizations
and Individual Members

General provisions

Rule 325. (a) No member or member organization doing any business with others than members or member organizations or doing a general business with the public, except a member or member organization subject to supervision by State or Federal banking authorities, shall permit, in the ordinary course of business as a broker, his or its Aggregate Indebtedness to exceed 2000 per centum of his or its Net Capital, which Net Capital shall be not less than $50,000 in the case of a member organization carrying any accounts for customers and shall be not less than $25,000 in the case of any other member or member organization subject to this rule, unless a specific temporary exception is made by the Exchange in the case of a particular member or member organization due to unusual circumstances.

The initial Net Capital of a member corporation shall be at least 120% of the Net Capital required to be maintained by this rule.

The Exchange may at any time or from time to time in the case of a particular member or member organization prescribe greater requirements than those prescribed herein.

Each member or member organization shall promptly notify the Exchange if his or its Net Capital does not equal or exceed the minimum required by this rule.

Definitions

(b) For the purpose of this rule—

(1) The term "proprietary accounts" shall include capital accounts of partners or sole proprietor, investment and trading accounts, participations in joint accounts, accounts of partners which are covered by agreements, approved by the Exchange, providing for the inclusion of equities therein as partnership property and borrowings covered by subordination agreements approved by the Exchange;

(2) the term "aggregate indebtedness" shall include the total money liabilities of the member or member organization in all accounts other than customers' and brokers' accounts for commodity future contracts; plus equities in customers' and brokers' accounts for commodity future contracts; plus the market value of securities borrowed (other than for delivery against customers' sales) for which no equivalent value is paid or credited, exclusive of the following:

(A) money borrowed (adequately collateralized) on securities, spot commodities or other assets owned by the member, member firm

¶ 2325   Continued

or general partner thereof, or a member corporation and on those subordinated to general creditors;

(B) money payable against securities loaned which are owned by the member, member firm or general partner thereof, or a member corporation and those subordinated to general creditors;

(C) money payable against securities failed to receive in connection with transactions for the account of the member, member firm or general partner thereof, or a member corporation and for accounts subordinated to general creditors;

(D) money borrowings adequately collateralized by securities exempted from registration under the Securities and Exchange Act of 1934, otherwise than by action of the Securities and Exchange Commission;

(E) liabilities subordinated to general creditors pursuant to a separate agreement approved by the Exchange;

(F) equities in customers' commodity accounts segregated under the Commodity Exchange Act;

(G) equities in general partners' commodity accounts and credit balances in other accounts of general partners; and

(H) liabilities on open contractual commitments.

(3) The term "net worth" shall be the excess of total assets over total liabilities, after provision for current dividends declared and unpaid by a member corporation (except that credit balances and equities in "proprietary accounts" shall not be considered as liabilities) with securities, spot commodities, commodity future contracts in "proprietary accounts" and all other assets marked to market or fair value. A loss, at market, in an individual contractual commitment shall be deducted in determining Net Worth and a profit shall not be included. (See (c)(10) "Special Provisions" below.)

(4) the term "net capital" shall be Net Worth, less the following:

Debit Items

(A) Amounts included in Net Worth for:

(i) Memberships, furniture and fixtures, real estate and other fixed assets;

(ii) the value of securities which have no ready market;

(iii) unsecured loans and advances to partners and deficits in partners' accounts including those unsecured (see (c)(10) below);

(iv) deficits in customers' accounts including unsecured accounts and notes receivable (see (c)(9), (10) and (11) below); and

(v) prepaid rent, insurance and expenses and unsecured advances to employees and salesmen.

(vi) Debit balance in each customer's spot (cash) commodity account other than the result of a tender made on a futures contract within the past 90 days and evidenced by warehouse receipt(s) issued by a warehouse licensed by a commodity exchange. (See (c)(11) below.)

¶ 2325   Rule 325   © 1964, Commerce Clearing House, Inc.

Long Positions

(B) 30% of the market value of securities and spot commodities long in "proprietary accounts" and in customers' accounts in deficit (10% of the market value of spot commodities if they are hedged). (See (c) Special Provisions below.)

Excess Short Positions

(C) The amount determined on the excess of the market value of short positions in securities over the market value of long positions in "proprietary accounts." The excess of the market value of short positions shall be determined separately for each percentage group set forth in this rule and in (c) "Special Provisions" thereof, except that bonds and stocks shall be considered separately. The amount of this debit item shall be 30% of the excess market value of short positions or the lesser percentage indicated in (c)(1) through (8) below. (See (c)(10) below.)

Commodity Futures—Proprietary Accounts

(D) 30% of the market value of all long and all short future commodity contracts (other than those contracts representing spreads and straddles in the same commodity and those contracts offsetting or hedging any spot commodity positions) in "proprietary accounts."

Credit Lines

(E) Total of credit lines granted on open commodity contracts in "trade" accounts with net long positions or in "trade" accounts with net short positions, whichever is greater, plus any credit lines granted on open commodity contracts in "trade" accounts with no net long or net short position. (In computing the credit line granted in the case of each account, deduct the amount of the equity or the amount of the deficit therein, provided such amount is not in excess of the credit line granted, and the deficit, if any, is comprehended in other "Debit Items.") (See (c)(9) below.)

Commodity Futures—Customers' Accounts

(F)(i) Total amount by which the daily limit fluctuation of all future commodity contracts carried for a customer's account or accounts controlled by a customer exceeds 10% of the net worth of the member organization. Contracts in each customer's account representing purchases and sales of a like amount of the same commodity in the same market and in the same crop year may be eliminated. The daily limit fluctuations for future contracts effected in foreign markets is to be considered the same as if such contracts had been effected in a domestic market. (See (c)(11) below.)

(ii) 1½% of the market values of the greater of either the total long or total short future contracts in each commodity carried for all customers. Contracts in each customer's account representing purchases and sales of a like amount of the same commodity in the same market and in the same crop year may be eliminated. (See (c)(11) below.)

¶ 2325   Continued

Cash Margin Deficiency

(G) Cash required to provide proper margin in customers' un-dermargined accounts in accordance with Rule 431 [¶ 2431]. (See (c)(9) and (11) below.)

(H) Cash required to provide margin equal to:

(i) the amount required to restore the original margin required by the pertinent commodity exchange or the clearing house requirement, per contract, whichever is greater, when the original margin has been depleted by 50% on all future commodity contracts in each customer's account. Cash required should be exclusive of liquidating deficits. (See (c)(9) and (11) below.)

(ii) 20% of the market value in each customer's account in equity containing spot commodity positions, evidenced by a warehouse receipt, issued by a warehouse licensed by a commodity exchange, which are the result of future contracts tendered through an exchange within the past 90 days, but not hedged by future contracts in the same commodity. (See (c)(9) and (11) below.)

(iii) 10% of the market value in each customer's combined account in equity when such account contains spot commodity positions, evidenced by a warehouse receipt issued by a warehouse licensed by a commodity exchange, which are the result of future contracts tendered through an exchange within the past 90 days, and hedged by future contracts in the same commodity. (See (c)(9) and (11) below.)

Other

(I) Any other amounts rightly to be comprehended as "Debit Items" in the computation of Net Capital.

Special provisions

U. S. Government and Municipal Bonds

(c)(1) In the case of obligations of:

(A) The United States or any agency thereof and obligations guaranteed as to principal or interest by the United States or any agency thereof the following percentages of market value shall be deducted:

(i)   Less than one year to maturity............... 0%
(ii) One year but less than two years to maturity.. 1%
(iii) Two years but less than three years to maturity 1½%
(iv) Three years but less than four years to maturity.. 2%
(v)   Four years but less than five years to maturity.. 2½%
(vi) Five years or more to maturity.............. 3%

(B) A State, territory or possession of the United States or any political subdivision thereof and obligations guaranteed as to principal or interest by such State, territory, possession or political subdivision thereof, which are not in default as to interest, the following percentages of market value shall be deducted:

(i)	Less than one year to maturity...............	0%
(ii)	One year but less than two years to maturity..	1%
(iii)	Two years but less than three years to maturity...	2%
(iv)	Three years but less than five years to maturity..	3%
(v)	Five years or more to maturity:	

a) covered by the 1st and 2nd ratings by any of the nationally known statistical services............ 4%

b) covered by the 3rd rating by any of the nationally known statistical services.................. 5%

c) covered by other ratings or not rated........ 10%

(C) Any authority, commission or agency of a State, territory or possession of the United States or any political subdivision thereof which are payable as to principal and interest solely from specified revenues and which are not in default as to interest, the following percentages of market value shall be deducted:

(i)	Less than one year to maturity...............	1%
(ii)	One year but less than two years to maturity...	2%
(iii)	Two years but less than three years to maturity	3%
(iv)	Three years or more to maturity:	

a) covered by the 1st and 2nd ratings by any of the nationally known statistical services............ 5%

b) covered by the 3rd rating by any of the nationally known statistical services.................. 7½%

c) covered by other ratings or not rated........ 10%

Other Government Obligations

(2)—*Deleted—Included in (1) above, effective December 1, 1958.*

Redeemable Securities

(3) In the case of obligations or preferred stocks which the issuer has officially declared will be redeemed within ninety days, the full market value or the cash redemption value, whichever is lower, shall be included in computing Net Worth and Net Capital.

Preferred Stocks

(4) In the case of preferred stocks (other than those above) on the "exempt" list shown in the NYSE GUIDE and senior nonconvertible preferred stocks of issuers whose interest bearing obligations are covered by the first three ratings by any of the nationally known statistical services, 20% of the market value shall be deducted.

Non-Convertible Bonds

(5) In the case of interest bearing obligations which do not have a conversion or exchange feature, covered by the first four ratings by any of the nationally known statistical services, the following percentages of market value shall be deducted: First rating—5%; second and third ratings—10%; fourth rating—15%, except that, in the case of such obli-

¶ 2325 Continued.

gations having five years or less to maturity, covered by the first three ratings, the following percentages of market value shall be deducted: Maturity one year or less—1%, two years—2%, three years—3%, four years—4% and five years—5%.

Convertible Bonds

(6) Interest bearing obligations which have a conversion or exchange feature and which are covered by the first four ratings by any of the nationally known statistical services, may be included in the computation of Net Capital at the lower of 100% of the principal amount or the market value less the applicable percentage designated for bonds which do not have a conversion or exchange feature.

Exchangeable Securities

(7) In the case of securities which are exchangeable or convertible, a security sold shall be considered, in computing Net Worth, as a sale of a security held, after adjustment of the cost or proceeds of such securities for any money to be paid or received in connection with such exchange or conversion provided the security held is, without restriction other than the payment of money, exchangeable or convertible into the security sold within a period not exceeding thirty days. With respect to a case involving a longer period of time, the Department of Member Firms will consider a written application for permission to deduct a percentage of the proceeds of sale (in lieu of 30% or some other percentage of the market value of the security held).

Preferential Treatment Upon Application

(8) In the case of securities coming within the scope of any of the following clauses, the Department of Member Firms will consider a written application for permission to deduct a lesser percentage of the market value than heretofore provided.

(A) Interest bearing obligations and serial equipment trust certificates which are to be the subject of a primary distribution but for which a published rating is not yet available;

(B) obligations of any authority, commission or agency of a State, territory or possession of the United States or any political subdivision thereof which are payable as to principal and interest solely from specified revenues and which are not in default as to interest, which have less than nine months to maturity.

(C) obligations of a State, territory or possession of the United States or any political subdivision thereof or any authority, commission or agency thereof which are not rated by any of the nationally known statistical services.

Exclusion

(9) Exclusive of bona fide cash transactions for customers in issued securities and after application of current outstanding calls for margin, marks or other deposits.

¶ 2325 **Rule 325**

Contractual Commitments

(10) Net Worth and "Debit Items" (A)(iii), (A)(iv), (B) and (C) of paragraph (b)(4) of Rule 325 should be adjusted for open contractual commitments which will include delayed delivery, underwriting and "when issued" contracts, endorsements of puts and calls and commitments in foreign currencies and spot (cash) commodity contracts but will not include open commodity future contracts and uncleared regular way purchases and sales of securities, by applying the amounts due thereon and any valuation of securities involved as though such amounts and valuations were actual, except that this treatment of any individual commitment shall not operate to increase Net Worth or Net Capital. A series of contracts of purchase or a series of contracts of sale, of a stated amount of the same security conditioned, if at all, only upon issuance shall be treated as an individual commitment and the profit, at market, in each individual commitment used to reduce the debit item (B) or (C) relating to that commitment.

Accounts Not Covered By Agreements

(11) Accounts of partners which are not covered by agreements, in form approved by the Exchange, providing that the securities and equities therein are to be included as partnership property, accounts of officers and accounts of holders of stock of a member corporation shall be considered as customers' accounts.

Amendments.
Rule 325(c)(1), (2) and (8)(B) amended October 16, 1958, effective December 1, 1958. Rule 325(b)(4) amended March 19, 1964, effective May 1, 1964.

● ● ● *Supplementary Material:*

.10   Computation of net capital under Rule 325.—

Credits:

(1) Credit balances in accounts for Capital stock........ $........

(2) Net credit balances in accounts for surplus and undivided profits (after provision, in the case of a corporation, for current dividends declared and unpaid).... ....

(3) Credit balances in "proprietary accounts".......... :.......

(4) Net profits, at market, in future commodity Exchange contracts carried for "proprietary accounts"........ ....

(5) Market value (or value indicated by accompanying instructions) of securities and spot commodities long in "proprietary accounts"........................ ....

(6) Reserves (other than liability reserves) which are available as capital ....

(7) Total credits .... $=====

¶ 2325.10   Continued

Debits:

(8)   Surplus deficit and undivided losses .... $........

(9)   Debit balances in "proprietary accounts"........... ....

(10) Deficits in customers' accounts (other than bona fide cash accounts) after application of current outstanding calls for margin, marks or other deposits........ ....

(11) Market value of securities short in "proprietary accounts" ....

(12) Net losses, at market, in future commodity Exchange contracts carried for "proprietary accounts" ....
      [Net worth is equal to total of credits (1) through (6) (*i. e.*, item (7)), less total of debits (8) through (12) .... $........]

(13) Debit balances in accounts for fixed assets, prepaid items etc. such as:
      Memberships .... $........
      Furniture, fixtures & Equipment....... ....
      Prepaid expenses ....
      Profits and commissions receivable from syndicates ....
      Real estate (See Instruction 10)........ ....
      Miscellaneous advances and receivables ....
      Dividends receivable—non-current (See Instruction 8) ....
      ....
      ....
      ....
      ....
      ....
      ....

      Total of Item (13)........................ $........

(14) 30% (or pertinent percentage of market values indicated in Rule 325 [¶ 2325] or (c)(1) through (8) thereof or as indicated in the accompanying instructions) of the market values of all securities and spot commodities long in "proprietary accounts" and in customers' accounts in deficit (other than bona fide cash accounts and after application of current outstanding calls for margin, marks or other deposits):

¶ 2325.10   **Rule 325**   © 1964, Commerce Clearing House, Inc.

Market values etc.	*Percentage charge*	*Amount of charge*
$........	30%	$........
....	20	....
....	15	....
....	10	....
....		....
....		....
....		....
....		....
....		....
....		....

Total Amount of Charge .... $........

(15) The amount determined on the excess of the market value of short positions in securities over the market value of long positions in "proprietary accounts" (See Debit Item (C) Rule 325 [¶ 2325]. See also Instruction 23 at .15, below.) .... $........

(16) 30% of the market value of all long and all short future commodity contracts (other than those representing spreads or straddles in the same commodity or hedging any spot commodity positions) carried for "proprietary accounts" .... $........

(17) Total of credit lines granted (See Instruction 24).... $........

(18) (a) Total of amount by which the daily limit fluctuation of all future commodity contracts carried for a customer's account or accounts controlled by a customer exceeds 10% of the net worth of the member organization. (See Instruction (25) (a)) ....

(b) 1½% of market values of total long or total short future contracts in each commodity. (See Instruction (25)(b)) ....

(19) Cash required to provide margin in accordance with Rule 431 [¶ 2431] after application of current outstanding calls for margin, marks or other deposits...... ....

(20) (a) Debit balance in each customer's spot (cash) commodity account other than the result of a tender made on a futures contract within the past 90 days and evidenced by warehouse receipt(s) issued by a warehouse licensed by a commodity exchange.. ....

(b) Cash required to provide margin in customers' commodity accounts in accordance with Rule 325 (b)(4)(H) after application of current outstanding calls for margin ....

(21) Total Debits .... $======

(22) Net Capital (item 7 less item 21) .... $======

¶ 2325.10—Continued

    (23) Aggregate Indebtedness per Rule 325 [¶ 2325], Section (b)(2):

        Total liabilities per Section (b)(2) .... $........

        Less exclusions per Section (b)(2)

            (a) .... $........

            (b) ....

            (c) ....

            (d) ....

            (e) ....

            (f) ....

            (g) ....

            (h) ....

        Total exclusions ....

        Aggregate Indebtedness .... $........

    (24) Minimum capital required to be maintained or 1/20th of item 23, whichever **greater** .... $

    (25) Net Capital in excess of minimum requirements (item 22 less item 24) .... $

    (26) Ratio of Aggregate Indebtedness to Net Capital (item 23 divided by item 22) .... %

Instructions

.15   **General.—**

    (1) Questions as to the computation of Net Capital or the treatment of items entering into such computation should be directed to the Department of Member Firms or phone HAnover 2-4200, extensions 325 or 326.

    (2) The term "proprietary accounts" includes capital accounts of partners or sole proprietor, investment and trading accounts, participations in joint accounts, accounts of partners which are covered by agreements, approved by the Exchange, providing for the inclusion of equities therein as partnership property and borrowings covered by subordination agreements approved by the Exchange.

    (3) Individual accounts of limited and general partners of a member firm which are not covered by "equities" agreements approved by the Exchange and those of holders of stock of a member corporation shall be considered as customers' accounts. However, **equities in general partners' commodity accounts and credit balances in other accounts of general partners shall not be included in Aggregate Indebtedness.**

    (4) If a limited partner contributes securities as capital and the partnership agreement limits his liability to an amount other than the market value thereof, enter in item (3) the lower of the amount to which his liability is limited or the market value reduced by the percentage to be deducted in accordance with ¶ 2325(c)(1) through (8). Do not include the value of such securities in item (5) or (14).

¶ **2325.15**   **Rule 325**   © 1964, Commerce Clearing House, Inc.

(5) Any borrowing for capital purposes which has not been approved by the Exchange, shall not be considered as a credit in computing Net Capital.

(6) Shares of the Board of Trade Clearing Corporation (Chicago) shall be considered as a current asset at the amount for which they can be sold to the Clearing Corporation. The excess of such amount over the ledger balance in the account for such shares shall be included in item (3). Any excess of the ledger balance over the current value shall be included as a debit in item (9).

(7) Cash surrender value of life insurance policies, which have been approved by the Exchange or which, in the opinion of firm's counsel, meet the requirements of the Exchange, shall be considered as a current asset. Any excess of such cash surrender value over the ledger balance shall be included as a credit in item (3). Any excess of the ledger balance over the cash surrender value shall be included as a debit in item (9).

(8) Dividends receivable recorded after the ex-dividend date shall be considered as a current asset unless they represent claims which are not readily collectible.

(9) Good faith deposits on commitments in securities shall also be considered as a current asset.

(10) The debit balance for Real Estate shown in item (13) may not be reduced by the amount of mortgages thereon unless such procedure has been approved by the Department of Member Firms.

(11) If non-exempt securities of customers are pledged against a borrowing of "Exempt" securities, the market value of the securities borrowed shall be included in Aggregate Indebtedness.

(12) Unrecorded assets and liabilities, other than contractual and contingent items, should be treated as though recorded when computing Net Capital and Aggregate Indebtedness. Consideration should also be given to sufficiency of liability reserves in connection with any lawsuits pending, accommodation endorsements, rediscounted notes, guarantees or any other contingent liability.

Long and short positions, endorsed puts and calls—proprietary accounts

(13) If a firm does no business with others than members or member organizations, the market value of all readily marketable securities in "proprietary accounts" shall be included in items (5) and (14). The percentage charge and amount of charge in items (14) and (15) shall be zero.

(14) In the case of long securities which have no ready market, no value should be included in items (5) or (14).

(15) In the case of obligations or preferred stocks which the issuer has officially declared will be redeemed within 90 days, enter in item (5) the full market value or the cash redemption value, whichever is lower. Do not enter in item (14).

(16) In the case of interest bearing obligations having a conversion or exchange feature which are covered by the first four ratings by any of the nationally known statistical services, include the market value thereof in item (5) and item (14). Include in item (14) as the "Amount of charge," the excess of market value included in item (5), over the principal amount or over the market value less the applicable percentage for bonds which

¶ 2325.15—Continued

do not have a conversion or exchange feature, whichever amount is greater. For example, if convertible bonds with maturities exceeding five years, have a second rating, the "Amount of charge" would be determined as follows:

(A)	Market value included in item (5)		$115,000
(B)	Principal amount	$100,000	
(C)	Market value $115,000 less 10% for second rating	103,500	
	Lower of (B) or (C) ....;..		100,000
	Amount of charge item (14)		$ 15,000

(A)	Market value included in item (5)		$105,000
(B)	Principal amount	$100,000	
(C)	Market value $105,000 less 10% for second rating	94,500	
	Lower of (B) or (C)		94,500
	Amount of charge item (14)		$ 10,500

On convertible bonds selling at 142⅞ or over, the maximum "Amount of charge" in item (14) will be 30% of market value as Rule 325 [¶ 2325] does not require a charge in excess of 30% of the market value of readily marketable securities.

(17) In the case of securities which are exchangeable or convertible, a security sold may be considered as a sale of a security held, after adjustment of the cost or proceeds of such security for any money to be paid or received in connection with such exchange or conversion, provided the security held is, without restriction other than the payment of money, exchangeable or convertible into a security sold within a period not exceeding 30 days. The proceeds of such securities, after adjustment, should be included in item (3) or used to reduce the debit in item (9). If the period exceeds 30 days and the Department of Member Firms has granted permission to include a percentage of the proceeds of sale, only the amount determined in accordance with such percentage, reduced by any amounts to be paid or increased by any amounts to be received in connection with such exchange or conversion, shall be included in item (3) or used to reduce the debit in item (9). Do not include the market value of the long securities in item (5) or the market value of securities sold in item (11).

(18) If the Department of Member Firms has, upon written application, granted permission to deduct a lesser percentage of the market value of a security than the percentage specifically provided by Rule 325 [¶ 2325], include the market value of such securities in item (5). Also include the market value in item (14), the percentage charge and the amount of charge.

¶ 2325.15   Rule 325   © 1964, Commerce Clearing House, Inc.

(19) In the case of a long security against which the firm has sold a call and bought a put endorsed by a member firm (conversion account), such security shall be valued at the lower of the put or call price in lieu of the market price and such value included in item (5). Such value shall also be included in item (14) and 15% thereof shall be included in the amount of charge.

(20) If a call has been sold against a security held for "proprietary accounts" the market value of the security shall be included in items (5) and (14). The amount of charge in item (14) should be at 30% (or pertinent percentage) *provided* the contract amount of the call is greater than 70% (or pertinent percentage) of the market value. If the contract amount of the call is less than 70% (or pertinent percentage) of the market value then the excess of the latter over the contract amount should be included in item (9).

(21) If a put has been sold against a short position in "proprietary accounts" the excess of the contract value over the market value shall be included in item (9).

(22) Where a put or a call has been endorsed and there is no offsetting security position, each such put or call shall be considered separately. The contract value of a put shall be included in item (9). The market value of the securities represented by the put shall be included in item (5). The market value and the amount of charge based on the pertinent percentage should be included in item (14). If the market value included as a credit in item (5) exceeds the debit included in item (9) plus the amount of charge included in item (14), such excess shall be included as a debit in item (9). In the case of a call, the amount by which the market value exceeds the contract value shall be included in item (9). However, if a put and a call have been sold for the same number of shares of the same security, only the option resulting in the greater reduction in Net Capital should be considered as a contractual commitment.

(23) The amount required by item (15), relates to "excess" short positions in securities in "proprietary accounts" and is determined in the following manner:

The actual positions long and short in such accounts are adjusted for open contractual commitments. There should be eliminated from the resulting long and short positions:

(A) All long and short positions, actual and contractual, bonds and stocks, which will be cleared by eventual conversion of such long securities for delivery of such securities sold;

(B) long positions and all puts and calls in "conversion" accounts where a security is purchased, a call is sold and a put is held which has been endorsed by a member firm;

(C) short positions and all puts and calls in "conversion" accounts where a security is sold, a put is sold and a call is held which has been endorsed by a member firm;

(D) long positions and calls where a security is held and a call has been sold.

(E) a put and a call sold for the same number of shares of the same security.

[The next page is 3537-3.]

Also, in regard to item (15), a put sold by the firm should not be used to eliminate a short position nor should the put be considered as a long position.

A put or call owned by the firm should be disregarded for the purpose of determining long or short positions.

After the above eliminations have been made for the purpose of item (15), the valuations of long and short positions should be determined separately for stocks and for bonds and separately for each percentage category.

The market value of longs in a category is compared with the market value of shorts in that category for purposes of item (15). In each category where the short values exceed the long values, a charge results based on the percentage charge in that category applied to the excess short value. An example follows:

		— *Market Values* —		
Category	Long	Short	Excess Short	Amount of Charge
Common and Pfd.				
Stocks 30%	$100,000	$120,000	$20,000	$6,000
Preferred Stocks 20%	30,000	—	—	—
Bonds 30%	50,000	—	—	—
Bonds 15%	10,000	15,000	5,000	750
Bonds 10%	100,000	—	—	—
Bonds 5%	50,000	—	—	—
Bonds 2%	—	50,000	50,000	1,000

Total Debit, Item (15) $7,750

The excess long values in a category should not be used to offset excess short values in another category.

The above relates only to charges on "excess" short positions in the accounts covered by item (15). It does not affect the charges on long positions in such accounts or the determination of any other debit item or credit item.

"Customers' Commodity Account Charges"

(24) The amount required by item (17), total of credit lines granted, is determined by multiplying the number of contracts in an account, on which credit has been granted, by the amount of credit granted on each such open contract. From the amount so determined, deduct the equity or deficit in that account (after application of current outstanding margin calls). The deduction, however, cannot exceed the amount of credit granted.

After the amount of credit granted has been determined for each customer's account, the amounts are totalled for accounts which have net long positions and separately for accounts which have net short positions. The amount required by the accounts with net longs or with net shorts, whichever amount is greater, is used. To this amount is added the amount determined for accounts with no net positions.

If an account has open positions in only one commodity, the number of contracts determines the net position. If it has a net long position in

¶ 2325.15—Continued

one commodity and a net short position in a different commodity, the market value determines the net position.

(25)(a) The amount by which the daily limit fluctuations of all future commodity contracts carried for a customer's account exceed 10% of the net worth of the member organization may be determined by eliminating from each customer's account or group of accounts controlled by a customer, purchases of a commodity in one contract month and sales of the same commodity in a different contract month provided such contracts are in the same crop year and were made in the same market.

After such eliminations, the remaining number of contracts long and short is multiplied by the amount of the daily limit fluctuation prescribed by the pertinent commodity exchange for each contract in the respective commodity.

The total of the amounts determined for each commodity, in a customer's account or group of accounts controlled by a customer, is then compared with an amount equal to 10% of the net worth of the member organization. (The net worth at the end of a month or accounting period may be used for the succeeding month or accounting period not to exceed five weeks.) The amount of the charge is the excess of the amount of the daily limit fluctuation over 10% of the net worth as in the following example:

Account of John Smith

	Number of Contracts		Daily Limit Fluctuation Per	
	Long	Short	Contract	Total
Cocoa	1,000		$ 300	$ 300,000
Cotton*	100	100	1,000	200,000
Soybean Oil	500		600	300,000
Sugar	300		560	168,000
Wheat	300		500	150,000

$1,118,000

10% of $10,000,000—Net Worth $1,000,000

Amount of Charge .... $ 118,000

*Straddle not in same crop year. The customer's equity in this account is not considered for the purpose of computing the amount of this charge.

(25)(b) The amount required by (18)(b), $1\frac{1}{2}\%$ of market values of the total long or total short future contracts in each commodity, may be determined by eliminating from each customer's account purchases of a commodity in one contract month and sales of the same commodity in a different contract month provided such contracts were made in the same market and in the same crop year.

After such eliminations, the total market values of the remaining contracts long and short in all customers' accounts are determined separately for each commodity. The greater of the long value or short value of each commodity enters into the computation of $1\frac{1}{2}\%$ as in the following example:

	Market Value		Greater of Long or Short
	Long	Short	
Coffee	$ 200,000	$ 100,000	$ 200,000
Cotton	1,500,000	1,000,000	1,500,000
Sugar	300,000	200,000	300,000
Corn	500,000	700,000	700,000
Oats	150,000	150,000	150,000
Wheat	1,000,000	1,300,000	1,300,000

$4,150,000

Amount Required, $1\frac{1}{2}\%$ of Total .... $ 62,250

Contractual Commitments

For Proprietary accounts and customers' accounts in deficit

(26) Debit and credit items shall be adjusted for contractual commitments other than uncleared regular way purchases and sales of securities.

¶ 2325.15—Continued

(27) A position in each security shall be considered as actual. The net cost of a long position should be included in item (9). The market value of a net long position should be included in item (5). Such market value and the amount of charge based on the pertinent percentage should be included in item (14). If the market value included as a credit in item (5) exceeds the debit included in item (9) plus the amount of charge included in item (14), such excess shall also be included as a debit in item (9). Where no position exists, any loss should be included in item (9) and any profit disregarded. In the case of a short position any excess of the short position, at market, over the net proceeds should be included in item (9) and any profit, at market, disregarded.

If when issued transactions will be consummated within 30 days, they may be considered as actual without restriction.

Spot (cash) commodities contracts

(28) A position in each commodity shall be considered as actual and treated the same as when issued contracts. Net sales should be considered as hedges of any spot position in the same commodity which is included in item (14).

Commitments in foreign currencies

(29) Any loss, at market, in each foreign currency shall be included as a debit in item (9). Any profit, at market, shall be disregarded.

Joint trading and investment accounts in which the firm participates

(30) Include firm's portion of debit or credit balance (without adjustment for any deposit) in item (9) or item (3) respectively. Include its portion of short position, at market, in item (11). Include in item (5) its portion of the market value of long securities. Such market value of long securities and the amount of charge at the pertinent percentage should be included in item (14). Any margin deposit is not to be included as a debit in computing capital.

Joint foreign and domestic arbitrage accounts in which the firm participates

(31) Money balances and securities positions carried by the firm and by a participant may be combined and considered on a net basis (offsetting positions in the same security may be eliminated). Adjustments may be made where different clearance dates apply to transactions made on the same day in the same security.

Include firm's portion of net debit or credit balance in item (9) or item (3) respectively. Include its portion of short positions, at market, in item (11). Include in item (14) its portion of the market value of long securities and the amount of charge at the pertinent percentage. Do not include, in item (19), any cash margin deficiency in connection with the participant's share of such account carried by the firm.

© 1964, Commerce Clearing House, Inc.

Information Regarding Capital Requirements

.16 **Applications for higher percentage treatment.**—Applications under .10 of Rule 325 [¶ 2325] should be submitted in writing to the Department of Member Firms. Such applications, in addition to clearly reciting the nature of the request for higher percentage treatment, should include the following information:

(1) Complete description of the security, including the number of shares of stock or principal amount of bonds involved;

(2) statement as to whether the shares of stock or principal amount of bonds are presently reflected in proprietary accounts. If not, an indication should be made as to the date on which the security is to be purchased or on which there will be a contingent commitment to purchase; and

(3) the rating assigned the security by a nationally-known statistical service and the name of such statistical service. If a rating is not available, it should be so stated.

.17 **General partners' securities and equities in computation of net capital.**—

No securities and equities in partners' individual accounts will be included as partnership property in computing the Net Capital of a member firm unless the partnership articles of the firm or some supplemental agreement specifically provide for such inclusion.

The phraseology of such provisions will necessarily vary as between different firms and therefore no standard form has been prescribed. However, a suggested form, containing the essential features of such provisions may be obtained from the Division of Documents, Department of Member Firms. Member firms are particularly cautioned to consider this suggested form merely as a guide and to consult their own counsel before adopting it or any other form of agreement, since substantial rights of the firm and of the individual partners may be affected. Before adopting any particular wording, member firms are urged to submit their proposed form of agreement to the Division of Documents, Department of Member Firms, in order to ascertain whether or not it is satisfactory from the Exchange's point of view.

If the partnership articles or supplemental agreement merely subordinates the claim of a partner to the claims of creditors of the partnership arising out of any matters occurring before the partner ceases to be a partner in the firm, the Exchange, in the event of the death of such partner, will immediately upon his death have to disallow the securities and equities in the partner's individual accounts in computing the firm's Net Capital. If the partner desires to have such equities and securities treated as firm capital after his death the agreement which is in effect at his death must specifically provide that the securities and equities in his account at the time of his death are to continue as capital of the firm at the risk of the business for a stated period of time after his death and all claims of the estate of the deceased partner must be subordinated to the claims of all present and future creditors of the firm arising out of any matters occurring prior to the end of the stated period.

.18 **Deceased or withdrawing partner's interest in continuing firms.**—

I.

Where the partnership articles of a member firm do not include specific and legally adequate provisions to the effect that the claim of the personal representative of a deceased partner to the partner's interest in the firm shall be

¶ 2325.18   Information Regarding Capital Requirements.—Continued
subordinated to the claims of all present or future creditors of the continuing firm (or any successor firm) arising out of matters occurring subsequent to the partner's death, the Exchange cannot, upon the partner's death, regard his interest as continuing to be part of the Net Capital of the continuing or successor firm.

Provisions in a deceased partner's Will permitting executors to continue a partner's capital interest at the risk of the business should not be relied upon as being effective immediately upon the partner's death, inasmuch as such provisions cannot, in any event, be availed of for a considerable period thereafter. Unless there are appropriate provisions in the partnership articles subjecting such capital to the risk of the business during the interim, the Exchange upon the partner's death cannot treat his interest as part of the firm's Net Capital. In many cases such a situation might render it necessary for the continuing firm to find additional capital immediately upon the death of the partner in order to meet the Exchange's capital requirements.

While the inclusion in the partnership articles of provisions continuing a deceased partner's interest at the risk of the business after his death is a matter to be determined in every case by the wishes of the partners, if it is the desire and intention of the partners of any firm that the interest of a deceased partner shall be considered, without interruption after his death, as a part of the capital of the continuing or successor firm for a specified period, the partnership articles should effectively provide in substance:

(1) That the payment of the deceased partner's interest in the firm to his estate be deferred for a stated period; and

(2) that until such payment, the interest of the deceased partner shall remain at the risk of the business of the continuing or successor firm and shall be considered as capital of such firm in the same manner and to the same extent as capital contributed by a limited partner; and

(3) that any claim of the personal representative of the deceased partner to such interest shall be subordinated in right of payment and subject to the prior payment or provision for payment in full of claims of all present and future creditors of the continuing firm (and any successor firm) arising out of any matters occurring before the end of the stated period.

If the partnership articles provide that such provisions are not effective unless affirmatively consented to by the personal representative of the deceased partner or if the personal representative is given the right, either to withdraw the capital or to terminate the continuing or successor firm before the end of the stated period, the deceased partner's capital can not be allowed by the Exchange in computing the firm's net capital after the date when the personal representative's consent is required or when the withdrawal of the capital or termination of the firm may be made effective except as follows: If the partnership articles give the personal representative the right to withdraw the capital prior to the end of the period during which it is otherwise kept at the risk of the business, all of such capital will not necessarily be disallowed by the Exchange from and after the date when such withdrawal might be effected, if the following additional conditions exist:

(1) The right to give notice (which may not be less than on 30 days) of a future withdrawal of capital may not accrue prior to the

¶ 2325.18   **Rule 325**   © 1958, Commerce Clearing House, Inc.

expiration of at least three months following the date of the personal representative's appointment.

(2) The personal representative shortly prior to the time when he may first give notice of withdrawal (whether he intends to give such notice or not) should submit to the Exchange an affidavit setting forth the known and estimated liabilities of the estate (including taxes), the estimated value of the estate's assets, a statement showing whether any income tax returns of the decedent have not yet been audited by the tax authorities and a statement that to the best of his knowledge and belief, the decedent made no gifts during his lifetime which might be construed as being subject to estate or inheritance taxes, and the Exchange must be satisfied that the indications are that the estate will prove solvent.

(3) The Will of the deceased partner must contain specific affirmative authority to the personal representative to leave the deceased's capital in the firm in the executor's discretion, notwithstanding his option of withdrawing it.

(4) The representative and the firm should both undertake to advise the Exchange promptly upon discovery that there appears to be any substantial increase in the estate's liabilities or decrease in its assets as compared with the figures given in the affidavit which might indicate a greater possibility than theretofore of estate insolvency.

Even if all of the foregoing conditions are fully met, a right of withdrawal in the personal representative will necessitate disallowance by the Exchange of the deceased partner's capital if one or more of the representatives of the deceased partner is also a partner in the firm. In any case, the Exchange reserves the right, in its sole discretion, to disallow the deceased partner's capital at any time.

In drafting provisions for inclusion in partnership articles, it should be borne in mind that if the partnership has a stated termination date and the capital of a deceased partner is placed at the risk of the business until the end of the partnership term, the death of a partner near the end of the term might necessitate a disallowance by the Exchange of his capital interest within a very short time. In order to avoid this difficulty, it may be desirable to make appropriate provision for the continuation of the capital at the risk of the business of a successor firm for a further stated period after the termination of the firm of which the deceased partner was a member.

If the surviving partners (rather than the personal representatives of the deceased partner) are to be given the right to elect whether or not the capital of a deceased partner is to be continued at the risk of the business of a continuing or successor firm, it may be desirable to provide that the capital is left absolutely at the risk of the business for a specified period, with the right in the surviving partners, prior to the expiration of such period, to elect to continue it for a longer time. Such a provision should obviate the necessity of making such an election immediately upon the death of the partner. If any of the surviving partners are also executors or administrators of the deceased partner the Exchange may not, for capital purposes, be able to give effect to such election.

If it is the desire of the partners to have a deceased partner's capital continued for a stated period immediately following his death, with the option in his personal representatives (rather than the partners) to continue it for

¶ 2325.18 Information Regarding Capital Requirements.—Continued
a longer period under the provisions of the deceased partner's Will, it is
suggested that the stated period in the partnership agreement be made
sufficiently long so as to permit the conditions discussed below with respect to
testamentary provisions to be complied with.

II.

With respect to provisions in a deceased partner's Will (as distinguished
from those in a partnership agreement) providing that the personal representative shall or may become a limited partner in the firm or subordinate the
claim of the estate to decedent's interest to the claims of firm creditors who
become such after the decedent's death, the Exchange's determination whether
or not to allow a deceased partner's capital interest in computing the Net
Capital of the firm will depend on the facts and circumstances of each case as
they exist at the time of such determination. However, in no case will such
testamentary provisions be considered as effective in connection with the Exchange's computation of Net Capital unless at least the following conditions
are met:

(1) The Will must contain provisions specifically authorizing the
personal representative of the deceased partner either to continue the deceased's capital interest in the firm as limited capital, or otherwise to
subordinate the estate's claims against the firm to the claims of creditors.
Moreover, unless a change in the personnel of the successor firm is to
terminate such authority, the Will must provide that the capital can be
continued at the risk of the business of the continuing or successor firm
despite changes in personnel in that firm.

(2) The period prescribed by law within which creditors of the decedent are required to file their claims against the estate must have expired.

(3) The Exchange must be furnished with affidavits setting forth the
financial status of the decedent's estate.

(4) The Exchange must be furnished with a satisfactory opinion of
counsel to the estate, to the effect that (A) the personal representative is
duly authorized to become a partner in the firm or otherwise to subordinate the deceased partner's capital interest, (B) that there is no State tax
lien on the decedent's interest, (C) that the decedent's interest is at the
risk of the business for a stated period, and (D) that any claim which any
legatees or creditors of the decedent may have is subordinated in right of
payment to the claims of all firm creditors arising during the stated period.

(5) The Exchange must be furnished with a release of the Federal
Estate Tax lien or satisfactory evidence that such tax has been paid in
full and that there are no further claims against the estate in connection
therewith.

(6) The personal representative of the decedent must have taken
appropriate action either to become a limited partner in the firm or to
subordinate the capital interest of the deceased partner as indicated above.

III.

In view of the fact that many partners of member firms may be serving in
the Armed Forces, with the possibility that receipt of any knowledge of death

may be considerably delayed, it is suggested that member firms having partners in the Armed Services consider the inclusion of provisions in their partnership articles continuing such partner's capital interest at the risk of the business until official notice of death is received and for an adequate length of time thereafter. It may also be desirable to specify the effect of an official notice that a person is "missing", e. g., that for the purposes of the articles such a notice shall be deemed the equivalent of notice of death or, on the other hand, that such a "missing" notice shall not be deemed notice of death until confirmation of actual death is received.

IV.

In drafting partnership articles, it is suggested that consideration be given to the question of whether or not appropriate provisions should be included with respect to the disposition and status of a partner's capital interest upon his withdrawal from the firm (as distinguished from his death). It is desirable to specify when his capital is to be repaid to him and whether or not, until such payment, it is to remain at the risk of the business of the continuing or successor firm.

V.

It is recommended that member firms consult their own counsel with respect to the advisability of incorporating in their partnership articles provisions of the sort discussed in this Section. Any member firm which decides to adopt such provisions should submit the proposed provisions, prior to execution, to the Division of Documents, Department of Member Firms. Such member firm will then be advised whether, upon the adoption of such provisions and in the event of the death of a partner, the Exchange will be in a position to consider his interest in the firm as part of its net capital for the specified period following his death.

Information regarding the procedure followed by the Exchange in connection with indicating the interest, if any, of a deceased partner in a member firm in the listing of member organizations in the "Member Organizations" Section of the Directory, Vol. 1, N. Y. S. E. Guide, may be obtained from the Office of the Secretary.

.19 Borrowings of cash and securities by members, partners and stockholders of member organizations for capital purposes.—All borrowings, regardless of size or description, and whether collateralized or not, of cash or securities, where the proceeds represent or will represent capital of an individual member or a member organization under Rule 325 [¶ 2325], should be reported promptly to the Exchange.

As a matter of policy, the Exchange requires that the documents which evidence these borrowings for capital purposes conform to certain standards and that copies be submitted to the Department of Member Firms before the cash or securities involved may qualify as capital acceptable for inclusion in the computation of net capital under Rule 325 [¶ 2325].

The character of the documents varies, depending upon whether the lender is an individual, a member of a national securities exchange, bank, estate, trust, corporation, partnership, etc.

Borrowings for capital purposes should be executed on a time basis of at least six months' duration or, preferably, for a longer period of time. Capital borrowings of shorter duration are not acceptable unless, due to exceptional circumstances, they have received the prior approval of the Exchange.

¶ **2325.19   Information Regarding Capital Requirements.**—Continued

It is, therefore, important that borrowers of cash or securities for capital purposes communicate with the Department of Member Firms (Extension 229, 387 or 455) prior to the consummation of any such borrowing to be sure the terms of the arrangement will permit the borrowed funds to be considered as capital under Rule 325 [¶ 2325].

A change in the amount or in any of the terms of a borrowing should be reported promptly to the Department of Member Firms in order that the Exchange will at all times have a current record of the status of such borrowed capital.

With respect to borrowings by a member organization on a subordinated basis, where the proceeds are to be considered in the computation of net capital under Rule 325 [¶ 2325], see .20, below.

.20   Subordinated borrowings by member organizations.—All subordinated accounts and all subordinated borrowings by a member organization—whether of cash or securities or both—where the proceeds are to be considered in the computation of net capital under Rule 325 [¶ 2325] must receive prior approval of the Exchange. Such borrowings may be arranged with anyone acceptable to the Board of Governors and are subject to the following provisions:

(1) Subordinated borrowings of cash

(A) The lender may be paid interest not exceeding 8%.

(B) If the lender is

(i) a member of the family of one of the borrowing organization's general partners or holders of voting stock, or of a deceased general partner or holder of voting stock;

(ii) an estate of or trust established by or for one of the borrowing organization's general partners or holders of voting stock;

(iii) one of the borrowing organization's employees or the employee pension, retirement or profit-sharing plan of the borrowing organization; or

(iv) a limited partner or holder of non-voting stock of the borrowing organization

he may also share in organization profits to a reasonable extent.

(2) Subordinated borrowings of securities; subordination of equities in customers' accounts

(A) If the lender is a person listed in (1)(B) above, he may be paid interest not exceeding 8%. He may also share in organization profits to a reasonable extent.

(B) If the lender is anyone other than those listed in (1)(B) above

(i) the lender's major account shall have been with the borrowing organization for at least two years, unless the lender had not been a customer of any organization for two years.

(ii) the number of such borrowings by a member organization shall be reasonable in relation to the size of the organization, and the total dollar amount of such borrowings shall not constitute more than 25% of the total capital of the borrowing organization.

(iii) compensation for the loan or subordination of the account shall not exceed 4% on the value of the securities.

(3) Application of the borrowing member organization shall be filed with the Exchange together with application signed by the lender, in form prescribed by the Exchange, which shall contain at least the following information:

(A) name of the lender; (in the case of subordinated borrowings of securities or of subordination of equities in accounts, identify the relationship of the lender to the organization or one of its general partners or holders of voting stock).

(B) amount of borrowing;

(C) effective date;

(D) expiration date;

(E) compensation for the subordinated loan or subordination of the account, and

(i) interest rate, if fixed, or

(ii) details as to how it is to be calculated if it is to be measured by profits of the firm or by any direct or indirect interest in the distribution of the profits of the corporation.

(4) At the time the application for approval to make a subordinated borrowing is submitted to the Exchange for posting, there should accompany such application:

(A) signed copy of the subordination agreement in form prescribed by the Exchange;

(B) opinion of counsel to the borrowing organization stating that the subordination agreement is binding and enforceable in accordance with its terms upon the lender,

(C) check of the applying member organization for $100 covering Exchange fee for consideration of the application. While the fee is payable at the time of posting, a member organization may request that the charge be placed on the regular quarterly statement from the Exchange.

(5) A statement of a proposed lender for approval to make a subordinated loan to a member organization is ordinarily not acted upon by the Board of Governors until after notice of the proposal has been posted on the Bulletin Board of the Exchange for a period of two weeks. Such notice is posted upon submission, in proper form, of all required papers in connection with the proposal.

(6) The minimum time basis for a subordinated loan by a member organization shall ordinarily be at least one year, except that (A) in the case of a member firm, if the partnership agreement provides that limited partners may withdraw their capital contributions upon written notice of 90 days or less, and (B) in the case of a member corporation, the Certificate of Incorporation authorizes the redemption of the non-voting stock upon written notice of 90 days or less, provision may be made for payment in full of principal and interest prior to the expiration of the loan 90 days after written demand.

¶ 2325   Information Regarding Capital Requirements.—Continued

.30   **Disclosure of subordinated borrowings in financial statements to customers.**—Subordinated liabilities of member organizations shall be disclosed in the body of condensed financial statements issued to customers and such disclosure shall not be made solely by means of footnotes to such statements.

The subordinated liabilities may be shown in a separate section on the liability side of the statement following current liabilities and preceding net worth or capital or may be shown, for example, as follows:

* Subordinated Liabilities and Capital:

  Liabilities subordinated to claims of general
      creditors . . . . $. . . . .

  Capital (net worth or other acceptable title). . .   . .

* If desired, this caption may be eliminated.

If any subordinated liability is covered by an agreement which will expire within a short time and which will not be renewed, the time of expiration of such agreement should be clearly shown.

(See Rule 419 [¶ 2419] for requirements re financial statements to customers.)

[The next page is 3571.]

Non-member Corporations and Associations

(Rules and Policies Administered by the
Department of Member Firms.)

¶ 2331   Disapproval of Business Connections

Rule 331. Whenever it shall appear that a member, member organization or participant therein has such a business connection with a corporation or association, that the corporation or association dominates the business of the member or member organization, or controls the policy of such business, the Board of Governors may require the discontinuance of such business connection.

¶ 2332   Member Acting as Broker for Controlled Corporations

Rule 332. Unless the prior written consent of the Exchange is obtained, no member or member organization shall act as a broker for any corporation or association in the purchase or sale of securities if such corporation or association is controlled through stock ownership or otherwise by such member or member organization or by a participant or participants therein and is itself engaged in the business of buying and selling securities as broker for others.

¶ 2333   Participation in Commissions

Rule 333. If a member or a participant in a member organization is an officer, director or employee of any corporation or association engaged in the business of buying and selling securities for its own account or as broker for others, or if he or his organization is a stockholder in any such corporation or association, neither he nor the member organization shall participate in any commission paid by such other corporation or association unless either he or the member organization is engaged in a general brokerage business and in connection with such business actively participates in the transaction on which such commission is paid, or such participant is actively engaged in business as a floor broker.

¶ 2334   Joint Offices

Rule 334. Unless the prior written consent of the Exchange is obtained, no member or member organization shall permit any corporation or association engaged in the business of buying and selling securities for its own account or as broker or agent for others to use as its office the office or any branch office of such member or organization, or to employ in its business the same business organization as that employed by such member or member organization, nor voluntarily permit any such corporation or association to conduct its business under a name that does not clearly differentiate such corporation or association from such member or member organization.
(*See* ¶ 2343.10, 2343.11 *for permissible office space arrangements.*)

¶ 2335   Responsibility for Controlled Corporations

Rule 335. If a member or member organization or a participant or participants therein control, directly or indirectly through stock ownership or otherwise, a corporation or association engaged in the business of

¶ 2335—Continued

buying and selling securities for its own account or as broker or agent for others, such member, participants or organization shall be responsible to the Exchange for any fraud committed by such corporation or association or for any act or proceeding of such corporation or association contrary to just and equitable principles of trade or detrimental to the interest or welfare of the Exchange, or tending to defeat the purpose of the commission law of the Exchange or any provision of the Constitution of the Exchange or of a Rule, to the same extent and in the same manner as though such fraud or act or proceeding had been the fraud, act or proceeding of such member, participants or organization and such member, participants or organization shall be under the same duty to produce the books, records and papers of any such corporation or association for the examination and inspection of the Board of Governors or of any committee, or of anyone acting under the authority of the Board or any such committee, and to furnish evidence in regard to the acts and proceedings of such corporation or association, and shall be subject to the same penalties for the neglect of such duty, as if such books, records, papers, acts and proceedings were the books, records, papers, acts and proceedings of such member, participants or organization.

[The next page is 3585.]

Offices and Employees

(Rules and Policies Administered by the
Department of Member Firms.)

¶ 2341   Addresses of Members

Rule 341. Every member shall register with the Secretary of the Exchange an address and subsequent changes thereof where notices may be served. The registered address of every member who personally transacts business on the Floor must be in the vicinity of the Exchange.

¶ 2342   Offices—Approval, Supervision and Control

Rule 342. (a) Each office, department or business activity of a member or member organization (including foreign incorporated branch offices) shall be under the supervision and control of the member or member organization establishing it and of the personnel delegated such authority and responsibility.

The person in charge of a group of employees shall reasonably discharge his duties and obligations in connection with supervision and control of the activities of those employees related to the business of their employer and compliance with securities laws and regulations.

(b) The general partners or voting stockholders of each member organization shall provide for appropriate supervisory control and shall designate from among their own number a person or group of persons to assume overall authority and responsibility for internal supervision and control of the organization and compliance with securities' laws and regulations. This person or group shall:

(1) delegate to qualified principals or employees responsibility and authority for supervision and control of each office, department or business activity, and provide for appropriate procedures of supervision and control.

(2) establish a separate system of follow-up and review to determine that the delegated authority and responsibility is being properly exercised.

(c) The prior consent of the Exchange shall be obtained for each office established by a member or member organization, other than a main office.

(d) Qualified persons acceptable to the Exchange shall be in charge of:

(1) any office of a member or member organization,

(2) any regional or other group of offices,

(3) any other organizational group of registered representatives.

(e) The amounts and types of credit extended by a member organization shall be supervised by members or allied members qualified by experience for such control in the types of business in which the member organization extends credit.

Amendment.
April 16, 1964.

● ● ● *Supplementary Material:*

.10 **Annual fee.**—Each office of a member organization or corporate affiliate, other than the main office of the member organization, shall be subject

¶ 2342.10—Continued

during its existence to a registration fee of $50 for each calendar year or part thereof, unless specifically exempted by the Exchange.

(*See* ¶ 2321.10-.34 *for corporate affiliate requirements.*)

.11 **Registered representative operating from residence.**—With the prior approval of the Exchange, a registered representative may operate from his residence. His home address and telephone number may be advertised in any normal manner (such as business cards, local newspapers, stationery, etc.) but, in such event, the residence address shall be considered as constituting an office of his employer.

.12 **Foreign branch offices.**—With prior approval and under conditions set by the Exchange, a member organization may establish a foreign branch office in corporate form, provided all the stock of the corporation is owned by the member organization. The Department of Member Firms will furnish information concerning these conditions. Continuance of the arrangement is subject to any changes in the Constitution, Rules and Regulations of the Exchange as may be thereafter adopted.

.13 **Acceptability of supervisors.**—Any member, allied member or employee who is a candidate for acceptability under (d) above should have a creditable record as a registered representative or equivalent experience, and is expected to pass either the Allied Member Examination or the Branch Office Manager Examination.

.14 **Experience of senior management.**—Member organizations without experienced senior principals may be subject to agreements with the Exchange appropriately limiting their scope of activity.

.15 **Small offices** may be in charge of a qualified principal or manager who is either resident or non-resident in that area. In the event that such a qualified supervisor is non-resident, a resident registered representative may be designated for subsidiary authority and is not required to meet a manager's examination and experience requirements.

.16 **Supervision of registered representatives.**—For responsibilities for supervision of customer accounts, see also Rule 405. Suggestions are included in the separately published guide to "Supervision and Management of Registered Representatives and Customer Accounts". Duties of supervisors of registered representatives should ordinarily include at least approval of new accounts and review of correspondence of registered representatives, transactions, and customer accounts. Appropriate records should be maintained evidencing the carrying out of supervisory responsibilities such as a written statement of the supervisory procedures currently in effect and initialing of correspondence, transactions, blotters, or statements reviewed in the supervisory process.

¶ 2343   Offices—Sole Tenancy, Hours, Display of Membership Certificates, Expenses

Rule 343. (a) Each office of a member or member organization, or foreign incorporated branch, shall be used solely for said business and, except as permitted by the Exchange, shall not be occupied jointly with any other member or non-member.

(*See* ¶ 2321.10, 2321.34 *for corporate affiliate requirements.*)

6-64
Report 90
Rules of Board—Officers and Employees
➤➤➤ Administered by Department of Member Firms.
3587

(b) Unless otherwise permitted by the Exchange, the main office of every member or member organization shall remain open for business on every full business day during the trading hours on the New York Stock Exchange.

(c) Members and member organizations maintaining customers' offices are required to display in each such office a certificate of membership provided by the Exchange. Such certificate shall be at all times the property of the Exchange, and every such certificate shall be returned upon demand of the Exchange or upon termination of the office or of the member's status as a partner, voting stockholder or member.

(d) The person in charge of any office of a member or member organization shall not be paid a gross sum for the expenses thereof, such as rental, clerk hire or other expenses, but all expenses of such office shall be borne directly by the member or member organization.

Amendment.
April 16, 1964.

● ● ● *Supplementary Material:*
Information Regarding Office Space Arrangements

.10 The Exchange, under Rule 343, above, permits the following office space arrangements:

.11 **Member—Non-member.**—A member or member organization may:

(1) Furnish office space free of charge or on a rental basis to their own corporate affiliates; or

(2) furnish office space free of charge to a non-member customer provided the non-member does not conduct a business with the public from such space. A non-member who operates discretionary accounts on a fee or other compensation basis is deemed to be conducting a business; or

(3) sublease space to non-members at rentals reasonably comparable to the going rate for like space, provided

(A) such space is separated by ceiling-high solid walls from the space occupied by the member organization; and

(B) such space has direct access to a public hall, main corridor or street; and

(C) the name of the non-member is placed on the door to such space; and

(D) there are no connecting doors or windows between the space to be occupied by the non-member and that occupied by the member; and

(E) the name of the non-member is not listed under the same telephone number as that of the member, and the telephone number of the member is not used on letterheads or in any advertising of the non-member.

No facilities within the offices of such non-member may be paid for by the member, except as provided in Rule 369(E) [¶ 2369].

The fulfillment of the foregoing conditions is not required if the non-member is a fellow member of another exchange and the arrangement is not contrary to the rules of such other exchange, and the non-member limits his

¶ 2343.11—Continued

business to Floor brokerage on the other exchange and/or the introduction to the member of this Exchange, on a disclosed basis, of accounts trading in securities or commodities dealt in on the other exchange, and the non-member does not regularly solicit or service such customer business.

Applications for permission to enter into any of the above arrangements should be submitted to the Department of Member Firms.

(*See* ¶ 2334 *for joint office requirements.*)

.12   Keeping books of non-member.—Without the prior approval of the Exchange, no member organization may do any of the bookkeeping for a non-member.

.13   Member-Member.—Clearing member organizations may furnish office space, telephone, ticker and other facilities, or any of them, to non-clearing member organizations, provided

(1) All of the business of the non-clearing organization, where possible, is introduced to, or cleared through, the clearing organization which is furnishing the subsidy.

(2) The clearing organization shall at any time be prepared to demonstrate to the Exchange

(A) that the split of commissions on introduced listed business is at least greater than the minimum clearance rate, by the amount of the subsidy, and

(B) in respect of other types of business done by the introducing organization, whether on a principal or a brokerage basis, the clearing organization shall receive a clearing fee of not less than the prescribed minimum rates of the Exchange where the securities or commodities are dealt in; clearing charges on unlisted securities to be by mutual agreement.

12-64
Report 97
Rules of Board—Offices and Employees
➡➡→ *Administered by Department of Member Firms.*
3589

(3) The Exchange will not require the demonstration mentioned above if the clearing organization's split is

(A) on stock commission business, either listed or unlisted,

(i) 40% or better, where Floor brokerage is borne by the clearing organization, or

(ii) 25% or better, where Floor brokerage is borne by the subsidized organization.

(B) on bond commission business, 50% or better to the clearing organization, and if

(C) on primary or secondary stock distributions, the clearing charge is 25% or better, of minimum non-member commission rates on listed securities of similar value.

(D) on principal business in unlisted securities, the clearing charge is not less than the minimum member clearing rates on listed securities of similar value.

(E) on principal business in listed securities, the clearing charge is not less than the prescribed minimum rates, and if

(F) on securities or commodities business on other exchanges, the split or clearing charge, as the case may be, is not less than minimum rates prescribed by such other exchanges.

A non-clearing member organization which has been afforded facilities of a clearing member organization as provided above, may permit its registered employees to perform their regular duties in the board room of the clearing organization, only if such employees of the non-clearing organization wear badges identifying them as employees of the non-clearing organization. It is the duty of the clearing organization to see that this requirement is observed.

Applications for permission to enter into any of the above arrangements should be submitted to the Department of Member Firms.

¶ 2344   Supervisory Analysts

Rule 344. Supervisory analysts required under rule 472 shall be acceptable to, and approved by, the Exchange.

Adopted.
June 18, 1964.

● ● ● *Supplementary Material:*

.10 In order to show evidence of acceptability to the Exchange as a supervisory analyst, a member, allied member or employee may do one of the following:

(1) Before September 30, 1964, submit to the Exchange a statement from a principal of his employing member organization that on July 1, 1964, the applicant was responsible for approval of all or part of said member organization's analytical securities research, either as a member or allied member exercising approval of research under rule 472, or as a supervisory analyst. Alternately, an applicant may submit a statement from a principal of a member organization that for a period of at least

¶ 2344.10—Continued

two years subsequent to January 1, 1960, the applicant held a position within either of the two classes of supervisors mentioned above within this subparagraph.

(2) Present evidence of appropriate experience and pass an Exchange Supervisory Analysts Examination.

(3) Present evidence that he has earned a Chartered Financial Analyst designation, and pass only that portion of the Exchange Supervisory Analysts Examination dealing with Exchange rules on research standards and related matters.

In addition, if not a member, allied member or registered representative, the candidate is subject to Exchange investigation of character and conduct and should submit personal information on Form RE-1 for this purpose.

The Exchange publishes a Study Outline for the Supervisory Analysts Examination. Examinations are requested and given under the procedures described in Para. 2345.15 for registered representative examinations.

¶ 2345   Employees—Registration, Approval, Records, Discipline

Rule 345. (a) No member or member organization shall

(1) permit any person to perform regularly the duties customarily performed by a registered representative, unless such person shall have been registered with and is acceptable to the Exchange, or

(2) employ any registered representative or other person in a nominal position because of the business obtained by such person.

(b) The Exchange may disapprove the employment of any person.

(c) (1) If the Exchange determines that any employee or prospective employee of a member or member organization (1) has violated any provision of the Constitution or of any rule adopted by the Board of Governors, (2) has violated any of his agreements with the Exchange, (3) has made any misstatement to the Exchange, or (4) has been guilty of (i) conduct inconsistent with just and equitable principles of trade, (ii) acts detrimental to the interest or welfare of the Exchange, or (iii) conduct contrary to an established practice of the Exchange, the Exchange may withhold, suspend or withdraw its approval of his employment by a member or member organization; may fine such employee or prospective employee $1,000 for each such violation, or misstatement; and may direct that he be censured. The Exchange shall disclose publicly withdrawals of approval or suspensions of registered representatives, employees or non-registered employees. The Exchange may in its discretion, disclose publicly censures and fines, censures or fines. The total of the fines imposed pursuant to this Rule, for which Board approval is not required, upon any such person at any one time shall not exceed $5,000. However, the Board of Governors may impose fines in excess of the limitations herein set forth.

(2) An accusation, charging a registered representative, non-registered employee or prospective employee with having committed a violation shall be in writing; it shall specify the charge or offense with reasonable

detail and inform the person charged that he is entitled to request an appearance before a panel of the staff of the department bringing the charges. A copy of the charge or charges shall be served upon the person charged by delivering or by mailing it to him at his office address or at his place of residence. The person charged shall have ten days from the date of such service to answer the same, or such further time as the Exchange may deem proper. The answer and request for an appearance shall be in writing, signed by the person charged and filed with the department bringing the charge. A panel composed of three members of the department shall meet to consider the charge or charges. Notice of this hearing shall be sent to the said person charged; he shall be entitled to be present personally to examine and cross-examine all witnesses produced before said panel and also to present such testimony, defense, explanation or witnesses as he may deem proper. If said person charged should decline, refuse or neglect to request a personal appearance at this hearing, the determination of the panel shall be made on the basis of the charges and the written answer, if any, of the person charged. After hearing all witnesses and the person charged, if he desires to be heard, the panel shall determine whether the person charged is guilty of the offense or offenses. Notice of the finding and the penalty imposed by the Exchange and that such person may require a review by the Board of Governors in accordance with Rule 345(d), shall be mailed to said registered representative, non-registered employee or prospective employee in the manner hereinbefore provided.

(d) Any present or prospective employee of a member or member organization may require a review by the Board of Governors of any determination made under this Rule by filing with the Secretary of the Exchange a written demand therefor within 20 days after such determination has been rendered.

Amended
September 17, 1959.
January 24, 1963.
December 3, 1964, effective January 1, 1965.

(*See Rule* 10 [¶ 2010] *for definition of registered representative.*)

● ● ● *Supplementary Material:*

Registration of Employees

.10 **Employees required to be registered.**—(See Rule 345, above, and definition of "registered representative" contained in Rules 9 [¶ 2009] and 10 [¶ 2010]).

.11 **Types of registration and application.**—There are two types of registration, as follows:

(a) *Full registration,* which entitles the registrant to handle any and every type of securities business on behalf of his member firm employer.

(b) *Limited registration* for the sale of mutual fund shares and/or the Monthly Investment Plan. This type of registration is a device for carefully controlled on-the-job training in securities customer service. A limited registrant may solicit or service only transactions involving mutual fund shares and/or Monthly Investment Plans from a securities list specifically provided by his firm for this purpose. He may not even

¶ 2345.11—Continued

transmit from customer to firm an unsolicited order involving other securities. A limited registration may be continued only for a period of up to seven months, during which the trainee must spend at least half his business time preparing to qualify for full registration.

Applications for the employment of a "registered representative" should be submitted to the Department of Member Firms on Form RE-1, copies of which will be supplied by the Department of Member Firms on request. This form should be completed and filed during the early part of the candidate's training period in order that Exchange investigation may be completed by the time the training period is finished.

Applications for the employment of "Limited Registered Representatives" should be accompanied by (1) a detailed description of the methods the firm will use to control the activities of the proposed limited registrant in order to insure his operating within the permissible limits described in the second preceding paragraph above and (2), a statement signed by a partner or holder of voting stock explaining the firm's limited training program in detail.

.12 Members of the Exchange.—An employee who also is a member of the Exchange is not required to qualify as a registered representative. However, every such employment arrangement must be reported to the Department of Member Firms for its information, and may be disapproved by the Exchange.

.13 Termination of employment.—The discharge or termination of employment of any registered representative, together with the reasons therefor, shall be reported promptly to the Department of Member Firms.

.14 Transfer of registered representative.—Prompt notice shall be given to such Department of the transfer of a registered representative to another office.

(*See Rule 342 [¶ 2342] and supplementary material for information re other offices.*)

.15 Acceptability.—In determining a candidate's acceptability for registration the Exchange looks for evidence of:

(1) The integrity of the candidate and his record of high standards of business conduct, as shown in the investigations and observations of his member firm employer, previous employers, educational institutions attended, etc.

(2) His potential ability to perform creditably the duties of a registered representative, as shown by an employment period of specific training for these duties in a member firm office or equivalent other experience in the securities business.

(3) His preparation in the areas of knowledge necessary for a registered representative as demonstrated in an Exchange examination.

Age.—A candidate for registration must be at least 21 years of age.

Training.—The usual requirements for training candidates without previous actual experience are:

(a) for full registration—six months;

(b) for limited registration—three months.

(c) for full registration via limited registration—eight months.

The training period may be reduced or waived by the Exchange if the candidate for registration has had some previous actual experience in the securities business as a principal or employee, or in a closely allied field (such as a bank trust officer).

During the training period, each trainee should undertake actual "on-the-job" training in appropriate departments of the firm, supplemented by organized study to prepare for his registered assignment. Limited registrants must spend at least half their business time in preparation for full registration. The entire training program is under the direct supervision of member firm employers, but a firm may assign its trainees to an approved university or institute course for the formal study part of its training program.

3 5 9 2   Rules of Board—Offices and Employees   6-65
Report 103
➡→ *Administered by Department of Member Firms.*

¶ 2345.15—Continued

Examinations—Near the close of the training period, candidates for registration are normally required to pass a qualifying Exchange examination. One limited registration examination is offered. The work of most registered representatives demands a depth of knowledge of corporate securities especially stocks. The Standard Examination for full registration, through which all but a very few candidates qualify, is designed to meet this demand. It tests on a broad range of securities knowledge, and in depth on corporate stocks. Other full registration examinations may be authorized for persons trading or specializing exclusively or predominantly in bonds. The only such examination currently available is on Municipal Bonds. It covers the entire range of broad basic securities knowledge but emphasizes depth on municipal bonds rather than corporate securities. Similar special examinations may be arranged for persons whose principal work is in unusual fields.

The Exchange and the NASD conduct a joint examination program for the candidates for registration with both organizations. Under this program, the Exchange accepts the NASD Examination in partial fulfillment of its own examination requirement, adding to it an NYSE Section and scoring candidates on their answers to the combined total. In combining, the Exchange will accept qualifying NASD scores made within one year of the end of the required training period. However, if a candidate fails to receive a passing grade on this combined basis, any re-examination will include both the NYSE and the NASD Sections. A Study Outline for Registration Examinations describes the qualifying examinations in detail.

Firms must apply for examination of candidates on the "Examination Request" Form supplied for this purpose. All examinations are administered by the NASD in their network of test centers. The regularly scheduled sessions will accommodate most candidates. Special sessions can be arranged for foreign examinations and in the United States to meet extraordinary circumstances.

Training Courses.—Many member firms have organized comprehensive internal training programs. The Exchange publishes a suggested 26-week training program for general use. The following Exchange trainee programs are recommended for guided study of a major part of a complete formal study plan. The Exchange will waive examination for candidates who have started one of the following programs before January 1, 1962 and have satisfactorily completed both parts with a grade of 75 or equivalent before December 31, 1963.

NEW YORK CITY—New York Institute of Finance: Work of the Stock Exchange and Brokerage Office Procedures; Security Analysis, I and II.

New York University, Graduate School of Business Administration: In. 254, Organized Security Markets; In. 241-242, Investment Analysis; Advanced Security Analysis.

City College of New York, Baruch School of Business and Public Admin.: No. 166, The Securities Markets; In. 163-263, Principles of Investment; Advanced Investment Analysis.

PHILADELPHIA—Univ. of Pennsylvania, Wharton School of Finance and Commerce: NYSE Program: Securities Markets, Securities and Their Analysis.

BOSTON—Boston University: NYSE Program: Stock Exchange and Brokerage House Operations, Investment Analysis.

CHICAGO—Northwestern University: Special IBA and NYSE Program: Stock Exchange Operations; Fundamentals of Investment Banking.

¶ **2345.15   Rule 345**   © 1965, Commerce Clearing House, Inc.

LOS ANGELES—Los Angeles Institute of Finance: Securities Market Practices; Investment Analysis; given in cooperation with the University of California in Los Angeles.

MIAMI—University of Miami, Finance Department: NYSE Program for Registered Representative Trainees.

ST. LOUIS—St. Louis University, School of Commerce and Finance: Institute of Finance: (a) Security Markets and Procedures; (b) Security Analysis.

SAN FRANCISCO—University of California, Business Administration Extension: NYSE Program for Registered Representative Trainees.

CORRESPONDENCE—New York Institute of Finance: Work of the Stock Exchange and Brokerage Office Procedure; Investment and Security Analysis.

University of Wisconsin, University Extension Division (partial program only): Fundamentals of Investment Banking (Commerce A67), presented in cooperation with IBA.

If the candidate is advanced in years, or suffers from a physical infirmity or health condition which might be seriously aggravated by a required examination, the examination requirement may be waived at the discretion of the Exchange, provided the firm certifies that the candidate has been adequately trained.

.16 Fee.—Each application for the employment of any individual as a registered employee shall be subject to a fee of $35. A reexamination fee of $10 is charged (a) for reexamination not less than 30 days after a failure, (b) in the event that a candidate does not appear for a scheduled examination without notifying the examiner in advance.

.17 Agreements.—Each prospective registered representative shall sign the following statements:

(A) "I authorize and request any and all of my former employers and any other person to furnish to the New York Stock Exchange any information they may have concerning my character, ability, business activities and reputation, together with, in the case of former employers, a history of my employment by them and the reasons for the termination thereof; and I hereby release each such employer and each such other person from any and all liability of whatsoever nature by reason of furnishing such information to the New York Stock Exchange.

(B) I authorize the New York Stock Exchange to make available to any prospective employer, or to any Federal, State or Municipal agency, any information it may have concerning me, and I hereby release the New York Stock Exchange from any and all liability of whatsoever nature by reason of furnishing such information.

(C) I agree that the decision of the New York Stock Exchange as to the results of any examinations it may require me to take will be accepted by me as final, and that the approval of my employment may be denied or, if granted, may be suspended or withdrawn by the Exchange at any time if, in the opinion of the Exchange, I have

(1) made any misstatements in this application or in any supplemental information given by me relating thereto;

(2) violated any of my agreements herein contained;

(3) been guilty of conduct or proceeding inconsistent with just and equitable principles of trade; or

¶ 2345.17—Continued

(4) been guilty of any act detrimental to the interest and welfare of the Exchange.

(D) I have read the Constitution and Rules of the Board of Governors of the New York Stock Exchange and, if approved, I hereby pledge myself to abide by the Constitution and Rules of the Board of Governors of the New York Stock Exchange as the same have been or shall be from time to time amended, and by all rules and regulations adopted pursuant to the Constitution, and by all practices of the Exchange."

Further, each registered representative, in consideration of the Exchange's approving his application, shall sign the following statements:

(A) "That I will not guarantee to my employer or to any other creditor carrying a customer's account, the payment of the debit balance in such account, without the prior written consent of the Exchange.

(B) That I will not guarantee any customer against loss in his account or in any way represent to any customer that I or my employer will guarantee the customer against such losses.

(C) That I will not take or receive, directly or indirectly, a share in the profits of any customer's account, or share in any losses sustained in any such account.

(D) That I will not make a cash or margin transaction or maintain a cash or margin account in securities or commodities, or have any direct or indirect financial interest in such a transaction or account, except with a member organization or with a bank. I understand and agree that no such transaction may be effected and no such account may be maintained without the prior consent of my member or member organization employer, and that except for Monthly Investment Plan transactions such employer must receive promptly, directly from the carrying member organization or bank, duplicate copies of all confirmations and statements relating to such transactions or account. I further understand and agree that I shall receive no compensation for commissions or profits earned on any transaction or account in which I have a direct or indirect financial interest, except with the approval of my employer and in accordance with the rules of the Exchange.

(E) That I will not rebate, directly or indirectly, to any person, firm or corporation any part of the compensation I receive as a registered representative, and I will not pay such compensation, or any part thereof, directly or indirectly, to any person, firm or corporation, as a bonus, commission, fee or other consideration for business sought or procured for me or for any member of the Exchange, firm or corporation registered thereon.

(F) That at any time, upon the request of the Department of Member Firms, or of any Committee or other Department of the New York Stock Exchange, I will appear before such Committee or Department and give evidence upon any subject under investigation by any such Committee or Department, and that I will produce, upon request of the Exchange, all of my records or documents relative to any inquiry being made by the Exchange.

¶ **2345.17   Rule 345**   © 1965, Commerce Clearing House, Inc.

(G) I understand that any changes in compensation in any form, or additional compensation in any form, may be subject to disapproval by the New York Stock Exchange, and that I may not be compensated for business done by or through my employer after the termination of my employment except as may be permitted by the Exchange.

(H) I agree that I will not take, accept, or receive, directly or indirectly, from any person, firm, corporation or association, other than the member or member organization with whom I am registered, compensation of any nature, as a bonus, commission, fee, gratuity or other consideration, in connection with any securities or commodities transaction or transactions, except with the prior written consent of the Exchange.

(I) I will notify the Department of Member Firms promptly if, during the tenure of my employment by the applicant member or organization herein named, I become involved in any litigation or if any judgments are found against me; or if my registration or license to sell or deal in securities or to function as an investment advisor is ever refused, suspended or revoked; or if I become enjoined, temporarily or otherwise, from selling or dealing in securities or from functioning as an investment advisor; or if I am arrested, summoned, arraigned or indicted for a criminal offense; or if I become involved in bankruptcy proceedings.

(J) I agree that any controversy between me and any member or member organization arising out of my employment or the termination of my employment by and with such member or member organization shall be settled by arbitration at the instance of any such party in accordance with the Constitution and rules then obtaining of the New York Stock Exchange."

General Information Regarding Employees

.18 Power of Exchange over all employees.—The Exchange may require at any time that the name, terms of employment, and actual duties of any person employed by a member or member organization shall be stated to the Exchange, together with such other information with respect to such employee as it may deem requisite.

.19 Investigations and Records.—Members and member organizations should make a thorough inquiry into the previous record and reputation of persons whom they contemplate employing. The background and reputation check should, whenever possible, include at least personal conversations with all employers during the previous 3 years and verification before or promptly after employment of business history for the previous 10 years. Further inquiry should be made where appropriate in the light of background information developed, the position for which the person is being considered, or other circumstances. In the case of proposed registered representatives the Exchange makes the 10-year verification check as a service to member firms, but the check of employers during the last 3 years is a member firm responsibility. Verifying and investigation should be done by a partner or voting stockholder, or by an authorized person under their supervision.

Members and member organizations should obtain at the time of employment, and keep on file during employment and for a minimum period of 3 years after termination of employment, at least the following information concerning all personnel whether registered with the Exchange or not: (1) Name; (2) home address; (3) social security number; (4) starting date of employment or other association with member organization; (5) date of birth; (6) title or position; (7) recent photograph; (8) signature; (9) the educational institutions attended and whether or not graduated therefrom; (10) a complete consecutive statement of all business connections for at least the preceding ten years, including reason for leaving each prior employment, and whether employment was part-time or full-time, with all time accounted for including periods of unemployment and residence while unemployed; (11) a record of any arrests, indictments or convictions for any felony or any misdemeanor except minor traffic offenses; (12) a record of any other name or names by which he has been known or which he has used; (13) a record of any previous or current surety bonds under which applicant may have been covered. Also whether such a bond has ever been denied, revoked, or surety paid because of applicant; (14) a record of any denial of membership or registration, and of any disciplinary action taken, or sanction imposed, upon him by any federal or state agency, or by any national securities exchange or national securities association, including any finding that he was a cause of any disciplinary action or had violated any law; (15) a record of any denial, suspension, expulsion or revocation of membership or registration of any member, broker or dealer with which he was associated in any capacity when such action was taken; (16) a record of any permanent or temporary injunction entered against him or any member, broker or dealer with which he was associated in any capacity at the time such injunction was entered.

The above record-keeping requirements, when signed by an authorized person, include compliance with Rule 17a-3 and 17a-4 under the Securities Exchange Act of 1934.

If any employee is registered with the Exchange, a duplicate copy of the registration application form signed by an authorized person shall satisfy all the record-keeping requirements of this paragraph except the recent photograph.

Amendment.
July 15, 1965.

¶ 2346   Employees—Fixed Duties

Rule 346.   Every registered representative of a member or member organization shall devote his entire time during business hours to the business of the member or member organization employing him, and shall not at any time be engaged in any other business or be employed by any other corpora-

¶ 2346—Continued

tion, firm or individual, or serve as an officer or director of another corporation without the prior consent of the Exchange.

No non-registered employee, without the prior approval of the Exchange, shall be engaged at any time in any other financial or securities or kindred business, or be connected by employment or otherwise (in any but a purely part-time clerical capacity which does not conflict with his normal duties and full-time hours of employment with his regular member organization employer) with any other corporation, firm or individual engaged in such business. For the purpose of this Rule, investment companies, investment trust management companies and investment advisors shall be considered to be engaged in the securities business. (See ¶ 2350)

● ● ● *Supplementary Material:*

.10 Writing and Broadcasting.—Consent of the Exchange will not be required for outside writing or broadcasting activities by members, allied members and employees of member organizations, when all of the following conditions are met:

(1) The total number of articles or appearances by any one such person published or broadcast in any calendar year does not exceed four, or the media is in the nature of a trade publication addressed primarily to persons or groups within the securities industry (such as the Analysts Journal or the Bulletin of the Association of Customers' Brokers).

(2) The subject is in the field of finance, any compensation is nominal, and the activity does not interfere with the performance of full-time duties for the member organizations.

(3) A member or member organization approves the activity and assumes responsibility for adherence to Exchange standards in articles or broadcasting scripts prepared by personnel of that organization, and for information supplied for such articles or broadcasts; a general partner or a holder of voting stock of the member organization assigned responsibilities in this area approves material prepared by an employee in advance of publication or broadcast.

(4) The author is identified with the material, and it is made clear that the author is associated with a securities firm.

(5) The article or broadcast is broadly educational.

The term "outside writing and broadcasting activities" refers to activities other than those engaged in by the member, allied member or employee of the member organization in the conduct of his or its securities business.

.11 Permission for Writing and Broadcasting Activities.—The Exchange may grant permission in individual cases for outside writing or broadcasting activities not meeting all conditions in ¶ 2346.10 above, upon application, where conditions in sub-paragraphs (2), (3) and (4) of ¶ 2346.10 are met, plus the following:

(1) The Exchange is satisfied that the nature of the commentary, the media and the audience are such that the author or broadcaster will continue to be identified in the public eye primarily as a member of the securities community, and will not become generally identified as a writer or broadcaster;

(2) in cases where the nature of the writing or broadcasting ceases to be broadly educational and tends more toward current commentary:

(a) in the case of broadcasts, no recommendations are made to buy, sell, switch or retain investments, whether labeled as such or not;

(b) in the case of articles, where recommendations may be made, they are clearly identified as those of the author or of the author's member organization, whose name shall be stated in that case;

(c) the Exchange is satisfied with the general format and purpose of the article or broadcast.

.12 Speaking and Teaching Activities.—Approval of the Exchange will not be required for single talks, courses or lecture series on investment subjects given by members, allied members and other member organization personnel as outside speaking activities before community groups and institutions, when all of the following conditions are met:

(1) Consent for each such talk or lecture has been given by a general partner or holder of voting stock, or by a branch office manager acting for the partner or voting stockholder in charge of speaking activities for the member organization;

(2) the member organization assumes responsibility for the general content of each talk or lecture and the speaker's educational approach;

(3) in the case of talks and lectures, no more than $25.00 is to be charged as admission, registration or tuition, or is to be paid to the speaker as a total fee by the sponsoring organization; in the case of courses at accredited colleges or universities, the charges and payment to the teacher are not more than the educational institution's normal fees and payments.

The term "outside speaking activities" refers to activities other than those engaged in by the member, allied member or employee of the organization in the conduct of *his or its* securities business.

12-64
Report 96   Rules of Board—Offices and Employees   **3597-3**
⟫⟫→ *Administered by Department of Member Firms.*

.13 Permission for Speaking Activities.—In individual cases of outside speaking activities where fees may be greater than specified in sub-paragraph (3) of paragraph above, specific approval of the Exchange will be required.

.14 Standards and Guideposts.—All outside writing, broadcasting or speaking activities by members, allied members and other member organization personnel, whether requiring specific Exchange approval or not, must comply with standards established in Rules 471, 472 and 473 and in Supplementary Material to these Rules. Copy and clippings for articles, radio-TV scripts, and a log of all speaking engagements must be retained by the member or member organization for three years for delivery to the Exchange on request.

.15 Director or Officer.—Consent of the Exchange will not be required for the following activities, provided the member or member organization employer wishes to have the employee so serve and the activities do not interfere with the performance of full-time duties of the registered representative:

(1) Director of up to three corporations not in the securities business, including chairman of the board of directors of one corporation if not chief executive officer.

(2) Director of a bank or trust company in compliance with state and federal banking laws.

(3) Officer of an operating company not in the securities business, if duties are nominal and non-operational.

The Exchange will consider on their individual circumstances any requests for outside activities which do not conform with the above conditions.

.16 Leave of Absence.—Consent of the Exchange will not be required for leave of absence, provided all of the following conditions are met:

(1) The member or member organization employer retains a written record of the leave.

(2) The registered representative is not physically present at any office of his employer, and does not act as a registered representative of his employer.

(3) The registered representative does not use the leave to engage in any other business, or be employed by any other corporation, firm or individual, or serve as a partner, officer or director of any other partnership or corporation.

(4) The total time on leave of absence does not exceed one year.

(5) The registered representative receives no compensation from the firm other than maintenance of fringe benefits such as medical insurance, etc.

The Exchange will consider on their individual circumstances any requests for leave of absence which do not conform with the above conditions.

¶ 2347   Compensation
Rule 347. (a) Pursuant to Section 1 of Article XV of the Constitution [¶ 1701], registered representatives may be compensated as follows:

(1) registered representatives—on a salary or a commission basis,

(2) branch office managers—on a salary or a commission basis; also, with the prior approval of the Exchange, they may receive a percentage of the net profit of the branch office,

¶ 2347—Continued

(3) a registered representative who is also head of a department of the organization—may, with prior approval of the Exchange, receive a percentage of the net profit of his department, and

(4) bonuses—registered representatives may participate, with the prior approval of the Exchange, in bonus distributions.

Controversies as to employment or termination of employment

(b) Any controversy between a registered representative and any member or member organization arising out of the employment or termination of employment of such registered representative by and with such member or member organization shall be settled by arbitration, at the instance of any such party, in accordance with the arbitration procedure prescribed elsewhere in these rules.

Rule 347(b) adopted.
April 17, 1958.

¶ 2348   Registered Representative—Limit of Credit on Own Accounts

Rule 348. Compensation to a registered representative, based on commissions and profits earned by his employer on accounts accredited to such registered representative, may include recognition on the regular basis for commissions and profits earned on accounts in which he has a personal interest, but only to the extent that commissions and profits on such accounts in which he has a personal interest shall not exceed 10% of the total commissions and profits on all other accounts accredited to such registered representative, computed on an annual basis.

Adopted.
January 19, 1956, effective February 13, 1956.

● ● ● *Supplementary Material:*

.10 **Compensation.**—Any plan for an employee to share in the profits of a department, branch office or the member firm as a whole requires prior written consent of the Exchange.

A registered representative who has retired and is not otherwise employed or engaged in business may be paid a percentage of commissions on "live" mutual fund contracts and "live" M. I. P. contracts.

On request of a member or member organization, the Exchange may permit payments to a widow or orphan of a deceased registered representative either in a lump sum or in fixed amounts over a reasonable period of time. In either case the proposed payments should be consistent with the length of service and average earnings of the deceased registered representative.

¶ 2349   Representatives of the Press

Rule 349. No member, member organization or participant therein, shall employ any representative of the press for the purpose of obtaining advance or confidential information.

¶ 2350   Compensation or Gratuities to Employees of Others

Rule 350.   (a) No member, allied member, member organization or employee thereof shall:

(1) employ or compensate for services rendered, except as specified below or with the prior written consent of the employer and the Exchange, or

(2) give any gratuity in excess of $25 per person per year to any principal, officer, or employee of the Exchange or its subsidiaries, another member or member organization, financial institution, news or financial information media, or non-member broker or dealer in securities, commodities, or money instruments.

A gift of any kind is considered a gratuity.

(b) Compensation for services rendered of up to $100 per person per year may be paid with the prior written consent of the employer, but not of the Exchange, to operations employees of the following types:

(1) A telephone clerk on the NYSE Floor who provides courtesy telephone relief to a member's clerk, or handles such a member's orders over the member's own wire.

(2) Employees who make out commission bills or prepare Exchange reports for members.

(3) A specialist's Floor clerk who maintains records for a specialist other than his employer, or provides courtesy relief to another specialist's clerk.

(4) When the service rendered by the employee exceeds that which the primary employer is obligated to furnish,

(a) A telephone clerk who handles a member's orders transmitted over the wire of the clerk's employer.

(b) Odd-lot clerks assigned to assist an Associate Odd-lot Broker.

(c) A telephone clerk who handles orders directed by the clerk's employer to the member who receives them.

(d) Operations employees of a carrying or clearing firm assigned by their employer to give a major amount of service to a member or member organization introducing accounts to, clearing through, corresponding with, or making an office with the employer firm.

(c) *Records* shall be retained for at least three years of all such gratuities and compensation for inspection by Exchange examiners.

Amendment.
April 16, 1964.

● ● ● *Supplementary Material:*

.10 When close relatives work in different financial organizations, gifts arising from the family relationship are not considered subject to Rule 350.

Employment of or gratuities to personnel working on the Floor of other exchanges and approved by the other exchange under a rule similar to Rule 350 are not considered subject to Rule 350.

New York Stock Exchange Guide   **Rule 350   ¶ 2350.10**

3 6 0 0   Rules of Board—Offices and Employees   8-65
Report 106
➢➢➢ *Administered by Department of Member Firms.*

¶ 2350.10—Continued

Requests for Exchange consent under Section a(1) of this Rule should be addressed as follows, and sent at least 10 days in advance of the proposed date of employment:

(A) Exchange employees—Attention: Personnel Department

(B) Floor employees of other members or member organizations—Attention: Floor Department

(C) All Others—Attention: Department of Member Firms

Consents under a(1) or (b), above, should include name and position of proposed employee, amount of proposed compensation, name and title of person giving consent for employer, and nature of proposed duties of employee. Approvals under a(1) will not be given in December.

Requests for exceptions to Section a(2) above will be considered only under very unusual circumstances.

In general, approval to employ an Exchange employee outside of the hours of regular employment by the Exchange will be limited to employment of a routine or clerical nature. Approval will not be given for the employment of an Exchange employee in an advisory or professional capacity with reference to Exchange operations or policies.

When the Exchange has granted permission for part-time employment of an employee of the Exchange or of another member or member organization no approval is required for a subsequent gratuity or bonus to such person provided it is in proportion to gratuities given full-time employees of the employing organization.

[The next page is 3611.]

Private Wire and Other Connections

*(Rules and Policies Administered by the
Department of Member Firms.)*

**¶ 2356   Discontinuance by Exchange of Any Means
of Communication**

Rule 356. The Exchange may require at any time the discontinuance of any means of communication whatsoever in or between the offices of a member or member organization. The Exchange may also deprive any member or member organization of the privilege of using any public telephone or means of communication installed by the Exchange for the use of members and member organizations.

(See Rule 36 [¶ 2036] in connection with wires to Floor of the Exchange.)

Amendments.
September 20, 1961.

¶ 2357   Retention of Communications

Rule 357. Members and member organizations shall keep on file, for at least two weeks, all communications sent and received over private wires, for possible inspection by the Exchange.

(See also S. E. C. Regulation § 240.17a-4 [¶ 4584].)

¶ 2358   Wire Costs for Joint Account Arbitrage

Rule 358. When wire costs are borne by a member or member organization and:

   (1) The wire is used exclusively for joint account arbitrage, the entire cost of such wire shall be charged to the joint account;

   (2) the wire is used for joint account arbitrage and also for other business, the member or member organization shall ascertain the proportionate share of the cost of the wire applicable to the joint account and shall charge such proportionate share to the joint account.

(See Rule 369(3)(E) [¶ 2369], re cost of transmitting orders as prohibited arrangement.)

(See ¶ 2381.19 for commissions to be charged on joint account arbitrage.)

¶ 2359   Communications with Non-members

Rule 359. (a) No member or member organization shall establish or maintain any private wire connection, private radio, television or wireless system, between his or its offices and the office of any non-member which is to be used for the transmission of the Exchange's continuous quotations unless the non-member has entered into an agreement in form prescribed by the Exchange for the protection of the Exchange's interest in its quotations.

   (b) Notification regarding a private means of communication with a non-member and the signed agreement, when necessary, shall be submitted to the Department of Member Firms. This notification, by a member or allied member, may be in form supplied by the Exchange or in letter form.

¶ 2359   Continued

(c) Each member or member organization shall submit annually to the Department of Member Firms a list of non-members with whom private means of communication are maintained.

Amendments.
Adopted September 20, 1961.

● ● ● *Supplementary Material:*

Wire and Other Connections—Ticker Service

.10 **Sharing cost of wires.**—A private wire connection between the offices of a member or member organization and a non-member shall not be used by a non-member to effect a through connection between the non-member and (1) a branch office of said non-member or (2) another non-member unless the non-member contributes towards the cost of such private wire connection in proportion to his use thereof, with a minimum of 10%. Commission or principal business received from the non-member by the member or member organization may not be regarded as payment by the non-member of his proportionate use of the private wire connection. In computing the proportionate use attributable to the non-member, the idle as well as the used time on the wire shall be considered.

Where a non-member requests a member organization to obtain or transmit quotations or orders in securities between the non-member and other organizations over a wire paid for by the member organization and the member organization, instead of effecting the transactions, gives up the name of the non-member who confirms directly with the other party, the member organizations must make a per share charge in connection with the transactions.

(*See Rule* 369(7) [¶ 2369].)

.11 Telephone listings.—A member or member organization may not permit a non-member to list the telephone number of a line terminating in a switchboard of the member or member organization in any type of telephone directory under the name of the non-member.

.12 Ticker service.—Applications by non-members for ticker service should be addressed to the New York Stock Exchange. The Exchange may require letters of recommendation of the applicant from two members or member organizations.

.13 Prohibited wire connections.—No member, allied member or member organization may utilize any private or public wire connection or any other means of communication whatsoever to transmit any business directly or indirectly with or for:

(1) Any illicit or illegal organization;

(2) any organization, firm or individual making a practice of dealing on differences in market quotations; or

(3) any organization, firm or individual engaged in purchasing or selling securities for customers and making a practice of taking the side of the market opposite to the side taken by the customers.

.14 Wire costs.—A New York member organization may pay for the cost of transmitting to New York orders for the account of another member organization or its customers provided

(1) Agreements covering such arrangements are submitted to the Exchange for approval, and

(2) the member making the payment

(A) executes the orders or causes them to be executed, and

(B) clears the business itself, and

(C) charges for such services the minimum rates for execution and clearance where a principal is not given up, as prescribed in Section 2(b) or 3(b) of Article XV [¶ 1702, 1703], or

(3) in the event the business of such out-of-town organization is cleared by mail through the facilities of the Stock Clearing Corporation, the member organization paying for the wire

(A) executes the orders or causes them to be executed, and

(B) charges each correspondent served by such wire or wires

(i) (for execution)—the minimum rates prescribed for execution where a principal is given up, as set forth in Section 2(c) or 3(c) of Article XV [¶ 1702, 1703], and

(ii) (for the service of transmittal and report)—additional fees to cover the cost of the wire.

(*See Rule* 369(7) [¶ 2369].)

.16 Give-ups on wire business—Time for effecting.—See ¶ 2411.70.

[The next page is 3625.]

Commissions

*(Rules and Policies Administered by the
Department of Member Firms.)*

¶ 2365   Collecting Commissions on "Give-ups"

Rule 365. (a) When a member or member organization executes an order for the purchase or sale of a security admitted to dealings on the Exchange and gives up another member or member organization the responsibility for collecting the full commission prescribed by Article XV [¶ 1701-1712] of the Constitution shall rest with the member or member organization clearing the transaction.

(b) When two members of the Exchange maintain a joint trading account, or where a joint specialist trading account is operated between two members and/or member organizations, the member or member organization effecting the Floor execution for such an account has performed a Floor brokerage service for such account and the executing member or member organization must charge the joint account with the Floor brokerage or, if the transaction has been cleared as well as executed, with the clearance commission.

¶ 2366   Transactions Made Outside of United States or Canada

Rule 366. (a) When a member or member organization accepts an order, from a customer within the United States or Canada, for the purchase or sale of a security admitted to dealings on the Exchange and causes the same to be executed in a market outside the United States or Canada, during the time the Exchange is open for the transaction of business, such member or member organization shall charge and collect, in addition to any commission payable to the party or parties executing such order in said market, a sum not less than the minimum member or non-member commission rate, as the case may be, prescribed by Article XV [¶ 1701-1712] of the Constitution.

(b) When a member or member organization accepts and clears, for a customer within the United States or Canada, a transaction arising from a purchase or sale of a security admitted to dealings on this Exchange effected by said customer in a market outside the United States or Canada, during the time the Exchange is open for the transaction of business, such member, or member organization shall charge and collect, in addition to any commission payable to the party or parties executing such transaction, a sum not less than the minimum member or non-member commission rate, as the case may be, prescribed by Article XV [¶ 1701-1712] of the Constitution.

Amendment.
November 19, 1964.

¶ 2367   Deliveries on Privileges

Rule 367. When securities are received or delivered for an allied member or a non-member on a privilege, full non-member commissions shall be charged and collected.

¶ 2368   Clearing Charges

Rule 368. Except as provided in Section 4 of Article XV [¶ 1704] of the Constitution, when a member or member organization receives and delivers securities for another member or member organization, the clearing charge for such service may be as mutually agreed, provided that such charge is based upon a stipulated sum of money for each 100 shares of stock or $1,000 principal amount of bonds.

¶ 2369   Prohibited Arrangements, etc.

Rule 369. While not in any way limiting the meaning or effect of Section 1, Article XV [¶ 1701] of the Constitution, prohibiting rebates of commission, a member, allied member or member organization may not make any of the following arrangements, agreements or payments:

Unusual interest rates or money advances

(1) An arrangement with a customer whereby special and unusual rates of interest are given or money advanced upon unusual terms for the purpose of obtaining or retaining business.

Interest on short sales

(2) An allowance of interest on short sales at more than the loan market rates for the stocks borrowed or used for such short sales.

Stamp taxes, etc.

(3) The assumption, by agreement or otherwise, of any part of

(A) any stamp tax imposed by the United States or any State on transfers, sales, loans, or borrowings for the account of a customer;

(B) any charge upon the sale of securities upon the Exchange because of the registration fee imposed upon national securities exchanges by the Securities Act of 1934;

(C) any commission payable upon transactions in commodities or securities dealt in upon another exchange;

Bank charges for handling securities

(D) any charge made by a bank or trust company for such services as handling a draft with securities attached which is deposited with them for collection; safekeeping of securities for the account of a customer; receiving securities with or without draft attached, against payment or against receipt; delivering securities against receipt or payment; effecting transfer, registration, subscription, or exchange of securities, *provided* that if the amount of such charge on all transactions for one customer on a single day is less than $1.00, the charge may be waived by the member or member organization;

Office expenses of non-members

(E) any expense pertaining to the office of a non-member except the cost of maintaining a private means of communication with the non-member provided that such cost is not in contravention to the provisions of ¶ 2359.10 Private Wires and Other Connections;

Statistical and investment advisory services

(F) any expense for services rendered to a non-member which is in contravention to the provisions of Statistical and Investment Advisory Services (¶ 2440A);

(G) any charge for shipping securities to or from a non-member or correspondent which is in contravention to the provisions of paragraph (c), Shipping and Postage Charges (¶ 2381.11).

Contracts of a customer

(4) The assumption of a contract made for a customer after a loss has been established and ascertained unless (A) the contract was made in error or (B) the consent of the Exchange has been obtained.

(See Rule 411 [¶ 2411] re Erroneous Reports.)

Office space arrangements

(5) An arrangement involving the furnishing of office space to members, member organizations and non-members which is in contravention to the provisions of Rule 343 [¶ 2343] and allied material, Office Space Arrangements.

Gratuities to employees

(6) The payment of any gratuity to any employee of the (A) Exchange or subsidiary thereof, (B) a member or member organization, (C) a non-member which is in contravention to the provisions of Rule 350 [¶ 2350] and allied material, Employees.

Cost of transmitting orders

(7) The payment of the cost of transmitting orders for the account of another member or member organization or non-member or his or its customers which is in contravention to the provisions of ¶ 2359.10 and 2359.14, Private Wire and Other Connections.

¶ 2370   Temporary Absence from the Floor

Rule 370. Commissions must be charged and collected on purchases and sales of securities dealt in upon the Exchange under all circumstances. This includes orders executed for other individual members during even a temporary absence from the crowd.

¶ 2371   Reverse Operations

Rule 371. In respect of transactions in bonds and those stocks which are exempt from the provisions of Rule 394 [¶ 2394], the difference between the purchase and sale prices, where a reverse operation is made upon the Exchange at or about the same time, must be not less than the commission prescribed by Article XV [¶ 1701-1712] of the Constitution on such a purchase or sale.

● ● ● *Supplementary Material:*

.10 "Reverse operation" for member's own account.—When the "over-the-counter" transaction is made by a member or member organization with an allied member or a non-member, and a reverse operation is made upon the

Exchange at or about the same time, the commission charged should be the full non-member commission.

When such "over-the-counter" transaction and reverse operation is made by a member or member organization with another member, or member organization, the commission charged should be the clearance commission.

¶ 2372   "Bunched" Orders

Rule 372. No member or member organization shall, without charging the required commission, execute "bunched" orders, i.e., a combination of orders accepted from several principals, whether members, allied members, or non-members, and executed as one lot.

(See Information Regarding Conduct of Accounts for information re bunching odd-lot orders [¶ 2411.10].)

● ● ● *Supplementary Material:*

.10 With reference to the above Rule, when a member organization executes an order for any of the principals specified therein and, in accordance with instructions received from such principal, sends two or more confirmations, each covering a portion of the total amount of the shares or bonds which the order represents, each confirmation is regarded as covering a separate order for the amount of securities which it represents and requires that the member organization charge the prescribed minimum commission on each portion, notwithstanding the fact that only one execution was actually effected on the Floor.

The same principle applies where a single order is entered by a trustee with instructions to apportion the securities among two or more trust accounts and therefore the member organization shall charge the prescribed minimum commission on each portion covered by a confirmation.

¶ 2373   Investment Trust Units

Rule 373. On transactions involving the purchase or sale of Investment Trust Units, the minimum commission prescribed by Article XV [¶ 1701-1712] of the Constitution shall be charged on each component part of the Unit.

¶ 2374   Joint Accounts with Non-Members

Rule 374. Full non-member rates of commission shall be charged on all transactions in joint accounts in listed securities, in which allied members or non-members are interested, when such accounts are carried on the books of a member organization whether the transactions in question take place on the Floor or "over the counter".

¶ 2375   Missing the Market

Rule 375. A member or member organization who has accepted an order for execution and who, by reason of neglect to execute the order or otherwise, takes or supplies for his or its own account, the securities named therein is not acting as a broker and shall not charge a commission, without the knowledge and consent of the customer.

¶ **2372   Rule 372**   © 1964, Commerce Clearing House, Inc.

¶ 2376   Payment of Give-Up Commissions

Rule 376. Unless otherwise agreed by the parties concerned, all payments between members on account of commissions on business when a principal is given up shall be made through Stock Clearing Corporation as prescribed by its By-Laws and Rules.

¶ 2377   Special Commission

Rule 377. Unless otherwise determined by the Exchange, the following special commission rates are fixed pursuant to Section 3 of Article XV [¶ 1703] of the Constitution:

U. S. Government bonds, etc.

(1) On bonds of the United States, Puerto Rico, Philippine Islands and States, territories and municipalities therein, and upon obligations of any international authorities in which the United States is a participant, the rate of commission to members, allied members, or non-members shall be such rate as may be mutually agreed upon.

Amendments.
March 7, 1963.

Short term bonds—Maturity in less than six months

(2) On bonds which will mature in less than six months, or are to be redeemed, pursuant to call or otherwise, in less than six months, and are selling at not less than 96% and not more than 110% of their redemption price, and on bonds which may be specifically designated under this paragraph by the Board of Governors, the rate of commission to members, allied members or non-members shall be such rate as may be mutually agreed upon.

Short term bonds—Maturity in six months to five years

(3) On bonds which will mature in not less than six months and not more than five years, or are to be redeemed, pursuant to call or otherwise, in not less than six months and not more than twelve months, and are selling at not less than 96% and not more than 110% of their redemption price, and on bonds which may be specifically designated under this paragraph by the Board of Governors, the rate of commission per $1,000 of principal shall be not less than the following:

	Rate per $1,000 of Principal
To allied members and non-members	$1.25
To members when a principal is not given up	0.625
To members when a principal is given up	0.375

Other bonds

(4) On bonds not included in (1), (2) or (3) above, the rate of commission shall not be less than that prescribed by Section 3 of Article XV [¶ 1703] of the Constitution.

Amendments.
March 29, 1956, effective April 2, 1956.

● ● ● *Supplementary Material:*

.10 Commission on bonds selling "flat."—On bonds, referred to in paragraphs (2) and (3) above which are traded in "flat," the regular rates of commission called for in Section 3(a), (b) and (c) of Article XV [¶ 1703] shall apply.

¶ 2378   Special Commission—Called Stocks

Rule 378. The following special commission rates are fixed pursuant to paragraph (f) of Section 2 of Article XV [¶ 1702] of the Constitution:

(1) On stocks which pursuant to call or otherwise are to be redeemed within twelve months, selling at not less than 96% and not more than 110% of the redemption price, the rate of commission to members, allied members, or non-members shall be such rate as may be mutually agreed upon.

(2) On such stocks selling below 96% or above 110% of the redemption price, the rates of commission to members, allied members or non-members shall be the rates prescribed in Section 2 of Article XV [¶ 1702] of the Constitution, unless the Board of Governors shall have determined special rates on any of such securities.

¶ 2379   Collection of Over-Riding Commission, Service Charge or Fee

Rule 379. No member or member organization shall undertake to collect for the account of a non-member an over-riding commission, service charge or other fee.

Amendments.
April 9, 1953, effective June 1, 1953.

● ● ● *Supplementary Material:*

.10   **Exception to rule.**—The Board of Governors has determined that Rule 379, above, shall not apply to over-riding commissions, service charges or other fees related exclusively to commodity transactions, where approved by the appropriate commodity exchanges, provided:

(1) The customer has given written authorization indicating:

(A) The precise charges which are to be made, and

(B) knowledge on the customer's part that such charges are over and above, and not a part of, the charge of the member organization carrying the account;

(2) the charge so made and collected for the non-member is shown separately as such on the confirmation of every transaction; and

(3) the customer recognizes in writing that the non-member for whom the fee is to be collected is the agent of the customer and not the agent of the member organization.

¶ 2380   Special Commission Rates—Rights and Warrants Selling Below 50¢

Rule 380. Pursuant to Section 5 of Article XV [¶ 1705] unless otherwise determined by the Board of Governors, on rights and warrants which are admitted to dealings upon the Exchange, whether on an issued or when issued basis, and which are selling below 50¢ per right or warrant, the following special rates of commission shall apply:

(1) On business for non-members or allied members, including joint account transactions in which any such person is interested, the commission shall be as mutually agreed.

¶ 2378   Rule 378

(2) On business for members of the Exchange when a principal is not given up:

Price	Rate per Share (cents)
1/256	.05
1/128	.1
1/64 and above, but under 2/32	.2
2/32	.2
Over 2/32, but under 4/32	.2
4/32 and above, but under 8/32	.5
8/32 and above, but under ½	.5

(3) On business for members of the Exchange when a principal is given up:

Price	Rate per Share (cents)
1/256	.05
1/128	.1
1/64 and above, but under 2/32	.1
2/32	.1
Over 2/32, but under 4/32	.1
4/32 and above, but under 8/32	.25
8/32 and above, but under ½	.25

¶ 2381   Collection of Commissions on "When Issued" or "When Distributed" Transactions

Rule 381. Pursuant to Section 5 of Article XV [¶ 1705] of the Constitution, although commissions are ordinarily charged and collected upon the execution of an order, nevertheless in respect of a transaction involving "when issued" or "when distributed" securities, the commission shall be charged and collected not later than when the transaction is settled for costs or proceeds and if a "when issued" or a "when distributed" contract is cancelled the commission shall be waived.

• • • *Supplementary Material:*

Information Regarding Commissions

.10 Charges for handling securities or drafts.—Various banks and trust companies make a service or handling charge for each draft with securities attached which is deposited with them for collection, or for the safekeeping of securities or for other services. Such services include receiving securities, with or without draft attached, against payment or against receipt; delivering securities against receipt or payment; and effecting transfer, registration, subscription or exchange of securities.

The absorption of any part of any such charge by a member or member organization is contrary to Section 1 of Article XV [¶ 1701] of the Constitution; however, if the amount of such charge on all transactions made on a single day for a single customer is less than one dollar, the collection thereof may be waived by the member organization.

¶ 2381 Information Regarding Commissions.—Continued

.11 Shipping and postage charges.—(a) The charging of a customer's or correspondent's account with the cost of shipping securities by mail to or from a customer or correspondent in connection with transactions executed on this Exchange for the account of such customer or correspondent, shall be left to the discretion of the member firm executing the transaction, except that the customer or correspondent must be charged when the amount involved is $1.00 or more. The cost of shipping securities as referred to in this paragraph shall include postage, insurance and split-up or transfer charges. The foregoing does not apply in the case of transactions in a special offering approved by the Exchange.

(b) Prorating Not Permitted in Bulk Shipments. In every instance where a charge to the customer or correspondent is required under (a) above, the charge for all such shipments shall be not less than the necessary cost of the direct shipment of the securities to and from the customer or correspondent. In any case, where securities of more than one customer or correspondent are shipped together, shipping charges to or from each customer or correspondent involved shall be based on the necessary cost of the direct separate shipment of the securities of each and the cost of the combined shipment may not be prorated among them.

(c) Bulk Shipment by New York City Correspondent. When a New York correspondent of an out-of-town member firm ships securities in bulk to the out-of-town firm by mail, including both negotiable and non-negotiable securities, the cost of such shipment shall be charged pursuant to the terms of the above paragraphs (a) to (b), inclusive.

(See Rule 369(G) [¶ 2369], Commissions.)

.12 Intra-office transactions.—When securities are transferred from one account to another in an office for a valuable consideration, the transaction constitutes a purchase and sale within the meaning of the Constitution and a buying and selling commission shall be charged.

A valuable consideration includes, but is not limited to (1) a credit to the transferor's account and/or debit to the transferee's account, or (2) a receipt for the transferor's account of another security and a delivery of such security from the transferee's account.

To avoid possible misunderstanding, the Exchange suggests that a client contemplating such a transfer be apprised of these rulings prior to effecting the transaction.

If a member or member organization is in doubt as to the necessity of charging a commission or feels that the circumstances surrounding a certain transaction warrant an exception to the above requirement, complete details covering each such transaction should be submitted to the Department of Member Firms.

.13 Firm bids, offers and orders.—No member or member organization shall make firm bids or offers, off the Exchange, without the prior consent of the Exchange. The practice of a member or member organization making firm bids or offers, or giving orders, as principal, in listed stocks, during the hours that the Exchange is open or otherwise, to a non-member either within the continental United States or elsewhere, is contrary to Article XV [¶ 1701-1712] of the Constitution and is therefore forbidden, unless the bid, offer or order is at a price less or greater than the last bid or offer on the Exchange, as the case may be, by an amount equal to the appropriate non-member commission and taxes; except that this ruling shall not apply in the event of news or circumstances which become known after the close of the Exchange. A separate record must be maintained by members or member organizations of any bids, offers or orders made in the light of such unusual news or circumstances.

.14 Computation of non-member commission charges on stocks.—In accordance with Section 2 of Article XV [¶ 1702], commissions on stocks selling at $1 per share and above are to be computed on the basis of the amount of money involved in a transaction. The schedule of rates should be applied to each single transaction, as defined in Section 2(d), involving 100 shares or less.

The Constitution sets forth the minimum commission as follows:

2% on first $400 of money involved, plus 1% on next $2,000 of money involved, plus ½% on next $2,600 of money involved, plus 1/10% on money involved above $5,000, plus $3.00 for a round lot or plus $1.00 for an odd lot.

In determining the minimum non-member commission on stocks selling at $1.00 per share and above, the following formula may be used:

Amount of Money Involved	*Commission*
Under $100	As mutually agreed
$ 100 to $ 399	2% plus $ 3.00
$ 400 to $2,399	1% plus $ 7.00
$2,400 to $4,999	½% plus $19.00
$5,000 and above	1/10% plus $39.00

Odd Lot—$2 Less

The minimum commission is not more than $1.50 per share or $75 per single transaction (100 shares or less), but not less than $6.00 per single transaction.

Some illustrations and comments concerning the computation of commissions under the new schedule are set forth below:

(1) If the transaction involves less than $100, the commission may be as mutually agreed.

(2) Where the money value of the transaction is $100 or over:

(A) In the case of round lots, determine the money value for each 100 shares. The commission for 100 shares may then be computed from the formula above. The commission charge on a transaction involving multiples of 100 shares, e.g., 200, 300, 400, etc., shares is determined by multiplying the applicable 100 share commission by 2, 3, 4, etc., respectively, as the case may be.

Examples: (1) 100 shares at $37.50 per share. Money involved, $3,750. Commission $37.75, computed as follows, as stated in the Constitution:

2% on first $ 400 =	$ 8.00	
1% on next $2,000 =	20.00	
½% on $1,350 =	6.75	
plus	3.00 for round lot	
	————	
	$37.75	

or from the formula:

½% of $3,750 ($18.75) plus $19.00

¶ 2381.14   Information Regarding Commissions.—Continued

(2) 400 shares at $41.75 per share. Money involved in 100 shares, $4,175. Commission on 100 shares, $39.88 (computed from formula). Commission on 400 shares, $159.52 ($39.88 × 4).

(B) In the case of an odd lot, determine the money value by multiplying the number of shares by the price and compute the commission from the formula. Note that the rates for odd lots are $2.00 less than round lot rates. If the commission amounts to more than $1.50 per share, the $1.50 per share minimum rate shall apply, unless such commission amounts to less than $6, in which event $6 is the charge; the minimum commission on any odd lot shall not exceed $75.

Examples: (1) 35 shares at $40 per share. Money involved, $1,400. Commission $19, computed as follows:

2% on first $ 400 =	$ 8.00	
1% on $1,000 =	10.00	
plus	3.00	
	$21.00	
less	2.00 for odd lot	
	$19.00	

(2) 10 shares at $150 per share. Money involved, $1,500. Commission $15.00. (Under the formula, the commission is $20.00; since this exceeds $1.50 per share, the $1.50 per share rate applies.)

(3) 3 shares at $175 per share. Money involved $525. Commission $6.00. (The $1.50 per share rate is less than the money involved rate, but the $6.00 minimum per transaction applies.)

(C) In the case of 100 share unit stocks, if an order is entered for a combination of a round lot and an odd lot, e.g., 130 shares, the commission for the 100 shares and the commission for the 30 shares should be determined separately, as indicated in B and A above. The commission for the 130 shares is then the total of the round lot commission plus the odd lot commission.

(D) In the case of 10 share unit stocks, in an order not exceeding 100 shares, the money value of all shares executed in the transaction shall be the basis upon which the commission is to be determined. For one or more units of trading, with or without an odd lot, the commission is computed from the round lot formula. If there is only an odd lot (less than 10 shares) the commission is computed from the formula using the odd lot deduction.

The precise computation of commissions on partial executions is left to the individual firm, so long as the calculation is related to the minimum commission applicable to the entire order for 100 shares or less.

.15   Clearances—Section 4, Article XV [¶ 1704].—On trades made and closed out the same day, the fees to be charged for the round turn shall be those specified in the first paragraph of Section 4 of Article XV [¶ 1704]; on trades made on one day and closed out on any succeeding day the fees to be charged shall be 1½ times such rates.

¶ 2381.15   **Rule 381**

Examples:

> (1) 100 shares XYZ bought and sold on Friday at a price above $50 per share-clearance charge $3.

> (2) 100 shares XYZ bought on Friday and sold on the following Monday (or thereafter) at a price above $50 per share-total clearance charge $4.50. In this case, it is customary to bill $3 on the "in" transaction and $1.50 on the closing or "out" transaction.

The Exchange has determined that on the types of transactions described below the proper clearance charges shall be as indicated:

> (1) On a purchase or sale of stock where there is no countering or offsetting transaction, but where instead the transaction is completed by the receipt or the delivery of the stock from or to the member or member organization who made the transaction, the clearance charge shall be the appropriate overnight rate.

> *Example:* On a purchase of 100 shares of stock at 45, with no offsetting transaction, the overnight rate is $4.13 ($2.75 × 1½).

> (2) On a purchase of rights and the subsequent countering of the transaction by the sale of the equivalent related stock; involving the receipt of the rights; the tender of the rights to the issuer; the receipt of the equivalent related stock, as well as the subsequent delivery of the stock, the clearance charge shall be the appropriate overnight rate on each side of the transaction, that is, on the purchase of the rights as well as on the sale of the stock.

> *Example:* On a purchase of 700 rights at 7/8, the overnight rate is $3.15 ($.30 × 1½ × 7). On the sale of 100 shares of the related stock at 47, the overnight rate is $4.13 ($2.75 × 1½), making a total clearance charge for the transaction of $7.28 ($3.15 + $4.13).

> (3) On the purchase of a convertible stock and the subsequent countering of the transaction by the sale of the securities into which the first securities were convertible, involving the receipt of the bought stock; the tender of that stock for conversion; the receipt of the new security, and the delivery of the new security on the sale thereof, the clearance charge shall be the appropriate overnight rate on each side of the transaction, that is, on the purchase of the one stock as well as on the sale of the new stock.

> *Example:* On a purchase of 100 shares of a preferred stock at 117, the overnight rate is $4.50 ($3.00 × 1½). On the sale of 300 shares of common stock, into which the preferred stock was converted, at 39¼, the overnight rate is $12.39 ($2.75 × 1½ × 3), making a total of $16.89 for the entire transaction ($4.50 + $12.39).

.16 Computation of fee to be charged under Section 4, Article XV [¶ 1704].
—There may be occasions in connection with "in" and "out" transactions when the transaction which establishes the position will be made in one fee bracket and the "evening out" transaction in another. The price of the shares

¶ 2381.16   Information Regarding Commissions.—Continued

in the transaction which originally establishes the position shall govern in determining the fee to be charged.

.17   **Clearances—Disclosure of status as principal or agent.**—Section 4 of Article XV [¶ 1704] provides that "when a member or member organization having made or caused to be made a contract for his or its own account on the Floor of the Exchange" has the contract cleared by another member or member organization, the clearing organization shall charge a certain prescribed minimum clearance fee. The Exchange has determined that the same fee shall apply for clearing a contract made on the Floor of the Exchange for the account of a member or member organization as principal when the execution on the Floor has been effected by a third member or member organization. Thus, if "A", for his or its own account, gives "B" an order with instructions to execute it on the Floor and to give up "C" for clearing, "B" would charge "A" Floor brokerage under Section 2(c) [¶ 1702] and "C" would charge "A" for clearing under Section 4 [¶ 1704]. Likewise, if "A" gives an order to "B" for the purchase or sale of securities for "A's" own account and instructs "B" to clear the transaction, the charges by "B" against "A" would be made up of Floor brokerage under Section 2(c) [¶ 1702] and clearance, under Section 4 [¶ 1704].

In each instance, therefore, where a member or member organization clears a transaction for another member or member organization, the clearing organization must be informed as to whether such transaction is for a customer's account or for the account of the member or member organization as principal, so that the proper charges may be made.

.18   **Clearance charges—Non-member brokers and dealers.**—Member organizations effecting receipts and deliveries of securities for non-member brokers and dealers, other than those which are made in connection with transactions on which commissions are charged, or in which the member organization has bought or sold the securities as principal, shall charge for such services at not less than the following rates:

Stocks

Price per share	Rates per share cents
Up to 50¢	As mutually agreed
50¢ and above but under $ 1	0.45
$ 1 and above but under $ 5	1.125
$ 5 and above but under $10	1.50
$10 and above but under $50	4.125
$50 and above	4.50

Bonds (Except upon obligations of the United States, Puerto Rico, Philippine Islands and States, Territories and Municipalities therein, which may be mutually agreed upon.)

Number of Bonds	Rate per $1000 of principal
1M to 49M	25¢
50M to 99M	17½¢
100M and over	12½¢

¶ **2381.17**   **Rule 381**   © 1957, Commerce Clearing House, Inc.

The rates specified cover a completed receipt and delivery, and each member organization may determine for itself whether it will make the necessary charge, as a practice, on every receipt or every delivery.

For the purposes of this section, the receipt of securities from a non-member broker or dealer with instructions to transfer them into one or more names and to return the securities to the non-member broker or dealer, except where such transfers are part of a current transaction on which commissions are charged, or in which the member has sold the security as principal, shall constitute a "clearance" of the securities and the applicable rate shall be charged.

.19 Joint account arbitrage.—In joint account with allied members or non-members only the party to said account who effects or causes to be effected within his own field of operation a transaction in any security, whether or not listed on this Exchange, for such account, shall charge a commission to such account on such transaction, which commission shall be at the minimum rate prescribed by Article XV [¶ 1701-1712] of the Constitution for non-members on securities which are listed on this Exchange; except that if the minimum commission rate prescribed by the stock exchange of which the correspondent is a member exceeds the minimum rate prescribed by this Exchange for non-members, then the commission shall be at the minimum rate prescribed by the exchange of which the correspondent is a member.

Except as provided herein for joint accounts with allied members or non-members, the member or member organization shall pay commissions only on transactions in securities effected for his or its account by the correspondent with third parties. Such commissions shall be at rates not greater than the minimum rates prescribed by the exchange on which the transaction takes place, and on unlisted securities not greater than the rates customary in the market where the transaction is effected.

.20 Sale of profitable options owned by customers.—When a member organization sells for the account of a customer, or buys from such customer, a profitable option, the member organization shall charge such customer two commissions.

[The next page is 3651.]

Special Procedures Regarding Blocks of Listed Securities and Off-Floor Transactions

¶ 2390A   Blocks Not Susceptible of Normal Processing

● ● ● *Supplementary Material:*

.10 **Basic philosophy.**—It is a basic concept of the Exchange Constitution that all transactions in listed stocks be effected on the Floor of the Exchange in the regular auction market. Any transaction, except one in a security contained in the Exempt List of guaranteed and preferred stocks (¶ 2394.10), not made in the regular auction market requires prior approval of the Exchange. Every transaction proposed to be made in other than the auction market should be reviewed in the light of the factors involved, including the market on the floor, the price, and the size, so that whenever possible the transaction may be effected on the floor of the Exchange.

.12 **Special procedures for handling blocks not susceptible of normal processing.**—The following procedures are provided by the Exchange to facilitate the handling of blocks of listed securities which cannot be absorbed or supplied in the regular auction market within a reasonable time and at a reasonable price or prices:

> Exchange Acquisitions
> Exchange Distributions
> Special Bids
> Special Offerings
> Secondary Distributions
> Specialist Block Purchases
> Specialist Block Sales

Applications and details in respect of Specialist Block Purchases and Specialist Block Sales are to be submitted to The Floor Department (HAnover 2-4200, Ext. 202 or 236) ; all others are to be submitted to the Department of Member Firms (HAnover 2-4200, Ext. 215 or 361). A member or member organization may discuss any application for any of the above procedures with a Floor Governor, as well as an application for an Off-Board transaction in stocks and rights, through HAnover 2-4200 by asking for the "Money Desk" extension and then asking for a Floor Governor.

The following pages contain rules and information governing the special procedures other than Specialist Block Purchases and Specialist Block Sales. (See Rule 107(a) and (b) [¶ 2107] and ¶ 2107.10 for information concerning Specialist Block Purchases and Specialist Block Sales.)

[The next page is 3655.]

Special Offerings, Exchange, and Secondary Distribution

*(Rules and Policies Administered by the
Department of Member Firms.)*

¶ 2391 Special Offerings and Special Bids

Rule 391. (a) Notwithstanding the provisions of Rules 45 to 110 [¶ 2045—2110], inclusive, the Exchange may, subject to the conditions specified in paragraph (c) hereof and to compliance with the provisions specified in paragraphs (c) to (i), inclusive, permit a "Special Offering" or a "Special Bid," as defined in paragraph (b) hereof, to be made through the facilities of the Exchange, provided that the Exchange (with the concurrence of a Governor who is active on the Floor of the Exchange) determines that the regular auction market on the Floor of the Exchange cannot, within a reasonable time and at a reasonable price or prices, absorb or supply the block of a security which is to be the subject of such Special Offering or Special Bid, as the case may be. In making such determination the following factors may be taken into consideration, viz.:

(1) Price range and volume of transactions in the security on the Floor of the Exchange during the preceding month;

(2) attempts which have been made to dispose of or acquire the security in the regular auction market on the Floor of the Exchange;

(3) the existing condition of the specialist's book and Floor quotations with respect to the security;

(4) the apparent past and current interest in the security in the regular auction market on the Floor; and

(5) the number of shares or bonds and the current market value of the block of the security proposed to be covered by such Special Offering or Special Bid.

Except in special circumstances a "Special Offering" or "Special Bid" will not be permitted unless it involves, in the case of stock, at least 1,000 shares having an aggregate market value of $25,000; and in the case of a bond, at least $15,000 principal amount having an aggregate market value of $10,000.

(b) A "Special Offering" is defined as an offering (designated as a fixed price offering) by one or more members or member organizations acting for his or its own account or for the account of one or more other persons, for sale of a block of a listed security through the facilities of the Exchange at a price not in excess of the last sale of such security or the current offer of such security in the regular market on the Floor of the Exchange, whichever is the lower, but not lower than the current bid for such security in such market, unless otherwise specifically permitted by the Exchange, whereby the offeror agrees to pay a special commission to such members and member organizations as may accept all or any part of such Offering for the account of his or their customers.

A "Special Bid" is defined as a bid designated as a fixed price bid by one or more members or member organizations acting for his or its own

¶ 2391   Continued

account or for the account of one or more other persons, for the purchase of
a block of a listed security through the facilities of the Exchange at a price
not below the last sale of such security or the current bid for such security in
the regular market on the Floor of the Exchange, whichever is the higher, but
not higher than the current offer of such security in such market, unless otherwise specifically permitted by the Exchange, whereby the bidder agrees to pay
a special commission to such members and member organizations as may
accept all or any part of such Bid for the account of his or their customers.

(c) No Special Offering or Special Bid shall be made unless all of the
following conditions are complied with:

(1) The person for whose account the Special Offering or Special
Bid is to be made shall at the time of the Offering or Bid be the owner
of or a bidder for (as the case may be) the entire block of the security to
be offered or purchased, except that, for the purpose of stabilizing or for
the purpose of covering sales made for the purpose of stabilizing the
bid, there also may be sold or purchased (as the case may be) for such
person's account, or for the account of any member organization offering
or bidding for the block of securities on his behalf, as part of the Special
Offering or Special Bid, an amount not to exceed 10% of the shares or
bonds owned and originally offered in the Special Offering or to be purchased and originally bid for in the Special Bid by such person.

(2) The person for whose account such Special Offering or Special
Bid is to be made shall include within the Offering or Bid all of the
security which he then intends to offer or bid for within a reasonable
time, and there shall be furnished to the Exchange before the Offering
or Bid is made a written statement by the offeror or by the bidder to that
effect or a written statement by his broker stating that the broker has
been so advised by the offeror or bidder.

(3) A Special Offering or a Special Bid shall be automatically
suspended as long as an offering or bid exists "regular way" at a price
which would permit a purchase at a lower net cost than in the Special
Offering or which would permit a sale at higher net proceeds than in the
Special Bid. Unless otherwise specifically exempted by the Exchange,
every Special Offering and Special Bid shall remain open for a minimum
period of 15 minutes, inclusive of any period during which it is suspended
by operation of the above provision. A Special Offering or a Special Bid
which has not been completed in the 15 minute minimum period shall not
be withdrawn before completion without the approval of the Exchange.

(4) The person for whose account such Special Offering or Special
Bid is made shall agree that, during the period such Offering or Bid is
open, he will not offer or bid for, in the regular market on the Floor of the
Exchange, any securities of the issue which is the subject of such Special
Offering or Special Bid, unless the prior permission of the Exchange is
first obtained.

(5) The special commission referred to in (b) above in the case of a
stock shall not exceed $1 per share on offerings or on bids at a price of $50

or less per share, or 2% of the offering price or of the bid price on offerings or on bids at a price in excess of $50 per share; and in the case of a bond shall not exceed 2½% of the offering or bid price. The special commission shall in no case be less than a single non-member commission based upon the per share rate of 100 shares at the price of the Special Offering or Special Bid.

(6) No member or member organization shall directly or indirectly receive any part of the special commission referred to in (b) above in connection with any purchase or sale, as the case may be, for his or its own account or the account of a partner thereof or a stockholder therein or for the account of any other member or member organization or partner thereof or stockholder therein, made pursuant to a Special Offering or Special Bid, except that a member or member organization may accept and retain such special commission for his or its own account in respect of securities purchased or sold as principal for the bona fide purpose of distribution or acquisition from others, as the case may be, even though such member organization has been unable to distribute or acquire the securities.

(7) A Special Offering or a Special Bid shall not be made unless it can be accepted in a lesser amount or amounts than the total of the securities offered or bid for, as the case may be.

(8) A Special Offering or Special Bid shall be made for acceptance in round lots or in odd lots, without preference, and in the case of an odd lot purchase or sale no differential shall be added to or deducted from the gross sale price of the Special Offering or Special Bid as the case may be.

(9) The Offeror or the Bidder may, at the time of the announcement of a Special Offering or Special Bid, as the case may be, allot on a firm basis, to member organizations engaged in the distributing business, not more than 50% of the securities involved in the offering or bid. When buying orders in a Special Offering or selling orders in a Special Bid exceed the amount of the offering or bid, as the case may be, the remainder of the offered securities or the bid for securities will be allocated in reasonably proportionate amounts.

(d) A Special Offering or Special Bid, when approved, shall become effective upon announcement by the Exchange on the tape of the terms and conditions of such Offering or Bid.

(e) The terms of a Special Offering or Special Bid shall be printed on the tape before it is effective, with a statement, if such be the fact, that stabilizing transactions have been effected or are contemplated and that it is intended to over-allot in the case of a Special Offering as permitted in (c)(1) above or that it is intended to over-buy in the case of a Special Bid within the limitations of (c)(1) above. Transactions effected pursuant to a Special Offering or Special Bid shall, when feasible, be printed currently on the tape, and the tape shall show the gross price and the special commission in a legend such as "SP OFF (BID) 100 XYZ 40 COM ½," as well as the number of orders involved in such transaction where more than one order is involved; and after the close of the market, any unprinted remainder of such transactions executed during the day shall be so printed. When the Offering or Bid is terminated an announcement to that effect shall be printed on the tape; and when the intention to stabilize is terminated, such fact shall be announced

¶ 2391   Continued

on the tape, together with a statement that stabilizing transactions have been effected, if such be the fact.

(f) Transactions effected pursuant to a Special Offering or Special Bid shall not elect the execution of any outstanding odd lot orders.

(g) A Special Offering or Special Bid may be approved and made only if the person or persons for whose account it is proposed to be made shall have specifically authorized such offering or bid and its terms.

(h) A member or member organization:

(1) Effecting for the account of a customer a purchase pursuant to a Special Offering or a sale pursuant to a Special Bid shall confirm such transaction to such customer at the offering price or at the bid price and shall not charge to or collect from such customer any commission on account of such transaction.

The confirmation by a member organization to a buyer or seller in either a Special Offering or a Special Bid shall state in full the terms and conditions of the Special Offering or Special Bid. The confirmation to the buyer or the seller, as the case may be, shall state at least:

(A) that the purchase or sale was part of a Special Offering or Special Bid;

(B) that no commission is to be charged to the customer;

(C) that the seller or buyer, as the case may be, is to pay a special commission to the member organization if such be the fact;

(D) the amount of such special commission;

(E) the information printed on the tape regarding stabilizing transactions or the intention to stabilize; and

(F) the nature of the member organization's interest in the Special Offering or Special Bid, if any, other than its interest as a recipient of the special commission.

(2) Soliciting purchase orders for execution pursuant to a Special Offering or sales orders for execution pursuant to a Special Bid shall advise the person so solicited of the terms and conditions of such Offering or Bid, as the case may be, before effecting any transaction for such person pursuant thereto. Such disclosure shall include at least the items described in subparagraphs (A) through (F) of Rule 391(h)(1), above.

(3) With an order for the purchase of a security which is the subject of a Special Offering or with an order for the sale of a security which is the subject of a Special Bid, shall effect such purchase or sale in the regular market whenever a "regular way" offering or bid, as the case may be, is available which would permit such purchase at a lower net cost than in the Special Offering or permit such sale at higher net proceeds than in the Special Bid. Every order for purchase in a Special Offering and every order for sale in a Special Bid shall be accepted pursuant to the above condition.

¶ 2391   **Rule 391**

(i) A member or member organization acting as broker for the offeror of a Special Offering or acting as broker for the bidder of a Special Bid shall charge and collect from such offeror or bidder, as the case may be, the commissions as prescribed in Article XV of the Constitution, and the provisions of such Article XV with respect to clearance and give-up commissions on transactions between members and member organizations shall apply to all such transactions effected in connection with or pursuant to a Special Offering or Special Bid.

Amendment:
October 11, 1957.

● ● ● *Supplementary Material:*

.10 **Information regarding Special Offerings and Special Bids.**—It is not the purpose of this rule to supersede the auction market or supplant approved secondary distributions, but to provide means for the handling of blocks of listed securities through the facilities of the Exchange, where such blocks, under current conditions, cannot readily be absorbed or acquired in the auction market within a reasonable time and at a reasonable price.

Rule 391 [¶ 2391] is intended primarily to provide for Special Offerings and Special Bids on an agency basis by members, or member organizations in behalf of their nonmember customers. However, the rule does not prohibit a Special Offering or a Special Bid by a member, or member organization for his or its own account.

Rule 391(a) [¶ 2391] places a general limitation on the size of the Special Offerings and Special Bids, except in special circumstances. Such an exception might apply to a stock located at Post 30.

.11 **Preliminary information required.**—The broker for the offeror or the bidder will be required to furnish the following information to the Department of Member Firms prior to the announcement of the Special Offering or the Special Bid on the tape:

(1) Name of the security and ticker symbol.

(2) Number of shares or principal amount of bonds.

(3) Special Offering or Special Bid price.

(4) Special commission.

(5) Current bid and offer and last sale.

(6) Name of the Offeror or Bidder.

(7) Daily price range and volume of transactions on the New York Stock Exchange, in the security which it is proposed to offer or bid for, for a period of one month prior to the date of the proposed offering or bid.

(8) Description of efforts to dispose of or acquire the security in the auction market on the Floor of the Exchange.

(9) Written assurance of the Offeror or Bidder, or of the broker upon advice from the Offeror or Bidder, that the shares or bonds contained in the Offering or Bid are all of the security which he then intends to offer or bid for within a reasonable time, as required in Rule 391(c)(2) [¶ 2391].

(10) Assurance of agreement of Offeror or Bidder to terms of Offering or Bid.

¶ 2391.11   Continued

(11) Statement as to whether stabilizing operations will be engaged in to facilitate the Special Offering.

(12) Statement as to whether the Offeror or his agent intends, for the purpose of stabilizing, to sell shares or bonds in the Special Offering in excess of that owned and included in the original offer as permitted by Rule 391(c)(1) [¶ 2391].

(13) Statement that the shares or bonds covered by the application for the Special Offering do or do not require registration under the Securities Act of 1933, together with explanation thereof.

This information should be given to the Department of Member Firms as soon as possible in advance of the time it is proposed to make the Special Offering or the Special Bid. Announcement will not be made on the tape of the Special Offering or the Special Bid (and the Special Offering or Special Bid thus cannot become effective) until the Department of Member Firms has the requisite information and has approved it.

.12   **Ownership.**—The offeror in a Special Offering must be the owner (as defined in ¶ 2440B.14) of the entire block of the security offered except for sales, for the purpose of stabilizing, as permitted by Rule 391(c)(1) [¶ 2391].

.13   **"Piecemeal" or "all or none" Special Offering or Special Bid.**—"Piecemeal" or successive offerings or bids of the same security by the same offeror or bidder, and offerings or bids on an "all or none" basis, will not be permitted.

.14   **Minimum period of offering.**—Rule 391(c)(3) [¶ 2391] provides in part that unless otherwise specifically exempted by the Exchange, every Special Offering or Special Bid shall remain open for a minimum period of 15 minutes. Exception from this minimum requirement is specifically given to any offering or bid which has been announced on the New York Stock Exchange ticker tape at least one hour before the offering or bid becomes effective. An offering or bid so exempted from the minimum 15-minute requirement shall not be closed without the approval of the Exchange.

.15   **Other offers by offeror or other bids by bidder.**—It should be noted that, under Rule 391(c)(4) [¶ 2391] an offeror or bidder may not, while his Special Offering or Special Bid is open, offer or bid for any of the same security in the regular auction market, without prior permission of the Exchange.

.16   **Orders after close.**—Orders accumulated after the close shall be completed on the Floor of the Exchange at the opening of the next market session.

.17   **Handling of Special Offering or Special Bid Transactions.**—Purchases against Special Offerings and sales against Special Bids must be completed on the Floor of the Exchange at the Post or Crowd where the security is dealt in. The handling of the Floor end of the business, on either the purchase or the offering side, may be entrusted to a Floor broker or specialist in the same manner as in the case of regular commission orders. In reference to Rule 391 [¶ 2391] attention is directed to the fact that in connection with a

Special Offering the broker for the buyer, and in connection with a Special Bid the broker for the seller, is acting in an agency capacity and the agency obligation to buy or sell at the most advantageous price to the customer shall be observed.

.18   **Stabilizing.**—The right to sell an amount not to exceed 10 per cent of the number of shares or bonds owned and originally offered in the Special Offering, for the purpose of stabilizing and as part of a Special Offering, is subject to the prior approval of the Exchange. Stabilizing operations in connection with Special Offerings must be discussed in advance with the staff of the Department of Member Firms.

.19   **Stop orders—Odd-lot orders.**—Transactions effected pursuant to Special Offerings or Special Bids shall not elect stop orders or open odd-lot orders for execution in the regular auction market.

.20   **Reports.**—In respect of a Special Offering the applicant shall submit to the Exchange at the close of each day a report of all transactions in the offered security effected for the account of any person having an interest as seller or as agent, offering the block of the security on the seller's behalf in the Special Offering. Such reports shall cover the period beginning with the date of commencement of the offering or the stabilizing, whichever is earlier, and ending with the date on which the short position has been covered or the Special Offering account has been terminated, whichever is later.

In respect of a Special Bid, the applicant similarly shall submit to the Exchange at the close of each day a report of all transactions in the security bid for effected for the account of any person having an interest as buyer or as agent, buying the block of the security on the buyer's behalf in the Special Bid. Such reports shall cover the period beginning with the date of commencement of the Special Bid and ending with the date on which the Special Bid has been terminated.

.21   **Confirmations.**—Rule 391(h)(1) [¶ 2391] details the type of information required to be shown on confirmations in respect of Special Offerings and Special Bids. If the information is inserted in or made a part of other printed matter on the confirmation, it should be in type no smaller than the surrounding material, and in no event smaller than 8-point. The information may be added to an ordinary confirmation by being impressed thereon with a rubber stamp, or attached thereto by adhesive, staple or other fastening device. If this latter method is used the size of type utilized shall be no smaller than 8-point. If there is insufficient space on the face of the confirmation it may be shown on the reverse side provided there is stamped or printed on the face "Important —See Reverse Side" in type no smaller than the following:

IMPORTANT—SEE REVERSE SIDE

¶ 2391.21   Continued

CONFIRMATION FORMS

The following are suggested forms of statements to be made on the appropriate confirmations. These are herewith reproduced in 8-point type, as required by the preceding paragraph. These statements relate to confirmations on purchases. Confirmations on sales may likewise be appropriately worded.

FORM A

(For use by the agent for the buyer where no stabilization is involved.)

> This purchase by you constitutes part of a Special Offering. No commission is being charged to you as the purchaser. A special commission of $.......... per share is being paid to this firm (corporation) by the offeror.

FORM B

(For use by the agent for the buyer where stabilization is involved.)

> This purchase by you constitutes part of a Special Offering. No commission is being charged to you as the purchaser. A special commission of $.......... per share is being paid to this firm (corporation) by the offeror.
>
> To facilitate the offering certain transactions ☐ may be ☐ have been ☐ have been and may further be effected to stabilize the price of this security. This statement is not an assurance that any or all of such transactions may not be discontinued at any time or that they will accomplish the intended purpose.

FORM C

(For use by the agent for the buyer when he is also agent for the seller where no stabilization is involved.)

> This purchase by you constitutes part of a Special Offering. No commission is being charged to you as the purchaser. A special commission of $.......... per share is being paid to this firm (corporation) by the offeror.
>
> In addition to receiving the special commission referred to above, this firm (corporation) was interested in the distribution as agent for the offeror, and as such received an additional commission not in excess of $........ per share.

FORM D

(For use by the agent for the buyer when he is also agent for the seller where stabilization is involved.)

> This purchase by you constitutes part of a Special Offering. No commission is being charged to you as the purchaser. A special commission of $.......... per share is being paid to this firm (corporation) by the offeror.
>
> To facilitate the offering certain transactions ☐ may be ☐ have been ☐ have been and may further be effected to stabilize the price of this security. This statement is not an assurance that any or all of such transactions may not be discontinued at any time or that they will accomplish the intended purpose.
>
> In addition to receiving the special commission referred to above, this firm (corporation) was interested in the distribution as agent for the offeror, and as such received an additional commission not in excess of $........ per share.

FORM E

(For use by organization in confirming sales to its own customers where organization sells to customer as principal and no stabilization is involved.)

> This purchase by you constitutes part of a Special Offering in which our firm (corporation) was the offeror.
>
> A special commission of $.......... per share is being paid by us to the brokers for buyers.

FORM F

(For use by organization in confirming sales to its own customers where organization sells to customer as principal and stabilization is involved.)

> This purchase by you constitutes part of a Special Offering in which our firm (corporation) was the offeror.
>
> To facilitate the offering certain transactions ☐ may be ☐ have been ☐ have been and may further be effected to stabilize the price of this security. This statement is not an assurance that any or all of such transactions may not be discontinued at any time or that they will accomplish the intended purpose.
>
> A special commission of $.......... per share is being paid by us to the brokers for buyers.

.22   **Other interest to be shown.**—Rule 391 (h)(1)(f) [¶ 2391] requires that
any other interest in the special offering be disclosed. Such an instance might
be where a member or member organization, although not acting as the offeror
or as the agent for the offeror, in addition to receiving the special commission
on sales in a special offering, has received a fee or commission as a member
of a so-called "stand by" group. In such a case the confirmations to purchasers should disclose this fact, and the amount of the fee.

Example:

John Doe & Co., as agent for the seller, is making a special offering of
10,000 shares XYZ at 50, special commission $1.00. John Doe & Co. is receiv-
ing a selling commission of 30¢ per share. John Doe & Co. has organized a
"stand by" group consisting of four other firms, each "standing by" for 2,000
shares. John Doe & Co. will pay a "stand by" fee of 15¢ per share to the
members of the "stand by" group. John Doe & Co. in confirming to purchasers, in accordance with forms "C" or "D," in addition to showing the
special commission of $1.00 per share, would disclose that it had received a
selling commission of 30¢ per share as agent for the seller. The other four
firms, comprising the "stand by" group, in confirming to purchasers, in
addition to showing the special commission of $1.00 per share, would disclose
"In addition our firm has received from the agent for the sellers a 'stand by'
fee or commission of 15¢ per share on 2,000 shares."

¶ 2392   Exchange Distributions and Exchange Acquisitions

Rule 392.   To effect an "Exchange Distribution" or an "Exchange Acquisition" of a block of a listed security, a member or member organization, for his or its own account or the account of a customer, may make an
arrangement with one or more other members or member organizations
under which:

(1) The members or member organizations, with whom the arrangement is made, solicit others to purchase the security in the case of an
Exchange Distribution or solicit others to sell such security in the case of
an Exchange Acquisition; and

(2) the selling or buying member or member organization, as the
case may be, pays to the members or member organizations, with whom
the arrangement is made, a special commission which is mutually agreeable but not lower than the applicable commission prescribed in Article XV
of the Constitution; and

(3) the members or member organizations, with whom the arrangement is made, may pay a special commission to their registered representatives; and/or

(4) pay a special commission to his or its registered representatives
for soliciting orders to purchase or to sell such security, as the case may be.

An "Exchange Distribution" or "Exchange Acquisition" may be made
only with the prior approval of the Exchange (given with the concurrence of
a Governor who is active on the Floor of the Exchange). Such a Distribution
or Acquisition shall not be approved unless the Exchange shall have determined that the regular market on the Floor of the Exchange cannot, within a
reasonable time or at a reasonable price or prices, otherwise absorb or supply,

as the case may be, the block of securities which is to be the subject of the "Exchange Distribution" or "Exchange Acquisition." In making such determination, the following factors may be taken into consideration, viz.:

(1) Price range and volume of transactions in the security on the Floor of the Exchange during the preceding month;

(2) attempts which have been made to dispose of or acquire the security in the regular auction market on the Floor of the Exchange;

(3) the existing condition of the specialist's book and Floor quotations with respect to the security;

(4) the apparent past and current interest in the security in the regular auction market on the Floor; and

(5) the number of shares or bonds and the current market value of the block of the security proposed to be covered by such "Exchange Distribution" or "Exchange Acquisition."

No "Exchange Distribution" or "Exchange Acquisition" shall be made unless all of the following conditions are complied with:

(1) The person for whose account the Distribution or Acquisition is to be made shall, at the time of the Distribution, be the owner of the entire block of the security to be so distributed or, at the time of the Acquisition, be a bidder for the entire block of the security to be so acquired;

(2) the person for whose account the Distribution or Acquisition is to be made shall include within the Distribution or Acquisition all of the security which he then intends to offer or to purchase, as the case may be, within a reasonable time and there shall be furnished to the Exchange, before the Distribution or Acquisition is made, a written statement by the offeror or bidder to that effect or by his broker stating that the broker has been so advised by the offeror or bidder;

(3) the person for whose account the Distribution or Acquisition is made shall agree that, during the Distribution, he will not bid for or purchase or, during the Acquisition, he will not offer or sell, any of the security for any account in which he has a direct or indirect interest;

(4) The members and member organizations who are parties to the arrangement for the Distribution or Acquisition shall not, during the period the Distribution or Acquisition is being made, bid for or purchase or offer or sell, as the case may be, any of the security for an account in which they have a direct or indirect interest;

(5) No member shall be granted approval to effect an "Exchange Distribution" or an "Exchange Acquisition" of a block of a security for an account in which he has a direct or indirect interest, if he is registered as a specialist in such security, unless the Exchange has determined that such member has been unable, within a reasonable period of time, to dispose of or obtain, as the case may be, the block of the security in the ordinary course of his dealings as a specialist. Such approval shall stipulate that the specialist may not deal directly with the public but must make an arrangement with one or more members or member organizations to solicit others to purchase or sell the security, as the case may be, and pay a special commission to such other members and member organizations as provided in the first paragraph of this Rule;

(6) Each member or member organization soliciting purchase or sell orders, as the case may be, for execution in the Distribution or Acquisition shall advise the person so solicited, before effecting any transaction for such person that the securities being offered or being bid for are part of a specified number of shares or bonds being offered or bid for, in an "Exchange Distribution" or an "Exchange Acquisition", as the case may be, and that he or it

      (A) is acting for the seller or buyer, and will receive a special commission from the seller or buyer or his brokers; or is acting as a principal, and

      (B) is charging the buying or selling customer, as the case may be, the regular commission, the equivalent of the regular commission, or is making the sale or purchase at a net amount.

(7) No "short" sale may be made in connection with an Exchange Distribution. However, securities may be borrowed to make delivery where the person owns the securities sold and intends to deliver such securities as soon as is possible without undue inconvenience or expense.

The conditions set forth in (2), (3) and (4) above shall not apply to transactions effected on the Exchange, for the purpose of maintaining a fair and orderly market, by a member in a security in which he is registered as a specialist and which is the subject of an "Exchange Distribution" or "Exchange Acquisition" for an account in which he has an interest except that:

      (1) During such Distribution he shall not bid for or purchase such security on the Exchange for an account in which he has an interest at a price above the preceding sale (i. e., A "plus" tick) or at a price above the next preceding different sale price (i. e., A "zero plus" tick) or

      (2) during such Acquisition he shall not offer or sell such security on the Exchange for an account in which he has an interest at a price below the preceding sale (i. e., A "minus" tick) or at a price below the next preceding different sale price (i. e., A "zero minus" tick).

The conditions set forth in (3) and (4) above shall not apply to purchases or sales necessitated solely in connection with "crossing" orders pursuant to the Distribution or Acquisition.

In effecting an "Exchange Distribution" or an "Exchange Acquisition", the orders for the purchase or sale—as the case may be, of the securities being distributed or acquired must be sent to the Floor together with an order to sell or buy an equal amount to be "crossed" in accordance with the rules applicable to the crossing of orders on the Floor, and such transactions shall be printed on the ticker tape.

The member or member organization selling or buying securities in an "Exchange Distribution" or buying securities in an "Exchange Acquisition" shall report to the Exchange all transactions in such securities effected by him or it for any account in which the seller or the buyer, as the case may be, had a direct or indirect interest, commencing with the time arrangements for the Distribution or Acquisition were made and ending with the time the Distribution or Acquisition was completed.

● ● ● *Supplementary Material:*

.10 Prints on the tape of transactions made on the Exchange as the result of an Exchange Acquisition or an Exchange Distribution will be preceded with the symbol "ACQ" (in the case of Exchange Acquisitions) or with the symbol "DIST" (in the case of Exchange Distributions). Such transactions are regular way transactions, and the designation "ACQ" or "DIST" is merely for the purpose of identification.

(*See also* ¶ 2390A.10.)

.11 The provisions of this rule apply whether the member or member organization is arranging an Exchange Distribution or Acquisition alone or with one or more other members or member organizations.

¶ 2393   Secondary Distributions

Rule 393. With the prior approval of the Exchange, member organizations may make and members and member organizations may participate in an "over-the-counter" or "off-board" secondary distribution of a security admitted to dealing on the Exchange.

● ● ● *Supplementary Material:*

.10 Application, in form acceptable to the Exchange, shall be made to the Department of Member Firms, well in advance of the contemplated offering, by the member or non-member organization making or managing the offering.

Approval may be granted if the Exchange, after consultation with, and with the concurrence of, a Governor who is active on the Floor of the Exchange, determines (1) that the regular auction market on the Floor of the Exchange cannot, within a reasonable time and at a reasonable price or prices, absorb the particular block of securities which is to be the subject of such Secondary Distribution, and (2) that a Special Offering or Exchange Distribution is not feasible.

In making such determination, the following factors may be taken into consideration, viz.:

     (1) Price range and volume of transactions in the security on the Floor of the Exchange during the preceding 30 days;

     (2) attempts which have been made to dispose of the security in the regular market on the Floor of the Exchange;

     (3) the existing condition of the specialist's book and Floor quotations with respect to the security;

     (4) the apparent past and current interest in the security in the regular auction market on the Floor, and

     (5) the number of shares or bonds and the current market value of the block of the security proposed to be offered in the Secondary Distribution.

Application shall be made in form prescribed by the Exchange.

.11 A Secondary Distribution is defined as an offering by one or more members or member organizations, or non-member organizations, acting as agent or principal, of a block of a listed security off the Floor, at a price (except with the express permission of the Exchange) not exceeding the last sale price of the security on the Floor at the time of offering, except that, with the specific approval of the Exchange, and provided the offering price is so represented, there may be added to such offering price, per share, if it is at such last sale, an amount equal to the minimum non-member commission applicable to 100 shares of stock, or one bond, determined at the price of such last sale.

A Secondary Distribution may be represented to be "at the market", "at a price related to the market" or at a fixed price.

.12   A Secondary Distribution, when approved, shall become effective upon announcement by the Exchange on the ticker tape of the terms and conditions of the distribution, including information as to stabilization and over-allotment, except that if a distribution is to become effective at a time when Exchange tickers are not in operation, announcement of such terms and conditions may be made by the distributing firm by such means as may be approved by the Exchange. Prior announcement of an expected Secondary Distribution may be made on the Exchange ticker.

.13   In each Secondary Distribution of a block of securities by a non-member of the Exchange, except (1) where the offeror takes a risk position prior to the offering, or (2) where the seller is required by an agency of the United States Government to invite competitive bids for the security to be sold, there shall be a difference between the offering price and the price paid by the underwriters, if the security is underwritten, or between such offering price and the amount received by the seller, if the distribution is made on an agency basis of not less than twice the minimum non-member commission per share applicable to 100 shares of stock, or one bond, determined at the last sale or the offering price if it is lower than the last sale.

.14   The dealer discount per share or per bond shall be not less than a single non-member commission at the rate applicable to 100 shares of stock or one bond at the offering price.

.15   (a) When a Secondary Distribution becomes effective after the close of the market, the distributor, unless otherwise prohibited by rules of a securities dealers association organized pursuant to Section 15A of the Securities Exchange Act of 1934 for at least one-half hour after the secondary distribution becomes effective, shall make and keep available to members of the Exchange, through the specialist in the security, a sufficient quantity of the security being distributed to fill all bids represented on the Floor at the close of the market at or above the offering price. The price at which such security is made available to member organizations shall be the offering price less at least an amount equal to the applicable non-member commission so that a customer buying the security through a member organization, after paying the minimum commission, shall obtain the security at the same actual cost he would have if he had bought it from the distributor or a member of the selling group.

(b) When a Secondary Distribution is in effect during market hours, the distributor must make the security available on the Floor of the Exchange in sufficient quantity to permit the maintenance of an orderly market.

.16   A Secondary Distribution may be made on a principal or an agency basis.

Confirmations and comparisons used by underwriters or selling group members in connection with Secondary Distributions must clearly describe the capacity in which the broker or dealer is acting.

.17   The distributor shall make daily reports to the Department of Member Firms giving all details of transactions made over-the-counter and on the Exchange and, at the termination of the distribution, a final report in form prescribed by the Exchange summarizing all transactions and listing all participants in the selling group.

¶ **2393.12   Rule 393**

4-65
Report 101
Rules of Board—Special Offerings, etc.
➤➤→ *Administered by Department of Member Firms.*
3669

.18 The Exchange may withdraw its approval of a Secondary Distribution at any time.

.19 If the terms of distribution are changed in any way, the Department of Member Firms shall be notified promptly, and the continuation of the Secondary Distribution shall be subject to the Exchange's approval of such change in terms.

.20 The distributor or syndicate manager shall keep his books open to receive member or member organization subscriptions for at least one-half hour after announcement of the Secondary Distribution, unless prior announcement of an expected distribution has been made at least one-half hour before the distribution in accordance with the last sentence of .12 above.

¶ 2394   Off-Floor Transactions in Listed Stocks

Rule 394. Except as otherwise specifically exempted by the Exchange, members and member organizations must obtain the permission of the Exchange before effecting a transaction in a listed stock off the Exchange, either as principal or agent.

(*See Rule 371 [¶ 2371] regarding "reverse operations."*)

● ● ● *Supplementary Material:*

.10 List of guaranteed and preferred stocks exempt from Rule 394 [¶ 2394].
    —The following guaranteed and preferred stocks have been exempted from the provisions of Rule 394, above. However, because of the basic concept of the Exchange Constitution that all transactions in listed stocks be executed on the Floor, every proposed transaction in these securities should be reviewed in the light of the factors involved, including the market on the Floor, the price, and the size, so that whenever possible the transaction may be effected on the Floor.

(*Note: This list is effective until the issuance of the next regular supplement to the New York Stock Exchange Guide.*)

GUARANTEED STOCKS

Allegheny & Western Railway Company...Capital (6% guaranteed)
Beech Creek Railroad Company...Capital (4% guaranteed)
Canada Southern Railway Company, (The)...Capital
Carolina, Clinchfield & Ohio Railway...Common
Cleveland & Pittsburgh Railroad Company, (The)...Gtd. 7% Capital
    ...Special Gtd. Betterment 4%
Erie & Pittsburgh Railroad Co....Capital
Northern Central Railway Co., (The)...Capital
Pittsburgh, Ft. Wayne & Chicago Ry. Co....7% Pfd.
Pittsburgh, Youngstown & Ashtabula Ry. Co., (The)...7% Non-Cum. Pfd.
Southern Railway Co., Mobile & Ohio...Stock Trust Ctfs.
Wheeling & Lake Erie Railway Co....Common

¶ 2394.10—Continued

PREFERRED STOCKS

A

Allied Stores Corporation...4% Cum. Pfd.
American Can Company...7% Cum. Pfd.
American Machine & Foundry Company...3.90% Cum. Pfd.
American Radiator & Standard Sanitary Corporation...7% Cum. Pfd.
American Snuff Company...6% Non-Cum. Pfd.
American Tobacco Company, (The)...6% Cum. Pfd.
Anchor Hocking Glass Corp....$4 Cum. Pfd.
Armstrong Cork Company...$3.75 Cum. Pfd.
Atlantic City Electric Co....4% Cum. Pfd.
Atlantic Refining Company, (The)...Cum. Pfd. 3.75% Series B

B

Baltimore Gas & Electric Co....4½% Cum. Pfd., Series B
   ...4% Cum. Pfd., Series C
Beatrice Foods Co....4½% Cum. Pfd.
Borg-Warner Corporation...3½% Cum. Pfd.
Bristol-Myers Company...3¾% Cum. Pfd.

C

Central Illinois Light Company...4½% Pfd. (Cum.)
Cincinnati Gas & Electric Co....4% Cum. Pfd.
   ...4¾% Cum. Pfd.
Cluett, Peabody & Co....7% Cum. Pfd.
Colgate-Palmolive Company...$3.50 Pfd.
Consolidated Edison Company of New York, Inc....$5 Cum. Pfd.
   ...4.65% Ser. C, Cum. Pfd. $100 par value.
Consumers Power Co....$4.16 Pfd.
   ...$4.50 Cum. Pfd.
   ...$4.52 Cum. Pfd.
Container Corporation of America...4% Cum. Pfd.
Continental Can Company, Inc....$3.75 Cum. Pfd.
Corning Glass Works...3½% Cum. Pfd.
   ...3½% Cum. Pfd., Ser. of 1947
Crane Co....3¾% Cum. Pfd.
Crown Zellerbach Corporation...$4.20 Cum. Pfd.

D

Dana Corporation...Cum. Pfd. 3¾% Ser. A
Dayton Power & Light Company, (The)...Pfd. 3.75% Ser. A
   ...Pfd. 3.75% Ser. B
   ..Pfd. 3.90% Ser. C
du Pont de Nemours, (E. I.) & Co.   Pfd. $3.50 Ser.
   ...Pfd. $4.50 Ser.
Duquesne Light Co....3.75% Pfd. (Cum.)
   ...4% Pfd.
   ...4.15% Pfd.
   ...4.20% Pfd.
   ...4.10% Pfd.
   ...$2.10 Pfd.

PREFERRED STOCKS—Continued

E

Endicott Johnson Corporation...4% Ser. Cum. Pfd.

F

Flintkote Company (The)...$4 Cum. Pfd.
Food Fair Stores, Inc....$4.20 Cum. Pfd. Series of 1951

G

General Motors Corporation...Pfd. Stk. $3.75 Ser.
   ...$5 Cum. Pfd.
General Telephone Company of Florida...$1.30 Cum. Pfd. Series B.
Grant (W. T.) Company...3¾% Cum. Pfd.
Gulf States Utilities Co....$4.20 Pfd.
   ...$4.40 Pfd.
   ...$4.44 Div. Pfd.
   ...$4.52 Div. Pfd.
   ...$5.00 Div. Pfd.
   ...$5.08 Div. Pfd.

H

Harbison-Walker Refractories Co....6% Cum. Pfd.
Heinz (H. J.) Co....3.65% Cum. Pfd.
Helme Products, Inc....7% Non-Cum. Pfd.
Hercules Powder Company...5% Cum. Pfd.
Hooker Chemical Corporation...$4.25 Pfd.
   ...$5 Div. 2nd Pfd. Ser. C
Household Finance Corporation...3¾% Cum. Pfd.
   ...4% Pfd.
   ...4.40% Pfd.

I

Illinois Power Co....4.08% Cum. Pfd.
   ...4.26% Cum. Pfd.
   ...4.70% Cum. Pfd.
   ...4.42% Cum. Pfd.
   ...4.20% Cum. Pfd.
Ingersoll-Rand Co....Pfd. 6% Cum.
International Harvester Co....7% Cum. Pfd.
International Paper Company...$4 Cum. Pfd.

J

Jewel Tea Co., Inc....3¾% Pfd.

K

Kaiser Aluminum & Chemical Corp....4¾% Pfd.

3 6 7 2　　　Rules of Board—Special Offerings, etc.　　　4-65
Report 101
➠→ *Administered by Department of Member Firms.*

¶ 2394.10　Continued

PREFERRED STOCKS—Continued

Kansas City Power & Light Co.. ..3.80% Cum. Pfd.
...4% Cum. Pfd.
...4.35% Cum. Pfd.
...4.50% Cum. Pfd.
...4.20% Cum. Pfd.
Koppers Company, Inc.　..Cum. Pfd. Stock 4% Series

L

Liggett & Myers Tobacco Co.. ..7% Cum. Pfd.
Long Island Lighting Co.. ..Pfd. 5% Series B
...Pfd. 4.25% Series D
...Pfd. 4.35% Series E
Lorillard, (P.) Company...7% Cum. Pfd.

M

May Department Stores, (The)...$3.75 Cum. Pfd.
...$3.40 Cum. Pfd.
...$3.75 Cum. Pfd. 1947 Ser.
Merck & Co., Inc.. ..$3.50 Cum. Pfd.
Metropolitan Edison Company...Cum. Pfd. 3.80% Series
...Cum. Pfd. 3.90% Series
...Cum. Pfd. 4.35% Series
...Cum. Pfd. 3.85 %Series
...Cum. Pfd. 4.45% Series
Morris (Philip) & Co., Ltd., Inc.. ..Cum. Pfd. 4% Ser.
...Cum. Pfd. 3.90% Ser.

N

Newberry (J. J.) Co.. ..3¾% Cum. Pfd.
New Jersey Power & Light Co.. ..Cum. Pfd. 4% Series
N. Y. State Electric & Gas Corp.. ..3.75% Pfd. (Cum.)
Niagara Mohawk Power Corp.. ..Pfd. 3.40% Ser. (Cum.)
...Pfd. 3.60% Ser. (Cum.)
...Pfd. 3.90% Ser. (Cum.)
...Pfd. 4.10% Ser.
...Pfd. 4.85% Ser.
...Pfd. 5.25% Ser.
Norfolk & Western Ry. Co.. ..4% Non-Cum. Adj. Pfd.
Northern Natural Gas Company...5½% Cum. Pfd.
...5.80% Cum. Pfd.
...5.60% Cum. Pfd.
Northern States Power Co.. ..Cum. Pfd. $3.60 Series
...Cum. Pfd. $4.10 Series
...Cum. Pfd. $4.08 Series
...Cum. Pfd. $4.11 Series
...Cum. Pfd. $4.16 Series
...Cum. Pfd. $4.56 Series

PREFERRED STOCKS—Continued

O

Ohio Edison Company...4.40% Cum. Pfd.
   ...3.90% Cum. Pfd.
   ...4.56% Cum. Pfd.
   ...4.44% Cum. Pfd.
Oklahoma Gas & Electric Co....4% Cum. Pfd.
   ...4.24% Cum. Pfd.

P

Pacific Telephone & Telegraph Co....Pfd. 6% Cum.
Panhandle Eastern Pipe Line Co....4% Cum. Pfd.
Pennsylvania Power & Light Co....4½% Cum. Pfd.
   ...4.40% Ser. Cum. Pfd.
Pet Milk Company...4½% Cum. Pfd.
Philadelphia Electric Company...3.8% Cum. Pfd.
   ...4.4% Cum. Pfd.
   ...4.3% Cum. Pfd.
   ...4.68% Cum. Pfd.
Public Service Company of Indiana, Inc....3½% Cum. Pfd.
   ...4.16% Cum. Pfd.
   ...4.32% Pfd.
Public Service Electric & Gas Co....4.08% Cum. Pfd.
   ...4.18% Cum. Pfd.
   ...4.30% Cum. Pfd.
   ...5.05% Cum. Pfd.
   ...5.28% Cum. Pfd.

Q

Quaker Oats Co....6% Cum. Pfd.

R

Reynolds, (R. J.) Tobacco Co....Preferred 3.60% Series

S

Scott Paper Company...$3.40 Cum. Pfd.
   ...$4 Cum. Pfd.
Scoville Manufacturing Co....3.65% Cum. Pfd.
Sherwin-Williams Company (The)...Cum. Pfd., 4% Series
Standard Brands, Incorporated...$3.50 Cum. Pfd.
Standard Oil Company (The), (Ohio)...3¾% Cum. Pfd. Series A
Stauffer Chemical Company...3½% Cum. Pfd.

T

Thompson Ramo Wooldridge, Inc....4% Cum. Pfd.
Tidewater Oil Company...$1.20 Pfd.

U

Union Electric Company...Pfd. $4.50 Ser.
   ...Pfd. $4 Ser.
   ...Pfd. $3.70 Ser.
   ...Pfd. $3.50 Ser.
   ...Pfd. $4.56 Ser.

3 6 7 4   Rules of Board—Special Offerings, etc.   6-65
                                                                Report 103
    ➡️ *Administered by Department of Member Firms.*

¶ 2394.10   Continued

PREFERRED STOCKS—Continued

Union Pacific Railroad Co....4% Non-Cum. Pfd.
United Shoe Machinery Corp....6% Cum. Pfd.
United States Gypsum Company...Pfd. (7% Cum.)
United States Plywood Corporation...3¾% Cum. Pfd., Series A
United States Steel Corp....7% Cum. Pfd.
United States Tobacco Co....7% Non-Cum. Pfd.

V

Virginia Electric & Power Co....$5 Div. Pfd.
    ...$4.20 Div. Pfd.
    ...$4.12 Div. Pfd.
    ...$4.04 Div. Pfd.
    ...$4.80 Div. Pfd.

W

West Penn Power Co. (The)...4½% Cum. Pfd.
    ...4.20% Cum. Pfd., Series B
    ...4.10% Cum. Pfd., Series C
West Virginia Pulp and Paper Company...4½% Cum. Pfd.
Westinghouse Electric Corp....3.80% Cum. Pfd., Ser. B
Wisconsin Electric Power Company...6% Pfd. (Cum.)

¶ 2395   Off-Floor Transactions in Listed Rights

"Rights", places of executions

Rule 395.   Unless otherwise determined by the Exchange, all transactions
            by members and member organizations in subscription rights
admitted to dealings on the Exchange, whether for the account of customers
or for the account of such members or organizations, shall be made only on
a national securities exchange on which such subscription rights are admitted
to dealings.

● ● ● *Supplementary Material:*

.10   Exemptions from Rule 395 [¶ 2395].—The Exchange has determined
    upon the following specific exemptions from Rule 395, above:

    (1) In respect of rights to subscribe to bonds, the Exchange has
determined that members and member organizations may deal for their
own account, off the Floor of the Exchange, with other members, non-
member brokers and dealers, and institutions.

    (2) In connection with rights to subscribe to preferred stocks, the
Exchange may consider requests for exemptions to permit the purchase
of rights over-the-counter in blocks of a size sufficient to subscribe to not
less than $100,000 of the securities subject to the rights, (and in respect
of issues amounting to less than $7,500,000 the size of the wholesale lot
might be proportionately reduced) provided the purchase is for the purpose of subscribing to the issue.

¶ 2395   **Rule 395**   © 1965, Commerce Clearing House, Inc.

(3) Members and member organizations may deal for their own account, off the Floor of the Exchange, with other members, non-member brokers and dealers, and institutions in rights to subscribe to certain preferred stocks which are included or which the Exchange has determined to include, in the special list of preferred stocks in which transactions may be made off the Floor of the Exchange without specific permission of the Exchange.

(4) The Exchange may give consideration to requests for exemptions in respect of private negotiations for the purchase over-the-counter of large blocks of rights to subscribe to preferred stocks or common stocks (A) in relation to the size of the issue, provided that the purchase is for the purpose of subscribing to the issue or (B) where because the size of certain blocks is so large that in the opinion of the Exchange the orderly process of the market might otherwise be disturbed, provided the purchase is for the purpose of subscribing to the issue.

(5) Member organizations may effect purchase transactions in rights admitted to trading on the Exchange, for own account, off the Floor of the Exchange, on a principal basis, in any number in a single transaction where the amount involved is less than $2; and in not more than 5 rights in a single transaction where the money involved is more than $2 but not more than $15; provided any sale of rights so purchased is made on a national securities exchange.

A member organization, having purchased rights in the manner described above, shall send the seller a principal confirmation and pay the proceeds to him either in cash or by check. No separate ledger account need be opened for such transaction provided the member organization makes and maintains a record containing the complete details of the transaction, including the name and address of the person from whom the rights were purchased. This procedure will be in compliance with Regulation § 240.17a-3 [¶ 4583] of the Securities and Exchange Commission.

(6) In some instances, issuers of rights have made arrangements with a particular bank or trust company to handle orders of stockholders to buy or sell so-called "overage" rights. This involves buying:

(A) From a stockholder whose rights are insufficient to subscribe to one share, all of such rights; or

(B) from a stockholder who is subscribing to the offering, any excess rights insufficient to subscribe to one share,

or selling:

(A) To a stockholder who is subscribing to the offering but who has received from the issuing company rights in an amount insufficient to subscribe to one share, the minimum number of rights necessary to enable him to subscribe to one share; or

(B) to a stockholder who is subscribing to the offering but who has received from the issuing company rights in excess of a number exactly sufficient for subscription, the minimum number of rights necessary to enable him to subscribe to one additional share.

Daily, after balancing off purchases and sales of the "overage" rights, the bank or trust company may have a remaining "breakage." Member organizations may purchase from the bank or trust company in such cases, off the

Floor of the Exchange, on a principal basis, the rights represented by such "breakage," provided any sale of rights so purchased is made on a national securities exchange.

¶ 2396   Off-Floor Transactions in Bonds

"Nine-bond" rule

Rule 396. Unless the prior consent of the Exchange has been obtained, every order for the purchase or sale of bonds, whether on a principal or agency basis, shall be sent to the Floor for execution except:

(1) When the order calls for the purchase or sale of ten bonds or more; or

(2) after a market on the Floor has been diligently sought and it has been ascertained that the order may be executed at a better price elsewhere; or

(3) in the case of an agency transaction (including intra-office cross transactions), when the customer specifically directs that the particular order shall not be executed on the Floor; but no member or member organization shall solicit such instructions before sending the order to the Floor and diligently seeking a market thereon; or

(4) when the order calls for the purchase or sale of securities of the United States, Puerto Rico, the Philippine Islands, or States, Territories or Municipalities therein, or of bonds which, pursuant to call or otherwise, are to be redeemed within twelve months.

Amendments.
March 29, 1956, effective April 2, 1956.

● ● ● *Supplementary Material:*

.10   Information regarding "Nine-bond rule."—In order to comply with the provisions of Rule 396, above, that a market on the Floor be "diligently sought," the following requirements must be observed:

(1) A bid or offer must actually be made on the Floor at a price before a purchase or sale at the same price may be made off the Exchange.

(2) (A) The bid or offer must be entered promptly on the Floor for the full amount of the order and must be maintained on the Floor for at least one hour or, if received less than one hour before the close, until the close.

(B) When prior to the expiration of the minimum time required in (A) above, a purchase or sale is made on the Floor of less than the full amount bid for or offered pursuant to (A) above, and a balance of the original order remains unfilled, the bid or offer for the entire amount of such unfilled balance must be maintained on the Floor until the expiration of the minimum time requirement applicable to the original order.

For information regarding dealings in rights to subscribe to bonds see ¶ 2395.10, Off-Floor Transactions in Listed Rights.

[The next page is 3695.]

Conduct of Accounts

*(Rules and Policies Administered by the
Department of Member Firms.)*

¶ 2401   Business Conduct

Rule 401. Every member, allied member and member organization shall at
all times adhere to the principles of good business practice in the
conduct of his or its business affairs.

¶ 2402   Restrictions on Pledge of Customers' Securities

Rule 402. (a) No agreement between a member organization and a customer authorizing the member organization to pledge securities
carried for the account of the customer either alone or with other securities,
either for the amount due thereon or for a greater amount, or to lend such
securities, shall justify the member organization in pledging or lending more
of such securities than is fair and reasonable in view of the indebtedness of
said customer to said member organization, except as provided in paragraph
(d) of this Rule.

Agreements for Use of Customers' Securities

(b) No member organization shall lend, either to itself as broker or to
others, securities held on margin for a customer and which may be pledged
or loaned under paragraph (a) hereof, unless such member organization shall
first have obtained a separate written authorization from such customer permitting the lending of such securities by such member organization.

Restrictions on Delivery of Customers' Securities

(c) No general agreement between a member organization and a customer shall justify the member organization in delivering securities carried
for the customer on sales made by the member organization for any account
in which such member organization or any partner thereof or stockholder
therein is directly or indirectly interested.

Free or Excess Margin Securities

(d) No securities held by a member organization for the account of a
customer, whether free or representing excess margin, may be loaned to itself
as broker, or to others, or delivered on sales made by the member organization
for any account in which the organization or any partner or stockholder has
a direct or indirect interest unless a specific written agreement designating
the particular securities to be loaned is first obtained from the customer.

● ● ● *Supplementary Material:*

Segregation of Securities

.10 **Wholly-owned and excess margin securities—Individual identification.—**
When a member organization holds securities that have been fully paid
for or holds securities in excess of the amount which can be pledged under
Rule 402, above, such securities should be segregated and marked in a manner which clearly identifies the interest of each individual customer. When
such securities are in the actual custody of the organization, this may be

¶ 2402.10 Segregation of Securities.—Continued

accomplished by placing them in separate envelopes bearing the customers' names or by attaching tags or labels, similarly marked, to the securities or by some other means which produces the same result. The date as of which a particular certificate is segregated should be clearly indicated either on the tag, label or envelope bearing the customer's name. When such securities are not in the actual custody of the organization, their location and the means by which they may be identified as belonging to the customers should be indicated on the books of the organization. The foregoing applies both to odd lots and full lots.

.20 Wholly-owned and excess margin stocks—Suggested bulk method.—Any member organization adopting the following method of segregation should notify the Department of Member Firms.

I

.30 General practice of brokerage offices.—In the general practice of brokerage offices, instructions for the segregation of customers' securities originate in the margin department and are carried out by the cashier. In the case of "free" (fully paid) and excess margin stocks, the cashier places the stock certificates in a separate box and annexes to each certificate a small linen or paper tab giving the name of the specific customer as owner. If a customer having "free" securities buys stock on margin or has a margin account which needs additional margin, the margin clerk directs the cashier to transfer from the box containing customers' "free" and excess margin securities the certificates that are required as margin. These certificates are then placed in the box of the organization containing "usable securities", that is, securities which the organization may use as margin. In case a less amount of stock is required as margin or if the balance of a customer's margin account is paid in full, the margin department directs the cashier to release the shares from the box containing the "usable securities" and they are returned to the box containing the customers' "free" and excess margin securities.

II

.40 Segregation for out-of-town branch offices and correspondents.—In the case of out-of-town branch offices of brokerage houses and in the case of their correspondents, the present system under which "free" and excess margin shares are identified and allotted to the particular customer involves the daily report by telegraph to out-of-town branches and correspondents of the numbers of the specific certificates segregated.

III
Card Plan

The card plan of identifying the segregated stocks will comprise:

.51 Requisition card.—(1) A "requisition card" indicating the name or account number of the person for whom the shares have been segregated, the number of shares, the name of the corporation and two spaces to be filled in by

(a) the margin clerk who orders it, and

(b) the security clerk who accomplishes the segregation.

This card will be substantially as follows:

¶ 2402.20   **Rule 402**   © 1957, Commerce Clearing House, Inc.

REQUISITION CARD

FIRM (CORPORATION) NAME		
Segregated for: *LANDEN, WALTER*		
Quantity	Security	
15	*U. S. STEEL*	
Remarks	Ordered by	Accomplished by
	A. B. Margin Clerk	*W. Z.* Security Clerk
	Date	Date
	(Rubber stamp)	(Rubber stamp)

.52 Removal card.—(2) A "removal card" will provide for the removal of shares from segregation giving the name or account number of the owner and the shares to be released. It will be initialed by the margin clerk who orders the removal of the shares and also by the security clerk who releases them. This card will be substantially as follows:

REMOVAL CARD

(Red Print) FIRM (CORPORATION) NAME		
Remove from segregation for: *SMITH, F.*		
Quantity	Security	
1,000	*U. S. STEEL*	
Remarks	Ordered by	Accomplished by
	D. E. Margin Clerk	*W. Z.* Security Clerk
	Date	Date
	(Rubber stamp)	(Rubber stamp)

.53 Summary card.—(3) A "summary card" will be headed with the name of the stock, and will show the total quantity of the shares segregated, the number of wholly-owned and excess margin shares belonging to custom-

¶ 2402.53   Card Plan.—Continued

ers, and also the number of shares to be segregated or the number of shares in excess of outstanding segregation instructions. This card will be substantially in the following form:

SUMMARY CARD

U. S. STEEL CORPORATION					
FIRM (CORPORATION) NAME					
Summary segregation record					
Date	Customer Shares	To be Segreg'd	Excess Segreg'n	Total in Segreg'n	Approved by
June 1	300		200	500	
2	700	200		500	
3					
6					
7					
8					
9					
10					

.54   Operation details of bulk method.—Under this plan, the margin department will as heretofore give direction to the cashier to place in the box containing the customer's "free" and excess margin shares the shares which are not required to finance the customer's indebtedness. The margin clerk will also fill out and initial the "requisition card" which will direct the security clerk to segregate (by placing in the "free" and excess margin box) the shares allotted to the specific customer on the requisition card. The security clerk will initial the card after he has placed the stock certificates in the box containing the "free" and excess margin shares.

If after this segregation is accomplished the margin department determines to order the removal of any "free" or excess margin shares from the segregated securities, the margin department will make out and initial the "removal card" directing the security clerk to remove certain shares from segregation. After the security clerk has removed the shares he will initial the "removal card."

Thus it is proposed to treat all one hundred share certificates of the same stock in the box of segregated "free" and excess margin shares as the equivalent of every other one hundred share certificate (or as "fungible") and the cards will control and identify the shares and will be the evidence of title on behalf of the persons whose names are on the cards.

The security clerk or a supervisory employee will be completely responsible for the box containing the segregated shares and must at all times have sufficient shares to cover all amounts called for by the cards in the "Total in Segregation" column of the "summary card."

¶ **2402.54   Rule 402**   © 1957, Commerce Clearing House, Inc.

The "summary card" will enable brokers to determine from day to day the total number of shares segregated. Although the "summary card" illustrated on the previous page provides space for recording the shares to be segregated on the basis of outstanding and unaccomplished instructions such column may be eliminated if the member organization's system does not necessarily require a "To be Segregated" column. The daily entries of amounts will be initialed by the security clerk or a supervisory employee.

The "requisition," "removal" and "summary" cards must be kept for a period running back to the date of last answer to the Stock Exchange Financial Questionnaire but at least six months in any event.

(*See also S. E. C. Regulation* § 240.17a-4 [¶ 4584].)

IV

.60 Securities registered in customers' names not to be put in segregated box.—If the above described method of segregation is used, all securities segregated must be registered either in the broker's name, the name of one of its nominees, or "street" names. *No securities registered in the names of customers may be put into the segregated box.* Each customer whose securities are to be transferred out of his name for the purpose of making such securities usable in the bulk segregation, should be given prompt notice of the transfer of his free or excess margin securities, or his consent in writing to do so obtained. In case a customer refuses to give such consent, or objects to the transfer, such of his securities shall be identified and segregated separately.

Note: The above plan would not apply to securities not of a "fungible" nature, such, for example, as callable bonds. Such securities would require separate identification and segregation, as heretofore. (See "Callable Bonds" at .80, below.)

.70 Segregation of excess margin securities.—With respect to the segregation of customers' securities representing excess margin as required under Rule 402(a) [¶ 2402], a member organization should segregate that portion of the stocks in a customer's account having a market value in excess of 140% of the debit balance therein. The foregoing applies solely to a customer's account which contains only stocks. When a customer's account contains bonds, the basis upon which the organization is borrowing or can borrow on such bonds should be taken into consideration in determining the amount of securities to be segregated.

.80 Callable bonds.—Member organizations which have in their possession or under their control bonds of issues which are callable in part, whether held in safekeeping or otherwise, shall so identify each such bond that their records shall clearly show for whose account it is held. However, this ruling need not be followed in the case of bonds, interest upon which has not been paid for at least two interest periods. In the event there is any call, in part, of such bonds not so identified, the member organization shall not allocate any such called bonds to any account in which it or its partners or stockholders have an interest until all customers' positions in such bonds have been satisfied.

.90 Approval.—Any proposed system devised by a member organization for the segregation of customers' securities in bulk which does not follow the exact procedure above described should be presented to the Department of Member Firms for approval.

¶ 2403   Bucket Shops, etc.

Rule 403. No member, allied member, or member organization shall be
directly or indirectly interested in or associated in business with,
or have his or its office directly or indirectly connected by public or private
wire or other method or contrivance with, or transact any business directly
or indirectly with or for:

(1) Any bucket-shop; or

(2) any organization, firm or individual making a practice of dealing
on differences in market quotations; or

(3) any organization, firm or individual engaged in purchasing or
selling securities for customers and making a practice of taking the side
of the market opposite to the side taken by customers.

(See ¶ 2358.13 re Private Wires.)

¶ 2404   Individual Members Not to Carry Accounts

Rule 404. No member, doing business as an individual, shall carry accounts
for customers, except as provided in Rule 316 [¶ 2316].

¶ 2405   Diligence as to Accounts

Rule 405. Every member organization is required through a general partner
or an officer who is a holder of voting stock to

(1) Use due diligence to learn the essential facts relative to every
customer, every order, every cash or margin account accepted or carried
by such organization and every person holding power of attorney over
any account accepted or carried by such organization.

Supervision of Accounts

(2) Supervise diligently all accounts handled by registered representatives of the organization.

Approval of Accounts

(3) Specifically approve the opening of an account prior to or
promptly after the completion of any transaction for the account of or
with a customer, provided, however, that in the case of branch offices, the
opening of an account for a customer may be approved by the manager
of such branch office but the action of such branch office manager shall
within a reasonable time be approved by a general partner or an officer
who is a holder of voting stock in the organization. The member, general
partner or officer approving the opening of the account shall, prior to giving his approval, be personally informed as to the essential facts relative
to the customer and to the nature of the proposed account and shall indicate his approval in writing on a document which is a part of the permanent records of his office or organization.

• • • Supplementary Material:

.10 Application of Rule 405(1) and (3) [¶ 2405].—In the case of a margin
account carried by a member organization for a non-member corporation,
definite knowledge should be had to the effect that the non-member corporation
has the right under its charter and by-laws to engage in margin transactions
for its own account and that the persons from whom orders and instructions are
accepted have been duly authorized by the corporation to act on its behalf.
It is advisable in each such case for the carrying organization to have in its

¶ 2403 **Rule 403**   © 1960, Commerce Clearing House, Inc.

possession a copy of the corporate Charter, By-laws and authorizations. Where it is not possible to obtain such documents, a member or allied member in the member organization carrying the account should prepare and sign a memorandum for its files indicating the basis upon which he believes that the corporation may properly engage in margin transactions and that the persons acting for the corporation have been duly authorized to do so.

In the case of a cash account carried for a non-member corporation, the carrying member organization should assure itself through a general partner or an officer who is a holder of voting stock that persons entering orders and issuing instructions with respect to the account do so upon the proper authority.

When an agency account is carried by a member organization its files should contain the name of the principal for whom the agent is acting and written evidence of the agent's authority.

When Estate and Trustee accounts are involved or when a husband is acting as agent for his wife, a member organization should obtain counsel's advice as to the documents which should be obtained.

In the case of accounts which are introduced by one member or member organization to another and are carried on a disclosed basis, the introducer will not be held to any responsibility under Rule 405(1) and (3) [¶ 2405] when the essential facts concerning a particular customer are obtained directly by the clearing organization and the opening of the account is approved by a member or allied member in the clearing organization "prior to or promptly after the completion of any brokerage transaction" and that is the understanding between the two.

As an alternative method of handling the investigation and approval of such accounts the clearing organization may treat the introducing organization, for the purposes of Rule 405(1) and (3) [¶ 2405], as though it were its branch office. Under these circumstances, the introducer will learn the essential facts with respect to each customer, and a general partner or an officer who is a holder of voting stock in the introducing organization will give an approval for the opening of the account. The information obtained must subsequently be passed upon by a member or allied member in the clearing organization and any further inquiry which the clearing organization might feel is desirable should be made. However, the mere fact that the account is being introduced by another member, or member organization is not sufficient information to permit a member or allied member in the carrying organization to approve the opening of the account.

Information as to the country of which a customer is a citizen is deemed to be an essential fact.

¶ 2406   Designation of Accounts

Rule 406. No member organization shall carry an account:

(1) On its books in the name of a person other than that of the customer, except that an account may be designated by a number or symbol, provided the organization has on file a written statement signed by the customer attesting the ownership of such account.

[The next page is 3701-3.]

Accounts of Members and Allied Members in Other Member Organizations

(2) For a member or allied member of another member organization without the prior written consent of another general partner or officer who is a holder of voting stock in such other organization. Duplicate reports and monthly statements shall be sent to a general partner or an officer who is a holder of voting stock (other than the member or allied member for whom the account is carried) designated in such consent.

All clearance transactions for a member or allied member of another member organization shall be reported by the clearing organization to a general partner or officer who is a holder of voting stock in such other organization who has no interest in such transactions.

¶ 2407   Transactions—Employees of Exchange, Member Organizations, or Certain Non-Member Organizations

Rule 407.   No member or member organization shall, without the prior written consent of the employer, make:

(1) A cash or margin transaction or carry a margin account in securities or commodities in which an employee of another member or member organization is directly or indirectly interested. Except in connection with transactions of an employee in Monthly Investment Plan type accounts, duplicate reports and statements shall be sent promptly to the employer.

(2) A cash or margin transaction or carry a margin account in securities or commodities in which an employee of the Exchange, or of any corporation of which the Exchange owns the majority of the capital stock, is directly or indirectly interested.

(3) A margin transaction or carry a margin account in securities or commodities in which an employee of a bank, trust company, insurance company, or of any other corporation, association, firm or individual engaged in the business of dealing, either as broker or as principal, in stocks, bonds, or other securities in any form, bills of exchange, acceptances, or other forms of commercial paper, is directly or indirectly interested.

Amendments.
June 16, 1960, effective July 1, 1960.

● ● ● *Supplementary Material:*

.10 Employees of Exchange.—An employee of the Exchange or any of its affiliated companies who wishes to open a securities or commodities account should apply for permission from the Secretary of the Exchange. A form of application can be obtained in the Office of the Secretary.

.20 Application of Rule 407(3).—Rule 407(3) applies to all employees of insurance companies without regard to whether they are compensated on a salary or commission basis. However, it is not considered applicable to independent insurance agents.

For the purpose of Rule 407(3), a person who is clearly designated by the Charter or By-Laws of a bank, trust company, insurance company, etc., as an officer of such institution is not considered an "employee".

¶ 2408   Employees' Discretion as to Customers' Accounts

Rule 408. No member or member organization shall permit any of his or its employees or any employee of another member or member organization to exercise discretion in the handling of a transaction for a customer of such member organization and no member, member organization, partner or stockholder therein shall delegate to any such employee any discretionary power vested by a customer in such member, organization, partner or stockholder, unless in either case the prior written authorization of the customer has been received and, if such discretionary authority runs, directly or by redelegation, to an employee of another member or member organization, the carrying organization must obtain the prior written consent of the employer of the individual authorized to exercise discretion. A member or allied member in the carrying organization shall approve and initial each discretionary order entered by an employee of such organization or of another member or member organization on the day the order is entered. The provisions of this Rule shall not apply to discretion as to the price at which or the time when an order given by a customer for the purchase or sale of a definite amount of a specified security shall be executed.

¶ 2409   Statements of Accounts to Customers

Rule 409.   (a) Except with the permission of the Exchange, member organizations shall send to their customers statements of account showing security and money positions and entries at least quarterly to all accounts having an entry, money or security position during the preceding quarter. *(See also SEC Rule 15c3-2 concerning quarterly notices of free credit balances on statements.)*

(b) No member organization shall address confirmations, statements or other communications to a non-member customer

(1) in care of a person holding power of attorney over the customer's account unless either (A) the customer has instructed the member organization in writing to send such confirmations, statements or other communications in care of such person, or (B) duplicate copies are sent to the customer at some other address designated in writing by him; or

(2) at the address of any member, member organization, or in care of a partner, stockholder or employee of any member organization.

The Exchange may upon written request therefor waive these requirements.

Amendment.
October 15, 1964, effective January 1, 1965.

● ● ● *Supplementary Material:*

.10   Exceptions to Rule 409(b) [¶ 2409].—The provisions of Rule 409(b), above, are not considered applicable to the following:

(1) General or special partners or holders of voting or non-voting stock of member organizations.

(2) Employees of member organizations.

(3) Persons who maintain desk space at the office of a member or member organization and who thereby establish such office as their place of business.

(4) Corporations of which partners, stockholders or employees are officers or directors, and corporation accounts over which such persons have powers of attorney, provided, in each such case, the partner, stockholder or employee is duly authorized by the corporation to receive communications covering the account.

(5) Trust accounts, when a partner, stockholder or employee of a member organization is a trustee and has been duly authorized by all other trustees to receive communications covering the account.

(6) Estate accounts, when a partner, stockholder or employee of a member organization is an executor or administrator of the estate and has been duly authorized by all other executors or administrators to receive communications covering the account.

(7) A wife's account with respect to which the husband acts as agent.

(8) Upon the written instructions of a customer and with the written approval of a member or allied member, a member organization may hold mail for a customer who will not be at his usual address for the period of his absence, but (a) not to exceed two months if the organization is advised that such customer will be on vacation or travelling or (b) not t' exceed three months if the customer is going abroad.

¶ 2410   Records of Orders

Rule 410. Every member or his organization shall preserve for at least three years a record of:

Transmitted to Floor

    (1) every order transmitted directly or indirectly by such member or organization to the Floor, which record shall include the name and amount of the security, the terms of the order, the time when it was so transmitted, and the time at which a report of execution was received.

Carried to Floor

    (2) every order received by such member, either orally or in writing, and carried by such member to the Floor, which record shall include the name and amount of the security, the terms of the order, the time when it was so received and the time at which a report of execution was received.

Cancellation

    (3) the time of the entry of every cancellation of an order covered by (1) and (2) above.

By Accounts

Before any order covered by (1) or (2) above is executed, there shall be placed upon the order slip or other record of the member, or his organization the name or designation of the account for which such order is to be executed. No change in such account name or designation shall be made unless the change has been authorized by the member or another member or allied member in his organization who shall, prior to giving his approval of such change, be personally informed of the essential facts relative thereto and shall indicate his approval of such change in writing on the order.

Exceptions

Under exceptional circumstances, the Exchange may upon written request waive the requirements contained in (1) and (2) above.

¶ 2411   Erroneous Reports

Rule 411. The price at which an order is executed shall be binding notwithstanding the fact that an erroneous report in respect thereto may have been rendered. A report shall not be binding if an order was not actually executed but was in error reported to have been executed; an order which was executed, but in error reported as not executed, shall be binding; provided, however, when a member who is on the Floor reports in good faith the execution of an order entrusted to him by another member or member organization and the other party to that transaction does not know it, the member or member organization to whom such report was rendered and the member broker who made the report shall treat the transaction as made for the account of the member who made the report, or the account of his member organization, if the price and size of the transaction were within the price and volume of transactions in the security at the time that the member who made the report believed he had executed the order. A detailed memorandum of each such transaction shall be prepared and filed with the Exchange by the member assuming the transaction.

    (Form DK2 can be obtained at Money Desk on the Floor.)

Amendments.
January 19, 1956, effective February 13, 1956.
June 28, 1957, effective July 1, 1957.

(See Rule 369 [¶ 2369] re Assumption of Customers' Contracts.)

● ● ● *Supplementary Material:*

INFORMATION REGARDING CONDUCT OF ACCOUNTS

.10 "Bunching" odd-lot orders.—A member or member organization shall not combine the orders given by several different customers to buy or sell odd lots of the same stock, into a round-lot order without the prior approval of the customers interested.

When a person gives, either for his own account or for various accounts in which he has an actual monetary interest, buy or sell odd-lot orders which aggregate 100 shares or more, such orders shall, as far as possible, be consolidated into full lots, except that selling orders marked "long" need not be so consolidated with selling orders marked "short."

(See Rule 372 [¶ 2372] for commissions on execution of bunched orders.)

.20 Confirmations to customers.—Confirmations of all transactions (including those made "over-the-counter" and on other exchanges) in securities admitted to dealings on the Exchange, sent by members or member organizations to their customers, shall bear the name of the securities market on which the transactions were made. This requirement also applies to confirmations or reports from an organization to a correspondent, but does not apply to reports made by floor brokers to the member or member organization from whom the orders were received.

It is urged that stationery be imprinted with a suitable legend or rubber stamps be used to indicate the required information on all confirmations. The exact form of legend and the manner of affixing the same is in the discretion of each member organization, except that the information in each case shall be clearly set forth.

.30 Wire messages.

(See Rules 355—357 [¶ 2355—2357], Private Wire and other connections; See also S. E. C. Regulation § 240.17a-4 [¶ 4584].)

.40 Recording of transactions in accounts.—Transactions in securities shall be recorded in accounts as of settlement dates and interest shall be computed accordingly.

.50 Monthly statements of guaranteed accounts.—Member organizations carrying margin accounts for customers should send duplicate copies of monthly statements of guaranteed accounts to the respective guarantors unless such guarantors have specifically declared in writing that they do not wish such statements sent to them.

.60 Give-ups on wire business; method of handling.—When a member or member organization receives an order from a customer of another member or organization, with instructions to give up that other member or organization, the member or organization originally receiving the order in New York shall on the same day send a written confirmation of the order as received to the office of the other member or organization.

The member or organization executing such an order shall confirm the execution thereof on the same day in writing to the office of the New York member or organization for whose account it was executed.

¶ 2411   Information Regarding Conduct of Accounts.—Continued

These confirmations shall be in addition to any report which may be made on the Floor.

The member or organization executing such an order shall clear the transaction unless otherwise consented to by the member or organization carrying the customer's account. If such member or organization is not a Clearing Member he shall cause the transaction to be cleared or settled for him by a Clearing Member.

.70   **Give-ups on wire business; time for effecting.**—The limit of time within which the executing member or organization must report to the member or organization carrying the customer's account shall be 4:15 p. m.

[The next page is 3721.]

Financial Statements and Reports

*(Rules and Policies Administered by the
Department of Member Firms.)*

¶ 2415   Accounts and Securities

Rule 415. When a member organization commences to carry accounts or
          hold securities for customers it shall immediately so notify the
Exchange in writing.

¶ 2416   Financial Questionnaire

Rule 416. Each member and member organization shall file with the Ex-
          change, at such times as may be designated, an answer to a
financial questionnaire in such form as may be prescribed.

[The next page is 3721-3.]

¶ 2417   Audit

Rule 417. The Exchange may require any member or member organization to cause to be made as of the date of an answer to a financial questionnaire an audit, by an independent public accountant, of his or its accounts and assets, including securities held for safekeeping, in accordance with such regulations as shall be prescribed and to file a statement to the effect that such audit has been made and whether it is in accord with the answer to the questionnaire. Such statement shall, in the case of each member not a partner or a stockholder in a member organization, be signed by such member and, in the case of each member organization, shall be signed by each member and allied member thereof unless, for good cause shown, the signature of one or more of them is waived by the Exchange provided, however, that the signatures of only two members or allied members shall be required if the answer to such financial questionnaire is made available to all members and allied members of the organization. Such statement shall in all cases be attested by the auditors, and the original report of the audit signed by the auditors shall be retained as part of the books and records of the member or organization.

Amendments.
December 19, 1955, effective January 4, 1956.

● ● ● *Supplementary Material:*

REGULATIONS PRESCRIBED FOR AUDIT UNDER AUTHORITY OF RULE 417 [¶ 2417]

(Identical With Those Prescribed by the Securities and Exchange Commission Pursuant to Regulation § 240.17a-5 [¶ 4585])

.10 The audit shall substantiate the stated assets and liabilities as of the date of the financial questionnaire and the scope and comprehensiveness thereof shall be such as would enable the independent public accountant to express an opinion as to the stated financial condition of the respondent as of that date.

The scope of the audit shall include at least the following:

(1) Comparison of ledger accounts with the trial balances obtained from the general and private ledgers and proofs of the aggregates of subsidiary ledgers with their respective controlling accounts.

(2) Physical examination and comparison with the books and records of all securities, currencies, tax stamps, warehouse receipts, and other such assets on hand, in vault, or in box, or otherwise in physical possession.

(3) Verification of securities in transit or in transfer.

(4) Balancing of positions in all securities and spot and future commodities as shown by the books and records.

(5) Obtaining of written confirmations with respect to the following (See note):

(a) bank balances; (In addition to the reconcilement and confirmation of bank balances as of the date of the audit, the independent public accountant shall, at a later date, after giving ample time for clearance of outstanding checks and transfers of funds, obtain from depositaries cancelled checks and statements of the bank accounts as of such date, and reconcile the balances shown thereon with the balances shown by the books of the respondent.)

(b) open contractual positions and deposits of funds with clearing corporations or associations;

(c) money borrowed and detail of collateral;

(d) accounts, commodities, securities, and commitments carried for the respondent by others;

(e) details of: (i) securities borrowed (ii) securities loaned (iii) securities failed to deliver (iv) securities failed to receive (v) when issued contracts (vi) delayed delivery and other similar open contracts and (vii) open commodity contracts with others;

(f) customers', partners', officers', directors' and respondent's accounts; (Confirmation of these accounts may be in the form of a written acknowledgment of the accuracy of the statement of balances, security positions, and open contractual commitments, other than uncleared regular way purchases and sales, accompanying the first request for confirmation mailed by the independent public accountant.)

(g) guarantees in cases where required to protect accounts guaranteed as of audit date; and

(h) all other accounts which in the opinion of the independent public accountant should be confirmed.

(*Note.—Compliance with requirements for obtaining written confirmation with respect to the above accounts shall be deemed to have been made if requests for confirmation have been mailed by the independent public accountant in an envelope bearing his own return address and second requests are similarly mailed to those not replying to the first requests, together with such auditing procedures as may be necessary; provided, however, that with respect to periodic investment plans sponsored by member firms of a national securities exchange, whose members are exempted from Regulation § 240.15c-1 [¶ 4482] by paragraph (b)(2) thereof, the independent public accountant examining the financial statements of the originating member firm may omit direct written confirmation of such plan accounts with customers when, in his judgment, such procedures are not necessary if (1) the originating member firm does not receive or hold securities belonging to such plan accounts and does not receive or hold funds for such accounts, except the initial payment which is promptly transmitted to the custodian; (2) the custodian is a member firm of such national securities exchange and files certified reports complying with Regulation § 240.17a-5 [¶4585] in connection with which the customers' accounts are confirmed by an independent public accountant; and (3) funds and securities held by the custodian for each such customer's account are reconciled with the records of the originating member firm as of the date of the most recent audit of the custodian.*)

(6) A written statement should be obtained from the proprietor, partner (if a partnership) or officer (if a corporation) as to the assets, liabilities, and accountabilities, contingent or otherwise, not recorded on the books of the respondent.

(7) The independent public accountant shall review the methods of internal accounting control of the respondent and its procedures for safeguarding securities.

SPECIAL INSTRUCTIONS

.11 Any condition disclosed by the audit that would cause the Net Capital or net worth of the member, member firm or member organization to be less than that prescribed by the Board of Governors shall be reported to the Department of Member Firms by the member organization immediately upon the ascertainment of such facts.

A written report, addressed to the member organization shall be submitted by the independent public accountant in which he shall attest that THE REQUIREMENTS OF THE AUDIT REGULATIONS HAVE BEEN OBSERVED IN THE CONDUCT OF THE AUDIT, and specifically comment in such report:

(1) That he has made a review of the methods of internal accounting control of the member organization; and

(2) That he has reviewed its procedures for safeguarding securities.

Not later than forty-five days after the date of audit, *the independent public accountant shall forward* a signed copy of such report in a sealed envelope addressed to

Chief Examiner
New York Stock Exchange
Department of Member Firms
11 Wall Street, New York 5, N. Y.

A copy of the answer to each financial questionnaire and all working papers and memoranda covering the answer should be retained for at least three years. (Working papers, etc., if in the custody of the independent public accountant, must be available for audit and review by a representative of the New York Stock Exchange.)

¶ 2418   "Surprise" Audits

Rule 418. Each member organization doing any business with others than members and member organizations is required to have an annual audit of its affairs conducted, in accordance with the audit regulations of the Exchange by independent public accountants at a date to be selected by such accountants without prior notice to the member organization, and to have such accountants prepare an answer to the financial questionnaire of the Exchange based upon such audit.

● ● ● *Supplementary Material:*
Information Regarding Audits

.10 Each member organization subject to Rule 418, above, shall select an independent public accountant to make such an audit at least once in each calendar year and shall notify the Department of Member Firms of the selection before January 10th of each year, submitting, at the same time, *a signed copy* of an agreement obtained from such accountant(s).

The required agreement should read substantially as follows although additional provisions may be contained therein:

. . . .
(Name of member organization)

Gentlemen:

You have selected us (me) to conduct an audit of your affairs as of a date during the calendar year 19...., in accordance with the audit regulations of the New York Stock Exchange, and to prepare an answer to its financial questionnaire based upon such audit.

We (I) agree

(1) to make an audit of the affairs of your firm (corporation) as of a date during the calendar year 19...., to be selected by us (me) without prior notice to your firm (corporation), in accordance with the audit regulations of the New York Stock Exchange;

(2) to notify the Department of Member Firms promptly that the audit has been commenced;

(3) to prepare an answer to its financial questionnaire based upon such audit;

(4) to submit to the Department of Member Firms a copy of such answer accompanied by a signed attestation in form prescribed by the Exchange;

(5) to submit to the Department of Member Firms a copy of our (my) report which will include an attest that the requirements of the audit regulations have been observed in the conduct of the audit, and specific statements that a review has been made of: (i) the methods of internal accounting control of the firm (corporation); and (ii) the firm's (corporation's) procedures for safeguarding securities.

Very truly yours,

. . . .
(Name of independent public accountant(s))

Under this procedure the accountant(s) will select a date during the year without discussion or consultation with the member organization. Therefore, the first indication which a member organization will receive that an audit is is to be made of its affairs will be the appearance of the accountant(s) at the office of the member organization. The accountant(s) will not be precluded from starting his inspection a few days prior to the audit date for the purpose of accomplishing preliminary work. Upon receipt by the Department of advice from the independent public accountant(s) that he has commenced such an audit of a member organization or the preliminary work in connection therewith, instructions with respect to the preparation and submission of the answer to the financial questionnaire and the regulations to be followed in conducting the audit and an attestation form will be forwarded promptly to the member organization for delivery to the independent public accountant(s).

¶ 2419   **Financial Statements to Customers**

Rule 419. Each member organization, except one subject to supervision by State or Federal banking authorities, shall make available to any customer of such organization at his request a statement of its financial condition as of the date of its most recent answer to the financial questionnaire of the Exchange or as of a date subsequent thereto. The financial statement shall be one which in the opinion of the organization fairly presents the financial condition of such organization.

Each monthly statement sent to a customer shall bear a legend reading as follows:

"A financial statement of this firm (corporation) is available for your personal inspection at its offices, or a copy of it will be mailed upon your written request."

Within thirty-five days of the date after which each annual audited financial questionnaire is required to be filed with the Exchange, each customer shall be sent either:

(1) A financial statement of the organization based upon such audit, which statement in the opinion of the organization fairly presents the financial condition of the organization, or

(2) a notice, with a return post card, reading as follows if the audit has been completed:

(A) "A financial statement of this firm (corporation) based on an audit by an independent public accountant is available for your personal inspection at its offices, or a copy of it will be mailed upon your written request. For your convenience in making such a request a return post card is enclosed."

or, in lieu of paragraph (A) above, in the event the audit is still in process, a notice with a return post card, reading as follows:

(B) "A financial statement of this firm (corporation) based on an audit now being conducted by an independent public accountant will be available upon completion for your personal inspection at its offices, or a copy of it will be mailed upon written request. A return post card is enclosed for your convenience in advising us whether (1) you wish a copy of the financial statement mailed to you, or (2) you wish to be advised when the financial statement is available for inspection at our offices."

(Note: The term "customer" as used in the above Rule means any person who either at the time of requesting such a financial statement or at the time of the distribution of such annual notice has an open account with the member organization.

Each member organization shall file with the Department of Member Firms of the Exchange, promptly after completion of the required annual audit, an exact copy of the financial statement, based upon such audit, which the firm intends to submit to its customers. Statements made available or distributed to customers at other times during the year shall follow in form the statements based upon the annual audits. However, copies of such other statements are not to be filed with the Department of Member Firms unless the organization has not been in existence a sufficient length of time to have had such a required annual audit.)

(See ¶ 2325.30 for disclosure of subordinated borrowings in financial statements to customers.)

¶ 2420   **Reports of Loans**

Rule 420. Each member, allied member and member organization shall promptly report to the Exchange:

(1) All borrowings regardless of their size or nature where the proceeds are placed in an account representing working capital of such member or member organization and all personal loans as follows:

(A) Each loan obtained in the amount of $2,500 or more (whether of cash or securities) regardless of the source of such borrowing;

(B) Each loan made in the amount of $2,500 or more (whether of cash or securities) to any member or member organization, member or allied member therein;

(C) Aggregate totals to the nearest thousand dollars of all loans obtained and all loans made, when such aggregate figures exceed $2,500. These totals should include loans which do not individually amount to $2,500 as well as loans reported under (A) and (B) of paragraph (1) of this Rule.

(2) Each change in a loan previously reported.

(3) However, no report shall be required with respect to:

(A) Any loan fully secured by readily marketable collateral, so long as such loan remains so secured;

(B) Any loan of securities made by the borrower for the purpose of effecting delivery against a sale where money payment equivalent to the market value of the securities is made to the lender and such contract is marked approximately to the market;

(C) Any loan on a life insurance policy which is not in excess of the cash surrender value of such policy;

(D) Any loan obtained from a bank, trust company, monied corporation, or fiduciary on the security of real estate;

(E) Any loan transaction between members and/or allied members in the same member organization.

● ● ● *Supplementary Material:*

Loans and Borrowings

.10 All loans obtained where any part of the proceeds are used to supply working capital to the borrower's member organization are reportable regardless of the exceptions granted under Rule 420, Section (2), to loans obtained for other purposes.

Reports are to be in letter form, addressed to the Department of Member Firms, and should contain the following information with respect to each loan or borrowing covered by Rule 420, above:

(1) The name of the lender;

(2) The name of the borrower;

(3) The amount of the loan or borrowing; (If securities, describe each security and give its current market value)

¶ **2420**   **Rule 420**

(4) The rate of interest;

(5) The date the loan or borrowing was made;

(6) The date of maturity; (If on demand, so state)

(7) Description of any collateral held or given;

(8) A copy of any agreement or note given in connection with the loan or borrowing should be submitted with the communication;

(9) In the case of borrowings, a statement by the borrower indicating whether or not the borrowed funds are to be contributed to the working capital of his organization. For information regarding the submission of applications and other documents with respect to any proposed borrowings by member organizations on a subordinated basis, where the proceeds are to be considered when computing the net capital of a member organization under Rule 325 [¶ 2325], see ¶ 2325.20.

Reports are to be made at the time a reportable loan or borrowing is made and the details of any change in data previously reported should promptly be brought to the Department's attention. It should be kept in mind that each new borrowing or loan or the cancellation of an old borrowing or loan will require that the report contain a statement indicating the revised aggregate total of borrowings or of loans.

New members, allied members and member organizations having information to report in connection with Rule 420, above, should make such reports as promptly as possible after the date of their admission.

¶ 2421   Periodic Reports

Rule 421. Member organizations and individual *direct clearing* members shall submit, as required by the Exchange, periodic reports with respect to

(1) Short positions in listed securities;

(2) obligations in respect of security underwritings and net positions resulting therefrom;

(3) total of collateral loans from banks, trust companies and other lenders in the United States excluding borrowings from other members of national securities exchanges;

(4) customers' debit and credit balances

(*See* ¶ 2440D *for other reports to be filed with the Exchange.*)

● ● ● *Supplementary Material:*

.10   Short positions (Form MF-2).—Member organizations and individual *direct clearing* members are required to report on Form MF-2 total "short" positions, including odd lots, in each stock listed on the Exchange. Such reports must be made as of the close on the settlement date falling on the 15th of each month, or, where the 15th is a non-settlement date, on the preceding settlement date.

"Short" positions to be reported on Form MF-2 are those resulting from "short" sales as defined in the Securities and Exchange Commission's Regulation § 240.3b-3 [¶ 4235], but excluding positions resulting from sales specified in clauses (1), (6), (7) and (8) of paragraph (d) of the Commission's Regulation § 240.10a-1 [¶ 4324]. Also to be excluded are "short" positions carried for other members and member organizations reporting for themselves.

3 7 2 8   Rules of Board—Financial Statements and Reports   8-65
Report 106
➤➤➤ *Administered by Department of Member Firms.*

¶ **2421.10** Continued

Each member and member organization required to report will receive a complete set of cards—one card for each stock listed on the Exchange. Respondent identification and the name of the stock will be imprinted on the cards, which will be in alphabetical order. These cards are to be considered as a permanent file to be kept up-to-date as described below.

To report a short position it is only necessary to select the proper card, enter the number of shares short in the space provided and forward it to the Stock Clearing Corporation.

Use only one card for each stock. If more than one "account" has a short position in the same stock, the combined aggregate should be reported.

Each card sent in will be replaced and cards for new listings will be supplied before the next reporting date to keep the file current.

Blank cards are provided in case the permanent file does not contain a card imprinted with the name of the stock to be reported or an imprinted card is spoiled or mislaid. In such cases, in addition to entering the number of shares short in the proper box, insert the NYSE stock ticker symbol immediately below the box.

Prepare and file MF-2 Summary Form, which will be furnished monthly. Complete only *one* section of this form. If another NYSE member reports your short positions for you, complete Section II, giving the name of the reporting member. In all other instances, complete Section I, showing the total shares short in *all* NYSE listed stocks (that is, the total of the shares reported on the individual cards) or if you have no short positions to report, write or print the notation "None".

Reports should be submitted *as soon as possible* but *not later than noon on the second business day after the reporting settlement date.*

Send reports to Stock Clearing Corporation, Settlement Department, 44 Broad Street, New York, N. Y. 10004.

Inquiries should be directed to the Statistical Division, telephone HAnover 2-4200, extension 568.

NOTE: A member organization which does not carry customers' margin accounts and does not clear its own transactions may obtain an exemption from reporting on Form MF-2 by notifying the Department of Member Firms in writing.

.20 Underwritings (Form MF-3).—Each member organization is required to submit weekly, using Form MF-3, the information indicated on the form with respect to commitments and positions of the organization resulting from underwritings, as of the close of business on each Friday. The reports of New York organizations are to be submitted by noon of each Wednesday. Out-of-town organizations should endeavor to have such reports received by the Exchange as promptly as possible after that hour.

Reports should be sent in a sealed envelope addressed to the New York Stock Exchange, Department of Member Firms, 11 Wall Street, New York 5, N. Y.

Each member organization must submit a report weekly unless an exemption has been obtained. When a member organization has no information to submit, a report should be returned with a notation thereon to that effect.

In lieu of the use of a formal report, the Exchange will accept tabulated listings of securities which may be prepared on business machines, provided all of the necessary information, called for in Form MF-3, is therein detailed.

¶ **2421.20   Rule 421**   © 1965, Commerce Clearing House, Inc.

Any organization which does not as a matter of policy make any commitments in underwritings, either actual or contingent, may obtain an exemption from submitting reports by making a written request to the Exchange for such exemption setting forth the reasons therefor.

.30 **Money borrowed (Form MF-4).**—Member organizations carrying margin accounts for customers are required to submit on Form MF-4 the total of money borrowed from banks, trust companies, and other lenders in the United States, excluding borrowings from other members of national securities exchanges, as of the close of business on the last Wednesday of each month as follows:

(1) Money borrowed from banks, trust companies, etc., on direct obligations of or obligations guaranteed as to principal or interest by the U. S. Government.

(2) Money borrowed from banks, trust companies, etc., on all other collateral.

(3) Total of that portion of money borrowed included under (2) above which represents the amount borrowed on customers' securities only.

Reports should include borrowings made by main and branch offices on securities collateral, commercial paper, "spot" commodities, etc.

Each member organization carrying margin accounts for customers, unless specifically exempted by the Exchange, is required to submit a report each month. When a member organization has no information to submit, a report should be filed with a notation thereon to that effect.

Reports are due as promptly as possible after the last Wednesday of the month, but not later than the second full business day thereafter. For information regarding the filing of these reports telephone HAnover 2-4200, Ext. 568.

.40 **Customers' debit and credit balances (Form MF-5).**—Member organizations carrying margin accounts for customers are required to submit on Form MF-5, as of the close of business on the last business day of each month the following information:

(1) Total of all net debit balances in accounts carried for customers. Include all securities accounts, both long and short, commodity accounts, and all other accounts. Do not include debit balances of other organizations which are members of national securities exchanges, of your own organization, or of members or allied members of your own organization.

(2) Total of that portion of each debit balance included under (1) above which represents the amount of credit extended to each customer secured by direct obligations of or obligations guaranteed as to principal or interest by the U. S. Government.

(3) Total cash on hand and in banks.

(4) Total of customers' free credit balances. Include free credit balances in all commodity accounts. Do not include free credit balances of other organizations which are members of national securities exchanges, of your own organization, or of members or allied members of your own organization.

Each reporting member organization is also required to indicate the number of open margin accounts in securities at the end of each month. This will

¶ 2421.40   Continued

include only margin accounts with debit balances or with credit balances other than free credit balances. All the margin accounts of one person or organization are to be counted as one account. Cash accounts, even though the customer has signed a loan, hypothecation, or so-called customer's agreement, and omnibus accounts of correspondents who are members of the Exchange, are not to be included.

Each member organization carrying margin accounts for customers, unless specifically exempted by the Exchange, is required to submit a report each month. When a member organization has no information to submit, a report should be filed with a notation thereon to that effect.

Reports are due as promptly as possible after the last business day of the month, but not later than the eighth full business day of the following month. For information regarding the filing of these reports telephone HAnover 2-4200, Ext. 568.

¶ 2422   Loans of and to Governors, etc.

Rule 422. Without the prior consent of the Board of Governors no member of the Board of Governors or of any committee of the Exchange, and no officer or employee of the Exchange shall make any loan of money or securities to or obtain any such loan from any member, member organization, partner or stockholder in a member organization, unless such loan be (a) fully secured by readily marketable collateral, or (b) made by a governor or committee member to or obtained by a governor or committee member from the member organization of which he is a partner or a stockholder or from a partner or a stockholder therein.

¶ 2423   Participations in Joint Accounts

Rule 423. No member, member organization, or partner or stockholder therein, shall, directly or indirectly, hold any interest or participation in any joint account for buying or selling any security on the Exchange, unless such joint account is reported to and not disapproved by the Exchange. Such reports, in form prescribed, shall be filed with the Exchange before any transaction is completed on the Exchange for such joint account.

● ● ● *Supplementary Material:*

.10   Joint accounts.—Each member and member organization is required to file a report of the existence of every joint account (including joint arbitrage accounts, joint accounts between specialists and joint accounts between odd-lot dealers) formed for the purpose of dealing in any listed security on the Exchange, in which such member or member organization, or any allied member is a participant. Such reports are to be made in letter form, addressed to the Department of Member Firms, and must be filed prior to the completion of any transaction for such account.

The report should contain the following information for each account:

(1) Name of the account, with names of all participants and their respective interests in profits and losses;

(2) a statement regarding the purpose of the account;

¶ 2422   **Rule 422**   © 1964, Commerce Clearing House, Inc.

(3) name of the member organization carrying and clearing the account;

(4) a copy of any written agreement or instrument relating to the account.

Any changes which take place in a joint account in respect of the information filed should be reported at once to the Department.

¶ 2424   Reports of Options

Rule 424. Each member and member organization shall report to the Exchange such information as may be required with respect to any substantial option relating to listed securities in which such member, member organization or partner or stockholder therein is directly or indirectly interested or of which such member, member organization or partner or stockholder has knowledge by reason of transactions executed by or through such member or organization.

The Exchange may disapprove of the connection of any member, member organization or partner or stockholder therein with any such option which it shall determine to be contrary to the best interest or welfare of the Exchange or to be likely to create prices which will not fairly reflect market values.

• • • Supplementary Material:

.10   Options.—Each member and member organization is required to report all options, selling agreements and kindred arrangements (excluding purchase warrants, puts and calls) relating to securities listed on the Exchange, in which options they are directly or indirectly interested, or of which they have knowledge by reason of transactions executed by or through them. Such reports are to be made in letter form, addressed to the Department of Member Firms, and must be filed as soon as such interest therein or knowledge thereof has been acquired.

The report should contain the following information for each option:

(1) The name of the security; if a stock, the number of shares; if a bond, the principal amount thereof;

(2) the duration and terms of the option;

(3) the names of the grantors and grantees;

(4) the names of all persons entitled as of the date of the report to exercise such option; and

(5) copies of any agreements or instruments in writing relating to the option thus reported.

Only an initial report of each option is required unless changes occur in the terms thereof, in which case such changes should be reported at once to the Department.

¶ 2425   Income and Expense Report

Rule 425. Each member organization carrying accounts, or introducing accounts on a fully disclosed basis, for public customers shall file an income and expense report and additional financial information in the type, form, manner and time prescribed by the Exchange.

Adopted.
July 15, 1965.

[The next page is 3751.]

Margins

*(Rules and Policies Administered by the
Department of Member Firms.)*

¶ 2431   Margin Requirements

Initial margin rule

Rule 431.   (a) For the purpose of effecting new securities transactions and commitments, the margin deposit shall be an amount equivalent to the requirements of paragraph (b) of this Rule, with a minimum equity in the account of at least $1,000 except that cash need not be deposited in excess of the cost of any security purchased. The foregoing minimum equity and cost of purchase provisions shall not apply to "when distributed" securities in cash accounts and the exercise of rights to subscribe.

For the purpose of this Rule, the term customer shall include any person or entity for whom securities are purchased or sold or to whom securities are sold or from whom securities are purchased whether on a regular way, when issued, delayed or future delivery basis. It will also include any person or entity for whom securities are held or carried. The term will not include a broker or dealer from whom a security has been purchased or to whom a security has been sold for the account of the member organization or its customers.

Withdrawals of cash or securities may be made from any account which has a debit balance, "short" position, or commitments, provided that after such withdrawal the equity in the account is at least the greater of $1,000 or the amount required by the maintenance requirement of this Rule.

Maintenance margin rule

(b) The margin which must be maintained in margin accounts of customers, whether members, allied members, member organizations or non-members, shall be as follows:

(1) 25% of the market value of all securities "long" in the account; plus

(2) $2.50 per share or 100% of the market value, in cash, whichever amount is greater, of each stock "short" in the account selling at less than $5.00 per share; plus

(3) $5.00 per share or 30% of the market value, in cash, whichever amount is greater, of each stock "short" in the account selling at $5.00 per share or above; plus

(4) 5% of the principal amount or 30% of the market value, in cash, whichever amount is greater, of each bond "short" in the account.

Exceptions to rule

(c) The foregoing requirements of this Rule are subject to the following exceptions:

(1) *"Long" and "Short" Positions in Exchangeable or Convertible Securities.*—When a security carried in a "long" position is exchangeable or

[The next page is 3751-3.]

convertible within a reasonable time, without restriction other than the payment of money, into a security carried in a "short" position for the same customer, the minimum margin on such positions shall be 10% of the market value of the "long" securities. In determining such margin requirement "short" positions shall be marked to the market.

(2) *Exempted Securities.*

(A) *Positions in United States Government Obligations.*—The minimum margin on any positions in obligations issued or unconditionally guaranteed as to principal or interest by the United States Government shall be 5% of the principal amount of such obligations, unless the Exchange, upon written application to the Department of Member Firms, grants a lower requirement in the case of a particular issue.

(B) *Positions in "Exempted Securities" Other Than Obligations of the United States Government.*—The minimum margin on any positions in such obligations shall be 15% of the principal amount of such obligations or 25% of the market value, whichever amount is lower, unless the Exchange, upon written application to the Department of Member Firms, grants a lower requirement in the case of a particular issue.

(The term "exempted securities" has the meaning given it in section 2(e) of Regulation T of the Board of Governors of the Federal Reserve System.)

(C) *Cash Transactions With Customers.—Special Provisions.*— When a customer purchases an issued "exempted" security from or through a member organization, in a cash account, full payment shall be made promptly. If, however, delivery or payment therefor is not made promptly after the trade date, a deposit shall be required as if it were a margin transaction, unless it is a transaction with a bank, trust company, insurance company, investment trust or charitable or non-profit educational institution.

In connection with any net position resulting from any transaction in issued "exempted" securities made for a member organization, or a non-member broker-dealer, or made for or with a bank, trust company, insurance company, investment trust or charitable or non-profit educational institution, no margin need be required and such net position need not be marked to market. However, where such net position is not marked to the market, an amount equal to the loss at the market in such position shall be considered as cash required to provide margin in the computation of the Net Capital of the member organization under the Exchange's Capital Requirements.

(3) *Joint Accounts in Which the Carrying Organization or a Partner or Stockholder Therein Has an Interest.*—In the case of joint accounts carried by member organizations, in which such organizations, or a partner or partners or a stockholder or stockholders therein participate with others, the interest of each participant other than the carrying member organization shall be margined by each such participant pursuant to the provisions of this Rule as if such interest were in a separate account.

¶ 2431   Continued.

The Exchange will consider requests for exemption from the provisions of this paragraph; provided

(A) the account is confined exclusively to transactions and positions in exempted securities, as defined in Section 2(e) of Regulation T of the Board of Governors of the Federal Reserve System; or

(B) the account is maintained as a Special Miscellaneous Account conforming to the conditions of Section 4(f)(4) of Regulation T of the Board of Governors of the Federal Reserve System; or

(C) the account is maintained as a Special Miscellaneous Account conforming to the conditions of Section 4(f)(5) of Regulation T of the Board of Governors of the Federal Reserve System and is confined exclusively to transactions and positions in

(i) serial equipment trust certificates, or

(ii) interest-bearing obligations which are the subject of a primary distribution and which are covered by the first four ratings of any nationally known statistical service

and each other participant margins his share of such account on such basis as the Exchange may prescribe.

(4) *Offsetting "Long" and "Short" Positions in the Same Security.*— No margin shall be required on either position if delivery has been made by the use of the "long" securities. Otherwise the minimum margin shall be 10% of the market value of the "long" securities. In determining such margin requirement "short" positions shall be marked to the market.

(5) *International Arbitrage Accounts.*—International arbitrage accounts for non-member foreign correspondents who are registered with and approved by the Exchange shall not be subject to this Rule. In computing, under the Exchange's Capital Requirements, the Net Capital

of any member organization carrying such an account which is not margined in accordance with the maintenance requirements hereof, the Exchange will consider as a debit item any difference between the minimum amount of margin computed in accordance with those requirements and the margin in such account.

(6) *Specialists' Accounts.*—

(A) The account of a member in which are effected only transactions in securities in which he is registered and acts as a specialist may be carried upon a margin basis which is satisfactory to the specialist and the member organization. The amount of any deficiency between the margin deposited by the specialist and the margin required by the other provisions of this Rule shall be considered as a debit item in the computation of the Net Capital of the member organization under the Exchange's Capital Requirements.

(B) In the case of joint accounts carried by member organizations for specialists, in which the member organizations participate, the margin deposited by the other participants may be in any amount which is mutually satisfactory. The amount of any deficiency between the amount deposited by the other participant, or participants, based upon their proportionate share of the margin required by the other provisions of this Rule, shall be considered as a debit item in the computation of the Net Capital of the member organization under the Exchange's Capital Requirements.

Other provisions

(d)(1) *Determination of Value for Margin Purposes.*—Active securities dealt in on a recognized exchange shall, for margin purposes, be valued at current market prices. Other securities shall be valued conservatively in the light of current market prices and the amount which might be realized upon liquidation. Substantial additional margin must be required in all cases where the securities carried are subject to unusually rapid or violent changes in value, or do not have an active market on a recognized exchange, or where the amount carried is such that it cannot be liquidated promptly.

(2) *Puts, Calls and Other Options.*—No put or call carried for a customer shall be considered of any value for the purpose of computing the margin required in the account of such customer.

The issuance or guarantee for a customer of a put or a call shall be considered as a security transaction subject to paragraph (a) of this Rule.

For the purpose of paragraph (b) of this Rule such puts and calls shall be considered as if they were exercised.

Each such put or call shall be margined separately and any difference between the market price and the price of a put or call shall be considered to be of value only in providing the amount of margin required on that particular put or call.

If both a put and a call for the same number of shares of the same security are issued or guaranteed for a customer, the amount of margin required shall be the margin on the put or call whichever is greater.

Where a call is issued or guaranteed against an existing "long" position or a put is issued or guaranteed against an existing "short" position,

¶ 2431 Continued.

no margin need be required on the call or put, provided such "long" or "short" position is adequately margined in accordance with this Rule. In computing margin on such existing stock position carried against a put or call, the current market price to be used shall not be greater than the call price in the case of a call or less than the put price in the case of a put.

When a member, or member organization issues or guarantees an option to receive or deliver securities for a customer, such option shall be margined as if it were a put or call.

(3) *"When Issued" and "When Distributed" Securities.*

(A) *Margin Accounts*

The minimum amount of margin on any transaction or net position in each "when issued" security shall be the same as if such security were issued.

Each position in a "when issued" security shall be margined separately and any unrealized profit shall be of value only in providing the amount of margin required on that particular position.

When an account has a "short" position in a "when issued" security and there are held in the account securities in respect of which the "when issued" security may be issued, such "short" position shall be marked to the market and the balance in the account shall for the purpose of this Rule be adjusted for any unrealized loss in such "short" position.

(B) *Cash Accounts*

In connection with any transaction or net position resulting from contracts for a "when issued" security in an account other than that of a member organization, non-member broker or dealer, bank, trust company, insurance company, investment trust, or charitable or non-profit educational institution, deposits shall be required equal to the margin required were such transaction or position in a margin account.

In connection with any net position resulting from contracts for a "when issued" security made for or with a non-member broker or dealer, no margin need be required, but such net position must be marked to the market.

In connection with any net position resulting from contracts for a "when issued" security made for a member organization or for or with a bank, trust company, insurance company, investment trust, or charitable or non-profit educational institution, no margin need be required and such net position need not be marked to the market. However, where such net position is not marked to the market, an amount equal to the loss at the market in such position shall be considered as cash required to provide margin in the computation of the Net Capital of the member organization under the Exchange's Capital Requirements.

The provisions of this sub-paragraph shall not apply to any position resulting from contracts on a "when issued" basis in a security

(i) which is the subject of a primary distribution in connection with a *bona fide* offering by the issuer to the general public for "cash", or

(ii) which is exempt by the Exchange as involving a primary distribution.

The term "when issued" as used herein also means "when distributed."

(4) *Guaranteed Accounts.*—Any account guaranteed by another account may be consolidated with such other account and the required margin may be determined on the net position of both accounts, provided the guarantee is in writing and permits the member organization carrying the account, without restriction, to use the money and securities in the guaranteeing account to carry the guaranteed account or to pay any deficit therein; and provided further that such guaranteeing account is not owned directly or indirectly by (a) a partner or a stockholder in the organization carrying such account or (b) a member, member organization or partner or stockholder therein having a definite arrangement for participating in the commissions earned on the guaranteed account. However, the guarantee of a limited partner or of a holder of non-voting stock, if based upon his resources other than his capital contribution to or other than his interest in a member organization, is not affected by the foregoing prohibition, and such a guarantee may be taken into consideration in computing margin in the guaranteed account.

(5) *Consolidation of Accounts.*—When two or more accounts are carried for any person or entity, the required margin may be determined on the net position of said accounts, provided the customer has consented that the money and securities in each of such accounts may be used to carry, or pay any deficit in, all such accounts.

(6) *Time Within Which Margin, Deposit or "Mark to Market" Must Be Obtained.*—The amount of margin, deposit or "mark to market" required by any provision of this Rule shall be obtained as promptly as possible and in any event within a reasonable time.

(7) *Practice of Meeting Margin Calls by Liquidation Prohibited.*—No member or member organization shall permit a customer to make a practice of effecting transactions requiring margin and then either deferring the furnishing of margin beyond the time when such transactions would ordinarily be settled or cleared, or meeting such demand for margin by the liquidation of the same or other commitments in his account.

Amendments.
January 19, 1956, effective February 13, 1956.
January 21, 1954.

● ● ● *Supplementary Material:*

.10 Request for exemption from Paragraph (c)(3) of Rule 431, above.—
Requests for exemption from the provisions of paragraph (c)(3) should be submitted in writing to the Department of Member Firms and, in addition to indicating the names and interests of the respective participants in the joint account, should contain a statement that the conditions described in clause (A), (B), (C)(i) or (C)(ii) actually obtain.

In the case of an account conforming to the conditions described in clause (C), the application should also include the following information as of the date of the request:

(A) Complete description of the security;

(B) cost price, offering price and principal amount of obligations which have been purchased or may be required to be purchased;

¶ 2431.10   Continued

  (C) date on which the security is to be purchased or on which there will be a contingent commitment to purchase the security;

  (D) approximate aggregate indebtedness;

  (E) approximate net capital; and

  (F) approximate total market value of all readily marketable securities (i) exempted, and (ii) non-exempted, held in organization accounts, partners' capital accounts, partners' individual accounts covered by approved agreements providing for their inclusion as partnership property, accounts covered by subordination agreements approved by the Exchange and customers' accounts in deficit.

.11   Transactions and positions in "conditional rights to subscribe."—For the purposes of the initial and maintenance margin requirements of Rule 431 [¶ 2431], no value shall be given to any "long" position in "conditional rights to subscribe," until such time as the conditions relating to the effectiveness of the rights to subscribe are met.

  The proceeds of sales of "conditional rights to subscribe" in margin accounts may not be given consideration in computing the margin required by the Rule, nor may the proceeds of the sale be withdrawn, until the conditions relating to the effectiveness of the rights to subscribe are met. (Note: A subsequent withdrawal may be made only if the withdrawal is permissible at the time of the withdrawal.)

  The proceeds of sales of "conditional rights to subscribe" in cash accounts may not be withdrawn, or given consideration for other transactions, until the conditions relating to the effectiveness of the rights to subscribe are met.

  A member organization shall obtain from a customer additional funds or collateral to "mark to the market" any loss resulting from a sale of "conditional rights to subscribe" when the securities, on which the "conditional rights to subscribe" accrue, are not registered in the name of the organization carrying the account, or its nominee, and the "conditional rights to subscribe" are not in the organization's possession.

  Funds or securities deposited as "marks to market" are not to be considered when determining the status of a customer's margin or cash account from the standpoint of Rule 431 [¶ 2431].

¶ 2432   Daily Record of Required Margin

Rule 432. (a) Each member organization carrying securities margin accounts for customers shall make each day a record of every case in which, pursuant to the rules of the Exchange or regulations of the Board of Governors of the Federal Reserve System, initial or additional margin must be obtained in a customer's account because of the transactions effected in the account on that day. The record shall be preserved for at least twelve months, and shall show, for each account, the amount of margin so required and the time when and manner in which the margin is furnished or obtained. The record shall be maintained in a manner satisfactory to the Exchange.

Margin met by liquidation

  (b) No such organization shall permit a customer to make a practice of effecting transactions requiring such initial or additional margin and then furnishing the margin by liquidation of the same or other commitments; except that the provisions of this paragraph (b) shall not apply to any account maintained for another broker or dealer in which are carried only the commitments of the customers of the other broker or dealer exclusive of his partners or stockholders, provided the other broker or dealer

(1) Is a member organization, or

(2) has agreed in good faith with the member organization carrying the account that he will maintain a record equivalent to that referred to in paragraph (a) of this Rule, or

(3) is not subject to the regulations of the Board of Governors of the Federal Reserve System.

(c) Each member organization shall report to the Exchange such information as may be required, with respect to each margin requirement which resulted from transactions effected in a customer's account and which was met by the liquidation of the same or other commitments.

● ● ● *Supplementary Material:*

Information Regarding Rule 432 [¶ 2432]

.10 Form of record.—The Exchange has not prescribed a form for use in making and maintaining the record.

Individual entries will be deemed a "record" within the meaning of Rule 432(a) [¶ 2432], and such entries need not be combined and kept as a separate record.

.20 Place where record is to be maintained.—A member organization whose customers' accounts are carried on books located only at its main office should maintain the record at its main office. An organization whose customers' accounts are carried on books located at two or more offices should keep the record at each of such offices with respect to the customers' accounts carried on the books of such office. The record must be kept available for inspection at the office at which it is maintained.

.30 Omnibus accounts—special agreement.—The exemption provided for by clause (2) of paragraph (b) of Rule 432 [¶ 2432] may be availed of only if the prescribed agreement is in writing and is on file in the office of the member organization where the account is carried.

.40 Meaning of the term "customer."—For the purpose of Rule 432 [¶ 2432], the term "customer" includes members, member organizations, partners and stockholders therein, as well as non-members.

Margin Requirements Met by Liquidation. (Form MF-1)

.50 Persons who must submit reports; form of report.—Each member organization carrying margin accounts for customers is required to submit to the Department of Member Firms promptly after each quarterly period ending March 31, June 30, September 30 and December 31, of each year, a report showing certain information relevant to every margin requirement in a customer's account which has been met by liquidation, other than those in omnibus accounts exempted under Rule 432(b) [¶ 2432]. The prescribed information is part of the record required to be kept pursuant to Rule 432(a)

¶ 2432.50 Margin Requirements Met by Liquidation.—Continued
[¶ 2432] of the Board of Governors and should be submitted on Form MF-1 in the manner described herein. (Reports temporarily suspended.)

.60 **Contents of MF-1 report—Column 1.**—Enter the name of each customer, other than exempted omnibus customers (see below), in whose account liquidation has had the effect of furnishing all or part of the margin which was required by Rules of the Exchange or regulations of the Board of Governors of the Federal Reserve System as a result of transactions effected in the account. Customers' surnames should be given first: e. g., "Adams, William B."; "Brown, Mary"; etc. An account that is designated on the ledger in a manner other than by the customer's name, such as by number or abbreviation, should be entered in the manner in which it appears on the ledger. If the designation of an account is changed, both the old and new designations should be given in Column 1 on the first occasion when such account appears on the report after such change takes place. Accounts should be listed alphabetically according to customers' surnames or in numerical order if they are so designated on the ledger.

If items involving different trade dates are to be reported in connection with a particular account, a separate line of the report should be devoted to each such item.

Omnibus accounts not subject to the provisions of paragraph (b) of Rule 432 [¶ 2432], i. e., those falling within any of the three categories described in the Rule, are not to be reported on Form MF-1. Other omnibus accounts are not exempt from paragraph (b) of the Rule and therefore are to be reported.

If the account in which margin was furnished by liquidation is carried for an individual member of the Exchange, a general partner or a holder of voting stock in a member organization, it should be identified on the report by the use of the letter "M", "P" or "S" after his name or the account designation to indicate whether the customer concerned is a "member", a "general partner" or a "voting stockholder."

Column 2.—Enter in Column 2 each trade date of transactions requiring margin which was furnished by liquidation.

Column 3.—In Column 3 there should be entered the total amount of initial or additional margin necessitated (pursuant to Regulation T or the rules of the Exchange, whichever amount is greater) by the transactions effected in the account on the date shown in Column 2 (trade date).

Column 4.—Enter in Column 4 the trade date of the liquidating transactions effected either upon the customer's order or as a "sell-out" by the broker.

Column 5.—In Column 5 should be shown the amount of margin released by the liquidating transaction, e. g., the sale of registered, non-exempted securities in a margin account realizing net proceeds of $1,000 would release $400 which amount should be shown in Column 5.

Column 6.—If part but not all of the required margin is furnished by liquidation, indicate in Column 6 whether cash or securities or both were deposited to furnish the balance of the margin. The amounts of margin furnished in each such manner should be shown; in the case of security deposits, it is the maximum loan value of such securities that will be recorded.

In each case where an extension of time has been granted, state in Column 6 by what exchange it was granted and give its expiration date.

¶ **2432.60   Rule 432**   © 1957, Commerce Clearing House, Inc.

Enter in the space provided at the bottom of the form the total number of instances during the period in which, pursuant to the rules of the New York Stock Exchange or Regulation T, transactions effected in customers' accounts resulted in requirements of initial or additional margin (this figure should include requirements met by liquidation as well as those met by deposit).

.70 Miscellaneous Instructions Regarding Form MF-1.—(a) If margin is obtained on more than one date, all dates on which liquidation was effected should be shown in Column 4 with corresponding entries in Column 5 and all dates on which cash or securities were deposited in connection with a margin requirement should be shown in Column 6 with the amounts of cash or maximum loan value of securities clearly indicated.

(b) This report includes only cases where margin which was required as a result of transactions in an account was furnished by liquidation. It does not include cases where margin which was demanded by a member organization solely because of depreciation of a customer's equity in an account and not because of transactions in such account, has been furnished by liquidation.

(c) If liquidation in a customer's account has been effective in satisfying all or part of the margin required by transactions on a previous day but, within the four full business day period prescribed by Regulation T, cash or securities are deposited by the customer in the amount of the requirement and not withdrawn the same day, no entry need be made on Form MF-1 in connection with that item.

(d) The report should be signed by a partner or an officer who is a holder of stock in the reporting organization, or with an authorized signature; but if the record is maintained at a branch office that is not in charge of a resident partner or such an officer, the report may be signed by the branch office manager.

(e) If more than one sheet of Form MF-1 is required for a particular report, the sheets should be numbered serially in the lower right-hand corner, and only the final one need be signed.

(f) If there are no reportable items for a particular period, "None" should be written across the form and it should be dated and signed and promptly submitted.

(g) The report must be legibly prepared and a duplicate copy thereof retained in the office of the reporting member organization.

.80 Period Covered by Report; When To Be Sent.—Each report should cover all margin requirements if such requirements were met by liquidation and resulted from transactions effected on trade dates during a particular three-month period. Reports should be forwarded as soon as they contain all necessary entries.

It is important that all envelopes containing reports should be plainly marked "Form MF-1" in the lower left-hand corner.

Organizations are requested to forward promptly each completed report and not to delay such forwarding for the reason that a report of any of its other accounting points is either incomplete or not at hand. Where an extension of time has been properly granted, transmittal of the report is to be postponed until the outstanding margin requirement has been satisfied.

[The next page is 3775.]

Miscellaneous Rules and Provisions

*(Rules and Policies Administered by the
Department of Member Firms.)*

¶ 2435   Miscellaneous Prohibitions

Rule 435.   No member, member organization, partner or stockholder therein
shall:

Excessive trading by members

(1) Effect on the Exchange purchases or sales for any account in
which he or it is directly or indirectly interested, which purchases or
sales are excessive in view of his or its financial resources or in view of
the market for such security.

Excessive trading in discretionary accounts

(2) Execute or cause to be executed on the Exchange purchases or
sales of any stock for any account with respect to which he or it or
another partner or stockholder therein is vested with any discretionary
power, which purchases or sales are excessive in size or frequency in
view of the financial resources in such account.

Successive transactions by members

(3) Execute or cause to be executed on the Exchange the purchase
of any security at successively higher prices or the sale of any security
at successively lower prices for the purpose of creating or inducing a
false, misleading or artificial appearance of activity in such security, or
for the purpose of unduly or improperly influencing the market price of
such security, or for the purpose of making a price which does not reflect
the true state of the market in such security.

Manipulative operations

(4) Directly or indirectly participate in or have any interest in the
profits of a manipulative operation or knowingly manage or finance a
manipulative operation.

For the purpose of paragraph (4), (A) any pool, syndicate or joint account, whether in corporate form or otherwise, organized or used intentionally
for the purpose of unfairly influencing the market price of any security by
means of options or otherwise and for the purpose of making a profit thereby
shall be deemed to be a manipulative operation; (B) the soliciting of subscriptions to any such pool, syndicate or joint account or the accepting of
discretionary orders from any such pool, syndicate or joint account shall be
deemed to be managing a manipulative operation; and (C) the carrying on
margin of either a "long" or a "short" position in securities for, or the advanc-
ing of credit through loans of money or of securities to, any such pool, syndicate or joint account shall be deemed to be financing a manipulative operation.

Circulation of rumors

(5) Circulate in any manner rumors of a sensational character.

Report shall be made to the Exchange of any information which comes
to his or its notice as to the circulation of such rumors.

Short sales of odd lots

(6) Effect on the Exchange any short sale of a stock in an amount
less than the unit of trading, unless such sale is based upon a sale, in

the unit of trading, the price of which (A) is higher than the price of the last "regular way" sale on the Exchange of such stock in the unit of trading, or (B) is the same as the price of such last sale and such price was higher than the last different price of a "regular way" sale on the Exchange of such stock in the unit of trading.

The provisions of this Paragraph (6) shall not apply to any sale if made (i) by an odd-lot dealer in a stock in which he is registered; (ii) for a special arbitrage account by a person who then owns another security by virtue of which he is, or presently will be, entitled to acquire an equivalent amount of stock of the same class as the stock sold; provided such sale, or the purchase which such sale offsets, is effected for the bona fide purpose of profiting from a current difference between the price of the stock sold and the security owned and that such right of acquisition was originally attached to or represented by another security or was issued to all the holders of any class of securities of the issuer; or (iii) for a special international arbitrage account for the bona fide purpose of profiting from a current difference between the price of the stock on a securities market not within or subject to the jurisdiction of the United States and on the Exchange; provided the seller at the time of the sale knows, or by virtue of information currently received has reasonable grounds to believe that an offer enabling him to cover such sale is then available to him in such foreign securities market and intends to accept such offer immediately. (*Note: For the purpose of clause (iii) of this paragraph, a depositary receipt for a security shall be deemed to be the same security as the security represented by such receipt.*)

(*See* ¶ 2440B *for information regarding the short selling rule of the Securities and Exchange Commission and* ¶ 2085.20, 2085.70 *for handling of short selling orders on Floor of Exchange.*)

Reopening a contract

(7) Reopen a contract which is subject to a transfer tax for the purpose of allowing another member or member organization to intervene in such transaction, or for the purpose of making a contract in his or its own interest at a different price.

Loans for account of non-members

(8) Loan money upon the security of stocks, bonds or other investment securities for the account of any non-banking corporation, partnership, association, business trust, other entity or individual.

¶ 2436   Interest on Credit Balances

Rule 436. No member organization, unless subject to supervision by State banking authorities, shall pay interest on any credit balance created for the purpose of receiving interest thereon. Credit balances arising out of transactions in securities or commodities or incidental to any business regularly carried on by a member organization prior to August 2, 1933, shall not be subject to the provisions of this Rule unless it appears that such credit balances have been increased solely for the purpose of receiving interest thereon.

¶ 2437   International Arbitrage

Rule 437. Members and member organizations which propose to operate in international arbitrage shall first obtain the permission of the Exchange.

¶ 2436   Rule 436

12-64
Report 96
Rules of Board—Miscellaneous Rules and Provisions
➡➡ *Administered by Department of Member Firms.*
3777

● ● ● *Supplementary Material:*

Information Regarding the Conduct of International Arbitrage

.10 Definition.—The term "International Arbitrage in Securities" means the business of buying or selling securities in one market with the intent of reversing such transactions in a market in a country different from that in which the original transaction has taken place, in order to profit from price differences between such markets, and which business is not casual but contains the element of continuity.

.11 Permission.—Members and member organizations which propose to engage either in international joint account arbitrage or in international arbitrage for their own account shall, before initiating any transaction in connection therewith, secure the permission of the Exchange. Application for permission shall be made to the Department of Member Firms for own account.

.12 Notice of discontinuance.—Members and member organizations discontinuing dealings in international arbitrage shall give prompt notice of such discontinuance to the Department.

.13 Accounting.—Separate accounts shall be kept by the member or member organization for each arbitrage authority granted by the Exchange and he or it shall require from his or its correspondents copies of similar special, separate accounts, at least monthly, and daily transaction slips describing purchases, sales and collateral entries thereto which shall specify separately commissions and brokerages. Said accounts shall show all debits and credits relating to said business and no others.

The member or member organization shall retain in his or its American office these accounts and documents, together with copies of all communications relating to the account, for a period of at least three years, which shall be available at all times for inspection by the Exchange.

.14 Agreements.—Copies of all agreements, and subsequent changes therein, between the member or member organization and his or its correspondents relating to the arbitrage for which authority is requested, or has been granted, shall be filed with the Department of Member Firms.

.15 Arbitrage accounts carried in dollar currency.—Foreign arbitrage accounts carried in dollar currency on the correspondent's books or carried in foreign currencies on the books of the member or member organization (other than control accounts) shall be closed out by reasonably prompt payment of debit balances.

.16 Brokerages.—On transactions actually effected for the account, members and member organizations may permit debits to the account for brokerages incurred by the correspondent and paid to third parties at rates not greater than those customary in the market where the transaction is effected.

.17 Commissions.—See Information Regarding Commissions, joint account arbitrage at ¶ 2381.19.

.18 Firm bids, offers and orders.—During the time the Exchange is open for business, no member or member organization shall effect:

(1) In the United States, a transaction in a listed security for the purpose of subsequently accepting a firm bid or offer originating outside the United States, or

¶ 2437.18 Information Regarding the Conduct of International Arbitrage.—Continued

(2) outside the United States, a transaction in a listed security for the purpose of subsequently accepting a firm bid or offer originating from an allied member or a non-member within the United States,

unless the net profit to the member or member organization resulting from such transaction, after deduction of all expenses connected therewith, including stamp taxes, is at least equal to the minimum non-member commission prescribed by Article XV of the Constitution [¶ 1701-1712].

Whenever a person has the right to accept a bid or offer either immediately or within a specified time, such person shall be deemed to have a firm bid or offer.

For the purpose of this definition, any order, whether at a specified price or without price limitation, executed through the medium of an international arbitrage account, shall be deemed to be a firm bid or offer.

The practice of a member or member organization making or transmitting firm bids or offers in listed securities, while the Exchange is either open or closed for business, to a non-member customer outside of the United States from whom he or it receives commission business, for the purpose of giving such non-member an undue advantage, shall be deemed an indirect rebate of commissions.

.19 Foreign exchange.—No member or member organization shall permit foreign exchange to be debited to the account at rates higher, or credited to the account at rates lower, than those current at the time exchange is bought or sold.

.20 Interest.—No member or member organization shall permit interest to be debited to the arbitrage account at rates higher, or credited to the account at rates lower, than those prevailing in the respective markets for similar financial transactions during the periods for which interest is charged or credited.

.21 Miscellaneous charges.—The member or member organization may permit debits to the account by the correspondent for cost of stamp taxes and such charges relating to the transactions and paid to others as are imposed by any governmental authority or by the authority of any stock exchange.

The member or member organization may also permit debits by the correspondent to the account for costs of communication, shipping, insurance and similar related charges in amounts as actually incurred and paid to others.

In joint account with allied members or non-members the member or member organization shall charge to such account the cost of stamp taxes relating to the transactions and paid to others by him or it as are imposed by any governmental authority, or by the authority of any stock exchange, as well as costs of communication, shipping, insurance, and similar related charges, in amounts as actually incurred by him or it and paid to others.

Income taxes payable by a party to the account shall not be charged to the account, but shall be borne by such party.

.22 Participations in international arbitrage joint accounts.—Only the registered parties to an international arbitrage joint account shall in any way participate therein; except that a participation in the net profit (remaining after the deduction of all charges in accordance with the "Information

¶ 2437.19 Rule 437 © 1964, Commerce Clearing House, Inc.

Regarding the Conduct of International Arbitrage") resulting from a particular transaction may be permitted to an outside party to such transaction, provided prompt report thereof is made to the Department of Member Firms.

.23 Reporting transactions.—Members and member organizations shall require their correspondents to report to them, as promptly as reasonably possible, all transactions made for their account.

Transactions once originated for the account shall not be cancelled or assumed by another account or principal.

All securities purchased or sold by a party to the account shall be reported at the actual price at which the transaction occurred.

.24 Wire costs.—See Rule 358 [¶ 2358], Private Wire and Other Connections.

.25 Written agreement from non-members.—Members and member organizations operating in joint account with allied members or non-members shall file with the Department of Member Firms a letter from each correspondent reading:

"I/We have read 'Information Regarding the Conduct of International Arbitrage,' as contained in ¶ 2437.10—2437.26 of the NEW YORK STOCK EXCHANGE GUIDE, and understand that all arbitrage business to which you are a party must be conducted in accordance therewith."

.26 Registration of international arbitrage non-member correspondents.—A foreign non-member correspondent of a member organization may be registered as an International Arbitrage Correspondent upon compliance with the following requirements:

(1) The member organization shall file with the Department of Member Firms a letter to the effect

(A) that it requests registration of the correspondent, whose name, business address, and the name of the stock exchange of which said correspondent is a member, shall be stated;

(B) that the correspondent conducts an international arbitrage business, in which the member organization has no interest as a principal, but for which said organization executes orders for a commission charge and carries positions in securities;

(C) that the account is such as may be properly described as international arbitrage because the correspondent is engaged in the business of buying or selling securities in one market with the intent of reversing such transactions in a market in a country different from that in which the original transaction has taken place, in order to profit from price differences between such markets, and which business is not casual but contains the element of continuity;

(D) that all transactions pertaining to said described business, and no others, will be entered in a special account which shall be designated as Special International Arbitrage Account of the correspondent and on which account reference shall be made to the date on which the registration of such correspondent was approved by the Exchange;

¶ **2437.26   Information Regarding the Conduct of International Arbitrage.**—
Continued

(E) that the member organization has secured the assurance of the correspondent and believes that the account is not to be used for the purpose of evading or circumventing the provisions of Regulation T of the Board of Governors of the Federal Reserve System, but only for *bona fide* international arbitrage transactions in securities;

(F) that the member organization will report to the Department of Member Firms quarterly, whether or not it has received monthly statements, as described in paragraph (2)(C) of the agreement of the non-member, from each non-member vostro arbitrage correspondent and whether or not it has found that all transactions effected through it in such account have been countered or offset within five full business days, as specified in paragraph (2)(B) of the agreement of the non-member;

(G) that the applicant member organization agrees that, should the nature of the Special International Arbitrage Account alter at any time, prompt notice will be given to the Department of Member Firms.

(2) With its application the member organization shall file a letter from the correspondent to the applicant, stating in effect

(A) that the account shall be used only for *bona fide* international arbitrage transactions, and that for this purpose international arbitrage shall be deemed to be the business of buying or selling securities in one market with the intent of reversing such transactions in a market in a country different from that in which the original transaction has taken place, in order to profit from price differences between such markets, and which business is not casual but contains the element of continuity;

(B) that he also agrees that if, at any time, securities bought or sold for the Special International Arbitrage Account have not, within the period of five full business days thereafter, been sold or bought (in order that each transaction shall be offset by a counter transaction and the position thereby balanced or made even) such transaction shall not be deemed to be of the nature of *bona fide* arbitrage transactions, and he will give instructions to the member organization to remove such transaction from the Special International Arbitrage Account;

(C) that he also agrees to furnish to the member organization monthly statements showing in each instance the date on which each transaction effected through the international arbitrage vostro account with the member organization has been countered or offset, the name of the security, the number of shares or bonds involved and the name of the counter party; except that if the counter party to such a transaction is a member of an established stock exchange, in lieu of reporting the name of such counter party on said monthly statement, it may be reported that such counter party is a member of .... stock exchange;

(D) that he agrees to supply at least the minimum margin which members and members organizations of the Exchange are required to demand on such accounts.

¶ **2437.26   Rule 437**

¶ 2438   Advertising in Quotation Sheets

Rule 438. Members and member organizations may list their names in quotation sheets having a strictly professional clientele showing "bid wanted" or "offer wanted" with respect to inactive listed securities but may not publish actual prices of bids or offers and may not show both "bid wanted" and "offer wanted" with respect to the same security on the same day. This Rule does not apply to obligations of the United States, Puerto Rico, Philippine Islands and States, Territories and Municipalities therein, or to bonds or notes which, pursuant to call or otherwise, are to be redeemed within twelve months.

¶ 2439   "Unit," "Group" or "Package" Plans, Participations

Rule 439. No member or member organization may participate in the offering of any so-called "unit," "group" or "package" plan on a dealer basis. No member or member organization may participate in the formation, sponsorship or management of any such plan or in the distribution thereunder, on a brokerage basis, unless such plan contains at least the following features:

(1) At the time of initial offering, the total price of the package to the investor, including charges, must be not less than $500.

(2) There must be reasonable diversification.

(3) Not less than five (5) shares of the stock of any one company must be included in each such offering.

(4) The total charges in addition to the round-lot price of the included shares must not be in excess of 10% of such round-lot price. This charge must include odd-lot differentials, commissions, transfer taxes, transfer charges, if any, and costs of distribution.

For the purposes of this Rule, the mere execution by members and member organizations of orders for the purchase or sale of securities for non-members who are operating "unit," "group" or "package" plans, will not be deemed to be a participation in the formation, sponsorship or management of such plans or in the distribution thereunder.

¶ 2440   Books and Records

Rule 440. Every individual member and every member organization shall make and preserve for at least three years such books and records as the Exchange may prescribe.

● ● ● *Supplementary Material:*

.10 Business transacted with members and member organizations.—An individual Exchange member or a member organization transacting business solely with members or member organizations shall make and preserve for at least three years records supporting all income and expenses relating to securities and commodities and details of all transactions in securities and commodities for any account in which such member or organization has an interest.

Those records shall consist, at least, of the following:

(1) Bank statements, cancelled checks and information as to source of deposits;

(2) statements of account and confirmations received from others;

(3) records reflecting assets and liabilities, income and expenses and proprietary interests; and

(4) copies of all reports rendered to any regulatory body including national securities exchanges and state and federal authorities.

(*See Rules* 121 *and* 123 [¶¶ 2121, 2123] *for records of orders to be kept by Exchange members. See Rule* 410 [¶ 2410] *for records of orders to be kept by member organizations.*)

.20 Business transacted with others than members and member organizations.—A member organization transacting business directly with others than members or member organizations shall make and preserve the records prescribed by Regulations §§ 240.17a-3 [¶¶ 4583] and 240.17a-4 [¶¶ 4584] of the Securities and Exchange Commission.

(*Note:* S. E. C. requires retention of certain records for at least six years. See [¶¶ 4584].)

¶ 2440A   Statistical and Investment Advisory Services

● ● ● *Supplementary Material:*

[*Also see Rule* 369(3)(F) (¶ 2369).]

.10 To whom furnished.—A member or member organization may furnish:

(1) To a professional non-member (i.e., broker-dealer in securities or commodities, insurance company, investment advisor, investment manager, bank, trust company, foundation, professional trustee, or one engaged in any closely allied activity), statistical and investment advisory services:

(A) Prepared by the member or member organization; or

(B) prepared by others and reissued by the member or member organization in his or its own name with the consent of the original issuer or publisher, provided the reissuing member or member organization is not required to pay for such consent.

(*Exception: This policy does not prohibit the furnishing by a member or member organization to a non-member professional (i.e., broker-dealer in securities or commodities, insurance company, investment adviser, investment manager, bank, trust company, foundation, professional trustee, or one engaged in any closely allied activity), of publications of nominal cost, i.e., aggregating not more than approximately $30 per year, per non-member professional.*)

(2) To another member or member organization or to a non-member customer who is a non-professional, statistical or investment advisory services

(A) prepared by the member or member organization, or

(B) prepared by others and reissued by the member or member organization.

The meaning of "statistical and investment advisory services" above is restricted to publications or services intended to aid professional or non-professional clients of member organizations in investment decisions concerning securities or commodities. All such publications or services must be clearly and prominently identified as being a publication or service of the original issuing member organization. (The name of the original issuing member organization may be omitted if the distributing member organization clears its listed business through the issuing member organization.)

.11 Fees.—Such service which is prepared or reissued by the member or member organization consistent with .10 above, may be furnished by the member or member organization to another member or member organization or to a non-member, either free of cost or on a fee basis. If such service is furnished on a fee basis, the fee may be adjusted in accordance with commission business received from the other member or member organization or from the non-member.

The fee for investment advisory service may be based on a percentage of the principal amount of the funds involved but may not be based upon the profits realized.

Different fees may be charged to different customers for the same or equivalent statistical service.

.12   Commissions to employees.—A commission of a fixed proportion of the
fee received by the member or member organization from the non-
member may be paid to employees of the member or member organization.

.13   Office space.—Occupancy of a member's or member organization's quarters by a non-member engaged in the business of rendering any type
of statistical or investment advisory service is in contravention of the office
space rules of the Exchange.

.14   Disclosure of interest.—If a member or member organization, or any
organization in which the member or any of his or its partners or holders
of voting stock have an interest furnishes statistical or investment advisory
service, and the member or member organization or any of his or its partners
or holders of voting stock is substantially interested in any security recommended, a full description of such facts shall be made to customers who
subscribe to the service.

.15   Exceptions.—The rules outlined in items (1), (2), (3), (4) and (5) above
do not apply to the occasional information supplied by a member or
member organization to another member or member organization or to a
non-member customer, upon request, such as individual corporation analyses,
specific excerpts from recognized standard statistical services, etc.

.16   Other services.—Except as provided in ¶ 2344.11 and 2344.12, member
firms may offer to non-member professionals other types of services, provided that the cash compensation for such services is sufficient to cover all
direct and indirect costs of the service. Such services may be so offered contingent on the non-member also giving the member firm commission business,
provided that all promotional literature, order forms and bills contain a direct
statement that the cash charge covers all costs of creating, producing and distributing the service.

.17   Services prepared by other members or member organizations.—A member or member organization may subscribe, for his or its own use, to a
service prepared by another member, member organization or non-member.
The fee paid for such service shall be commensurate with the service rendered
and with the fee charged by other organizations for the same or similar services, and commensurate with the fee charged by the issuing organization to
other subscribers for the same or similar services.

¶ 2440B   Short Sales

● ● ● *Supplementary Material:*

Interpretations of Securities and Exchange Commission Rules
(See Regulations §§ 240.10a-1 and 240.10a-2 of Securities
and Exchange Commission [¶ 4324, 4325])

.10   General rule.—In general, the rule prohibits any "short sale" of a security on a national securities exchange, (1) below the last regular way sale price of such security on such exchange, or (2) at such price unless it was above the last previous regular way different price of such security on such exchange. A "short sale" is defined as (1) any sale of a security which the seller does not own; or (2) any sale which is consummated by the delivery of a security borrowed by or for the account of the seller. Thus, a sale of a security which is owned by the seller becomes a "short sale" if delivery to the purchaser is made by the use of borrowed securities. This may often be the case if the original security is not available in or near New York in negotiable form at the time of sale.

Although the term "short sale" may thus include many sales which would ordinarily be regarded as long sales, the prohibition of the general rule does not apply to (1) any person, whether a member or a non-member, selling a security which he owns and intends to deliver as soon as is possible without undue inconvenience or expense; or (2) any *member* executing for an account in which he has no interest a sell order *marked* "long" (see .13 below); or (3) any sale of an odd lot. (Rule 435 (6) [¶ 2435] of the Board of Governors imposes comparable restrictions on the price at which a short sale of an odd lot may be made on the Exchange.) Certain additional transactions are exempted by paragraph (d) of Regulation § 240.10a-1 [¶ 4324].

The general prohibition referred to above has the effect of a criminal law. Any person, including any member or any customer, who effects for his own account or for any other account any "short sale" in violation of the rule may be guilty of a criminal offense.

.11   Securities subject to the rule.—The rule applies, generally speaking, to all securities dealt in upon any national securities exchange, other than U. S. Government or municipal securities.

.12   Place of transaction.—The rule applies to any short sale effected on a national securities exchange. In consequence, it covers all short sales (other than odd lots and other sales exempted by the rule itself) made upon the Exchange, of any security subject to the rule. The rule does not apply, however, to sales not made on any national securities exchange.

.13   Marking of orders: customer's written agreement regarding designation of sell orders.—Every sell order (including odd lots) in a security subject to the rule, which is executed on the Exchange, whether originated or handled by a member, must be marked to indicate whether it is "long" or "short." The abbreviation "L" or "S" may be used. A member (including any Floor broker) or any employee may mark an order "long" only if (1) the customer's account is "long" the security involved; or (2) the member or employee is informed that the seller owns the security and will deliver it as soon as is possible without undue inconvenience or expense. If a sell order is to be marked "long" pursuant to (2) above, the information prescribed therein must

¶ 2440B.13   Continued

actually be obtained in some manner.   To obviate the necessity of hurriedly obtaining the information specified in Regulation § 240.10a-2 [¶ 4325], it is advisable for the member when he receives the order also to obtain information from the seller as to the practicability of then delivering the security.   As a method of obtaining such information with respect to an order to sell, a member (including any Floor broker) may enter into any *bona fide* written agreement with his customer that the customer, when placing "short" sell orders, will designate them as such, and that the designation of a sell order as "long" is a representation by the customer to the member that the customer owns the security, that it is then impracticable to deliver the security to such member and that the customer will deliver it as soon as is possible without undue inconvenience or expense.

The Exchange is advised that in the opinion of the Securities and Exchange Commission's staff a member is not justified in marking a sell order "long" on the basis of an agreement with the customer that the absence of any designation of a sell order constitutes a representation by him to the member that the conditions described in Regulation § 240.10a-1(c)(2) [¶ 4324] obtain; the mere omission of any designation of the order whatsoever may not be considered as effectively conveying the required information.   Therefore, in order to accomplish its purpose, namely, to avoid the necessity of obtaining the required information with each individual order to sell a security "long" which is not in the customer's account, a written agreement with the customer must provide not only that all "short" sell orders will be designated as "short" but also that "long" sell orders will be specifically designated as "long."   In addition, the agreement should further provide that the actual designation "long" is to be taken as a representation that the conditions specified in the rules as described above actually obtain.

For the information of members there is given below a form of written agreement which is considered by the staff of the Securities and Exchange Commission to provide a suitable method of obtaining the information required in connection with the rules under discussion.   This is, of course, not the only form which a proper agreement may take but is given here merely as one example of a suitable form.

"Having in mind the rules promulgated by the Securities and Exchange Commission under Section 10(a) of the Securities Exchange Act of 1934 [¶ 4322], which you have called to our attention, we hereby undertake and agree to designate all sell orders as either 'long' or 'short,' unless the security to be delivered after sale is carried in the account for which the sale is to be effected, and that the designation by us of an order as a 'long' sell order shall be a certification by us that the security ordered to be sold is owned by the seller and that either (1) such security has been forwarded to such account or (2) it is then impracticable to deliver such security to such account, but that the seller will deliver such security to such account as soon as is possible without undue inconvenience or

¶ 2440B.13

expense. If there is carried in the account for which the sale is to be effected a security which can be delivered in satisfaction of the sale, you are authorized and directed to deliver such security from such account.

"Will you kindly evidence your concurrence in this understanding and arrangement by signing and returning to us the enclosed carbon copy of this letter."

In the case of a member who executes selling orders for a foreign customer with whom he communicates in a code which does not employ words having normal meanings, the Exchange is informed that in the opinion of the Commission's staff it would be appropriate to include in the written agreement with such a customer, in addition to the material quoted above, the following arrangement in regard to the code, or its equivalent:

"We desire hereby also to agree with you that in addition to the meanings assigned to the respective words relating to sales on pages .... of the .... code book which we use in communicating with each other, said words shall, unless otherwise noted, be interpreted to include a certification by us that the security ordered to be sold is owned by the seller and that either (1) such security has been forwarded to such account or (2) it is then impracticable to deliver such security to such account, but that the seller will deliver such security to such account as soon as is possible without undue inconvenience or expense.

"For the purpose of further evidencing the additional meanings hereby assigned to the said code words, you and we will affix to the said pages of the said code book in our respective possession an appropriate endorsement or legend expressly setting forth the aforesaid additional meanings. The text of such legend is:

'In addition to the meanings assigned on this page to the respective words relating to sales, said words shall, unless otherwise noted, also mean that the security ordered to be sold is owned by the seller and that either (1) such security has been forwarded to such account or (2) it is then impracticable to deliver such security to such account, but that the seller will deliver such security to such account as soon as is possible without undue inconvenience or expense.'"

Paragraph (b) of the Securities and Exchange Commission's Regulation § 240.10a-1 [¶ 4324] provides that "No member of a national securities exchange shall, by the use of any facility of such exchange, execute any sell order unless such order is marked either 'long' or 'short'."

Therefore, members on the Floor who receive sell orders from other members, whether in full or odd lots of stock, or in bonds are required to take particular care to see whether such orders are marked either "long" or "short," and whenever any member on the Floor receives from another member or member organization any sell order which is not marked either "long" or "short" such order should not be filled or executed but should be returned for proper marking to the member or organization from whom it was received.

.14 **Ownership of securities.**—A person is deemed to own a security if (1) he or his agent has title to it; or (2) he has purchased or has entered into an unconditional contract, binding on both parties, to purchase it but has not yet received it; or (3) he owns a security convertible into or exchangeable for it and has tendered such security for conversion or exchange; or (4) he has an option to purchase or acquire it and has exercised such option; or (5) he

¶ 2440B.14   Continued

has rights or warrants to subscribe to it and has exercised such rights or warrants.   He is not deemed to own a security if he owns securities convertible into or exchangeable for it but has not tendered such securities for conversion or exchange, or if he has an option or owns rights or warrants entitling him to such security, but has not exercised them.

Within the meaning of the rules a person "owns" securities only to the extent that he has a net long position in such securities.   Thus, if a person maintains two accounts and is short 1000 shares of a security in one and long 1000 shares of the same security in another, any sales of such security by such person are "short sales" and are subject to the provisions of the rules.

.15   **Price at which short sales may be made.**—A short sale may not be made below the price of the last regular way sale, but may be made at the price of the last regular way sale, provided that the previous different regular way sale price was lower than the price of the last sale, irrespective of whether such prices were established on the same day or some earlier day.   If the previous different price was higher than the price of the last sale, a short sale may be made only at a price which is higher than the price of the last sale. Therefore, a member with an order to sell short must ascertain the price of the last regular way sale and (unless the bid is above the price of the last sale) also the previous different regular way price, regardless of when the transactions occurred, in order to determine the price at which a short sale may be made.   A member with an order to sell 500 shares short may either sell the entire quantity in one lot at a price permitted by the rule, or sell 500 shares in smaller lots at such price, provided no intervening sales occur which change the price basis as above described.   In determining the price at which a short sale may be effected after a security goes ex-dividend, ex-right, or ex- any other distribution, all sale prices prior to the "ex" date may be reduced by the value of such distribution.

> **EXAMPLES:**
>
> (1) **When no distribution is involved:**
>
> If the last sale was at 50 and the last previous different price was at 50⅛, a short sale may be made only at 50⅛ or above;
>
> If the last sale was at 51½ and the previous different price was at 51⅜, a short sale may be made at 51½ or above;
>
> If the last sale was at 52 and the previous different price was at 52¼, a short sale may be made at 52⅛ or above;
>
> If the last sale was at 49¾ and the previous different price was at 49½, a short sale may be made at 49¾ or above.
>
> (2) **When a distribution is involved:**
>
> The value of a dividend, right or other distribution may be deducted from all last sale prices made in securities prior to the "ex" date to determine the price at which a short sale in such "ex" securities may be effected.   Thus, if the value of a dividend, right or other distribution was $1.50 and:
>
> If the last sale price prior to the "ex" date was at 51½ and the previous different price was at 51⅜, by deducting the $1.50 value the last sale price would be regarded to be 50 and the previous different price to be 49⅞, a short sale may be made at 50 or above;
>
> If the last sale price prior to the "ex" date was at 48⅝ and the previous different price was at 48¾, by deducting the $1.50 value the last sale price would be regarded to be 47⅛ and the previous different price to be 47¼, a short sale may be made at 47¼, or above;

¶ 2440B.15

If the last sale price prior to the "ex" date was at 53 and the previous different price was at 53¼, by deducting the $1.50 value the last sale price would be regarded to be 51½ and the previous different price to be 51¾ a short sale may be made at 51⅝ or above;

If the last sale price prior to the "ex" date was at 52¾ and the previous different price was at 52½, by deducting the $1.50 value the last sale price would be regarded to be 51¼ and the previous different price to be 51, a short sale may be made at 51¼ or above.

When a security is dealt in on two or more national securities exchanges, the last regular way sale price on the particular exchange involved is controlling. Thus, if on a given day a mutually listed stock closes at 35 on the New York Stock Exchange, with the previous different price 34⅞ but closes at 34 on another national securities exchange, short sales at the opening on the next day may not be made below 35 on the Exchange except, as explained and illustrated above, when a distribution is involved.

Initial sale may be short sale.—A ruling has been made by the Division of Trading and Exchanges that the initial sale of a security newly listed on a national securities exchange may be a short sale. Subsequent sales at the same price may also be short sales provided there is no intervening transaction at a different price. Once a transaction at a different price takes place the regular operation of the short selling rules becomes effective.

In the case of securities dealt in at variations of less than ⅛, the price at which short sales may be made under the rule is determined by the minimum variation permitted; e. g., if a bond is dealt in at variations of 1/32, the last sale having been 100 and the previous different price 100 2/32, a short sale may be made at or above 100 1/32.

.16 "When issued" and "when distributed" securities.—The rules apply to the sale of "when issued" and "when distributed" securities in the same manner as issued securities. In the case of a sale of a "when issued" or "when distributed" security, the last "regular way" sale price means the last price at which the "when issued" or "when distributed" security has sold on the Exchange, and the "next preceding different price" means the last previous different price at which a sale of such "when issued" or "when distributed" security took place on the Exchange. A person is deemed to be the owner of a "when issued" or "when distributed" security if he has entered into a contract to purchase the same binding on both parties and subject only to the condition of issuance or distribution or, by virtue of his ownership of an issued security, will be entitled to receive, without the payment of consideration, the "when issued" or "when distributed" security, to the extent that he has not already disposed of such "when issued" or "when distributed" security.

.17 Covering transactions.—If on the due date of delivery of a security sold pursuant to an order marked "long," the member has not received the security from the customer, he must cover the open position unless he knows or has been informed by the seller either (1) that the security is in transit to him; or (2) that the seller owns the security, that it is then impracticable to deliver it and that it will be delivered as soon as is possible without undue inconvenience or expense. If the member has received the security at his main or branch office, or if he knows or has been informed by the seller that either (1) or (2) is the case, he may at his option either fail to deliver or make delivery with borrowed securities. If, however, he neither knows nor is informed by the seller that either of these situations exists, and has not

¶ 2440B.17   Continued

received the security, either he must cover the transaction by buying in for "cash," for the account of the customer, the security sold, or if such buy-in for "cash" is rendered necessary by the discovery, after the sale took place, of a *bona fide* error, he must make application for an exemption from the provisions of Regulation § 240.10a-2(a) [¶ 4325] to the exchange upon which the sale was effected. Information concerning the method to be used in submitting requests for exemptions and the circumstances under which such requests may be favorably acted upon is contained in .19 below.

Buy-ins for the purpose of obviating violations of Regulation § 240.10a-2(a) [¶ 4325] are not to be sent to The Floor Department for execution, but are to be effected by the member directly or through an agent of his own choosing. If on the date when delivery upon the original contract is due, the member receives the security so bought in, or knows that it is in transit to him, he may make delivery upon the original contract with the security so received, or with borrowed securities, or may fail to make delivery thereon.

The provisions of this paragraph apply to odd lots as well as to full lots.

.18   Loans of securities between members.—A member may, without regard to the restrictions imposed by Regulation § 240.10a-2 [¶ 4325] and without inquiry as to the purpose of the loan, lend a security to another member. The lending member may none the less be criminally liable for a violation of the short selling rules if he knows that the borrower intends to violate such rules.

.19   Exemptions from the requirements of Regulation § 240.10a-2(a) [¶ 4325].
—Under amended Regulation § 240.10a-2 [¶ 4325], if a broker discovers prior to delivery date that a sale was effected pursuant to an order which through error was incorrectly marked "long," the requirements of Regulation § 240.10a-2(a) [¶ 4325] will not apply provided the exchange on which the transaction took place is satisfied as to the existence of the conditions described in (i), (ii) and (iii) of Regulation § 240.10a-2(b)(2) [¶ 4325].

Members should submit all requests for exemptions to the Floor Governors as promptly as possible after discovery of the errors involved. Such requests may be made in writing, or by telephone or telegraph provided they are promptly confirmed in writing by the member or member organization. Out-of-town organizations may submit their requests through their New York correspondents.

In order that the Exchange may make a proper determination in each case, it is imperative that all requests contain sufficient information to indicate clearly that the conditions described in (i), (ii) and (iii) actually obtain.

.20   Approval of short sale which is exempted by Regulation § 240.10a-1(d)(6) [¶ 4324] of the Securities and Exchange Commission.—Floor Officials have been authorized by the Board of Governors to approve transactions by members in accordance with Regulation § 240.10a-1(d)(6) [¶ 4324] of the Securities and Exchange Commission. Before applying to a Floor Official for the Exchange's approval, a member wishing to make a short sale of the type exempted from the price restrictions by item (6) of paragraph (d) of the Securities and Exchange Commission's Regulation § 240.10a-1 [¶ 4324] should fill out one of the appropriate forms, which may be obtained at the Information Desk. If approval of the short sale is obtained, the form, properly signed by the approving Floor Official should be delivered to a supervisor on the Floor by the member who makes the application.

¶ 2440B.18

9-64
Report 93
Rules of Board—Miscellaneous Rules and Provisions **3 7 8 9**
➤➤➤ *Administered by Department of Member Firms.*

.21 **"Short-exempt" sell orders.**—The Commission's short selling rules require, in effect, that all sell orders must be marked either "long" or "short." A member may not mark a sell order "long" except in the circumstances described in paragraph (c) of Regulation § 240.10a-1 [¶ 4324]. Although the Commission's short selling rules do not specifically prescribe a special marking of short selling orders which are subject to the exemption provided by paragraph (d) of Regulation § 240.10a-1 [¶ 4324], the Exchange understands that it is appropriate for a member to mark as "short exempt" any short selling order which properly comes within the provisions of clause (4), (5), (6), (7), (8) or (9) of paragraph (d) of Regulation § 240.10a-1 [¶ 4324].

Clauses (4), (5), (6), (7), (8) and (9) of paragraph (d) of Regulation § 240.10a-1 [¶ 4324] read as follows:

"(4) any sale by an odd-lot dealer to offset odd-lot orders of customers;

"(5) any sale by an odd-lot dealer to liquidate a long position which is less than a round lot, provided such sale does not change the position of such odd-lot dealer by more than the unit of trading;

"(6) any sale of a security on a national securities exchange effected with the approval of such exchange which is necessary to equalize the price of such security thereon with the current price of such security on another national securities exchange which is the principal exchange market for such security;

"(7) any sale of a security for a special arbitrage account by a person who then owns another security by virtue of which he is, or presently will be, entitled to acquire an equivalent number of securities of the same class as the securities sold; provided such sale, or the purchase which such sale offsets, is effected for the bona fide purpose of profiting from a current difference between the price of the security sold and the security owned and that such right of acquisition was originally attached to or represented by another security or was issued to all the holders of any class of securities of the issuer;

"(8) any sale of a security on a national securities exchange effected for a special international arbitrage account for the bona fide purpose of profiting from a current difference between the price of such security on a securities market not within or subject to the jurisdiction of the United States and on such national securities exchange: *Provided,* The seller at the time of such sale knows or, by virtue of information currently received, has reasonable grounds to believe that an offer enabling him to cover such sale is then available to him in such foreign securities market and intends to accept such offer immediately; or

"(9) any sale of a security on a national securities exchange effected in accordance with a special offering plan declared effective by the Commission pursuant to Regulation § 240.10b-2(d) [¶ 4328]."

"For the purpose of clause (8) hereof, a depositary receipt for a security shall be deemed to be the same security as the security represented by such receipt."

When members or member organizations transmit for execution sell orders which are originated by their customers or themselves and which are entitled to the exemption provided by clause (4), (5), (6), (7), (8) or (9) of paragraph (d) of Regulation § 240.10a-1 [¶ 4324], such members and organiza-

¶ 2440B.21   "Short-exempt" sell orders.—Continued

tions should, for their own protection, make a record of the clause which is applicable to each such order, and should preserve such record at the point of origin of such order for a period of at least twelve months.

Any order which falls in any category other than the above should not be marked "short-exempt."

¶ 2440C   Deliveries Against Short Sales

• • • *Supplementary Material:*

.10   **Failure to deliver.**—No member or member organization should "fail to deliver" against a short sale of a security on a national securities exchange until a diligent effort has been made by such member or organization to borrow the necessary securities to make delivery.

¶ 2440D   Reports to the Exchange

• • • *Supplementary Material:*

.10   **List of periodic reports.**—Below is a list of periodic reports which members and member organizations are required to submit to the Exchange unless specific exemptions have been obtained. The list also indicates in each case where detailed information with respect to such reports may be found.

Daily:	*Subject of Report*	*Paragraph*
1.	Reports by Registered Traders of On-Floor Transactions for Accounts in Which They Have an Interest (Form 82-A)	2112.30
Weekly:		
2.	Underwriting Commitments and Positions (Form MF-3)	**2421.20**
3.	Transactions by Members and Member Organizations for Own Account (Form 121)	2440G.10
4.	Total Sales Transactions Effected on Exchange (Form 120)	2440F.10
4A.	Transactions Made by a Specialist's Public Customers in Stocks in Which the Specialist Is Registered (Form SPA)	2111.10
Monthly:		
5.	Money Borrowed (Form MF-4)	2421.30
6.	Customers' Debit and Credit Balances (Form MF-5)	2421.40
7.	Foreign Reports (Forms S-1/3 and S-4 of the Federal Reserve Bank of New York)	2440E.10
8.	Registration Fee (Form 120-A)	2440H.10
9.	Net Commissions Received and Retained on Floor Transactions (Form 600)	2440I.10
9A.	Odd Lot Transactions by Odd Lot Dealers (Form 600A)	2440J.10
10.	Short Positions (Form MF-2)	2421.10
10A.	Bona Fide Arbitrage, Errors, Difficult Market Situations (Form 82-B)	2111(c)
Periodically as Requested:		
11.	Margin Requirements Met by Liquidation (Form MF-1)	**2432.50**
12.	Financial Questionnaire (Rule 416 [¶ 2416])	**2416**
13.	Specialists' Dealings in Stocks in Which They Are Registered (Form 81)	2104A.50
14.	Discretionary Transactions	2095.10
15.	Prepayments	2440K.10
Promptly After Reportable Information Is Acquired:		
16.	Joint Accounts (No form furnished)	2423
17.	Options (No form furnished)	2424
18.	Loans and Borrowings (No form furnished)	2420
19.	Specialists' Borrowings (Form SPC) (Monthly after initial report)	2104.40

¶ 2440C   © 1964, Commerce Clearing House, Inc.

¶ 2440E   Foreign Reports

• • • *Supplementary Material:*

Reports on Forms S-1/3 and S-4

.10 Requirements for filing.—Every member organization, unless specifically exempted, whose principal place of business is located in the Second Federal Reserve District should file the following reports with the Exchange or with the Federal Reserve Bank of New York:

Form S-1/3—Purchases and sales of "long term" securities by "foreigners."

Form S-4—Foreign debit and credit balances.

Firms and corporations whose principal place of business is located in some other Federal Reserve District should file their reports directly with the Federal Reserve Bank of the District in which their principal place of business is located and should advise the Exchange in writing as to which Federal Reserve Bank they are reporting.

Every firm and corporation having domestic branch offices should consolidate the figures for all its domestic offices on one set of report forms so that no firm or corporation will report to more than one Federal Reserve Bank.

Period covered by report.—Reports on Form S-1/3 should cover transactions for an entire calendar month and the reports on Form S-4 should show balances as of the close of business each June 30 and December 31.

Reports should be forwarded to Stock Clearing Corporation, Central Receiving Department, 8 Broad Street, New York, N. Y., in the case of Form S-1/3 not later than the fifteenth day following the end of the month covered by the report and, in the case of Form S-4, the fifteenth day following the report dates.

Duplicate copies of the report should be retained in the files of each reporting firm.

Exemptions from reporting.—The Department of Member Firms will consider written requests for exemption from filing reports on Forms S-1/3 and S-4. Such exemptions will be granted on the basis that the business of the firm or corporation is such that it will have no information of a reportable nature to submit.

Inquiries.—Inquiries regarding the preparation of Forms S-1/3 and S-4 should be submitted to the Federal Reserve Bank of New York. Questions regarding the filing of reports may be directed to the Department of Member Firms of the Exchange.

Additional forms.—Additional report forms may be obtained from the Balance of Payments Division of the Federal Reserve Bank of New York or from the Mailing Division, 11 Wall Street, New York 5, N. Y.

¶ 2440F   Total Sale Transactions Effected on the Exchange

• • • *Supplementary Material:*

Reports on Form 120

.10 Requirements for filing.—Every member firm and member corporation clearing or settling transactions is required by the rules of the Exchange to file weekly on Form 120 a report of the total **ROUND-LOT** sale transactions and total **ROUND-LOT** short sale transactions in stocks for each day, effected on the New York Stock Exchange, which were or are to be cleared or settled by the reporting firm or corporation.

General Instructions.—

(1) Report by **TRADE** (not blotter) **DATES.**

(2) Stocks include deposit and other certificates therefor.

(3) Transactions include, "Regular Way", "Cash", "When Issued" and "Seller's Options" on date of trade.

(4) The term "Round-Lot" means 100 shares or 10 shares or multiples thereof depending on the unit of trading in the stocks reported. In the case of a special offering do not report transactions or portions of transactions of less than 100 shares or 10 shares depending on the unit of trading.

(5) The sale transactions referred to above may result from sales of stocks made for the accounts of: (a) customers, (b) reporting firm or corporation, (c) non-clearing firms or corporations, or members who cleared or settled through the reporting firm or corporation, (d) customers of non-clearing firms or corporations clearing or settling through the reporting firm or corporation, (e) partners, stockholders or correspondents, etc., of the reporting firm or corporation or firms or corporations which cleared through the reporting firm or corporation, (f) arbitrage and hedging accounts, (g) error account, and (h) the amount of any stock sales for joint accounts cleared or settled by the reporting firm or corporation.

(6) In the event that a reporting firm or corporation does not have reportable transactions during a given week, a report on Form 120 should be submitted endorsed "No Transactions."

(7) File this report with the Statistical Division, 8 Broad Street, New York 5, New York, not later than 12 noon on the fourth business day following the week covered by the report.

(8) Inquiries should be addressed to the Department of Research & Statistics, Statistical Division, Telephone HAnover 2-4200, Ext. 457.

(9) Additional copies of this form may be obtained from the Mailing Division, 11 Wall Street.

Specific Instructions.—

(1) For the purpose of this report, "short sales" are those defined in the Securities and Exchange Commission's Rule X-3B-3, but do not include any sale exempted by paragraph (d) of Rule X-10A-1. The classification of a sale as "short" should be determined by either the manner in which the order was marked, or the basis on which a sale "initiated on the floor," was executed. However, in the case of an order erroneously marked and so executed, the resulting transaction should be classified in accordance with its correct status.

(2) Short sales for hedging accounts and short sales executed as such for arbitrage accounts should be included in the report of short sales as well as in the report of total sales. Sales made on a "short-exempt" basis for arbitrage accounts should not be included in the total of short sales but such transactions should be included in the report of total sales.

¶ 2440F.10   © 1962, Commerce Clearing House, Inc.

(3) Exclude from the report the following:

(a) All purchase transactions;

(b) all odd-lot transactions;

(c) all transactions in rights and other warrants;

(d) all transactions in bonds;

(e) transactions cleared or settled for you by another firm or corporation;

(f) stocks loaned or borrowed;

(g) transactions executed in over-the-counter markets or on other exchanges;

(h) all or any part of transactions for any joint account which will be reported by another member firm or member corporation.

¶ 2440G   Transactions by Members and Member
Organizations for Own Account

● ● ● *Supplementary Material:*

Reports on Form 121

.10   Requirements for filing.—Every member organization and every member who is not a partner in a member firm or a holder of stock in a member corporation, unless specifically exempted, is required by the rules of the Exchange to file weekly on Form 121 a daily report of total **ROUND-LOT** purchase and sale transactions and total **ROUND-LOT** short sale transactions in all listed stocks effected as dealer on the Exchange for own account. Transactions effected as broker should be excluded. Provision has been made on Form 121 for reports of transactions made by specialists in stocks in which registered, and by all members and member organizations when the reportable transactions were respectively initiated on and off the floor.

Instructions.—

(1) Report by **TRADE** (not blotter) **DATES.**

(2) Stocks include deposit and other certificates therefor.

(3) Transactions include, "Regular Way", "Cash", "When Issued", "When Distributed", and "Seller's Options" on date of trade.

(4) The term "Round-Lot" means 100 shares or 10 shares or multiples thereof depending on the unit of trading.

(5) The term "partners" includes general, special and limited partners, and the term "stockholder" includes holders of voting and non-voting stock.

(6) The figures required on this report are the daily number of shares of listed stocks bought and sold and sold short in round-lots as principals for own account on the New York Stock Exchange for the following accounts:

(a) reporting member, firm or corporation;

(b) partners thereof and stockholders therein;

(c) the proportionate share of any joint account in which the reporting member, firm, or corporation or any partners thereof or stockholders therein, had a direct or indirect interest.

Member organizations should file only one report each week containing a combined record of all reportable transactions for the organization account and for the accounts of all partners or all stockholders of the corporation. Partners and stockholders should not file individual reports.

(7) For the purpose of this report, short sales are those defined in the Securities and Exchange Commission's Regulation § 240.3b-3 [¶ 4235], but do not include any sale exempted by paragraph (d) of Regulation § 240.10a-1 [¶ 4324]. The classification of a sale as "short" should be determined by either the manner in which the order was marked, or the basis on which a sale "initiated on the floor" was executed. However, in the case of an order erroneously marked and so executed, the resulting transaction should be classified in accordance with its correct status.

(8) **EXCLUDE** the following transactions:

(a) in rights and other warrants;

(b) in bonds;

(c) for customers other than partners of the reporting firm or stockholder of the reporting corporation;

(d) in odd-lots;

(e) all agency transactions;

(f) stocks loaned or borrowed;

(g) transactions in the over-the-counter market and on other exchanges;

(h) by odd-lot dealers and specialist odd-lot dealers in stocks in which they were registered as odd-lot dealers when the round-lot transactions were effected to offset transactions in odd lots on the New York Stock Exchange.

(9) A transaction for own account is regarded as having been initiated on the floor when the order for such transaction was not received over the wire or otherwise from a locality off the trading floor regardless of whether the order was executed by the originating member or by another member of the Exchange. Such transactions, unless made by specialists in stocks in which registered while running the book, should be reported in Box #2 of Form 121.

(10) A transaction for own account is regarded as having been initiated off the floor when the order for such transaction was received over the wire or otherwise from a locality off the trading floor regardless of the identity of the executing member. Such transactions should be reported in Box #3.

(11) Report in Box #1 of Form 121, as regular or as relief specialist, only those transactions made for own account in the stocks in which you were registered as specialist and executed either by you, or by a partner of your firm or a stockholder in your corporation, or by a member with whom you acted as specialist in joint account while you or they were running the book.

(12) Report in Box #2, as regular or as relief specialist, transactions made for own account which were initiated on the floor either by you or by a floor partner of your firm or a floor member stockholder in your corporation, or by a member with whom you acted as specialist or otherwise in joint account in stocks in which you or they were registered as specialist, and

¶ 2440G.10

executed while you or they were not running the book. All specialists should report in Box #2 all transactions made for own account which were initiated on the floor in stocks in which not registered as specialists.

(13) In the event that a reporting member, firm or corporation does not have reportable transactions during a given week, a Form 121 report should be submitted endorsed "No Transactions".

(14) The Department of Research & Statistics will consider written requests for exemption from filing reports on Form 121. Such exemptions may be granted on the basis that the business of the member, member firm or member corporation has been and will be such that there will be no reportable information to submit.

(15) File this report with the Statistical Division, 8 Broad Street, New York 5, New York, not later than 12 noon on the Friday following the week covered by the report.

(16) Inquiries should be addressed to the Department of Research & Statistics, Statistical Division, Telephone HAnover 2-4200, Ext. 437.

(17) Additional copies of this form may be obtained from the Mailing Division, 11 Wall Street.

¶ 2440H   Registration Fees

● ● ● **Supplementary Material:**

Report on Form 120-A

.10   **Statutory requirements.**—Section 31 of the Securities Exchange Act of 1934 [¶ 4721] imposes upon every national securities exchange the payment of a fee of 1/500th of 1 per centum of the aggregate dollar amount of the sales of securities transacted on such exchange, except in respect of transactions in securities which are direct obligations of or obligations guaranteed as to principal or interest by the United States, or such securities issued or guaranteed by corporations in which the United States has a direct or indirect interest as may be designated for exemption therefrom by the Secretary of the Treasury.

The Exchange has issued the following directions:

(1) Every member, or member organization engaged in clearing or settling transactions effected upon the Exchange shall maintain a daily record of the aggregate dollar amount of the sales of securities made upon the Exchange and cleared or settled by him or it. The amount of money shall be computed upon the actual sales price, disregarding commissions, taxes or accrued interest on bonds. Blotter dates shall be used throughout. All sales of securities on the Exchange shall be included, except securities which are direct obligations of or obligations guaranteed as to principal or interest by the United States, or such securities issued or guaranteed by corporations in which the United States has a direct or indirect interest as may be designated for exemption therefrom by the Secretary of the Treasury. Odd-lot dealers shall record both the full lots and the odd lots which they sell on the Exchange. If a member organization clears and settles a transaction for a member or member organization that in turn clears it for another principal, only the member organization settling the transaction shall include it in its record. Monthly reports (Form 120-A) of the daily totals above referred to shall be submitted to the Exchange in the manner described below.

           ¶ 2440H.10

(2) At or before 10:30 a.m. on the 10th day of each month each member or member organization required to report shall submit to the Controller's Department a report on Form 120-A showing: aggregate dollar sales volume; the Registration Fee due thereon; principal amount of bonds; number of shares of stock and number of rights to subscribe.

(3) Every such reporting member or member organization shall pay to the Exchange a sum equal to one cent for each $500 or fraction thereof of the total aggregate dollar sales volume reported monthly. The total amount payable as shown on the reports on Form 120-A submitted during the quarter will appear on the next quarterly bill as rendered by the Exchange.

(4) With respect to all transactions which are required by these directions to be included in the foregoing report, the member, firm or corporation responsible for reporting any transaction to the Exchange shall charge to the account, as billed, for which such transaction was made the sum of one cent for each $500 or fraction thereof represented by such transaction.

Whenever the account against which such charge is made is that of a member, member firm or member corporation who is acting for a principal, such member, firm or corporation shall withhold from the sum credited to the account of such principal, as billed, an amount equal to one cent for each $500 or fraction thereof represented by the transaction made for such principal.

(5) In rendering to customers confirmations of sales made on the Exchange for their account, the charge required by these directions either shall be shown separately or be treated in the same manner as transfer taxes. In either case the confirmation shall contain an explanatory legend.

(6) Members, firms or corporations that cease the clearing or settling of security transactions shall promptly render reports for any interim period resulting from such change, and shall pay promptly any sum due under the above directions.

(7) When sales are made on the Exchange for a customer each item reported in writing to the customer must be separately used as the basis for computing the fee appertaining thereto. If the written report shows as a single item the sale of two or more lots of the same security at the same price on the same day, the fee may be computed upon the total of such lots as a unit; otherwise each sale, whether reported together with others or separately, must be independently made the basis for computing the fee relating thereto.

(8) Members, firms or corporations who settle transactions for other members, firms or corporations and who consequently are required to report sales on the Exchange and pay a fee thereon pursuant to paragraphs 1 and 2 above must charge the account of the member, firm or corporation for whom they act on the same basis as is prescribed above with respect to transactions made for customers. This applies also to firms and corporations carrying accounts of floor traders, specialists, and non-clearing members, firms or corporations both in New York City and elsewhere.

(9) The use of daily, weekly, or any similar totals of transactions made for a particular customer or for a particular account as a basis for computing the fee chargeable to such customer or account, whether member or non-member, is prohibited.

¶ 2440H.10

(10) When differences in the computation of the fee arise in good faith, such as when a firm or corporation has rendered to a customer a single report covering two or more lots of the same security at the same price, and, because of "give-ups" or otherwise, it is necessary to bill or record the transaction as two or more separate lots, or when similar differences arise between a main office and a branch office, such differences may be adjusted by those involved by mutual agreement.

¶ 24440 I   Net Commissions Received and Retained
on Floor Transactions

• • • *Supplementary Material:*

Reports on Form 600

.10   When and by whom reports are to be submitted.—

(1) Each member organization and each individual member who is not a general partner of a member firm or a holder of voting stock in a member corporation is required to submit to the Controller's Department a report of commissions on business done on the Exchange during the preceding month.

(2) When a member or member organization has no information to report, a signed report should be submitted with a notation thereon to that effect.

(3) These reports are to be made on Form 600 and are to be filed on or before the 18th day following the month covered by the report unless the Exchange is closed on such day, in which event the report is to be filed on the next business day.

(4) Member organizations with branch offices must submit one report monthly for all offices.

(5) A member who transfers his membership or a member organization which dissolves will be required to file a report covering commissions previously unreported.

(6) A member who retires as a general partner in a member firm or ceases to be a holder of voting stock in a member corporation and does not immediately become a general partner in another member firm or a holder of voting stock in another member corporation is required to file a report for the period commencing the next business day following such event. (The first report and subsequent reports are to be filed in accordance with instruction 3 above.)

(7) An individual member (including special and limited partners in member firms and holders of non-voting stock in member corporations) who would not as a rule have anything to report on Form 600 may obtain permission to submit only an annual report (to be filed on or before December 15 of each year for the period ending November 30) by making a written request to the Controller of the Exchange for such permission, setting forth the reasons therefor.

.20   Contents of report.—

Item (1) on Form 600.—Report the total of all commissions received or receivable on business for members, member organizations, non-members, and allied members, pursuant to Sections 2, 3, and 5 of Article XV of the Constitution (including special offerings and odd-lot transactions). If commissions are charged on such business at rates in excess of the minimums prescribed by these sections, such excess shall also be included in the amount reported. Clearing charges, pursuant to Section 4 of Article XV, are not to be included in Item 1.

All "brokerage" earned on the Floor of the Exchange by a member who is a general partner of a member firm or a holder of voting stock in a member corporation shall be included in the report rendered by that member firm or member corporation.

Respondent's share of any commissions from accounts carried on a disclosed basis by another member firm or member corporation shall be included in the amount reported. This applies only to transactions effected on the Floor of the Exchange.

Gross commissions earned on Monthly Investment Plan accounts (without reduction for the service charge made by the odd lot firms) are to be included in Item 1. Also to be included are respondent's share of commissions received from other member organizations at the direction of Mutual Funds and other customers on transactions effected on the Exchange for the account of such customers.

Item (2) on Form 600.—Report the total of all commissions paid or payable to other members or member organizations with respect to transactions, the commissions on which have been reported in Item 1. Items of this nature may include commissions paid to correspondents carrying omnibus accounts for respondent firm; commissions paid to member organizations or individual members for whom accounts are carried on a disclosed basis, and floor "brokerage."

Do not include in Item 2 commissions paid or payable to other members or member organizations on transactions for firm or personal account, unless commissions on such transactions are also included in Item 1.

.30 Miscellaneous instructions regarding Form 600.—

(1) Information reported in Items 1 and 2 on Form 600 may be based either on trade or on settlement dates.

(2) The charge, pursuant to Section 2 of Article X of the Constitution, will be computed in the Controller's Department from the information reported on Form 600 and will appear on the next quarterly bill rendered by the Exchange. For example, charges computed from reports submitted in July, August, and September for the calendar months of June, July, and August will appear on bills dated September 30th.

(3) A report submitted by a member organization should bear the individual signature of a general partner in that firm, or an officer who is a holder of voting stock in that corporation, and a report submitted by an individual member should bear his signature.

(4) Additional copies of Form 600 may be obtained at the Mailing Division.

¶ 2440J   Odd Lot Transactions by Odd Lot Dealers

● ● ● *Supplementary Material:*

Reports on Form 600-A

.10 When and by whom reports are to be submitted.—

(1) Each member organization and each individual member who is not a general partner of a member firm or a holder of voting stock

¶ **2440I.30**   © 1964, Commerce Clearing House, Inc.

in a member corporation who makes transactions on the Floor of the Exchange as an odd lot dealer is required to submit to the Controller's Department a report showing the aggregate share volume of his or its odd lot purchases and sales effected on the Exchange during the preceding month.

(2) These reports are to be made on Form 600-A and are to be filed on or before the 18th day following the month covered by the report unless the Exchange is closed on such day, in which event the report is to be filed on the next business day.

(3) A member who transfers his membership or member organization which dissolves will be required to file a report covering transactions previously unreported.

.20 Contents of report.—

Item (1) on Form 600-A.—Report the total of all odd lot purchases effected on the Floor of the Exchange as an odd lot dealer.

Item (2) on Form 600-A.—Report the total of all odd lot sales effected on the Floor of the Exchange as an odd lot dealer.

.30 Miscellaneous instructions regarding Form 600-A.—

(1) Information reported on Form 600-A may be based either on trade or on blotter dates. The method elected should be followed on all monthly reports.

(2) The charge, pursuant to Section 9 of Article X of the Constitution, [¶ 1452] will be computed in the Controller's Department from the information reported on Form 600-A and will appear on the next quarterly bill rendered by the Exchange. For example, charges computed from reports submitted in July, August, and September for the calendar months of June, July, and August will appear on bills dated September 30th.

(3) A report submitted by a member organization should bear the individual signature of a general partner in that firm, or an officer who is a holder of voting stock in that corporation, and a report submitted by an individual member should bear his signature.

(4) Additional copies of Form 600-A may be obtained at the Mailing Division.

¶ 2440K   Prepayments on Sales

● ● ● *Supplementary Material:*

.10 Maintenance of Reports.—Each office of a member firm which does business with the public shall prepare monthly and, if it is a branch office, send promptly to the main office of the member organization, in a form prescribed by the Exchange, a report containing information regarding any prepayment to a customer of the proceeds of sales of listed securities.

For purposes of internal control, a general partner or holder of voting stock of the member organization shall review promptly each such report, and if necessary, take appropriate action.

Such reports shall be retained by the member organization in a readily accessible place for a period of one year.

¶ 2440L   Recovery of Exchange Expenditures in Connection with the Liquidation of Ira Haupt & Co.

● ● ● *Supplementary Material:*

The charges imposed by Sec. 9, Art. X of the Constitution apply to transactions effected on the Exchange on and after February 1, 1964 and remain in effect until the Exchange recovers its expenditures in connection with the liquidation of Ira Haupt & Co.

Reports on Form 601

.10   When and by whom reports are to be submitted.—

(1) Each member organization and each individual member who is not a general partner of a member firm or a holder of voting stock in a member corporation is required to submit a report on Form 601 to the Controller's Department.

(2) Reports on Form 601 (which are combined with Form 600) are to be filed on or before the 18th day following the month covered by the report unless the Exchange is closed on such day, in which event the report is to be filed on the next business day.

(3) A member who transfers his membership or a member organization which dissolves will be required to file a report covering the period previously unreported.

(4) A member who retires as a general partner in a member firm or ceases to be a holder of voting stock in a member corporation and does not immediately become a general partner in another member firm or a holder of voting stock in another member corporation is required to file a report for the period commencing the next business day following such event.   (The first report and subsequent reports are to be filed in accordance with instruction 2 above.)

(5) An individual member (including special and limited partners in member firms and holders of non-voting stock in member corporations) who would not as a rule have anything to report on Form 600 may obtain permission to submit only an annual report on Forms 600 and 601 (to be filed on or before December 15 of each year for the period ending November 30) by making a written request to the Controller of the Exchange for such permission, setting forth the reasons therefor.

.20   Contents of report.—

Line 5(A).—Enter on this line ½ of 1% of the Net Commissions Received and Retained for the month covered by the report.

Line 5(B).—(To be filled in by individual members who are not general partners of member firms or holders of voting stock in member corporations.) Enter the minimum charge of $62.50 per month, or $2.08 for each day (including Saturdays, Sundays and holidays) covered by the report if such report covers less than a full month.

Special Credit.—Limited partners of member firms and nonvoting stockholders of member corporations who participate in the profits of such member organizations, and who are subject to the minimum charge at the rate of $750 per year, may claim a credit against such minimum for their percentage of the Haupt liquidation expenses paid by the member organization in which they are limited partners or non-voting stockholders. Show this credit as a

¶ 2440L   © 1964, Commerce Clearing House, Inc.

subtraction from the minimum charge entered on Line 5(B). If such special credit exceeds $62.50 in any month, the excess will be carried forward and applied against the minimum charge for subsequent months.

Line 5(C).—(To be filled in by member organizations.) Enter the minimum charge of $62.50 per month for *each Exchange member* who was a general partner or holder of voting stock for the full month covered by the report. Enter $2.08 per day (including Saturdays, Sundays and holidays) for *each Exchange member* who was a general partner or voting stockholder for part of the month covered by the report.

Enter as Line 5 the highest of (A) (B) or (C).

Note:—Members and member organizations who ordinarily would report the minimum charge may, in some months, be subject to a higher charge at the rate of ½ of 1% on net commissions reported for the month. If, however, the aggregate commissions reported for the entire year do not require more than the minimum charge (at the annual rate of $750 per member), the Exchange will make an adjustment after the close of the year and will allow any overpayment as a credit against subsequent charges.

Line 6.—Credit (if any).—Members and member organizations who have prepaid all or part of their estimated share of the Haupt liquidation expenses should enter on Line 6 a deduction equal to the charge appearing on Line 5 (or equal to the unapplied balance of their prepayment, if less than Line 5).

.30 Miscellaneous information regarding Form 601.—

(1) Individual members who have been given permission to file annual reports on Forms 601 (and Form 600) will be required to file these annual reports in December of each year. During the year, however, such members will automatically be billed for the minimum charge of $62.50 per month for their share of the Haupt liquidation expenses.

(2) The charge, pursuant to Section 9 of Article X of the Constitution, (¶ 1459), and any applicable credits, will appear on the next quarterly bill rendered by the Exchange. For example, information shown on reports submitted in April, May and June for the calendar months of March, April and May will appear on bills dated June 30.

(3) A report submitted by a member organization should bear the individual signature of a general partner in that firm, or an officer who is a holder of voting stock in that corporation, and a report submitted by an individual member should bear his signature.

(4) Additional copies of Form 601 may be obtained at the Mailing Division.

¶ 2440M   Recovery of Exchange Expenditures in Connection with the Liquidation of Ira Haupt & Co.

● ● ● *Supplementary Material:*

The charges imposed by Sec. 9, Art. X of the Constitution apply to transactions effected on the Exchange on and after February 1, 1964 and remain in effect until the Exchange recovers its expenditures in connection with the liquidation of Ira Haupt & Co.

Reports on Form 601A

.10 When and by whom reports are to be submitted.—

(1) Each member organization and each individual member who is not a general partner of a member firm or a holder of voting stock in a member corporation who makes transactions on the floor of the Exchange as an odd lot dealer is required to submit a report on Form 601A to the Controller's Department.

(2) Reports on Form 601A (which are combined with Form 600A) are to be filed on or before the 18th day following the month covered by the report unless the Exchange is closed on such day, in which event the report is to be filed on the next business day.

(3) A member who transfers his membership or a member organization which dissolves will be required to file a report covering the period previously unreported.

.20 Contents of report.—

Line 5(A).—Enter on this line $\frac{1}{16}$ of 1¢ per share on the total odd lot purchases and odd lot sales effected on the Floor of the Exchange as an odd lot dealer for the month covered by the report.

Line 5(B).—(To be filled in by individual members who are not general partners of member firms or holders of voting stock in member corporations.) Enter the minimum charge of $62.50 per month, or $2.08 for each day (including Saturdays, Sundays and holidays) covered by the report if such report covers less than a full month.

Special Credit.—Limited partners of member firms and non-voting stockholders of member corporations who participate in the profits of such member organizations, and who are subject to the minimum charge at the rate of $750 per year, may claim a credit against such minimum for their percentage of the Haupt liquidation expenses paid by the member organization in which they are limited partners or non-voting stockholders. Show this credit as a subtraction from the minimum charge entered on line 5(B). If such special credit exceeds $62.50 in any month, the excess will be carried forward and applied against the minimum charge for subsequent months.

Line 5(C).—(To be filled in by member organizations.) Enter the minimum charge of $62.50 per month for *each Exchange member* who was a general partner or holder of voting stock for the full month covered by the report. Enter $2.08 per day (including Saturdays, Sundays and holidays) for *each Exchange member* who was a general partner or voting stockholder for part of the month covered by the report.

Enter as Line 5 the highest of (A), (B) or (C).

Note:—Members and member organizations who ordinarily would report the minimum charge may, in some months, be subject to a higher charge at the rate of $\frac{1}{16}$ of 1¢ per share on odd lot purchases and sales reported for the month. If, however, the aggregate amounts reported for the entire year do not require more than the minimum charge (at the annual rate of $750 per member), the Exchange will make an adjustment after the close of the year and will allow any overpayment as a credit against subsequent charges.

Line 6.—Credit (if any).—Members and member organizations who have prepaid all or part of their estimated share of the Haupt liquidation expenses should enter on Line 6 a deduction equal to the charge appearing on Line 5 (or equal to the unapplied balance of their prepayment, if less than Line 5.)

.30   Miscellaneous information regarding Form 601A.—

(1) The charge, pursuant to Section 9 of Article X of the Constitution (¶ 1459), and any applicable credits, will appear on the next quarterly bill rendered by the Exchange. For example, information shown on reports submitted in April, May and June for the calendar months of March, April and May will appear on bills dated June 30.

(2) A report submitted by a member organization should bear the individual signature of a general partner in that firm, or an officer who is a holder of voting stock in that corporation, and a report submitted by an individual member should bear his signature.

(3) Additional copies of Form 601A may be obtained at the Mailing Division.

[The next page is 3805.]

Proxies

(Rules and Policies Administered by the Department of Stock List.)

Applicability of proxy rules.—Rules 450 to 460 [¶ 2450-2460], inclusive, apply to both listed and unlisted securities, unless the context otherwise limits application.

The term "unregistered company" as used in Rules 456 to 459 [¶ 2456-2459] means a company not registered under the Public Utility Holding Company Act or the Investment Company Act, or one not having securities registered on a national securities exchange.

The term "member" as used in connection with Rules 456 to 459 [¶ 2456-2459] includes a member, allied member, member firm, member corporation and employee thereof.

¶ 2450   Restriction on Giving of Proxies

Rule 450. No member organization shall give a proxy to vote stock registered in its name, except as required or permitted under the provisions of Rule 452 [¶ 2452], unless such member organization is the beneficial owner of such stock.

¶ 2451   Transmission of Proxy Material

Rule 451. (a) Whenever a person soliciting proxies shall furnish a member organization:

(1) Copies of all soliciting material which such person is sending to registered holders, and

(2) satisfactory assurance that he will reimburse such member organization for all out-of-pocket expenses, including reasonable clerical expenses, incurred by such member organization in connection with such solicitation,

such member organization shall transmit to each beneficial owner of stock which is in its possession or control the material furnished; and

(b) such member organization shall transmit with such material either:

(1) a request for voting instructions and, as to matters which may be voted without instructions under Rule 452 [¶ 2452], a statement to the effect that, if such instructions are not received by the tenth day before the meeting, the proxy may be given at discretion by the owner of record of the stock; provided, however, when the proxy soliciting material is transmitted to the beneficial owner of the stock twenty-five days or more before the meeting, the statement accompanying such material shall be to the effect that the proxy may be given fifteen days before the meeting at the discretion of the owner of record of the stock; or

(2) a signed proxy indicating the number of shares held for such beneficial owner and bearing a symbol identifying the proxy with proxy records of such member organization, and also a letter informing the

¶ 2451   Continued

    beneficial owner of the necessity for completing the proxy form and for-
warding it to the person soliciting proxies in order that the shares may
be represented at the meeting.

This rule shall not apply to beneficial owners outside the United States.

● ● ● *Supplementary Material:*

.10   **Annual reports to be transmitted.**—The annual report shall be transmitted to beneficial owners under the same conditions as those applying
to proxy soliciting material under Rule 451 even though it is not proxy-solicit-
ing material under the proxy rules of the Securities and Exchange Commission.

.20   **Forms of letters to clients requesting voting instructions.**—There appear
below specimens of letters containing the information and instructions
required pursuant to the proxy rules to be given to clients in the circumstances indicated in the appropriate heading. These are shown as examples
and not as prescribed forms. They have also been published in the NYSE
Company Manual as a matter of information for companies having securities
listed on this Exchange, although, normally, member organizations will be
expected to supply their own letters.

    These letters are designed to permit furnishing to clients the actual
proxy form for use in transmitting instructions to the member organization.

When Broker May Vote on All Proposals Without Instructions

To our Clients:

    We have been requested to forward to you the enclosed proxy material
relative to shares carried by us in your account but not registered in your
name. Such shares can be voted only by us as the holder of record.

    We shall be pleased to vote your shares in accordance with your wishes,
if you will execute the enclosed proxy form and return it to us promptly in the
self-addressed, stamped envelope, also enclosed. It is understood that, if you sign
without otherwise marking the form, the shares will be voted as recommended
by the management on all matters to be considered at the meeting.

    Should you wish to have a proxy covering your shares issued to yourself
or others, we shall be pleased to issue the same.

    The rules of the New York Stock Exchange provide that if instructions
are not received by the tenth day before the meeting, the proxy may be given
at discretion by the holder of record of the shares.

When Broker May Not Vote on Any Proposals Without Instructions

To our Clients:

    We have been requested to forward to you the enclosed proxy material
relative to shares carried by us in your account but not registered in your name.
Such shares can be voted only by us as the holder of record.

    In order for your shares to be represented at the meeting, it will be necessary
for us to have your specific voting instructions. Accordingly, please give your
instructions over your signature on the enclosed proxy form and return it to us
promptly in the self-addressed, stamped envelope, also enclosed. It is understood
that, if you sign without otherwise marking the form, the shares will be voted
as recommended by the management on all matters to be considered at the
meeting.

    Should you wish to have a proxy covering your shares issued to yourself
or others, we shall be pleased to issue the same.

When Broker May Vote on Certain But Not All of the Proposals
Without Instructions

To our Clients:

We have been requested to forward to you the enclosed proxy material relative to shares carried by us in your account but not registered in your name. Such shares can be voted only by us as the holder of record.

We wish to call your attention to the fact that, under the rules of the New York Stock Exchange, we cannot vote your shares on one or more of the matters to be acted upon at the meeting without your specific voting instructions.

Accordingly, in order for your shares to be voted on all matters, please give your instructions over your signature on the enclosed proxy form and return it to us promptly in the self-addressed, stamped envelope, also enclosed. It is understood that, if you sign without otherwise marking the form, you wish us to vote the shares as recommended by management on all matters to be acted upon at the meeting. If we do not hear from you by the tenth day before the meeting, we may vote your shares in our discretion to the extent permitted by the rules of the Exchange.

Should you wish to have a proxy covering your shares issued to yourself or others, we shall be pleased to issue the same.

.30 Forwarding of signed proxy.—The following conditions shall be met by a member organization adopting the procedure of sending signed proxies to customers:

(1) Each signed proxy sent to a customer shall contain a code number for identification and the exact number of shares held of record for the account of the customer.

(2) Signed proxies sent to customers shall be accompanied by appropriate instructions to the customer for transmitting his vote to the company.

(3) The member organization shall advise the company of the number of proxies sent to customers and the identifying numbers and shares represented by such proxies.

(4) When requested by a company, the member organization shall send a follow-up request to customers whose proxies have not been received by the company.

(5) Records of the member organization covering the solicitation of proxies shall show:

(A) The date of receipt of the proxy material from the issuer or other person soliciting the proxies.

(B) Names of customers to whom the material and proxies are sent, and the date of mailing.

(C) The number of shares covered by each proxy.

(D) The code number of each customer's proxy.

.40 Forms of letters to clients to accompany signed proxies.—There appear below specimens of letters containing the information and instructions required pursuant to the proxy rules to be given to clients in the circumstances indicated in the appropriate heading. These are shown as examples and not as prescribed forms. They have also been published in the NYSE Company Manual as a matter of information for companies having securities listed on the Exchange, although, normally, member organizations will be expected to supply their own letters.

[The next page is 3807-3.]

When Proxy Contains No Proposals To Be Voted On

To our Clients:

We have been requested to forward to you the enclosed proxy material relative to shares carried by us in your account but not registered in your name.

If you wish your stock to be voted at the meeting, it will be necessary for you to date and forward the enclosed proxy form, which has been signed by us as the holder of record, in the self-addressed, stamped envelope which is furnished for the purpose.

We urge you to send your proxy in promptly to assure the largest possible representation of stockholders at the meeting.

When Proxy Contains Proposals To Be Voted On

To our Clients:

We have been requested to forward to you the enclosed proxy material relative to shares carried by us in your account but not registered in your name.

If you wish your stock to be voted at the meeting, it will be necessary for you to complete and forward the enclosed proxy form, which has been signed by us as the holder of record, in the self-addressed, stamped envelope which is furnished for the purpose.

Please note that you may direct the manner in which your shares will be voted by marking the appropriate spaces in the signed proxy form. If you forward the proxy without indicating the manner in which you wish your shares to be voted, the proxy will be voted as recommended by the management on all matters to be considered at the meeting.

We urge you to send your proxy in promptly to assure the largest possible representation of stockholders at the meeting.

.50 Method to be used in transmission of proxy material.—First class mail should be used to facilitate the obtaining of voting instructions or forwarding signed proxies, unless another method is specified by the persons for whom the material is transmitted.

.60 Duty to transmit even when requested not to.—The proxy material must be sent to a beneficial owner even though such owner has instructed the firm not to do so.

.70 Non-applicability to beneficial owners outside the United States.—Proxy material need not be sent to beneficial owners outside the United States. However, member organizations may do so if they so desire.

.80 Duty of out-of-town member organization.—If securities are held in an omnibus account for an out-of-town or non-clearing member organization, it is incumbent upon the out-of-town or non-clearing member organization to see that the necessary proxy material is transmitted to the beneficial owners and that the proper records relative thereto are kept.

.90 Schedule of approved charges by member organizations in connection with proxy solicitations.—The Exchange has approved the following as fair and reasonable rates of reimbursement of member organizations for all out-of-pocket expenses, including reasonable clerical expenses, incurred in connection with proxy solicitations pursuant to Rule 451 and in mailing interim reports or other material pursuant to Rule 465:

40¢ for each set of proxy material, plus postage, with a minimum of $3.00 for all sets mailed;

¶ 2451.90—Continued

10¢ for each copy, plus postage, for interim reports or other material, with no minimum.

Member organizations are required to mail out such material as provided by Rules 451 and 465 when satisfactory assurance is received of reimbursement of expenses at such rates; provided, however, that a member organization may request reimbursement of expenses at lower rates than those mentioned above or, if agreed to by the person soliciting proxies or the company, at higher rates.

(See ¶ 2465.30 for form of bill to be used.)

                              © 1964, Commerce Clearing House, Inc.

¶ 2452   Giving Proxies by Member Organization

Rule 452. A member organization shall give a proxy for stock registered in its name, at the direction of the beneficial owner. If the stock is not in the control or possession of the member organization, satisfactory proof of the beneficial ownership as of the record date may be required.

Voting member organization holdings as executor, etc.

A member organization may give a proxy to vote any stock registered in its name if such member organization holds such stock as executor, administrator, guardian, trustee, or in a similar representative or fiduciary capacity with authority to vote.

Voting procedure without instructions

A member organization which has transmitted proxy soliciting material to the beneficial owner of stock and solicited voting instructions in accordance with the provisions of Rule 451 [¶ 2451], and which has not received instructions from the beneficial owner by the date specified in the statement accompanying such material, may give a proxy to vote such stock, provided the person signing the proxy has no knowledge of any contest as to the action to be taken at the meeting and provided such action is adequately disclosed to stockholders and does not include authorization for a merger, consolidation or any other matter which may affect substantially the rights or privileges of such stock.

Instructions on stock in names of other member organizations

A member organization which has in its possession or control stock registered in the name of another member organization, and which has solicited voting instructions in accordance with the provisions of Rule 451(b)(1) [¶ 2451], shall

    (1) Forward to the second member organization any voting instructions received from the beneficial owner, or

    (2) if the proxy-soliciting material has been transmitted to the beneficial owner of the stock in accordance with Rule 451 [¶ 2451] and no instructions have been received by the date specified in the statement accompanying such material, notify the second member organization of such fact in order that such member organization may give the proxy as provided in the third paragraph of this rule.

Signed proxies for stock in names of other member organizations

A member organization which has in its possession or control stock registered in the name of another member organization, and which desires to transmit signed proxies pursuant to the provisions of Rule 451(b)(2) [¶ 2451], shall obtain the requisite number of signed proxies from such holder of record.

• • • *Supplementary Material:*

Giving a Proxy To Vote Stock

.10 When member organization may vote without customer instructions.— Rule 452, above, provides that a member organization may give a proxy to vote stock provided that:

    (1) It has transmitted proxy soliciting material to the beneficial owner of stock in accordance with Rule 451 [¶ 2451], and

¶ 2452.10   **Giving a Proxy To Vote Stock.**—Continued

(2) it has not received voting instructions from the beneficial owner by the date specified in the statement accompanying such material, and

(3) the person signing the proxy has no knowledge of any contest as to the action to be taken at the meeting and provided such action is adequately disclosed to stockholders and does not include authorization for a merger, consolidation or any matter which may affect substantially the rights or privileges of such stock.

.11   **When member organization may not vote without customer instructions.**—In the list of meetings of stockholders appearing in the Weekly Bulletin, after proxy material has been reviewed by the Exchange, each meeting will be designated by an appropriate symbol to indicate either (a) that members may execute a proxy without instructions of beneficial owners, (b) that members may not vote specific matters on the proxy, or (c) that members may not vote the entire proxy.

Generally speaking, a member organization may not give a proxy to vote without instructions from beneficial owners when the matter to be voted upon:

(1) is not submitted to stockholders by means of a proxy statement comparable to that specified in Schedule 14-A of the Securities and Exchange Commission;

(2) is the subject of a counter-solicitation, or is part of a proposal made by a stockholder which is being opposed by management (i.e., a contest);

(3) relates to a merger or consolidation (except when the company's proposal is to merge with its own wholly owned subsidiary, provided its shareholders dissenting thereto do not have rights of appraisal);

(4) involves right of appraisal;

(5) authorizes mortgaging of property;

(6) authorizes or creates indebtedness or increases the authorized amount of indebtedness;

(7) authorizes or creates a preferred stock or increases the authorized amount of an existing preferred stock;

(8) alters the terms or conditions of existing stock or indebtedness;

(9) involves waiver or modification of preemptive rights (except when the company's proposal is to waive such rights with respect to shares being offered pursuant to stock option or purchase plans involving the additional issuance of not more than 5% of the company's outstanding common shares (see Item 12));

(10) changes existing quorum requirements with respect to stockholder meetings;

© 1962, Commerce Clearing House, Inc.

(11) alters voting provisions or the proportionate voting power of a stock, or the number of its votes per share (except where cumulative voting provisions govern the number of votes per share for election of directors and the company's proposal involves a change in the number of its directors by not more than 10% or not more than one) ;

(12) authorizes issuance of stock, or options to purchase stock, to directors, officers, or employees in an amount which exceeds 5% of the total amount of the class outstanding;

(13) authorizes

a. a new profit-sharing or special remuneration plan, or a new retirement plan, the annual cost of which will amount to more than 10% of average annual income before taxes for the preceding five years, or

b. the amendment of an existing plan which would bring its cost above 10% of such average annual income before taxes.

Exception may be made in cases of

a. retirement plans based on agreement or negotiations with labor unions (or which have been or are to be approved by such unions) ; and

b. any related retirement plan for benefit of non-union employees having terms substantially equivalent to the terms of such union-negotiated plan, which is submitted for action of stockholders concurrently with such union-negotiated plan;

(14) changes the purposes or powers of a company to an extent which would permit it to change to a materially different line of business and it is the company's stated intention to make such a change;

(15) authorizes the acquisition of property, assets, or a company, where the consideration to be given has a fair value approximating 20% or more of the market value of the previously outstanding shares;

(16) authorizes the sale or other disposition of assets or earning power approximating 20% or more of those existing prior to the transaction.

(17) authorizes a transaction not in the ordinary course of business in which an officer, director or substantial security holder has a direct or indirect interest;

(18) reduces earned surplus by 51% or more, or reduces earned surplus to an amount less than the aggregate of three years' common stock dividends computed at the current dividend rate.

.12 Discretionary and non-discretionary proposals in one proxy form.—In some cases, a proxy form may contain proposals, some of which may be acted upon at the discretion of the member organization in the absence of instructions, and others which may be voted only in accordance with the directions of the beneficial owner. This should be indicated in the letter of transmittal. In such cases, the member organization may vote the proxy in the absence of instructions if it physically crosses out those portions where it does not have discretion.

.13 Cancellation of discretionary proxy where counter-solicitation develops.
—Where a discretionary proxy has been given in good faith under the rules and counter-solicitation develops at a later date, thereby creating a

¶ 2452.13　Giving a Proxy To Vote Stock.—Continued
"contest," the question as to whether or not the discretionary proxy should then be cancelled is a matter which each member organization must decide for itself. After a contest has developed no further proxies should be given except at the direction of beneficial owners.

.14　**Subsequent proxy.**—Where a member organization gives a subsequent proxy, it should clearly indicate whether the proxy is in addition to, in substitution for or in revocation of any prior proxy.

.15　**Signing and dating proxy—designating shares covered.**—All proxies should be dated and should show the number of shares voted. Since manual signatures are sometimes illegible, a member organization should also either type or rubber-stamp its name on such proxy.

.16　**Proxy records.**—Records covering the solicitation of proxies shall show the following:

(1) The date of receipt of the proxy material from the issuer or other person soliciting the proxies;

(2) names of customers to whom the material is sent together with date of mailing;

(3) all voting instructions showing whether verbal or written; and

(4) a summary of all proxies voted by the member organization clearly setting forth total shares voted for or against or not voted for each proposal to be acted upon at the meeting.

Verbal voting instructions may be accepted provided a record is kept of the instructions of the beneficial owner and the instructions are retained by the member organization. The record shall also indicate the date of the receipt of the instructions and the name of the recipient.

.20　**Retention of records.**—All proxy solicitation records, originals of all communications received and copies of all communications sent relating to such solicitation, shall be retained for a period of not less than three years, the first two years in an easily accessible place.

¶ 2453　　　　　Proxy to Show Number of Shares

Rule 453.　In all cases in which a proxy is given by a member organization the proxy shall state the actual number of shares of stock for which the proxy is given.

¶ 2454　　　　　Transfers to Facilitate Solicitation

Rule 454.　A member organization, when so requested by the Exchange shall transfer certificates of a listed stock held either for its own account or for the account of others, if registered in the name of a previous holder of record, into its own name, prior to the taking of a record of stockholders, to facilitate the convenient solicitation of proxies.

The Exchange will make such request at the instance of the issuer or of persons owning in the aggregate at least ten per cent. of such stock, provided, if the Exchange so requires, the issuer or persons making such request agree

to indemnify member organizations against transfer taxes, and the Exchange
may make such a request whenever it deems it advisable.

¶ 2455   Rules Apply to Individual Members and Nominees

Rule 455.   Rules 450 through 454 [¶ 2450-2454] shall apply also to individual
             members and to any nominees of member organizations or indi-
vidual members. They shall apply also to voting in person.

¶ 2456   Representations to Management

Rule 456.   Before a member, allied member, member organization or employee
             thereof states to the management of a registered or unregistered
company that he represents stockholders in making demands for changes in
management or company policies, he must have

(1) Received permission of such stockholders to make such demands,
and
(2) if an unregistered company is involved, filed with the Exchange
the information required by Schedule B.

*(Note: In the case of a registered company the member may be a participant under
Regulation § 240.14a-11 of the Securities and Exchange Commission [¶ 4445] and
required to file Schedule 14-B with the Commission.)*

¶ 2457   Filing Participant Information (Schedule B)

Rule 457.   A member, allied member, member organization or employee
             thereof must file with the Exchange the information required by
Schedule B before he engages, alone or with others, in any of the following
activities relating to a present or prospective proxy contest involving an
unregistered company:

(1) Requests more than 10 security holders:

(A) to sign a proxy (other than in the normal course of transmission of another's proxy material as required by Rule 451 [¶ 2451]);
or

(B) to vote for or against, or abstain from voting on any
proposal;

(2) requests another security holder:

(A) to join in calling a meeting of security holders;

(B) to join in litigation against an issuer; or

(C) to join or assist in the formation of a security holders'
committee;

(3) becomes a nominee for director;

(4) becomes a member of a security holders' committee or group; or

(5) contributes funds toward the cost of a prospective or present
proxy contest.

¶ 2458   Filing of Proxy Material (Schedule A)

Rule 458.   A member, allied member, member organization or employee thereof
                 must file with the Exchange the information called for by Sched-
ule A before he, acting alone or with others, requests more than ten security
holders, in connection with a proxy contest involving an unregistered company:

(1) To sign a proxy (other than in the normal course of transmission
of another's proxy material as required by Rule 451 [¶ 2451]) ; or

(2) to vote for or against, or abstain from voting on any proposal;
and a copy of such information must be furnished to each person of whom
such request is made.

● ● ● *Supplementary Material:*

.10 **Securities and Exchange Commission proxy rules.**—Members who intend
     to become active in a proxy contest involving a registered company
should familiarize themselves with the provisions of Regulations § 240.14 of
the Securities and Exchange Commission [¶¶ 4436—4445].

Attention is drawn to the following interpretation:

Voting advice.—We understand it to be the position of the Securities and
Exchange Commission that on the unsolicited request of a customer, a member
may advise him how to vote in a proxy contest without becoming a participant
and having to file under Securities and Exchange Commission rules. However, if a member volunteers advice to customers on how to vote a proxy, he
may have to file with the Commission.

¶ 2459   Other Persons to File Information When Associated
                           with Member

Rule 459.   No member, allied member, member organization or employee
                 thereof shall join with any other person in requesting more than
ten security holders, in connection with a proxy contest involving an unregistered company:

(1) To sign a proxy; or

(2) to vote for or against, or abstain from voting on any proposal,
unless such other person agrees to:

(A) file with the Exchange Schedules A and B, and

(B) furnish a copy of the information contained in Schedule A
to each person of whom such request is made.

● ● ● *Supplementary Material:*

.10 **Public information.**—All information filed with the Exchange under these
     policies will be public.

After the section which lists the meetings of stockholders in the Weekly
Bulletin there will appear a title "Election Contests" which will be followed
by a statement reading: "Companies as to which proxy solicitation material
filed with the Exchange indicates that there is a counter-solicitation of proxies

for the election of directors:". There will then follow a list of such companies where counter-proxy solicitation material has been filed with the Exchange.

Copies of Schedules A and B may be obtained upon request from the Department of Member Firms.

¶ 2460   Specialists Participating in Contests

Rule 460.   (a) No member who is a specialist, no partner of a member firm in which such member is a partner, no stockholder in a member corporation in which such member is a stockholder, no such firm or corporation, nor any employee of any of them, shall participate in a proxy contest of a company if such member specializes in the stock of that company.

Specialists as Directors

(b) No member who is a specialist, no partner of a member firm in which such member is a partner, no stockholder in a member corporation in which such member is a stockholder, nor any employee of any of them, shall be a director of a company if such member specializes in the stock of that company.

● ● ● *Supplementary Material:*

.10   **Control relationships—Business transactions—Finder's fees.**—No specialist should be in a control relationship with any company in whose stock he is registered. This applies not only with respect to the ownership of 10% or more of the stock in such a company, but also to business transactions of any kind with such companies; for example, loans, etc. A specialist must not accept a finder's fee from a company in whose stock he is registered.

Company Reports to Stockholders

(Rules and Policies administered by the Department of Stock List.)

¶ 2465   Transmission of Interim Reports and Other Material

Rule 465. A member organization, when so requested by a company, and upon being furnished with:

(1) copies of interim reports of earnings or other material being sent to stockholders, and

(2) satisfactory assurance that it will be reimbursed by such company for all out-of-pocket expenses, including reasonable clerical expenses,

shall transmit such reports or material to each beneficial owner of stock of such company held by such member organization and registered in a name other than the name of the beneficial owner.

This rule shall not apply to beneficial owners outside the United States.

● ● ● *Supplementary Material:*

.10 **Application of rule.**—This rule applies to both listed and unlisted companies. (See ¶ 2451.10 for transmission of annual reports.)

.20 **Mailing charges by member organizations.**—The Exchange has approved the following as fair and reasonable rates of reimbursement of member organizations for all out-of-pocket expenses, including reasonable clerical expenses, incurred in connection with proxy solicitations pursuant to Rule 451 and in mailing interim reports or other material pursuant to Rule 465:

40¢ for each set of proxy material, plus postage, with a minimum of $3.00 for all sets mailed;

10¢ for each copy, plus postage, for interim reports or other material, with no minimum.

Member organizations are required to mail out such material as provided by Rules 451 and 465 when satisfactory assurance is received of reimbursement of expenses at such rates; provided, however, that a member organization may request reimbursement of expenses at lower rates than those mentioned above or, if agreed to by the person soliciting proxies or the company, at higher rates.

.30   Form of bill to be used by member organizations.—

TO:				DATE:
Expenses incurred in connection with mailing of following material:	No. Sets Mailed	Service Fee	Postage Expense	Total Charges
ANNUAL REPORT PROXY SOLICITING MATERIAL INTERIM REPORT POST MEETING REPORT STOCKHOLDER LETTER OTHER:				
FOR CORPORATION RECORDS DATE PAID CHECK NO.				

NEW YORK STOCK EXCHANGE
COMMUNICATIONS WITH THE PUBLIC

. . . rules of Board of Governors dealing with advertising, market letters, research reports, sales literature, radio, television and telephone reports, writing and speaking activities . . .

TABLE OF CONTENTS

Advertising, Market Letters, Sales Literature, Radio, Television and Telephone Reports

Communications with the Public

Advertising, Market Letters, Research Reports, Sales Literature, Radio, Television and Writing and Speaking Activities

(Rules and Policies Administered by Public Relations.)

¶ 2471   Advertising

Rule 471.   Members and member organizations shall submit to the Exchange —before publication—all advertisements for approval of manner and form of presentation, unless the copy is in a general form previously approved.

Amendments.
March 20, 1958.

● ● ● *Supplementary Material:*

.10 Information regarding advertising.—Routine advertisements in a general form previously approved do not have to be submitted to the Exchange. These include: (a) business cards; (b) announcements stating that specific unlisted securities are bought, sold and quoted; (c) announcements of dissolution; (d) approved firm or corporation formations; (e) approved partnership or stockholder changes; (f) approved new offices; or (g) approved employment of registered representatives.

Underwriting ads do not have to be submitted to the Exchange unless a member organization in advertising with a non-member wishes to identify itself in the ad as a member of the New York Stock Exchange.

All other advertisements should be submitted to Department of Public Relations, in duplicate, prior to publication. One copy will be returned with an indication of approval or suggested changes in manner or form of presentation.

.20 Requirements administered by SEC for over-the-counter brokers and dealers.—Unless an over-the-counter broker or dealer is registered with the Commission under Section 15(b) of the Securities Exchange Act (see law at ¶ 4453, and following), he may not advertise through the facilities of interstate commerce, except in the case of securities specifically exempted by Regulations §§ 240.15a-1 [¶ 4452], 240.15a-2 [¶ 4452A] and 240.15a-3 [¶ 4452B].

¶ 2472   Market Letters, Sales Literature, Research Reports and Writing Activities

Rule 472.   Each market letter, research report and all sales literature prepared and issued by a member or member organization for general distribution to customers or the public shall be approved in advance by such member or by a general partner or a holder of voting stock in such organization or by a competent delegate authorized by him to act in his behalf.

In addition, research reports shall be prepared or approved by a supervisory analyst acceptable to the Exchange under the provisions of rule 344. In the event that the member organization has no principal or employee qualified with the Exchange to approve such material, it shall be approved by a qualified supervisory analyst in another member organization by arrangement between the two member organizations.

Market letters, sales literature and research reports which refer to the market or to specific companies or securities, listed or unlisted, shall be retained for at least three years by the member or member organization which prepared the material. The copies retained shall contain the name or names of the persons who prepared the material and the name or names of the persons approving its issuance, and shall at all times within the three-year period be readily available.

Amendments.

October 20, 1955, effective November 1, 1955; September 19, 1963, effective October 15, 1963; June 18, 1964.

● ● ● *Supplementary Material:*

.10 Information regarding market letters, research reports and sales literature.—The requirement for three-year retention of such material applies only to members and member organizations which prepared it for distribution.

The term "market letter" refers to any publication, printed or processed, which comments on the securities market or individual securities and is prepared for general distribution to the organization's customers or to the public. It also includes material on investment subjects prepared by a member or personnel of a member organization for publication in newspapers and periodicals.

The term "research report" refers to printed or processed analyses covering individual companies or industries.

The term "sales literature" refers to printed or processed material interpreting the facilities offered by a member organization or its personnel to the public, discussing the place of investment in an individual's financial planning, or calling attention to any market letter, research report or sales literature, which is prepared for and given general distribution.

Internal wires, memoranda and other written communications to branch offices or correspondent firms which refer to securities, industries or the market in general and which are shown or distributed to the public are subject to these standards; internal sales communications to be used in making recommendations to customers are also subject to these standards. All such material should be approved in advance by a general partner or a holder of voting stock, or his authorized delegate, and retained by the firm for three years subject to review by the Exchange.

Internal wires and memoranda carrying flash news, or in response to specific inquiries are exempt from these standards. Wires marked "For Internal Use" or "Confidential" are also exempt if their distribution is actually internal. However, close supervision must be exercised to be sure that these communications are used only for internal purposes.

¶ 2473   Radio, Television, Telephone Reports

Rule 473. Members and member organizations desiring to broadcast New York Stock Exchange quotations in radio or television programs, or in public telephone market reports, or to make use of radio or television broadcasts for any business purpose, shall first obtain the consent of the Exchange by submitting an outline of the program and an example of the script to be used.

The text of all commercials, used on radio and television or in telephone reports, must be approved in advance by the Exchange. Program material (except lists of market quotations) used by members or member organizations on radio, television or public telephone market reports, or program

¶ **2472.10   Rule 473**   © 1964, Commerce Clearing House, Inc.

material supplied to these media shall be retained by the firm for at least a year and be available to the Exchange upon request.

Amendments.

October 20, 1955, effective November 1, 1955.

● ● ● *Supplementary Material:*

.10 **Information regarding radio, etc., reports.**—A single copy of the text of commercials and program material (except lists of quotations) sponsored or supplied by the membership on radio, television and telephone market reports will be adequate.

¶ 2474A Standards for Advertising, Market Letters, Sales Literature, Research Reports, Radio, Television and Writing Activities

● ● ● *Supplementary Material:*

.10 **General.**—Truthfulness and good taste are the traditional standards of the Exchange community in any form of communication with the public. Rules can never take the place of good judgment in such communications. Under some circumstances what is left out may be just as important as what is included.

Member organizations, of course, can never overlook basic characteristics of investments—that prices can go down as well as up; that dividends can be cut, omitted or increased; that there is some degree of risk in any security; that investments can not be depended upon to produce a certain return in terms of purchasing power or in dollars.

In reviewing member organization material—as specified in Rules 471, 472 and 473—the New York Stock Exchange is concerned with the manner— or form—in which information and opinions are presented. The Exchange can not, of course, be responsible for the accuracy and completeness of factual information, nor the opinions of member organizations, in the material reviewed.

Some of the guideposts established by the Exchange for written communications with the public include:

(1) **Recommendations.** A recommendation (even though not labeled as a recommendation) must have a basis which can be substantiated as reasonable.

When recommending the purchase, sale or switch of specific securities, supporting information should be provided or offered.

The market price at the time the recommendation is made must be shown.

(2) **Disclosure.** When market letters, sales literature or research reports recommend the purchase or sale of a specific security, member organizations must disclose the following information, if such conditions exist:

(a) that the firm usually makes a market in the issue being recommended.

(b) that the member organization or its partners hold options in any securities of the recommended issuer.

(c) that some or all of the recommended securities are to be sold to or bought from customers on a principal basis by the member organization or its partners (unless covered by (a) above).

(d) that the member organization was manager or co-manager of the most recent public offering (within 3 years) of any securities of the recommended issuer.

It has been the experience of some firms that disclosure of directorates or other insider relationships is a good way of avoiding difficulties in this area. When such disclosure is made, however, the firm should be careful to avoid exploiting these relationships by implying that the recommendation is based directly or indirectly on privileged information.

(3) Past Recommendations. Material promoting past records of research recommendations, in connection with purchases or sales, is acceptable if it covers all of the following:

(a) At least a 1-year period.

(b) A list of all of the issues in a specific "universe"—or clearly definable area which can be fully isolated and circumscribed—recommended during the period. The list may be given or offered.

(c) The date and price of each recommendation at the recommendation date and at the end of the period or when sale was suggested, whichever is earlier.

(d) The number of issues recommended, the number that advanced and the number that declined, in the event a list is offered but not included in the material.

It must be made clear that—

(a) There is no implication in any such published record of comparable future performance or that a customer can't lose by following the firm's recommendations.

(b) The period covered was one of a generally rising market, if such is the case.

(c) If a record is averaged, or otherwise summarized, such results would have been obtained only if each issue had been purchased when recommended and then sold at the end of the period covered or when sale was recommended. The purchase price of a given number of shares—such as a round lot—of each of the recommended securities must be shown. Commissions must be mentioned.

If such a record is started and published, and publication is subsequently discontinued for any reason, resumption will be permitted only when the intervening period is included in the published record.

A file of all the original recommendations on which the record is based must be kept by the firm and be available to the Exchange on request for three years.

A statement in a market letter, for example, that a particular security was recommended at a specific price and is now selling at a higher price is unacceptable if the intent or the effect is to show the success of a past recommendation. In such a case, all of the above qualifications would have to be met.

¶ **2474A.10   Rule 473**   © 1964, Commerce Clearing House, Inc.

11-64
Report 95
Rules of Board—Communications with the Public
➡➡ *Administered by Public Relations and Market Development.*
4 0 2 9

(4) Testimonials. In using testimonials, the following points must be clearly stated in the body copy of the material:

(a) The testimonial may not be representative of the experience of other clients.

(b) The testimonial can not be indicative of future performance or success.

(c) If more than a nominal sum is paid, the fact that it is a paid testimonial must be indicated.

(d) If the testimonial concerns a technical aspect of investing, the person making the testimonial must have adequate knowledge and experience to form valid opinion.

(5) Projections and Predictions. Past records, charts, tables or other material can not, of course, be used to promise future profits or income from securities.

Projections and predictions should be clearly labeled as estimates. A reference to the bases of the estimates should be given or must be available on request.

(6) Periodic Investment. In mentioning the benefits of dollar-cost-averaging, it should be made clear that periodic purchases in a fixed dollar amount must be continued through fluctuations in the market price, that such a plan does not protect against loss in a declining market, and that the price at which the shares are sold must be more than their average cost, in order to realize a profit.

If the low cost of buying securities under any periodic investment plan is emphasized, it is important to state whether there are commissions for the purchase and sale.

In showing total value of prior investments including reinvested dividends, the amount of the reinvested dividends should be stated separately. Commissions, taxes or other costs should also be mentioned.

(7) Language. Statements which are promissory, exaggerated, flamboyant or contain unwarranted superlatives are to be avoided.

(8) Comparisons. Any comparison of one firm's service, personnel, facilities or charges with those of other firms must be factually supportable.

(9) Claims for Research. For purposes of these standards, investment research encompasses the organized collection and analysis of information obtained in oral or written form from primary or secondary sources, which is concerned with securities, industries, the market or the economy in general and has the purpose of assisting member organizations and their customers in evaluating securities.

A member organization which advertises or promotes its research services or capabilities must have a reasonable basis for any claims it makes.

A market letter, research report or similar publication should not carry a research department by-line, or by implication give the impression of originating within a research department, unless it did originate there.

(10) Dating Reports. All market letters, research reports and similar publications must be appropriately dated. Any significant information that is

Rule 473 ¶ 2474A.10

not reasonably current (usually not more than 6 months old—depending on the industry and circumstances) should be noted.

(11) Identification of Sources. A market letter or research report not prepared under the direct supervision of the research department of the distributing firm or its correspondent member organization should show the person (by name and appropriate title) or outside organization which prepared the material.

In distributing market letters or research reports prepared under the direct supervision of the research department of a correspondent member organization, the distributing firm should mention this fact, although it may not be necessary to identify the correspondent by name. (See ¶ 2440A.10)

Releases prepared and published by or for a corporate issuer or its public relations counsel and distributed by member organizations should be clearly identified as such.

(12) Portfolio Analysis. Portfolio Analysis is defined as the appraisal of an investor's present holdings of securities, individually and collectively, for the purpose of offering investment recommendations consistent with his stated objectives and general financial status.

Persons engaged in Portfolio Analysis should be adequately supervised and they should not undertake analysis which is not commensurate with their experience and training.

¶ 2474B   Standards for Speaking Activities

(1) Prior consent must be obtained from a general partner or a holder of voting stock, or from a branch office manager acting for the partner or voting stockholder responsible for the member organization's communications with the public, for each speech or lecture course. (For Exchange approval of outside speaking activities see rules 318 and 346.)

(2) The member organization assumes responsibility for the general content of each such speech or lecture.

(3) A log of all single talks and lecture series given by a member or member organization personnel should be kept by the member or member organization for at least three years for delivery to the Exchange upon request. The log should contain the following information for each speaking assignment: (a) the name of the sponsoring group, (b) its presiding officer (or program chairman) and his mailing address, (c) the subject discussed, (d) the date, (e) approximate attendance and (f) the speaker's name.

All talks and lecture courses by members and member organization personnel, whether represening their own firm or cooperating with other firms as Investors' Information Committees, should be conducted in an educational manner.

In talks and lectures sponsored by public or private groups, such as clubs, lodges, colleges, evening adult schools, community centers, libraries, employee organizations, military bases, and professional societies, members and member organization personnel should not recommend specific securities, industries, or methods of investing. In such talks, any sales literature supplied should be made available on a pick-up or request basis rather than by general distribution to the audience.

In talks and lectures sponsored by member organizations themselves, or in other lectures where it may be pertinent to discuss specific securities, industries, or methods of investing, speakers are to follow the Standards in ¶ 2474A.

When members or member organization personnel invite guest speakers to participate in speaking programs, the member or member organization assumes responsibility for the content and manner of presentation.

NEW YORK STOCK EXCHANGE
ARBITRATION

. . . rules of Board of Governors administered through the facilities of the Exchange prescribing the procedure to be used in arbitration . . .

TABLE OF CONTENTS

Arbitration

Arbitration

*(Rules and Policies Administered by the
Office of the Secretary.)*

¶ 2481   Initiation of Proceedings

Statement of claim

Rule 481. A member, a member organization, a participant in a member
organization, or a non-member who wishes to institute proceedings pursuant to the provisions of Article VIII of the Constitution [¶¶ 1351-1357] against any such person or organization shall file with the Arbitration Director a concise statement of claim or controversy.

Where the parties to a controversy have previously entered into an agreement to arbitrate future disputes in accordance with the procedure of the Exchange, or a court has issued an order directing such an arbitration, proceedings may be instituted by either party filing with the Arbitration Director a concise statement of claim or controversy, together with a copy of the agreement providing for arbitration or court order and moving papers.

The statement of claim or controversy shall specifically set forth the matters to be arbitrated and, if possible, the amount claimed.

Reply and counterclaim

A copy of the statement filed by the party initiating the proceeding shall be furnished by the Arbitration Director to the opposing party for reply. Said reply shall be filed with the Arbitration Director within ten days of the receipt by such opposing party of said statement, or such longer period as may be granted by the Exchange. In the event that the opposing party wishes to assert a counterclaim, said reply shall contain a statement of counterclaim, which shall specifically set forth the matter to be arbitrated and, if possible, the exact amount of said counterclaim. The initiating party shall be given the same opportunity to reply to the counterclaim as was given the opposing party in the case of the original statement of claim or controversy.

Submission

If the Exchange does not decline to accept jurisdiction, a copy of the statement of claim or controversy and the reply, and counterclaim if any, and reply to the counterclaim, shall be attached to a form of submission prescribed by the Exchange, which shall be sent to the parties and shall be executed and acknowledged by the parties before an officer duly authorized by law. Said submission shall be promptly filed with the Arbitration Director.

Where a copy of an agreement between the parties to arbitrate future disputes in accordance with the procedure of the Exchange, or a copy of a court order directing such an arbitration, has been filed with the Exchange, the Exchange may accept such agreement or order in lieu of requiring the execution of a submission.

(See: ¶ 2492A *for form of submission.)*

New York Stock Exchange Guide   **Rule 481**   **¶ 2481**

¶ 2482   Costs

Rule 482.   The maximum amount chargeable to the parties as costs to cover the expense of the hearings shall not exceed the following, which amount shall be deposited with the Exchange by the party initiating a proceeding upon institution of proceedings or prior to each subsequent hearing, as the case may be, unless such requirement is waived by the Exchange for a non-member party.

Where the amount (exclusive of interest and costs) involved in the controversy is:

	Member Controversy	Non-Member Controversy
$500 or less	$ 60	$ 25
More than $500 but not more than $1000	60	50
More than $1000 but less than $2500	60	60
$2500 or more but less than $5000	90	90
$5000 or more but less than $10,000	90 per hearing	90 per hearing
$10,000 or more	120 per hearing	120 per hearing

Where the controversy does not involve a money claim, the costs and the amount to be deposited, shall be such amount as may be fixed in advance by the Exchange, except that such amount shall not exceed $120 per hearing.

¶ 2483   Representation by Attorney

Rule 483.   A party is not required to be represented by an attorney at any stage in an arbitration including the hearings. However, a party has a right to be represented by an attorney and may claim such right at any time as to any part of the arbitration or hearings which have not taken place. A party who is to be represented by an attorney shall so notify the Arbitration Director and shall also furnish him with the attorney's name and address in the statement of claim or reply or reply to a counterclaim, as the case may be, or if the right to representation by an attorney is claimed subsequent to the filing of the statement of claim or reply or reply to a counterclaim, by a written notice to the other party or parties and the Arbitration Director. After the Arbitration Director has received such notification from a party, subsequent papers in the proceeding to be served on such party shall be served upon his attorney.

¶ 2484   Election of Arbitrators

Rule 484.   If the non-member party to a proceeding does not signify in the statement of claim or the reply, as the case may be, or within five days after he is requested to do so by the Exchange, whichever is later, whether he elects to have the controversy adjudicated by Arbitrators selected from the Panels of the Exchange or by members of the Board of Arbitration, he shall be deemed not to desire to make the election permitted him under Article VIII, Section 6, of the Constitution [¶ 1356] and the Arbitrators shall be selected by lot from the Panels of the Exchange, pursuant to said section.

¶ 2485   Time and Place of Hearing

Rule 485. Subsequent to the receipt of the submission, duly executed by the parties, or where a submission is not required pursuant to the provisions of Rule 481 [¶ 2481], subsequent to the receipt of the statements of the parties, the Arbitrators shall appoint a time and place for the hearing and shall cause notice thereof to be given to each of the parties as provided in Rule 487 [¶ 2487] of the Board of Governors. If any of the parties, after due notice, fails to be present or represented at a hearing or any adjourned hearing, the Arbitrators may, nevertheless, in their own discretion, proceed with the adjudication of the controversy.

Procedure at hearing

At the hearing, the statements of the parties shall be read to the Arbitrators, unless such reading shall be specifically waived by the parties or their attorneys-in-fact or counsel; each of the parties or his attorney-in-fact or counsel shall be permitted to make an opening statement, present witnesses and documentary evidence, and present closing arguments orally or in writing as may be determined at the hearing by the Arbitrators. Witnesses shall be subject to examination by the opposing party or his attorney-in-fact or counsel. The hearings shall be formally declared closed by the Arbitrators. Such hearings may, in the discretion of the Arbitrators, be reopened at any time prior to the making of an award.

Amendments to claims or counterclaims

At any time during the hearings or before the hearings are declared closed, any party may move the amendment of his claim or counterclaim, and, if the Arbitrators shall permit, such amendment shall be incorporated forthwith in an amendment to the submission to be executed by the parties in the same manner as in the case of the original submission, or, where a submission was not required, in an amendment to the statement of claim or counterclaim, as the case may be.

Adjournments

The Arbitrators may adjourn the hearings from time to time upon the application of either party or at their own instance.

¶ 2486   Award of Arbitrators—Costs

Rule 486. The award of the Arbitrators shall be made in writing and shall be acknowledged in like manner as a deed to be recorded.

The Arbitrators in the award shall fix the amount of costs chargeable to the parties to cover the expense of the hearings, and shall determine the manner in which and by whom such costs shall be borne.

¶ 2487   **Notices and Communications**

Rule 487. Notices may be given to the parties by the Arbitration Director or otherwise as the Arbitrators may direct.

Notices of hearings shall be given to the parties or their attorneys-in-fact or counsel in writing personally or by registered or certified mail at least ten days in advance of such hearing, unless such notice is waived by the parties or their attorneys-in-fact or counsel. Notice of an adjourned hearing may be given orally by the Arbitrators at any preceding hearing.

All other notices, orders, papers and communications, including a copy of the award, may be served on any party by delivering or mailing the same to the party or his attorney-in-fact or counsel.

¶ 2488   **Oaths of Arbitrators and Witnesses**

Rule 488. Before proceeding with an Arbitration, an oath shall be administered to the Arbitrators in the presence of the parties, except where the parties or their attorneys-in-fact or counsel continue the arbitration without objection to the failure of the Arbitrators to take the oath, or where the oath is waived in writing by the parties to the submission or their attorneys-in-fact or counsel.

Witnesses shall be sworn before testifying, unless the taking of an oath is waived by the parties or their attorneys-in-fact or counsel.

¶ 2489   **Subpoenas**

Rule 489. The Arbitrators and any attorney of record in the arbitration proceeding shall have such powers of subpoena as may be provided by law, but so far as it is possible for them to do so, the parties shall produce witnesses and present proofs without the issuance of subpoena.

¶ 2490   **Constitution and Rules Part of Submission**

Rule 490. The provisions of Article VIII of the Constitution [¶ 1351-1357] and of Rules 481-491 [¶ 2481-2491] of the Board of Governors shall be deemed to be a part of the submission and the parties shall be bound thereby, except that, with the prior consent of the Exchange, the parties may otherwise agree, in so far as the Rules of the Board are concerned.

¶ 2491   **Interpretation of Rules**

Rule 491. During the course of proceedings, the Arbitrators in a particular case shall have the power to interpret and apply Rules 481-491 [¶ 2481-2491] of the Board of Governors and the provisions of the submission and such interpretation shall be binding upon the parties.

¶ 2492A   Form of Submission
NEW YORK STOCK EXCHANGE

In the Matter of the Arbitration between }SUBMISSION

We, the undersigned parties, hereby submit to arbitration by five Arbitrators selected in accordance with Paragraph $\left\{ \begin{array}{l} \text{IV. A.} \\ \text{IV. B. 1.} \\ \text{IV. B. 2.} \end{array} \right\}$ of the within submission the matter in controversy between us and all the matters, claims and counterclaims relating thereto, set forth in the statements of the parties, annexed hereto, and we agree to abide by and perform any award rendered pursuant to this agreement, and we do further agree that a judgment of ....
.... may be entered on said award and to that end do voluntarily submit ourselves to the jurisdiction of said court.

We further agree that the above entitled arbitration shall be held at a place to be designated by said Arbitrators in the City of .... and State of ...., and shall be conducted in accordance with the following:

(Here is set forth the text of Article VIII of the Constitution [¶¶ 1351-1357])

RULES AND PROCEDURE
I. Institution of Proceedings
(Here is set forth the text of Rule 481 [¶ 2481] of the Board of Governors)

II. Costs
(Here is set forth the text of Rule 482 [¶ 2482] of the Board of Governors)

III. Counsel
(Here is set forth the text of Rule 483 [¶ 2483] of the Board of Governors)

IV. Arbitrators

A. Member Controversies. In the case of a controversy between members, allied members, member firms or member corporations, the Arbitrators shall be five members of the Board of Arbitration.

B. Non-Member Controversies. In the case of a controversy between a non-member and a member, allied member, member firm or member corporation, the Arbitrators shall be

1. five persons selected from the panels of the Exchange, as provided in Section 6 of Article VIII of the Constitution [¶ 1356]; or, at the election of the non-member, made in the submission,
2. five members of the Board of Arbitration.

(Here is set forth the text of Rule 484 [¶ 2484] of the Board of Governors)

V. Place of Hearings

A. Member Controversies. Controversies between members, allied members, member firms or member corporations shall be heard in New York City.

B. Non-Member Controversies. Controversies between a non-member and a member, allied member, member firm or member corporation, shall be heard in New York City, except, where controversies involve any parties who are located outside of New York City, the Exchange may, at the request of the non-member, designate some other place in the United States.

VI. Hearings

(Here is set forth the text of Rule 485 [¶ 2485] of the Board of Governors)

VII. Award

(Here is set forth the text of Rule 486 [¶ 2486] of the Board of Governors)

VIII. Notices and Communications

(Here is set forth the text of Rule 487 [¶ 2487] of the Board of Governors)

IX. Oath of the Arbitrators and Witnesses

(Here is set forth the text of Rule 488 [¶ 2488] of the Board of Governors)

X. Subpoenas

(Here is set forth the text of Rule 489 [¶ 2489] of the Board of Governors)

XI. Constitutional Provisions and Rules Part of Submission

(Here is set forth the text of Rule 490 [¶ 2490] of the Board of Governors)

XII. Interpretation of Rules

(Here is set forth the text of Rule 491 [¶ 2491] of the Board of Governors)

XIII. Amendment to Rules

The Board of Governors may from time to time amend, alter or repeal any of the Rules of the Board with respect to arbitration, either generally or in reference to a particular case, as it in its sole discretion may find expedient.

> [*There are attached to the submission, prior to its execution, the statements of claim and the reply. The submission form contains provision for the signatures of the parties and proper acknowledgment of such signatures.*]

NEW YORK STOCK EXCHANGE
LISTING AND DELISTING OF SECURITIES

... procedures and policies relating to the listing of securities on the Exchange, and to removal of securities from the list ...

TABLE OF CONTENTS

NEW YORK STOCK EXCHANGE

LISTING AND DELISTING OF SECURITIES

...procedures and policies related to the listing
of securities on the Exchange, and to removal
of securities from the list.

TABLE OF CONTENTS

Listing Policies and Procedures

Listing and Delisting of Securities
Listing Policies and Procedures

> The following consists of an excerpt of that portion
> of the NYSE Company Manual which sets forth the Ex-
> change's general listing policies. Detailed data contained
> in that Manual and other information regarding specific
> policies or procedures will be furnished upon request of
> the Department of Stock List.
>
> (Complete copies of the Manual are on file with the
> Secretaries of all companies having securities listed on
> the Exchange and with the law firms and accountants serv-
> ing such companies.)

¶ 2495A   Standards of Eligibility for Listing

● ● ● **Supplementary Material:**

.10   **General qualifications.**—The Exchange welcomes inquiries from company officials where the numerical standards outlined below have been met.

There are, of course, other factors which must necessarily be taken into
consideration. The company must be a going concern or be the successor to
a going concern. While the amount of assets and earnings and the aggregate
market value are considerations, greater emphasis is placed on such questions
as the degree of national interest in the company, the character of the market
for its products, its relative stability and position in its industry, and whether or not
it is engaged in an expanding industry with prospects for maintaining its position.

Companies are urged to take advantage of an informal preliminary review of eligibility (which is done on a confidential basis) in order that all
factors may be considered. These would include such matters as voting rights
of shareholders, any voting arrangements which may be present, pyramiding
of control, and other subjects of a similar nature as further outlined below and
in Section A—15 of this [NYSE Company] Manual relating to voting rights.

Amendments.
Effective April 15, 1965.

¶ 2495B   Minimum Numerical Standards

● ● ● **Supplementary Material:**

.10   Distribution and value.—

Number of stockholders	
Total	2,000
Holders of 100 shares or more	1,700
(The number of beneficial holders of stock held in the name of NYSE member organizations will be considered in addition to holders of record)	
Number of shares	
Total outstanding	1,000,000
Publicly held	700,000
Market value publicly-held shares	$12,000,000
(Net tangible assets should be $10,000,000 al-though greater emphasis is placed on market value)	

Demonstrated earning power under competitive conditions
(normally for at least 3 years)

Pre-Tax .... $ 2,000,000
Net income .... $ 1,200,000

Where there is an indication of a lack of public interest in the securities
of a company—evidenced for example by low trading volume on another exchange, lack of dealer interest in the over-the-counter market, unusual geo-
graphic concentration of holders or shares, slow growth in the number of
shareholders, low rate of transfers, etc.—higher distribution standards may be
required to be met. In this connection, particular attention will be directed
to the number of holders of from 100 to 1,000 shares and the total number of
shares in this category.

Amendments.
Effective April 15, 1965.

¶ 2495C   Confidential Preliminary Review of Eligibility

● ● ● *Supplementary Material:*

.10 Procedure.—Upon request, the Exchange will be pleased to conduct an
informal and confidential review of eligibility. This review should be
completed prior to announcement in the press, annual report, prospectus, etc.,
of a company's intention to file a listing application.

The following is a general outline of the information needed for this purpose:

1. The Charter and By-laws.

2. Specimens of bonds or stock certificates.

3. Copies of the annual reports to stockholders for the last five years.

4. The latest prospectus covering an offering under the Securities
Act of 1933 (where available).

5. The proxy statement for the most recent annual meeting.

6. A stock distribution schedule on the Exchange's form (See page
B—102 of the NYSE Company Manual).

7. Supplementary data to assist the Exchange in determining the
character of the share distribution and the number of publicly-held shares:

(a) Identification of 10 largest holders of record, including beneficial owners (if known) of holdings of record by nominees.

(b) List of holdings of 1,000 shares or more in the names of Exchange member organizations.

(c) Number of transfers and shares transferred during the last
two years. (Over-the-counter companies only.)

(d) Summary, by principal groups, of stock owned or controlled by:
(1) Officers or directors and their immediate families.
(2) Other concentrated holdings of 10% or more.

(e) Estimates of number of employees owning stock and the
total shares held.

(f) Company shares held in profit-sharing, savings, pension, or
other similar funds or trusts established for the benefit of officers, employees, etc. Details as to the method followed in soliciting proxies
and voting such shares.

8. It is recognized that in a closely-held company, situations involving the personal interests of officers, directors, or principal shareowners

¶ 2495C.10

are sometimes regarded as advantageous or convenient. Usually, the character and appropriateness of these relationships is reconsidered when a company seeks the benefits of broader public ownership. Accordingly, the Exchange would look for information on any such relationships; for example, the leasing of property to or from the company, interests or options in subsidiaries, interests (other than ordinary investments in widely-held, publicly-owned companies) in businesses that are competitors, suppliers, or customers of the company.

Amendments.
Effective April 15, 1965.

¶ 2495D   Formal Application for Listing

• • • Supplementary Material:

.10   **Report of Application.**—If informal approval is given and a signed application is subsequently filed (See Section B—2 of the NYSE Company Manual), the Exchange will report the receipt of the application through the press and in its next weekly Bulletin.

.20   **Processing Time.**—Action will be taken by the Exchange on an application as soon as practicable after any necessary revisions have been made, the file of supporting documents completed, and a convenient time schedule worked out with the company. While the time element varies from company to company, it is customary to formally present the application to the Board of Governors about three or four weeks after receipt of the signed application. Approval by the Board of Governors of the Exchange is required for all original listings. Action by the Board is publicly announced. Admission to trading normally takes place about 30 days after Board action in order to permit registration under the Securities Exchange Act of 1934 to become effective.

¶ 2495E   Listing and Registration Under Securities Exchange Act of 1934 Both Requisite

• • • Supplementary Material:

.10   **Listing and registration both requisite.**—Before securities may be admitted to trading on the Exchange, they must be authorized for listing by the Exchange and, in addition, must be registered under the Securities Exchange Act of 1934.

Listing is effected by the submission to, and approval by, the Exchange of an application supported by certain supplemental documents prepared and signed by the company in conformity with the rules of the Exchange.

Registration under the Securities Exchange Act of 1934 requires filing with both the Exchange and the Securities and Exchange Commission of a registration statement conforming to the rules of the Commission, and certification by the Exchange, to the Commission, that it has received what purports to be a registration statement and has approved the particular securities for listing and registration. Registration becomes effective automatically thirty days after receipt, by the Commission, of the Exchange's certification, but may become effective within a shorter period, by order of the Commission, upon request made by the company of the Commission. The Exchange will concur in the company's request for acceleration when its concurrence seems appropriate.

4228   Rules of Board—Listing Policies and Procedures   6-65
Report 103
➠→ *Administered by Department of Stock List.*

Registration of banks is effected in a similar manner through the filing of registration statements with the appropriate Federal banking agency.
Amendments.
Effective April 15, 1965.

¶ 2495F   The Listing Application

● ● ● *Supplementary Material:*

.10 **Preparation.**—The application for original listing is designed to serve the dual purpose of placing before the Exchange the information essential to its determination as to the suitability of the securities for public trading on the Exchange and, equally important, of providing for the investing public such information as it may reasonably be presumed to require as an aid to its judgment as to the merits of the security.

The application for listing of additional securities is designed to give full information as to the purpose for which such securities are to be issued and the consideration to be received therefor, and to bring up to date significant data given in previous applications of the company.

No prepared or blank forms are used for the application itself. Instead, the data should be set forth in narrative form, supplemented by financial statements. It should be so drawn as to provide a comprehensive summary description of the company and of the securities as to which listing is being requested and, as to unissued securities for which listing is sought, the terms and conditions under which they are to be issued.

While a certain degree of uniformity in substance and form is desired in all applications, the specific data to be included in the application will necessarily vary as between industries, and possibly even as between different companies in the same industry, where some unique feature or circumstance seems to warrant such variation. Detailed directions for preparation of applications for original listing are contained in Section B 2 of the [NYSE Company] Manual, and for subsequent listings in Section B 3 of the [NYSE Company] Manual. Reference to several recently approved listing applications also will be found helpful as a guide to the form of the application. The Department of Stock List will be pleased to furnish several such specimen applications upon request.

.20 **Exchange assistance in preparation.**—The Exchange employs a staff of Representatives who will welcome the opportunity to assist and advise the company in the preparation of the listing application and in related matters.

In cases where it is desired that the application proceed according to an exact time schedule as, for example, in the case of an offering to stockholders, it is urged that the Exchange be consulted at the earliest possible moment.

.30 **Submission of application.**—Four draft copies of the application (which may be typewritten) should be submitted to the Department of Stock List of the Exchange at least two weeks in advance of the date on which it is desired to have the application acted upon, to allow time for preliminary examination and revision. A longer period is desirable, particularly in the case of original listings. Every effort should be made to have the application in substantially its final revised form (and the file of required supporting documents complete) at least one week in advance of the date it is to be acted upon.

It should be noted that, before an additional amount of a listed class, issue or series of security may be issued, such additional amount must be authorized to be listed by the Exchange. Companies undertaking any financing, recapitalization or other program, pursuant to which they may be com-

5-64
Report 89
Rules of Board—Listing Policies and Procedures
➤➤➤ *Administered by Department of Stock List.*
4229

mitted to issuance of such additional amount on a stipulated date, should allow sufficient time to permit the Exchange to take action on the listing application in due course.

¶ 2495G   Outside Directors

• • • *Supplementary Material:*

.10 Full disclosure of corporate affairs for the information of the investing public is, of course, normal and usual procedure for listed companies. Many companies have found that this procedure has been greatly aided by having at least two outside directors whose functions on the board would include particular attention to such matters. Companies not having outside directors are urged to consider the desirability of doing so, particularly where the stock has been closely held.

[The next page is 4235.]

Delisting of Securities

(Rules Administered by the
Department of Stock List.)

¶ 2498A   General

● ● ● *Supplementary Material:*

.10   General.—The New York Stock Exchange seeks to provide the foremost
      auction market for securities of well-established companies that have kept
pace with the expanding economy and in which there is a broad public interest.

In considering the appropriateness of a security for continued dealing and
listing on the Exchange, many factors must be taken into account by the
Exchange and each case must be considered on its own merits. Among these
are the degree of national interest in the company, its standing in its particular field, the character of the market for its products and whether it is
engaged in an expanding industry with prospects of maintaining or improving
its relative position.

Action taken by a company or others may sometimes affect the appropriateness
of the company's securities for continued dealing and listing on the Exchange.
Any action which substantially reduces the size of the company, the nature or
scope of its operations, the value or amount of its securities available for the
market or the number of its shareholders may have that effect. This would
include the sale, destruction, loss or abandonment of a substantial portion of
its business or assets, spin-offs or other distributions of its investments or
assets as dividends or otherwise, steps toward liquidation, repurchase or
redemption of its common stock, or discontinuance of all or a substantial part
of its operations for whatever reason.

¶ 2499   Suspension from Dealings or Removal from
                 List by Action of the Exchange

Rule 499.   Securities admitted to the list may be suspended from dealings or
             removed from the list at any time.

● ● ● *Supplementary Material:*

.10   Criteria.—The appropriateness of continued listing on the Exchange can-
       not be measured mathematically. However, under present circumstances,
there are some criteria which usually lead to a re-examination of a security's
eligibility for continued dealings on the Exchange. It must be remembered,
however, that the Exchange may at any time suspend or delist a security if
the Exchange believes that continued dealings in the security on the Exchange
are not advisable, whether the security meets or fails to meet any of the criteria
set forth in this section.

WHEN A COMPANY FALLS BELOW ANY OF THESE CRITERIA,
THE EXCHANGE MAY GIVE CONSIDERATION TO ANY DEFINI-
TIVE ACTION THAT A COMPANY WOULD PROPOSE TO TAKE
THAT WOULD BRING IT *IN LINE WITH ORIGINAL LISTING
STANDARDS*. ON THE OTHER HAND, CHANGES THAT A COM-
PANY MIGHT CONSIDER OR MAKE THAT WOULD BRING IT
ABOVE THE DELISTING CRITERIA BUT NOT IN LINE WITH
ORIGINAL LISTING STANDARDS WOULD NORMALLY NOT BE
ADEQUATE REASON TO WARRANT CONTINUED LISTING.

The Exchange would normally give consideration to suspending or re-
moving from the list a security of a company when:

¶ 2499.10—Continued

1. Number of shareholders is less than:
   Total 800
   Holders of 100 shares or more 700
   The number of beneficial holders of stock held in the name of NYSE member organizations will be considered in addition to holders of record.

2. Number of publicly-held shares* less than 300,000

3. Aggregate market value of publicly-held shares* less than $2,500,000
   * Shares held by officers, directors, or their immediate families and other concentrated holdings of 10% or more are excluded in calculating the number of publicly-held shares.

4. { Aggregate market value of shares outstanding (excluding treasury stock) is less than $5,000,000
     and
     Average net income after taxes for past 3 years is less than .... $ 400,000

5. { Net assets available to common stock are less than .. $5,000,000
     and
     Average net income after taxes for past 3 years is less than .... $ 400,000

6. Bonds**
   Aggregate market value or principal amount of publicly-held bonds is less than .... $ 200,000

7. Preferred Stock, Guaranteed Railroad Stock and Similar Issues**
   Aggregate market value of publicly-held shares less than .... $ 400,000
   or
   Publicly-held shares are less than 10,000

8. Principal Operating Assets and/or Scope of Operations Reduced. —The principal operating assets have been substantially reduced such as by sale, lease, spin-off, distribution, discontinuance, abandonment, destruction, condemnation, seizure or expropriation, or the company has ceased to be an operating company or discontinued a substantial portion of its operations or business for any reason whatsoever.

9. Liquidation Authorized.—Where liquidation has been authorized by stockholders and the company is committed to proceed, the Exchange will normally await the initial liquidating distribution if made within one year.

10. Authoritative Advice Received Security is Without Value.—Advice has been received, deemed by the Exchange to be authoritative, that the security is without value. In this connection, it should be noted that the Exchange does not pass judgment upon the value of securities.

** Effect on Other Listed Securities of an Issuer when Consideration is Given to Delisting its Common Stock.

When consideration is given to the suspension or delisting of the common stock of a company, the Exchange will usually consider the appropriateness of the continued listing of other securities of the issuer, whether or not such other securities meet the delisting criteria otherwise applicable to them, and may determine, in the light of all of the circumstances, to continue such other securities on the list or to suspend and proceed to remove from the list such other securities where it seems to be advisable.

11. Registration No Longer Effective.—The registration or exemption from registration pursuant to the Securities Exchange Act of 1934 is no longer effective for any reason.

12. A Class of Non-Voting Common Stock is Created.—This does not apply to a non-voting class of stock which in the opinion of the Exchange has normal and appropriate preferences which entitle it to be regarded as a preferred stock.

13. Proxies are not Solicited for All Meetings of Stockholders.— Actively operating companies currently filing applications to list on the Exchange must agree to solicit proxies from stockholders. Companies soliciting voluntarily, although not under agreement to solicit, which hereafter discontinue the practice, must agree to resume solicitation within one year after failure to solicit.

This does not apply where the issuer is not an actively operating company. Exception may be made where applicable law precludes or makes virtually impossible the solicitation of proxies in the United States.

14. Agreements are Violated.—Company, its transfer agent or registrar, violates any of its, or their, listing or other agreements with the Exchange.

15. Payment, Redemption or Retirement of Entire Class, Issue, or Series.—Whenever the entire outstanding amount of a listed class, issue, or series is retired through payment at maturity, or through redemption, reclassification or otherwise, the Exchange, at a time which is appropriate in consideration of the circumstances of the particular case, may suspend dealings in the security and give notice to the Commission, on the Commission's Form 25, of intention to remove such security from listing and registration, as required by Rule 12d2-2 of the Commission.

In the case of a security redeemed or retired through cash payment (whether upon maturity or otherwise), dealings may be suspended immediately the redemption or retirement funds are made available to holders of the security, unless such security is convertible and its market price is at, or close to, the conversion price. In the latter case, suspension of the security being redeemed or retired may be deferred until the opening of the market on the day on which the conversion privilege expires, or until conversions cease to be active, or until the amount of the security outstanding has been so reduced as to make further dealings therein inadvisable in the opinion of the Exchange. As provided by Rule § 240.12d2-2 [¶ 4394] of the Securities and Exchange Commission, the removal from listing and registration becomes effective on the date specified in the Exchange's notice (to the Commission) of its intention to remove the security from listing and registration, but not less than ten days after such notice is sent to the Commission. Ordinarily, the Exchange will send such notice on the day that dealings in the security are suspended and will specify the fifteenth day thereafter as the date on which it is intended to remove the security from listing and registration.

If the retirement occurs through reclassification or other procedure pursuant to which the instruments representing the securities comprising the entire class come to evidence, by operation of law or otherwise, other securities in substitution for the securities so retired, the Exchange may suspend the security so retired at the opening of the market on the day on which it receives notice that such reclassification is effective (or on

¶ 2499—Continued

the business day following), depending upon the time of day at which such notice is received. In such case notice is given the Commission (on Form 25) of the Exchange's intention to remove the security from listing and registration approximately fifteen days thereafter, unless the successor security (succeeding the security retired by reclassification) is to be admitted to dealings as a security temporarily exempt from registration under the Securities Exchange Act of 1934. In the latter case, the security retired by reclassification is not removed from listing and registration until the successor security is removed from its exempt status through registration becoming effective.

The Exchange should be notified as to the payment of the security at maturity, or as to the redemption or other retirement of the security as set forth in Section A 10 of this [NYSE Company] Manual, entitled *Redemption-Tender Offers,* and particularly in the sub-section headed *Redemption of Entire Class, Issue, or Series—Stock or Bonds.*

16. Redemption or Retirement of Part of Class, Issue or Series.— When only a part of a listed class, issue or series is to be redeemed, or otherwise retired, the amount thereof authorized to be listed will be reduced by the number of shares, or face amount of bonds, to be so retired or redeemed. In the case of redemption, the reduction will occur as soon as the redemption funds become available to holders of the redeemed security, unless the class, issue or series is convertible, in which case the reduction in the amount authorized to be listed will be deferred until conversion occurs or the conversion right expires. In the case of retirement, such reduction will occur as soon as the Exchange receives notice of the retirement.

However, under the rules of the Exchange, stock certificates or registered bonds called for redemption are not deliverable in settlement of contracts after the record date (or closing of the transfer books) for determination of the certificates or registered bonds to be redeemed, except in respect to transactions in "called" securities dealt in specifically as such. Coupon bonds are not deliverable in settlement of contracts on and after the date of first publication of notice of the call for redemption except in respect of transactions in "called" bonds dealt in specifically as such.

No action by the company is necessary to effect withdrawal of the amount redeemed or retired from listing, except for giving notice of such redemption or retirement to the Exchange, as set forth in Section A 10 of this Manual, entitled *Redemption-Tender Offers,* and particularly in the sub-sections thereof entitled *Partial Redemption—Stock* and *Partial Redemption—Bonds.*

However, if the outstanding amount of the issue or class has been reduced, through one or more transactions not previously reported by the company to the Commission, by an amount in excess of 5% of the outstanding amount of the issue or class, a Form 8-K report should be filed with the Securities and Exchange Commission and the Exchange on or before the tenth day of the month following that in which said percentage is reached, as required by the Commission's rules. Such report need not be made in respect of reductions due to ordinary sinking fund operation, conversion or similar periodic reductions made pursuant to the terms of the constituent instruments relating to the security.

¶ 2499.10   Rule 499

Except for the filing of the Form 8-K report, the foregoing procedure does not apply to listed securities reacquired for purposes other than retirement, as such reacquired securities remain listed and registered so long as the outstanding balance of the issue remains listed and registered.

17. Reduction or Cancellation of Authorization of Listing Upon Notice of Issuance.—The Exchange's authorization of the listing and registration, upon official notice of issuance for a specified purpose, of a particular amount of any class, issue or series, is effective only as to that part of such amount as issued for such specified purpose.

If it becomes evident, through occurrence of some event or through lapse of time, that the amount as to which listing and registration was so authorized is in excess of the amount actually issued, or to be issued, for the specified purpose, the Exchange may cancel the listing authorization in respect of the excess amount.

It is the practice of the Exchange to give the company prior notice of its intention to cancel the listing authorization. If, at that time, the company has plans which will result in issuance of the excess amount for another purpose, the Exchange may defer the cancellation for a reasonable period, pending receipt of an application from the company for a change in the listing authorization so as to make it applicable to such other purpose.

No action by the company is necessary to effect the reduction in, or cancellation of, authority for listing upon notice of issuance under this procedure, except to furnish such notice or information as the Exchange may request.

.20 Effect on other listed securities of the issuer when its common stock is suspended from trading or removed from the list by action of the Exchange.—When consideration is given to the suspension or delisting of the common stock of a company, the Exchange will usually consider the appropriateness of the continued listing of other listed securities of the issuer, whether or not such other securities meet the delisting criteria otherwise applicable to them, and may determine, in the light of all the circumstances, to continue such other securities on the list or to suspend and proceed to remove from the list such other securities where it seems to be advisable.

.30 Public hearings.—The Exchange may hold a public hearing in connection with its consideration of suspension of a security from dealings.

.40 Information furnished by company.—No action by the company concerned is required in connection with a delisting action initiated by the Exchange except for the furnishing of such information or notice as the Exchange may request.

Amendments.
April 15, 1965.

¶ 2500   Removal from the List Upon Request of the Issuer

Rule 500. In the absence of special circumstances, a security considered by the Exchange to be eligible for continued listing will not be removed from the list upon request or application of the issuer, unless the proposed withdrawal from listing is approved by the security holders at a meeting at which a substantial percentage of the outstanding amount of the

4240   Rules of Board—Delisting of Securities   6-65
Report 103
➤➤➤ *Administered by Department of Stock List.*

particular security is represented, without objection to the proposed withdrawal from a substantial number of individual holders of the particular security; provided, however, that the Exchange will not oppose delisting action by the issuer of a security listed on the Exchange if

(1) The Exchange shall have denied the listing of an additional amount of such security within the preceding 30 days, and

(2) following such action by the Exchange, delisting has been approved by a majority of the company's directors then in office and the company has notified stockholders, in form satisfactory to the Exchange, of the proposed delisting prior to the filing of the delisting application and at least 30 days in advance of the date delisting is effected.

Amendments.
June 21, 1956.

● ● ● *Supplementary Material:*

.10 Minimum requirement.—In applying the provisions of Rule 500, above, relating to approval by security holders, the Exchange, in the absence of special circumstances, will consider approval of the proposed withdrawal from listing by 66⅔% of the outstanding security, together with a failure of 10% of the individual holders thereof to object, as the minimum requirement.

.11 Purpose of clause (2) in Rule 500.—The purpose of the second clause in Rule 500 is to permit a listed company to effect delisting, without the necessity to secure the stockholder vote otherwise required, in those instances in which the Exchange is unwilling to authorize the listing of an additional amount of a security under the circumstances of the proposed issuance.

A company's listing agreement would, of course, remain fully effective until the completion of any delisting action under this rule. Accordingly, where the company proceeds to delist in order to issue the additional securities, the time of issuance would be governed by the time required to effect delisting under the rules of the Securities and Exchange Commission.

.20 Voluntary transfer of listing to another Exchange.—Where a company falls below the criteria for continued listing, the Exchange will permit the company, by action of its Board of Directors, to voluntarily transfer its listing to another registered Securities Exchange and cooperate with the company and the other Exchange in order to avoid any interruption in trading. Where the listing of the common stock of a company is transferred in this manner, it would normally be expected that any other securities of the company listed on the Exchange would likewise be transferred to the other exchange, although each such case would be considered on its merits.

¶ 2501A Withdrawal from Listing and Registration Under Securities Exchange Act of 1934

● ● ● *Supplementary Material:*

.10 Section 12(d) of the Securities Exchange Act of 1934 provides, among other things, as follows: "A security registered with a national securities exchange may be withdrawn or stricken from listing and registration in accordance with the rules of the exchange and, upon such terms as the Commission may deem necessary to impose for the protection of investors, upon application by the issuer or the exchange to the Commission;—"

The applicable regulations of the Securities and Exchange Commission are Regulations §§ 240.12d2-1 [¶ 4393] and 240.12d2-2 [¶ 4394].

STOCK CLEARING CORPORATION

... the full text of its Certificate of Incorporation, By-Laws and Rules, together with supplementary explanatory information ...

TABLE OF CONTENTS

STOCK CLEARING CORPORATION
Certificate of Incorporation

¶ 3001   **Preamble**

We, the undersigned, desiring to form a corporation under the Laws of the State of New York pursuant to the provisions of the Business Corporation Law, all being of full age, at least two-thirds being citizens of the United States, and at least one of us a resident of the State of New York, do hereby make, sign, acknowledge and file this Certificate for that purpose as follows:

¶ 3002   **Name**

First: The name of the proposed corporation is STOCK CLEARING COR-PORATION.

¶ 3003   **Purposes**

Second: The purposes for which it is to be formed are to provide members of the New York Stock Exchange and other persons, firms and corporations for whom it may act with facilities for clearing contracts between them and for delivering stocks and securities to and receiving stocks and securities from each other and for procuring the transfer of stocks and securities upon the books of the corporations or associations issuing the same and for procuring the exchange of any stocks or securities for any other stocks or securities and for receiving or paying any amounts payable to or payable by such members, persons, firms and corporations in connection with any of the foregoing transactions or in connection with any loans made by or to them; to act for such of the members of the New York Stock Exchange and such other persons, firms and corporations as shall employ it upon terms and conditions satisfactory to it, as agent, in clearing contracts between such members, persons, firms and corporations and in delivering stocks and securities to and receiving stocks and securities from such members, persons, firms and corporations and in procuring the transfer of stocks and securities upon the books of the corporations or associations issuing the same and in procuring the exchange of any stocks or securities for any other stocks or securities and in receiving from and paying to such members, persons, firms and corporations any amounts payable to or payable by them in connection with any of the foregoing transactions or in connection with any loans made by or to them; to enter into all such contracts and to do all things necessary or proper to carry out the foregoing purposes.

Amendment.
May 28, 1928.

¶ 3004   **Capital Stock**

Third: The amount of the capital stock is Five Hundred Thousand Dollars ($500,000).

¶ 3005   **Number and Par Value of Shares**

Fourth: The number of shares of which said capital shall consist is Five Thousand (5,000) of the par value of One Hundred Dollars ($100) each and the amount of capital with which said Corporation shall begin business is Ten Thousand Dollars ($10,000).

¶ 3006   Principal Office

Fifth: The location of its principal office is in the Borough of Manhattan, City of New York and State of New York.

¶ 3007   Duration

Sixth: Its duration is to be perpetual.

¶ 3008   Directors

Seventh: The number of Directors of the Corporation shall be fixed from time to time by the By-Laws of the Corporation, but shall be not less than five (5) nor more than nine (9). No director need be a stockholder of the Corporation. Any Director may be removed at any time by the holders of the majority in amount of the capital stock issued and outstanding in such manner as may be provided in the By-Laws.

Amendments.
May 6, 1938; May 19, 1955.

¶ 3009   Initial Directors

Eighth: The names and the post office addresses of the Directors for the first year and the term of office of each are as follows:

* * *

¶ 3010   Subscribers

Ninth: The names and post office addresses of the subscribers to this Certificate and a statement of the number of shares of stock which each agree to take in the Corporation are as follows:

* * *

¶ 3011   By-Laws

Tenth: The Corporation may adopt By-Laws for the management of its affairs and the regulation of its business and it may alter and amend the same as therein provided and in and by said By-Laws the Corporation may provide for the appointment of an Executive Committee which in the intervals between the meeting of the Board of Directors may exercise such of the powers of the Board as may be lawfully delegated. All transactions of the Corporation and its members shall be conducted in accordance with such By-Laws and shall be deemed to have been entered into subject to all the provisions thereof.

(SIGNATURE, ETC., OMITTED.)

[The next page is 4551.]

Stock Clearing Corporation
By-Laws

ARTICLE I
Meetings of Stockholders

¶ 3025   Annual Meeting

SEC. 1. The annual meeting of stockholders for the election of Directors and for such other business as may properly come before said meeting shall be held at 11:15 o'clock in the forenoon (New York City Time) on the fourth Monday in May of each year or if such be a day on which the New York Stock Exchange is closed, on the next succeeding day on which the New York Stock Exchange is open.

¶ 3026   Special Meetings

SEC. 2. Special meetings of stockholders may be held at any time and may be called either by resolution of a majority of the Board of Directors of the Corporation or by the President or by the written request of stockholders owning at least one-third of the outstanding stock of the Corporation.

¶ 3027   Place of Meetings

SEC. 3. All meetings of stockholders shall be held at 11 Wall Street in the Borough of Manhattan, City of New York, or at such other place in the State of New York as shall be fixed by the Board of Directors or by the President and stated in the Notice of Meeting.

¶ 3028   Notice of Meetings

SEC. 4. Notice of the time and place of holding any meeting of stockholders and stating the purpose for which it is called, shall be in writing signed by the President, a Vice-President, the Secretary or an Assistant Secretary and shall be given either personally or by mail to each stockholder of record, entitled to vote at said meeting, not less than 10 days and not more than 40 days before the time fixed for said meeting. If mailed, such Notice shall be deemed to have been given when posted, its postage prepaid, addressed to each stockholder to his address of record on the stock books of the Corporation or to such other address to which the Corporation has been duly requested to send Notices for such stockholders.

¶ 3029   Quorum

SEC. 5. At each meeting of stockholders there must be present to constitute a quorum for the transaction of business, except when otherwise required by statute, in person or by proxy, holders of record of a majority of the outstanding shares of capital stock, entitled to be voted thereat. If a quorum be lacking, the stockholders present and entitled to vote, by a vote of a majority in interest, may from time to time adjourn the meeting not beyond one month at any one time.

¶ 3030   Voting

SEC. 6. At each meeting of stockholders every stockholder of record of shares shall be entitled to one vote for each share held and may be present and vote said shares in person or by proxy appointed by an instrument of proxy signed by such stockholder or by such stockholder's authorized attorney-in-fact. Such instrument of proxy shall be filed with the Secretary of the meeting at which the proxy votes thereunder. No instrument of proxy shall be voted on after eleven months from its date, unless it expressly provides that it shall remain valid for a longer period. The voting at any meeting of stockholders need not be by ballot (unless so required by statute) but it shall be by ballot, if any qualified voter present so requests. Each ballot shall be signed by the stockholder voting or in his name and by his proxy and shall state the number of shares voted thereby. Shares of its own stock belonging to the Corporation shall not be voted either directly or indirectly. All matters, except the election of Directors and those for which other provision is expressly made by statute or in the Corporation's certificates of incorporation or in these By-Laws, which shall properly come before any meeting of stockholders, shall be decided thereat by the vote of a majority in interest of the stockholders present, a quorum being then present.

¶ 3031   List of Stockholders

SEC. 7. A list of the stockholders shall be open to inspection by stockholders at every meeting of stockholders.

Amendment.
May 25, 1955.

ARTICLE II

Board of Directors

¶ 3051   Number and Election

SEC. 1. The Board of Directors shall consist of five Directors elected by a plurality of the votes cast at the annual meeting of stockholders. Each Director shall be elected to hold office for one year and until his successor shall have been elected and qualified or until his death, resignation, disqualification or removal. No Director need be a stockholder.

Amendment.
June 9, 1964.

¶ 3052   Time and Place of Meetings

SEC. 2. Upon the adjournment of the annual meeting of stockholders, the Board of Directors shall meet for the purpose of the election of a Chairman, a Vice-Chairman and a President for the ensuing year. Regular meetings of the Board of Directors may be held at such times as may be fixed from time to time by the Board. At any time special Meetings of the Board of Directors shall be held when called by the Chairman of the Board or by the President or by a writing signed by any two Directors. The Directors may hold such meetings and may keep an office and maintain books of the Corporation, except as otherwise provided by statute, in such place or places in the State of New

York or outside the State of New York as the Board of Directors may from time to time determine.

¶ 3053   Notice

SEC. 3. No Notice need be given of the organization meeting or any regular meeting of the Board of Directors. Notice to each Director of the time and place of holding each special meeting of the Board of Directors shall be given by mail, postage prepaid, at least one day before the time fixed for said meeting or by personal service, prepaid telegraph or telephone, at least one hour before time fixed for said meeting. If mailed, such Notice shall be deemed to have been given when posted, its postage prepaid, addressed to each Director at his residence or usual place of business or to such other address to which the Corporation has been duly requested to send Notices for such Director.

¶ 3054   Quorum and Manner of Acting

SEC. 4. Three Directors must be present to constitute a quorum for the transaction of business at any meeting of the Board of Directors. The act of a majority of the Directors present at a meeting at which a quorum is present shall constitute the act of the Board of Directors.

¶ 3055   Resignations

SEC. 5. A Director may resign at any time by giving written notice of his resignation to the President or to the Secretary and such resignation, unless specifically contingent upon its acceptance, will be effective as of its date or as of the effective date specified therein.

¶ 3056   Removal

SEC. 6. A Director may be removed, with or without cause, by the vote of a majority in interest of the stockholders present entitled to vote, at any meeting of stockholders called for such purpose.

¶ 3057   Vacancies

SEC. 7. Vacancies in the Board of Directors may be filled for the unexpired portion of the term of office vacant, by the vote of a majority of the Directors remaining in office although the remaining Directors are less than a quorum. If the number of Directors shall be increased, such increase shall be deemed to create vacancies in the Board of Directors which may be filled as aforesaid. Any vacancies occurring in the Board of Directors by action of the stockholders, however, may be filled by the stockholders, at the same meeting at which such action was taken, in the same manner as for the election of Directors at an annual meeting of stockholders.

¶ 3058   Interest of Directors and Officers in Transactions of the Corporation

SEC. 8. In the absence of fraud, no contract or transaction between the Corporation and any other corporation, association or partnership shall be affected by the fact that any of the directors or officers of the Corporation are interested in or are directors, officers or members of such other corporation, association or partnership and no such contract or transaction of the Corporation with any other corporation, association or partnership shall be affected by the fact that any director or officer of the Corporation is in any way connected with such other corporation, association or partnership; and any director of the Corporation who is also a director, officer or member of such other corporation, association or partnership may be counted in determining the existence of a quorum for the purpose of, and may vote upon the question of, authorizing or approving any such contract or transaction. Each and every person who may become a director or officer of the Corporation is hereby relieved from any liability that might otherwise exist by reason of thus contracting with the Corporation for the benefit of any corporation, association or partnership in which he may be in anywise interested; provided that, except in respect of contracts or transactions between the Corporation and parent, subsidiary or affiliated corporations or associations, the fact and nature of any such relationship or interest shall be disclosed, or shall have been known, to at least a majority of the Board of Directors.

Amendment.
May 31, 1956.

ARTICLE III

Officers

¶ 3075   Appointment

SEC. 1. A Chairman, a Vice-Chairman and a President shall be chosen by the Board of Directors from among its members to hold office for one year and until their respective successors are chosen and qualified. In addition, with the approval of the Board of Directors, the President may appoint one or more Vice-Presidents, a Treasurer, a Secretary and such other officers of the Corporation as he from time to time may determine are required for the efficient management and operation of the Corporation and fix the duties, responsibilities, terms and conditions of employment of such officers and, subject to like approval, he may terminate their employment at any time. All such officers shall be responsible to the President for the proper performance of their duties.

¶ 3076   Powers and Duties

SEC. 2. The powers and duties of the Chairman of the Board of Directors, the Vice-Chairman of the Board of Directors and the President, subject to the supervision and control of the Board of Directors, shall be those usually appertaining to their respective offices and whatever other powers and duties are prescribed by these By-Laws or by the Board of Directors.

(a) The *Chairman of the Board of Directors* shall preside at all its meetings and at all meetings of the stockholders.

(b) The *Vice-Chairman of the Board of Directors* shall, in the absence or disability of the Chairman of the Board of Directors, perform the duties of the Chairman of the Board of Directors.

(c) The *President* shall be the chief officer and shall have general control over the affairs and business of the Corporation and supervision of its several officers appointed by him.

¶ 3077   Removal

SEC. 3.   The Chairman, the Vice-Chairman and the President, or any of them, may be removed with or without cause by resolution of the Board of Directors adopted by a majority of the Directors then in office and any other officer may be so removed or he may be removed with or without cause by the President, as provided in Section 1 subject to the approval of the Board of Directors.

¶ 3078   Vacancies

SEC. 4.   Vacancies shall be filled in the same manner as for original appointment to office.

Amendment.
May 25, 1955.

ARTICLE IV

Compensation of Officers

¶ 3091   Salaries

SEC. 1.   The compensation, if any, of the President shall be fixed by a majority (which shall not include the President) of the whole Board of Directors. Salaries of all other officers shall be fixed by the President with the approval of the Board of Directors and no officer shall be precluded from receiving a salary because he is also a Director.

Amendment.
May 25, 1955.

ARTICLE V

Clearing Members

¶ 3101   Limitation to Members

SEC. 1.   Except as hereinafter provided in Article VI, Stock Clearing Corporation shall act only for member organizations (qualified member firms or member corporations of the New York Stock Exchange) who apply to Stock Clearing Corporation to act for them, whose applications are approved by Stock Clearing Corporation and who have contributed to the Clearing Fund as provided in Article VII of the By-Laws. It may at any time in its discretion cease either temporarily or definitively to act for any such member organization and shall definitively cease to act when notified in writing to do so by member organization except in so far as provision is made in the Rules of the Stock Clearing Corporation for pending transactions. The member organizations for whom the corporation acts and who have contributed to the Clearing Fund, as provided in Article VII of the By-Laws, shall, until the Corporation definitely ceases to act for them, be known as Clearing Members. Clearing Members for whom it has temporarily ceased to act shall be known as retired Clearing Members.

A member organization whose application to become a Clearing Member has been approved by the Stock Clearing Corporation shall pay to the Stock

Clearing Corporation its original contribution to the Clearing Fund determined in accordance with the provisions of Article VII hereof and shall sign and deliver to the Stock Clearing Corporation an instrument in writing whereby such applicant shall agree:

(a) That the Clearing Member will clear or settle through the Stock Clearing Corporation directly or through another Clearing Member every contract and transaction to which he may be a party and which the By-Laws or Rules of the Stock Clearing Corporation may require to be cleared or settled through the Stock Clearing Corporation.

(b) That the Clearing Member will abide by the By-Laws and Rules of the Stock Clearing Corporation and shall be bound by all the provisions thereof including the provisions prescribing the liens which the Stock Clearing Corporation shall have upon stocks and securities which are the subject of transactions had for his account, and the Stock Clearing Corporation shall have all the liens, rights and remedies contemplated by said By-Laws and Rules of the Stock Clearing Corporation.

(c) That said By-Laws and Rules of the Stock Clearing Corporation shall be a part of the terms and conditions of every contract or transaction which the Clearing Member may make or have with the Stock Clearing Corporation and of every contract or transaction into which the Clearing Member may enter and which the By-Laws or Rules of the Stock Clearing Corporation may require to be cleared or settled through the Stock Clearing Corporation.

(d) That the Clearing Member will not clear or settle through the Stock Clearing Corporation any contract or transaction unless the By-Laws and Rules of the Stock Clearing Corporation are a part of the terms and conditions of such contract or transaction.

(e) That the Clearing Member will pay to the Stock Clearing Corporation the compensation provided for by the By-Laws and Rules of the Stock Clearing Corporation for clearing and other services rendered and such fines as may be imposed in accordance with such By-Laws and Rules of the Stock Clearing Corporation for the failure to comply therewith.

(f) That the Clearing Member will pay to the Stock Clearing Corporation any amounts which pursuant to the provisions of Article VII hereof shall become payable by the Clearing Member to the Stock Clearing Corporation.

(g) That in case the Clearing Fund together with the other resources of the Stock Clearing Corporation applicable to the payment of its liabilities incurred or growing out of the transactions of a Clearing Member are insufficient to enable it to meet such liabilities, the Clearing Member will contribute toward such deficiency a sum bearing the same proportion thereto that the Clearing Members' contribution to the Fund (as fixed at the time or times when the liabilities are incurred or the transactions occur) bears to such Fund, not exceeding however the amount of such contribution.

(h) That the Clearing Member's books and records shall at all times be open to the inspection of the duly authorized representatives of the Stock Clearing Corporation and that the Stock Clearing Corporation shall be furnished with all such information in respect to the

Clearing Member's business and transactions as it may require, provided that if he shall cease to be a Clearing Member the Stock Clearing Corporation shall have no right to inspect his books and records or to require information relating to transactions wholly subsequent to the time when he ceases to be a Clearing Member.

(i) That the determination of the Stock Clearing Corporation by its Board of Directors of all questions affecting the charges to which the Clearing Members contribution to the Clearing Fund are or may be subject shall be final and conclusive.

(j) That the Clearing Member will be bound by any amendment to the By-Laws or Rules of the Stock Clearing Corporation with respect to any transaction occurring subsequent to the time such amendment takes effect as fully as though such amendment were now a part of the By-Laws and Rules of the Stock Clearing Corporation, provided however that no such amendment shall affect the Clearing Member's right to cease to be a Clearing Member or alter the provisions of Article VII of the By-Laws of Stock Clearing Corporation unless before such amendment becomes effective the Clearing Member is given an opportunity to give written notice to the Stock Clearing Corporation of his election that it shall definitively cease to act for him.

Amendments.
August 23, 1939; August 1, 1946; May 1, 1953; May 25, 1955; July 15, 1965.

¶ 3102 Clearance of Contracts

SEC. 2. Except as hereinafter provided in Article VI, Clearing Members only shall be entitled to clear or settle contracts through the Stock Clearing Corporation. A Clearing Member who clears, settles or carries out through the Stock Clearing Corporation any contract or transaction for a member organization who is not a Clearing Member shall, so far as the rights of the Stock Clearing Corporation and all other Clearing Members are concerned, be liable as principal.

¶ 3103 Particular Transactions

SEC. 3. The Stock Clearing Corporation, without ceasing to act for a Clearing Member, may decline to act in respect to any particular transaction or class of transactions.

¶ 3104 Pending Transactions

SEC. 4. In so far as provision is made in the Rules of the Stock Clearing Corporation for transactions pending when the Stock Clearing Corporation ceases to act for a Clearing Member, the Clearing Member shall be bound by action of the Stock Clearing Corporation taken pursuant to said Rules of the Stock Clearing Corporation.

¶ 3105 Notice to Members

SEC. 5. Any notice from the Stock Clearing Corporation to a Clearing Member shall be sufficiently served on such Clearing Member if the notice is in writing and is delivered to the Clearing Member's office address or is given as required by the Rules of the Stock Clearing Corporation.

ARTICLE VI

Lists To Be Maintained

¶ 3125   Cleared Securities

SEC. 1. The Stock Clearing Corporation shall maintain a list of the stocks, bonds, notes, rights to subscribe and other securities, rights or interests which may be the subject of contracts cleared through the Stock Clearing Corporation and which are hereinafter called "cleared securities" and may from time to time add to such list or remove therefrom stocks, bonds, notes, rights to subscribe or other securities or rights.

¶ 3126   Lenders

SEC. 2. The Stock Clearing Corporation shall maintain a list of banks, bankers, trust companies and other lenders of money approved by it, who have entered into an agreement, in form prescribed by it, to comply with its regulations, so that it may act for Clearing Members in delivering to them and receiving from them stocks and securities and receiving from them and paying to them amounts payable in connection with such receipts and deliveries; and it may from time to time add names to such list and remove names therefrom.

¶ 3127   Clearing Members, Non-Clearing Members

SEC. 3. The Stock Clearing Corporation shall maintain lists of such Clearing Members and other member organizations as shall apply to the Stock Clearing Corporation to act for them and who shall have entered into an agreement in form prescribed by it to comply with its By-Laws and Rules, so that it may act for them in clearing or settling any contract or transaction which the Stock Clearing Corporation shall undertake to clear or settle and for which it shall make rules.

¶ 3128   Non-Member Banks, Non-Members

SEC. 4. The Stock Clearing Corporation shall maintain a list of banks, bankers, trust companies and other non-members who have been approved by the Stock Clearing Corporation and have entered into an agreement, in form prescribed by it, to comply with its regulations, so that it may act for Clearing Members in delivering to such banks, bankers, trust companies and other non-members and receiving from them stocks and securities and receiving from them and paying to them amounts payable in connection with such receipts and deliveries; and it may from time to time add names to such list and remove names therefrom.

Amendments.
August 23, 1939; May 1, 1953.

ARTICLE VII

Clearing Fund

¶ 3151   Contributions

SEC. 1. The contribution of each Clearing Member to the Clearing Fund shall be fixed by the Stock Clearing Corporation in its discretion at the time of the Clearing Member's application for membership and may thereafter from time to time be increased or diminished by the Stock Clearing Corporation but the minimum contribution to be made by a Clearing Member shall be Ten Thousand Dollars.

The Stock Clearing Corporation may permit a part of a Clearing Member's contribution to the Clearing Fund to be evidenced by an open account indebtedness secured by unmatured bearer bonds which are direct obligations of, or obligations guaranteed as to principal and interest by, the United States or unmatured bearer bonds which are general obligations of, or obligations guaranteed by, a State or political subdivision thereof which are in the first or second ratings of any nationally known statistical service, having a market value not less than the amount of such open account indebtedness. Such bonds shall be pledged to Stock Clearing Corporation on such terms and conditions as it shall require. The Stock Clearing Corporation shall fix the minimum amount of each Clearing Member's cash contribution to the Clearing Fund and may from time to time increase or diminish such minimum amount. Each Clearing Member shall forthwith pay all or such part of its open account indebtedness as Stock Clearing Corporation may request. The bonds pledged by a Clearing Member to secure its open account indebtedness may be held by Stock Clearing Corporation or for its account by a Bank or Trust Company.

¶ 3152   Use of Fund

SEC. 2. The Clearing Fund may be used by the Stock Clearing Corporation for the purposes of its business as defined in its Articles of Incorporation, and in the discretion of its Board of Directors may from time to time be partially or wholly invested by the Corporation for its account in securities issued or guaranteed by the United States and to the extent not so invested shall be deposited by the Stock Clearing Corporation in a special account or accounts in its name in such depository or depositories in the City of New York as may be selected by the Stock Clearing Corporation. Any securities in which the Clearing Fund is invested shall be the property of the Stock Clearing Corporation, may be used by it for the purposes of its business and may be pledged by it as security for loans made to it and for its other obligations.

Any interest paid by the depositories of cash in the Clearing Fund or paid on securities in which the Fund or any part thereof may be invested shall belong to the Stock Clearing Corporation. No interest shall be paid to the Clearing Members on the amounts contributed by them to the Clearing Fund.

¶ 3153   Discharge of Liability of Member

SEC. 3. If any Clearing Member shall fail to discharge duly any liability to the Stock Clearing Corporation, the amount of his contribution or so much thereof as is necessary shall forthwith be applied toward the discharge of such liability and such Clearing Member shall immediately upon demand make good the deficiency in the amount of his contribution resulting from such application.

¶ 3154   Loss in Excess of Contribution

SEC. 4. If the Stock Clearing Corporation suffers a loss in excess of a Clearing Member's contribution to the Clearing Fund by reason of his default, or suffers a loss as a result of clearing or settling or carrying out any contract or transaction for a Clearing Member, or by reason of the insolvency of a depository, or larceny, or embezzlement, such excess loss, or such loss, as the case may be, shall to the extent of the surplus of the Stock Clearing Corporation be made good therefrom, but to the extent that said surplus is insufficient to make it good it shall be made good out of the Clearing Fund and charged pro rata against the contributions as fixed at the time of transaction from which the loss results of the Clearing Members other than the Clearing Member, if any, primarily liable.

In so far, however, as a loss sustained through the default of a Clearing Member in any contract or transaction with another Clearing Member or other Clearing Members is under the Rules of the Stock Clearing Corporation made good by such other Clearing Member or Clearing Members, it is not to be deemed a loss sustained by the Stock Clearing Corporation within the meaning of this section.

¶ 3155   Liabilities Guaranteed

SEC. 5. All liabilities of the Stock Clearing Corporation shall be guaranteed by the Clearing Fund which so far as necessary shall be applied to the discharge of such liabilities. Amounts paid out of the Clearing Fund to discharge liabilities of the Stock Clearing Corporation shall be made good out of the existing surplus of the Stock Clearing Corporation, and if such payment does not represent a loss of the character specified in Section 4 of this Article, then, in so far as the surplus is insufficient to make the same good, it shall be made good out of the capital of the Stock Clearing Corporation. Amounts paid out of the Clearing Fund, and not made good as herein provided, shall be charged pro rata against the contributions as fixed at the time of the transactions from which the liabilities result of the Clearing Members other than those, if any, primarily liable.

¶ 3156   Return of Contribution

SEC. 6. Whenever a Clearing Member definitively ceases to be such, the amount of his contribution shall be returned to him or his representatives, but not until all transactions open at the time he ceases to be a Clearing Member from which losses or payments chargeable to the Clearing Fund might result have been closed and all amounts chargeable against his contribution on account of transactions had while he was a Clearing Member have been deducted or, with the approval of the Stock Clearing Corporation, another Clearing Member has been substituted on each such transaction.

¶ 3157   Increase of Contribution

SEC. 7. If the contribution to the Clearing Fund to be made by a Clearing Member is increased, such increase shall not become effective until he is given an opportunity to give written notice to the Stock Clearing Corporation of his election that it shall definitively cease to act for him. If, however, he does not give such written notice before the time specified in the notice to him of the increase in the amount of his contribution at the time when the same becomes effective, he shall contribute to the Stock Clearing Corporation the amount of the increase and the liability of his contribution for losses and his additional personal liability under his agreement with the Stock Clearing Corporation shall thereafter be fixed and determined by the amount of his contribution as increased. If a pro rata charge against any Clearing Member's contribution is made pursuant to the provisions of Section 4 or Section 5 of this Article, he may at any time within two days after notice to him of such charge give written notice to the Stock Clearing Corporation of his election that it shall definitively cease to act for him. If he gives such notice the amount of the pro rata charge against his contribution shall nevertheless be deducted from the amount of his contribution and such pro rata charge shall not affect the amount of the liability of his contribution or his additional personal liability on account of other transactions occurring before he ceases to be a Clearing Member; but the aggregate amount of the liability of his contribution and his additional personal liability by reason of such pro rata charge and such other transactions shall not exceed the amount of his contribution plus One Hundred per cent. thereof, except that he must carry out any obligation to make good the deficiency in the amount of his contribution resulting from a previous pro rata charge.

¶ 3158   Decrease of Contribution

SEC. 8. If a Clearing Member's contribution to the Clearing Fund after having been fixed by the Stock Clearing Corporation and paid in by the Clearing Member is thereafter decreased by the Stock Clearing Corporation, the difference shall be paid to the Clearing Member as soon as all transactions open at the time of such decrease from which losses and payments chargeable to the Clearing Fund might result have been closed and after the amount if any to be charged against his contribution on account of transactions previously had have been made good by him.

¶ 3159   Recovery of Loss

SEC. 9. If a loss charged pro rata against the contributions of Clearing Members is afterward recovered by the Stock Clearing Corporation, in whole or in part, the net amount of such recovery shall be credited to the Clearing Members against whose contributions the loss was charged in proportion to the amounts charged against their respective contributions whether or not they are still Clearing Members.

¶ 3160   Surplus and Dividends

SEC. 10. The net annual earnings of the Stock Clearing Corporation in excess of six per cent. of the amount of its capital stock shall be carried to surplus until the surplus equals $500,000. After the surplus equals $500,000, all or any part of the net annual earnings may be distributed as dividends.

Amendments.

August 23, 1939; February 7, 1947; January 14, 1949; January 1, 1951; May 1, 1956; May 23, 1960.

ARTICLE VIII

Rules

¶ 3175   Controlling Rules

The Board of Directors shall prescribe and from time to time amend the Rules of the Stock Clearing Corporation. Said Rules shall determine what contracts and transactions between Clearing Members shall be cleared or settled through the Stock Clearing Corporation and may regulate the clearing or the settlement of such contracts and transactions and the receipt and delivery of stocks and securities on contracts and transactions between Clearing Members and the payment therefor and the delivery and receipt by the Stock Clearing Corporation for account of Clearing Members of stocks and securities to and from banks, bankers, trust companies and other non-members named in the lists for which provision is made in Sections 2 and 4 of Article VI hereof, and the receipt from and payment to said banks, bankers, trust companies and other non-members of the amount of loans made by them to Clearing Members and the other amounts payable in connection with such receipts and deliveries and may also prescribe the terms and conditions on which the Stock Clearing Corporation will act for Clearing Members in procuring the transfer of stocks or securities on the books of the corporations or associations issuing the same. Said Rules may also prescribe the terms and conditions on which the Stock Clearing Corporation will act for such Clearing Members and such non-members named in the lists for which provision is made in Section 3 of Article VI hereof in regard to the clearing or settling of any contract or transaction and the terms and conditions on which it will act for Clearing Members in any matters in which it may act for them under its Certificate of Incorporation, and shall prescribe and define the duties and obligations of Clearing Members in connection with all matters in which the Stock Clearing Corporation may act for Clearing Members and shall also prescribe and define the manner in which pending transactions of Clearing Members for whom it ceases to act or who die or are suspended or expelled from the New York Stock Exchange or who become insolvent shall be dealt with. The Board of Directors may by special rules, adopted from time to time, make provision for special clearances of any contracts between Clearing Members having to do with any stocks, bonds, notes, rights to subscribe or other securities or rights. The Rules of the Stock Clearing Corporation, made in accordance with these By-Laws, shall have the same force and effect as though a part hereof, and may define the rights and remedies of the Stock Clearing Corporation on account of amounts that may be paid out by it for account of a Clearing Member or for which the Clearing Member may be otherwise indebted to it, and its liens, rights and remedies with respect to stocks, securities or moneys received by it for account of a Clearing Member or which are the subject of transactions in which it is concerned, and may prescribe the procedure to be followed in case of default of a Clearing Member in the performance of his obligations to the Stock Clearing Corporation or in case of his default upon his contracts, which are subject to the clearing or otherwise and may prescribe the extent to which any losses resulting from such procedure and not made good by the defaulting Clearing Member are to be charged against his contribution to the Clearing Fund and how far and in what manner such losses shall be borne by and charged against the other Clearing Members with whom the defaulting Clear-

¶ **3175   SCC Art. VIII**   © 1960, Commerce Clearing House, Inc.

ing Member's contracts have been made. The Rules of the Stock Clearing Corporation may provide that the Stock Clearing Corporation may borrow money and may pledge for the re-payment thereof all or any part of the securities held by it for account of a Clearing Member either alone or together with stocks or securities held by it for accounts of other Clearing Members or otherwise and whether or not the amounts for which such stocks and securities are so pledged shall exceed the indebtedness of the Clearing Member to the Stock Clearing Corporation. The Rules of the Stock Clearing Corporation may prescribe the charges to be paid for services rendered by the Stock Clearing Corporation to Clearing Members and the fines or other penalties to which Clearing Members will be liable for violation of the Rules of the Stock Clearing Corporation or its By-Laws and may contain any other regulations and provisions which are consistent with the Articles of Incorporation and these By-Laws and which in the opinion of the Board of Directors are necessary to carry out the purposes of the Stock Clearing Corporation.

The Board of Directors of Stock Clearing Corporation shall have power to interpret the Rules adopted pursuant to the provisions of this Article VIII and any and all amendments or changes therein and additions thereto and any such interpretation so made shall be final and conclusive.

Amendments.
August 23, 1939; August 1, 1946.

ARTICLE IX
Corporate Instruments and Obligations

¶ 3191   Deeds, Leases, Contracts, etc.

SEC. 1. All leases and contracts made in the ordinary course of business, authorized by the Board of Directors, shall be signed on behalf of the Corporation by the President or a Vice-President or by such other person as may from time to time be designated by the Board of Directors. All deeds, when authorized by the Board of Directors, shall be signed by the President or a Vice-President. Whenever the corporate seal shall be affixed to any instrument the same may be attested by the Secretary or an Assistant Secretary.

¶ 3192   Checks, Drafts and Endorsements

SEC. 2. All checks, drafts or other orders for the payment of money, notes, acceptances or other evidence of indebtedness issued in the name of the Corporation shall be signed by such officers or agents and in such manner as shall be determined from time to time by resolution of the Board of Directors. Endorsements for deposit to the credit of the Corporation in any of its duly authorized depositaries may be made by hand-stamped legend in the name of the Corporation or by written endorsement without countersignature.

¶ 3193   Sale or Transfer of Securities

SEC. 3. Stock certificates or bonds or other securities owned or held by the Corporation may be sold or otherwise disposed of and transferred pursuant to resolution (either general or special) of the Board of Directors and, when so authorized to be sold or otherwise disposed of, may be transferred from the name of the Corporation by the signature of the President or a Vice-President or the Treasurer or an Assistant Treasurer.

¶ 3194   Proxies

SEC. 4. The President, a Vice-President or the Treasurer may attend in person and act and vote on behalf of the Corporation at any meeting of the stockholders of any corporation in which the Corporation holds stock or by his signature may appoint in the name and on behalf of the Corporation a proxy to attend and act and vote in respect of such stock at any such meeting.

Amendment.
May 25, 1955.

ARTICLE X

Corporate Seal

¶ 3201   Corporate Seal

The seal of the Corporation shall be circular with the name of the Corporation written in full thereon and with the legend "State of New York 1919" in the center thereof.

Amendment.
May 25, 1955.

ARTICLE XI

Capital Stock

¶ 3211   Certificates

SEC. 1. Certificates for shares of capital stock of the Corporation shall be in form approved by the Board of Directors. Such certificates shall bear the seal of the Corporation (which may be engraved or printed) and shall be signed by the President and the Secretary or an Assistant Secretary or the Treasurer or an Assistant Treasurer.

¶ 3212   Record of Stockholders

SEC. 2. The stockholders of record entitled to vote at any meeting of stockholders or entitled to receive payment of any dividend or to any allotment of rights or to exercise the rights in respect of any change or conversion or exchange of capital stock shall be determined according to the Corporation's record of stockholders and, if so determined by the Board of Directors in the manner provided by statute, shall be such stockholders of record (a) at the date fixed for closing the stock transfer books, (b) at the date fixed as a date of record, or (c) at the time of the meeting. In the absence of such determination the stockholders of record at the time of the annual meeting of stockholders shall be the stockholders entitled to vote at such meeting.

¶ 3213   Transfers

SEC. 3. Transfers of shares shall be made upon the stock books of the Corporation by the stockholder of record of said shares or by the authorized attorney-in-fact of such stockholder, upon surrender of the certificate or certificates therefor. The person in whose name at any time shares stand of record upon the stock books of the Corporation shall, so far as the Corporation is concerned, be deemed the holder of said shares.

¶ 3214   Lost, Stolen or Destroyed Certificates

SEC. 4. Lost, stolen or destroyed certificates may be replaced by the Corporation by new certificates for the same number of shares; provided, however, that the Corporation shall have received due and prompt notice of the loss, theft or destruction and provided, further, that the Corporation shall have been furnished with satisfactory evidence of such loss, theft or destruction or with security sufficient, in the determination of the Board of Directors, to indemnify the Corporation against any claim which might be made by reason of the issue of new certificates for the same shares.

Amendment.
May 25, 1955.

ARTICLE XII
Notice—How Waived

¶ 3225   Attendance at Meetings

SEC. 1. Attendance at any meeting of the Board of Directors or stockholders, or written waiver of notice of any such meeting, signed either before or after the holding thereof, by any person entitled to notice of such meeting or in the case of meetings of stockholders by the attorney-in-fact or proxy of any such person shall constitute a waiver of notice of the time and place of holding such meeting and of the purpose thereof and of any requirement for the publication of such notice.

¶ 3226   Notice of an Adjourned Meeting

SEC. 2. Notice of an adjourned meeting need not be given, if notation has been made in the corporate minute book of the date to which the meeting was adjourned. At such adjourned meeting the same business may be transacted which might have been transacted at the meeting originally called.

Amendment.
May 25, 1955.

ARTICLE XIII
Miscellaneous

¶ 3241   Books of Account and Corporate Records

SEC. 1. Books of account and corporate records shall be open to the inspection of stockholders or others only, if at all, to the extent authorized or permitted by the Board of Directors, except that stock ledgers and stock transfer books shall be open to the inspection of stockholders to the extent required by statute.

¶ 3242   Fiscal Year

SEC. 2. The fiscal year of the Corporation shall be the calendar year.

¶ 3243   Amendments

SEC. 3. Amendments to these By-Laws or their repeal may be authorized by the vote of a majority in interest of the stockholders present entitled to vote at any meeting or by resolution of the Board of Directors, adopted by a majority of its total number then in office; provided, however, that notice of the proposed amendment or modification of these By-Laws shall have been included in the notice of the meeting at which such action is authorized and provided, further, that if any By-Law regulating an impending election of Directors is adopted or amended or repealed by the Board of Directors, there shall be set forth in the Notice of the next meeting of the members of the Corporation for the election of Directors the By-Laws so adopted or amended or repealed, together with a concise statement of the changes made.

Amendment.
May 25, 1955.

[The next page is 4575.]

© 1957, Commerce Clearing House, Inc.

Stock Clearing Corporation
General Information

¶ 3251 **Executive Office**

Entrance

44 Broad Street, New York, N. Y. 10004

¶ 3252 **Principal Departments**

Entrances

Central Delivery Department

Member Deliveries to other Members, Non-Member Banks and Non-Members shall be made to Central Delivery Department at windows located in 40 New Street .... 40 New Street

Non-Member Deliveries to other Non-Members, Members and Non-Member Banks shall be made to Central Delivery Department at windows located in 40 New Street .... 40 New Street

Non-Member Bank Deliveries to other Non-Member Banks, Members and Non-Members shall be made to Central Delivery Department at designated window or windows.......... 40 New Street

Central Receiving Department .... 40 Broad Street

Clearance—Data Processing Department ...... 44 Broad Street

Direct Clearing Department .... 44 Broad Street

Distributing Department .... 40 Broad Street

Settlement Department .... 40 Broad Street

Hours

Entrances at 40 Broad Street and 40 New Street will be open between the hours of 8:00 A. M. and 5:00 P. M. on business days. (Will remain open later if the Central Receiving and Distributing Departments' time schedules are extended.)

Night Telephone Connections

Executive Office .... HA 2–4265
Central Delivery Department .... HA 2–4282
Central Receiving Department .... HA 2–4267
Clearance—Data Processing Department .... HA 2–4266
Direct Clearing Department .... HA 2–4288–89–90
Settlement Department .... HA 2–4282

¶ 3253   General

Representatives of Clearing Members holding regular Stock Clearing Corporation passes issued in accordance with the provisions of Rule 23 will be admitted during any business day at all entrances to the premises occupied by Stock Clearing Corporation, when open.

Representatives of member organizations holding identification cards issued in accordance with the provisions of Rule 23 will have access between hours of 8:00 A. M. and 1:30 P. M. only to the Distributing Department and from 1:30 P. M. to 5:00 P. M. will have access to either the Distributing Department or the Settlement Department.

Neither pass nor identification card will be required of those representatives of firms making deliveries to the Central Delivery Department at the chute located in the 40 New Street entrance.

Holders of the special types of passes issued to representatives of Non-Member Banks and Non-Members will be admitted during any business day at all entrances to the premises occupied by Stock Clearing Corporation, when open.

[The next page is 4601.]

© 1965, Commerce Clearing House, Inc.

Stock Clearing Corporation
Rules

*(Adopted, August 29, 1946, Pursuant to Article VIII
of the By-Laws of Stock Clearing Corporation)*

¶ 3301   Definitions and Descriptions

Rule 1.   Unless the context requires otherwise, the terms defined in this Rule
shall, for all purposes of the Rules, have the meanings herein specified.

The Exchange

The term "the Exchange" means the New York Stock Exchange.

The Corporation

The term "the Corporation" means Stock Clearing Corporation.

Security

The term "security" or "securities" includes stocks, bonds, notes, certificates of deposit or participation, trust receipts, rights, warrants and other
similar instruments which may be the subject of contracts and transactions
with which the Corporation has to do.

By-Laws

The term "By-Laws" means the By-Laws of the Corporation as the same
may be amended from time to time.

Board of Directors

The term "Board of Directors" means the Board of Directors of the Corporation.

Cleared Securities

The term "Cleared Securities" means securities included in the list for
which provision is made in Section 1 of Article VI of the By-Laws.

Non-Cleared Securities

The term "Non-Cleared Securities" means securities traded on the Exchange other than cleared securities.

Clearing Members

The term "Clearing Members" means member organizations of the Exchange who have qualified pursuant to the provisions of Article V of the
By-Laws.

Non-Clearing Members

The term "Non-Clearing Members" means member organizations of the
Exchange who have not qualified pursuant to the provisions of Article V of
the By-Laws but who have entered into an agreement with the Corporation
pursuant to the provisions of Section 3 of Article VI of the By-Laws.

¶ 3301 Continued

Non-Member Banks

The term "Non-Member Banks" means banks and trust companies which are members of the New York Clearing House Association, named from time to time on one of the lists for which provision is made in Section 4 of Article VI of the By-Laws.

Non-Members

The term "Non-Members" means all persons, firms and corporations other than Clearing Members, Non-Clearing Members or Non-Member Banks, named from time to time on one of the lists for which provision is made in Section 4 of Article VI of the By-Laws.

He, him, his

The words "he", "him" and "his", when used with respect to all Members, shall include partnerships and corporations as well as individuals, when the context so requires.

Business day

The term "business day" means any day on which the Exchange is open for business. In accordance with the Rules of the Exchange, however, on any business day that the banks, transfer agencies and depositories for securities in New York State are closed, no deliveries shall be made.

Clearance Operation

The term "Clearance Operation" covers all the operations having to do with Cleared Securities to which these Rules are applicable up to and including the issuance of balance orders by the Clearance Department of the Corporation directing the receipt and delivery of securities. Such orders shall be deemed to have been issued when they are available to Clearing Members, although they may not in fact have been distributed to such Clearing Members.

Clearing House Comparison service

The term "Clearing House Comparison service" covers all the operations having to do with the supplementary comparison service provided for in Section 8 of Rule 4 up to and including the issuance of orders by the Clearance Department of the Corporation directing the receipt and delivery of securities. Such orders shall be deemed to have been issued when they are available to Clearing Members, although they may not in fact have been distributed to such Clearing Members.

Special Clearances and Special Intermediate Clearances

The terms "Special Clearances" and "Special Intermediate Clearances" cover all the operations having to do with special clearances of any contracts, as provided for in Article VIII of the By-Laws, up to and including the issuance of orders by the Corporation directing the receipt and delivery of security balances, or the discontinuance of the Clearance.

Settlement of Contracts

The term "Settlement of Contracts" covers all other ordinary operations to which these Rules are applicable.

¶ 3301   **SCC Rule 1**

Debit Balance

The term "Debit Balance" as used in these Rules in respect to a Clearing Member means the amount which the Corporation has paid out or is obligated or may become obligated to pay out for his account pursuant to these Rules and the amounts payable by such Clearing Member to the Corporation on account of fines and penalties or for services rendered, less the credits to which such Clearing Member has become definitively entitled pursuant to these Rules. The Clearing Member's contribution to the Clearing Fund and the amount payable to the Clearing Member or payable by him under the provisions of the By-Laws relating to the Clearing Fund do not enter into the debit balance.

[The next page is 4603-3.]

[The next page is 495-37]

All Members

The term "All Members" means Clearing Members, Non-Clearing Members, Non-Member Banks, and Non-Members of Stock Clearing Corporation.

Settling Members

The term "Settling Members" means Clearing Members, Non-Clearing Members, and Non-Member Banks of Stock Clearing Corporation.

Amendments.

August 24, 1946; March 25, 1947; May 1, 1947; July 18, 1947; August 4, 1948; November 1, 1948; January 14, 1949; March 3, 1952; September 29, 1952; May 1, 1953; February 1, 1954; September 20, 1961.

¶ 3302   General Provisions

Cleared Transactions

Rule 2. SEC. 1. Unless it is otherwise stipulated in the bid or offer or the parties otherwise agree, a receive exchange ticket covering the buy side and a deliver exchange ticket covering the sell side of each contract between Clearing Members made on the Exchange calling for delivery of Cleared Securities shall be sent for comparison to the Central Receiving Department of the Corporation; such contracts shall be cleared through the Clearance Department; delivery shall be made through the Central Delivery Department, and payment shall be made through the Settlement Department. Such comparison, clearance, delivery and payment shall be effected as hereinafter prescribed in these Rules or in such regulations with respect thereto as the Corporation may from time to time adopt.

When issued and when distributed cleared transactions shall be settled and payment therefore made at such time, in such manner, and by the delivery of securities and/or other property as the Corporation may determine, or shall be cancelled and thereafter shall be null and void if the Corporation determines that the plan or proposal pursuant to which the securities were to be issued or distributed has been abandoned or materially changed.

The Corporation, notwithstanding anything herein contained, may in its discretion decline to act in respect to any transaction or class of transactions.

Duties of Clearing Members

SEC. 2. Every Clearing Member shall maintain an office at a location in the vicinity of the Exchange approved by the Corporation. A Clearing Member may use for the purposes hereof the office of another Clearing Member, provided such use is pursuant to a written agreement approved by the Corporation.

There shall be present at said office on every business day, between the hours of 9:15 A. M. and 3:00 P. M., a representative of the Clearing Member authorized in the name of the Clearing Member to sign all instruments and transact all business requisite in connection with the operations of the Corporation. If the representative of the Clearing Member is not a general partner in the Clearing Member's firm, or is not an officer of the Clearing Member's corporation, such representative shall, in the case of a firm, be authorized to act by written power of attorney, or in the case of a corporation by resolution by the Board of Directors of such corporation. Such power of attorney or resolution, as the case may be, shall be in form approved by the Corporation.

There shall be present at said office on every business day from 9:00 A. M. until 5:30 P. M., some person authorized on behalf of the Clearing Member to correct errors and to perform such other duties as may be required under these Rules.

Clearing Members shall file with the Corporation the signatures of the members of their firms or the officers of their corporations and of the representatives of such firms or corporations who are authorized to sign checks, agreements, receipts, orders and other papers necessary for conducting business with the Corporation together with the powers of attorney or other instruments giving such authority.

The Corporation may require Clearing Members who are to receive its checks or other instruments to prepare them for execution by it by filling them out in whole or in part and to identify them by the signatures of their representatives.

Notices to all Members that the Corporation has ceased to act for a Clearing Member or that a Clearing Member is insolvent shall be sufficient if sent out on the ticker service of the New York Quotation Company, but so far as practicable such notices in the cases of Non-Member Banks and Non-Members shall be supplemented by telephone or other speedy means of communication.

All Members will be allotted a number which must appear on the face of all forms used by him in connection with the operations of the Corporation.

The official date of the Clearance Operation and of the Settlement of Contracts is the day on which contracts are due and the securities are to be delivered and all exchange tickets, summaries, security balance orders, stamp bills, checks and drafts, except as may be otherwise directed by the Corporation, either in general or in particular instances, shall bear that date even though they may be issued on a preceding day.

Clearing Member Acting as Agent for Another Clearing Member

SEC. 3. A Clearing Member may appoint another Clearing Member as his agent with respect to all contracts or transactions cleared, settled, delivered or carried out through or by the Corporation and all matters relating thereto, provided that such appointment has been consented to by the Corporation and is evidenced by such appointments, authorizations, certifications and other agreements in such form as may be required by the Corporation.

Amendments.
July 18, 1947; January 14, 1949; March 3, 1952; September 29, 1952; May 1, 1953; March 1, 1957; August 29, 1963; September 3, 1964.

● ● ● *Supplementary Material:*

.10 **Cleared Securities.**—The list of Cleared Securities shall consist of all listed stocks, rights, warrants and when issued or when distributed bonds in round lots and multiples thereof.

.11 **For account of insolvent banks.**—The Corporation directs that transactions in any cleared security sold for the account of an insolvent bank in liquidation be made ex-Central Receiving and ex-Clearance Departments.

¶ **3302.10 SCC Rule 2**   © 1964, Commerce Clearing House, Inc.

We are advised that Transfer Agents, in transferring such stock when accompanied by a tax free sales ticket require the actual certificate representing the securities actually sold.

Clearing Members may handle these transactions by using all Central Delivery Department and Settlement Department facilities but not those of the Central Receiving and Clearance Departments.

The seller of such securities should promptly notify each buyer so that both contracting parties may know that the transaction is ex-Central Receiving and ex-Clearance Departments.

This ruling applies to cleared securities only when same are sold for the account of an insolvent bank in liquidation as per Internal Revenue rulings.

.12 For account of any foreign sovereignty.—Extracts from a circular issued by the Department of Floor Procedure of the Exchange under date of November 5, 1948, follow:

"The attention of members is directed to an opinion dated April 9, 1947, of the Attorney General of the State of New York regarding the application of Article 12 of the Tax Law relating to the stock transfer tax to sales of securities in New York by the British Government. It is believed that the opinion would be equally applicable to sales by any foreign sovereignty.

"The effect of the opinion is that the amendment of Section 270, subdivision 3, of the Tax Law in 1945, placing the duty of paying the stock transfer tax on the transferee as well as the transferor, did not alter the exemption or immunity of individual parties but places the obligation of paying the tax on the party who is not exempt or immune. Consequently a non-exempt transferee purchasing stock from a foreign government is liable for the New York transfer tax.

"Inasmuch as all regular contracts on the New York Stock Exchange are based upon the payment by the seller of the necessary Federal and New York State transfer taxes, members are advised that in making a sale of stock for the account of a foreign government, when it is contemplated that the New York State transfer tax will not be paid by the seller, the condition that the buyer pay the necessary New York State transfer tax shall be specified in the order and announced by the selling broker in connection with his offer."

In the aforementioned circumstances the facilities of Central Delivery and Settlement Departments of Stock Clearing Corporation may be used in such transactions, but not those of the Central Receiving and Clearance Departments.

¶ 3303   **Distributing Department**

Functions of Distributing Department

Rule 3. The Corporation will maintain a Distributing Department, the facilities of which may, subject to such regulations as the Corporation may from time to time prescribe, be used by All Members for the distribution of tickets, checks, papers, documents and other material incidental to the ordinary course of business, except that exchange tickets, advisory notices and deletion notices covering transactions in Cleared Securities and exchange tickets covering transactions subject to the Clearing House Comparison service shall be delivered to the Central Receiving Department.

¶ 3303 Continued

The Corporation assumes no responsibility whatever for the form or content of any tickets, checks, papers, documents or other material placed in the locked boxes in the Distributing Department and assigned to each subscriber, nor for any improper or unauthorized removal therefrom of any such tickets, checks, papers, documents or other material.

All Members shall send an authorized representative to the Distributing Department at frequent intervals for any documents or material placed in his locked box. No such documents or material shall be permitted to remain in such boxes overnight.

The Distributing Department will remain open from 8:00 A. M. to 5:00 P. M. on business days; except that these hours may be extended on any given day by the Corporation.

Amendments.

July 1, 1947; January 14, 1949; September 29, 1952; August 9, 1954; September 20, 1961; September 3, 1964.

● ● ● *Supplementary Material:*

.10 **Locked box.**—A locked box is assigned without application to each Clearing Member, Non-Member Bank and Non-Member.

Any Non-Clearing Member Organization of the Exchange may upon written application (on own stationery) obtain such a locked box.

The locked boxes are to be used for the distribution of tickets, checks, papers, documents and other material incidental to the ordinary course of business.

.11 **Extension of time.**—In the event the volume of transactions on any business day requires that the Central Receiving Department remain open beyond the normal hours a notice announcing an extension of time will apply, in like manner, to the Distributing Department.

¶ 3304 **Central Receiving Department**

Reports, tickets, etc.

Rule 4. SEC. 1. Reports, tickets and other documents required by the Rules to be delivered to the Corporation, shall, except as may otherwise be prescribed by the Rules, be delivered to and will be handled by the Central Receiving Department.

Comparisons of transactions

SEC. 2. The Central Receiving Department will, in accordance with the following sections of this Rule 4, handle comparisons of transactions effected by Clearing Members.

Exchange tickets

SEC. 3. On each transaction between Clearing Members (unless otherwise agreed) calling for the delivery of Cleared Securities, the buying and selling Clearing Members shall, as the Corporation may from time to time direct, send to the Central Receiving Department on the business day following the transaction an exchange ticket in the form prescribed by the Corporation,

¶ **3303.10 SCC Rule 4** © 1964, Commerce Clearing House, Inc.

addressed to the other Clearing Member party to the transaction. Such exchange tickets shall be delivered to the Central Receiving Department on the business day following the transaction in accordance with time schedules established or from time to time determined by the Corporation.

Summaries

SEC. 4. At the same time as the delivery to the Corporation of exchange tickets, as provided in Section 3 of this Rule, there shall be delivered two summaries, in form prescribed by the Corporation, one showing the total number of shares and the total contract value for regular way transactions the other the total number of shares or total par value and the total contract values for when issued and/or when distributed transactions covered by all such exchange tickets.

Signatures

SEC. 5. The name of a Clearing Member printed, stamped or written on any exchange ticket, confirmation of cleared or compared transactions, confirmation of when issued or when distributed cleared transactions, or advisory notice or deletion notice issued by him shall be deemed to have been adopted by him as his signature and shall be valid and binding upon him in all respects as though he had manually affixed his signature to such confirmation, ticket or notice.

Comparisons—Contract lists

SEC. 6. From the exchange tickets received by the Central Receiving Department as provided in Section 3 of this Rule, the Corporation will effect comparisons of buy and sell transactions to the extent that they are comparable and enter same in the Clearance Operation as compared trades on the respective Clearing Members' contract lists; all or any part of such transactions that are not so compared will be entered as uncompared transactions on the submitting Clearing Members' contract lists and as advisory data on the addressee Clearing Members' contract lists. The Corporation will prepare, with respect to each Clearing Member, four contract lists, one of which will show the purchases and one the sales of Regular Way Cleared Securities and one the purchases and one the sales of When Issued and/or When Distributed Cleared Securities effected for the Clearing Member on the date to which such lists relate, the numbers of the other Clearing Members with whom such transactions were effected and such other information and/or forms as the Corporation may deem advisable. Such contract lists and such forms as the Corporation may from time to time determine will be placed in the Clearing Members' boxes in the Distributing Department by 8:00 A. M. on the second business day succeeding the day of the transactions included in such lists, and shall be called for by Clearing Members not later than 9:15 A. M. on the day on which they are so made available. Each Clearing Member shall promptly check each contract list he receives. It shall be the duty of both the buying and the selling Clearing Member immediately to advise by telephone the Clearing Member on the opposite side of any item requiring change for any reason whatsoever which has not been resolved through the medium of advisory notices.

Corrections—Deletions—Supplemental lists

SEC. 7. (a) Each Clearing Member will be furnished with a notice, in form prescribed by the Corporation, for each transaction appearing in the

¶ 3304 Continued

advisory data section of each contract list as provided in Section 6 of this Rule. Each Clearing Member receiving such notice, if he knows the trade exactly as printed on the notice and wishes to have it added to his compared contracts shall so indicate by imprinting his name and number stamp on Parts #1 and #2 and sending both parts to the Corporation within such time limits as set forth from time to time by the Corporation. The Corporation will on the receipt of Parts #1 and #2 add the transaction to the compared contract section of the contract lists of both Clearing Members and distribute Part # 2 to the addressee Clearing Member named therein.

(b) Transactions not compared under Section 6 or Section 7(a) of this Rule shall be submitted to the Corporation by the selling Clearing Member, after agreement with the opposite side, for comparison and clearance in the form of, at such times and under such conditions as prescribed by the Corporation from time to time.

(c) Transactions compared under Section 6 and Paragraphs (a) and (b) of this Section 7 will be deleted in whole or in part (in multiples of the unit of trading) and excluded from the clearance by the Corporation on its receipt of a deletion notice (in form prescribed by the Corporation) from either the buying or selling Clearing Member at such times and under such conditions as determined from time to time by the Corporation. An item so deleted, unless compared through the Clearing House Comparison service, shall be adjusted directly between the parties or settled in accordance with the applicable Rules of the Board of Governors of the Exchange.

(d) Supplemental contract lists will be distributed to Clearing Members on which will be shown the additions and deletions of compared transactions made by the Corporation pursuant to Paragraphs (a), (b) and (c) of this Section 7, as well as such other information as the Corporation may deem advisable.

Clearing House Comparison service

SEC. 8.   For transactions in either Cleared Securities or Non-Cleared Securities as the Corporation in its sole discretion may choose, the Central Receiving Department will provide a Clearing House Comparison service for the comparison of items not resolved between the buying and selling Clearing Members as provided and within the times specified in Section 6 and Section 7 of this Rule, and other transactions in either Cleared or Non-Cleared Securities. With respect to all such transactions to be compared through the Clearing House Comparison service, the selling Clearing Member shall, between the hours of 1:00 P. M. and 3:00 P. M. on the third business day following the transaction, send to the Central Receiving Department a deliver exchange ticket in the form prescribed by the Corporation addressed to the buying Clearing Member, and, between such hours, the buying Clearing Member shall send to the Central Receiving Department a receive exchange ticket in the form prescribed by the Corporation addressed to the selling Clearing Member. At the same time as the delivery to the Corporation of exchange tickets there shall be delivered a summary in form prescribed by the Corporation, showing the total number of shares and the total contract value for transactions covered by all such exchange tickets.

From the exchange tickets so received by the Central Receiving Department as provided in this Section, the Corporation will effect comparison of

¶ 3304   SCC Rule 4   © 1964, Commerce Clearing House, Inc.

buy and sell transactions to the extent that they are comparable and enter same as compared trades (excluded from the Clearance Operation) on the respective Clearing Members' contract lists; all or any part of such transactions that are not so compared will be entered as uncompared transactions on the submitting Clearing Members' contract lists and as advisory data on the addressee Clearing Members' contract lists. The Corporation will prepare, with respect to each Clearing Member, two contract lists, one of which will show the purchases and the other the sales of securities effected for the Clearing Member on the date to which such lists relate, the numbers of the other Clearing Members with whom such transactions were effected and such other information as the Corporation may deem advisable. Such contract lists will be placed in the Clearing Members' boxes in the Distributing Department by 8:00 A. M. on the fourth business day succeeding the day of the transactions included in such lists, and shall be called for by Clearing Members not later than 9:15 A. M. on the date on which they are so made available. Any transaction listed in the uncompared or advisory section of the contract list shall be adjusted directly between the parties or settled in accordance with the applicable Rules of the Board of Governors of the Exchange.

Appropriate receive and deliver security orders will be issued by the Corporation in connection with the Clearing House Comparison service and such orders shall have the same status as security balance orders issued in connection with the regular Clearance Operation and will be subject to all Rules pertaining to such security balance orders unless otherwise specified by the Corporation.

Confirmations

SEC. 9. Each Clearing Member who has received any contract list provided for in this Rule shall affix on each page of said contract lists and supplemental contract lists a facsimile firm signature, or the signature of a general partner or attorney in fact, and shall retain same for a period of at least six years and further shall not later than 12:00 Noon on the third business day following the transaction, deliver to the Central Receiving Department two written confirmations one for regular way transactions and transactions compared in the Clearing House Comparison service which have the same settlement date and the other for when issued and/or when distributed transactions thereby confirming and acknowledging each transaction appearing on such purchase and/or sale contract lists as may be amended and corrected on supplemental contract lists.

Amendments.
July 18, 1947; May 17, 1948; July 21, 1948; March 22, 1951; March 3, 1952; February 1, 1954; September 20, 1961; September 3, 1964.

● ● ● *Supplementary Material:*

.10 General—Time schedules.—

From Stock Clearing Corporation to Clearing Members:

Contract Lists. 6:00 P. M. of business day following transaction.

Advisory Notices Part 2. 11:30 A. M. on 2nd business day following transaction.

Supplementary Adds Part 2. 1:30 P. M. on 2nd business day following transaction.

¶ 3304.10   Continued

Deletion Notices Part 2. 2:30 P. M. on 2nd business day following transaction.

Clearing House Comparison service security orders and contract lists. 8:00 A. M. on established settlement date.

From Clearing Members to Stock Clearing Corporation:

Receive and Deliver Exchange Tickets & Summaries. 1:00 P. M. on business day following transaction.

Advisory Notices. 11:00 A. M. on 2nd business day following transaction.

Supplementary Adds. 1:00 P. M. on 2nd business day following transaction.

Deletion Notices. 2:00 P. M. on 2nd business day following transaction.

Confirmations of Transactions. 12:00 Noon on 3rd business day following transaction.

Clearing House Comparison service receive and deliver exchange tickets and summary Form 089. 1:00 P. M. to 3:00 P. M. on business day prior to established settlement date.

In the event that any of the above time limits are extended, a special notice announcing such extension will be placed in each Clearing Member's Distributing Department box.

.20   **Exchange Rule re "give-ups."**—The attention of Clearing Members is directed to Rules 138 and 139 of the Rules of the Board of Governors of the Exchange in connection with "give-ups," excerpts of which follow:

"Rule 138. * * *:

"Such give-ups shall be effected either at the time of the transaction or within one hour and a half after the time of the trasanction; except that the time limit for effecting give-ups on any day shall be one hour after the closing of the Exchange on the day of the transaction. Give-ups effected at any time other than at the time of the transactions, on transactions which are not to be cleared through Stock Clearing Corporation, shall be in writing and delivered to the party on the other side of the transaction.

"* * *.

"Rule 139:

"When names are given up on transactions, members or member organizations so given up or receiving such give-ups shall immediately record such names on their blotters or other records, and shall use the names, so given up, on exchange tickets and comparisons, or when exchanging contracts."

.30   **Suggested procedure.**—Clearing Members are particularly requested to observe, and endeavor to have others observe, the following suggestions made by the Department of Floor Procedure of the Exchange:

(a) Give-ups should be effected on the Floor at the time of trade whenever possible.

(b) When a large block of stock is traded and the Specialist reports or states "names later," the broker trading with the Specialist should include such statement in his report so that receive and deliver exchange tickets or comparisons will not be sent out until the give-up names are received.

(c) Official abbreviated firm names should be used on all Floor reports. In view of the similarity of names of many firms, ticket clerks should be furnished with a list of all such firms.

¶ **3304.20   SCC Rule 4**   © 1964, Commerce Clearing House, Inc.

(d) Floor reports should be written as legibly as possible to avoid receive and deliver exchange tickets or Comparisons being sent out which are not correct as to name, symbol or price.

(e) Specialists and other Members who deal for their own accounts on the Floor should send reports to their own offices or that of their clearing agents as promptly as possible.

.41 Form of exchange tickets.—Each Clearing Member is required to supply his own exchange tickets. Form of such exchange tickets must be submitted to Stock Clearing Corporation for approval before being printed.

Clearing Members with the facilities to do so, may, by special arrangement, send to the Corporation a pre-punched card or magnetic tape suitable for use in the Corporation's computers, instead of the aforesaid exchange tickets.

Amendment.
July 15, 1965.

.42 Preparation and submission of exchange tickets.—Each ticket must be legible, the required information must be shown in the proper space provided on the form, and each ticket must show:

The Clearing number of the Clearing Member to whom it is addressed, quantity of shares, official Exchange ticker symbol, value and the Clearing number of the executing broker or organization (account of).

(Note: Abbreviated firm title or Clearing Member's full name and abbreviated or full name of Cleared Securities may also be shown if desired, but not required.)

Receive and deliver tickets must be kept separate and sorted alphabetically by the first letter of each ticker symbol and delivered to the Central Receiving Department in special envelopes provided by the Corporation.

Do not send *DUPLICATE* exchange tickets to the Central Receiving Department at any time.

Stamp Bills

.43 Cleared securities.—Clearing Members are reminded that the regulations of the Federal and New York State transfer tax authorities in connection with Cleared Securities are as follows:

Every broker executing or effecting a sale, delivery or transfer where the taxes are paid through a clearing corporation shall impress by rubber stamp (1) on the certificate of stock or other corporate certificate where such certificate is delivered pursuant to a balance order issued by the clearing corporation, (2) on each page of a copy of the sale contract list and supplemental sale contract list retained by the broker, and (3) on the confirmation notices filed with the clearing corporation, covering sales of cleared securities made with their clearing brokers a certificate in substantially the following form:

New York State and Federal stamp taxes paid through

. . . .

(Insert name of clearing corporation.)

. . . .

Member Securities Exchange

¶ 3304 Continued

.44 **Non-cleared securities.**—In the case of all non-cleared contracts the seller must continue to deliver to the buyer a form of stamp bill on which must appear a rubber stamp imprint regarding the payment of Federal and New York State transfer taxes through the Corporation.

.45 **Trading on legal holidays in New York State.**—When the Exchange is open for business on a holiday in New York State, transactions in Cleared Securities made on such day shall be combined with those made on the preceding business day for the purposes of Clearance and Settlement; but each such day shall be treated separately for the purposes of comparison.

¶ 3305   Clearance Department

Clearance operation

Rule 5. Sec. 1. The Clearance Department will effect a separate Clearance Operation, based on the data received by it from the Central Receiving Department, for transactions effected on each business day.

Settlement prices

Sec. 2. The Corporation shall establish Settlement Prices for each Clearance Operation.

Clearance cost adjustment

Sec. 3. From the data received from the Central Receiving Department and the established Settlement Prices, the Corporation, through its Clearance Operation shall, with respect to each Clearing Member, ascertain the debit or credit balance in money, which is the difference between the amounts computed on the basis of the contract prices and the amounts computed on the basis of the Settlement Prices and shall charge or credit, as the case may be, such balance to the account of the Clearing Member in the Settlement Department on the day of the settlement for such Clearance Operation; provided, however, the Corporation may at any time, in its discretion, charge or credit to the account of a Clearing Member any balance so ascertained.

Balance orders

SEC. 4. From the resultant security balances established through the Clearance Operation, the Clearance Department will prepare and issue to Clearing Members a separate deliver balance order for each delivery of each security to be delivered, showing the Settlement Price established by the Corporation. The Clearance Department will similarly prepare and issue to Clearing Members receive balance orders showing the Settlement Price established by the Corporation.

Amendments.

May 1, 1947; July 18, 1947; May 17, 1948; June 21, 1948; September 29, 1952.

• • • *Supplementary Material:*

Explanatory Notes Regarding Clearance Operation

.10 **Clearance statement.**—Following the completion of each Clearance Operation the Clearance Department will issue to each Clearing Member a statement (Form 086 consisting of two parts, each part consisting of two sections, namely: Clearance Statement and Settlement Statement).

The Clearance section of said statement will show as to each Clearing Member the contract values of all transactions in Cleared Securities included in such Clearance Operation and the total amounts to be paid or received upon delivery of the resultant balances of securities computed at Settlement Prices.

The Settlement section of said statement will show as to each Clearing Member the clearance cash adjustment, debit or credit as the case may be.

¶ 3306   Central Delivery Department

Clearing Member and Non-Member Bank Division

Rule 6.   SEC. 1. The Central Delivery Department will receive envelopes, of the type approved by the Corporation, from Clearing Members and Non-Member Banks addressed to Clearing Members and Non-Member Banks on business days. Such envelopes will be sorted and made available to the authorized representatives of the Clearing Members and Non-Member Banks to whom they are addressed as provided in this Section 1.

Deliveries of envelopes (time schedule)

1. Deliveries of envelopes to the Central Delivery Department shall be made in accordance with the following schedule:

Classification of Deliveries	Final Delivery Time	Final Reclamation Time
Non-Member Bank to Clearing Member	12:00 M.	12:30 P. M.
Clearing Member to Clearing Member	12:00 M.	12:30 P. M.
Clearing Member to Non-Member Bank	12:30 P. M.	1:30 P. M.
Non-Member Bank to Non-Member Bank	1:30 P. M.	2:00 P. M.

Contents of envelopes

2. An envelope delivered to the Central Delivery Department shall contain only securities; tickets relating to securities contained in the envelope; or

¶ 3306   Continued

tickets covering "transfer as directed" items, or such other items as the Corporation may from time to time permit.

Credit lists

3. The envelopes shall be accompanied by a credit list, in duplicate, in form prescribed by the Corporation. The form of credit list to be used by Clearing Members when making deliveries shall be different from that to be used by Non-Member Banks. The credit list shall list each of the envelopes delivered with it and shall show the number of the Clearing Member or Non-Member Bank to whom each envelope is addressed and the total money value, if any, of the items contained in that envelope, and each credit list shall be totaled.

Accompanying tickets

4. Each separate item in an envelope shall be accompanied by tickets or orders, in duplicate, containing such information as may be necessary for the receiving Clearing Member or Non-Member Bank to identify the item. An envelope containing more than one item must also contain an adding machine tape of the money value of the items included in such envelope. The total shown on such tape must be the same as the money value recorded on the credit list for that envelope.

Stamping of credit lists

5. All envelopes delivered to the Central Delivery Department will be checked against the credit list which accompanies them to see that each envelope on the credit list has been received. If the envelopes delivered are properly listed on the accompanying credit list, the Corporation will stamp the duplicate credit list and make it available to the Clearing Member or Non-Member Bank who issued it. Receipted credit lists will be immediately available to the Non-Member Bank representative making the delivery. All envelopes listed on a credit list shall be deemed to have been accepted by the Corporation when the Corporation stamps the duplicate credit list on which such envelopes are listed, and at the time of such stamping the envelope shall be deemed for all purposes to have been delivered to the receiving Clearing Member or Non-Member Bank. Prior to the stamping of the credit list, envelopes will be held by the Corporation for the delivering Clearing Member or Non-Member Bank and after stamping for the receiving Clearing Member or Non-Member Bank.

Delivery of envelopes to receiver

6. The Corporation will sort the envelopes accepted by it and, subject to the right of the Corporation to hold property as security for the obligations of Clearing Members and Non-Member Banks, will deliver such envelopes at the Central Delivery Department to the authorized representatives of the Clearing Members or Non-Member Banks to whom they are addressed. The Corporation will not examine the contents of the envelopes nor verify the amounts of money shown on the credit list, and it shall not be responsible with respect thereto, except to deliver the envelopes accepted by it to the authorized representatives of the Clearing Members or Non-Member Banks to whom they are addressed.

¶ **3306   SCC Rule 6**

Accountancy

7. The Corporation when it stamps a credit list is authorized to, and will, credit the delivering Clearing Member's or Non-Member Bank's account with the amount shown on such stamped credit list and debit the receiving Clearing Member's or Non-Member Bank's account with the same amount.

Time schedule

8. Each Clearing Member shall send to the Central Delivery Department at frequent intervals and at 12:00 Noon and 1:30 P. M. on business days a representative authorized, pursuant to Rule 23, to receive envelopes delivered through the Central Delivery Department. Each Non-Member Bank shall send to the Central Delivery Department at frequent intervals and at 12:30 P. M., 1:30 P. M., and 2:00 P. M. on business days, a representative authorized, pursuant to Rule 23, to receive and receipt for envelopes delivered through the Central Delivery Department.

Reclamations

9. In case of any irregularity in an item, the receiving Clearing Member or Non-Member Bank may return such item to the delivering Clearing Member or non-member banks by putting such item in an envelope and delivering the envelope in the same manner as provided by this Section 1 for the delivery by Clearing Members and Non-Member Banks, except that the tickets in the envelope and the credit list accompanying the envelope, which are used in connection therewith, shall bear the legend "RECLAMATION." If such delivery of returned items is to be made through the Corporation it shall be made at Central Delivery Department on the day received in accordance with the schedule contained in Paragraph 1 hereof.

Designated value

10. The Corporation, upon receipt of an envelope addressed to a Non-Member Bank, the total money value of which as listed on the accompanying credit list is of $100,000.00 or more, will indicate such amount on the envelope. A Non-Member Bank's authorized representative will be advised, upon appearing at the Central Delivery Department to receive envelopes, of the approximate aggregate value of such envelopes as so indicated.

Lien for debit balance

11. The Corporation shall have a lien for any debit balance due it by a receiving Clearing Member on any property delivered to the Corporation or which may come into its possession as a result of deliveries made by other Clearing Members or Non-Member Banks through the Corporation and may exercise in respect thereof all the rights reserved to the Corporation under Rule 13 hereof.

Lien on property

12. The Corporation shall have a lien on any and all property which may be in its possession or under its control from time to time in which a Non-Member Bank has any interest whatsoever, for any and all amounts due or which may become due to it from such Non-Member Bank under the provisions of this Section 1 and with respect to said lien, the Corporation shall have and may exercise any and all rights and remedies to which it would be entitled under its Rules, (including, but without limitation, Rule 13), in the

¶ 3306   Continued

same manner and to the same extent as though such Non-Member Bank were a Clearing Member.

Crediting

13. Amounts which the Corporation has agreed to credit to a Clearing Member or to a Non-Member Bank on account of deliveries made to other Clearing Members or Non-Member Banks, pursuant to this Section 1, shall be credited in the Settlement Department from time to time during each business day and shall be included in the settlement for that day, pursuant to Rule 7.

Non-Member Division

Sec. 2.   The Central Delivery Department will, up to 12 Noon on business days, receive sealed envelopes, of a type approved by the Corporation, from Clearing Members and Non-Member Banks addressed to Non-Members and from Non-Members addressed to other Non-Members, Clearing Members and Non-Member Banks, and will sort such envelopes and make them available to the authorized representatives of Clearing Members, Non-Member Banks and Non-Members to whom they are addressed, as provided in this Section 2.

Contents of envelopes

1. An envelope delivered to the Central Delivery Department may contain only securities; tickets relating to securities contained in the envelope; checks; or such other items as the Corporation may from time to time permit.

Prescribed list

2. The envelopes must be accompanied by a list, in duplicate, in form prescribed by the Corporation. The list shall list each of the envelopes delivered with it and shall show the Clearing number of the Participant to whom each envelope is addressed.

Responsibility

3. The Corporation will not examine or verify the contents of the envelopes and it shall not be responsible with respect to such contents, its sole duty being to make the envelopes available to the Participant to whom they are addressed.

Value of envelopes

4. No envelope delivered to Central Delivery Department pursuant to this Section 2 shall contain securities or other property having aggregate value of more than Fifty Thousand Dollars.

Stamping of lists

5. All envelopes delivered to the Central Delivery Department, as provided in this Section 2, will be checked against the list which accompanies them to verify that each envelope on the list has been received. If the envelopes delivered are properly listed on the accompanying list, the Corporation will stamp the duplicate list and make it available to the Deliverer who issued it. All envelopes listed on such list shall be deemed to have been accepted by the Corporation when the Corporation stamps the duplicate list on which such envelopes are listed. Prior to the stamping of such list the envelopes

will be held by the Corporation for the Deliverer. After such stamping, (a) an envelope addressed to a Clearing Member or Non-Member Bank shall be deemed for all purposes to have been delivered to such receiving Clearing Member or Non-Member Bank and (b) an envelope addressed to a Non-Member will be held by the Corporation for the delivering Clearing Member, Non-Member Bank or Non-Member until 12:00 Noon and thereafter such envelope shall be deemed for all purposes to have been delivered to the receiving Non-Member.

Sorting of envelopes

6. The Corporation will sort the envelopes accepted by it and will make such envelopes available at the Central Delivery Department to authorized representatives of the Receiver to whom the envelopes are addressed.

Time schedules

7. Each Clearing Member, Non-Member Bank and Non-Member shall send to the Central Delivery Department at frequent intervals and at 12 Noon on business days, a representative authorized, pursuant to Rule 23, to receive envelopes delivered through Central Delivery Department.

Delivery of payment

8. The Corporation will not act with respect to the settlement for any items delivered pursuant to this Section 2 and has no responsibility whatsoever for the payment of such items. Checks in payment for such items may be placed in envelopes and such envelopes may be delivered to the Central Delivery Department by Clearing Members, Non-Member Banks and Non-Members in the same manner as a delivery as provided in this Section II. After 12 Noon on business days such checks may be delivered through the locked boxes located in the Distributing Department of the Corporation.

Certified checks

9. All checks in the amount of Three Thousand Dollars or more shall be certified before they are delivered to the Central Delivery Department or delivered through the locked boxes located in the Distributing Department, and all checks must be delivered before 2:00 P. M. on business days.

Withdrawal of Corporation

10. The Corporation may, in its discretion, at any time cease to act for a Non-Member, either with respect to a particular transaction or transactions or to transactions generally.

Amendments.
May 1, 1947; July 1, 1948; August 4, 1948; October 24, 1949; September 29, 1952; August 9, 1954.

¶ 3307   Settlement Department

Settlement of money payments

Rule 7. Settlement of Money payments between the Corporation and Settling Members and between Settling Members arising out of or based upon transactions or matters covered by Rules 5, 6, 9, 10, 11, 12, 20, 21 and 22 shall be made through the Settlement Department as provided in this Rule. The Corporation, through the Settlement Department shall debit or credit itself, and Settling Members with the amounts payable and receivable in accordance with the provisions of such Rules.

If at the close of any business day, a balance is due the Corporation from a Settling Member, a check on a bank or trust company in the vicinity of the Exchange, payable through the New York Clearing House Association, drawn to the order of Stock Clearing Corporation for the amount of such balance shall be delivered to the Corporation at the Settlement Department before 3 P. M. on business days. The check shall be certified if for $5,000 or over, unless it is the check of a bank which is a Non-Member Bank. If the check is in payment of a balance due by a Clearing Member, or Non-Clearing Member, it shall be a check of a member organization of the Exchange.

If at the close of any business day a balance is due a Settling Member by the Corporation, a memorandum of such balance in such form as the Corporation shall require shall be presented to the Corporation before 3 P. M. on business days. The Corporation shall make available to the Settling Member its check for the amount of such balance at the Settlement Department not later than 3 P. M. on business days.

A Settling Member shall pay Stock Clearing Corporation the whole or any part of his debit balance at any time on its demand. At the request of the Corporation, a Clearing Member or a Non-Clearing Member shall immediately furnish it with such assurances as it shall require of his ability to finance his commitments and shall conform to any conditions which the Corporation deems necessary for its protection and the protection of other Clearing Members.

Amendments.
August 4, 1948; September 29, 1952; May 1, 1953; August 9, 1954.

● ● ● *Supplementary Material:*

Explanatory Notes Regarding Settlement Operation

.10 **Settlement statement.**—The Settlement Statement (Form 086), showing the Clearance Cash Adjustment, furnished by the Corporation must be retained in the office of the Clearing Member until the day of the settlement for each such Clearance Operation. On the day of settlement, each Clearing Member shall complete and present to the Settlement Department before 3:00 P. M. Part 1 of such Settlement Statement showing the amount due to or due from the Corporation as the result of that day's Settlement Operation.

¶ 3308   Failure to Deliver on Security Balance Orders

Delivery of securities

Rule 8. If a Clearing Member shall not make delivery of all the securities to be delivered pursuant to a security balance order by 12 Noon on business days, the Clearing Member to whom the securities are to be delivered may cause such securities as are not so delivered to be bought in as provided for in the Rules of the Board of Governors of the Exchange.

If a Clearing Member shall refuse to receive all the securities deliverable to him pursuant to a security balance order and such refusal shall continue up to 12 Noon on business days, the securities the receipt of which is refused may be sold out as provided for in the Rules of the Board of Governors of the Exchange.

¶ **3307.10   SCC Rule 8**

If the delivery of securities under a securities balance order is not completed by 12 Noon on business days, the parties to deliver and receive respectively may enter into a new contract with respect to such transaction, or, if such securities are not bought in or sold out as hereinabove provided, and no such new contract is entered into, such parties shall be deemed to have entered into such a new contract which shall mature on the next business day. In either case, such parties alone shall be liable on such new contract, and the same shall not be included in any future Clearance Operation and any delivery and payment pursuant to such new contract shall be effected in the same manner as though the security was a Non-Cleared Security.

Amendments.
January 14, 1949; September 29, 1952.

¶ 3309   Marking to the Market

Exchange contract for the borrowing or loan of securities

Rule 9. SEC. 1. (a) Whenever both parties to an Exchange contract for the borrowing or loan of securities are Clearing Members and one of such parties makes a demand that such contract be marked to the market, pursuant to the Rules of the Board of Governors of the Exchange, he shall notify the other party of such demand by delivering such forms as may be prescribed by the Corporation to such other party through the Central Delivery Department up to Final Delivery time on business days, as prescribed by Rule 6. If such other party elects to have the amount so demanded charged to his account with the Corporation, he shall authorize such charge to be made on the form so prescribed. Such charge shall thereupon be effected by the Settlement Department by charging the amount so demanded and authorized to the account of the party from whom it is demanded and crediting the same to the account of the party making the demand.

In case of any irregularity in a Mark to Market, under this Section 1(a), the receiving Clearing Member shall make reclamation against the delivering Clearing Member in the same manner as provided in this Section 1(a) for the delivery of Marks to Market between Clearing Members except that the form or ticket shall bear the legend "Reclamation." Deliveries on reclamations may be made at Central Delivery Department not later than thirty minutes after the final time set for making deliveries.

(b) After Final Delivery time as above provided on business days, Clearing Members demanding such mark to market shall deliver to the office of the party upon whom the demand is made forms prescribed by the Corporation. If such party elects to have the amount so demanded charged to his account with the Corporation he shall authorize such charge on the prescribed form and the form with such authorization shall be presented to the Settlement Department at or before 2:45 P. M. Such charge shall thereupon be effected by the Settlement Department by charging the amount so demanded and authorized to the account of the party from whom it is demanded and crediting the same to the account of the party making the demand.

Exchange contracts other than contracts for the borrowing or loan of securities

SEC. 2. Whenever both parties to an Exchange contract (other than a contract for the borrowing or loan of securities) are Clearing Members and one of such parties makes a demand that such contract be marked to the market, pursuant to the Rules of the Board of Governors of the Exchange, he shall notify the other party on such forms as may be prescribed by the Corporation. If such other party elects to deposit the difference so demanded with the Corporation, he shall acknowledge the forms received from the first party and such forms shall be delivered in the manner prescribed in such forms to the Settlement Department at or before 2:45 P. M. on business days. Thereupon the deposit so demanded shall be effected by the Settlement Department's charging the account of the party from whom it is so demanded. The Corporation shall thereupon deposit the amount so charged in one or more special accounts in its name in banks or trust companies selected by it and all deposits made pursuant to this Section 2 by Clearing Members may be treated by the Corporation as a single fund and may be combined in one or more of such special accounts. All funds deposited in accordance with the foregoing shall be at the risk of the respective parties to the contract so marked.

The Clearing Member in whose favor a deposit with respect to a contract is made may, with the consent of the Corporation, assign such deposit or part thereof to another Clearing Member who assumes such contract for the purpose of marking to the market the identical transaction in question, and any such assignment made with the consent of the Corporation shall thereafter be deemed to be a deposit to the credit of the Clearing Member in whose favor the assignment is made. When either the contract has been consummated or there has been a change in market value reducing the amount of the deposit necessary, the deposit or part thereof shall be returned upon the request of the Clearing Member depositing the same. The Corporation before complying with a request for the return of a deposit or of part thereof may require the consent of the party in whose favor the deposit was made or his assignee or evidence satisfactory to it that the return of the deposit is authorized.

In case of default on an Exchange contract on which such deposit has been made, the Corporation shall apply such deposit, so far as it has not been withdrawn at the time of default, in such manner as in its judgment will protect the party in whose favor it was made or his assignee from any loss by reason of such default and it shall return any balance to the party making the deposit or to his legal representatives.

Amendments.
December 4, 1947; January 14, 1949; September 29, 1952.

¶ 3310   Federal and New York State Transfer Taxes

Regulations for Clearing Members

Rule 10.   SEC. 1. With respect to such Federal and New York State stock transfer taxes as are or may be payable pursuant to applicable laws and regulations by Clearing Members through the Corporation, each Clearing Member shall on each business day, at or before 10:00 A. M., file with the Settlement Department a report, on such form as may be prescribed by the Corporation, of the amount of such taxes on transactions of such Clearing Member and of others for whom he may be acting, which are due for settlement on that day. If no such taxes are so payable, a report so stating shall be filed at or before the time above provided.

The Settlement Department will debit the account of such Clearing Member with the amounts of taxes payable as shown in such reports and will in accordance with the applicable laws and regulations, remit or pay such amounts to the appropriate tax authorities.

Applications by Non-Clearing Members to have their names appear on list

SEC. 2. Member Organizations of the Exchange who are not Clearing Members may make application to the Corporation to have their names placed upon a list maintained by the Corporation, pursuant to Sec. 3 of Article VI of the By-Laws of the Corporation, of Non-Clearing Members for whom the Corporation will act in respect of the payment through the Corporation of Federal and New York State stock transfer taxes, such application to be accompanied by an agreement, in form prescribed by the Corporation, providing for the Corporation's so acting for the applicant in accordance with the provisions of this Rule.

Regulations for Non-Clearing Members

SEC. 3. (a) With respect to such Federal and New York State transfer taxes as are or may be payable pursuant to applicable laws and regulations by Non-Clearing Members whose names appear on the list provided for by Sec. 2 of this Rule, each such Non-Clearing Member shall at such times as may be prescribed by the Corporation, file with the Settlement Department a report, on such form as may be prescribed by the Corporation, of the amount of such taxes on transactions of such Non-Clearing Member, *other than transactions the taxes on which are included in the report of a Clearing Member as provided in Sec. 1 of this Rule.*

(b) Such a Non-Clearing Member may authorize a Clearing Member to sign the Non-Clearing Member's name and to file in his behalf the reports provided for by the foregoing Paragraph (a) and such Clearing Member may authorize the Corporation to debit his account in the Settlement Department with the amount of taxes payable as shown in the reports filed by him on behalf of the Non-Clearing Member.

(c) Each report filed by the Non-Clearing Member shall be accompanied by a check to the order of the Corporation for the amount of such taxes shown on such report, and each report filed by a Clearing Member in the name of a Non-Clearing Member shall be accompanied by such a check, unless the Clearing Member has authorized such amount to be debited to his account with the Corporation.

(d) The Corporation, upon receipt of such checks or upon making such debits to the account of such Clearing Member, will, in accordance with applicable laws and regulations, remit or pay the amounts so received or debited to the appropriate tax authorities.

Method of stamp bill delivery

SEC. 4. The Corporation may, from time to time, prescribe the method by and the manner in which a selling Clearing Member shall deliver a stamp bill to the buying Clearing Member.

Amendments.
December 4, 1947; May 1, 1953; February 1, 1954.

¶ 3311   Special and Special Intermediate Clearances

Contracts between Clearing Members having to do with securities

Rule 11. Subject to such special rules, regulations and directions as the Corporation may adopt or issue in any particular instance, this Rule shall be
applicable to such Special and Special Intermediate Clearances with respect to
contracts between Clearing Members having to do with any securities, as the
Corporation may from time to time undertake to handle.

Such Special and Special Intermediate Clearances shall be conducted
under the following conditions:

Responsibility of original parties

SEC. 1. Responsibility of original parties to cleared contracts shall remain
unaffected, except that original parties shall not have the right to have cleared
contracts marked to market; but parties ordered, as a result of these special
intermediate clearances, to deliver and receive balances of securities shall
have the right to require that such balances be adjusted to a new delivery
price through the Corporation, either through a general adjustment or through
separate individual adjustments, at the discretion of the Corporation. Clearing
Members may be substituted in these special intermediate clearances at the
discretion of the Corporation.

Obligation of participating parties

SEC. 2. Parties by participating in an intermediate clearance shall be obligated to participate in any further intermediate clearance or adjustment of
security balances to a new delivery price or final clearance by the Corporation,
and the orders to deliver and receive security balances resulting from intermediate clearances shall be entered on the clearing sheets of the parties
participating in each subsequent intermediate or final clearance.

Debit and credit cash balances

SEC. 3. Each party having a debit cash balance as a result of an intermediate clearance or an adjustment of security balances to a new delivery price
shall make a cash deposit to cover such debit balance, as directed by the Corporation. Such moneys shall be deposited by the Corporation as hereinafter
provided and shall be retained by it until there is a subsequent intermediate
clearance, adjustment of security balances to a new delivery price, final settlement, discontinuance of the clearance or until the Corporation determines that
the plan has been abandoned; in any case, cash so deposited shall be dealt with
in accordance with the rights of the parties to the clearance as may be determined by the Corporation. Credit cash balances due to parties to the clearance
shall be carried as credits to the parties by the Corporation until there is a
further intermediate clearance, adjustment of security balances to a new
delivery price, final settlement, discontinuance of the clearance, or until the
Corporation determines that the plan has been abandoned.

The Corporation may permit all or part of a Clearing Member's debit cash
balance to be evidenced by an open account indebtedness secured by unmatured
bearer bonds which are direct obligations of, or obligations guaranteed as to
principal and interest by, the United States, or unmatured bearer bonds which
are general obligations of, or obligations guaranteed by, a State or political subdivi-

¶ **3311   SCC Rule 11**   © 1960, Commerce Clearing House, Inc.

sion thereof, which are in the first or second ratings of any nationally known statistical service, having a market value not less than the amount of such open account indebtedness and having maturity dates as the Corporation may determine. Such bonds shall be pledged to the Corporation on such terms and conditions as the Corporation shall require.

The Corporation may fix the minimum amount of each Clearing Member's debit cash balance which must be deposited in cash and may from time to time increase or diminish such minimum amount. Each Clearing Member shall forthwith pay in cash all or such part of its open account indebtedness as the Corporation may request. The bonds pledged by a Clearing Member to secure its open account indebtedness may be held by the Corporation or for its account by a bank or trust company at the risk of the parties to the clearances. In case of loss of any such bonds, such loss shall be apportioned by the Corporation among the parties to the clearances in such manner and proportion as it shall deem equitable, and any such apportionment shall be conclusive on all parties to the clearances.

Deposits received by Corporation

SEC. 4. The aggregate amount of deposits received by the Corporation pursuant hereto shall be deposited by the Corporation in a special account or special accounts in its name in one or more banks or trust companies selected by it, but shall be at the risk of the parties to the clearances. In case of loss through insolvency of a depository or otherwise such loss shall be apportioned by the Corporation among such parties to the clearances and in such manner and proportion as it shall deem equitable, and any such apportionment shall be conclusive on all parties to the clearances.

Interests in cash deposits and pledged securities

SEC. 5. No party to such a clearance shall, without the prior written consent of the Corporation, sell, assign, transfer or in any manner pledge or encumber his interest in any such cash deposit or pledged securities.

Delivery of securities

SEC. 6. If the delivery of securities under a security balance order is not completed by delivery time limit, on a date subsequently to be determined by the Corporation, the failure to deliver shall be subject to and governed by the provisions of Rule 8.

Discontinue clearances

SEC. 7. The Corporation, at its discretion, may discontinue any clearance at any time.

Governing rules

SEC. 8. The same rules and principles, so far as applicable, shall govern the special clearance, including matters connected therewith arising out of the insolvency of a party thereto, as in the case of a regular clearance; and the judgment of the Corporation as to the applicability of such rules and principles shall be conclusive on all parties concerned in all respects.

Amendments.
October 6, 1959, effective October 9, 1959; May 23, 1960.

[The next page is 4621-3.]

¶ 3312   Settlement of Commissions

Regulations on Commissions

Rule 12. All payments of commissions due on business when a principal is given up between Clearing Members and Non-Clearing Members shall be settled monthly as follows:

(1) Each Payee shall make up bills in the customary form for all commissions due on business when a principal is given up and shall make out and sign a ticket, in form prescribed by the Corporation, showing the total amount due from and the name of each Payer.

(2) Each Payee shall deliver such ticket with the customary commission bill to each Payer on or before the 5th day of each month if a business day; otherwise the next succeeding business day.

(3) Each Payer shall promptly verify such bill and shall not later than 12 noon on the 10th day of each month, if a business day; otherwise on the next succeeding business day, deliver such tickets to the Settlement Department, accompanied by such forms as the Corporation may prescribe.

(4) The Corporation shall upon completion of the clearance of such tickets, debit and credit the respective Payers and Payees with resulting amounts plus or minus the charges for services rendered for which provision is made in Rule 20.

If, as a result of such clearance of commissions, a Non-Clearing Member shall be indebted to the Corporation, such Non-Clearing Member shall pay the amount due to the Corporation through the Settlement Department on or before the settlement day of each month, as determined by the Corporation. If such Non-Clearing Member shall be entitled to a credit, the Corporation will pay the same by check deliverable through the Settlement Department as soon as practicable.

If, as a result of such clearance of commissions, a Clearing Member shall be indebted to the Corporation or entitled to a credit, such debits and credits shall be included in the final settlement of the accounts of such Clearing Member in the Settlement Department for such day as the Corporation may determine.

The Board of Directors of the Corporation shall have power to determine the amounts received by it in the settlement of commissions and the persons entitled thereto and any determination so made shall be final and conclusive upon all parties to the settlement.

In case any commissions on business when a principal is given up shall be due to or from a member organization of the Exchange who is not a Clearing or Non-Clearing Member, all such commissions shall be paid or collected through a Clearing Member or a Non-Clearing Member.

Amendments.
January 14, 1949; May 1, 1953; February 1, 1954.

¶ 3313   Rights of the Corporation in Respect to Securities and Other Property Held

Lien on securities or property

Rule 13. The Corporation shall have a lien on any and all securities and other property held by it at any time or from time to time for the account of a Clearing Member for all amounts due or which may from time to time become due to it from said Clearing Member under its By-Laws or Rules. It shall have the right to borrow money and pledge for the repayment thereof all or any part of the securities or other property held by it for account of a Clearing Member, either alone or together with securities and other property held by it for account of other Clearing Members or otherwise and whether or not the amounts for which such securities or other property are so pledged shall exceed the debit balance of the Clearing Member. In case a Clearing Member shall become insolvent, as defined in Rule 16, or shall fail to pay his debit balance by the time required under the Rules or on demand, or in case the securities and other property held for his account by the Corporation shall become in its opinion insufficient to afford adequate security for his obligations to it or he shall fail on its demand to furnish additional collateral, the Corporation may, in its discretion, cause all or any of the securities or other property held by it for his account to be sold. Such sale may be made on the Exchange or on any other available market or at public auction or by private sale and may be made without further demand or notice to the Clearing Member. If the sale is made on the Exchange, or any other exchange, or in the over-the-counter market, or if the sale is at public auction, the Corporation may purchase for its own account the securities or other property sold.

The proceeds of sale shall be applied by the Corporation to the payment of the Clearing Member's debit balance and any surplus shall be paid over to the Clearing Member or his legal representative.

Amendments.
January 14, 1949; August 9, 1954.

¶ 3314   When the Corporation Declines to Act for a
Clearing Member Other than in
Cases of Insolvency

Refusal to act for Member
Responsibility of Corporation

Rule 14. SEC. 1. The Corporation may, in its discretion, at any time cease to act for
a Clearing Member either with respect to a particular transaction or transactions or to transactions generally. When it ceases to act for a Clearing Member with respect to a particular transaction or transactions, it will notify such
Clearing Member and such other Clearing Members, Non-Clearing Members,
Non-Member Banks and Non-Members as it deems proper and will determine
what steps are to be taken in the comparison operation, pending Clearance
Operation, Settlement or other transactions, in view of its so ceasing to act
for such Clearing Member. When the Corporation ceases to act for a Clearing
Member in transactions generally, it will notify such Clearing Member, other
Clearing Members, Non-Clearing Members, Non-Member Banks and Non-
Members. The notice that it has ceased to act for a Clearing Member given
by the Corporation shall state in general terms how pending transactions will
be affected.

Notice given before issuance of security balance orders

SEC. 2. (a) If notice that the Corporation is ceasing to act for a Clearing
Member in transactions generally, is given before the security balance
orders in a pending Clearance Operation have been issued, the Corporation
may, in its discretion, either eliminate from the comparison operation, or
such Clearance Operation, or both, all transactions to which the Clearing
Member to whom such notice is applicable is a party, or the Corporation
may complete either, or both of such operations, as though no such notice
had been given. If the Corporation eliminates such transactions from the
comparison operation, the exchange tickets covering such transactions
shall be made available for return to the Clearing Member from whom
they were received and such transactions shall be compared as provided
by the Rules of the Board of Governors of the Exchange. If the Corporation eliminates such transactions from the Clearance Operation, such
transactions shall be settled between such Clearing Member and the other
parties to the contracts and not through the Corporation. If the Corporation determines to complete the pending Clearance Operation, security
balance orders shall be issued by the Clearance Department as though
no such notice had been given and deliveries pursuant to such orders
and payments for securities delivered thereon shall be governed by the
provisions of Section 3 of this Rule.

Notice given after issuance of security balance orders

(b) If the notice that the Corporation has ceased to act is given after
the security balance orders have been issued, deliveries pursuant to such
orders and payment for securities delivered thereon shall be governed by
the provisions of Section 3 of this Rule.

Method of obtaining payment

SEC. 3. (a) After the Corporation has ceased to act for a Clearing Member
generally, it may accept from him envelopes to be delivered to other

Clearing Members (whether such deliveries are pursuant to security balance orders issued by the Corporation or are otherwise provided for in the Rules) or it may decline to accept any such deliveries, in which case such Clearing Member may make such deliveries to other Clearing Members and obtain payment therefor as provided in the Rules of the Board of Governors of the Exchange.

(b) After the Corporation has ceased to act for a Clearing Member generally, it shall decline to accept from other Clearing Members or from Non-Members and Non-Member Banks envelopes or orders to be delivered to such Clearing Member, in which case such other Clearing Members may make such deliveries to such Clearing Member and obtain payment therefor as provided for in the Rules of the Board of Governors of the Exchange and such Non-Member Banks and Non-Members may make such deliveries to such Clearing Member and obtain payment therefor as may be agreed between such Non-Member Banks and Non-Members respectively and such Clearing Member.

Rights and remedies of Corporation

SEC. 4. After the Corporation has ceased to act for a Clearing Member either in respect to a particular transaction or transactions generally, the Corporation shall nevertheless have the same rights and remedies in respect to any debit balance due from such Clearing Member or any liability incurred on his behalf as though it had not so ceased to act for him.

Clearing member insolvency

SEC. 5. The provisions of this Rule shall not apply in a case where a Clearing Member is insolvent, as defined in Rule 16, and in such cases the provisions of such Rule 16 shall govern.

Amendments.
July 18, 1947; January 14, 1949.

¶ 3315   Death, Expulsion or Suspension (Other than for Insolvency) of Sole Exchange Member of a Clearing Member Firm or Member Corporation

Clearing Member status

Rule 15. If the sole Exchange Member of a member firm which is a Clearing Member or the sole Exchange Member who is a director of a member corporation which is a Clearing Member, dies, or is expelled or suspended by the Exchange, other than for insolvency, the Corporation shall, upon receipt of notice thereof, cease to act for such Clearing Member, firm or corporation with respect to transactions generally, as provided in Rule 14, subject, however, to the provisions of the next paragraph of this Rule.

In the case of the death of the sole Exchange Member of a member firm which is a Clearing Member or the sole Exchange Member who is a director of a member corporation which is a Clearing Member, the Corporation shall not cease to act for such firm or corporation if and for so long as such member firm or member corporation is permitted by the Board of Governors of the

Exchange, pursuant to the provisions of Section 13 of Article IX of the Constitution of the Exchange, to have the status of a member firm or member corporation; subject, however, to the right of the Corporation to cease to act at any time as provided in Rule 14. The Corporation shall so cease to act upon any termination of such status in the same manner and to the same extent as though the death of such sole Exchange member had occurred at the time when such termination becomes effective.

Amendments
May 1, 1953; July 15, 1965.

¶ 3316   Insolvency of a Clearing Member

General provisions as to insolvency

Rule 16. Sec. 1. (a) A Clearing Member who fails to perform his contracts or is insolvent shall immediately inform the Corporation in writing that he is unable to meet his engagements.

(b) A Clearing Member shall be deemed to be and shall be treated in all respects as insolvent in the event specified in Paragraph (a) of this Section 1, or if he is suspended as a member firm or member corporation of the Exchange pursuant to the provisions of Section 1 or 2 of Article XIII of the Constitution of the Exchange.

(c) As used in this Rule, the phrase "time of insolvency" shall mean (i) the time when the Corporation receives notice from the Clearing Member that he is unable to meet his engagements, or (ii) the time when he is suspended pursuant to Section 1 or 2 of Article XIII of the Constitution of the Exchange, as the case may be.

(d) From and after the time of insolvency of a Clearing Member, the Corporation shall cease to act for him, except as hereinafter provided in this Rule. The Corporation shall as soon as possible after the time of insolvency notify the insolvent Clearing Member, other Clearing Members, Non-Clearing Members, Non-Member Banks and Non-Members that it has ceased to act for the insolvent Clearing Member pursuant to the provisions of this Rule and such notice shall state, in general terms, how pending matters will be affected and what steps are to be taken in connection therewith.

Effect of insolvency on Clearance Operations

Sec. 2. (a) All transactions of an insolvent Clearing Member effected on the day on which the time of insolvency occurs shall be excluded from the Clearance Operation with respect to that day's transactions and all exchange tickets covering such transactions which have been delivered to the Corporation shall be returned to the Clearing Members who issued the same.

(b) If the time of insolvency occurs when a Clearance Operation covering transactions effected by the insolvent Clearing Member on a day prior to that on which the time of insolvency occurs has not been completed, the Board of Directors, in its discretion, may determine either (i) that such transactions shall be excluded from such incompleted Clearance Operation, in which case the exchange tickets covering such transactions which have been delivered to the Corporation shall be returned to the Clearing Members who issued the same, or (ii) that such of the transactions of the insolvent Clearing Member as have been compared by the Corporation shall be included in such incompleted Clearance Operation and that such Operation shall be completed by the

¶ 3316 Continued

Corporation, in which case the provisions of Section 3 of this Rule shall apply to the security balance orders and the actions to be taken with respect thereto when the same are issued on completion of such Clearance Operation.

Close outs on account of insolvency

SEC. 3. (a) All transactions of the insolvent Clearing Member which are excluded from an incompleted Clearance Operation pursuant to the provisions of Sub-paragraphs (a) or (b)(i) of Section 2 of this Rule shall be closed out and the securities deliverable to or deliverable by such insolvent Clearing Member on each such transaction shall be sold out or bought as provided in the Rules of the Board of Governors of the Exchange.

(b) All transactions of an insolvent Clearing Member which have been or are included in a Clearance Operation as a result of which security balance orders have been or are issued by the Corporation shall not be closed out as provided in Sub-paragraph (a) of this section but securities deliverable to or deliverable by the insolvent Clearing Member pursuant to such security balance orders (except such securities as shall at the time of insolvency have been delivered pursuant to such orders) shall be sold out or bought in by the Clearing Members named in such security balance orders as provided in the Rules of the Board of Governors of the Exchange for the closing of contracts of an insolvent.

Accounting for profits and losses resulting from close outs on security balance orders

SEC. 4. (a) Separate accountings as to each business day, as hereinafter provided in Paragraph (b) of this Section 4, shall be had with respect to the profits and losses of other Clearing Members (computed on the basis of the Settlement Prices shown on the security balance orders) resulting from the buying in or selling out (as provided in Section 3) of securities deliverable to or by the insolvent Clearing Member under security balance orders calling for such delivery on such day; provided, however, that there shall not be included in any such accounting, profits or losses where the securities bought in or sold out should, pursuant to a security balance order, have been delivered prior to the time of insolvency.

(b) As to each separate accounting specified in Paragraph (a) of this Section 4:

(1) If a profit (other than a profit to be excluded from the accounting as provided in Paragraph (a)) results from the selling out or the buying in of securities deliverable to or deliverable by the insolvent Clearing Member under a security balance order, the Clearing Member realizing such profit shall at once send a statement of the transaction to the Corporation and shall pay over such profit to it. Such profit shall be applied by the Corporation to the payment of losses incurred by such Clearing Member or by other Clearing Members in selling out or buying in securities deliverable to or deliverable by the insolvent Clearing Member under other security balance orders calling for delivery on the same day.

(2) If a loss (other than a loss to be excluded from the accounting as provided in Paragraph (a)) results from the selling out or the buying in of securities deliverable by the insolvent Clearing Member under a security balance order, the Clearing Member sustaining such loss shall at once

© 1965, Commerce Clearing House, Inc.

send a statement of the transaction to the Corporation, which shall pay him the amount of the loss in the manner and to the extent hereinafter provided.

· (3) (i) If, in the aggregate, the selling out and buying in of securities deliverable to or deliverable by the insolvent Clearing Member under security balance orders calling for delivery on the same day results in a profit, said profit shall be credited to the account of the insolvent Clearing Member with the Corporation.

(ii) If in the aggregate, the selling out and buying in of securities deliverable to or deliverable by the insolvent Clearing Member under security balance orders calling for delivery on the same day results in a loss, the Corporation in its discretion may (1) pay the same or any part thereof to the Clearing Members sustaining such losses, and debit the net amount to the account of the insolvent Clearing Member with the Corporation or (2) pay the amount of the loss or such part thereof as the Corporation may not have paid pursuant to preceding clause (1), after the collection by it from other Clearing Members of the pro rata assessments for which provision is hereinafter made. If the Corporation determines to make such assessments, then those Clearing Members with whom the insolvent Clearing Member had the transactions included in the particular Clearance Operation (as hereinafter defined) which would have shown a loss to the insolvent Clearing Member if such transactions had been closed out under the provisions of Rules of the Board of Governors of the Exchange at the price at which the security balances were closed out, shall each pay to the Corporation a sum up to the amount of such loss, as soon as notice fixing such sum is received by them respectively from the Corporation. In the case of transactions in any security where there is no resulting security balance, the nearest even price to the last quotation at the time when it would have been closed out under the provisions of Rules of the Board of Governors of the Exchange is to be taken as the settlement price. The amounts so paid to the Corporation shall be credited to a special account, to which shall also be credited the profits resulting from the closing out of security balances deliverable to or deliverable by the insolvent Clearing Member. The amounts to the credit of said special account shall be applied in the following order: *first,* to reimburse the Corporation for differences paid out for account of the insolvent Clearing Member in connection with the particular Clearing Operation; *second,* to reimburse Clearing Members for losses sustained by them in closing out security balances deliverable to or deliverable by the insolvent Clearing Member on security balance orders of the Corporation; *third,* to reimburse the Corporation for any loss sustained by it by reason of the insolvency for which it will not otherwise be reimbursed by the remedies provided by these Rules or by the By-Laws; *fourth,* to reimburse pro rata the Clearing Members as herein provided for amounts paid by them to the Corporation on account of losses which would have been sustained in closing out transactions between them and the insolvent Clearing Member had such transactions in fact been closed out; *fifth,* if any amount shall remain, the same shall be paid over to the insolvent Clearing Member or his legal representative.

¶ 3316 Continued

The term "the particular Clearance Operation", as used in this Rule, shall mean the Clearance Operation as a result of which those security balance orders were issued, the profits or losses from the closing out of which are included in the particular separate accounting.

Amendments.
May 1, 1947; July 18, 1947; January 14, 1949; May 1, 1953; July 15, 1965.

¶ 3317   Loss from Insolvency of Non-Member Bank

Proration of losses

Rule 17.   If, in any transaction for the account of Clearing Members, the Corporation suffers a loss by reason of the insolvency of a Non-Member Bank the amount thereof shall be pro rated among the Clearing Members for whose account the Corporation was acting in such transaction, and each such Clearing Member shall pay to the Corporation on demand his pro rata part of such amount.

If any such loss so paid pro rata by Clearing Members is afterwards recovered by the Corporation in whole or in part, the net amount of such recovery shall be paid to such Clearing Members in proportion to the amounts paid by them, whether or not they are still Clearing Members.

Amendments.
January 14, 1949.

¶ 3318   Suspension of Rules

Extensions and waivers

Rule 18.   The time fixed by the Rules for the doing of any act or acts may be extended or the doing of any act or acts required by the Rules may be waived or any provision of these Rules may be suspended by the Board of Directors whenever, in its judgment, such extension, waiver or suspension is necessary or expedient.

¶ 3319   Action by the Corporation

Officers who may act for Corporation

Rule 19.   Except where action of the Board of Directors is specifically required by the Rules, the Corporation may act by its President or Vice President or by such other person as may be designated by the Board of Directors from time to time.

¶ 3320   Charges for Services Rendered

Charges to Clearing Members

Rule 20.   Sec. 1.   (a) Each Clearing Member who is a Clearing Member as of the close of business on the first business day of any month shall pay, as a basic service charge for such month, the sum of $40.00.

(b)(i) For every ten shares of stock recorded in each purchase and sale contract list 5/10ths of one cent, for every $1,000 par value of bonds two cents.

(ii) Where a Clearing Member submits to the Corporation pre-punched tabulating machine cards or magnetic tape in form acceptable to and approved by the Corporation, the charge in Sub-paragraph (i) above shall be reduced to 3½ 10ths of one cent for every ten shares of stock recorded on each sales contract list.

(c) For every ten shares of stock to be received and delivered as shown by the security balance orders issued by the Corporation 5/10ths of one cent, for every $1,000 par value of bonds two cents.

(d) For each Clearing Member and Non-Member Bank delivery envelope received and delivered through the Central Delivery Department five cents.

(e) For each Non-Member delivery envelope received and delivered through the Central Delivery Department three cents.

(f) For each mark to market debited or credited to his account five cents.

(g) For conducting special and special intermediate clearances

(1) For every ten shares of stock to be cleared on deliver exchange tickets, receive exchange tickets, and for every ten shares of stock on balances to receive and balances to deliver resulting from final clearance, 3/10ths of one cent.

(2) For every $1,000 par value of bonds to be cleared on deliver exchange tickets, receive exchange tickets, and for every $1,000 par value of bonds on balances to receive and balances to deliver resulting from final clearance, two cents.

(h) For each Commission Bill ticket debited or credited to his account, two cents.

(i) Notwithstanding the provisions of Paragraphs (a) to (g), inclusive, of this Section 1;

(1) if the aggregate of the debits and of the credits made during a calendar month in the Settlement Department pursuant to the provisions of Rule 6, Section 1 (hereinafter referred to in this Paragraph (i) as "aggregate debits and credits") to the account of a Clearing Member shall exceed $10,000,000.00, and

(2) if the aggregate of the charges for such calendar month due by such Clearing Member pursuant to Paragraphs (a) to (g), inclusive, shall be less than a sum computed on the basis of two dollars and fifty cents for each $100,000.00 (or fraction thereof) of such Clearing Member's aggregate debits and credits,

then, in lieu of the charges imposed for such month on such Clearing Member by the provisions of said Paragraphs (a) to (g), inclusive, such Clearing Member shall pay a charge for such month computed on the basis of two dollars and fifty cents for each $100,000.00 or fraction thereof of his aggregate debits and credits in such month.

(j) In cases of Cleared Securities consisting of rights or warrants, where the selling price is less than $1.00 per right or warrant, the charges under Paragraphs (b), (c), and (g)(1) of this Section 1 shall be at such rates (not in excess of the rates specified in such paragraphs) as the Corporation may determine in each case, in lieu of the rates specified in such paragraphs.

Charges to Non-Clearing Members

SEC. 2. (a) For the use of Distributing Department boxes, five dollars per month, payable annually.

(b) For services rendered in payment of Federal and New York State stock transfer taxes, five dollars per month, payable annually.

(c) For each Commission Bill ticket debited or credited to his account, two cents.

Charges to Non-Member Banks

SEC. 3. (a) Basic service charge for each month or any part thereof, $25.00.

(b) For each Clearing Member and Non-Member Bank delivery envelope received and delivered through the Central Delivery Department, five cents.

(c) For each Non-Member delivery envelope received and delivered through the Central Delivery Department, three cents.

Charges to Non-Members

SEC. 4. (a) Basic service charge for each month or any part thereof, $15.00.

(b) For each Non-Member delivery envelope received and delivered through the Central Delivery Department, three cents.

Charge for unusual expenses

SEC. 5. A Clearing Member or a Non-Clearing Member may be charged for any unusual expenses caused directly or indirectly by such Clearing Member or Non-Clearing Member, including but without limitation, the cost of producing records pursuant to a court order, or other legal process in any litigation or other legal proceeding to which such Clearing Member or Non-Clearing Member is a party or in which such records relating to such Clearing Member or Non-Clearing Member are so required to be produced, whether such production is required at the instance of such Clearing Member, Non-Clearing Member, or of any other party.

Amendments.
January 14, 1945; May 2, 1949; June 1, 1949; February 1, 1954; August 9, 1954; July 15, 1965.

● ● ● *Supplementary Material:*

.10 "Ten shares of stock."—For the purposes of Paragraphs (b), (c) and (g)(1) of Sec. 1, above, the term "ten shares of stock" shall be deemed to include ten rights or similar securities other than stock.

¶ 3321   Fines

Imposition of fines

Rule 21. The Corporation may impose a fine on a Clearing Member or a Non-Clearing Member for a violation of the Rules or for errors, delays, or other conduct embarrassing the operations of the Corporation, or for not providing adequate facilities for his transaction with the Corporation, provided, however, that no fine for any given offense shall exceed the sum of $250.00.

Such fine may be imposed and the amount thereof fixed by the President or First Vice President of the Corporation, provided, however, that a Clearing or Non-Clearing Member on whom a fine has been so imposed may within two business days after its imposition request that the matter be reviewed by the Board of Directors, which, if requested, shall give such Clearing or Non-Clearing Member a hearing and shall render a decision thereon which shall be final and conclusive. The Board of Directors may, whether or not a review is requested, reduce or remit a fine imposed by the President or Vice President.

¶ 3322 Bills Rendered

Submission of bills

Rule 22. The Corporation will render bills to Clearing Members for charges on account of the business of any month and for fines imposed during any month on or before the tenth day of the succeeding month and will charge the accounts of Clearing Members with the amounts thereof on or before such tenth day.

The Corporation will render such bills to Non-Clearing Members on or before the tenth day of such succeeding month and such bills shall be paid within ten days after such bills are rendered.

Such bills to Clearing and Non-Clearing Members shall not include the charges for settlement of commissions specified in Paragraph (i), Section 1, and Paragraph (c), Section 2, of Rule 20, for the payment of which charges provision is made in Rule 12.

Amendments.
January 14, 1949.

¶ 3323 Admission to Premises of the Corporation— Powers of Attorney, etc.

Presentation of credentials

Rule 23. No person will be permitted to enter the premises of the Corporation as the representative of Any Member unless he has first been approved by the Corporation and has been issued such credentials as the Corporation may from time to time prescribe and such credentials have not been cancelled or revoked. Such credentials must be shown on demand, and may limit the portions of the premises to which access is permitted thereunder. Any credentials issued pursuant to this Rule may be revoked at any time by the Corporation in its discretion, and prompt notice of such revocation shall be given to the employer of the person whose credentials have been so revoked.

Every person to whom, as the representative of a Clearing Member, Non-Member Bank or Non-Member, credentials have been or may hereafter be issued by the Corporation authorizing such person to have access, during the hours when securities or envelopes are to be received and delivered, to the portion of the Corporation's premises in which the Central Delivery Department is located, shall be deemed to have been authorized by such Clearing Member, Non-Member Bank or Non-Member to receive and deliver securities or envelopes in behalf of such Clearing Member, Non-Member Bank or Non-Member.

All Members shall, if any person in their employ to whom any credentials have been issued pursuant to this Rule or to whom a power of attorney or other authorization has been given to act for them in connection with the work of the Corporation shall for any reason cease to be so employed, give to the Corporation immediate notice in writing of such termination of employment and if any such power of attorney or other authorization is otherwise revoked or cancelled, shall likewise give to the Corporation immediate notice in writing of such revocation or cancellation. All credentials issued pursuant to this Rule shall be immediately surrendered to the Corporation upon their revocation by the Corporation or by the employer or upon the termination of the employment of the holder thereof.

Unless revoked by the Corporation, all credentials, authorizations, and powers of attorney issued pursuant to this Rule or in connection with the work of the Corporation shall remain in full force and effect until the Corporation shall have received written notice of the revocation thereof or of the termination of the holder's employment.

Amendments.
August 4, 1948; January 14, 1949; May 1, 1953; August 9, 1954.

• • • Supplementary Material:

Procedures for Obtaining Regular and Special Passes and Cards of Identification

.10 **Credentials.**—The Corporation will provide representatives of All Members with necessary credentials for entering its premises, as provided in Rule 23, subject to the following regulations:

(1) Regular Passes marked "S. C. C." will be issued upon application only to representatives of Clearing Members. Applications shall be made on prescribed forms and must be presented in person by the representative named in the application to the Corporation.

(2) Special Passes marked "Bank" will be issued upon application to representatives of Non-Member Banks. Applications shall be made on prescribed forms and must be signed by an officer of the Non-Member Bank, and presented to the Corporation in person by the representative named therein.

(3) Special Passes marked "N M" will be issued upon application to representatives of Non-Members. Applications shall be made on prescribed forms and must be presented in person by the representative named in the application to the Corporation.

(4) Cards of Identification will be issued upon application to representatives of Clearing Members not holding regular passes issued under (1) above and to representatives of Non-Clearing Members. Applications for such identification cards must be on own stationery and must be signed by the employer or by a person duly authorized by the employer under a power of attorney filed with the Corporation.

One or more names may be included in any one application. Supply the full name and a specimen signature of each representative for whom application is made. Applicants must appear in person.

All passes and cards will be issued promptly upon receipt of applications.

The Corporation may, in its discretion, limit the number of Regular Passes or Special Passes issued to representatives of any one Clearing Member, Non-Member Bank or Non-Member.

¶ 3324   Forms

Issuance of forms

Rule 24. In connection with any transactions or matters handled through, with or by the Corporation under or pursuant to the Rules, such forms of tickets, lists, notices and other documents shall be used as the Corporation may from time to time prescribe, and additions to, changes in and elimination of any such forms may be made by the Corporation at any time in its discretion.

● ● ● *Supplementary Material:*

Explanatory Notes and Information Regarding Form of Tickets, Lists,
Notices and Other Documents Prescribed in the Rules for
Use in Connection with Transactions Through,
with or by the Corporation

.10 **Prescribed forms.**—The principal forms prescribed for use in connection with the operations of the Corporation are furnished by the Corporation. Those forms which are not so furnished or which may be supplied by All Members, providing they are in acceptable form, are as follows:

03   Deliver Exchange Ticket
04   Receive Exchange Ticket
045   Deliver Ticket (For deliveries through Central Delivery Department)
615   Envelopes (For Member-to-Member Deliveries)
616   Envelopes (For Non-Member-Bank Deliveries)
617   Envelopes (For Non-Member Deliveries)

.11 **Supplies.**—Prescribed forms which are required to be completed in the offices of All Members may be obtained by listing requirements on Form 226, and delivering same before 2:00 P. M. on business days at the Stationery Window on the main corridor, 8 Broad St. The supplies will be placed in the locked boxes in the Distributing Department.

NEW YORK STOCK EXCHANGE
INDEX TO CONSTITUTION AND RULES

. . . a detailed topical index to the Constitution
of the New York Stock Exchange and to the Rules
of its Board of Governors—also a cross-reference
list from old to new Rule numbers . . .

TABLE OF CONTENTS

INDEX TO
CONSTITUTION AND RULES

References are to paragraph (¶) numbers

A

5 5 1 2   Index to Constitution and Rules   8-65
Report 106
➠➤ *References are to paragraph numbers.*

Affiliated companies of member organizations—continued
. disclosure of transactions to member organization 2321.32
. endorsement of obligations by member organization 2321.22
. form of organization............2321.11
. functions 2321.25
. name 2321.12
. new issues 2321.31
. non-voting stockholders 2321.16
. off-board transactions 2321.34
. offices 2321.26
. place of organization...........2321.11
. reports 2321.21
. severance of connection with....2321.33
. stock classes 2321.14
. stockholders' agreement 2321.17
. transactions with member organization 2321.29
. voting stockholders 2321.15

Age
. membership requirement 2301.10

Aggregate indebtedness
. computation 2325.10
. defined 2325
. limitation 2325
. partners' accounts 2325.15

Agreements
. A-B-C (See A-B-C agreement)
. arbitrage (See Arbitrage)
. audit (surprise) by accountants..2418.10
. borrowings, subordinated 2325.20
.. commission, prohibited 2369
. corporate
.. disposition of stock...........2312.21
.. documents 2312.28
.. "float" of net profits......2314.11(8)
.. non-assignment of stock......2313.24
.. stock ownership by non-member
........................2313.24
.. use and proceeds of seat......2314.20
. corporate affiliate
.. severance 2321.33
.. stockholders 2321.17
. customer (See Customer)
. indemnity, applicant for Exchange membership 2301.22
. loan, subordinated 2325.20
. partnership
.. articles (documents), submission of proposed 2312.26
.. continuing interest of deceased partner 2325.18
.. equities of partners..........2325.17

Agreements—continued
. partnership—continued
.. "float" of net profits......2314.11(8)
.. sole board member..........2314.28
.. use and proceeds of seat......2314.20
. registered representative 2345.17
. subordination (See Subordination Agreement)
. wires, private (See Wire and wireless connections)

Alarm, Civil Defense—procedure....2299A

All or none order 2013

Allied members
. business connections 2312.14
. cessation of status as general partner or holder of voting stock.....1512
. connection with former member corporation 1407
. death 1510
. defined 1003; 2002
. election as President of NYSE...1511
. examination 2312.12
. exclusion from floor..............1411
. expulsion 1510
. fixed interest in business..........2314
. Governors
.. rights 1051
. interest in business.......2314; 2314.11
. liability for acts of firm..........1666
. non-payment of fines............1513
. number allowed 1401
. outside activities 2318.11
. partners in member firm.........1408
. pledge 2312.18
. procedure for becoming..........1409
. qualifications 2312.12
. rights and privileges 1410
. sponsors 2312.20
. supervision by Board of Governors.1106
. transfer 1509
. voting stock in member corporation..1408

Alterations
. acknowledgments—noted by signing officer 2215
. assignment of securities
.. explanation 2197
.. signatures 2198
. instruments—explanation 2197
. powers of substitution
.. explanation 2197
.. signatures 2198

Alternates for members
. designation of 2303.20
. procedure 1414; 1415

Age

8-65
Report 106

Index to Constitution and Rules
➠ References are to paragraph numbers.

5513

Banks and bankers
. Stock Clearing Corporation list...3126; 3128

Beneficiaries
. Gratuity Fund 1753; 1754

Bids and offers
. acceptance binding 2079
. arbitrage 2437.18
. arbitrage, bona fide 2108
. below best bid—above best offer...2070
. binding 2079; 2085.32
. bonds other than convertible and
    U. S. Government...............2068
. cabinet securities
. . acceptance—what constitutes..2085.32
. . better bid or offer, recognition.2085.38
. . sequence of orders..............2085
. . special bids and offers........2085.41
. called securities 2072
. combining with orders.........2108.10
. commissions 2115.20
. convertible bonds 2067
. "crossing" orders 2076; 2076.10
. "delayed delivery" bond trades..2068.10; 2069
. disputes, how settled..... 2075; 2075.10
. "fourth-day" bond trades..2068.10; 2069
. less than trading unit......2061; 2061.10
. limitation on members'............2108
. members
. . parity 2108
. . precedence based on size........2108
. memberships 2301.21
. more than trading unit.....2061; 2061.20
. odd-lot dealers 2108; 2109
. odd lots 2061
. offsetting transaction made in
    error 2108; 2109
. one or two points or more away
    from last sale 2079A.30
. oral 2085; 2085.60
. . orders
. . written 2117
. parity
. . members 2108
. . registered traders ....2112(c); 2112.24
. . specialists ....2112.24(b)
. precedence 2071; 2072; 2072.10
. . bids equaling or exceeding offer..2072
. . bids for less than offer...........2072
. . free bonds 2072.30
. . members 2108
. . registered traders ....2112(c); 2112.24
. . specialists ....2112.24(b)
. priority 2072.10
. priority of first bid................2072

Bids and offers—continued
. prohibited dealings 2077
. publicity 2074
. quotation cards 2079A.50
. recognized quotations 2061
. registered traders
. . parity ....2108; 2112(c); 2112.24
. . precedence based on size 2108; 2112C; 2112.24
. reporters 2079A.70
. request to make better bid or
    offer 2079A.10
. round lots 2061
. sale removes bids from Floor......2072
. . subsequent bids 2072
. sell and buy orders coupled at same
    price 2078
. "seller's option" 2073
. simultaneous bids 2072
. special 2390A.12
. . after close of Exchange......2391.16
. . all or none 2391.13
. . authorization 2391
. . bonds 2391
. . conditions 2391
. . confirmations 2391; 2391.21
. . handling of transactions.2391; 2391.17
. . intent of rule................2391.10
. . limitation 2391
. . minimum period 2391; 2391.14
. . odd-lot orders 2391.19
. . other offers by bidder...2391; 2391.15
. . piecemeal 2391.13
. . preliminary information
    required 2391; 2391.11
. . reports 2391.20
. . special bid, defined............2391
. . stock 2391
. . stop orders 2391.19
. splitting 2072.20
. stocks
. . "cash" 2064
. . less than 100-share-unit........2065
. . "regular way" 2064
. . "seller's option" 2064
. tape 2079A.20
. transactions at wide variations.2079A.40
. transactions within ring.......2079A.60
. transfer of priority, parity and
    precedence 2072
. transmission of names of bidders,
    offerors, buyers or sellers.......2080
. U. S. Government bonds ..2062.10; 2066
. variations
. . bonds 2062
. . government bonds 2062.10
. . "part-redeemed" bonds 2062.20
. . stocks 2062

Bil

C

Con

Duties and powers
. Board of Governors.............1101
. chairman, Board of Governors....
                    ....1151-1154; 1156
. Emergency Committee 1831

Duties and powers—continued
. President 1251-1257
. vice-chairman, Board of Governors
 1201

E

Elections
. annual 1301
. Board of Governors
. . chairman
. . . eligibility for reelection.......1051
. . Governors
. . . eligibility for reelection.......1051
. . officers 1103
. . public representatives 1103
. . vice-chairman 1103
. eligibility for reelection
. . Chairman of Board.............1051
. . Governors 1051
. nominating committee 1302, 1303
. nominees
. . arrangement of ballot..........1304
. . death, withdrawal or disqualifica-
      tion of 1304
. . petition 1304
. positions to be filled.............1301
. postponement 1307
. President 1103
. public representatives, Board of
    Governors 1103
. quorum 1309
. tellers, appointment of...........1153
. terms of office..................1301
. tie vote 1305
. vacancies in board..............1306
. vice-chairman, Board of Governors
 1103
. votes required to elect...........1305
. voting privileges 1308

Emergency Committee
. composition 1832
. meetings 1833
. Special Committee 1101
. vesting of powers...............1831

Employees
. after-hours employment....2350; 2350.10
. bonding 2319
. closing of contracts—names of em-
    ployees authorized to close con-
    tracts 2054.10
. director or officer.............2346.15
. Floor employees (See Floor em-
    ployees)

Employees—continued
. members, allied members, member
    firms and member corporations
. . gratuities 2350; 2369
. . investigation before hiring 2345.19
. . nominal positions 2345
. . non-registered employees, duties
      and restrictions 2346
. . office in residence............2342.11
. . outside activities 2346.10
. . power of exchange over employees
      ....2345.18
. . press representatives 2349
. . records 2345.19
. . registered employees, duties and
      restrictions 2346
. . registration 2345
. . transactions with member or mem-
      ber organization ....<.....2407
. New York Stock Exchange
. . compensation or gratuities from
      members 2350
. . gratuities 2350; 2369
. . loans to or by.................2422
. . transactions with member or mem-
      ber organizations 2407
. non-members
. . compensation or gratuities from
      members 2350
. . transactions with member or mem-
      ber organization 2407
. officer or director.............2346.15
. powers of attorney (See Powers of
    attorney)
. records 2345.19
. Stock Clearing Corporation
. . compensation or gratuities from
      members 2350

Endorsed bonds
. delivery 2221
. reclamation 2269

Equipment trust certificates
. net capital computation...........2325

Erroneous
. reports—execution price of order..2411
. reports of orders.............2123A.45
. statement—specialists' orders..2123A.35

8-65
Report 106
Index to Constitution and Rules
5 5 3 3
➡️ *References are to paragraph numbers.*

5534 Index to Constitution and Rules 8-65
Report 106
➡️ *References are to paragraph numbers.*

L

M

Machine imprinted facsimile signatures
. forms of acknowledgment—member
     organizations ....pp. 2853-2857
. use by member organizations in as-
     signment of securities 2200.30

Maintenance margin requirements (See Margin)

Managers, branch offices of member organizations (See Branch offices)

Manager, branch office
. defined 2009

Manipulative operations
. members and member organizations
    2435

Margin
. accounts
. . report of customers' debit and credit
     balances 2421.40
. "conditional rights to subscribe,"
     transactions and positions in..2431.10
. consolidation of accounts.........2431
. customer, defined 2432.40
. daily record 2432
. . form 2432.10
. equity 2431
. exempted securities.......2431, 2431.10
. government obligations 2431
. guaranteed accounts 2431
. initial...........................2431
. international arbitrage accounts....2431
. joint accounts in which member has
     interest 2431
. "long" and "short" positions in ex-
     changeable or convertible securi-
     ties 2431
. maintenance margin rule 2431
. . exceptions 2431, 2431.10
. meeting margin calls by liquidation
     ....2431; 2432
. . report 2432.50-2432.80
. offsetting "long" and "short" posi-
     tions in same security..........2431
. omnibus accounts 2432.30
. puts, calls and other options......2431
. records
. . omnibus accounts, special agree-
     ment 2432.30
. . place maintained 2432.20
. specialists' accounts 2431
. . joint account carried by member
     organization 2431
. time within which obtained 2431

Margin—continued
. value determination for margin pur-
     poses 2431
. "when issued" and "when distrib-
     uted" securities 2431

Market
. advertising (See Advertising)
. conduct of members 2110
. demoralization of—penalty........1654
. making disclosure ....2474A.10(2)
. marking
. . clearing members 3309
. marking to market
. . demands 2165
. . . procedure 2166
. . deposits thru clearing members
    2167
. . failure to comply 2168
. . failure to comply with demand..2168
. . payment 2165
. missing the market 2091
. . commissions 2375
. orders (See Orders)

Market letters
. approval before distribution.......2472
. defined 2472.10
. standards 2474A.10

Market order—See also Orders
. broker's obligation 2123A.41
. defined 2013
. precedence over limited orders 2115A.20

Marking of orders (See Orders)

Marking to market (See, also, Market)
. amount
. . time for determination 2431

Matching
. specialists 2104A.10

**Means of communication (See Com-
munication, means of)**

**Mechanically reproduced facsimile sig-
natures**
. forms of acknowledgment—member
     organizations ....pp. 2853-2857
. use by member organizations in as-
     signment of securities ...2200; 2200.30

Meetings
. Board of Directors—Stock Clearing
     Corporation 3052-3053
. Board of Governors 1102
. . special meetings 1152, 1252

5 5 3 8   Index to Constitution and Rules   8-65
Report 106
➡ *References are to paragraph numbers.*

Mem

8-65
Report 106
Index to Constitution and Rules
➡ *References are to paragraph numbers.*
5539

New York Stock Exchange—continued
. membership requirements, etc. (See
  Membership)
. objects of 1002
. rules, Board of Governors (See Rules
  of Board of Governors)
. time—local New York City time...2023

Nine-bond rule
. off-floor transactions in bonds.....
  ....2396; 2396.10

Nominal positions—restrictions......2345

Nominal transfer of membership (See
  Membership)

Nominating committee
. composition of 1302
. meetings 1303

Nominees
. New York Stock Exchange offices..1304
.. death, withdrawal or disqualification 1304
. proxies 2455

Non-cleared securities (Stock Clearing
  Corporation)
. defined 3301
. stamp bills 3304.43

Non-clearing members (Stock Clearing
  Corporation)
. defined 3301

Non-delivery of securities (See Delivery
  of securities)

Non-members
. books kept by member.........2343.12
. clearance charges 2381.18
. defined 1003; 2002
. employees (See Employees)
. employees of, compensation or gratuities from members...........2350
. Governors
.. duties 1051
.. rights 1051
. joint accounts with, commissions..2374
. ticker service 2359.12
. wire, etc. connections.......2355; 2359

**Non-member corporations and associa-
  tions**
. business connections, disapproval..2331
. joint offices 2334
. member acting as broker for corporation controlled by 2332
. participation in commissions.....2333
. responsibility for controlled corporations 2335

Non-voting stock
. defined 1003; 2002

"Not held" orders
. broker's handling 2123A.44
. defined 2013

Notice
. application for approval of admission of participant in existing
  member organization 2312.24
. application for approval of formation and admission of member organization 2312.24
. arbitration proceedings...........2487
. bulletin board
.. application for approval of admission of participant in existing
  member organization 2312.24
.. application for approval of formation and admission of member
  organization 2312.24
.. proposed transfer of membership
  ....2301.26
.. transfer of membership........1502
. closing contracts
.. closed 2288
.. intention to close 2284
... successive parties 2285
. contract, seller's option 2179
. loans
.. money, return of 2160
.. securities, return of 2160
. member corporations to Exchange
.. proposed change in
... charter, certificate of incorporation, by-laws 2312
... directors or officers..........2312
... stockholdings 2312
. member organizations to Exchange
.. cessation 2312
.. commencing to carry accounts or
  hold securities 2415
. member organizations to Exchange—
  continued
.. dissolution of member organization 2312
. member to Exchange
.. death of partner..............2312
.. proposal to admit person as participant in member organization
 2311
.. proposal to become participant in
  member organization 2311
.. proposal to form member organization 2311
.. retirement of participant or officer
 2312
. proposed transfer of membership..2301.26
. seller's option contract 2179

P

Q

8-65
Report 106
Index to Constitution and Rules
5 5 4 5
➡➤ *References are to paragraph numbers.*

Quorum
. Board of Directors—Stock Clearing
  Corporation 3054
. Board of Governors..............1102
. Gratuity Fund—meetings of trus-
  tees 1804
. New York Stock Exchange elections. .1309
. stockholders—Stock Clearing Cor-
  poration 3029

Quotation sheets
. advertising 2438

Quotation wire service
. Exchange and member offices 2036;
                                  2036.10

Quotations
. advertising in quotation sheets.....2438
. Board of Governors, supervision...1106
. bonds, free 2079A.50
. broadcasting, radio and television. .2473
. cards—free bonds 2079A.50
. recognized quotations — bids and
  offers 2061
. request for quotations—method of
  handling 2123A.60
. specialist's quotation for own account 2104.10
. telephone quotation lines—installation or disconnection of......2036.10

R

Radio
. permission to broadcast........2346.10;
                              2473; 2473.10
. . standards 2474A
. private system
. . consent of Exchange.......2355; 2359
. . discontinuance by Exchange.....2356

Real estate
. net capital computation.........2325.15

Reclamation of securities
. defined 2265
. replacement of returns 2267
. time limit
. . called security 2273
. . endorsed bonds 2269
. . exchangeable certificates 2270
. . lost or stolen 2272
. . married women 2274
. . payment prohibited or restricted. .2272
. . questionable title 2272
. . security with irregularity...2266; 2268
. . special cases 2275
. . transfer prohibited or restricted. .2272
. . without time limit 2272
. . wrong security delivered 2271

Recording
. transactions in customers' accounts
  ....2411.40

Records (See also Books and records)
. cost of production 2025
. duty of members to keep 2440
. employee 2345.19
. failure to produce 1659; 1661
. margin accounts (See Margin)
. proxies 2451.30; 2452.16; 2452.20
. specialists' income 2104.50
. specialists' records of transactions..
  ....2091.10

Records—continued
. Stock Clearing Corporation........3241
. transactions
. . availability 2131

Redemption
. due-bills 2259
. securities called for redemption
. . delivery
. . . coupon bonds 2218
. . . registered bonds 2217
. . . stock 2217

Reduction of orders (See Orders)

Registered representative
. defined 2010
. leave of absence...............2346.16
. limit of credit on own accounts....2348
. supervision of 2342.16

**Registered Trader (See Floor trading
rules)**

Registration
. addresses of members 2341
. fees
. . branch offices 2342.10
. . report form 120A 2440H.10
. Floor employees 2035
. international arbitrage non-member
  correspondents.............2437.26
. odd-lot brokers and dealers 2101
. fee 2103.10
. registered traders ....2111(a)
. representatives—see Representatives
. securities
. . registration required under Securi-
    ties Exchange Act of 1934 before
    admission to trading 2495E.10
. specialists 2103; 2103.10

Regular specialists (See Specialists)

Regular way delayed delivery
. delivery of securities 2179

Release
. financing of memberships 2301.32

Released endorsed bonds
. delivery 2222
. reclamation .2269

Relief clerks
. badges 2035.30
. regulations 2035.20
. tickets 2035.10

Relief specialists (See Specialists)

Remission of penalties (See Penalties)

Removal
. chairman, Board of Governors. 1109
. Governors 1109
. President 1109
. securities from listing
. action of Exchange. 2499-2499.40
. . request of issuer 2500
. . Securities Exchange Act of 1934—
    provisions regarding delisting. .
    . . . . .2501A.10
. trustees, Gratuity Fund 1109

Reopening contracts
. restriction of—members and member
    organizations 2435
. transaction without order 2117.20

Reports
. affiliated companies of member or-
    ganizations 2321.21
. application for listing 2495D.10
. arbitrage, international 2437.23
. borrowings 2420; 2420.10
. collateral loans 2421.30
. commissions (form 600) . . . . .2440 I
. exchange distributions and acquisi-
    tions 2392
. financial information 2425
. foreigners, purchases and sales by
    . . . . .2440E
. handling 2123A.60
. "Haupt expenditures" recovery (form
    601) 2440L
. "Haupt expenditures" recovery (form
    601A) 2440M
. income and expense 2425
. joint accounts, participation in . . . . .
    .2423; 2423.10
. liquidations to meet margin calls
    (Form MF-1) . . . . . . .2432.50—2432.80
. loans 2420; 2420.10
. margin account debit and credit bal-
    ances 2421.40

Reports—continued
. margin—liquidation to meet (Form
    MF-1) 2432.50-2432.80
. notice by member organization com-
    mencing to carry accounts or hold
    securities .2415
. options—listed securities. . .2424; 2424.10
. periodic reports. 2421
. list 2440D
. registration fees (form 120A). . . .2440H
. secondary distributions 2393.17
. security underwritings 2421.20
. short positions 2421.10
. special bids 2391.20
. special offerings 2391.20
. specialists
. . financing on special basis (form
    SPC) .2104.40
. . public customers (form SPA). .2113.10
. . purchases and sales initiated on
    Floor (Form 81) 2104A.50
. "stopped" securities 2116.10
. temporary specialists 2104.17
. transactions
. . discretionary 2095.10
. . members to offices 2131
. . odd lots (form 600A). 2440J
. . own accounts 2440G.10
. . round lots 2440F.10
. transactions initiated or originated
    by members on Floor 2112.30

Representatives
. agreements 2345.17
. compensation 2347
. examinations 2345.15
. fee for application for employment
    . . . . .2345.16
. leave of absence. 2346.16
. limit on credit on own accounts. . . .2348
. members of exchange 2345.12
. nominal positions 2345
. office in residence 2342.11
. outside activities 2346.10
. press (see Employees)
. public, Board of Governors 1103
. . bonuses .2347
. registered
. . compensation 2347; 2348; 2348.10
. registered representative, defined. .
    . . . . .2009; 2010
. registration 2345
. . application 2345.11
. termination of employment 2345.13
. transfer .2345.14

Research reports
. approval before distribution. 2472
. defined .2472.10
. standards 2474A

S

8-65
Report 106

Index to Constitution and Rules
➤➤ References are to paragraph numbers.

5 5 4 9

8-65
Report 106
Index to Constitution and Rules
➡➡➤ *References are to paragraph numbers.*
5 5 5 1

5552

5 5 5 2   Index to Constitution and Rules   8-65
Report 106
➡➡ *References are to paragraph numbers.*

Stock Clearing Corporation—continued
. by-laws—continued
. . lists to be maintained
. . . cleared securities 3125
. . . clearing or settling contracts...3127
. . . deliveries, receipts and payments..3128
. . . lenders 3126
. . meeting of stockholders
. . . annual 3025
. . . list of stockholders open to
        inspection 3031
. . . notice 3028
. . . place 3027
. . . quorum 3029
. . . special 3026
. . . voting 3030
. . notice
. . . adjourned meeting 3226
. . . attendance at meetings 3225
. . officers 3075-3078
. . . appointment 3075
. . . compensation 3091
. . . removal 3077
. . . powers and duties 3076
. . . vacancies 3078
. . part of terms and conditions of
        contracts cleared or settled thru
        Corporation 1552
. . proxies 3194
. . rules, controlling 3175
. . . sale or transfer of securities....3193
. . signing of:
. . . checks, drafts, endorsements...3192
. . . deeds, leases, contracts.......3191
. . . surplus and dividends.........3160
. capital stock
. . certificates 3211
. . . lost, stolen, destroyed 3214
. . record of stockholders.........3212
. . transfers 3213
. central delivery department
. . clearing member division 3306
. . non-member bank division 3306
. . non-member division..........3306
. central receiving department
. . regulations 3304
. certificate of incorporation....3001-3011
. . by-laws 3011
. . capital stock 3004
. . . number and par value of shares..3005
. . directors 3008
. . . initial 3009
. . duration 3007
. . name 3002
. . preamble 3001
. . principal office 3006
. . purposes 3003
. . subscribers 3010

Stock Clearing Corporation—continued
. charges for services rendered
. . clearing members 3320
. . non-clearing members 3320
. . non-member banks 3320
. . non-members 3320
. . unusual expenses 3320
. clearance department
. . clearance operation 3305
. . statement 3305.10
. clearance of contracts 3102
. clearance operations
. . defined 3301
. . effect of insolvency 3316
. cleared securities
. . defined 3301
. . foreign sovereignty 3302.12
. . insolvent banks 3302.11
. . list 3302.10
. . stamp bills 3304.43
. cleared securities list 3125
. cleared transactions 3302
. clearing fund
. . contributions — cash; "exempt"
        bonds 3151
. . . decrease 3158
. . . increase 3157
. . . return 3156
. . liabilities guaranteed 3155
. . liability of member, discharge....3153
. . loss in excess of contribution....3154
. . recovery of loss 3159
. . use 3152
. Clearing House Comparison Service
        ....3301; 3304
. clearing members
. . defined 3301
. . duties 3302
. commissions 3312
. comparison of transactions...2132; 3304
. . central receiving department 3304
. . Clearing House Comparison Service
        ....3301; 3304
. . comparison notice 2132
. . contract lists 2132
. . deliver exchange tickets 2132
. contract lists 3304
. . confirmations 3304
. . deletions 3304
. contracts between clearing members..3311
. contracts, Exchange—cleared or set-
        tled thru Corporation
. . by-laws of Corporation deemed
        part of 1552
. . delivery and payment 1553

5 5 5 4
Index to Constitution and Rules
➡ *References are to paragraph numbers.*
8-65
Report 106

Stock Clearing Corporation—continued
. non-member banks
. . defined 3301
. non-members
. . defined 3301
. notice
. . Corporation ceasing to act for
    member 3314
. notice to members.................3105
. office, executive 3251
. officers
. . action for corporation 3319
. . appointment 3075
. . authorization in assignment of se-
    curities on behalf of members
    and member organizations.....2200
. . compensation 3091
. . duties 3076
. . powers 3076
. . removal 3077
. . restriction on NYSE member,
    making transaction in listed se-
    curity 2054
. . vacancies 3078
. orders for receipt or delivery of se-
    curities, effect 2143
. payment on delivery of securities..2183
. principal departments 3252
. proxies 3194
. quorum
. . Board of Directors 3054
. . meeting of stockholders........3029
. refusal to act for member.........3314
. refusal to act in clearance in partic-
    ular case 1553
. removal of members.............3315
. reports, delivery of..............3304
. resources limited to clearing mem-
    bers only 3101
. rules
. . applicability to closing of contracts
    —suspension for insolvency....2282
. rules—continued
. . part of terms and conditions of
    contracts cleared or settled thru
    Corporation 1552
. . suspension of 3318
. sales ticket—tax 2194
. securities
. . defined 3301
. . receipt or delivery of—orders....2143
. settlement department
. . money payments 3307
. . . statement .....!...........3307.10
. settlement of contracts
. . defined 3301
. settlement prices—clearance oper-
    ation 3305

Stock Clearing Corporation—continued
. settling members
. . defined 3301
. signatures of clearing members....3304
. special and special intermediate clear-
    ances 3311
. . defined 3301
. . deposits—cash; "exempt" bonds...3311
. . mark to new delivery price......3311
. stamp bills
. . method of delivery.............3310
. stockholders
. . list open to inspection..........3031
. . meetings 3025; 3026; 3027; 3028
. . quorum 3029
. . voting 3030
. summaries
. . central receiving department....3304
. surplus and dividends............3160
. suspension
. . individual clearing member......3315
. . sole Exchange member of a clear-
    ing member firm or corporation..3315
. suspension of rules 3318
. tickets, delivery of...............3304
. time schedules 3304.10
. transfer taxes
. . clearing members 3310
. . non-clearing members 3310
. use of securities or property.......3313
. vacancies
. . board of directors.............3057

Stock clerks
. badges 2035.30
. regulations 2035.20
. tickets 2035.10

**Stockholders—Stock Clearing Corpora-
tion** (See Stock Clearing Corporation)

Stockholders
. member corporations
. . agreement with Exchange.....2313.24
. . list 2313.23

Stop limit order 2013

Stop orders
. cabinet securities 2085.42
. defined 2013
. odd-lot 2100
. specialist's responsibility 2123A.40

"Stopped" securities
. agreement constitutes guarantee....2116
. bonds—bids or offers in cabinets.2085.43
. handling 2115A.20
. limitation 2116.20
. publication of transactions.....2125A.16
. report to customers............2116.10

T

8-65
Report 106
Index to Constitution and Rules
➡ *References are to paragraph numbers.*
5 5 5 7

W

Warrants
. commissions 2380
. ex-warrants 2236

"When distributed" securities
. bids and offers 2063
. cash accounts 2431
. commissions (See Commissions)
. contract form 2137A.30
. margin accounts 2431
. short sales 2440B.16

"When distributed" transactions
. commissions, collection 2381

"When issued" contracts
. net worth, effect 2325; 2325.15

When issued or when distributed contracts
. clearance of contracts............3302
. comparison of contracts..........3304
. exchange of contracts ...2137; 2137A.30

"When issued" securities
. bids and offers 2063
. cash accounts 2431
. commissions (See Commissions)
. contract form 2137A.30
. margin accounts 2431
. short sales 2440B.16

"When issued" transactions
. commissions, collection 2381

Wire and wireless connections
. agreement by non-member 2359
. consent of Exchange 2356
. costs
. . joint account arbitrage 2358
. . payment by member organization
   for other member organization
   ....2359.14
. . sharing 2359.10
. discontinuance by Exchange 2356
. Exchange and members' offices....
   ....2036; 2036.10
. file of communications—private wire
  2357
. give-ups 2359.16
. prohibited wire connections.....2359.13
. ticker service 2359.12

"Wire" business give-ups (See Give-ups)

Wire connections (See Wire and wireless connections)

Wire costs, sharing of (See Costs)

Writing activities ..
. consent of Exchange ...2318.11; 2346.10
. standards 2474A

Written orders
. member for member transaction...2117
. member to specialist..........2123A.20

[The next page is 5601.]

Cross-Reference List

(From Old to New, New York Stock Exchange Rule Numbers)

Former Rule	Current Rule	Par.	Former Rule	Current Rule	Par.	Former Rule	Current Rule	Par.
1	1	2001	131	80	2080	188	202	2202
2	2	2002	132	116	2116	189	203	2203
3	3	2003	133	78	2078	190	204	2204
4	4	2004	134	117	2117	191	205	2205
5	5	2005	135	118	2118	192	206	2206
6	6	2006	136	119	2119	193	207	2207
7	7	2007	137	46	2046	194	208	2208
8	8	2008	138	47	2047	195	Rescinded	
9	Rescinded		141	131	2131	196	Rescinded	
10	9	2009	142	132	2132	197	209	2209
11	10	2010	143	133	2133	198	210	2210
12	11	2011	144	134	2134	199	211	2211
13	12	2012	145	135	2135	200	212	2212
26	21	2021	146	136	2136	201	213	2213
27	22	2022	147	137	2137	202	214	2214
28	23	2023	148	138	2138	203	215	2215
29	25	2025	149	139	2139	204	216	2216
30	24	2024	150	140	2140	205	217	2217
100	45	2045	151	141	2141	206	218	2218
101	51	2051	152	142	2142	207	219	2219
102	52	2052	153	143	2143	208	220	2220
103	53	2053	160	175	2175	209	221	2221
104	54	2054	161	176	2176	210	222	2222
105	55	2055	162	177	2177	211	223	2223
106	56	2056	163	178	2178	212	224	2224
107	61	2061	164	179	2179	213	225	2225
108	63	2063	165	180	2180	214	200	2200
109	64	2064	166	181	2181	224	265	2265
110	66	2066	167	182	2182	225	266	2266
111	67	2067	168	183	2183	226	267	2267
112	68	2068	169	184	2184	227	268	2268
113	69	2069	170	185	2185	228	269	2269
114	65	2065	171	186	2186	229	270	2270
115	85	2085	172	187	2187	230	271	2271
116	79	2079	173	188	2188	231	272	2272
117	61	2061	174	189	2189	232	273	2273
118	70	2070	175	190	2190	233	274	2274
119	71	2071	176	191	2191	234	275	2275
120	72	2072	177	192	2192	250	151	2151
121	71	2071	178	193	2193	251	152	2152
122	72	2072	179	194	2194	252	153	2153
123	73	2073	180	195	2195	253	154	2154
124	74	2074	181	195	2195	254	155	2155
125	75	2075	182	196	2196	255	156	2156
126	62	2062	183	197	2197	256	157	2157
127	76	2076	184	198	2198	257	158	2158
128	123	2123	185	199	2199	258	159	2159
129	77	2077	186	201	2201	259	160	2160
130	122	2122	187	200	2200	260	161	2161

Cross-references

Former Rule	Current Rule	Par.	Former Rule	Current Rule	Par.	Former Rule	Current Rule	Par.
270	281	2281	366	121	2121	483	377	2377
271	282	2282	367	101	2101	484	378	2378
272	283	2283	368	102	2102	485	379	2379
273	284	2284	369	93	2093	486	380	2380
274	285	2285	370	95	2095	487	381	2381
275	286	2286	371	96	2096	490	391	2391
276	287	2287	372	108	2108	491	391	2391
277	288	2288	373	109	2109	492	391	2391
278	289	2289	374 Rescinded			493	391	2391
279	290	2290	375	110	2110	494	391	2391
280	291	2291	401	311	2311	495	391	2391
281	292	2292	402	312	2312	496	391	2391
282	293	2293	403	313	2313	497	391	2391
283	294	2294	404	314	2314	498	392	2392
290	165	2165	405	315	2315	500	401	2401
291	166	2166	406	316	2316	501	402	2402
292	167	2167	407	317	2317	502	403	2403
293	168	2168	408	318	2318	503	404	2404
300	235	2235	409	319	2319	504	405	2405
301	236	2236	409	320	2320	505	405	2405
302	237	2237	415	325	2325	506	405	2405
303	238	2238	416	325	2325	507	406	2406
304	239	2239	420	331	2331	508	407	2407
305	240	2240	421	332	2332	509 Rescinded		
306	241	2241	422	333	2333	510	407	2407
307	242	2242	423	334	2334	511	406	2406
308	243	2243	424	335	2335	512 Rescinded		
309	244	2244	430	341	2341	513	408	2408
310	245	2245	431	342	2342	514	409	2409
311	246	2246	432	343	2343	515	410	2410
312	247	2247	433	344	2344	516	411	2411
313	248	2248	434	345	2345	530	415	2415
314	249	2249	435	346	2346	531	416	2416
315	250	2250	436	347	2347	532	417	2417
316	251	2251	437	345	2345	533	418	2418
318	255	2255	438	349	2349	534	419	2419
319	256	2256	442 Rescinded			535	420	2420
320	257	2257	443	350	2350	536	421	2421
321	258	2258	444	350	2350	537	422	2422
322	259	2259	445	348	2348	538	423	2423
330	37	2037	460	355	2355	539	424	2424
331	38	2038	461	356	2356	550	431	2431
332	35	2035	470	365	2365	551 Rescinded		
333	36	2036	471	366	2366	552 Rescinded		
350	91	2091	472	367	2367	553	432	2432
351	106	2106	473	368	2368	608	435	2435
352	92	2092	474	369	2369	609	435	2435
353	107	2107	475 Rescinded			610	435	2435
360	120	2120	476	369	2369	611	436	2436
361	103	2103	477	371	2371	612	435	2435
362	105	2105	478	369	2369	613	435	2435
363	115	2115	479	369	2369	614	435	2435
364	94	2094	480	369	2369	615	435	2435
365	104	2104	481	375	2375			
			482	376	2376			

Former Rule	Current Rule	Par.	Former Rule	Current Rule	Par.	Former Rule	Current Rule	Par.
616	Rescinded		726	301	2301	761	491	2491
617	435	2435	727	302	2302	860	500	2500
618	Rescinded		728	303	2303	870	450	2450
619	437	2437	751	481	2481	871	451	2451
620	396	2396	752	482	2482	872	452	2452
621	396	2396	753	483	2483	873	453	2453
622	395	2395	754	484	2484	874	454	2454
623	438	2438	755	485	2485	875	455	2455
624	439	2439	756	486	2486	880	456	2456
625	Rescinded		757	487	2487	881	457	2457
701	471	2471	758	488	2488	882	458	2458
702	472	2472	759	489	2489	883	459	2459
703	473	2473	760	490	2490	884	460	2460